Cairo
Cosmopolitan

Cairo
Cosmopolitan

POLITICS, CULTURE, AND URBAN SPACE
IN THE NEW GLOBALIZED MIDDLE EAST

Edited by
Diane Singerman
and **Paul Amar**

The American University in Cairo Press
Cairo   New York

First paperback edition 2009

An earlier version of chapter 3 appeared as "Dimensions nouvelles de la métropolisation dans le Monde arabe: le cas du Caire." *Les Cahiers de la Méditerranée. Université de Nice*, No. 64, 119–66. Reproduced by permission.

Material in chapter 8 is drawn from Farha Ghannam, *Remaking the Modern: Space, Relocation, and the Politics of Identity in Global Cairo*. University of California Press, 2002. Reproduced by permission.

An earlier version of chapter 15 appeared as "When the Lights Go Down in Cairo: Cinema as Global Crossroads and Space of Playful Resistance." *Visual Anthropology* 10 (1998): 413–42. Reproduced by permission.

Dar el Kutub No. 4094/09
ISBN 978 977 416 289 3

Dar el Kutub Cataloging-in-Publication Data

Singerman, Diane
    Cairo Cosmopolitan: Politics, Culture, and Urban Space in the New Globalized Middle East /
Edited by Diane Singerman and Paul Amar.—Cairo: The American University in Cairo Press, 2009
        p.   cm.
        ISBN 978 977 416 289 3
        1. Culture and globalization   I. Singerman, Diane (ed.)   II. Amar, Paul (ed.)
        306

1 2 3 4 5 6 7 8   14 13 12 11 10 09

Designed by Fatiha Bouzidi/AUC Press Design Center
Printed in Egypt

To the courageous, hopeful, and creative people of Cairo
who have all taught us so much about their city

Contents

Cairo Celebratory Spaces and Vernacular World-Crossing

Contributors

Mona Abaza is professor of sociology at the American University in Cairo. Her recent publications include *Changing Consumer Cultures of Modern Egypt: Cairo's Urban Reshaping* (2006), *Debates on Islam and Knowledge in Malaysia and Egypt* (2002), *Islamic Education: Perceptions and Exchanges, Indonesian Students in Cairo* (1994), and *The Changing Image of Women in Rural Egypt* (1987).

Nezar AlSayyad is professor of architecture and planning and chair of the Center for Middle Eastern Studies, University of California, Berkeley. He is the author and editor of many books including *Cities and Caliphs* (1991), *Forms of Dominance* (1993), *Hybrid Urbanism* (2000), *Consuming Tradition, Manufacturing Heritage* (2001), and *Making Cairo Medieval* (2005).

Paul Amar, a political scientist and urban ethnographer, is an assistant professor in the Law and Society Program, University of California, Santa Barbara. His forthcoming publications include *The Security Archipelago: Human-Security States, Sexuality Politics, and the End of Neoliberalism*; *New Racial Missions of Policing*; and *Enforcement Globalizations*.

Walter Armbrust is the Albert Hourani Fellow of Modern Middle East Studies at St. Antony's College, University of Oxford. He is the author of *Mass Culture and Modernism in Egypt* (1996) and the editor of *Mass Mediations: New Approaches to Popular Culture in the Middle East and Beyond* (2000).

Vincent Battesti is a researcher in social anthropology at the Centre National de la Recherche Scientifique (CNRS) in Paris, Muséum National d'Histoire Naturelle, and formerly at the Centre d'Études et de Documentation Économiques, Juridiques et Sociales (CEDEJ) in Cairo where he led research on public spaces (parks and the downtown area). He is co-editing a vast volume on contemporary Egypt with François Ireton. His latest book is *Jardins au désert, Évolutions des pratiques et savoirs oasiens, Jérid tunisien* (2005).

Fanny Colonna is Director Emeritus of Research at the Centre National de la Recherche Scientifique (CNRS) in Paris, L'École des Hautes Études en Science Sociales (EHESS). Her publications include *Les versets de l'invincibilité* (1995), *Récits de la province égyptienne* (2004), "The Phantom of Dispossession: From the Uprooting to the Weight of the World" in *Bourdieu in Algeria, Colonial Politics, Ethnographic Practices, Theoretical Developments*, edited by Jane Goodman and Paul Silverstein (2009), and *Traces, désir de savoir et volonté d'être* (forthcoming).

Eric Denis is a researcher in geography at the Centre National de la Recherche Scientifique (CNRS) in Paris and presently heads the department of social sciences at the French Institute of Pondicherry, focusing on Indian urban and economic transformation. He was formerly in charge of the Observatoire urbain du Caire contemporain at CEDEJ (1997–2002). His publications focus on metropolitan and real-estate dynamics, illegal settlements, and access to services in Egypt and Sudan.

Dalila ElKerdany is a practicing architect and professor of architecture at the Faculty of Engineering, Cairo University. She is involved in research as well as practice in the fields of conservation, heritage, and design and is the recipient of many awards for architectural competitions.

Yasser Elsheshtawy is associate professor of architecture at the United Arab Emirates University. He has written about Middle Eastern urbanism in *Planning Middle Eastern Cities* (2004), *The Evolving Arab City* (2008), and *Dubai: Behind an Urban Spectacle* (2009).

Farha Ghannam is associate professor of anthropology at Swarthmore College and has written on globalization, spatial practices, displacement, migration, gender inequalities, and identity in *Remaking the Modern: Space,*

Relocation, and the Politics of Identity in a Global Cairo (2002) and *Health and Identity in Egypt* (2004).

Galila El Kadi is an urban planner and research director at the Institut de Recherche pour le Développement (IRD) in France. Her publications on urban planning and heritage conservation include *L'urbanisation spontanée au Caire* (1987), *L'urbain dans le Monde Arabe* (1998), *Rashid* (1999), *Architecture for the Dead* (with Alain Bonnamy, 2007), and *al-Tahaddur al-ashwa'i* (2009).

Anouk de Koning received her PhD from the University of Amsterdam. Her recent book *Global Dreams: Class, Gender, and Public Space in Cosmopolitan Cairo* (2009) examines the fate of the middle class in Cairo in the wake of economic liberalization.

Petra Kuppinger is associate professor of anthropology at Monmouth College and writes about issues of space, power, and globalization in Cairo. She edited a special issue of *City and Society* (2004) entitled "Gated Communities and Other Forms of Urban Segregation," which included her contribution, "Exclusive Greenery: New Gated Communities in Cairo."

Anna Madoeuf is professor of geography at Tours University and was formerly in charge of the Observatoire urbain du Caire contemporain at CEDEJ and has co-edited *Les pèlerinages au Maghreb et au Moyen-Orient: Espaces publics, espaces du public* (2005) and *Divertissements et loisirs dans les sociétés urbaines à l'époque moderne et contemporaine* (2005).

Catherine Miller is a fellow and researcher at the Institut de Recherche et d'Etudes sur le Monde Arabe et Musulman (IREMAM) in Aix en Provence where she specializes in Arabic urban sociolinguistics and anthropological linguistics, particularly in Sudan, Egypt, and Morocco. Her recent publications include *Arabic in the City* (2007) and a special issue of the journal REMMM on language, modernity, an religion in the Muslim region (2008).

Nicolas Puig is a researcher in anthropology at the Institut de Recherche pour le Développement (IRD) in France. He has written about social change in Tunisia in *Bédouins sédentarisés et société citadine à Tozeur* (2003) and is now studying the relationship between cultural production, identity, and urbanity among Palestinian refugees in Lebanon.

Said Sadek is an affiliate professor of sociology and political science at the American University in Cairo and the representative of the Finnish Institute in the Middle East (FIME) in Egypt. He has been a long-time media consultant for several international organizations and a freelance political commentator for Arab media.

Omnia El Shakry is an associate professor of history at the University of California, Davis. Her research interests relate to the history of social science in Egypt and the formulation of a postcolonial national modernity. Her publications include *The Great Social Laboratory: Subjects of Knowledge in Colonial and Postcolonial Egypt* (2007).

Diane Singerman is an associate professor of political science at American University. Her publications include *Avenues of Participation: Family, Politics, and Networks in Urban Quarters of Cairo* (1995), *Cairo Cosmopolitan: Politics, Culture, and Urban Space in the New Globalized Middle East* (co-edited with Paul Amar, 2006), and *Development, Change, and Gender in Cairo: A View from the Household* (co-edited with Homa Hoodfar, 1996). She is editor of *Cairo Contested: Governance, Urban Space, and Global Modernity* (2009).

Elizabeth A. Smith is an assistant professor of anthropology at the University of Vermont and works on tourism, national identity, and gender in the Middle East. She is the author of *Nubian Nostalgia: Race, Ethnicity, and Gender in Nubian Cultural Productions* (forthcoming).

Leïla Vignal is a geographer and currently a researcher at the Middle East Centre, St Antony's College, Oxford University. She is working on the impact of globalization on the Middle Eastern metropolis.

Caroline Williams is an independent scholar and has published extensively on Islamic art and architecture in Egypt, including *Islamic Monuments in Cairo: The Practical Guide* (sixth edition) and the four-part video "Cairo: 1001 Years of Art and Architecture."

Acknowledgments

Like many other intellectual projects, the idea for this book began as a discussion. Loosely or formally affiliated with CEDEJ (le Centre d'Etudes et de Documentation Economiques, Juridiques et Sociales) in the late 1990s, we launched this project to counter the simplistic meta-narratives of terrorism and extremism on the one hand, and apathy and immobility on the other that have so distorted the complexities of life and politics in Cairo, and the Middle East more generally. Over the years we built upon a dialogue with the original group of contributors from the CEDEJ cohort, and then scoured Egypt's capital and the world for specialists whose interests and methods would complement the vision of what would become the Cairo School of Urban Studies, and allow us to fulfill our objective—to produce a fresh, three-dimensional, grounded starting point for understanding, teaching, and producing knowledge about the Middle East. This book became an exciting and challenging experience in global cooperation, between the two editors, contributors, advisors, reviewers, publishers, and critics.

Along the way CEDEJ, the Fulbright Commission in Egypt, and the Social Research Center at the American University in Cairo backed up the research projects of this volume's co-editors as well as several contributors. Crucial research trips, conferences, and translations were made possible by the financial support of the School of Public Affairs and the Department of Government at American University, the University of California, Santa Barbara, the Centre National de la Recherche Scientifique (CNRS), France, and the Ford Foundation (Cairo).

Diane Singerman would like to thank her networks of colleagues, family, students, and friends in the United States and Egypt for inspiring her during this long process, which began on a sabbatical in Cairo at CEDEJ and the Social Research Center at the American University in Cairo. While this project did not benefit from the direct intervention of Paul Wapner, his intelligence, support, and care buoyed the possibility that it would be concluded. She would also like to thank her children, Lizzie and Zeke, who have reawakened again and again the creative, curious, and joyful in us all. Many thanks as well for creative support to Sue Katz-Miller, Nicole Salimbene-Bauman, Eva Bellin, Mort and Elinor Wapner, Homa Hoodfar, Leni Singerman, Phyllis Singerman, and Victorina Venzor. Dean William Leogrande and Saul Newman, her former department chair at American University, graciously supported this project.

Paul Amar would especially like to thank Janet Abu-Lughod, in whose "Global Cities" graduate seminar at the New School his passion for urban studies was born. He also would like to thank Andrew Ross, Michael Gilsenan, Charles Tilly, Miriam Cooke, Sharon Zukin, Essam Rifaat, Nawal Al-Saadawi, and Lisa Duggan, in whose courses and workshops his critical perspectives on cities and urban social contestations developed. And in particular, he would like to thank Timothy Mitchell for his intellectual guidance, generosity, and paradigm-melting insights. Paul would also like to thank his enthusiastic and loving father and mother, who gave unflinching moral support to his long soujorns alone through the risky areas of the Middle East and Mediterranean, carried out from age sixteen forward. And he thanks his brother Jeremy, sister-in-law Traci, and nephew Dakota for their solidarity and good humor as he passed many holidays editing, re-translating, and revising chunks of manuscript.

Producing an English-language volume out of an original set of drafts composed sometimes in French and Arabic required the effort of several translators, among whom we would especially like to thank Suzanne Braswell at the University of California Santa Barbara for her speedy and friendly services. Similarly, the management and editing of this volume was greatly enhanced by the wonderful contributions of Mary Breeding at American University. We would also like to thank Seda Demiralp at American University and Nadia Nader and Maria del Mar Logroño at University of California Santa Barbara for their assistance.

Several esteemed colleagues have been kind enough to review parts of the text and their advice has been constitutive of the Cairo School vision and the integrity of this book. In this light we would like to thank Anne Norton, Ann

Lesch, Marsha Pripstein Posusney, Nezar AlSayyad, Lisa Hajjar, Richard Falk, Omnia El Shakry, Eric Denis, and Catherine Miller.

It has been a pleasure to depend on a committed editor, Neil Hewison at the American University in Cairo Press, for this project and he has been patient, constructive, and supportive throughout this process—believing in the importance of the work of the Cairo School and tolerant of our desire to make this a comprehensive volume that would be attractive to, and affordable for a wide variety of publics. The tireless efforts and 'eagle eyes' of Nadia Naqib at the American University in Cairo Press are also greatly appreciated, as was the careful editing by Robin Dougherty. Jean Pierre Ribière was incredibly generous by allowing us to include many of his beautiful and poignant pictures in the volume.

Finally we would like to thank our brilliant contributors for their willingness to revise and re-frame their chapters in a spirit of interdisciplinary openness and intellectual solidarity, and for their patience in making this project a reality.

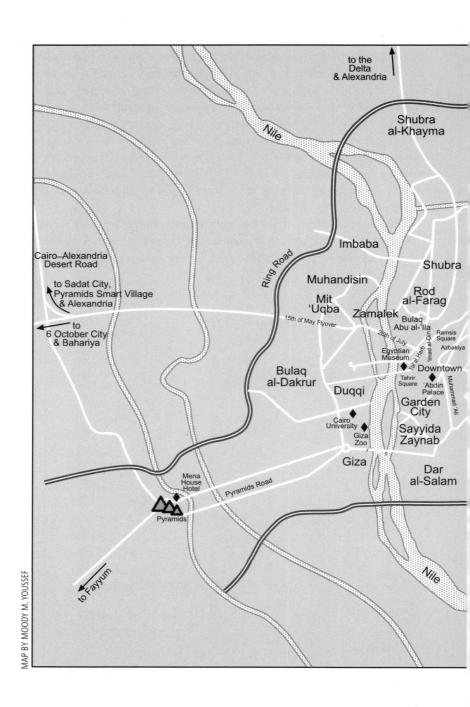

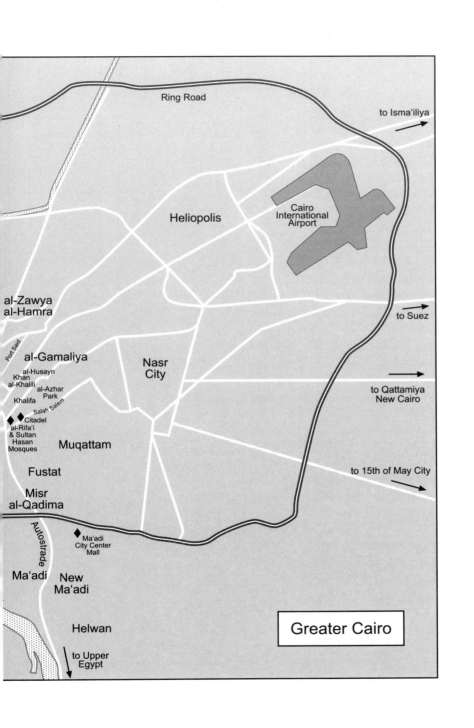

Ring Road

to Isma'iliya

Cairo
International
Airport

Heliopolis

al-Zawya
al-Hamra

to Suez

al-Gamaliya

Nasr
City

al-Husayn
Khan
al-Khalili
al-Azhar
Khalifa   Park
        Salah Salem
◆ ◆ Citadel
al-Rifa'i
& Sultan
Hasan   Muqattam
Mosques

to Qattamiya
New Cairo

Fustat

to 15th of May City

Misr
al-Qadima

◆ Ma'adi
City Center
Mall

Ma'adi   New
          Ma'adi

Helwan

Greater Cairo

to Upper
Egypt

Cairo
Introduction

Contesting Myths, Critiquing Cosmopolitanism, and Creating the New Cairo School of Urban Studies

Diane Singerman and Paul Amar

During the tumultuous spring and summer of 2005, the streets of Egypt's capital became a theater for challenging authoritarianism and saying "Enough!" to the crony forms of neo-liberalism that had come to define the contradictions of a new, globalized Cairo. Rising up to shape their own city and re-make their own history, the women and men of this densely populated metropolis organized themselves through community, university, union, syndicate, religious, human rights, feminist, and prisoner-advocacy groups. These mobilizations seized public space and demanded an end to the politics of brutality and hypocrisy that had suffocated local and regional politics for a generation. Although Cairo's tens of thousands of protestors and their movements' leaders may not (yet) constitute a broad-based popular or social revolution, they brought the world's attention to a set of dynamics and protagonists bustling at the urban crossroads of an assertive, outward-looking Middle East. This city and this region cannot be easily contained or understood through the rigid categories of the past.

Completed during the 2005 season of uprisings and elections in Cairo, this volume brings together the work of the newly coined 'Cairo School of

3

Urban Studies' and strives to capture the innovations of a generation of Cairo-centered scholars and critical thinkers who have rejected the narrow lenses of both mainstream politics (e.g. nationalism, fundamentalism, and security hysteria) and rigid social science methods (e.g. rationalism, positivism, and neo-orientalism). This introductory chapter aims to present some of our research collective's findings on the novelty and complexity of globalizing Cairo. Our hope is to help launch a set of questions that will lead to more productive, critical, and democratic approaches for producing knowledge about the Middle East. We will lay out the specificities of the Cairo School's agenda and methods, and, in particular, our critique and careful appropriation of cosmopolitanism. In brief, we recognize that cosmopolitanism has often been imbedded in transnationalist, normative, universalist, and imperialist discourses. Nevertheless, when reworked through critical scholarship and public action, cosmopolitanism may inform an emancipatory counter-ethic beyond the limits of nationalism, fear, and narrow identity politics, one that complements the Cairo School's experiments with post-positivist research methodologies. But first, we return to the events that confirmed Cairo's re-emergence as a critical site for action and inquiry, and which made the release of this set of studies timely.

In 2004 and 2005, an umbrella group of twenty-six human rights and civil society organizations, established originally to protest the U.S. occupation of Iraq, projected its bold message to the streets of Cairo and the world: "Enough for Mubarak" and "No to hereditary rule" (El-Dein 2004). More formally constituted as the "Egyptian Movement for Change," *Kifaya,* the Arabic word for 'enough,' became the nickname and frame for a panoply of protests, mobilizations, and coalitions that took place from late 2004 throughout 2005. In February 2005, amid the unrest, President Mubarak amended Article 76 of the 1971 constitution, allowing for direct contested presidential elections; this amendment was later ratified in a popular referendum. Nationally based pressure from the Kifaya movement and Cairo-based professional associations (particularly the Judges' Club and Journalists' Syndicate), combined with the United States' new democratization campaign in the Middle East, which placed some restrictions on the regime's penchant for naked coercion, produced slightly more open—and certainly more politically destabilizing and contentious—civil legislative elections. Kifaya and other mass movements, heirs to the momentum of the new Intifada and protests against the U.S. invasion of Iraq, routinely took to the streets between 2004 and 2005, precipitating a domino effect that stirred many groups including the Muslim Brothers, young people, students, the labor movement, the women's movement, and Nasserist forces. Although the government still used violence and intimidation in the parliamentary elections held in three stages, the Muslim Brothers were able to win almost a fifth of the seats in the next parliament. Oppositional secular, leftist, liberal, and feminist platforms also gained a public airing and established visible new leadership cohorts in the public eye.

These oppositional forms shed critical light on economic power structures in Cairo's urban space and in the globalized Middle-East region, and on the internationally embedded legal and political apparatuses of police states. They also identified the hindrances to and possibilities for new gender and religious mobilizations and identities, and the limits of rigid nationalisms. Cairo's explosion of social movement activity in 2005 began to express what we see as new kinds of 'cosmopolitan claims-making' that constitute the daily realities of the contemporary Middle-Eastern megacity explored in these pages.

From Liberal Genealogy to Critical Cosmopolitan Geography

For decades, the people of Cairo had been forced to squeeze their public expressions through the narrowest filters of cultural essentialisms—either conspiracy-theory nationalisms or puritanical moral crusades. The authoritarian, neo-liberal state in Egypt, with consistent encouragement from its patron, the United States, had spent the last thirty years repressing the economic claims of its citizens in the pursuit of brutal privatization and speculative projects of oligarchical economic restructuring. The state had criminalized the political voices of its citizens by crushing non-govermental organizations (NGOs) and social movements, and by using anti-terror laws, emergency provisions, and restrictive laws of association to justify the arrest of even the most moderate of dissident journalists, scholars, and activists. For example, Professor Saad Eddin Ibrahim, a well-known liberal-democracy activist and founder of the Ibn Khaldun Center for Development Studies, was arrested in 2000 and imprisoned for a year and a half due to the political activities of his NGO, and its receipt of financial support from regional and international institutions. A series of show trials against journalists, NGOs, and opposition party leaders in the past ten years have ravaged notions of citizenship and colonized the private and public bodies of Egypt's people—as well as of its political elites. More recently, similar tactics were used against the leader of the Tomorrow Party (al-Ghad), Ayman Nour (who was also a member of parliament). In the space of a single year he was stripped of his parliamentary immunity and imprisoned for allegedly forging signatures to launch al-Ghad. The presidential elections, in which Nour garnered the second-highest percentage of the presidential vote (about 7–8 %) were contested before he was returned to jail at the end of 2005. He has been sentenced to five years' imprisonment although appeals are pending ("Protests Mar Mubarak Win" 2005).

With the uprisings, protests, campaigns, and new popular alliances of 2005, Cairenes surprised many international and local observers not just for holding public demonstrations but for starting to assert a refashioned project of active citizenship that transcended the national/global-religious/secular polarizations and shrugged off the paranoia and self-consciousness that defined the previous era of moral panic and culture wars. At the very least, these forces were re-imagining the country's future with new tactics and strategies, which Engin Isin tells us, is itself an act of citizenship (2005).

In Cairo, 2005, a new urban-based, cosmopolitan, radical democracy agenda began to emerge, as the product of a three-year convergence trend within and between leftist, liberal, and Islamist groups, and a myriad of city and transnational advocates. Its development dates to the summer of 2002 when millions of individuals in Arab capitals, including Cairo, flooded the streets to rally in support of the Palestinian's new Intifada. On an equal scale in 2003, and joined by others across the globe, they battled their national security forces and took back the streets to protest the U.S. invasion of Iraq (Bayat 2003). A new, boldly assertive, pan-Arab, and globally aware collective sensibility had been materializing, but had not yet moved beyond protest expressions toward the articulation of a grounded national political agenda.

In October 2004, protests against foreign militarism began to be channeled into militancy against injustice and the abuse of human rights at home. Ex-judge Tariq al-Bishri penned a widely circulated manifesto calling on Egyptians to "withdraw their long-abused consent to be governed" and engage in mass civil disobedience (al-Ghobashy 2005). In December 2004, the legitimacy of the Egyptian state and other states in the region was eroded when a group of largely Cairo-based Arab intellectuals leaked their draft of the Arab Human Development Report, produced for the United Nations Development Program. In an unprecedented move, the U.S. had blocked the UN release of the report because the report held the Egyptian government, other authoritarian states in the region, Persian Gulf principalities, and U.S. foreign policy responsible for the lack of human health, education, and social and cultural development in the region, as well as for endemic poverty and social exclusion (Khoury 2004). The report was unique in its post-neoliberal insistence on refusing to separate poverty from politics, and to hold national and international actors accountable rather than retreat to technocratic fixes.

It seemed that a new era opened in Middle East political history when, early in 2005, university groups, labor syndicates, journalists, the Muslim Brotherhood (in Arabic, *al-Ikhwan al-Muslimin*, or simply *al-Ikhwan*), and even factions of Egypt's crony capitalist oligarchy formed a united front to apply pressure on President Muhammad Hosni Mubarak, forcing his party to allow other presidential candidates to run against him in the September 2005 elections. Internal and external pressures—including the Bush administrations 'democratization' initiative—did not allow for true political pluralism, yet, crucially, it did decriminalize opposition political rallies, making many politicized social movements and forms of public contention legal again.

Cairenes were asked to rubber-stamp Mubarak's initiative to permit someone to contest him in presidential elections on May 25, although his plan kept in place many other inequities and intimidation mechanisms built into the electoral process. Demonstrators from the seven opposition parties and the Kifaya movement, which had called for a boycott of this referendum, were set upon by plain-clothed thugs, who beat demonstrators as the police looked on, doing nothing. Unlike the typical violent attacks on demonstrators by armed and uniformed security forces in Cairo, plain-clothed thugs targeted female demonstrators, conspicuously tearing their clothes and stripping them as they attacked them. Within days, hundreds of women, rallied by progressive Islamist feminists, organized a day in black to protest the sexual molestation, and demanded that the Minister of Interior immediately resign. Despite further harassment the women did not back down but instead, formed *Shayfinkum* or 'we are watching you' to protest against what was termed Black Wednesday (May 25), political violence, and rigged elections (see *www. shayfeen.com*). Protest groups were making explicit cosmopolitan claims on the government, demanding accountability, legality, and respect for human rights. In similar ways, community collectives from slum neighborhoods and more privileged student groups began to cooperate, demanding fair elections and the constitution of a new public sphere, on their own terms.

During the U.S. Secretary of State's visit to Cairo on June 20, 2005, Egypt's government promised Dr. Rice that opposition rallies would enjoy freedom to gather and express themselves without fear of brutality. Nevertheless, the only change implemented was that plain-clothed police officers and paid thugs (the same ones that roam the streets intimidating voters on election days) rather than uniformed security troops did the dirty work. In late July, security forces continued to attack protestors. Senior leaders of the Kifaya movement were badly beaten, detained, and disappeared to a military camp at al-Darrasa in Cairo. Journalists, public observers, and social scientists witnessing the new level of conflict and this explosion of citizen assertiveness asked: where did this collective action come from? Does this moment in Cairo show where globalization or democratization is heading in the Middle East?

Shifts in alliances and explosions in social movement activity paralyzed mainstream media and many academic observers—squeezing them between sentiments of Western triumphalism and Islamophobic despair. Those that had been keeping an eye on the Middle East realized they were ignorant of the new logics of social and political patterns that characterize the Middle Eastern city and Arab protagonism of today. For example, in 2005, international neo-liberal and neo-conservative commentators rushed to characterize Cairo's protest dynamics as part of a Middle-East 'democratic spring.' U.S. President Bush and U.K. Prime Minister Blair—under attack for falsifying information about weapons of mass destruction in Iraq—had sought to replace the discredited doctrine of forcing disarmament with one of promoting democracy. Massive election irregularities and the strong showing of Islamists in elections in Egypt (as well as in Palestine, Iraq, and Lebanon) quieted triumphalist comparisons of Arab elections with the democratic revolutions of Eastern Europe or Latin America of the 1980s, or the more recent "Orange Revolution" in the Ukraine in 2003 ("Mideast Climate Change" 2005; "Something Stirs" 2005). But by overly lamenting the defeat of opposition-presidential candidates—or by assuming that the strong showing by the Muslim Brotherhood would increase fundamentalism or terrorism—liberal and neo-conservative observers ignored the dynamic changes that have made the new generation of activists, including Islamists, more pluralistic and democratic, thus creating common spaces of opposition consensus that partially embody the concerns of some leftists and feminists.

During the 1980s and 1990s the Muslim Brotherhood and other Islamist groups began to advocate political party pluralism, including the rights of secular parties to exist within a proposed Islamic state, and full rights of citizenship for Coptic Christians and for women. The West assumes that debates about the application of Shari'a law and gender control dominate Brotherhood politics—and certain populist factions of the Brotherhood do continue to obsess about the comportment, morals, and bodies of women and girls—but the political initiatives of the new generation's leadership spearheaded national efforts to confront police brutality, torture, state repression, prison conditions, and the illegality of the Emergency Law that have been in place since 1981 (al-Ghobashy 2005, 225, 374–79). Common cultural positions and worldviews between all opposition actors did not exist, but a shared sense of outrage about repression and the lack of democratic and social rights did place the Ikhwan within the democratic camp on these crucial issues at this momentous time. Kifaya's alliance revealed to Cairo and to the world the brutal, rusty mechanism of the ruling party's domination, and by revoking the popular mandate of the regime, their dissent had lasting implications. The largest mass protest of all was the refusal of 25 million registered voters, 77 percent of the total electorate, to go to the polls and vote in the presidential election, which denied the victor a national mandate ("Protests Mar Mubarak Win" 2005). Mubarak, in the end, won the election; but to do so he had to expose his illegal vote-controlling operations and thus give up, in the eyes of large sectors of the public, his claim on legitimacy and legality. But above all, despite the violence of the security forces and the ingenuity of the government in manipulating the elections, the courage of popular movement activities grabbed the spotlight.

Moving Beyond Old Visions

The summer of political challenges in Cairo in 2005 exposed the violent, repressive nature of what has come to be accepted as globalization and liberalism in the Middle-East region at large—that is, in the case of Egypt in particular, a state run in the interests of an elite, state-subsidized ring of Cairo-based capitalists who call themselves liberals or globalizers or democratizers because they facilitate foreign investment in the economic sphere, even as they insist on repression, the extension of the Emergency Law, and police-state practices in the political sphere. As Mona al-Ghobashy suggests, "The younger representatives of Egypt's ruling class may be technologically savvy, US-educated and American-accented, and properly deferential to private sector dominance and the laws of the market but when it comes to institutionalizing binding consultation of citizens or protecting citizens from arbitrary state power, their silence is palpable . . ." (al-Ghobashy 2005).

Cairo has long been a contested city, as increased regional and global flows of labor, investment, foreign aid, migration, media, and political and legal activism interact with its cultures, heritages, and social, political, and economic institutions. We have titled this volume 'Cairo Cosmopolitan' in recognition of the limitations of a nation-state scale of analysis, which minimizes the importance of border-crossing social, cultural, and political-economic flows. Here, we present evidence of vernacular, bottom-up cosmopolitanisms of enhanced agency and claims-making practices among more and more individuals and collective forces in Cairo. We see these critical cosmopolitanisms as publicly and visibly demanding justice, accountability, representation, citizenship, and political and social rights. The volumes' chapters work together to explain tensions surrounding politics, culture, and urban space in the new, globalized Middle East.

Normatively dedicated to moving beyond modernist dichotomies between local and global, this collection explores the ambivalent forces at work in contemporary Cairo, which both present opportunities and limitations. The studies we have compiled here offer evidence that Cairo and its residents are not only receivers of globalization, satellite media, consumer culture, or government repression. Cairene socio-cultural collectives, urban communities, popular movements—and even semi-autonomous state projects and renegade elite factions—act in contradictory ways. They move within, through, and against dominant state institutions and spatial and economic structures, articulating forms of subjectivity and agency, but under conditions not of their own choosing, and within relations of power that can radically dehumanize and militarize daily existence.

By grounding this collective study in real spaces and street-level contests we aim to survey the landscape of globalizing power and socio-political contestation in the Middle East, from the privileged location of Cairo. We collectively offer fresh standpoints from which to engage and appreciate classes of people, economies, and institutions at work, even if they only rarely attract the attention of those scholars and media outlets that generate familiar profiles of extremism, dictatorship, and violence in the region. Through researching and compiling this volume, we have rediscovered how the operations of the authoritarian state, city administration, social control agencies, and national identities are contingent, internally contested, often fragmented, and pregnant with multiple possibilities. Yet we do not offer a catalogue of resistance modes or utopian futures. Domination within Cairo is complex and dynamic, still undeniably cruel, hierarchical, and often violent. Nevertheless, in its fragmented contingent forms, domination never completely forecloses creativity and agency. And in this volume we highlight surprising turns of events and shifts in opportunity structures, by bringing experiments in political economy, social geography, and urban ethnography into engagement with the less adroit methodologies of rationalist and positivist social science.

Cairo as a Global City: Neo-Liberalism and Contests over Public Space and Resources

The summer of 2005's political turmoil must be understood within the context of larger changes in late twentieth-century and early twenty-first-century Cairo. These changes include the emergence of a new spatial economy, where globalization and structural adjustment have led to high unemployment, particularly among educated young people, and the selling off of the public patrimony (see Vignal and Denis in this volume) to enhance the private sector and to build exclusive, luxury, gated communities for a phantom luxury class.

In her contribution to this volume, Omnia El Shakry argues that the demonization of the demographic masses is linked to the state's embrace of a neo-liberal order. Since the beginning of the Sadat era in 1981, urban planners and policy elites argued that population density was consuming the promises of economic growth and the government deployed laws, investment strategies, industrial policies, and infrastructural investments to subsidize and build satellite cities in the desert to facilitate the "productive redistribution of the population."

Questions of Egyptian migration not only need to grapple with the hundreds of thousands of citizens who migrate to the Persian Gulf or Europe and the U.S., but also with internal migration to jobs in outlying satellite cities or to tourism zones where the need for jobs, wherever they might be, reconstitutes the social and cultural bonds of urban communities and remakes urban/transnational class, gender, and religious identities in the process. While Egypt's elite might feel safe in walled enclaves while managing franchises in the satellite cities' industrial zones, their abandonment of the urban core of Cairo is accompanied by what Denis calls a "security risk" discourse that identifies the city and its poorer residents with poverty, pollution, disorder, criminality, violence, and terrorism. This politics of risk enables and provides a cover-story for radical forms of repression and even racialization, as the "war on terror" and the "campaign against pollution" sieze the bodies and dwellings of working-class Cairenes and sub-Saharan African immigrants with ambivalent legal status.

As Elsheshtawy in this volume (chapter 7) reminds us, global trends in cities seem to be characterized by efforts to "wall some in and keep others out" (UN-Habitat 2001, 30). With globalization comes a "high degree of segmentation in the spheres of both production and consumption," where the economy, enmeshed in global flows and foreign franchises produces gendered pleasures and consumer-class distinctions along differentiated paths (see de Koning in this volume). Goods and services, as Vignal and

Denis explain in their chapter, are designed and produced for luxury markets or for the poor, with luxury malls—planned for those with more wealth and cars—on the outskirts of the city via the new Ring Road, while the informal economy and small artisanal and family enterprises produce and distribute second-order goods and services. All sectors of the economy are dependent, however, on low-wage workers, and to compete globally, the Egyptian state must ensure, as much as it can, that these wages stay low.

It is within the context of hierarchies of consumption, production, and access to services that the political turmoil in the summer of 2005 should be understood. It is not surprising that new and more widely articulated claims for political and social rights, legality, human rights, and citizenship and the ability to elect leaders and parliaments are being made within Cairo's new spatial political economy and violent transnationally articulated socio-cultural geography. It is equally surprising that these new claims, assertions, and formations are repressed with severity; but repression and exclusion have not eliminated the dynamics that impel continued contestation.

Throughout this long summer of activism, people transcended their status as merely dangerous classes seething on the so-called Arab street. Cairenes re-emerged as citizens, bearing the mantle of popular sovereignty, legality, and legitimacy. And, crucially, by claiming to redefine questions of democracy, legality, and social justice on the streets of the largest city, at the core of the world's most strategically sensitive economic, political, and religious region, the Middle East, the people of Cairo claimed a certain kind of cosmopolitan status and transnational agency.

For this volume, we ask readers to consider the new and changing spatial economy of the Middle East, as explored through Cairo-based case studies. We analyze those Cairenes who drive to and shop in new luxury malls built with Dubai financing and Gulf models, while others are kept out of these malls because the security guards find them too threatening or shabbily dressed. Some of the more elaborate malls have themselves become part of the large tourist sector, as Upper Egyptians and the provincial middle-class from the Delta use tour buses to experience their consumerist vision, theaters, entertainment, playgrounds, food courts, and endless shops. While luxurious malls continue to be built, others have gone bust or stand half empty, crippling the banking sector, as Mona Abaza explains in this volume. At a more individual level, Farha Ghannam describes the ways in which labor migrants become even more connected to their families when they work abroad, as they communicate with them constantly, channeling the financial hopes for the family and their future. According to Leïla Vignal and Eric Denis in this volume, close to two million Egyptians work in the Gulf countries, and their remittances inject income into Cairo's economy on parity with tourism revenues (US$ 3 billion against 4). These remittances have fueled the vast expansion of informal/unplanned housing communities, or 'ashwa'iyat, in peri-urban areas of Greater Cairo, which now house more than half of Cairo's residents and have satisfied 80 percent of housing needs for the last twenty years. The informal sector has also produced 40 percent of non-agricultural jobs (Denis and Séjourné, 2002).

The privatizing exclusivity of the neo-liberal model, sustained by low wages, is a product of this era, and it is a theme that many authors in this collection explore. The very definition of the public is quite ambivalent in Cairo today, as formerly public places and entire neighborhoods are cleansed of their populations and their historic monuments recklessly remade and often poorly renovated to attract international tourists and their "1001 Nights" visions of "Islamic Cairo," as Caroline Williams explains in her chapter. Similarly, Yasser Elsheshtawy examines the fate of a public square between the Sultan Hasan madrasa (a fourteenth-century religious school) and al-Rifa'i mosque (a nineteenth-century mosque), which was initially converted to pedestrian use in 1984 and had become popular with local residents since there were few public spaces in the older mixed-use neighborhoods of Cairo. Yet, by 2003, the government had fenced in and closed the gates to the square, since it viewed local residents as a threat to be contained and removed so that global tourists could enjoy a sanitized space (that is, one without Egyptians). The case of this public square between two great monuments of Islamic Cairo demonstrates how tourist sites in the contemporary era display Egyptianness only according to a carefully crafted script, oriented toward the global tourist trade. Metaphorically, whether governments decide to convert formerly open, pedestrian malls into touristic spaces, or private developers, backed by government-subsidized loans land sales, build gated communities isolated from the urban center, literal and metaphorical walls are being increasingly erected within the Greater Cairo Region (GCR).

City officials in many global cities are encouraging this "quartering of public space" (analyzed by Elsheshtawy, chapter 10, in this volume) to reap the awards from tourists and investors, yet this leaves sharper divisions between rich and poor that are not only economic in nature (see also Sassen 2001). This political and economic vision is egregiously clear in the new spatial layout of Cairo, and this collection tries, through grounded, detailed, largely ethnographic field work, to represent the ways in which structural adjustment, privatization, or globalization have been overlaid on the spatial political economy of Cairo. Petra Kuppinger's chapter, for example, describes the unsettling disparity between a Giza village without basic access to water and utilities, and the Pyramids Plateau nearby which funnels vast international and national investment to infrastructure, museums, and luxury hotels. The Pyramids are the quintessential symbol of Egyptian national heritage, and claim to be the iconic wonder of world civilization. Yet, more and more, the Pyramids and other popular tourist sites have become commodified as part of the global tourist economy and wholly dependent upon it. Does the Egyptian state invest in water for the lower-class urban quarters of Giza or does it try to raise US$ 350 million to build the world's largest archaeological museum—the Grand Egyptian Museum—to house select Egyptian artifacts in over a two-hundred acre complex? In the international tourist economy, as Elsheshtawy explains in chapter 10, cities themselves become brands; and mega-museums, world heritage sites, or neo-orientalist green spaces like the recently-built al-Azhar Park are but attempts to keep market share. A tourist economy demands that the Egyptian government remain solicitous to the needs, wants, and desires of its clients—international tourists—while official silences about problems within communities a few minutes away remain glaringly obvious to their residents.

Alternatively, Armbrust's study of film spectatorship in cinemas in downtown Cairo *(wust al-balad)* and Battesti's study of the Giza Zoo demonstrate how the popular classes have appropriated particular public spaces and created an ambience that celebrates density and crowds. Battesti reminds us that modernist meta-narratives that celebrated public hygiene are not new but date back to the nineteenth century when green spaces and ordered urban leisure norms were to discipline the crowd and cultivate bourgeois modern individuals. Today, these nineteenth-century discourses return in exclusionary rather than disciplinary form. For example, the recently opened al-Azhar Park, celebrated as a vast green oasis of neo-Islamic architecture, articulates Cairo's current drive to transform public patrimony into Islamicized gated enclaves. This park, like many new centers of consumption and entertainment, is filled with wealthy Gulf and Saudi tourists, particularly in the summer months; the spaces are designed to serve the needs of spectacular consumerism by subjects of rentier petroleum states rather than transform local urbanites into a productive bourgeoisie.

Puig discusses in this volume that a significant share of the market for musicians is now oriented to Persian Gulf tastes and preferences. Both Sadek and Puig explain how this growing Gulf Arab influence, as well as the influence of Egyptian labor circulating through Europe, and new flows of refugees, sub-Saharan Africans, and Levantine migrants to Cairo have diversified the artistic range of modern Egyptian music as it becomes more self-consciously cosmopolitan, incorporating Spanish, Nubian, Arabian, or South Asian melodic tunes.

Despite the density of transnational cultural flows traversing Egypt from Europe and the Gulf that Armbrust, Sadek, Abaza, and Ghannam discuss in this volume, Vignal and Denis question the degree to which Cairo can be seriously considered a 'global city.' They argue that in many ways Egypt remains on the 'ultra-periphery' of global financial flows, with a barely legible share in global stock markets (the volatile Egyptian stock market has been artificially inflated by the privatization and sale of public sector companies), disappointing levels of direct foreign investment, weak export growth, and a relatively small financial services and banking sector. In fact, Cairo's case presents a critique of much of the literature on global cities, because privatization and structural adjustment—and the global flows and networks they entail—have had a tremendous impact on Egypt's strong manufacturing and industrial sector, rather than the information/computer industries and financial and service sectors usually highlighted in the new economies. Egypt's large manufacturing sector has changed, often been privatized and consolidated, but remains strong, diversified, and geared toward the domestic market. This manufacturing sector in Cairo has triggered an explosion of "new social forces, grounded in inequalities and in elitist modes of consuming, displacement, and residence that strive to match cosmopolitan standards, while the living conditions of the many remain very localized, limited, impoverished and isolated" (Vignal and Denis in this volume). The new spatial political economy of Greater Cairo has transformed the city's landscape, configuring new circuits of distribution and transportation facilitated by new technologies and services. Along with these transformations, urban development plans, both industrial and residential, have grown increasingly bifurcated. There remains a consequential illegal and paralegal sweatshop manufacturing sector (between 27 percent and 40 percent of jobs, according to sources), which in some dense clusters of industrial activity are quite productive yet reliant on low-wage laborers, easily supplied by these densely populated areas. Neo-liberalism's new circuits of distribution and consumption have relocated important markets for wholesale food and textiles out of the urban core (Gertel 1997). As Williams explains in this volume, the Cairo governor proposed evicting 1,200 fabric merchants from al-Muski to a new mall in Abbasiya, near the police station, arguing that the noise, crowds, and pollution affect tourists in nearby Khan al-Khalili. A few years ago, the Egyptian government moved the wholesale food market from Rod al-Farag to the suburbs despite organized protests; but to date they have failed to force the textile merchants to a new location.

Cairo today is infused with emergent hierarchies of exclusion and reordered patterns of structural violence, which the scholarship in this collection highlights. Vignal and Denis suggest that Egypt, a country of "weak or modest technological capacities, of course owes its integration into the archipelago of great metropolises to its abundant and cheap manual labor" where all sectors of the economy function "on the basis of minimal salaries for work, and maximum subsidies for elite speculation." While manufacturers, often linked to international companies and government supporters, benefit from tax breaks and cheaper rents in the vast new satellite cities such as Sixth of October, or Tenth of Ramadan, (established 1979), workers commute long distances on minibuses, making it more difficult for women to gain these private sector jobs (Assaad 2004). The relationship between hierarchy, exclusion, and globalization, we suggest, is not emphasized enough in the literature on cosmopolitanism.

Hierarchies are reproduced through transnational flows and through the structures of the neo-liberal order in today's Cairo. When young men migrate abroad to finance the substantial costs of marriage in Egypt, they may spend years saving for and preparing their new marital abode (Singerman and Ibrahim 2001). As Ghannam shows in this volume, jobs in the Gulf for lower-income men are often the sole route to savings and their imagined dreams of prosperity. Yet even if they succeed in finding employment in oil-producing countries, once they return to Egypt, their desire for more income and new consumer goods remain shaped by the ideas, money, and products brought from these countries. There is a multiplicity of global influences in Cairo, and increasingly rigid and revanchist class distinctions are often how these global distinctions are naturalized and socially materialized. While some members of a family may enrich themselves by working in Libya or Kuwait, others are not able to secure visas, or positions abroad and thus, as Ghannam argues, "new forms of inequality [are] produced by global processes *within* the same city, the same neighborhood, and even the same family (emphasis added)." The migrants' access to wealth and promised prosperity comes without citizenship. Ironically "the club of Gulf exclusion for migrants reinforces longing and belonging back in Cairo," facilitated most recently by an explosion in international communications technology, according to Ghannam.

Circulation through and relocation to more rural areas does not necessarily mean a kind of exile or exit from cosmopolitan circuits. Whereas El Shakry in this volume describes 1960s Cairo as the master planner and command center for an essentially rural nation; smaller towns in the rural countryside in Egypt have now become sites of innovation and border-crossing access points that stimulate and remake the capital city. Fanny Colonna's chapter in this volume on provincial elites examines Cairo through the eyes of a television producer from Isma'iliya, who critiques the hegemonic role of the state media in Egypt, while leading one of the first, innovative provincial television stations. This new generation of media innovators "see attachment to and engagement with the provincial scale and local specificity as a necessary part of a broader sense of belonging, empowerment, and citizenship empowerment . . . aimed at transforming the whole of Egyptian society, to give it new voices and new groundings for the realities of its popular and provincial classes."

In this collection, we hope to explain why international tourism, for example, or government and private speculation and investment in gated communities can infuriate Cairenes and spark opposition, resistance, or simply further exacerbate economic or political exclusion. In Egypt, the issue of local control and the strategic objectives of urban planning are fundamentally influenced by a political system that is heavily centralized and authoritarian. Do the residents or merchants of El Tayyibin in Giza or from Fatimid Cairo, public sector housing residents in Zawiya al-Hamra or al-Rifa'i square have any means to protest government policy or investment strategies? Can provincial journalists and intellectuals create independent media programs that raise public issues and challenge the hegemony of Cairo over the rest of the nation? How do the small shop owners in *wust al-balad* (downtown Cairo), built in the late nineteenth and early twentieth centuries, compete with the proliferation of vast malls and foreign-owned superstores in the exurbs of Cairo? Will a new pedestrian mall and renovations of the belle époque-era Egyptian Stock Market in the area that El Kadi and ElKerdany discuss in this book succeed in retaining and attracting local customers or tourists to the area? The political dynamics of planning and local administration will be taken up more directly in the succeeding volume of this project, *Cairo Hegemonic: State, Justice, and Urban Social Control in the New Globalized Middle East.*

Seeking answers to these questions about popular and elite reappropriations of space, investor struggles, globalizing hierarchies, consumer-class polarization, new cosmopolitan claims, and national(ist) security politics has brought together the contributors to this volume, and generated a broad research agenda that has come to be called 'the Cairo School of Urban Studies.'

The Cairo School: Grounded Projects and Rooftop Plots

During the eventful summer of 2005, the two editors of this volume held final meetings with our contributors on hotel rooftop cafés in the heart of downtown Cairo. During the same period, stringer journalists based in Iraq, of every nationality, taking weekend leaves in Cairo, came in and out of conversations at dinners around town, weaving horrifying accounts of war and insurgency into the discussion, revealing exhilarating stories that never made it to print. Egyptian protestors and opposition candidates circulated through cafés and restaurants in order to not-so-subtly smuggle in illegal leaflets that revealed secret protest gathering-points. These rebel activists would show off cigarette burns and electrical shock scars they had picked up while in police interrogation. A war-time form of rebel cosmopolitanism had sparked to life in Cairo.

At this seeming worst of times, exiled leaders and defunct youth organizations and theater groups were rematerializing in Cairo. Our 'Cairo School of Urban Studies' seemed to find its place among them. This school, as we came to call it, represents an international research collective that asks new questions about cities and citizenship, elite domination, public policy, and subaltern politics. We focus on developing fieldwork tools that register and analyze contradictory street-level assertions that have survived and taken on surprising forms in the wake of state repression and economic restructuring. New globalizing strategies of domination have produced unpredictable and unstable effects, starkly evident in the daily life of the urban communities in the global south.

This volume asserts that the globalizing city of Cairo, at least as much as the wealthy metropoles of the global north, offers a laboratory for exploring and developing new forms of citizenship and contestation for facing the contradictions of power in a militarized and unequal world. Cairo has produced a new generation of intellectuals and activists (Egyptian, exile, and expatriate) who are evaluating these same contradictions with new urbanist lenses. The Cairo School hopes to disseminate new critical methodologies for qualitative social science as well as new perspectives on urban social movements, state forms, public policy, elite domination, and subaltern publics in the globalized Middle East. Our collective includes Egyptian, Arab, U.S., Iranian, African, and European specialists that first came together during Egypt's previous period of democratic openness in the mid-1990s. This volume represents one of the first published products of our experiments with methodologies grounded in down-to-earth fieldwork on contemporary border-crossing, street-level Middle-Eastern power relations, including those that undergird class conflict, gender/sexual formations, urban spaces, and political-economic structures.

Through workshops in Cairo and Paris, and at panels at Middle East Studies Association (MESA) conferences in the U.S., various clusters within our school came together to seek out ways to break out of rigid assumptions about Islamism, terrorism, and inequality. We sought to develop methodologies and research agendas that would work against the grain of the two dominant dualistic paradigms: the neo-liberal notion of dictatorial regimes locked in opposition to liberal middle-class civil societies, and the neo-imperialist 'Clash of Civilizations' vision that imagines the world split between elite Westernized secularist modernizers and backward Islamist fundamentalists. Our urban-transnational fieldwork offered alternative directions.

To develop our distinctiveness, we insisted on grounding our studies in particular urban intersections where state, global, local, community, and social protagonism would intersect in ways that did not allow for easy simplifications or quantifications. How are power, subjectivity, and voice enabled and reproduced? As we compared our case studies and ethnographies, our Cairo School came to highlight forms of agency, identification, mobilization, and creativity. Exploring the ambivalences of both cosmopolitanism and groundedness in Cairo—a highly unequal megacity at the core of an economically polarized and militarized Middle East—we focused on identifying new field-research experiments among both elite and subaltern world-making projects, and among both popular-class slums and luxury enclaves in Cairo. Bringing these studies into dialogue, we hoped to begin to reveal complexity and by implication, to challenge the necessity of repressive, exclusionary, hierarchical processes of globalization, neo-colonialism, and authoritarianism in the urban and transnational context.

As we finalized the volume, we recalled the limitations we have faced. A project that tries to represent and characterize a global metropolis is bound to be fraught with difficulties from the beginning—particularly one that tries to convey the diversity, agency, dynamism, and ambivalence of a city that is so regionally and nationally preeminent, and globally misrepresented. Traditionally, the dominant norms of social science would insist that analysis should begin with the particular and generalize universal patterns by moving farther away—shifting in the direction of national comparisons, global dialectics, or large-N data sets. This collection offers alternatives. We begin from very concrete qualitative analyses of daily life in a particular corner of contemporary Cairo and then move in even closer and closer. We move within and around our sites, carefully untangling how each of these 'local' patterns are neither artifacts of the universal nor necessarily analytically receptive to generalization. Rather, they are deeply connected, influenced by and reconstituting regional and global identities, relations, and forces.

Writing a Comprehensive Cairo

Our studies occupy a niche within an increasingly rich body of literature on Egypt's capital and its socio-cultural, geopolitical, and historical importance. Today's Cairo is the largest and most diverse metropolis of three intersecting world regions: the Middle East, the Mediterranean, and Africa.[1] The capital of Egypt is an entrepôt that hosts contact across borders, and a laboratory that generates new transnational concerns, state practices, socio-political mobilizations, and urban solutions. This strategic megacity serves as a point of origin, intersection, and experimentation. The local dynamics of this metropolis have global implications.[2]

Greater Cairo—referred to as the "City Victorious" and "Mother of the World," *Umm al-Dunya*—operates as the political capital of the Arab League and pan-African institutions, and as the guardian of a significant portion of humanity's architectural heritage. Modern discourses and practices that make up the contradictory essence of today's globalization—'mass tourism,' 'counter-terrorism,' and externally imposed 'fiscal adjustment'—were first tested and developed in and around colonized Cairo in the late 1800s. And in the twentieth century, the urban spaces of Egypt's capital have served as the cradle of modern revolutions, insurgencies, and solidarity movements: Nasserism, Arab Socialism, Islamism, Third Worldism, Mediterraneanism, the Non-Aligned Movement, Pan-Africanism, and so on.

Heir to these dynamics, the urban geography of contemporary Cairo as a whole has been the object of relatively few comprehensive treatments, although there has been a profusion of more targeted urbanist and disciplinary-located studies, many of them written by the authors in this collection.[3] But among non-academic publics, even visiting Western tourists, Cairo remains neglected. Many European tourists bypass the capital; their planes and trains and Nile cruise boats head directly for the so-called timeless zones of Luxor, Aswan, or the Red Sea. Academic visitors, political scientists, and journalists also detour around Cairo, in an analytical sense, ascending to the level of geopolitics, where Cairo is objectified, referred to as a monolithic strategic actor—the authoritarian ruler forcing along the impossibly skewed Middle East peace process or doing the West's dirty work in the war on terror. In this context, Cairo's thirteen to eighteen million inhabitants and the city's vital cultural spaces and socio-political institutions have been substantively ignored, pushed into the backstage of tourism, archaeology, or structural adjustment, or massed into the abstractions of the Arab Street or Islamist Militancy.[4] In fact, no comprehensive social science examination of contemporary Cairo has been published since Janet Abu-Lughod's *Cairo: 1001 Years of the City Victorious*. This classic was drafted in the 1960s at the high point of the turbulence and optimism of Gamal Abd al-Nasser's revolution.

This is not to say that there have not been many internationally available titles published on Cairo during the last generation. Yet, in the context of this blossoming of innovative writings on Cairo, a thorough analysis of the city's diversity of class, cultural, and socio-political protagonisms remained unwritten. Of course there are reasons for this. In the decades that have followed the Nasser era study, the fabric of neo-orientalist or neo-colonial meta-narratives draped themselves over the city of Cairo, closing in over the urban landscape. These obscuring legends or meta-narratives can be grouped, roughly, into two types: Cairo as a *bomb* and Cairo as a *tomb*.

Cairo Meta-narratives: The Bomb, The Tomb

The first myth of the city as an explosive device is familiar to most. Indeed, many academics, reporters, and international diplomats continue to stake their careers on incendiary images of the city: Cairo as a population bomb, a pollution epicenter, a laboratory for explosive terrorist cells, the flashpoint for communal Coptic-Muslim riots, or ground zero for insurgent solidarities such as anti-American protests, anti-IMF riots, pro-Palestinian or Islamic movements. In these representations, the people, spaces, public opinion, and state institutions of Cairo are projected onto fantasies about the Arab Street, a racist euphemism popular with journalists. In the nineteenth century the term 'street Arabs' referred to racialized, homeless hooligan boys and traffickers among the lumpenproletariat of London, New York, and Chicago, who were imagined to constitute the menacing core of anarchist cultures, vice zones, and dangerous classes. Jacob Riis in *How the Other Half Lives* dedicated a chapter to the phenomenon of the "street Arab" who "has all the faults and virtues of the lawless life he leads. Vagabond that he is, acknowledging no authority and owing no allegiance to anybody or anything, with his cunning fist raised against society wherever it tries to coerce him, he is as bright and shrewd as the weasel, which, among all the predatory beasts he most resembles" (Riis 1890).

Now in the twenty-first century, the term 'street Arab' has been flipped, and projected back into the post-colonial Middle East. When journalists and academics evoke the Arab Street today, they mean the worst kind of barbarous urban mob, threatening local and global orders such as the Camp David Accords or Free Trade and IMF-instituted structural adjustment (Bayat 2003). As Denis argues in this volume, real-estate developers and politicians exploit more and more the stigmatization of the street, spread by the media on a global scale, arguing that the Arab metropolis is a terrorist risk factory. This Islamist Peril, like the Red Peril of the Cold War era, legitimizes political de-liberalization (including repression, torture, election-rigging) while promoting a particular landscape of perverse economic liberalization (producing gates, walls, mass arrests, and surveillance systems rather than any social or labor equivalent of a free market). Where in these bomb images and Arab-street metaphors are the active subjects, the interests, the histories, the institutions, and the struggles that constitute Cairo and its peoples? Where are the real social, spatial, and new institutional actors that enable contemporary repression in the day-to-day life of the city?

Paradoxically, a second well-worn myth about Cairo proclaims the megacity to be anything but explosive. In the tomb myth, the city is hyper-passive—dead or ruthlessly repressed and thus quiescent. Often noting and blowing out of proportion the fact that some Cairenes reside in cemetery zones, internationals romanticize Cairo as 'The City of the Dead.' The city is depicted as a Saharan landscape of mummies and pyramid-crypts, an open-air museum of monuments, a veiled feminized site of submission, a seductive, deadly harem closed to outsiders, an impenetrable warren of Oriental alleyways and timeless urban peasant traditions, or a population of quiescent serfs ruled by despots. Middle Eastern dictators and kings, obsessed with national security and repressing internal diversity and dissent, strive to embody Arab states as rigid, monolithic national-security polities, and rarely critique these mythic bomb and tomb discourses. And so, fundamentalist jurists and millenarian religious extremists continue to preoccupy headlines, national policies, and research agendas worldwide. But just as political pundits depend on the bomb myth of Cairo's terroristic Arab street, so do the multi-billion dollar tourist and movie industries depend on the romantic myths of tombs and harems to lure visitors.

Neither of these meta-tropes or categories of popular narrative permit the development of a more nuanced recognition of the causes and contours of Cairo's activities, diversities, cruelties, contentions, and modern relevance. This lack of attention to Cairo's broader forms of agency has enabled the reproduction of essentialized misunderstandings of the larger Middle East region. As a result, global publics as well as those within the Middle East remain unfamiliar with the lives and concerns of many classes and forms of agency at work in the region, and incapable of imagining quotidian life and subjectivity. While inattention to the city and region abound, events in the last few years have challenged mythic meta-narratives, opened up scholarship on Cairo, and awakened international interest, leading to the development of richer, more grounded, more democratic investigations of the city, at least in the academic realm.

Shaking up and Rebuilding Qualitative Methodologies

In 1992 the devastating Cairo Earthquake temporarily shook some sense into international observers of the Middle East. The quake acted to tilt television cameras away from the geopolitics of war and fundamentalism, and down to the side streets of Cairo's urban communities. Starting with this quake coverage, global publics witnessed the spectacle of local NGOs, religious groups, and community networks rallying together to save individual homes and to reshape their shared, fractured, capital city. The Egyptian government feared this burst of autonomous effort and moved to shut down some of these highly efficient groups. But momentum for street-level change accelerated once again in 1994. In that year, Egypt's NGOs, Cairo's public spaces, and local religio-cultural debates attracted the world's spotlight as the United Nations World Conference on Population and Development (dubbed "the Cairo Conference") embraced the city. Alongside this momentary flourishing of globally articulated civil society in Egypt, several important critical movements blossomed within Egyptian and international academic circles, with Cairo as one of their key bases and research sites.

By the mid-1990s, Cairo had collected a large concentration of innovative researchers from across the region. As civil war, military siege, and repression made work very difficult in Algiers, Beirut, Khartoum, Baghdad, and Jerusalem, researchers, artists, and urbanists gathered in Cairo. U.S.-based researchers flooded Egypt as international funding and employment became more available following the Camp David Accords in 1978 and the Islamic revolution and war in Beirut closed off research in Iran and Lebanon. The French government also extended funding of urban studies and infrastructure projects in particular, as well as both traditional and more critical work on heritage, architecture, and culture. German research funding supported studies to redefine economic development, with greater attention to community agency, women's participation, and ecological concerns. Arab and Iranian intellectuals also gathered together in Cairo at this time, regenerating new, more dynamic Islamist, post-Islamist, as well as secular, feminist, and critical cosmopolitan frameworks.

These regrouped academics and activists, Arab scholars, and Middle East specialists who had resided in Cairo for many years, endowed with language skills, local knowledge, and experience in the region, attempted to counter the simplistic meta-narratives associated with 'the bomb and tomb,' as well as the stereotypes about Islamist extremism, veiled submission, and un-contested state repression. Many of the scholars that came together in the 1990s, some of whom formed this Cairo School were influenced by post-colonial studies where the agency of the colonized and those outside of the coteries of power were acknowledged in the context of a critical, engaged critique of spaces, power, institutions, and race/gender formations. Many participants were also influenced by post-modern and post-structuralist critiques that analyze power as circuits of practices, discourses, and disciplines that organize and animate societies, states, and subjectivities.

These scholars were also provoked by the contradictions of Egyptian life and meta-narratives, which they had to negotiate intellectually. As Susanne Rudolph reminds us, the interpretivist is likely "to present multiple takes on the truth or to make more modest claims about the level of confidence with which something can be known" (Rudolph 2005, 16). The Cairo School is comfortable with a certain amount of ambivalence in its representation and analysis of Cairene life. For example, while many would note the Egyptian state is omnipresent, with a huge civil service and military to enact its policies, at the same time it seems hopelessly incapable and enervated. While the agency of Cairenes might not lie within institutionalized arenas typically studied by political scientists, the residents of Cairo, in complicated and particular ways, have a history of influencing their surroundings, the identity of Cairo, and Egypt itself, despite the supposedly overwhelming presence and power of the central government (Singerman 1995).

There is an important link as well between our acknowledgment of ambivalence in the Cairo School and cosmopolitanism. Zygmunt Baumant argues that "Order and chaos are *modern* twins" (1991, 4). The dichotomy between order and disorder demands that the world be classified to achieve "a commodious filing cabinet that contains all the files that contain all the items that the world contains—but confines each file and each item within a separate place of its own . . . " (Bauman 1991, 2). This classificatory urge necessitates acts of inclusion which can by definition only occur in so far as other entities are excluded.

Ambivalence, "the possibility of assigning an object or an event to more than one category" utterly confuses and sabotages this modernist penchant for classification (Bauman 1991, 1). Bauman notes that "the other of the modern state is the no-man's or contested land: the under-or over-definition, the demon of ambiguity. Since the sovereignty of the modern state is the power to define and to make the definitions stick—everything that self-defines or eludes the power-assisted definition is subversive" (Bauman 1991, 8). James Scott's book, *Seeing Like a State* similarly notes the damning and destructive power of modernist planning and classificatory schemes (1999).

Cosmopolitanism, in one of its various incarnations, does have the potential to challenge category distinctions that wall the self off from class/national/gender/race others. Although we rigorously critique its elitist and neo-liberal incarnations, some perspectives on cosmopolitanism may still maintain a kernel of possibility—as a politics and ethics—bringing into the political sphere such notions as friendship, hospitality, cross-border interaction, equality with difference, peaceful cooperation, tolerance, extra-territoriality, and so on, which, when articulated with a thorough political-economic and social-history critique can have a mobilizing potential (Carter 2006).

Embracing ambivalence means privileging complexity and multiple frameworks and audiences, eschewing a variable-centric approach to social science where parsimony and universalism distort so much of our knowledge and judgment of the political world. It also sensitizes the social scientist to investigate, acknowledge, and represent the claims that marginalized communities are making. The massive public funds and international investment that have gone into promoting satellite and desert cities should not seduce us into ignoring the vast majority of Cairenes that live in 'ashwa'iyat or informal housing areas. The longevity of emergency law and the use of military courts to try civilians should not blind us to the complexity and autonomy of the Egyptian judicial system, which some brave lawyers and activists, from both secular and Islamist groups have used to strengthen their constitutional rights and political activism. An appreciation of ambivalence in the Cairo School allows us to understand both resurgent forms of monolithic Egyptian nationalism as well as the nascent Nubian identity movement. Elizabeth Smith argues that this movement is tackling racism in Egypt and the linguistic hegemony of Arabic, as Nubian intellectuals and writers open Nubian language schools and publish fiction in these dialects within a self-consciously *nationalistic* project of promoting the Egyptianness of Nubia.

It has been through qualitative social-science fieldwork, often historicized, that many of the scholars in this book have struggled to find new ways for learning about, analyzing, and spreading academic interest and public awareness about the new realities and challenges of contemporary Cairo. While long dominant in anthropology, research methods grounded in participatory fieldwork have been less accepted and encouraged in political science, economics, political economy, international relations, and some other social science sub-disciplines. One of the obvious benefits of fieldwork is that it goes beyond the textual record of official documents, journalism, and intellectual products, and allows researchers to hear and consider, with a critical, experienced ear, the perspectives of subaltern people whose voices and practices might not be recorded in official or public records, and whose practices might be misread, despised, criminalized, or ignored. We agree with critical science theorists like Flyvbjerg who see the social sciences as entirely dependent on contexts of interpretation, generating useful meaning rather than successful predictions. Thus our approaches move away from the reification of scientific knowledge or *episteme* and toward practical wisdom (an updated Aristotelian notion of *phronesis*) that is contextual, grounded in experience, and inextricably linked to the world and its concrete relations of power (Flyvbjerg 2001; Thiele 2000).

It is not that the voices of Cairenes are heard uncritically, since those voices are often as diverse, opaque, and contradictory as archival texts, statistical indicators, or political speeches may be. Rather, ethnography and even less intensive forms of field-based case studies encourage the researcher to explore and re-evaluate contexts for actions, behaviors, meanings, limitations, locations, and the structures through/under which people live. The emphasis on context and critical dialogue is essential to this approach and thus the Cairo School, and this volume, are inter-disciplinary. And our editorial process has insisted that each author's arguments and empirical material is accessible and understandable to those outside the author's field or national academic tradition.

Disciplinary Geopolitics

This collection emerged from a multi-national community of researchers who originally came together at the Centre d'études et de documentations économiques, juridiques et sociales (CEDEJ) in Cairo in the late 1990s. As a fraught, interdisciplinary collaboration, this volume reflects the locations, intersections, and collisions of divergent perspectives. Below the surface, this volume also reflects, occasionally, the national-security concerns that shaped research agendas in home countries. For example, U.S. scholars may start from the questions generated by the democratization studies paradigm, looking at civil society—theorized as a domain, between individuals and the state, of middle-class groupings, naturally inclined to push for liberal transformations. Or U.S. cultural scholars may start from the questions generated by the frameworks of human-rights advocacy, or the global movements for gender justice and sexual rights. French and Franco-Arab researchers are also a strong force within our group, building on their community's traditional strengths in urban planning, geography, 'space,' and sectarianism. These sub-disciplines in France did originate within colonial administrations; however, since the 1970s these fields have been radically reconstituted by Marxist geography and anti-colonial critical ethnography. Geographers trained in the French tradition do not accept 'public space' as a mere metaphor for bourgeois civil society, but insist on doing the detailed empirical fieldwork necessary to trace investment patterns, settlement flows, economic activities, and micro-political discourses that constitute the hierarchies and meanings of spaces and publics grounded in territories, bodies, and patterns of circulation. Researchers from other Arab countries, Iran, and Muslim Africa who contributed to this volume are also trained in and are aware of the uses and limits of European and American research agendas, but have pioneered in establishing distinct critical trajectories. Among this international group of Cairo-based researchers there is a new generation of Egyptian architects and planners, influenced by post-colonial studies, Islamic art and architecture studies, and the global-studies schools, as well as by movements critical of elite forms of globalization and essentialist and hypocritical forms of moral politics and revanchist nationalism.

This multinational, multidisciplinary Cairo School has aimed to forge a more nuanced, multi-level analysis of phenomena that strives to tie the mundane, common sensical, the everyday, and the local to global processes and flows without forgetting the geopolitics of war, terrorism, monopoly petro-capitalism, and resurgent Third World solidarity that make Cairo such a notorious, if misunderstood, megacity. The Cairo School challenges disciplinary divides between comparative politics and international relations, between anthropology and political science, and between urban planning, geography, and political economy. It is inter-disciplinary by nature, since the binaries of qualitative and quantitative research, the local and the global, the modern and the traditional impede understanding.

Spaces of Fieldwork
Within U.S. political science circles, a cyber movement has arisen in the last few years that shares many of the same commitments of the Cairo School. Sparked by a single anonymous e-mail manifesto in October 2000 from "Mr. Perestroika," the Perestroika movement is dedicated to freeing moribund political science from the domination of rational choice theory, formal theory, and quantitative and statistical methods (Norton 2002; Monroe 2005). This amorphous, uninstitutionalized movement, has critiqued the

privileging of large-N, statistical, theory-driven, and cross-national studies in political science, and the disparagement of studies that rely upon culturally specific ethnographic and qualitative field work, historical research, and/or normative research on contemporary problems. As Gregory Kasza explains, a "technicism—the tendency to treat the means of research as more significant than the ends—has infected the discipline" (Kasza 2002, 4). It also urges more "problem-driven" rather than "method-driven" research that builds on an incremental approach to knowledge and addresses political realities in useful ways, rather than exploring theory and generating method games that dismiss social, policy, and justice implications and commitments (Shapiro 2005).

On a parallel track, students in Europe launched the "post-autistic economics" movement and network (*www.paecon.net*) in protest against neo-classical economics, attacking the fundamentalism hiding behind the 'objective' number-crunching of the Washington Consensus and neo-liberal economic methods that serve as the backbone of World Bank and IMF prescriptions. The 'post-autistics' championed the return of qualitative, politically emancipatory methods, including structuralist/world-system analyses, dependency theories, etc. They argued that the "uncontrolled use" of neo-classical economics, and the treatment of mathematics as "an end in itself," led to economics becoming "an 'autistic science,' lost in 'imaginary worlds.'" This movement called for methodological pluralism, ethnographic political economy, and reforms to "rescue economics from its autistic and socially irresponsible state" (Fullbrook 2002). Whether in France, the United States, or Egypt, academic communities at the end of the twentieth century reacted to the universalist pretensions of hyper-rationalistic and neo-classical social sciences that ignored issues of cultural contestation, colonial histories and continuities, gender/race/sexuality formation, historical specificity, and social-geographic context. This volume, we hope, will offer both academic and non-academic audiences an example of the strengths of a set of normative projects inspired by the passions of the U.S. academic Perestroika movement, the European post-autistic economics movement, as well as much more dynamic approaches to vernacular space, urban inequality and socio-religious identity emerging from Egyptian, South Asian, and African academic milieus.

Cosmopolitanism: Conflicting Legacies and Methodologies in Cairo

It was Europe—a region repeatedly devastated and reconstituted by massive wars and the repercussions of disintegrating empires—that was the site for the most crucial world predicaments of the 20th century. But in the 21st century the fulcrum of world politics has shifted geographically to the Middle East (and secondarily to South Asia). As a result, a special challenge arises for progressive intellectuals: how should we, both as citizens of specific countries and as individuals dedicated to global justice, situate ourselves usefully in the problematics of the region, learning about and engaging with the struggles of the area in ways that encourage democratic tendencies and cosmopolitan appreciations, with a central goal of avoiding the tragedies of the last century during the twilight of a Eurocentric world order that featured the horrors of colonialism, war, fanatical nationalism, state terror on massive scale, and ideological extremism. Richard Falk (2005).

The phenomenon of labor migration, Dubai investment in shopping malls and media cities, international tourism in Egypt, and the cultural influence of Gulf media outlets and entertainers, are only some examples of the ways in which Cairo has become more cosmopolitan. But in a land still full of rage and resentment against forms of colonialism and imperialism that flaunted themselves as vehicles of cosmopolitan culture, what possible progressive use does the term have for us?

Nostalgic views of cosmopolitanism are resurgent in today's Middle East. Urban luxury developers and speculators, and well-intentioned liberals celebrate a golden age of nineteenth and early-twentieth century epochs of urban multicultural heritage. But they ignore or downplay the colonial contexts of these histories, and their antecedents in exoticist and racializing "world's fair" displays (Mitchell 1991). They also ignore the mechanisms of exclusion, violence, hierarchy, and exploitation that were naturalized through the construction of ethnic and cultural sub-group identity, which generated the rigid identity distinctions taken up by hyper-nationalism, pogroms, civil conflict, mass exodus, and even genocide and the evacuation of communities such as the Armenians, Kurds, or Jews across the Middle East (Öncü 2005). Today's celebration of cultural pluralism in Ottoman Istanbul or Beirut, or in the belle époque empires of Britain and France can risk repeating their violence if a thorough critique of cosmopolitanism is not engaged. However, this cannot end in justifying a return to vulgar forms of majoritarian nationalism or rigid nativism. Multiculturalism and cosmopolitanism have other futures in the Middle East.

Among the various forms of cosmopolitanism competing with 'multicultural heritage-ism' to define the culture of globalization in the region, we also find the powerful and sometimes overlapping discourse of Persian Gulf petrol-cosmopolitanism. Based in the Gulf Emirate of Dubai and the neighboring monarchies, and radiating throughout regional networks of planners, designers, satellite media, and consumer promotions, petrol-cosmopolitanism is grounded in a contradictory game. This form of cosmopolitanism advocates an aesthetic Islamism of architectural spaces and design motifs, while waging war against militarized Islamism and its socio-political agendas. Petrol-cosmopolitans advocate neo-Islamist architectural trends for elite consumers of villas, office parks, and shopping malls, while collaborating with the U.S. to ruthlessly repress Islamist radicalism (see Elsheshtawy, chapter 7, and Abaza in this volume). Exploiting a world of male labor migrants and female domestic workers, but dispensing with the concept of citizenship, petrol-cosmopolitan states maintain a system of guest-worker apartheid that the U.S. and France are now moving to emulate. It is not yet clear that Egypt wants to embrace this model, or can afford to. Heritage cosmopolitanism, multicultural nostalgia, and petrol-state globalisms dominate the new terrains in which Cairo persists today. But these forms do not exhaust post-nationalist politics, or foreclose the struggle to develop counter-hegemonic emancipatory cosmopolitanism.

This volume uses the term cosmopolitan in its title to draw attention to the world-scale cultural claims and nostalgia of elite projects, but also to shift debates toward questions of agency (of elites as well as subalterns), and to processes of vernacular world-making among Cairenes that may not constitute resistance at all, but which do reconstitute worlds that cross or challenge class, urban, and national borders. Today, Cairenes daily, literally, and virtually transcend national boundaries. They surf the internet, become migrants and interact with tourists, shop in global tax-free zones or in informal markets of pirated commodities, seek refuge from wars or volunteer to fight in them, learn foreign languages and internet technologies, drink cappuccinos in malls, eat at McDonald's, revolt against their government's alliance with Israel, and are tortured with the implicit help of U.S. military assistance and anti-terrorist intelligence services.

We do not use the term cosmopolitan in its classical sense, which referred to Kant's ideal of belonging to a world community, whose universalist humanitarian ideals would ensure peace (Robbins 1998, 2). We prefer Rabinow's understanding of the term since he emphasizes "an ethos of macro-interdependencies, with an acute consciousness (often forced upon people) of the inescapabilities and particularities of places, characters, historical trajectories, and fates" (Rabinow 1986, 258 as cited by Robbins, 1998, 1). In this sense, as Cairo becomes increasingly culturally porous, economically interdependent, and politically induced into more universalistic economic and legal orders (such as the international, bilateral, and regional conventions on trade, investment, intellectual property rights, or human rights law), it becomes more globalized—which raises new political opportunities for some, and exclusion or resistance for others. Labdaoui argues that universalist norms "impos[e] criteria of classification regardless of local will and interests. It is a grammar which crosses national frontiers and which is scornful of national, cultural, or political considerations" (Labdaoui 2003, 148).

An "emergent post-colonial cosmopolitanism" which Benita Parry sees as a result of the "'global flows' of transnational cultural traffic" is at the heart of Sadek's chapter in this book where he describes the rapid rise of Gulf satellite news and entertainment channels, such as Al Jazeera, or the stars from Saudi Arabia, Lebanon, and Morocco who still flock to Cairo to make their careers, but who now sing in their own dialects, and use stylists or dancers from Lebanon in their video-clips, which are then beamed by satellite to the region and the Arab diaspora market in Europe, America, or Africa (Parry 1991, 41 as cited by Robbins 1998, 1). Said argues in his chapter that a pan-Arabist union has been achieved culturally on the streets, websites, and billboards of Cairo and other Middle East metropolises.

Cosmopolitanism of Fools and Traitors?

Why has cosmopolitanism as a socio-political appeal, or a methodology for analyzing identity, been identified with colonial elitism? How can we get beyond this?

If patriotic security nationalism in the U.S. drove new forms of imperialism in the twenty-first century, is it possible that cosmopolitanism in Egypt can drive anti-imperialism today? We cannot forget that during the era of British colonialism in Egypt (1880s–1930s), considered the golden age of cosmopolitanism by some, the Middle Eastern "cosmopolis" was a city of legal and racial barriers and structural violence (see Zubaida 1999, Vitalis forthcoming). Yet, liberal nationalists in the 1920s and 1930s encouraged an embrace of Egyptian agency within cosmopolitanism, rediscovering proud histories of multiple, intersectional globalisms, such as their appreciation for a Mediterranean or pharaonic, or even Hellenistic identity (Zubaida 1999, 27). During the 1940s, cosmopolitanism was violated by the brutalities of World War II and betrayed by colonial powers and their allies, who forged utilitarian and strategic alliances with Israel. After Nasser and other post-colonial leaders came to power, international law was betrayed as the world community failed to implement UN resolutions relating to Israeli military occupation and the colonization of Egyptian, Syrian, Lebanese, and Palestinian lands, making it very difficult to combine the defense of Arab national dignity with faith in cosmopolitan justice and universal legal norms. In this context, those who battle for progressive cosmopolitanism are accused of foolishness, treason, and of prostituting the nation.

The debate about class and insider/outsider or foreign/native status, is certainly not new. De Koning suggests in this volume, "In Cairo, familiarity with the significant outside, *barra*, and the adoption of explicitly cosmopolitan styles has long since been a marker of elite status." Clearly, there is an emerging new cosmopolitan sense of belonging, whether that means the increased use of English in daily speech or product advertising as Abaza and de Koning note, or gender mixing in leisure activities, residence in gated communities, or watching films in expensive theaters, as Armbrust describes. Cairo is globalized for all of its citizens, but what this means is less a democratization of cosmopolitanism than the hardening of a new hierarchy of access to certain kinds of activities. Armbrust in this volume points out a seismic shift in the economic and political center of gravity in Cairo. In his research on popular culture, films, and film spectatorship, he finds that the "rituals of movie-going, dominated in downtown Cairo for a few brief decades by downwardly mobile middle class male youth, are gradually being set aside for a wealthier class defined by their access to Gulf or European economic standards. The fate of the downtown movie audience therefore is a microcosm for broader processes that marginalize everyone restricted to the national public sphere."

As the poverty line has risen in the 1990s, de Koning points to a new bourgeoisie and relatively affluent professional upper-middle class that "finds work in a small, yet significant internationally oriented top segment of the labor market" where "wages tend to be three to five times higher than those paid in similar occupations in the 'less modern' sectors of the formal economy, including the large public sector and civil service" (Assaad and Rouchdy 1999; Nagy 2001).

Egypt's demography is now shaped by a youth bulge and the largest cohort of adolescents (10–19 years of age) in its history; many young people are left on the lower rung of this cosmopolitan hierarchy as post-Infitah ('Open Door') economic policies leaves them among the most unemployed in the nation. The rate of youth unemployment in 1998 was triple that of total unemployment in Egypt and it is not surprising that young people have flocked to newly emerging protest movements (Yousef 2003, 14). Armbrust argues that after male youth took over the movie theaters in the late 1980s, the downtown film district had lost favor in the eyes of cultural gatekeepers. "Elites willfully mischaracterized these young men as a barbarian invasion of lower-class 'tradesmen,' thereby obfuscating a phenomenon that was, in reality, connected to a broad downgrading of middle-class fortunes in the post-Nasser era."

Nevertheless, surprisingly, after three generations of conflict, sixty years since the traumatic end of World War II, when the European powers betrayed their colonized Arab allies, making fools out of the advocates of Euro-cosmopolitan solidarity, the case is alive for more vernacular, less elitist, non-Eurocentric cosmopolitanisms in the Middle East. Cosmopolitan discourse is no longer limited to the circles of liberal elites spinning utopian Mediterranean heritage narratives, or to the bastions of neo-colonial millionaires justifying five-star contractor projects and consumer marketing schemes. Of course these forms of exclusive, cruel cosmopolitanism are stronger than ever. But also new forms of cosmopolitanism in the Middle East are crawling back to the margins of the public sphere in the shape of subversive, grounded, fierce, world-weary articulations.

Cosmopolitanism from Below: From Identity Politics to Critical Conviviality

In *The Wretched of the Earth*, Franz Fanon points us to the need to look for popular protagonism, and the process of socio-political change in a "series of local engagements [. . .] and none of these are decisive. [. . .] Consciousness slowly dawns upon truths that are only partial, limited and unstable [. . .] Each local ebb and tide will be used to review the question from the standpoint [. . .] of all political networks" (Fanon 1963, 140 as cited by Bhabha 2001, [39]).

Homi Bhabha in his essay, "Unsatisfied: Notes on Vernacular Cosmopolitanism," interprets Fanon as offering a glimpse of cosmopolitical praxis that does not strive for utopia (an elite transcendence of local attachments), nor for revolution (the elimination of all injustice through annihilation). Offering an alternative, Fanon insists that the "wretched" are agents positioned in a dynamic, structurally violent, but ultimately open fabric of power in which nuanced, crafty cultural politics is possible, and necessary. These efforts need to challenge the limits of rigid self-victimizing puritanism and reject the policing of narrow, fixed identities. Through Fanon, Bhabha sees a kind of active cosmopolitanism in the critical engagement of the living present, asking "How do we think this relation of locality whose every ebb and flow requires the re-inscription of global relations" (Bhabha 2001, 40)?

Certain critical cosmopolitan analyses of globalization stemming from transnational studies of migration and colonialism in Latin America and the Caribbean, for example, highlight the coloniality of globalization. Rather than fall back into a simple nationalist rejection of the foreign to rescue national identity, this school of critical cosmopolitan studies struggles to reclaim and decolonize the notion of conviviality, grounded in what Walter Mignolo calls "border thinking," that is, consciousness of how identities and differences are made, remade, embodied, culturally naturalized, and hierarchically organized (Mignolo 2000).

For Richard Sennett, this border thinking is not an obsession with limitation, but the precondition to human openness. In his darker cosmopolitan vision, concern for others, the possibility of conviviality "arises from recognizing the insufficiencies of the self . . . the fractures, self-destructiveness and irresolvable conflicts of desires within ourselves which . . . will prompt us to cross boundaries. . . . Openness to the needs of others comes from ceasing to dream of the world made whole" (1994, 13).

Paul Gilroy in *Post-colonial Melancholia* suggests that forms of border-thinking can allow urban communities, as well as socio-political theorists, to reach beyond the zero-sum game of divisive, essentialist multicultural identity politics that sometimes can reinforce the fetishistic legacies of racial colonial-modernity, without interrogating the power relations and hierarchies that reproduce and hide behind the masks of autarkic religious, racial and ethnic figurations (Gilroy 2005).

This new turn in the practice and analysis of identity politics—critically engaging the coloniality of identification—is very different from conservative, depoliticizing approaches that promote 'gender blindness,' 'race blindness,' or radically rejectionist, secular approaches to religious identity. Ignoring or repressing the real power of embodied identities, or encapsulating them in a pre-political realm of rigid multiculturalist cubicles, it seems, has the same effects as parallel attempts to keep religion or radicalism out of politics. Keeping identity in the realm of cultural purity rather than public creativity ensures that it remains a tool for internal colonialism, not emancipation.

Cosmopolitan Hierarchies, Egyptian Identities, and Heritage

The hierarchies structured by global processes, international dependency, and state policies in post-Infitah Egypt have not foreclosed dynamics of social and cultural contestation. Various subnational identities and critiques of forms of Egyptian national homogeneity promoted by the state and the official cultural establishment continue to emerge in Cairo, as Puig, Miller, Smith, Colonna, and Madoeuf suggest in this volume. Yet, these strategies to re-write Egyptian identity are not portrayed as local 'responses' to the global or national, but as themselves enmeshed in transnational processes, national popular movements and state factions, and urban geopolitics. For example, in Miller's chapter, Upper Egyptians are redefining their sense of 'asabiyya, or solidarity based on a common lineage, to celebrate their regional origin in the southern part of the country, which is not only the poorest and least developed, but typically lampooned by Cairenes as populated by backward, stupid, stubborn people. No matter how wealthy or politically powerful Upper Egyptians (Sa'idi) become, they are nevertheless collectively identified with poor unskilled migrants and with the stigmatized perception of the 'ashwa'iyat (informal housing settlements where they have largely settled in the post-Infitah era) as the locus of extremism, crime, and poverty. Yet, the regional identity that Upper Egyptians are embracing and promoting in their quest for political and communal leadership is itself also influenced by their experience of migration, since the Gulf urban model value in Saudi Arabia or Kuwait values the tribe as one of the most authentic and legitimate type of social organization and uses a tribal rhetoric that privileges blood origin and genealogy as a challenge to Egypt's modernist discourse, which ignores ethnicity and difference (Shryock 1997).

Both Miller and Smith in this volume point out that Egypt's strong centralist and nationalist identity, promoted by Nasserism as well as neoliberalism in different forms, has prohibited public expression and political expression of any kind of communalism, whether based on religion (the Copts for example), region (Upper Egypt), or ethnicity (non-Arab Nubians). Yet, Nubian intellectuals and activists, Upper Egyptians, working-class Cairenes, and even members of Sufi brotherhoods, struggle to assert themselves. They fight to have dark-skinned Egyptians and Nubians represented in the visual media, or veiled women for that matter, and to revive the Nubian languages of Kanzi and Fadicca, to promote an Upper Egyptian identity (honor, solidarity, piety, respect for elders, kin solidarity) as an antidote to the more Westernized, Cairene elite, or to continue the popular religious festivals (*mulids*) of Sufi brotherhoods despite the increasingly tight control of crowds that the police enforce. The celebrations of saints' birthdays by Sufi brotherhoods in Husayn or Sayyida Zaynab valorize neglected quarters of the city and enhance feelings of belonging; in a sense, as Madoeuf suggests, space is woven into the collective memory through these important annual festivals. Many of the six million men who are members of Sufi brotherhoods in Egypt pour into Cairo to participate, strengthening their own religious commitments and cultural practices, as well as remaking the streets of popular areas into an almost carnival-like atmosphere where social norms are temporarily suspended and where women and youth can carve out spheres for collective expression, pleasure, and identity transformation.

Outside the *mulid* season, Cairo's streets host a series of struggles and innovations in the musical and public sphere. Egyptians in the popular classes, many of whom live in *'ashwa'iyat* continue to buy the cassettes of their musical stars, who celebrate their identity and problems as they sing at weddings, street festivals, and parties, despite the condemnation of these popular musicians by the official cultural establishment, since they are seen as too vulgar or politically problematic. Nevertheless, their popularity "reinforces the cultural presence of the urban masses in the public sphere," as Puig suggests in this volume.

It is struggles over the public sphere, spatially, politically, and culturally which many of our chapters delineate. El Kadi and ElKerdany's chapter describes the way in which architects, intellectuals, state officials, urban planners, and scholars have revitalized Egypt's nineteenth- and early twentieth-century downtown *(wust al-balad)* by renovating and restoring its period buildings and seeking official protection, which serves to broaden and diversify Egypt's notion of its national heritage—into a sense of heritages. As they point out, the heritization process itself has always been very politicized, as distinct elite groupings and working-class communities identify with different historical epochs, monuments, and relics, and inhabit, use, and interact with them in different ways. These struggles with the state and contested identities have made important inroads where a rough cosmopolitanism from below emerges from a diverse set of activists, artists, scholars, intellectuals, entertainers, and community leaders in Cairo.

Conclusion

The ethnographic and case-study commitments of the Cairo School, discussed above, bring us back to the people in Cairo and Egypt that have taught us to understand this megacity, if only partially. All of us in this volume have spent years learning about Cairo, have lived there, and learned from its residents to understand its complexity and the nuances which surround our objects of study. The ability of Cairenes to negotiate their political, economic, and social worlds is remarkable. Yet, the obstacles that they face continue to be formidable. The ambivalence that we recognize in this collection restrains our ability to present firm conclusions or predictions about Cairo. We have to ask—Cairo, for whom, in whose interest, and in whose name? Grounding our questions in urban space brings debates about globalization and cartographies of redistribution, to use Omnia El Shakry's term, to a very concrete level. We can see the ways in which satellite cities have become an important hub of manufacturing industries, while workers still refuse to move there but continue to commute long distances from their homes in the urban core of Cairo or in the *'ashwa'iyat*. We can see the ways in which *'ashwa'iyat* have mushroomed in size and become more concentrated in the last few decades, though they still do not secure government services in proportion to the size of their populations. We can see how Dubai financing and models have created new industrial and commercial parks that ring Cairo, as well as luxury malls only accessible by car, for those who can afford one. We can see historic areas in Cairo being renovated to appeal to the lucrative tourist market that is a critical earner of foreign exchange, while people are fenced out of formerly public spaces. We can see how the economic logic and social fabric of old markets and industrial areas in Cairo is being radically altered to make way for tourist buses, the gaze of tourists, and their cultural aesthetics, without the support or participation of local communities.

Everyday decisions about the issues we have described are made by the Egyptian government, aid agencies, military and security agencies, foreign embassies, religious and financial institutions. The power of policy and the decision to deploy budget resources, investment, armies, police forces, expertise, media images, and mass fear takes a tremendous toll, of course, on those struggling to articulate alternatives. These deployments may also penetrate and reconstitute these subordinated alternatives. But this volume reveals this process of reconstruction as messy and open-ended. Nevertheless, changing these decisions and deployments, and making policy changes is a priority, and this research agenda hopes to facilitate the generation of alternatives.

While we have noted the agency and creativity of Cairenes, and the possibilities for alternatives, we have also outlined many of the obstacles to the ideals of cosmopolitanism. As Sheldon Wolin suggests, we are less concerned with prediction, than we are with posting warnings. While similar to predictions, in some respect, warnings differ in two important respects. "In the first place, a warning implies an unpleasant or undesirable consequence, while a scientific prediction is neutral. Secondly, a warning is usually made by a person who feels some involvement with the person or party being warned; a warning, in short, tokens a commitment that is lacking in predictions (Wolin 2004, 13–14). As national actors in our own countries and as scholars, we have the self-conscious obligation to communicate, to analyze, and to warn about the danger of sustained political and economic exclusion in Cairo supported by a militarized security state and its allies.[5]

We began this chapter with a somewhat optimistic assessment of the movement saying "Enough" to authoritarianism that embraced some of the ideals of democratic cosmopolitanism. The boisterous street demonstrations in 2005, built on earlier political organizing, nudged the Mubarak regime to allow presidential contestation and fairer parliamentary elections in November 2005. While the government's National Democratic Party prevailed in these elections, the Egyptian public did begin to articulate claims for legality, participation, and representation more persuasively, furthering its ability to mobilize supporters. But the security forces, autocratic political leadership, and the financial power of the state and international backers continued to divide and weaken emerging groups. Yet Cairenes became more savvy in exploiting ambivalence, contradictions, and political opportunities. As the façade of the omnipotent state cracked even further, many subnational, political, cultural, and religious sensibilities began to be able to articulate claims and goals.

We hope that these chapters will clarify why it makes no sense to think of Cairo either as a tomb or a bomb, or to read the street as a dangerous mob. These chapters interrogate the diversity of Cairo, the agency of its residents, and the interplay of global flows with a variety of other forces. Our authors have worked hard to explain the complexity of Cairo in a manner that is accessible and understandable, out of a concern that so much of the lives, struggles, and joys of people in the Middle East are so superficially understood, or recklessly mystified outside of the region. Our modest attempt is not to present a universalizing, comprehensive narrative of Cairo, but to suggest that vernacular cosmopolitanism is increasing in Egypt, despite the intense obstacles before Egyptians. Egyptians—and their assembled exiles, expatriates, and international allies—are repositioning themselves to struggle with the constantly shifting environment and build creative political strategies for their future. But economic, military, and spatial structures, and transnationally empowered mobilizations for increased speculation, autarky, fear-mongering, and repression are also on the rise. In the following chapters we hope to begin to make sense of the city that holds our local histories and global commitments, our Cairo Cosmopolitan.

Works Cited

AlSayyad, Nezar, Irene Bierman and Nasser Rabat. 2005. *Making Cairo Medieval*. New York: Lexington Books.

Anderson-Gold, Sharon. 2001. *Cosmopolitanism and Human Rights*. Cardiff: University of Wales.

Assaad, Ragui and Malak Rouchdy. 1999. "Poverty and Poverty Alleviation Strategies in Egypt." *Cairo Papers in Social Science* 22: 1.

Bauman, Zymunt. 1999. *Modernity and Ambivalence*. Ithaca, NY: Cornell University Press.

Bayat, Asef. 2003. "The 'Street' and the Politics of Dissent in the Arab World." *Middle East Report* (Spring). *<http://www.merip.org/mer/ mer226/226_bayat.html>*. Visited 10 October, 2005.

Beattie, Andrew. 2005. *Cairo: A Cultural History*. New York: Oxford University Press.

Bhabha, Homi. 2001. "Unsatisfied: Notes on Vernacular Cosmopolitanism." In *Postcolonial Discourses: An Anthology*, ed. Gregory Castle

Bianca, Stefano and Philip Jodido, eds. 2004. *Cairo: Revitalizing a Historic Metropolis*. Turin, Italy: The Agha Khan Trust for Culture.

Carter, April. 2006. *The Political Theory of Global Citizenship*. London: Routledge.

Denis, Eric and Séjourné Marion. 2002. *ISIS Information System for Informal settlements*. Draft report for the Urban Research Participatory Urban Management Program, Ministry of Planning & German Technical Co-operation (GTZ) & Observatoire urbain du Caire Contemporain (OUCC), unpublished.

"Egyptian Opposition Continues Sit-in." 2005. Aljazeera.net 31 July. *http://english.aljazeera.net/NR/exeres/1D78B343-BAD3-45C6-BBD2-DE3CCFBE5F06.htm. Visited 30 October 2005.*

Falk, Richard. 2005. Comments delivered at an Editorial Board Meeting of *Middle East Report*, in Santa Barbara California, May. Transmitted by personal communication.

Fanon, Franz. 1963. *The Wretched of the Earth*. New York: Grove Widenfeld.

Flyvbjerg, Bent. 2001. *Making Social Science Matter: Why Social Inquiry Fails and How it Can Succeed Again*. Cambridge: Cambridge University Press.

Fulbrook, Edward. 2002. "The Post-Autistic Economics Movement: A Brief History." *Journal of Australian Political Economy* 50 (December). *<http:// www.jape.org/jape200212.htm>*. Visited 11 November, 2005.

Gertel, Jorg. 1997. *Kairo. Nahrungssicherheit und Verwundbarkeit im Kontext der Globalisierung*. Unpublished Habilitation Thesis, University of Freiburg.

al-Ghobashy, Mona. 2005. "Egypt Looks Ahead to Portentous Year." *Middle East Report Online* 2 Feb 2005. *<http://www.merip.org/mero/mero020205. html>*. Visited 30 October, 2005.

Gilroy, Paul. 2005. *Post-colonial Melancholia*. New York: Columbia University Press.

Golia, Maria. 2004. *Cairo: City of Sand*. London: Reaktion.

Kasza, Gregory J. 2002. "Deserves Got Nothin' to Do with It: Perestroika and the Nature of Ideas in Today's Academy." Council on Comparative

Studies Working Paper #2, American University, 5 November. <*http://
www.american.edu/academic.depts/ccs/workingpaperkasza.pdf*>. Visited 10
October, 2005.

Khouri, Rami G. 2004. "Set up an Independent Arab Human Development
Center." *Beirut Daily Star,* 22 December. *http://www.dailystar.com.lb/article.
asp?edition_id=10&categ_id=5&article_id=11197* Visited 15 January, 2006.

Isin, Engin. 2005. "Bombs, Bodies, Bits: Acts, Claims, Struggle." Paper
presented at "Cities and Globalization: Challenges to Citizenship"
Conference. Heinrich Böll Foundation, Institute Français du Proche-
Orient. December 9–11, Beirut.

Ismail, Salwa. 2002. *Rethinking Islamist Politics: Culture, the State and Islamism*
London: I.B. Tauris.

Labdaoui, Abdellah. 2003. "Universality, Modernity and Identity: The Case
of Morocco." In *Cosmopolitanism, Identity and Authenticity in the Middle
East*, Roel Meijer, ed., 145–58. London: Routledge Curzon.

Mahmood, Saba. 2005. *Politics of Piety: The Islamic Revival and the Feminist
Subject*. Princeton, N.J.: Princeton University Press.

Malkki, Lisa. 1992. "National Geographic: the Rooting of Peoples and the
Territorialization of National Identity among Scholars and Refugees."
Cultural Anthropology 7 (February).

"Mideast Climate Change." 2005. *New York Times* 3 March. <*http://coranet.
radicalparty.org/pressreview/print_right.php?func=detail&par=12513*>
Visited 10 January, 2006.

Mignolo, Walter. 2000. "The Many Faces of Cosmo-Polis: Border Thinking
and Critical Cosmopolitanism." *Public Culture* 12 (Fall 2000): 723–41.

Mitchell, Tim. 1991. *Colonising Egypt*. Berkeley: University of California Press.
_____. 2002. *Rule of Experts: Egypt Techno-Politics and Modernity*. Berkeley:
University of California Press.

Monroe, Kristin. 1991. "Theory of Rational Action: What Is It? How Useful
Is It for Political Science?" In *Political Science: Looking to the Future, Vol. 1*,
ed. William Crotty. Evanston, IL: Northwestern University Press.

Monroe, Kristen Renwick. 2005. *Perestroika: The Raucous Rebellion in Political
Science*. New Haven, C.T.: Yale University Press.

Nagi, Saad Z. 2001. Poverty in Egypt: Human Needs and Institutional
Capacities. Lanham, MD: Lexington Books.

Nussbaum, Martha. 1994. "Patriotism and Cosmopolitanism." *Boston Review*
19 (October/November).

Öncü, Ayshe. 2005. "Global Discourses of Multiculturalism and Political
Claims to Istanbul's Present/Past." Paper presented at "Cities and

Globalization: Challenges to Citizenship" Conference. Heinrich Böll Foundation, Institute Français du Proche-Orient. December 9–11, Beirut.

Parry, Benita. 1991. "The Contradictions of Cultural Studies." *Transition* 53 (1991).

"Protests Mar Mubarak Win." 2005. Al-Jazeera.net 11 Sept *<http://english. aljazeera.net/NR/exeres/4BB84C5D-63A8-4B00-9CAC-09412FAF82E0.htm>*. Visited10 January, 2006.

Rabinow, Paul. 1986. "Representations are Social Facts." In *Writing Culture: The Poetics and Politics of Ethnography*, James Clifford and George Marcus, eds., Berkeley: University of California Press.

Raymond, André. 2000. *Cairo*. trans. Willard Wood. Cambridge: Harvard University Press.

Riis, Jacob. 1890. *How the Other Half Lives: Studies Among the Tenements of New York*. New York: Scribners.

Robbins, Bruce. 1998. "Introduction Part 1: Actually Existing Cosmopolitanism." In *Cosmpolitics: Thinking and Feeling beyond the Nation*, Pheng Cheah and Bruce Robbins, eds., 1–19. Minneapolis: University of Minnesota Press.

Rodenbeck, Max. 2000. *Cairo: The City Victorious*. New York: Vintage.

Rudolph, Susanne Hoeber. 2005. "Perestroika and Its Other." In *Perestroika: The Raucous Rebellion in Political Science*, Kristen Renwich Monroe, ed., 12–20. New Haven, C.T.: Yale University Press.

Said, Mohamed Sayyid. 2003. "Cosmopolitanism and Cultural Autarky in Egypt." In *Cosmopolitanism, Identity and Authenticity in the Middle East*, Roel Meijer, ed., 183–96. London: Routledge Curzon.

Sassen, Saskia. 2001. *The Global City*. Princeton, N.J.: Princeton University Press.

Scott, James C. 1999. *Seeing Like a State : How Certain Schemes to Improve the Human Condition Have Failed*. New Haven, C.T.: Yale University Press.

Sennett, Richard. 1994. "Christian Cosmopolitanism." *Boston Review* 19/5 (October/November): 13.

Shapiro, Ian. 2005. *The Flight from Reality in the Human Sciences*. Princeton, N.J.: Princeton University Press.

Sims, David. 2003. *"Cairo, Egypt. Understanding Slums: Case Studies for the Global Report on Human Settlements*. United Nations Human Settlements Programme *(UN-Habitat)* and the Development Planning Unit *(DPU)*, University College London. *<http://www.ucl.ac.uk/dpu-projects/Global_ Report/cities/cairo.htm>*. Visited 9 January, 2006.

Singerman, Diane. 1995. *Avenues of Participation: Family, Politics, and Networks in Urban Quarters of Cairo.* Princeton, N.J.: Princeton University Press.

Singerman, Diane and Barbara Ibrahim. 2001. "The Cost of Marriage in Egypt: A Hidden Variable in the New Arab Demography and Poverty Research." Special Edition on "The New Arab Family," Nick Hopkins, ed. *Cairo Papers in the Social Sciences*, 24 (Spring): 80–116.

Shryock, Andrew. 1997. *Nationalism and the Genealogical Imagination: Oral History and Textual Authority in Tribal Jordan.* Berkeley: University of California Press.

"Something Stirs." *The Economist* 3 March, 2005 *http://www.mafhoum.com/press7/230s21.htm.* Visited 13 January, 2006.

Thiele, Les. 2000. "Review of *Making Social Science Matter: Why Social Inquiry Fails and How it Can Succeed Again.*" *Journal of Politics* 64: 274–76.

Wolin, Sheldon S. 2004. *Politics and Vision : Continuity and Innovation in Western Political Thought.* Princeton, N.J.: Princeton University Press.

Yousef, Tarik. 2003. "Youth in the Middle East and North Africa: Demography, Employment, and Conflict." In *Youth Explosion in Developing World Cities: Approaches to Reducing Poverty and Conflict in an Urban Age,* eds. Blair A. Ruble, Joseph S. Tulchin, Diana H. Varat with Lisa M. Hanley, 9–24. Washington D.C.: Woodrow Wilson International Center for Scholars.

UN-Habitat. 2001. *Cities in a Globalizing World: Global Report on Human Settlements.* London: Earthscan Publications Ltd.

Vitalis, Robert. Forthcoming, 2006. "Alexandria Without Illusions." In *Cosmopolitan Alexandria*, Deborah Starr, ed. Syracuse, NY: Syracuse University Press.

Zubaida, Sami. 1999. "Cosmopolitanism in the Middle East." In *Cosmopolitan Identity and Authenticity in the Middle East*, ed. Roel Meijer, 15–34. London: Routledge Curzon.

Notes

1 Istanbul may have approached or surpassed the size of Greater Cairo; but the Turkish city in the early twenty-first century emphasized its place in the European region, downplaying its Middle-Eastern, Mediterranean, and other regional affinities.

2 A 'megacity' is an urban agglomeration (a city, suburbs, and greater metropolitan region) that includes more than ten million people.

3 See Raymond 2000; Rodenbeck 2000, Beattie 2005, Ahmed 2000, Golia 2004, Bianca and Jodido 2004, Myntti 2000, AlSayyad, Bierman, and Rabat 2005,

Mitchell 1991 and 2002, Singerman 1995, Ghannam 2002, Mahmoud 2005, Ismail 2002, Hoodfar 1997, and Kienle 2001.

4   Definitions of the metropolitan region of Greater Cairo vary considerably, leading to a wide variation in population estimates. Cairo's population makes up one-quarter of Egypt's total population. Thirty-three percent of Cairo's population is under the age of 15, and 48.8 percent are females. See Sims 2003, 3. "Cairo, Egypt" *Understanding Slums: Case Studies for the Global Report on Human Settlements* (UN-Habitat 2003). *<http://www.ucl.ac.uk/dpu-projects/Global_Report/ cities/cairo.htm>*. Visited 9 January, 2006.

5   This insight was made quite convincingly by Professor Mona Harb of the American University of Beirut in a concluding session of the "Cities and Globalization: Challenges to Citizenship" conference, Heinrich Böll Foundation, Institute Français du Proche-Orient. December 9–11, Beirut.

Cairo
The City Cosmopolitan

1 Cairo as Neoliberal Capital?

From Walled City to Gated Communities

Eric Denis

Insecurity and a Land of Dreams

Ahmed Ashraf al-Mansuri will not be slowed down too much by traffic this evening.[1] His chauffeur is without equal for sinuously extricating him from the agitation of the inner city. Blowing the horn and winking to the police, the driver climbs up the on-ramp and merges onto the new elevated beltway. He dashes quickly westward, toward the new gated city in the once-revolutionary Sixth of October settlement. Without so much as a glance, Mr. al-Mansuri has skimmed over that unknown world where peasants are packed into an inextricable universe of bricks, refuse, self-made tenements, and old state housing projects. When it occurs to him to turn his head, it is to affirm that he has made the right choice in moving far away from what he thinks of as a backward world that remains a burden for Egypt, and that diminishes and pollutes the image of Cairo. He knows that he has again joined the future of Egypt. At any moment, he thinks, this crowd could mutate into a rioting horde, pushed by who knows what manipulating sheikh's harangue.

Neither the heat, nor the muffled noise of the congested streets has penetrated his air-conditioned limousine. Ahmed Ashraf al-Mansuri considers the prospect of a round of golf, followed by a discussion at the club house with his friend Yasin from the Ministry of Finance, then a short stroll home. The stress of his day is already fading away.

Since 8 AM, shadows had begun to haunt Ahmed as he looked out from the eleventh-floor windows of the Cairo World Trade Center dominating the Ministry of Foreign Affairs and looming over the corniche that lines the Nile River. He is experiencing a downturn in his business transactions—that important monopoly on ice cream was not granted to him and the opportunity to buy an apartment building escaped him. 'Risky' remains his watchword. Would that it were owing only to this currency devaluation of which no one knows the way out, or the disappearance of foreign exchange. Fortunately, he has obtained a respectable distribution contract with an international chain of hotels to buy his cartons of milk that he packages in his small factory. He will have to go there tomorrow to accelerate production before going to the office. He has hardly the time to call his son who is in his third year in political science at SOAS (the School of Oriental and African Studies) in London. But in his car his anxieties fade away as he commutes away from downtown Cairo, past the Pyramids, into the desert. Then Mr. al-Mansuri arrives home, entering the gates of his new residential community, Dreamland.

There he passes Abu Muhammad, his usual caddy who, having finished his day, is waiting for the minibus that will take him to his small apartment of forty square meters, shared with some ten other waiters and workers living in the oldest quarters of the town of Sixth October, farther to the west on the desert plateau. His wife and children, having never migrated to the capital city, have remained in the village near the city of Mansura in the Delta.

The wife of Ahmed Ashraf al-Mansuri has not been to Cairo for more than two weeks. She comes only to visit a female cousin in Utopia, a near-by gated community. After her foray to the shopping center, she is late picking up her children. They are returning from an afternoon at the amusement park with Maria, the Ethiopian maid. The children are playing now in the pool, watched over by Mahmoud, the security guard. Maria, the Ethiopian maid, knows that she will return to her room—a small room without windows behind the kitchen—but only later that evening. There are the guests; she will have to help the cook after putting the children to bed.

New Risks and Privatized Exclusivity

With the above fictionalized narrative, we arrive on the desert plateaus bordering the city and suburbs of Cairo. To the east and to the west, for a dozen or more years, promotion of the construction of private apartment buildings has led to the acquisition of vast expanses of the public domain, putting them in the hands of development contractors. More than one hundred square kilometers are actually under construction, that is to say, a surface equivalent to more than a third of the existing city and suburbs, which has been fashioned and refashioned among the same founding sites for a thousand years. Dozens of luxury gated communities, accompanied by golf courses, amusement parks, clinics, and private universities have burgeoned along the beltways like their siblings, the shopping malls. (See Abaza, and Elsheshtawy (chapter 7) in this volume for analysis of the growth of luxury malls in Cairo.) Against an extremely compact 'organic' urban area, the model for the dense, non-linear 'Asiatic' city analyzed by orientalist geographers, is juxtaposed against the horizon of a new city more like Los Angeles, gauged from now on according to the speed of the automobile. This new dimension of Cairo is marked by a flight of the urban elites made more visible by the de-densification of the urban center.[2] This radical reformulation of the metropolitan landscape, which its promoters invite us to view as an urban renaissance or *nahda 'umraniya*, is completely in tune with the parameters of economic liberalization and IMF-driven structural adjustment.

To be sold, the gated communities brandish and actualize the universal myth of the great city where one can lose oneself in privatized domestic bliss. Promoters exploit more and more the stigmatization of 'the street,' spread by the media on a global scale, and finally of the Arab metropolis as a terrorist risk factory that is necessarily 'Islamic.' Far from being rejected, the Islamist peril is exploited by the Egyptian authorities to legitimize political deliberalization, while it promotes a particular landscape of economic restructuring. The current regime redirects and displaces the urgency of law and the immediate interests of Egypt's elites through the affirmation of market and security systems, of which the gated communities are a prominent feature.

Within this optic, the gated communities must appear as a privileged window onto the reality of liberalization in Egypt. Analysis of these settlements allows one to understand how mechanisms of risk control impose social exclusion (the reverse side of elitist globalization) and how they define the risks themselves. Urban ecology and the priorities of security are reversed to favor suburban desert colonies: defensive bastions against the lost metropolis. At the heart of this reversal, global/local developers and state agencies play out the transfer of power to businesspeople associated with the construction of a new hybrid, globalized Americano-Mediterranean lifestyle.

العزيزية

خان العزيزية

بجـوار الأهرامات

فتح باب الحجز
للمرحلة الثالثة

من ٢٠/ ١٦ الى ٧/ ٣٠
بإذن الله

والفنادق والمتحف المصرى الجديد

Advertisement
for a new gated
community
in Cairo that
appropriates neo-
orientalist/Islamic
models, (*al-Ahram*
1996, n.d.).

At the center of this new way of life are Egypt's elites, themselves connecting together the archipelago of micro-city communities that they administer as if they were so many experimental accomplishments of a private democracy to come. The gated communities, like a spatial plan, authorize the elites who live there to continue the forced march for economic, oligopolistic liberalization, without redistribution, while protecting themselves from the ill effects of its pollution and its risks. In the same way, these elites rejoin the transmetropolitan club of the worldwide archipelago of walled enclaves (Caldeira 2000). The potential guilty anxieties relative to the suffering of ordinary city dwellers are, then, masked by global rejection of the city, according to an anti-urban discourse that incorporates and naturalizes pollution, identifying it with poverty, criminality, and violent protests against the regime. In this elite perspective, Cairo has become a complex of unsustainable nuisances against which nothing more can be done, except to escape or to protect oneself. Urban risk, and, by the same token, urban ecology, are radically recomposed.

In the rest of this chapter, I will trace the material development of the gated communities, their promotion and appropriation. Then I will identify the risk discourses that create the foundation for, and enable the legitimation of, the renewed management of social distances. But first, it is appropriate to define what we mean by fear, risk, myth, and urban ecology.

Contouring Risk and Legitimacy in the Landscape

Risk is understood as a social and political construct that crystallizes, sorts, and normalizes dangers, fears, and anxieties that define and limit a given society (Hacking 2003). The formulation of risks allows one to focus on modalities of individual and collective action, and to determine strategies of habitation, in order to protect integrity and the sense of being among one's own, or, simply, diversity control. As places in which diversity and coexistence are maximized, metropolitan areas are, in their material, social, and political expressions, the product of responses and reactions to the dangers that are negatively associated with density and diversity. Dimissive fears, like those associated with pollution, nourish the procedures of self-definition and delimitation of a city community. They facilitate the creation of 'society' (Douglas 1966; Douglas and Wildavsky 1982). Like marginalities, fears define borders. They lie at the heart of the interactionist formulation of identity as relationships of domination.[3]

The specter of risks, projected through media and representational structures, normalizes collective fears (Weldes et al. 1999). It claims to validate legitimate worries and put aside superstitions that appear as backward. This work of definition authorizes a system of protection of individual or collective control, and the establishment of norms and institutions, such as insurance, legislation, armed forces, police, medicine, borders, architecture, urban planning, etc. Measures taken to acknowledge risk aim at replacing chance occurrences with predictable events.

Always present is the myth of the urban Babylon, portrayed as a prostitute and as a place of potentially unfathomable corruption and loss. As always, this image serves to reify diffuse anxieties that threaten the stability of a regime embedded in urban order. Risk myths allow the legitimation of borders and of territorial command. The definition of risk enters into the heart of procedures that stigmatize subordinate groups, designate 'scapegoats,' and map illegitimate territories (Girard 1982). It lies at the foundation of the designation of clandestine transients—those who do not have their place in the city and must be kept at a distance because they threaten its harmony.

It is, therefore, more than coincidental that, precisely in Egypt, the word 'ashwa'iyat, which derives from the Arabic root that signifies chance, appeared at the beginning of the 1990s to designate slums, shantytowns, and the self-made satellite cities of the poor, i.e. illegal and/or illegitimate quarters. By the end of the 1990s, the term came to describe not just spaces but peoples, encompassing a near-majority of the city as risky, 'hazardous,' errant figures. The figure of the errant is that which most frightens this urban society.

Seen as the invading silhouette of the decidedly peasant migrant from the provinces, the *fallah* (peasant) frightened and still frightens urban society. This designation also reanimates the classic Muslim opposition between the *fallah* and the *hadari* (the urban or 'civilised'), and between settled and nomad communities.

Today Egypt's globalizing metropolis finds itself at a point of instability, swaying between a society in which fatalism and malediction play a major role in the management of crises and catastrophes, and the 'society of risk' characterized by a lack of certainty, in which it becomes impossible to attribute uncertainty to external or ungovernable causes. In reality, the level of risk depends on political decisions and choices. It is produced industrially and economically and becomes, therefore, politically reflexive. Egypt, however, analyzed from the perspective of Ulrich Beck, reminds us that old modernization solutions are untenable, because religious radicalism and authoritarian practices are growing, but are always attributed to foreign plotting, denying the development of a reflexive national public and repressing internal debates (1992). In this context, risk remains an ambivalent object that produces exclusionary norms while ancestral myths and beliefs are reappropriated and remade in order to master and stabilize current forms of political monopoly.

Gated communities are one of the most striking and revealing products of this new ecology of risk and monopolization of politics. They reveal processes of disorganizing and reorganizing modes of living and cohabiting in the city, that is, the dynamics of spatializing a new neoliberal 'moral order' and justifying it through risk discourse (Park 1926).

The New Liberal Age and the Material Framework of Colonial Nostalgia

The state's offering of a new exclusive lifestyle ignited an explosion. From 1994, when the Ministry of Housing began on a massive scale to sell lots on the desert margins of Cairo, the number of luxury construction projects very quickly surpassed market absorption capacity. The region of Greater Cairo includes a limited number of middle-class families; not more than 315,000 families' current expenses exceed LE2,000 per month ($350 in 2005 dollars). And these are counted as the 9.5 percent most wealthy.[4] Yet within this limited market, 320 companies have acquired land and declared projects that, in potential volume, total six hundred thousand residences.[5] In the first years since the boom, no less than eighty gated city projects have been erected, with many sectors presold, and the first families settled. In 2003 alone these companies put some sixty thousand housing units of villas and apartments on the market. Where will all these rich families come from?

Utopia, Qattamiya Heights, Beverly Hills, Palm Hills, Belle Ville, Mena Garden City, Dreamland: these are some of the gated communities under development. These developments are marketed as the cutting edge of a post-metropolitan lifestyle, invented between the imaginaries of 'fortress America's' sprawling cities and the new risk-apartheid of Johannesburg (Blakely and Snyder 1997). However, if the ensembles of villas respond perfectly to the global concept of the protected city, encircled by a wall and assuring a totally managed autonomy, this is not just an importation of a universal model. There is also visible the influence of the Persian Gulf oil monarchies' taste for luxurious living. Gulf fashions are represented in the grand embellishments of baroque gilding, imposing balconies, and neoclassic colonnades. The architectural models and the forms of appropriation by residents are 'hybridized,' mixing local and Arab-regional influences as much as they correspond to values from global cities (AlSayyad 2001). The idea of the Mediterranean is also an essential referent framework for Egypt as a southern Mediterranean country, evoking idealized Greek village motifs, tiled roofs, Tuscan pine gardens, or the shimmering colors of Riviera resorts. The Mediterranean model has already been articulated through the Egyptian Riviera development experiment, on the coast west of Alexandria. This coastal model has since been adopted by potential inland Cairene buyers as an extension of a society perpetually on vacation under the sun. This positive Mediterranean image and the extravagant Persian Gulf styles are at least as visible as American/Western influences as Egypt renegotiates its international identity, reframing its primary Middle Eastern–Arab identity through touristic and residential commercialization.

Reference to the Mediterranean allows Cairo to negotiate and to attenuate Arab and Muslim values that are present architecturally, but made into folkloric consumer symbols. Islam and Arabness are referenced in a way closer to the iconography of Disney's Aladdin or Sinbad rather than to the culture of austerity, modesty, and self-discipline identified with contemporary Islamic populism and militance. The businessman Ahmed Bahgat even explains that it was after a visit to Celebration (the private ideal community built by the Walt Disney Corporation in Orlando, Florida) that he conceived of Dreamland ("Dreamland . . ." 1998). More than a collection of luxury residences, this gated community complex offers a view of the plateau of the pyramids of Giza, access to a golf course, and your own private amusement park. When, at the end of the nineteenth century, Khedive Isma'il conceived of a new city center for Cairo, he dreamt of a Haussmannian Paris of boulevards uniting public squares and apartment blocks. Today, a hybrid, Egyptianized version of the American dream predominates; but with a strong reference to the past and the khedival/colonial era itself. This new global reconstitution of nostalgia becomes an essential argument for selling and living in the desert, as inhabitants are faced with the uncertainty of the future and the instability of the present.

Exclusivity as Urban Renaissance

Before we aspire to the day when, as Toussaint Caneri asked in 1905, the Muqattam (the plateau to the east of Cairo) becomes a park sprinkled with villas, linked to the city by a tram, can we wish, at least, for a less egotistical attitude among the ruling classes? It is even in their own interests, if they do not wish to prepare a terrain of choice for the social experiments of tomorrow. Clerget 1934, 21; Caneri 1905.

Clerget, one of the first French urban geographers who was critical of some of the Orientalist real estate schemes and Khedival politics of the era, perceived the tensions and the risks induced by liberal luxury developments. He feared that building outside the margins of Cairo would rupture the tissue of urban space even though he also built some projects in the new areas. Today, a nostalgic view of a vanished late-nineteenth, early-twentieth-century 'liberal era' is common. This perspective invites us to view the connection between the two epochs of liberalization in modern Egypt, as well as their urban-development consequences. The late nineteenth and twentieth centuries were already a period of real-estate excess that marks, to the present day, the composition of the metropolis (Arnaud 1998). The promoters of the gated communities love to reflect back on the past in view of investing their own projects with the positive image of the belle-époque liberal age, that is, the age of Egypt's Khedive Isma'il, the era of British colonial occupation, of high debt, foreign investment and control, as well as of rampant speculation and luxury public and private construction. This colonial (a.k.a. khedivial or Isma'ilian) era is called by some "Egypt's liberal age" because it also featured the development of limited, elite-oriented, and colonially constrained liberal political and cultural institutions, and is remembered for the birth of democratic Western-leaning nationalism under Sa'd Zaghlul.

Today, many prominent Egyptian real-estate developers, like Tal'at Mustafa, do not hesitate to present themselves as heirs of Baron Empain (Kamal 1998), a Belgian settler and investor in Egypt who founded in 1905 the sumptuous urban oasis Heliopolis, then in the middle of the desert to the east of Cairo and linked to the city center by a tramway that he privately owned and profited from (Ilbert 1981; Garret 2001). Close to the family of president Anwar al-Sadat, Tal'at Mustafa built his fortune beginning in the 1970s through the construction of military infrastructure. Mustafa is currently mobilizing support for the construction of an entire satellite city, al-Rihab, to be situated to the east of Cairo and designed to welcome some 150,000 residents (Zaki 1999).

Similarly, the Belle Ville project—a gated community boasting a view of the pyramids of Giza to the west of Cairo—was promoted in the daily press and in magazines with photos that drew parallels between the irretrievable architectural prestige of the Isma'ilian center, allotted since 1870, and the emergence of a future according to the image of this new, glorious page of private urbanism. Mena Garden City was shown on television in an advertisement that made the villas of the former Garden City, an early twentieth-century bohemian and foreign-residence zone, fly away, carried by powerful cranes. The old Garden City was built at the beginning of the twentieth century on the banks of the Nile at the edge of the heart of the Isma'ilian center, promising its residents quiet, likened to the tranquility of a desert oasis. Now, the Garden City of the future blooms literally in the distant desert, while the old Isma'ilian Garden City is invaded by high-rise towers and militarized security checkpoints that protect the few foreign residents and embassies that remain there. Elsewhere, models of villas don the names of the Egyptian rulers of the nineteenth and twentieth centuries—Farouk, Isma'il, etc. Even the grandson of the original Baron Empain himself has participated in the promotion of a scheme for New Heliopolis.

If this reinscription of the past is henceforth possible, even invoked, it is then necessary that, like the rehabilitation of royalty, it allows the legitimation of the entrepreneurs who are partitioning and seizing the public lands in the desert. These enterprises then become vital to creating a new elite national patrimony, of the sort developed at the beginning of the twentieth century. They participate in the creation of a patina, that is, a nostalgic landscape built upon the reappropriation of an old framework, patrimonializing and historicizing the gated communities. This patina promotes a sense of authenticity and nostalgia for the present (McKraken 1988; Appadurai 2001). Not only does contemporary life appear historicized, but also as something already lost. Like fashion, a product of the tangle of worlds and a parable of accelerated circulation on a worldwide scale, the patina generates ephemerality. This effacement of the present for the commercial ends of promotion and consumption is akin to the visibilization of risk, in that they both create instability. They both invite self-protection, leading to demand for protections in the face of growing insecurity, and to destabilization of routines and relations.

The rehabilitation of the spirit and the city of royalty and colonial investors before the anticolonial struggle, before independence and before the Egyptian Revolution, is inscribed very clearly in the renovation of the old city center of Cairo. This spirit is reflected in the support for the idea of Hosni Mubarak crowning his own son as the next president, as a kind of khedivial successor. A legitimate façade of liberalization and adjustment is sought, paradoxically in the imaginary of the archaic colonized khedivial monarchy and its new/old luxury landscapes.

When, live on television's Channel One in May 1997, President Hosni Mubarak inaugurated a golf course and said that he saw there a green lung for the Cairene people, he validated a very exclusive enterprise as a national project. He sanctioned an elitist appropriation, closing off, and privatization of the once publicly owned deserts (and a seizing of the water needed to irrigate them) while cloaking it in the spirit of great open public projects realized in the national interest *(al-mashru' al-gama'i)*.

Advertisement for Belle Ville, a gated community near the Giza Pyramids, which celebrates its links to the colonial architecture of late nineteenth-century Cairo (*al-Ahram*, 1996, n.d.).

In a parallel process, the state tightly censors and controls all forms of citizen representation by political parties, and NGOs are suppressed by a mountain of disabling laws, police seizures, and bureaucratic penetration, all while businesspeople are highly regarded and cultivated by the state, notably in support for the formation of working groups and privileged lobbies given highest level access in the National Assembly. While press, NGOs, and social movements are crushed, commercial foundations and business associations flourish, like those regrouping the businesspeople from the industrial zones of the new cities. To conform to the new national 'ethics' of neoliberalism and structural adjustment that prohibit direct intervention by the state in the domain of construction, the alliance between entrepreneurs and those in service of the state is redefined: Those public contractors who previously performed the construction, en masse, of public housing, now operate as semiprivate contractors, developing luxury lots while benefiting from credit furnished by public banks, which is gauged according to the speculative and overvalued worth of land purchased at a very low price, with the state holding down the price for developers.

At the same time, charity again becomes an urban bourgeois value and a way of self-presentation essential to the image of a good citizen and a good Muslim. In particular, populist soup kitchens, which had not existed since 1952, have been reactivated, whereas the list of subsidized products is presently reduced to four articles (oil, sugar, flour, and bread), whose stocks are constantly shrinking (Korayem 2001). The ostentatious charity tables for the month of Ramadan, begun at the end of the 1980s, and a pure product of the reinvention of the Islamic tradition, are more and more in evidence. They now constitute an emblematic figure of the rapport between the bourgeoisie and the urban people. They embody the legitimate exhibition of wealth made manifest through the concern to have the largest table, the one that provides the most places. These tables dramatize the gift of scraps. Here, the state and religious practice, like the rewriting of monarchical/colonial-era national history, validate the pertinence of neoliberal change and reflect the 'best times' of social reformism and its benevolent organizations. This spectacle of social inequalities and alms can also be read in terms of risk, of the accentuated risk of uprising. Charity is imposed as the only relation to the poor and their only vehicle for social uplift, with the police as the last rampart. There are no other modalities allowed for the redistribution of the fruits of liberalization.

This mediatized work of the new urban world, affiliated with the liberal age before 1952, erases the period of national construction and of 'socialist' public, modernist, and integrative planning. The revolutionary, Arab nationalist,

Third-World Solidarity era of the 1950s—when Egypt won its independence—to the 1970s has since become represented as a dark period, identified by its visible lack of elegance, and its architectural and infrastructural stagnation, rather than by its social achievements. Parallels with real-estate speculation during the belle-époque era suggest that only private entrepreneurs, not revolutionary states, are able to create the city and to distinguish it in an enduring way. But it should be said that this parallel does not just romanticize the spirit of neoliberal free enterprise or certain elite aesthetic values and lifestyles, it also reconfigures modes of production. Indeed, in both elitist epochs, then and now, the state offers up its public patrimony. It opens vast expanses of territory to be divided up amongst a handful of private developers, while stimulating the flow of capital through the sale of land.

Today's parallel is not, then, just about style, façade, or a set of symbolic representations. It indicates a disillusionment with respect to the public, state, and national development, as well as the project of modernization dominant since 1952.

A sense of shifting priorities is also generally in the air. It corresponds in effect to the spirit of 'good urban and corporate governance' promoted by the World Bank. Does the structurally adjusted state in Egypt really have an alternative? Must it rebuild its alliances with cosmopolitan elite entrepreneurs in order to survive?

Entrepreneurial Spirit and the State

In 1991 Egypt signed a tripartite management agreement with the IMF and the World Bank. This Economic Reform and Structural Adjustment Program marks the entrance of Egypt into an active phase of reforms, transformations of the economic apparatus, and change in modes of government. Privatization was imposed as the privileged instrument of urban reform with the delegation of a network of public services.

Since 1991 the privatization of electricity has proceeded in the production sector and, more recently, in the power-distribution sector. The privatization of telecommunications and waste treatment are also well advanced. The state has privatized the building of parking garages, the subway system, roads, and tunnels through 'build, operate, and transfer' contracts (where private transnational companies, usually based in Europe or the United States, build infrastructure, profit from it by toll or fee collection, then much later transfer it to the Egyptian state and public).

From now on, underintegrated slums (informal or self-constructed quarters in which poor people reside), may be demolished, restructured, and 'managed' by a for-profit company as a state concession, providing that the firm guarantees in-place relocation or some compensation for residents, and that it builds infrastructure.

In 1997, the governor of Cairo, Dr. Ibrahim Shehata, explained his slum privatization plan: "Here, I have an informal quarter in which fifty thousand people live. The governorate of Cairo is interested in signing a development contract with a promoter, providing he furnish ten thousand residential units for those living there, a public garden, two clinics, and three schools. And he may develop the rest of the quarter according to his interests." And to this Dr. Shehata adds: "The volume of irrational use of urban land is insane. I would say, willingly, that all of Cairo is not appropriate to a logical, rational economic plan, with rare exceptions, like perhaps the Ramses Hilton [an international luxury tourist hotel that includes cinemas and a shopping mall for Egyptian upper-middle classes and Persian Gulf Arab visitors]." (See Ghannam's chapter in this volume for an analysis of the government's relocation of the residents around the Ramses Hilton to clear the way for its development.)

Hospital services are progressing toward privatization, and of course the state has moved to privatize and globalize most of the country's industrial base. The possibility of a private police force operating on the public highway has also been raised following violent incidents between union organizers. Finally, the gated communities assert their autonomy to provide 'free' sanitary drainage, potable water, and private security, guaranteeing quality services, free from ponderous state involvement. These communities benefit ungratefully from state-paid public infrastructure developed for the new cities. (See Vignal and Denis in this volume for further analysis of the manufacturing sector and structural adjustment.)

In this regard, we subscribe fully to the analysis advanced by Timothy Mitchell who argues that this neoliberalization does not in reality signify a retreat of the state (2002). Here, to account for the formal semblance of economic liberalization, it is necessary to recognize more fully the change of alliance modalities between entrepreneurs and the state. In fact, in addition to its huge irrigation projects—like the Peace Canal that is to be constructed near the shore of the North Sinai from Port Said to al-'Arish, or the other branch of the Nile, Tushka, to be carved out of the (public) Western Desert near Lake Nasser by state funds and labor, and then sold to global agrobusiness investors—the state continues to subsidize and construct housing that it calls 'social' or 'low cost' but which is in fact speculative and directed toward stimulating elite settlement. The explosion in private luxury construction within the gated communities also falls within the project to reformulate the paradoxical neoliberal, neomonarchical appearance of an alliance between entrepreneurs and public elites in support of industrial channels for cement, steel, and construction, which compromise the gigantic industrial engine at the heart of the system of wealth generation and speculation, controlled by a few families that monopolize both private and public power.

Political Deliberalization and Privatizing Democracy

Gated communities represent the socio-political result of economic neoliberalization. Here private democracy materializes. While estimating that public institutions cannot assure the well-being and the defense of the collective, a restrained community of like-minded people itself takes charge of the management of the protection of its own way of life. The community of residents of the gated community of Mena Garden City, for example, manages shared spaces, lighting, and the roadways from common funds that it places in the Cairo stock exchange.

This kind of private democracy flourishes in Egypt while on the national social scale, political exclusion and repression has intensified. The election of mayors *('umdas)* was suppressed in 1994 under the guise of the struggle against Islamism, replaced by a system of administrative appointment from above.

In April 2002, the election of local councils was marked by the attribution of 97 percent of the seats to the party in power! What is more, these representative, elected bodies, even in their highly constrained form, have always played a merely consultative role. The executive nominates the managers of the public administration who are typically drawn from the ranks of the army. The Cairo region is thus administered by three military governors named by presidential decree. Adding to this climate of 'political deliberalization' is the revision of the law on labor, which blocks the free constitution of labor unions and the right to strike. These prohibitions date to the declaration of the Emergency Law promulgated just after the assassination of President Sadat in 1981 (Kienle 2001). Similarly, nongovernmental organizations are more and more tightly controlled. Their modes of financing their own actions cannot be political.

The adherence by the elites to the political model of the gated community, a form of voluntary disaffiliation and exclusionary self-organization facilitated by the state and stock exchange, aims to constitute autonomous units in which it is possible to live in a directly participatory democracy without waiting for, or while blocking the arrival of, the substantive democracy for the country as a whole. The elite gated communities authorize the construction of private democracies when, all around on the outside, economic liberalization is accompanied by political deliberalization. Privatization of reform is extended into the privatization of politics, accelerating the downward spiral of exclusion, disenfranchisement, and poverty, dispossessing the rights and the potential of the workforce that is one of the primary resources Egypt possesses on the world market of goods and services.

Evasion of Risk or Inversion of Risk

Although it is apparently motivated by an escalation of urban risk, the move to live in the desert cannot be understood as a mere evasion of risk. The phenomenon of gated communities is a form of fixing worth, investing the unshared gains flowing directly from the liberalization and privatization process, and then fixing them in a new global/local hierarchy and landscape. These constructions are inscribed in stone and real estate, from wealth extracted from the public patrimony and from public lands in a context of inflation, certainly reduced in relation to the 1980s, but characterized by a strong monetary devaluation. Major public stakeholders give private actors access to land and property while avoiding market competition. These public actors include the Ministry of Defense, the Egyptian State Railways, the Ministry of Housing and New Communities, the Ministry of Agriculture and Land Reclamation, the Ministry of Religious Endowments *(awqaf)*, public insurance companies, etc.

To better understand this process, we turn to the field of structural geography and the "theory of takeover" *(théorie du rachat)* formulated by Rebour (2000) building upon the work of Desmarais and Ritchot (2000, 121):

Dysphorias emanating from urban areas marked by industrial concentration (insalubrity, social agitation . . .) were often invoked to explain the departure of bourgeois residents, conjoined to positions of contiguous assembly, for suburban villas and their country domains. These distant, sumptuous developments denote, however, something other than flight. They differentiate the urban expanse, break its homogeneity, and capture new values placed in charge by the dynamics of takeover [rachat] that feeds the economic system.

The social values of the metropolis are taken over, refixed, and thus inverted.

Thus, the Shatir clan, at the head of a farm-produce empire, enjoys a quasi-monopoly on the production of potato chips in Egypt. The family built factory units in the industrial zone of the new city of Sixth of October and then began to develop an ensemble of villas in a residential complex, of which the family is the proprietor. Up to the present time, they have not sold the seat of their company located in the commercial center of Cairo.

Negotiating Appearances

Living in the desert does not speak for itself. It also symbolizes the realm of the dead. The desert remains associated with the successive displacements of cemeteries and visits to the dead. To render the desert attractive supposes then, on the one hand, that the repulsion of the dense metropolis is intense and that a fundamentally distinctive change of desert soil has been effected. Ecological recomposition is at play in the tension between rejection and attractiveness and between stigmatization of the masses and over-valuation of the elite. Promoted for more than twenty years as a space for the relegation of polluting industries, and, with the new cities, of the working class, the deserts are no Garden of Eden, nor are they perfect sites for creating modern utopias (although one of the new gated cities of Sixth of October is called Utopia). The shift of perception is socially constructed through neoliberal discourses that redefine the desert as virgin terrain for the refoundation of Egyptian society.

After independence, the desert became the space to conquer and to populate, not only for reasons of de-densification and preservation of agricultural lands, but also, even above all, in view of producing a new peasant and a new urban resident, a veritable pioneer of a new society (Fanchette 1995; see also El Shakry in this volume). The gated communities, twisting this revolutionary perspective, are presented as inheritors of the national project for the conquest of the desert. Private investors, while substituting themselves for the state, restructure the nation in accordance with neoliberal modalities. Beside the promoters, who are lionized by the media for their efforts to populate the desert and to turn it green, the buyers of villas in the gated communities may see themselves as pioneers working for the expansion of inhabitable space, thus working for the valorization of the common good, embodied in Egyptian territory. Among the first residents of the gated communities, there are a good number of gentlemen-farmers who have first-hand experience with land improvement, allowing them to 'tame the desert.' The figure of the industrial pioneer—the hero, frontiersman, innovator—allows buyers and promoters to divert attention from the private and above all very exclusive appropriation of public lands, and therefore from the disappearance of space and resources around the capital. The will to express one's individual difference, to expose one's capital, to speculate without worrying about society or general national uplift is thus transmuted into a land of pioneering courage, and a kind of developmental innovation and entrepreneurial bravado.

From this point on, living in the desert is no longer conceived of as a departure toward the periphery, but as a relocalization of the city center and new focus on places of innovation. This acts as a visible show of the reconcentration of the spaces of power that in part accompanies the expansion of the gated communities.

Map showing the new gated community, Beverly Hills, on the fringes of Sixth of October City, a satellite city founded by President Sadat in the desert beyond the Pyramids (*al-Ahram*, 1996, n.d.).

This migration of the experimental spaces of a model society, of 'agricultural improvements,' to the new suburbs of Cairo is accompanied by the symbolic transfer of the power to innovate from the state's civil servants to the elites and entrepreneurs, and from the public to the private domain, which is made manifest by the marked exclusivity of the model.

This way of seeing development as pioneering makes personal success stories visible—stories that were masked in the heart of the metropolis and in the concepts of the public, national and social. In the city, such successes are effaced by the demands of density, proximity, and decency, which cohabitation, social diversity, and inequality impose. In the popular city, a lack of space makes ostentatious display of individual 'innovation' or distinction impossible without risk of friction. In the old metropolis, spectacles of individuality must be confined to private or semiprivate interior spaces, such as the large five-star tourist hotels, in order to conform with the norms of discretion associated with modern public space in twentieth-century Cairo.

In contrast, the desert offers distance and perspective. The expanse favors the expansion of view-scapes, of rites of approach and of passages that dramatize the grandeur of the new residences: successive thresholds are thus established between the exit from the agglomeration and the arrival at the colonnade and steps of the villa. First, there is the rupture in the landscape of the desert, followed by the monumental entrance of the new city, and finally the passage through guarded doors of the gated community.

Desert localization favors the exhibition of one's success with grandeur and ostentation. The architecture of the villas expresses this clearly through recourse to a panoply of cosmopolitan transcultural signs: the pool, the square, the neoclassic columns, the lawn, the pines, and the garage. The garage in turn refers of course to owning a car, which has long served as a projection of private space in the crowded urban space, the only vector expressing one's rank and success among the popular throng. Perfectly understood by the ensemble of the social body, the Mercedes in Cairo has been given a popular nickname, "the phantom." This term reflects a view of the elites as distant, menacing, ephemeral. Mercedes are also nicknamed "pig eyes" or "powder," the latter implying that only cocaine dealers can afford them.

Projection of the spectacle of elite distinction from city street to desert gated city enables speculation and spectacle in the same way as does the migration to summer resorts on the shore of the Mediterranean, or driving a tinted-glass Mercedes through a downtown traffic jam. It is through a double rapport that one must understand the adhesion of the elites to the program of the gated communities: they can have access to this space because they have these cars, and inversely, the distance allows them to enjoy the power of these automobiles. Living in the distant desert has become a luxury, while previously the new cities had been seen as a burden, where poor workers and ordinary citizens took long bus rides to reach their factory jobs.

Ostentation leads us to a duality of the model of gated communities, which are apparently sold according to the theme of protection and security. Nevertheless, far from the bunker architecture of South African villas or the compounds of Latin America, defenses here are somewhat expressively outward looking. Certainly, the settlements are closed, but the walls appear to be quite fragile, rather low, and especially open, with grillwork that allows one to glimpse the luxury of the villas from the outside. The buyer purchases a protected residence with a plan to create a sense of distance, of filtering; but he desires at the same time to be seen. Thus exposed, the security figure associated with the promotion of the gated communities expresses their fragility. The closure confirms the radical nature of the social rupture and clearly indicates the will of the promoters, like the buyers, to disassociate themselves voluntarily from the mass remaining behind in the dense areas of the city. But the model appears quite vulnerable. It responds to the demand for distinction and for exposure, but at the same time, it emphasizes insecurity rather than protecting from it. It produces risk in a city that remains perhaps quite over-confident.

Ecology, Liberalization, and Authoritarianism

Ecology appears on the Egyptian scene as a radically imported category that accompanies the process of economic liberalization in the same way as IMF/World Bank programs for mastering poverty. These are two major tools for the mastery and regulation of the effects of liberalization and adjustment. Ecology imposes a foreign expertise and reorganizes the industrial apparatus on the basis of imported procedures and technologies, transferred through foreign companies; the struggle against poverty fills the domain once occupied by welfare-state social services and abandons questions formerly posed in terms of redistribution.

In Egypt, the institutionalization of ecology remains at the center of USAID and Canadian aid programs. In 1992, a presidential decree launched the National Environment Action Plan (NEAP) carried by the Egyptian Environmental Affairs Agency (EEAA), instituted in 1982 to formulate environmental policy and to educate public and private sectors, and the population at large, to the dangers posed by pollution and the manner in which to combat them. In 1994, the parliament voted for Law No. 4, concerning environmental protection and instituting norms for water and air pollution. In 1997, Presidential Decree No. 275 led to the nomination of the first secretary of state for the environment, and in 1999, the government launched the first plan for environmental action. Ecology arrived in Egypt at the same moment and in the context of gated-city speculation (Hopkins, Mehanna, and el-Haggar 2001).

The state apparatus, while appropriating and instituting ecological discourse, confirms the largely shared sentiment of a global, ecological shift. It appropriates the monopoly on measuring and defining pollution, ignoring pollution from industrial, agricultural, and military sources, while directing attention to other kinds of pollution against which it is more convenient to fight. Measures then come to reinforce regulation and the new elite social order at the heart of the metropolis. For example, the policy on green spaces and gardens empowers organizations for clearing and de-densifying central and pericentral spaces, but does not allow the public or NGOs to enter or use these spaces.

Ecology also reveals itself to be an ideal tool for showcasing the transfer of competences that characterize liberalization. From the regime's point of view, 'good' environment is based on an alliance with businesspeople who know the issues at stake, whereas the people, completely incompetent, can only be polluters. Gated communities are emblematic of this transfer and of the commodification of the environmental question. Here, ecology plays the role that reformism played during Egypt's prerevolutionary liberal age. Ecology becomes one lever for putting into place the apparatus for taking charge of space and for population control.

Naturalizing the Urban Order

The appropriation of ecological discourse should merit more ample development and serious investigation. The alliance of the 'Greens' with right-wing Islamism reinforces the competences of authoritarian power. This alliance finds in ecology a new list of legitimate arguments to justify in the name of protecting the common good, their increased ascendance in society and politics. We find a despotic appropriation of ecological values according to modalities that resemble those promulgated by Luc Ferry in Europe: i.e., elite-defined 'nature' comes before the needs of the social order (1992). This kind of ecology favors the enlistment of the technocratic edifice and the authoritarian state apparatus. It offers to the state a new savant discourse and instruments of scientific domination. Cairo ecologism favors the construction of threats and constraints legitimating the maintenance of an authoritarian regime and of an exclusivist mode of redistribution.

This kind of ecologism differs in a certain sense from the old reformism: pretensions to ameliorating life conditions and to education are effaced because the concern is with non-human 'nature.' As some would say, "It is in their nature . . . , they are filthy, they are violent, fanatics. . . ." In other words, the people are neither educable nor reformable. These principles of natural inferiority, already present in the construction of the categories of colonial administration, again finds here a new political youth. This colonial-liberal continuity of modes of government and of ways of understanding the social totality, its limits and its excluded parties, questions the very idea of national construction and of an independent state that strives to develop a community of citizens. Similarly, gated communities reveal forms of disaffiliation and disinterest toward the life of the city, to the benefit of a privatized life. This neoliberal geography permits the management of elite social or familial networks and facilitates the continued privatization, mining, and exploitation of national resources while social redistribution is reduced to the minimum. Meanwhile membership in a transnationally articulated elite is fostered. The values conveyed in their time by colonial urbanism are reproduced, dissociating the people's city from the city of their masters.

Conclusions: Intersections of Neoliberal Risks and Justifications

The phenomenon of the gated community takes shape at the intersection of two kinds of justifying or legitimating arguments. The new exclusivist geography of neoliberal Cairo represents, on the one hand, a world showcase for a certain kind of liberalization, that which stimulates praise and affirmation far from Egypt, as the *Wall Street Journal* in 1997 blessed the new projects, remarking, "How far Egypt has gone" (*Wall Street Journal*, 14 April, 1997). On the other hand, this gated-city geography imposes a redefinition of risks. The so-called urban renaissance justifies and bears witness to the performativity of liberalization policy and to the new delegation of competences that will remake Egypt for transnational businesspeople. Further, these developments must be justified by the construction of risks corresponding to general principles associated with this lifestyle of living separately, among one's own class and clans, in elite microcollectives that are protected, subsidized, and 'democratically' self-run. This nascent mode of partititioning crystallizes the true logic of current neoliberal reforms, all the while hardening the social landscape against multiple countereffects, alternatives, and resistances.

Moments, Models, and Universality

In this context is it acceptable, from the perspective of urban studies, to define today's city, the very big globalizing city in particular, as a combination of mixed elements, of diversity, and of density, favoring cosmopolitanism and innovation?

We must reconcile this definition with the new facts, not less universal, that the object of new urban policies is to struggle against combinations of incongruous elements, eliminate diversity, and criminalize density, melange, and proximity. These policies separate and establish a hierarchy well beyond that which a simple functionalist perspective would require. The model of the European, cosmopolitan global city—without a doubt mythic, elitist, and ethnocentric in its own way—is not today a useful 'ideal' nor even a useful point of comparison. And maybe European and U.S. settler-colonial cities and postindustrial dystopias are more interesting points of comparison. Or perhaps Cairo is a city that 'models' neoliberal fashions in a way which is paradoxically and troublingly 'ideal' in a universal sense.

Egypt's gated communities are proposed as the ultimate figure of risk. Yet they generate by their very presence many profound forms of social risk, fragility, and general vulnerability that all the physical and discursive ramparts of neoliberal geography and luxury housing would like to block out. Walled communities realize, in fact, the national fragility and produce the generalized social risk they claim to secure.

If gated communities came to spectacularize Egypt's neoliberalization from 1990 to 2000, then it is not surprising that they lie at the heart of the post-2000 financial crisis in Egypt. The immense capitalization that was necessary for the exclusive subsidized development of these desert areas was evidently one of the major causes of the crisis in liquidity and the bursting of the building bubble that caused the collapse of property prices and the collapse of the national economy in general. The elite development model appeared at the center of the national crisis. And it came to stand, perhaps, for risk itself. The depreciation of speculative investments in the gated communities, sustained largely by many private as well as public banks, is reflected in all of economic headlines of the 2003–2004 period: the quasi-failure of the Bahgat group (whose proprietor was even imprisoned), the difficulties of the steel magnate Ahmad al-'Ezz, and the scandals that haunt the shadow of the minister of housing, Ahmed Soliman, responsible for the sale of lands on which the gated communities were implanted. Protections and alliances among businesspeople and public officials were reconstituted and purged through the crisis. Certainly, as Timothy Mitchell shows, it is important to see capitalism in action, a channeling of benefits and of credit toward the most irrational desires, which during the boom years took shape in land and stone, transforming the desert into an inhabitable place (2002). The bubble burst. The Egyptian economy collapsed after 2000. But the new liberal, neocolonial city, the embodiment of risk and exclusivism, had already taken shape to occupy, constrain, and remake the social world. Cairo has been radically altered.

Works Cited

AlSayyad, Nizar, ed. 2001. *Hybrid Urbanism*. Westport, Conn.: Praeger.

Appadurai, Arjun. 2001. *Après le colonialisme: les conséquences culturelles de la globalisation*. Paris: Payot.

Arnaud, Jean-Luc. 1998. *Le Caire: mise en place d'une ville moderne, 1867–1907*. Paris: Sindbad/Actes Sud.

Barth, Fredrich. 1969. "Introduction." In *Ethnic Groups and Boundaries*, ed. Fredrich Barth, 9–38. Boston: Little, Brown and Co.

Beck, Ulrich. 1992. *Risk Society: Towards a New Modernity*. Newbury Park, Calif.: Sage.

Blakely, Edward, and Mary Snyder, eds. 1997. *Fortress America: Gated Communities in the United States*. Washington, D.C.: Brookings Institution Press.

Caldeira, Teresa. 2000. *City of Walls: Crime, Segregation and Citizenship in São Paulo*. Berkeley: University of California Press.

Caneri, Toussaint. 1905. *La ville du Caire son présent et son arenir*. Cairo: Institut Francais d'Archéologie Orientale.

Clerget, Marcel. 1934. *Le Caire: étude de géographie urbaine et économique*. Cairo: Shindler.

Desmarais, Gaëtan, and Gilles Ritchot. 2000. *La géographie structurale*. Paris: L'Harmattan.

Douglas, Mary. 1966. *Purity and Danger: An Analysis of Pollution and Taboo*. London: Routledge & Kegan Paul.

Douglas, Mary, and Aaron Wildavsky. 1982. *Risk and Culture: an Essay on the Selection of Technical and Environmental Dangers*. Berkeley: University of California Press.

"Dreamland, the Urban Renaissance *(nahda 'umraniya)* during the Mubârak Era." 1998. *Mitr Murabba'a* (October): 10–14.

Fanchette, Sylvie. 1995. "Un village idéal pour une société nouvelle: l'expérience de la province de Tahrir dans le désert occidental." In *Entre réforme sociale et mouvement national*, ed. Alain Roussillon, 479–500. Cairo: CEDEJ.

Ferry, Luc. 1992. *Le nouvel ordre écologique: l'arbre, l'animal et l'homme*. Paris: Grasset.

Garret, Pascal. 2001. "Le passage à l'échelle urbaine: Héliopolis et ses mythes." In *Le Caire–Alexandrie: architectures européennes 1850–1950*, ed. Mercedes Volait, 109–20. Cairo: IFAO-CEDEJ.

Girard, René. 1982. *Le bouc émissaire*. Paris: Grasset.

Hacking, Ian. 2003. "Risk and Dirt." In *Risk and Morality*, eds. Richard Ericson and Aaron Doyle, 22–47. Toronto: University of Toronto Press.

Hopkins, Nicholas, Sohair Mehanna, and S. El-Haggar, eds. 2001. *People and Pollution: Cultural Constructions and Social Action in Egypt*. Cairo: The American University in Cairo Press.

Ilbert, Robert. 1981. *Héliopolis, 1905–1922, genèse d'une ville*. Marseille: Éditions du CNRS.

Kamal, 'Abdallah. 1998. "al-Ruju' Baron Empain!" *Ruz al-Yusuf*, 12 October.

Kienle, Eberhard. 2001. *A Grand Delusion: Democracy and Economic Reform in Egypt*. London: I.B. Tauris.

Korayem, Karima. 2001. "The Impact of Food Subsidy Policy on Low Income People and the Poor in Egypt." *Cairo Papers in Social Science* 23 (Spring): 69–125.

McKraken, Grant. 1988. *Culture and Consumption: New Approaches to the Symbolic Character of Consumer Goods and Activities*. Bloomington: Indiana University Press.

Mitchell, Timothy. 2002. "Dreamland." In *Rule of Experts: Egypt, Techno-Politics, Modernity*, ed. Timothy Mitchell, 272–304. Berkeley: University of California Press.

Park, Robert. 1926. "The Urban Community as a Spatial Pattern and a Moral Order." In *The Urban Community*, eds. Ernest Burgess and Robert Park, 122–38. Chicago: University of Chicago Press.

Rebour, Thierry. 2000. *La théorie du rachat: géographie, économie, histoire*. Paris: Publications de la Sorbonne.

Weldes, Jutta, Mark Laffey, Hugh Gusterson, and Raymond Duvall, eds. 1999. *Cultures of Insecurity: States, Communities and the Production of Danger*. Minneapolis: University of Minnesota Press.

Zaki, Mohed. 1999. *Egyptian Business Elites*. Cairo: Konrad Adenauer Stiftung and Arab Center for Development and Future Research.

Notes

1   Mr. al-Mansuri is not a real individual. Mr. al-Mansuri and this opening narrative represent a fictionalized composite of several individuals interviewed by the author during the past four years, and evoke the overall contours of their experience and vision of their new Cairo.

2   The agglomeration is marked by a clear depopulation of its center and even, for some twenty years, of its ancient inner-city suburbs; but the de-densification is entirely relative. Cairo remains one of the most densely populated metropolises in the world with, on average, more that 250 inhabitants per hectare and with quarters surpassing eight hundred inhabitants. Simply stated, extreme densities of population have left the historic center at the profit of unregulated peripheral areas, where, henceforth, the majority of Cairenes live. Up to the present, urban sprawl did not exist—the agglomeration remained extremely compact. Flight to the desert gated communities thus takes on a character which represents that much more of a rupture with the norms of habitation.

3   Here, we adhere to Fredrik Barth's approach to identity, which is understood as performative and elaborated through interaction; that is to say, in the encounter, even in confrontation, with others (1969). Thus, we distance ourselves from all

substantial definitions of culture, and the confusion between culture and identity. Ethnocultural identity uses culture, but rarely all culture. Culture is a resource whose composing elements are rewritten at present as a function of situations. Identity depends, therefore, on relationships with borders and not with a center. Admitted as a social construct born of and made dynamic through interaction, identity invites an interrogation of the following type: How, why, and by whom, at such a moment and in such a context, is a particular identity produced, maintained, or put into question?

4   These data are calculated from the 1995–1996 study of budget consumption of households and from census data taken between 1986 and 1996 on the number of households and their rate of growth. The study does not allow one to precisely identify the revenue and even less the property of the families studied. On the other hand, it provides a reliable distribution relative to current budgetary consumption, including housing expenses. These 315,000 families themselves represent more than 26 percent of current consumption, or as much as 50 percent of that of the poorest. Property may nevertheless be estimated with respect to the number of families possessing more than one residence in 1996, either 172,000 families or 6.6 percent of the families in the region of Greater Cairo (more than 8 percent in Cairo proper).

5   This is as many residences as were constructed in ten years in the Cairo region, all segments combined, between 1986 and 1996.

2 Cairo as Capital of Socialist Revolution?

Omnia El Shakry

It is not difficult to imagine the scene in Tahrir Province, the *definitive* land-reclamation project inaugurated under Gamal 'Abd al-Nasser, upon the arrival of a high-profile visitor—such as the January 1957 visit of the Yugoslavian ambassador or the September 1957 visits from the representatives of the newly formed National Assembly ("al-Safir al-Yugoslavi yaqul . . ." 1957; "Ma'a al-nuwwab . . ." 1957). Former peasants appeared now as citizens: men dressed in gingham shirts and overalls, and women dressed in white shirts, black skirts, and printed headscarves, looking quite 'picturesque' for the cameras. Early-morning visitors would no doubt witness the call to attention, the daily salutes, and nationalist songs sung in unison. Visitors would also surely note, as scholar Doreen Warriner did on her 1956 visit, that settlers had been subjected to "complete human reconditioning. . . . Every aspect of their lives was disciplined and standardized" (1961, 54). They might also have remarked upon the rows of new houses, each identical to the other, "consisting of two rooms, a hall, a kitchen, and a bathroom, . . . a front terrace and a backyard . . . carefully planned and built according to health conditions" (United Arab Republic, Institute of National Planning 1965, 34). The village itself, with its spacious and straight roads, and a main square situated in the center (with buildings for village administration, a cooperative center, school, nursery, and clubs for migrants and employees), would have appeared quite unlike any other 'typical' Egyptian village in the Delta (United Arab Republic, Institute of National Planning 1965, 34). An especially astute observer might have also noticed the peculiar absence of any children running around the village—all safely ensconced in day-care centers.

Exactly forty years later, if one were to step into a new desert city, such as Sixth of October, or further yet, Sadat City, one would find, much like the protagonist of Yousry Nasrallah's 1993 film *Mercedes* (who emerges from a mental hospital in the wake of the fall of the Berlin wall) that the world had become one in which socialism was passé. One would instead find relocated populations on the outskirts of Cairo living in close proximity to industrial zones inhabited by such familiar multinational corporations as Nestlé and General Motors. One would note the relative isolation of the residential zones, their intensely class-segregated subdivisions, and the near absence of public spaces geared toward communal life. The monotony of the five-story Khrushchev-style walk-ups, recurring in an endless repetition of Corbusian functionalism, would appear almost as a belated parody of modernism.

I evoke these two very different spectacles of modernity as illustrations of two contrasting spatial modes of regulation: a social-welfare mode of regulation for the period spanning the 1930s to the 1960s, and a neoliberal mode of regulation for the period after economic liberalization (Infitah), roughly beginning in the late 1970s. In what follows, I contend that the land-reclamation schemes inaugurated under Nasser (such as Tahrir Province), on the one hand, and the new desert settlements and Greater Cairo schemes promoted after Infitah, on the other, were each indicative of spatial practices enmeshed within the reproduction of a particular 'mode of regulation.'

To anticipate my argument, I suggest that the period of the 1930s to the 1960s was characterized by an emphasis upon social welfare, and the projects of horizontal land reclamation were imbued with what I am terming a *pioneering ethic*, geared toward the conquering of spatial boundaries and the expansion of a frontier, in order to form a community of settlers. Such a social-welfare framework sought to increase the health, wealth, and productivity of the population through rural reconstruction and land reclamation and resettlement schemes, which were holistic, comprehensive, and communal, as the above example of Tahrir Province illustrates. Within the rhetoric of postcolonial Egypt (Egypt achieved independence from the British in 1936 with the signing of the Anglo-Egyptian Treaty, but its postcoloniality is said to have begun with the 1952 revolution, led by Gamal 'Abd al-Nasser and organized around state socialism), social planners imagined Cairo as a revolutionary planning hub, in which rural space was privileged, and targeted for improvement, in the reconstitution of space. Nationalist discourse, and social reformers, posited the *city as the quintessential site of the modern* (the seat of rational state planning and the development of modern forms of power), and *the rural as the site of national identity* (with the peasantry as representative of the demographic masses). In a sense, throughout this period the city became the locus of government, while the countryside became the object of governance.

After the economic liberalization policies of Infitah a global shift occurred in which local and international agents (such as the representatives of the state bourgeoisie and landowning interests in the state apparatus, led by Anwar Sadat; global multinational corporations with local liaisons; and USAID) actively incorporated Egypt into a neoliberal capitalist regime in which socioeconomic development became the state's primary object of governance. Infitah led to the creation of a very different set of spatial practices, which emphasized a process that I am terming a *cartography of redistribution*, and specifically a funneling and cantonization, geared toward a deconcentration and a radiating out of the urban agglomeration of Cairo. After Infitah, the project of rural transformation was abandoned, and urban density, which was perceived as consuming economic growth, was targeted as urban and social reformers sought the "productive redistribution of the population" (Ministry of Planning 1978). The urban was thereby transformed from a product of benign neglect to the supreme object of governance.

People and Land under Reclamation

Adequate socialist planning is the only path which would ensure the complete use of our natural resources—material, natural and human—in a practical, scientific and humane manner that would enable us to achieve the welfare of the entire people and make a comfortable life available to them.
  Egypt's National Charter, 1962

Building factories is easy, building canals is easy, building dams is easy—but building men, that is the harshest difficulty.
  Gamal 'Abd al-Nasser
  (Ministry of Land Reclamation, 1969)

Land-reclamation projects were launched under Nasser to address the slow rate of expansion in cultivated land area in relation to rapid population growth. Government efforts focused upon both reducing population growth through the nascent family planning programs and expanding horizontally to reclaim land. Land reclamation and resettlement was primarily the purview of governmental agencies, such as the Permanent Organization for Land Reclamation, established in 1954 and in 1966 consolidated, along with several other agencies, into the Egyptian Authority for the Utilization and Development of Reclaimed Land (EAUDRL) (United Arab Republic 1960, 437; al-Abd 1979, 95). Numerous actors, institutional formations, and political blocs (in particular, the burgeoning technocratic elite of the Army Corps) competed to engineer the development and maintenance of land-reclamation projects such as Tahrir Province. Newly formed state agencies (such as the Organization for Land Reclamation), as well as reinvigorated ministries (such as the Ministry of Agriculture and the Ministry of Social Affairs), were actively involved in the development of social-welfare policies aligned with the new political orientation of the Nasserist regime. These agencies fostered the development of a technocratic elite (the hallmark of the Nasser era) and the cultivation of new forms of expertise, in fields ranging from agricultural engineering to social work.

The Tahrir Province project was itself figured by the revolutionary regime as its quintessential enterprise, "one of the major pioneering programs for the invasion of the desert" (United Arab Republic, Institute of National Planning 1965, 22). The project aimed to increase national production through the expansion of cultivable land, but more importantly, also attempted to create a "model rural community based on Socialist principles" and "give self-confidence to individuals by demonstrating their capacity to undertake large projects, especially that this project is total-ly undertaken and supervised by Arab technicians without any foreign assistance" (United Arab Republic 1960, 439). Located west of the Delta and south of Alexandria, this project began shortly after the revolution in 1952 under the supervision of Magdi Hassanein, himself a Free Officer from the small group that had led the Egyptian revolution of 1952 (Hassanein 1975). Hassanein became head of the Tahrir Province Organization, administering the province for several years, controversially, along a socialist-utopian model. In the words of Hassanein, the object of the project was to "accustom our people to the desert, to make the young intellectuals practically active in reclamation, and to give more work" (Hassanein as cited by Warriner 1957, 49). Hassanein also intended to demonstrate that the Arab world could compete with the much-vaunted Israeli 'colonization of the desert' (Hassanein 1975, 103).

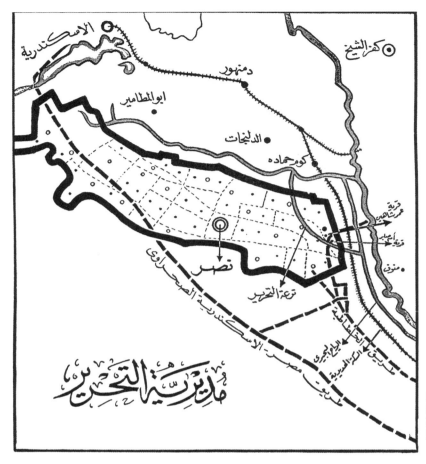

مديريّة التحرير

Map of Tahrir Province (from Ministry of Land Reclamation 1969, 77).

The process of settlement in Tahrir Province was by no means in-discriminate. The Migration Committee began a policy of migration after the completion of Omar Shahin, the province's second village, after which the committee relocated to Manufiya governorate (the most crowded governorate in the republic) in order to choose the first group of citizens to occupy the new community (Bassiouni 1972, 179–87). Settlers had to fulfill numerous requirements in order to qualify for migration, such as literacy, sound mental and physical health, a clear police record, and agricultural or manual experience (Abu-Zayd n.d., 55–57; al-Abd 1979, 94). Families were then selected by the agency for medical, psychological and occupational testing. Speaking on the selection of settlers in Tahrir Province, Doreen Warriner recounts the words of Major Gamal Zaki, director of the Social Affairs Department:

Settlers, he said, are selected scientifically on social, medical, and psychological tests. . . . Of 1,100 applicants so far, all had the right social qualifications, but only 382 families were accepted medically, because while most of the men were healthy enough, the women and children fell far short of standard. Only 180 families survived the psychological test. . . . Of these, 132 are now undergoing the six months' training, which includes a three-month probation period. 'We consider both people and land to be under reclamation'. Warriner 1957, 51, emphasis added.

The first transfer of families occurred on 22 October 1955, when 131 families were transferred to Tahrir Province, followed by thirty families on 1 February 1957 (Bassiouni 1972, 183). In the words of one of the first female settlers:

They selected a man and his wife to go and see the new places. We were selected and we went with the omda to Om Saber and Omar Shahin. We saw the buffaloes and the cows, the chickens and the houses. They fascinated us with the project. We saw the concrete red-brick houses in which we were to live instead of the mud-brick houses. We went back to the village amazed by what we had seen and we started to tell others about these new places, the cleanliness, the houses which have water and electricity, the furniture which we never had and most important the land, the five feddans which we will own. Sabea 1987, 34.

Upon their arrival the new citizens were trained in the village of Omar Shahin, after which they would be relocated to their new villages. Social specialists (including social workers and public health workers) organized

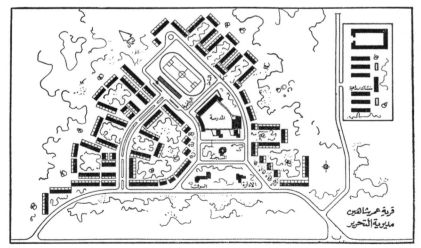

Plan of Omar Shahin village (from Ministry of Land Reclamation 1969, 79).

a comprehensive six-month training program for settlers to facilitate their mental and practical acclimation to their new environment. Social training took place on an individual, family, and group level, and was concerned with the introduction and acclimation of settlers to the principles of the revolution and of the new community and its way of life—through both practical and intellectual means, such as lectures, radio programs, cultural programs, and various publications (Abu-Zayd n.d., 54–67; El-Hammami 1999).

Training and instruction was to be fairly extensive and included the fields of primary and vocational education, childcare, house care, and hygiene, in Zaki's words: "Everything is disciplined, standardized, new." Settlers had a daily routine, wore uniforms, and all children left their mothers' care at the age of two to be placed in nurseries. The province contained a social services center, which aimed at providing inhabitants with the necessary training for "raising the standard of their production capacity," and social workers supervised virtually all aspects of social life—including athletics and the use of leisure time (Ministry of Land Reclamation 1969, 34–70; Abu Zayd n.d., 54–67; El-Hammami 1999).

Settlers received this 'total care' so as to help them acclimate to their new environment and foster self-help and governance. All aspects of life in the province, such as the daily salutes and singing, were attempts to foster group unity and a sense of shared principles and goals. Even the uniforms served a purpose—to efface differences and create a sense of equality (Abu-Zayd n.d., 61–62). Above all, the new society was to foster the principle of equality. Indeed, in the recollection of Ahmed El-Hammami, an engineer who worked on the project under Hassanein, the idea that women were equal partners in labor was among the most marked features of life in Tahrir Province (El-Hammami 1999). According to Hekmat Abu-Zayd, a prominent social scientist who worked extensively on the project and conducted a 1957 survey on social acclimation, settlers were meant to come to view the state differently. Not as the repressive apparatus familiar to them in the army, police, and courts, and in the spirit of domination *(ruh al-saytara)*; but rather, in the faces of vocational trainers, social workers, and agricultural engineers—all sharing the same goal of collective cooperation (n.d., 62). In the recollection of an early settler:

Mostafa explained that when they first moved there was a lot of care from the government officials. They knew the problems of the settlers and tried to solve them. There were regular gatherings after sunset where people used to sit together to get to know each other. Everybody started by introducing himself to small groups of ten people. Each told the others where he came from, why, about their families and so on. Then this group of ten met and exchanged ideas with other similar

groupings, until in the end everyone came to know everybody else in the village by
name and where he is from. Then there were collective gatherings for the whole
village in the theater. Each one talked and anybody facing a problem was given
a chance to share it with others and solutions were sought out collectively. Meals
were shared. . . . They gave people clothes . . . 'like people from the city.' There were
female social workers who went into the houses and taught women how to cook
and to keep the place clean. Hopkins et al. 1988, 68.

Magdi Hassanein's supervision of the project, however, was short-lived
and beset by administrative difficulties and political rivalries. In November
of 1957, following a heated debate in the inaugural session of the National
Assembly, Hassanein, the proponent of a socialist model loosely based on
Soviet models and the communal ownership of land, was ousted and replaced
by Sayed Marei, then head of the Higher Committee on Agrarian Reform
responsible for land redistribution, and the proponent of a far less radical
smallholder model (Springborg 1979, 55; El-Hammami 1999). Clearly, the
early days of Tahrir Province were an *experimental* attempt to create a new
rural community based on socialist principles. Although Hassanein was later
vilified by the press (accused of being a communist with bourgeois tastes),
many of the settlers poignantly recalled the days of Hassanein as among the
best in their lives, in an attempt to correct the historical record (El-Hammami
1999). In the words of a settler:

Hassanein did not stay long in Tahrir. In 1957 he left because of the conflict
that arose around him. The journalist Rawya Attiya made use of that and she
claimed he was creating a new republic in the Mudiriyah. *Because the settlers*
loved him and appreciated what he did for them, people outside the Mudiriyah
felt that he was mobilizing the peasants against the regime, that he was creating
an army in Tahrir to seize power. We were quite sad when he had to leave. He
did a lot for us and we are the only ones who could judge him and give him the
credit he deserves. Sabea 1987, 39.

Shortly after Marei's takeover, however, the pro-Leftist faction of the
regime (Ali Sabri and 'Abd al-Muhsin Abuel Nur) successfully challenged
Marei's leadership and regained control of the province in 1961 under Abuel
Nur's direction, following a Soviet state-farm model, and emboldened by Nikita
Khrushchev's May 1964 visit there (Springborg 1979, 55–60; El-Hammami 1999).
After Nasser's death, Sadat purged the pro-Leftist faction of the regime (such as
Ali Sabri) and began to experiment with various reclamation models (including

giving land grants to agricultural engineering graduates), but eventually EAUDRL was dissolved in 1976 and independent private-sector companies, such as the South Tahrir Company, were established to oversee land reclamation instead (Voll 1980, 139; Hopkins et al. 1988, 9). There were suggestions of simply selling the land to joint-venture agrobusinesses—indeed, one such venture, First Arabian Agribusiness (FAAB), located itself on ten thousand feddans in South Tahrir (Hopkins et al. 1988, 9–10). By the late 1970s the land reclaimed by the government had begun to be parceled off and sold in five- to twenty-five-feddan lots at subsidized prices, and eventually to sole or joint ventures, such as Coca-Cola, which leased large tracts for agrobusiness-style farms (Hinnebusch 1985, 143). Thus the emphasis during the Infitah period shifted from public to private ownership of land; but more significantly, away from a holistic model of building a community of settlers to reclaim land toward simply expanding cultivation to larger tracts of land via capital-intensive projects.

The Tahrir project, however, was an important *conceptual* model of land reclamation and social welfare under the revolutionary regime. What is most striking about Tahrir Province, and most distinctive about this particular phase of postcoloniality, is the accent placed upon scientific socialist planning and the extremely structured environment that was created for its inhabitants—much of it centered on welfare, health and hygiene, communitarianism, and cooperation. First and foremost, reclamation projects aimed to create new model communities of citizens, entailing "the addition of productive units to society"; the transformation of waste lands into productive resources; the creation of a happy family made of workers and peasants; and the inculcation of individuals with communitarian and socialist ethics (Ministry of Land Reclamation 1969, 7–8). In short, they aimed at 'building men' as much as building new societies. Further, the key to these new communities was the supervision of their composition and the direction of their development by the state—that is, their planned nature. Such features as the selection of settlers with the knowledge of the state *(bi-ma'rifat al-dawla)*; the organization of relations among citizens within the framework of social and economic institutions, in order to fulfill the goals of the state for a model community, were indeed innovations in state power (Ministry of Land Reclamation 1969, 24).

The Nasserist land-reclamation projects belong to a social-welfare mode of regulation, in which spatial projects were conceptualized in terms of the circulation of wealth, health, hygiene, and productivity through the body politic. The emphasis was on reconstructing bodies and minds: building and cleaning villages, homes, and children, and thus constructing a 'new Egyptian' through comprehensive social schemes that sought to regulate the daily life of peasants and women by instructing them in the care of their bodies, homes, and children. Multiple agents and actors (ranging from the elite intelligentsia to the state-sponsored initiatives of the Ministry of Social Affairs) engaged in the politics of 'social-welfare regulation.' The concern for social welfare is not meant to refer to an innocuous, benevolent process whereby the state shepherds its citizens in their own welfare. Rather, it refers, quite specifically, to the social and political process of reproducing *particular* social relations, such as those between the city and the countryside, in order to ensure the successful reproduction of labor power and to minimize class antagonisms—a 'happy family' of workers and peasants (Ministry of Land Reclamation 1969, 7). Within a social-welfare framework, urban-based social reformers and experts were to lead rural men and women (viewed as the source of national wealth and identity) to 'reformed' social practices (health, hygiene, and labor) to allow for a healthy, productive, and efficient population—appropriate to the progress of the modern world. Crucially, throughout this era state planners and technocrats conceived of 'population' itself as a national resource to be cultivated in the rural areas (from the technocratic nucleus of Cairo), rather than as a threat to be managed (Abu-Zayd n.d.; Hassanein 1975; Zaki n.d., 1964).

Urbanism under the Revolutionary State

Much has been written on the colonial heritage of Cairo—the moderate transformations under Muhammad 'Ali and the more wide-scale realignment of the physical structure and social space of the city under Khedive Isma'il's reign in the second half of the nineteenth century (or what some have referred to as the 'Haussmannization' of Cairo) (Abu-Lughod 1971; Agha Khan 1985, 91–113; Mitchell 1988). While the early literature on the turn-of-the-century transformations of Cairo posited a dual city—the construction of a modern European core section in contrast to the native traditional quarters—this scholarship has now begun to come into question (Fahmy 2002). Nevertheless, scholars agree that the century's turn was marked by the planning and development of numerous residential areas in Cairo, with a peak in construction activities—both large-scale projects initiated by foreign land-development companies, and smaller-scale projects by individual entrepreneurs—between 1890 and 1907 (Agha Khan 1985; Raymond 2000; Volait 2003). Among the major projects developed during this period were the elite residential districts of Qasr al-dubara (1890s); Garden City and Zamalek (1905–1907); Heliopolis (1906); and Maadi (1906) (Agha Khan 1985; Ilbert 1985; Raymond 2000; Volait 2003).

These developments were achieved through the influx and expansion of a foreign-funded infrastructural system of tramways, bridges, roads, and sewage and electricity networks; but also at the expense of the so-called "old city" and the lower-income populations (Agha Khan 1985, 95–97). By the early 1900s Cairo exhibited unevenly developed zones. The interwar period saw the rapid deterioration of housing conditions, with increased densities especially marked in the middle-class mixed zones and the traditional quarters (El Kadi 1990, 186–87). This deterioration, coupled with increased rural–urban migration and the increased embourgeoisement of the previously foreign sectors of Cairo, led to an uneven housing situation, in which the older quarters and the adjacent cemeteries were marked by nonexistent or inadequate infrastructure and overcrowding, in contrast to the newer sections of the city with their recently constructed buildings and services (Agha Khan 1985, 95–98; El Kadi 1990, 186–87).

In sum, the interwar period was marked by a negligible focus on urban areas; despite the creation of a Planning Higher Advisory Council in 1929 and the elaboration of a general town plan for Cairo, approved in 1932, plans were minimal in scope and deferred in their implementation (Volait 2003). Indeed, it would not be until 1949 that an autonomous urban municipality for Cairo would be in place (Volait 2003, 38; El Kadi 1990, 187). It is noteworthy that among the projects actually selected for implementation, such as that of Muhandisin, plans were intensive and extensive in scope—aimed not at containing the growth of the city, but rather at increasing zones of urban habitation (Volait 2003).

This urban crisis, perceived in the urban-planning literature as very much a crisis of governance, was the urban legacy that the Nasser regime took over. As such the first master plan of Cairo, begun in 1953 and completed in 1956, and put forth by several Egyptians trained in the U.S. and Great Britain, was explicitly addressed to the remedying of these urban problems (El Kadi 1990, 187–88). The idea of planning, and specifically the scientific nature of socialist planning, was one that gained great currency in the post-independence period under Nasser. The first master plan for Cairo was initiated in order to accumulate information regarding "the distribution of inhabitants, the location of industry, commerce, and other land uses, housing conditions, labor conditions, transport and communication problems, streets, and highways" (Abu-Lughod 1971, 229). The elaboration of a master plan for Cairo was part of the larger objective of improving knowledge of and exercising control over the urban reality Nasserism inherited (El Kadi 1990, 188). Conceptually, in a fashion similar to the interwar period, the plan was aimed less at containing the growth of the city, and more at increasing zones of urban habitation, through the development of industrial zones—a policy which would later be criticized by urban planners in the Infitah era.

The first master plan aimed at the creation of industrial areas in the immediate vicinity of Cairo; six satellite industrial zones (workers' cities) were planned in Helwan, Shubra al-Khayma, Imbaba, and Giza, and were to receive 50 percent of the industrial investment allocation under the first five-year plan (1960–65) (Agha Khan 1985, 97–98). "These six towns should be developed as satellite industrial towns, self-contained, with all their public facilities. Failing this it is feared that chaos will spread" (from the text of the master plan as cited in El Kadi 1990, 189–90). The satellite cities were aimed at addressing the problem of linking workers' place of living with their work without exacerbating already taxed traffic and transportation. The plans to develop industrial centers just outside of Cairo were coupled with recommendations to create new industrial centers around the Suez Canal region and the iron-ore mines in Upper Egypt (El Kadi 1990, 190). Government action, however, was taken for only one of the satellite towns: Helwan, which was transformed into a workers' city with a heavy industrial base and one of the largest public-housing projects in Egypt at the time (Abu-Lughod 1971, 231–32; El Kadi 1990, 191). Government involvement in investment in infrastructure as well as residential housing, and specifically the construction of popular-housing schemes, also began to be formulated during this time period. Programs for public housing were undertaken either in the form of rental units or cooperative ownership (Abu-Lughod 1971, 230–32; United Arab Republic 1960, 667–69; El Kadi 1990, 192). They consisted mainly of heavily subsidized low-cost housing located near the industrial centers (United Arab Republic 1960, 483–84).

The revolutionary state, then, defined itself as the provider of low- and middle-income housing units, previously unavailable to the mass of the population. The 1960–65 plan, as well as the publications of the Ministry of Housing (Wizarat al-iskan wa-l-marafiq), was quite explicit in its delineation of urban housing projects and in its condemnation of the prerevolutionary state's neglect to provide affordable and sanitary housing for citizens currently living under "abnormal housing conditions" (Ministry of Housing and Development 1965, 35–53). Urban planners linked the degeneration of the housing situation, on the one hand, to the dual processes of increased population growth and rural–urban migration, and on the other, to the profiteering motives of the private sector in establishing luxury and high-income housing units (Ministry of Housing and Development 1965, 35–36). The new public-housing buildings were most often styled along the lines of the so-called "Khrushchev blocks":

five- to six-story pre-fabricated walk-up flats, common to Soviet-bloc mass-housing projects (Castillo 1992, 281; Ministry of Housing and Development 1965, 60–71). (See Ghannam's contribution to this volume for a detailed discussion of the private and public housing project in al-Zawya al-Hamra.)

The other main urban project undertaken during the Nasser period was the development of Nasr City, planned in 1958 (Abu-Lughod 1971, 233). Planned on a desert plateau, it was intended to be a bureaucratic-administrative town, containing all the major ministries, with housing and community facilities for the growing technocratic-civil servant class (El Kadi 1990, 191–92). It thus *spatially* embodied the regime's conception of Cairo as a technocratic planning nucleus. The project was undertaken jointly by the ministries of housing and defense (Abu-Lughod 1971, 233–34). Architects (including Muhammad Riyad, former chief of the Cairo *baladiya*—municipality) constructed the site plan of the city along several communal 'general zones of use,' corresponding roughly to a concentration of (i) administrative-institutional (ministries, stadium, international fairgrounds); (ii) industrial, recreational and educational (factories, university campuses, recreational zones); and (iii) residential uses (combined worker and white-collar housing; multifamily housing for low- and middle-income groups) (Ministry of Housing and Development 1965, 54–71; Abu-Lughod 1971, 232–36).

The schemes to develop industrial cities and zones under Nasser were very much in keeping with the regime's aggressive attempts at industrialization, as well as agricultural expansion. The focus was upon the rational, efficient, and scientific management of production and consumption (administrative, agricultural, and industrial) within a social-welfare mode of regulation. The spatial strategies of the period all focus upon the efficient management of the relation between population growth and the organization of bodies and production in space. All the elements of a functionalist modernism are present: the rational ordering of space enabling a subsumability into more efficient circuits of production and the Corbusian house as a 'machine for living.'

In particular, the distinction between a social-welfare mode of regulation and the neoliberal mode, which emerges after Infitah, lay in the state's transformed relationship to urbanism, to demographic mass (the notion of 'population'), and to the rural hinterlands. Under a social-welfare mode of regulation, comprehensive land-reclamation projects, as well as urban housing projects, were geared toward the development of holistic communities (targeting the demographic masses—namely, peasants and workers) and the inculcation of individuals with communitarian or egalitarian ethics. State technocrats privileged rural expansion and development (viewed as the pivot of national wealth), while the urban became the product of benign neglect. Population resettlement policies shifted under Infitah, as a new set of local and international actors privileged urban economic productivity and socioeconomic development. In fact, after Infitah urban population density began to be radically targeted, as state technocrats and urban planners proposed the development of desert and satellite cities as a solution for the decentralization of Cairo. This shift was toward the building of new cities and the "productive redistribution of the population" (Ministry of Planning 1978). In sum, the transition to Infitah can be seen as a shift *from an ethics of rural expansion to an ethics of urban redistribution.*

Toward a Cartography of Redistribution

The demise of Nasserism was a complex product of both internal ideological and class contradictions within the regime's pursuit of socialism, and of external political conflicts, namely, the 1967 war with Israel. The liberalization policies of Egypt's Infitah were inaugurated by Anwar Sadat's Presidential Working Paper of October 1974, in an attempt to create a transition to a free-market economy (Hinnebusch 1985, 112–16). Infitah paved the way for a different (although not discontinuous) set of international and domestic relations, characterized by a general rapproachment with foreign capital (or what Malak Zaalouk refers to as a "delocalisation of capital") and a strengthening of the private sector through a series of governmental concessions, that is to say a dual internal and external process of liberalization (Zaalouk 1989, 75–94; cf. Boyer 1990; Harvey 1989; Lipietz 1986). Among the marked features of Infitah, enabled through a series of regulatory interventions as well as a shift in global conditions of capitalism, were: the creation of a favorable environment for foreign investment projects (usually in the form of joint ventures) through a new investment law containing various privileges (such as tax exemptions for foreign ventures); a decentralization and liberalization of foreign trade, signaling the end of the public-sector monopoly on foreign trade and the opening up of the economy to foreign goods through the private sector; an expansive influx of international aid; government liberalization of fiscal policy; the abolition of public holding companies previously in charge of planning, coordinating, and supervising the public sector and a concomitant decentralization in state economic planning; and the weakening of the state's control over public enterprise through a liberalization of wage and employment regulations, facilitated in part by a redefinition of the public sector, thereby leaving private-sector management with more autonomy (Dessouki 1991, 259–62; Zaalouk 1989, 75–94).

The predominant agents and architects of Infitah were a combination of members of the old industrial bourgeoisie who had managed to insinuate themselves into the state apparatus after the 1952 revolution; members of the state technocratic bourgeoisie that emerged under Nasser (the upper stratum of the bureaucratic and managerial elite, high-ranking civil servants, army officers and directors, managers of public-sector companies, etc.); and the emerging commercial bourgeoisie whose financial activities were opened up by Infitah—wholesale traders, contractors, importer-exporters, etc. (Zaalouk 1989). Infitah could not have been implemented, however, without the consolidation of new political and social discourses, specifically an ideological commitment to economic productivity and socioeconomic development. The new Infitah elite privileged the urban as the site of capitalist transformation— the location of elite commercial and speculative ventures par excellence (El Kadi 1990, 201).

The second master plan of Cairo, drawn up between 1966 and 1970 by the Greater Cairo Planning Commission (established in 1965), and approved by ministerial decree in 1974, introduced the concept of the Greater Cairo region and recommended the construction of planned desert cities (Gorgy 1985, 176–82; UN 1990, 9). This plan articulated the nascent shift in the regime of accumulation, which culminated in the Infitah policies. It marked itself off radically from the first phase of Cairo's planning, viewed in the urban-planning literature as anarchic: resulting in an uncontrolled urban expansion, attracting migrant labor and informal settlements to Cairo, consuming arable land, and ignoring infrastructure and service provision: in short as simply exacerbating the urban crisis (El Kadi 1990, 193–201; Agha Khan 1985, 98–99).

The plan recommended international migration and the development of satellite towns in order to reduce densities in 'saturated sectors'; the need to substitute large farms for subsistence agriculture in the rural periphery; and greater freedom to the private sector in housing and construction (El Kadi 1990, 193–201). The two most salient, and related, features of the plan were its recommendations for the construction of self-sufficient towns and the control of the existing urban agglomeration in order to end urban encroachment on arable land (Gorgy 1985, 178). Under Sadat's 1974 Presidential Working Paper, the idea of desert cities was supported as a means to preserve arable land and decentralize and depopulate Cairo (El Kadi 1990, 200; Hegab 1985, 172; UN 1990, 9).

It emphasized the need for an urbanization strategy which would remap the population of Egypt through the creation of new urbanized centers endowed with "new economic activities and better services so as to attract people to a new and productive life" built away from that "narrow green strip of land" (Hegab 1985, 172). Between 1975 and 1979, planning had begun for several new cities and in 1979 the government formed the New Urban Communities Authority (UN 1990, 9). Law No. 59 of 1979, codifying the new settlement policy, inaugurated the creation of eighteen new cities in Egypt, including relatively freestanding new towns (e.g., Sadat City, Tenth of Ramadan) and satellite cities (e.g., Sixth of October, Fifteenth of May); and created a favorable economic environment for private-sector investment and the use of foreign expertise. El Kadi 1990, 200.

Government efforts at *enticing* people to settle the desert cities entailed numerous incentives, such as doubled salaries for government employees, rent subsidies for industrial and residential units, and tax exemptions for new industries (UN 1990, 10). In the words of Ahmed, an operations office government employee who arrived in Tenth of Ramadan City in 1977:

The administration exerted . . . forces to push its own employees to move to the Tenth of Ramadan: One was attraction, a temptation in the form of an increase in salaries. Those who lived in a new city received a sixty percent increase to their original payment as a compensation for living in an undeveloped area. A forty percent increase was also added to the original salary of employees who agreed to work in any of the undeveloped sites. The employees who were in need of the extra monthly income agreed to this deal. Shafik 1991, 87.

The creation of these new cities was articulated directly in tandem with the question of housing, urban crowding, and food security (UNFPA 1980, 25). In fact, by the late 1970s the technocratic elite of the Sadat regime began to radically problematize Cairo's population density (or its 'absorptive capacity'), in keeping with the administration's establishment of its official National Population Policy and Population-Development Program beginning in 1973 (Sayed 1989; SCFPP 1980). According to the 1978–82 five-year plan:

Easing the burden of population on Egyptian cities and lowering the rate of population increase can be realized within the present area of Egypt: outside cities, in villages in the desert and on the seacoast. . . . Egypt currently suffers from a number of social and economic problems, but the most important among them is the problem of high population density . . . it is necessary to identify the true dimensions of the problem of population distribution within national boundaries. There are governorates densely populated to the point of suffocation, while other regions are almost devoid of inhabitants. . . . Development may bring about a reduction in the total population density on presently occupied land through productive redistribution of the population. Ministry of Planning 1978, 32, 70–71.

During the late 1970s urban planners began to construct a new image of the city of Cairo. It had undergone a shift from an image of overcrowding toward a radical assessment of the city as engulfing and consuming not only arable land, but economic growth as well (Kafafi 1980). In part to address the alarm at Cairo's rapid and uncontainable growth the General Organization for Physical Planning (a national agency for regional and urban planning established in 1973) set out to formulate yet a third master scheme for Cairo (El Kadi 1990, 201–2). By the end of the 1970s, government urban planners began to address urban density more systematically in terms of the availability of affordable housing and the spread of informal settlements, for example by upgrading existing areas (rather than embarking on large-scale public housing projects) with informal settlements being the prime target (Agha Khan 1985, 100).

Sadat City: Iconography (photograph by Omnia El Shakry, July 1996).

The 1983 master scheme was framed by two main objectives: economic growth and the improvement of the living environment (GOPP 1983, 2.2). The scheme retained the two main concepts of the 1970 master scheme, namely the containment and maintenance of an optimum size for Cairo (a sealing off) and the development of self-sufficient new communities (new settlements and satellite cities), with the 'residual population' of Cairo expected to be absorbed into the 'new settlements' (a funneling out). With respect to the Greater Cairo region itself, the plan put forth four new spatial concepts: urban region, homogeneous sectors, new settlements in the Greater Cairo region, and development corridors (GOPP 1983, 2.10–2.16). The concept of

Sixth of October, "Land of Culture and Science" (photograph by Omnia El Shakry, July 1996).

new settlements was reframed for the 1983 master scheme, as earlier new communities had proved too costly and at too great of an economic distance (Agha Khan 1985, 105; UN 1990, 12; Bécard 1985, 183–87; Observatoire urbaine 1993, 2). They encompassed: (i) *new towns* (independent cities at a sufficient distance from the center city that their residents will not commute to work); (ii) *satellite cities* (similar to new towns but situated closer to a city center in order to reduce public investment and permit them to benefit from the advantage of their location); and (iii) *new settlements* (areas of predominantly residential development which take advantage of existing employment bases and offer an alternative to living in the informal settlements) (Agha Khan 1985, 105–106; Observatoire urbaine 1993, 2).

What the new communities attempted to create was what Lefebvre refers to as "the lowest possible threshold of sociability—the point beyond which survival would no longer be possible because all social life would have disappeared" (Lefebvre 1991, 316). In newly built towns, such as Tenth of Ramadan, building standards were often quite low, particularly for those in a low-income group. In the words of Abdu, a driver for the Operations Agency of Tenth of Ramadan City:

I just want the responsible directors to come and visit my place and see how I survive with my wife and children. But when the authorities come to the city, it is broadcasted on television, and they visit the houses and apartments of directors and big bosses, they never see how the little people like us live. Shafik 1991, 143.

Further, many new towns were plagued by a hierarchical and divisive organizational layout, with clear segregation between high-, middle-, and low-income groups, oftentimes enforced and reproduced by the Operations Agency and inhabitants themselves. According to the wife of an administrator in the operations office of Tenth of Ramadan City:

It is inconceivable that the custodian lives in the same apartment building with us, these people have rural habits, they breed animals and poultry, they are unclean and the women and children are accustomed to hang around the streets all day. Shafik 1991, 140.

Tenth of Ramadan apartment block (photograph by Omnia El Shakry, July 1996).

Fifteenth of May apartment block (photograph by Omnia El Shakry, August 1996).

Hala, a social worker in Tenth of Ramadan, analyzes the division of the city into class-segregated neighborhoods:

It is very obvious through observing the planning rules of the city—the mere division of the city into districts which are supposed to represent social classes— that an implementation of the notion of class discrimination and social bias which initiates the class struggle has already been perpetuated. These districts are mainly characterized as high-class, a low standard and a workers' district. This segregation gave a certain nature to the character of the city. Shafik 1991, 142.

According to residents who live in the working-class district, such as Nada, the possibility of upward mobility is foreclosed—even for those who could afford it:

It is unfair . . . for some residents to live here and others live there, just because workers do not have a college degree. Do you know that even if one of the workers wants to move out of one of these deteriorating apartments and is ready to pay a higher rent in a better neighborhood, the operations office does not allow it. A prerequisite necessitates that a resident should have a college degree in order to apply for an apartment in the better neighborhoods. Shafik 1991, 151.

The individual experiences of those settled in the new communities reflect the wider shift in the mode of regulation from one in which the state actively sought to construct a new Egyptian (the project of "building men") through building new societies to one in which state and private efforts would turn to developing the economy, through a dual process of economic liberalization, and the reduction and redistribution of Egypt's population. The new communities of the Infitah era focus upon creating attractive centers, which will *entice* new settlers to move because of social and economic opportunities—a very different process than the *pioneering ethic* of the Nasser era, geared toward the conquering of spatial boundaries and the expansion of a frontier, in order to form a community of settlers imbued with communitarian or socialist ethics.

Seen through the trajectory of Egypt's spatial strategies, the shift which occurred around the late 1970s marks the entry into a mode of regulation which works not through holistic models of building communities of settlers to reclaim land (by delineating the specificity of health and hygiene practices to mothers, children, and peasants, or by reconstituting villages by reconstructing them). Rather, the mode of regulation works through the building of new cities, geared in a more specifically capitalist manner to the redistribution of Egypt's population, in order to increase economic productivity and absorb excess population. After Infitah, with the emphasis on rational economic productivity embodied in the new object of economic development, the holistic nature of the previous welfare emphasis is disaggregated into constituent components of economic development.

Conclusion

Studies of Cairo often focus on the microscopic transformations that have occurred within the urban fabric of the city. In particular, studies rooted in an urban-planning perspective often address questions such as the origins of the city's modernity (preceding or following colonialism); the origins of various urban-planning schemes (European or autochthonous); the consequences of various urban models (garden city or new town); or the existence of a dual city (elite and popular) (Abu-Lughod 1971, El Kadi 1990, Fahmy 2002, Raymond 2000, Volait 2003).

This paper has suggested an alternative analytic framework for understanding what I term Egypt's uneven relationship to urbanism in the twentieth century, one that privileges historical analysis. I have tried to sketch—rather schematically—what this historical framework for the development of 'urbanism' might look like. I argued that a historical framework for the study of Cairo in the twentieth century must take into consideration at least three interrelated factors—the historically changing relationship of the state to the rural hinterlands, to rational state planning, and to the subaltern demographic masses (Gramsci 1971; Guha 1982; cf. Hanna 2002). If the state's relationship to the subaltern masses (in Egypt's case, the peasantry), is foregrounded, then the focus on the urban space of Cairo within the twentieth century appears as a sporadic concern until well after the 1952 revolution—at which point urbanism begins to be the dominant concern among state, urban, and technocratic planners, to the exclusion of the problem of ruralism.

In fact, as I have tried to argue, an isolated focus on Cairo is, in effect, misguided. The development of urbanism cannot be understood except in conjunction with 'the rural question,' its privileging within the social-welfare mode of regulation of the 1930s to the 1960s, and its erasure under the Infitah neoliberal mode of regulation. Paradoxically, the contemporary megacity of Cairo can be seen as the product of two antiurbanization spatial modes of regulation. From the 1930s to the 1960s, rural Egypt was viewed as the pivot of national wealth and was privileged in the reconstitution of space, while Cairo was perceived as a revolutionary planning hub, its urban organization neglected. After Infitah, economic development, particularly of urban-based capitalist sectors, was privileged, while the urban density of Cairo (especially of the popular classes) was demonized. Social planners perceived urban density as consuming economic growth and the solution posited was that of creating relatively autonomous new desert cities.

During the Nasser era when the 'urban' was first systematically addressed, it was in terms of the coordination of efficient and rationally ordered systems of production, consumption, transportation, and leisure. The reconstituted spaces of the reconstructed villages, the administrative cities, and the hyperefficiency of the workers' cities were all aimed at the rational (functional and spatial) ordering of space. Such a spatial mode of regulation relied on the 'space of the people' (the demographic masses) to generate the dynamism behind the expansion and consolidation of the nation-building project. In contrast, the Infitah era's spatial mode of regulation took socioeconomic development as its object of governance, the problem of urbanism was privileged, rural transformation was abandoned, and economic growth was sought through "the productive redistribution of the population" (Ministry of Planning 1978).

Works Cited

al-Abd, Salah. 1979. "Land Reclamation and Resettlement in Egypt." In *Human Settlement on New Lands: Their Design and Development*, ed. Laila El-Hamamsy, 91–113. Cairo: Social Research Center/The American University in Cairo Press.

Abu-Lughod, Janet. 1971. *Cairo: 1001 Years of the City Victorious*. Princeton: Princeton University Press.

Abu Zayd, Hekmat. n.d. *al-Takayyuf al-ijtima'i fi al-rif al-misri al-jadid*. Cairo: Maktabat al-Anglo al-Misriya.

Agha Khan Program for Islamic Architecture. 1985. "Cairo, 1800–2000: Planning for the Capital City in the Context of Egypt's History and Development." In *The Agha Khan Award for Architecture. The Expanding Metropolis: Coping with the Urban Growth of Cairo*, 91–113. Cambridge, Mass.: Agha Khan Program for Islamic Architecture/MIT Press.

Aglietta, Michel. 1979. *A Theory of Capitalist Regulation: the U.S. Experience*. London: New Left Books.

Bassiouni, Muhammad Salah Abdel-Meguid. 1972. *Mudiriyat al-Tahrir ka-namuzaj lil-mujtama'at al-mukhattata*. M.A. thesis. Cairo: 'Ayn Shams University.

Bécard, Laurent. 1985. "New Settlements: A New Approach to Solving Housing and Urban Projects." In *The Agha Khan Award for Architecture. The Expanding Metropolis: Coping with the Urban Growth of Cairo*, 183–87.

Cambridge, Mass.: Agha Khan Program for Islamic Architecture/MIT Press.

Boyer, Robert. 1990. *The Regulation School: a Critical Introduction*. New York: Columbia University Press.

Brown, Nathan J. 1990. *Peasant Politics in Modern Egypt: The Struggle Against the State*. New Haven and London: Yale University Press.

Castillo, Greg. 1992. "Cities of the Stalinist Empire." In *Forms of Dominance: On the Architecture and Urbanism of the Colonial Enterprise*, ed. Nezzar Al-Sayyad, 261–88. Brookfield: Ashgate Publishing Company.

Dessouki, Ali. 1991. "The Public Sector in Egypt: Organization, Evolution, and Strategies of Reform." In *Employment and Structural Adjustment: Egypt in the 1990s*, eds. Heba Handoussa and Gillian Potter, 259–73. Cairo: The American University in Cairo Press.

Fahmy, Khaled. 2002. "An Olfactory Tale of Two Cities: Cairo in the Nineteenth Century." In *Historians in Cairo: Essays in Honor of George Scanlon*, ed. Jill Edwards, 155–87. Cairo: The American University in Cairo Press.

General Organization for Physical Planning (GOPP), Omnium Technique de l'Urbanisme et de l'Infrastructure (OTUI). Institut d'Aménagement et d'Urbanisme de la Région d'Ile de France (IAURIF). 1983. *Greater Cairo Region: Long Range Urban Development Scheme (Master Scheme)*. Cairo: Ministry of Development and State Ministry for Housing and Land Reclamation.

Gorgy, Michel Fouad. 1985. "The Greater Cairo Region: Land Use Today and Tomorrow." In *The Agha Khan Award for Architecture. The Expanding Metropolis: Coping with the Urban Growth of Cairo*, 176–82. Cambridge, Mass.: Agha Khan Program for Islamic Architecture/MIT Press.

Gramsci, Antonio. 1971. *Selections from the Prison Notebooks*. New York: International Publishers.

Guha, Ranajit. 1982. "On Some Aspects of the Historiography of Colonial India." In *Subaltern Studies I*, ed. Ranajit Guha, 37–44. Delhi: Oxford University Press.

El-Hammami, Ahmed. 1 May 1999. Personal interview.

Hanna, Nelly. 2002. "The Urban History of Cairo around 1900: A Reinterpretation." In *Historians in Cairo: Essays in Honor of George Scanlon*, ed. Jill Edwards, 189–201. Cairo: The American University in Cairo Press.

Harvey, David. 1989. *The Condition of Postmodernity: An Enquiry into the Origins of Cultural Change*. Oxford and Cambridge: Basil Blackwell.

Hassanein, Magdi. 1975. *al-Sahara': al-thawra wa-al-tharwa, qissat Mudiriyat al-Tahrir*. Cairo: al-Hay'a al-'Amma al-Misriya li-l-Kitab.

Hegab, Salah-Eddin Muhammad. 1985. "New Towns Policy." In *The Agha Khan Award for Architecture. The Expanding Metropolis: Coping with the Urban Growth of Cairo*, 171–75. Cambridge, Mass.: Agha Khan Program for Islamic Architecture/MIT Press.

Hinnebusch, Raymond. 1985. *Egyptian Politics under Sadat*. Cambridge: Cambridge University Press.

Hopkins, Nicholas, et al. 1988. *Participation and Community in the Egyptian New Lands: The Case of South Tahrir*. Cairo: Cairo Papers in Social Science.

Ilbert, Robert. 1985. "Heliopolis: Colonial Enterprise or Town Planning Success?" In *The Agha Khan Award for Architecture. The Expanding Metropolis: Coping with the Urban Growth of Cairo*, 35–42. Cambridge, Mass.: Agha Khan Program for Islamic Architecture/MIT Press.

El Kadi, Galila. 1990. "Trente ans de planification urbaine au Caire." *Revue Tiers Monde* 31 (121): 185–207.

Kafafi, Husayn. 1980. *Ru'ya 'asriya li-kharitat Misr: dirasa iqtisadiya wa-ijtima'iya*. Cairo: al-Hay'a al-'Amma al-Misriya li-l-Kitab.

Lefebvre, Henri. 1991. *The Production of Space*. Oxford: Blackwell.

Lipietz, Alain. 1986. "New Tendencies in the International Division of Labour: Regimes of Accumulation and Modes of Regulation." In *Production, Work, Territory: The Geographical Anatomy of Industrial Capitalism*, eds. M. Storper and A.J. Scott, 16–40. Boston: Allen and Unwin.

"Ma'a al-nuwwab fi Mudiriyat al-Tahrir." 1957. *al-Sahara'* 2 (20).

Ministry of Housing and Development. 1965. *Mashru'at al-iskan wa-al-marafiq fi zill al-thawra*. Cairo: Dar al-Tahrir.

Ministry of Land Reclamation. 1969. *Takwin wa tanmiyat al-mujtama'at al-jadida fi al-aradi al-mustasliha*. Cairo: Wizarat al-Istislah al-Aradi.

Ministry of Planning. 1978. *The Five Year Plan: 1978–1980*. Cairo: Ministry of Planning.

Mitchell, Timothy. 1988. *Colonising Egypt*. Cambridge: Cambridge University Press.

Observatoire urbaine du Caire contemporain. 1993. *Les "new settlements" du Caire*. Supplément à la *Lettre d'Information*, no. 33.

Raymond, André. 2000. *Cairo*. Cambridge and London: Harvard University Press.

Sabea, Hanan. 1987. *Paths of Rural Transformation: Stratification and Differentiation Processes in a New Lands Village*. M.A. thesis. Cairo: American University in Cairo.

"al-Safir al-Yugoslavi yaqul: Mudiriyat al-Tahrir min a'zam al-tajarib al-ijtima'iya fi al-'alam." 1957. *al-Sahara'* 1 (12): 17.

Sayed, H.A. 1989. "Population Policy in Egypt." *Cairo Demographic Center Annual Seminar.* Cairo: Cairo Demographic Center.

Selim, Samah. 2004. *The Novel and the Rural Imaginary in Egypt, 1880–1985.* New York and London: Routledge Curzon.

Shafik, Zeinab Youssef. 1991. *The Life-Structure of a New City: Egypt's Tenth of Ramadan.* Ph.D. diss. Ann Arbor: University of Michigan.

El Shakry, Omnia. 2005. "Barren Land and Fecund Bodies: The Emergence of Population Discourse in Interwar Egypt." *International Journal of Middle East Studies* 37 (3): 351–72.

Springborg, Robert. 1979. "Patrimonialism and Policy Making in Egypt: Nasser and Sadat and the Tenure Policy for Reclaimed Lands." *Middle Eastern Studies* 15 (1): 48–69.

Supreme Council for Family Planning and Population (SCFPP). 1980. *Itar al-istratijiya al-qawmiya li-l-sukkan w-al-mawadd al-bashariya wa birnamij tanzim al-usra.* Cairo: SCFPP.

United Arab Republic, Institute of National Planning. 1965. *Research Report on Employment Problems in Rural Areas of the United Arab Republic.* Report B: Migration in the U.A.R. Cairo: Institute of National Planning.

United Arab Republic. 1960. *The U.A.R. Yearbook 1960.* Cairo: Information Department.

United Nations Fund for Population Activities (UNFPA). 1980. *Arab Republic of Egypt: Background Paper for Population Assistance Needs Assessment Mission.* Cairo: UNFPA.

United Nations, Department of International Economic and Social Affairs (UN). 1990. *Population Growth and Policies in Megacities: Cairo: Population Policy Paper No. 34.* New York: United Nations.

Volait, Mercedes. 2003. "Making Cairo Modern (1870–1950): Multiple Models for a 'European-Style' Urbanism." In *Urbanism: Imported or Exported? Native Aspirations and Foreign Plans*, eds. Joe Nasr and Mercedes Volait, 17–50. West Sussex: Wiley-Academy.

Voll, Sara. 1980. "Egyptian Land Reclamation since the Revolution." *Middle East Journal* (34): 127–48.

Warriner, Doreen. 1957. *Land Reform and Development in the Middle East: A Study of Egypt, Syria and Iraq.* London and New York: Royal Institute of International Affairs.

———. 1961. *Agrarian Reform and Community Development in the U.A.R.* Cairo: Dar al-Ta'awun.

Zaalouk, Malak. 1989. *Power, Class, and Foreign Capital in Egypt.* London: Zed Books.

Zaki, Gamal. 1964. "Some Sociological Aspects of Planned Communities."
al-Majalla al-ijtima'iyah al-qawmiya / National Review of Social Sciences 1:
149–62.

_____. n.d. *Tanzim wa-tanmiyat al-mujtama'at.* Cairo: Dar al-Thaqafa wa-al-
'Ulum lil-Tiba'a wa-al-Nashr.

Notes

1   I am drawing here on the theory of the French regulation school, which
attempts to disaggregate Marx's concept of a mode-of-production and was
pioneered by Michel Aglietta's *A Theory of Capitalist Regulation* (1979), and
is familiar to most through the popularization of the concepts of *Taylorism,
Fordism,* and *Post-Fordism.* See Boyer (1990), Harvey (1989), and Lipietz (1986)
for useful introductions. Quite simply, a mode of regulation refers to the most
efficient manner for creating a population of governable subjects and citizens.
Subjects, that is, who are self-regulating individuals—physically and mentally
sound, economically productive, and socially adapted—to a particular phase of
capitalist production. Multiple agents and forces (such as international, state,
and private agencies, members of the intelligentsia, educators, the religious
establishment, etc.), interact in complex, often unconscious ways—consonant
with the reproduction of the national economy, polity, and society—to maintain
the *status quo.* It is the materialization of the mode of regulation (in the "form
of norms, habits, laws, regulating networks . . . [a] body of interiorized rules
and social processes") that defines a particular era, as well as the structures and
conditions of possibility that exist within it (Lipietz 1986, 19). However, as I hope
to demonstrate, the complex processes involved in the reproduction of *particular*
social relations (such as those between the city and the countryside) often led to
unintended, and unforeseen, consequences.

2   I develop this argument—on the étatist social-welfare orientation of the 1930s
to the 1960s—at length in my forthcoming book, *The Great Social Laboratory:
Reformers and Utopians in Twentieth-Century Egypt,* thereby contesting the
disjuncture usually presumed to have occurred with the 1952 revolution.

3   In stating that rural space was privileged in the period of the 1930s to the 1960s,
I do not mean to suggest that a concern for urbanism was completely absent.
Rather, I am suggesting that urbanism begins to be *the dominant* concern among
state, urban and technocratic planners only after the 1952 revolution. Prior to that
members of the state apparatus, and the urban elite intelligentsia, were concerned
primarily with questions of rural welfare and the "problem of the peasantry" (see
Brown 1990, El Shakry 2005, and Selim 2004).

4   One could argue that this targeting of the urban was simply related to the dramatic
increase in Cairo's population. However, beginning in the late 1930s, Cairo had
already begun to experience a marked increase in population that, nevertheless,
did not inhibit the state's focus on rural areas in tandem with urban modifications
(El Shakry 2005). Further, the entire question of rural–urban migration itself must
be understood in relation to the role of the state in cultivating, or abandoning, the
project of rural transformation.

3 Cairo as Regional/Global Economic Capital?

Leïla Vignal and Eric Denis

I had acquired the habit, since childhood, of calling it "Egypt" instead of "Cairo."
"I am going to go to Egypt," "I'm returning from Egypt," "I sent a courier to Egypt,"
"the young girls from Egypt."... Everyone refers to the capital city by saying
"Egypt" and not "Cairo," and nothing attests to its supremacy, its privileged
situation better than this designation.... Cairo is a microcosm of Egypt. It is the
heart of literature just as it is the heart of space and time.
     Gamal al-Ghitani (2001)

In less than ten years, Cairo has doubled its surface area. A new kind of unified and extensive city has come to surround and graft itself onto one of the world's densest agglomerations, leading to a bifurcation of urban development patterns. This bifurcation is linked to neoliberalization and global processes of recomposition, including the new international division of labor, the volatility and intensification of flows of information and capital, the conjunction of markets, and the emergence of a distinct, if limited, global-city role.

     This chapter discusses the radical transformation of economic and social metropolitan topographies in Cairo that have recently led to the inversion of polarities and values. Most importantly the city center has lost its prestige as the spatial economy, housing, and the demographic mass expands into the desert periphery and incorporates a métissage of pericentral zones into its confines. It is impossible and misguided to isolate any single cause for what we call this "new metropolitanization." Yet, this new profile of a national and regional capital paradoxically represents an apparent demographic trend toward dispersion of populations away from the capital while at the same time increasingly concentrating the capital's new productive capacities and command functions.

Significant transformations have resulted from this contradictory process of renewed metropolitan expansion, including new modes and sites of production, new forms and locations of residential quarters, new places and modes of consumption, and new circuits of mobility. We have also witnessed entire business sectors excluded and sometimes destabilized by this new spatial political economy. In particular, new as well as old sectors are subjected to a very unstable conjuncture of forces that allow little room for the creation of a sustainable city. Finally, this new spatial political economy does not foster expansion of the salaried worker sector since there is no stable support base in the neoliberal context for the long-term financing and maintenance of these new urban spaces.

These three factors—the bifurcation of the urban development cycle and of urban settlement forms, the development of new infra-urban topographies, and the reinforcement of Cairo's dominance of the nation, capture the landscape of the new metropolitanization in Egypt. This chapter will analyze this process of contradictory capital-city transformation, tracing its roots in urban-production logics that have integrated Egypt into global and regional processes of economic neoliberalization, restructuring, and globalization accelerating since the early 1990s. These defining forces of twenty-first-century Egypt are also relevant to many other Third World and Mediterranean cities.

The findings of this chapter rely on the analysis of socioeconomic information, both statistical and bibliographical, as well as on a spatial analysis of changes in urban Cairo including qualitative cartography, interviews, a review of the press, and field observation. On the statistical side, we used mainly the 1996 population, industrial and socioeconomical databases that are collected by the Central Agency for Public Mobalization and Statistics (CAPMAS). The spatial expression of the data has been possible through the GIS EGYPTE CEDEJ-CAPMAS (geographical information system covering Egypt, built through the cooperation between Le Centre d'Études et de

Documentation Économiques, Juridiques et Sociales (CEDEJ), the French research center in Egypt, and CAPMAS). We also used the 2000 Egyptian edition of the worldwide business directory of enterprises, KOMPASS, from which we extracted the information needed to follow the qualitative changes in industrial settlements.

Neoliberal Transition, the Global-City System, and Industrial Expansion

In 1991 the government of Egypt signed the Economic Reform and Structural Adjustment Program with the World Bank and the International Monetary Fund (IMF). This accord marked Egypt's entrance into an active phase of reforms that transformed economic apparatuses, modes of government, and state functions. The decade of the 1990s was marked by the gradual implementation of a program of economic liberalization and privatization. A new social contract gradually took shape between the public and private sectors as public expenditures were drastically adjusted. Imposing conformity with international commercial agreements led toward the gradual eradication of customs barriers. Conditions for the development of industrial activities and distribution were radically transformed as the emergence of a new landscape triggered the decline of old forms of concentration and circulation.

The restructuring of the manufacturing sector is strongly linked to the transformation of the way in which the capital city is organized. Other analysts of globalized cities, evaluating urban economies in transition, have often focused on the promotion of information/computer industries, financial sectors and 'new economies,' and on the metropolis' capacity to dominate, organize, and transmit flows of innovation and capital (Sassen 1996; Veltz 1996). However, these models, while appropriately encouraging a systemic analysis of the archipelago economies of globalizing cities and urban nodes, have also led toward a superficial understanding of the complexities of globalization in Third World cities. They do not adequately take into account the continuing, but transformed, industrial and manufacturing sectors of cities, by overly privileging the manifestations of financial and service sector activities. Thus, they overlook the resulting industrial, discursive, and spatial specificities that have triggered a global explosion of new social forces, grounded in inequalities and in elitist modes of consuming, displacement, and residence that strive to match cosmopolitan standards, while the living conditions of the many remain very localized, limited, impoverished, and isolated.

In the metropolises of the global South, this new kind of concentration and organization of activity within a national and regional urban system cannot create an economy of expansion and redeployment in the industrial sector. As Nigel Harris argues about Bombay, metropolitanization is an engine for skewed growth (1995). Moreover, works on the new urban economy in the United States demonstrate that the emergence of global cities always supposes an industrial expansion nearby (Castells 1989). For cities such as New York or Tokyo, the expansion into peripheral areas for innovative industries of software and telecommunications (military as well as civilian) was necessary to be able to master global flows of capital, goods, services, or labor. This kind of expansion was essential in the cases of Seoul and Singapore as well. The supposed deindustrialization of global cities is only a type of redeployment of their productive capacity and, on another level, the reformulation of the system of relations and hierarchies between cities.

In the case of Cairo, it is evident that this new metropolitanization is articulated around industrial transition away from the structure put into place by Nasser's revolutionary-socialist era of the 1960s, which enabled the creation of an independent national and Arab-regional industrial base. The transformations of the 1960s themselves were only the product of earlier extractive orientations characteristic of the tropical, colonial economies organized around cotton. Today's industrial parks that cluster together heavy industry and textile industries have become obsolete. More dynamic is the manufacturing sector oriented toward the assembly of consumer goods, processing farm produce, and producing intermediary goods (e.g., cement, ceramics, and steel) needed in the building and public-works sector which has seen the strongest growth in Egypt (10.5 percent of production value between the fiscal years of 1997–98 and 1998–99, heading the industrial sector which grew in general by 9.7 percent) (Central Bank of Egypt 1999/2000).

With the emergence a new kind of modern manufacturing sector in Cairo, the city landscape was transformed: first, because new circuits of distribution were transplanted there, and second, because this brought with it the development of services for enterprises and for new technologies, such as software engineering and information management.[1] These developments also brought a new distribution of transportation (cargo refrigeration, air freight, etc.). The rupture of the old model and its aging public sector left the new manufacturing sector and an innovating private sector to welcome capital and new imported technologies. It is also important to take into account a consequential illegal and quasi-legal 'sweatshop' manufacturing sector (between 27 percent and 40 percent of jobs, according to sources and whether double activity is counted or not). This important sector produced substandard consumer goods sheltered behind solid customs barriers. Today, with the reduction of these barriers in conformity with the GATT agreements, this informal sector is increasingly exposed to competition from products imported from China and India. In most cases, only the decrease in daily salary and the increase in child labor allow this sector to remain competitive.

Between the fiscal years 1991–92 and 1998–99, the private sector grew from 58.3 percent of industrial production to 81.8 percent (Central Bank of Egypt 1999/2000). This process was skewed from the start as the private sector took control through the privatization of the best-performing public enterprises, while on the other hand, without new investment the public sector saw its productivity steadily weaken. In 1996–97 the average value added (by worker and by year) in establishments with more than ten salaried workers was LE9,500 against LE21,300 for the private sector (CAPMAS 1996–1997).

By 1996 the public manufacturing sector still employed one quarter of Egyptian workers, of which close to 40 percent were working in the Greater Cairo region (CAPMAS 1996a). However, the surplus of workers in the public sector is estimated at 18 percent of the work force, according to the government, and at more than 40 percent, according to potential privatization buyers ("Round Up" 1997). Despite the elimination of 125,000 jobs since the launching of structural adjustment in 1991, the increasing profitability of public industries remains impossible due to the obsolescence of equipment and Egypt's lack of competitiveness in key international sectors like textiles. Most often, the value of public companies resides merely in the land their factories sit on. These properties are more likely to be razed than to survive since the land has risen considerably in value as the city has grown around these formerly peripheral areas. We shall detail the functional consequences of the recomposition of the production apparatus, but first, we will situate the 'metropolity' or the nodal character of Cairo within the system of the great world metropolises and Arab urban hierarchies, again noting some of the ambiguities surrounding a 'globalized' Cairo.

International Integration and Dependence

International indicators acknowledge the weakness of Egypt's integration in global economic networks as well as in the system of global cities. This modest level of integration on the global scale corresponds to an equally weak integration on the Arab-regional scale. Indeed, Middle Eastern metropolitan economies maintain little rapport among themselves, in terms of complementarities. However, as quantitatively marginal as these very small-scale economic indicators appear to be, they do have a visible impact on the national and metropolitan scales shaping the profound transformations occurring in Egypt and its capital.

Table 1: Gross Urban Product (GUP) in 1995

	GUP in USD thousands	Population in thousands	OPI*	GUP/ GDP in percent	GUP/ inhabitants in USD millions
Paris	361,416	9,513	1.515	24.9	37,992
Barcelona	65,900	3,892	1.287	12.4	16,932
Istanbul	49,889	8,383	2.134	29.1	5,951
Naples	39,983	2,964	0.705	3.6	13,490
Tel Aviv-Jaffa	32,172	1,920	1.080	36.7	16,756
Marseille	31,808	1,226	1.035	2.2	25,945
Athens	29,046	3,074	1.151	33.8	9,450
Kuwait	28,302	1,350	1.000	85.7	20,964
Riyad	23,961	3,446	1.000	18.4	6,954
Teheran	18,711	7,769	1.300	16.5	2,408
Cairo	12,929	10,801	1.439	22.5	1,003
Izmir	11,802	1,984	2.133	6.9	5,949
Baghdad	6,036	3,981	1.200	24.5	1,516
Beirut	5,089	1,405	1.300	54.7	3,623
Casablanca	4,682	2,970	1.300	14.5	1,576
Algiers	3,790	2,414	1.000	8.5	1,570
Tunis	3,530	1,633	1.200	21.8	2,162
Amman	3,339	2,022	1.109	52.7	1,651
Damascus	2,298	2,512	1.000	16	915

Source: Moriconi-Ebrard 2000, p. 227.

* Over Productivity Index (1 = national average)

Cairo's gross urban product (GUP) represents 22.5 percent of the national gross domestic product (GDP, see Table 1); the economic weight of Cairo is central without being macrocephalic. This kind of limited domination of the national territory, to about the same degree that Paris economically dominates France, reflects the diversification of the metropolitan economy at the heart of a national economy. Egypt's economy itself is relatively diversified and its important industrial base constitutes a remarkable exception among the countries of the Middle East. This indicator underscores that Cairo is not only the largest city in the Arab world, but above all, it is the capital of a vast country structured by several important secondary urban poles.

However, the gross wealth produced by Cairo is twenty-eight times *less* than that of Paris, and more than thirty-seven times less when we compare it to the number of inhabitants. At the heart of Arab countries, the Cairene GUP situates the metropolis well after the oil capitals of the Arab Gulf, but largely ahead of all the old metropolises of the not-exclusively-oil-producing Arab countries. However, Cairo is relegated almost to last place when one compares its GUP to the number of its inhabitants. It is a city that produces wealth, certainly, but too little to satisfy the relative needs of its population.

The Cairo Stock Exchange

After an eclipse of forty years, the place of Cairo's stock market, associated with that of Alexandria, reinscribed itself in the international system. This desire to stimulate investment in a moribund financial market was accompanied by a movement toward capturing currency, important to Cairo's front-line economic functions notably in the financial-services sector. This concentration of activity in Cairo's stock market is barely legible on the global scale, where Cairo has a good deal of trouble maintaining its credibility as an 'emerging market.' But on the national scale, the stock market reinforces Cairo's urban primacy, by way of channeling new functions of the global economy to the city.

On the international scale, the Cairo stock exchange concurrently holds, in effect, only 0.12 percent of the portion of world stock-market capitalization (Table 2). Moreover, the ensemble of stock markets in the Arab world is situated in an ultraperipheral area of global financial flows. These are principally made up of national assets produced by the privatization of public-sector enterprises or the sale of certain state-run monopolies (mobile-telephone franchises, for example). The general tendency toward the growth of regional stock markets over the course of the 1990s is particularly exemplary in Egypt: 573 enterprises were quoted there in 1990, against 1,033 in 2000; during the same period, stock-market capitalization rose from $1.8 billion to $32.8 billion. However, this rise in stock-market capitalization reflects a similar global pattern over the course of the 1990s, which Egypt is only following.

Table 2: Stock exchanges in the Arab world in 1996 (and comparison with non-Arab cities)

	Capitaliza-tion	Turnover ratio	Portion of global stock market capitalization		Regional part
	USD billions 1999	percent of GNP 1998	Capitalization/ exchanges 1999	percent 1999	percent 1999
Johannesburg	262.4	127.6	34.1	0.96	Non-Arab
Bombay	184.6	24.5	84.4	0.67	Non-Arab
Mexico	154.0	23.3	29	0.56	Non-Arab
Kuala Lumpur	145.4	136	39.8	0.53	Non-Arab
Istanbul	112.7	16.9	102.8	0.41	36.01
Tel Aviv	63.8	39.4	29.9	0.23	20.38
Riyad	60.4	33	28.8	0.22	19.3
Cairo	32.8	29.5	31.6	0.12	10.48
Teheran	14.9	13.1	9.3	0.05	4.76
Casablanca	13.7	44.1	17.6	0.05	4.38
Amman	5.8	79	9.4	0.02	1.85
Oman	4.3	29.4	33.8	0.02	1.37
Tunis	2.7	11.4	13.3	0.01	0.86
Beirut	1.9	13.8	9.3	0.01	0.61

Source: International Finance Corporation's (IFC) Emerging Market Database, 1999.

It must be also be noted that few offerings are truly active on the Egyptian market. In September 2000, for example, the thirty companies that had the largest stock-market capitalization represented 55 percent of market capital, and 93 percent of turnover (amongst a total of more than 1,000 registered enterprises). During the same month, the Mobinil cell-phone company had been, itself, the object of 36.5 percent of all stock-market transactions. Otherwise stated, this extremely speculative market does not allow productive investments to sit for the long term. The market nevertheless understands the dynamism of certain sectors of activity that, founded principally on national capital, participate in the redeployment of a new economy centered on and dominated by the Cairene metropolis. Indeed, private capital is mobilized mainly to back activities that accompany the recomposition of the production apparatus (Table 3), i.e. the manufacturing sector (consumer goods, food products) and construction relating to elite residences, tourism, and leisure activities.

At the same time, it is important to underscore the very great volatility of the Middle East regional markets, which have been fragile and subject to strong shake-ups since 1999 (which does not appear in Table 2). This instability is reflected in the crash in Istanbul in 1999, the severe liquidity crisis in Egypt at the same time, and the subsequent generalized regional recession. Thus, in Egypt, the Hermes index for Cairo's stock exchange, after a peak at the end of 1999, lost 58 percent of its value in less than six months, followed by stagnation (EFG-Hermes 2000). Foreign investors comprised 20 percent of buyers in 2000 yet they fell to 12 percent during the first six months of 2001, again suggesting the lack of foreign-investor confidence in Egypt and the volatility of the markets. In this light, even though stock-market indicators for 'emerging markets' appear to be productive in these 'transition economies,' they should be viewed with much skepticism.

In 1998 Egypt capitalized 0.41 percent of direct global investment in proportion to the country's 1 percent of the world's total population (Table 4). That is approximately the same relative level of capitalization as that of 1980, whereas the value of this capitalization (in millions of U.S. dollars) was multiplied by a factor greater than seven (by eight for global stocks).

The flow of foreign direct investment (FDI) toward Egypt (Table 5) also remains modest relative to the global scale (0.19 percent of global fluctuations in 1998), and without any significant increase since the 1980s (UNCTAD 2000). In addition, annual flows during the 1990s reflected the lack of investor confidence, regularly dampened by regional political shocks. These variations also take into account global-investment trends that fluctuate over the average term, and that always favor industrialized countries. Such is the direction of globalization. Egypt has not improved its capacity to attract investors and after a certain infatuation at the beginning of the decade, FDI flows destined for Egypt stagnated at an extremely modest level.

Table 3: Activity of companies registered on the Cairo Stock Exchange (February 2000)

Sector	Official	Unofficial*	Total
Financial services	4	133	137
Construction and public works	11	112	123
Housing	12	86	98
Commerce	5	85	90
Engineering	11	69	80
Food and drink	13	64	77
Travel and tourism	5	67	72
Textiles and manufacturing	14	40	54
Training services	6	47	53
Construction materials	4	48	52
Pharmaceutical products	10	35	45
Transportation and telecommunications	11	21	32
Paper and packaging	3	26	29
Agriculture	5	21	26
Chemical products	7	17	24
Gas and mines	1	12	13
Cement	6	6	12
Computers and information technologies	–	12	12
Mills	7	5	12
Distributors	5	4	9
Total	140	910	1050

Source: Cairo Stock Exchange, February 2000.

* That is to say, below the financial and statutory criteria required for official recording.

Table 4: Direct investment stocks in millions of dollars

	1980		1990		1998	
	in USD millions	percent	in USD millions	percent	in USD millions	percent
Egypt	2,257	0.45	11,039	0.62	16,700	0.41
Industrialized countries	373,658	73.76	11,394,853	78.87	2,785,449	68.14
Developing countries	132,945	26.24	370,644	20.96	1,219,271	29.83
World	506,602	100	1,768,456	100	4,088,068	100

Source: UNCTAD 2000.

Table 5: Fluctuation of foreign direct investment (FDI) between 1987 and 1998, in USD millions

	1987–92*	1993	1994	1995	1996	1997	1998
Egypt	806	493	1 256	598	636	891	1 076
Egypt/ World in percent	–	4.64	0.22	0.50	0.18	0.18	0.19
Industrialized countries	136,628	13,385	146,379	208,372	21,112	273,276	460,431
Developing countries	35,326	78,813	101,196	106,224	135,343	172,533	165,936
World	17,353	219,421	253,506	328,862	358,869	464,341	643,879

Source: UNCTAD 2000.

*Annual average

Financial contributions since the beginning of the 1990s have not, then, allowed investment interests along the banks of the Nile to be sustainable, nor have they strengthened an infrastructure that would be more favorable for future profitable investment. Nevertheless, more than a billion dollars has been invested each year in Egypt, putting the country at the head of those nations benefiting from global investment in the region, including Turkey, Algeria (an oil-producing nation), and Iran (UNCTAD 2000).

International Trade

The portion of manufactured products relative to Egyptian exports has clearly increased during the last decade of the century, passing from 41.5 percent of export value in 1985 to 63.7 percent in 1994, excluding oil products (or 28.5 percent of total exports, of which 12.5 percent are in textiles) (Ministry of Economy and Foreign Trade 2000). Nevertheless, this represents an extremely modest position on the global scale; in 1995 this part of production accounted for 0.06 percent of the international commerce of manufactured goods.

Egypt remains an economically dependent country, an exporter of raw or barely transformed materials (oil products, gases, phosphate, cotton) and an importer of high-value-added manufactured products and equipment. Expansion in exports of manufactured products has occurred, but at the price of heavy investment in imported technologies. Egypt does not have at its disposal a capacity for innovation and, simply put, does not have investment capacities that can support its domestic production potential. Weak export growth is due in part to the fact that local investment, even that matched by foreign capital, is directed toward production for the internal market, substituting for exports in ways that reveal little originality or appeal to external markets. The development of this industry does not constitute the basis for a radical transformation of the national economy's independent structure, as the discovery of new gas deposits or the next application of the GATT agreements might lead one to suppose. These accords will in effect irremediably condemn one part of the industrial base (textiles of course), but also some of the barely emerging industrial lines, such as automobile assembly and the pharmaceutical industry.

However, the very weak weight of Egypt on the international commercial scene must not eclipse the impact of this integration, as recent and as modest as it may be, on the country's economy and on that of its metropolis. Small degrees of global integration have a massive impact on the municipal and national arenas. On the one hand, Cairo suffers the effects of worsening commercial dependence, embodied in the lopsided Egyptian–American trade partnerships. Over the course of the 1990s, the United States became Egypt's premier commercial partner and quasi-exclusive supplier of wheat flour (that constitutes more than 95 percent of Egypt's imports). National wheat production assured only 40 percent of the population's needs (Gertel

1998). In the Middle East, however, Egypt is one of the rare countries in which locally produced products constitute the majority of consumed goods. But it is the new private sector of consumer industries, greatly bolstered by a power structure confronted by a declining public sector, that responds increasingly to domestic demand. And it does so according to a commercial logic and necessarily different pricing structures than those used by public enterprises and subsidized production lines. From this point on, consumer access is radically class differentiated by modes of production for different kinds of products and by stratified distribution networks.

The metropolis that has taken shape in this context of export-oriented logics and accrued dependence of Egypt on the United States has spatially concretized the increasing gap between an impoverished urban population and the tenants of the new, privatized productive city. The support structure for the urban poor is less and less secure, owing to the gradual retreat of state support for basic food products (bread, notably) and to inflation. Meanwhile, the more prosperous tenants of the newly reordered city enjoy exclusive semipublic spaces, such as shopping malls, or completely private gated communities. The face of poverty has changed with the passage from a society of shortages to a society of consumerism, without a redistribution of revenue that would enable either the growth or survival of the middle class. Cairo is tending toward decline, in accordance with a double standard: on the one hand, the popular majority focuses on survival, while on the other hand, a thin layer of city dwellers consumes on a world-class scale, affording a lifestyle that is increasingly similar to those in other international cities.[2]

Middle East Regional Node?

Clearly, with regard to production capacity—its capacity to drain capital and to finance modernization—Cairo is not a city of global stature. At best, one can conceive of it as a relay-city for the world economy, structured by the archipelago of the largest metropolises (Veltz 1996). But Cairo can also be understood as the capital of the Arab world. For more than two hundred years, Cairo has been recognized as the largest of the region's cities. In 1800 the city had twice the population of the second-largest city of that epoch, Tunis. Since then, its primacy continues to be reaffirmed, as well as its demographic weight, relative to Egypt's Mediterranean port of Alexandria, which is its second-largest city. However, the fact that Cairo dominates an ensemble of more than two thousand other cities in the region, and that it stands as the hub and political capital of the Arab League, does not mean that the Egyptian metropolis is the node for a system of cities. For this to be true, one would have to be convinced, on the one hand, of the importance of exchanges inside of what would have to appear to be an integrated network of Middle Eastern cities, and of the capacity of Cairo to dominate flows and control exchanges on a regional scale.

If one thinks about Cairo on the regional scale, it is easy to enumerate the indices of *cultural* centrality, whether in audiovisual publishing or production (Moriconi and Rateb 1996) (see Sadek in this volume). It is also easy to witness Cairo's capacity for concentrating Arab political interests around the Arab League, which returned to Cairo in 1990. Egyptian centrality on the Middle Eastern diplomatic scene is enacted in Cairo as governments work for the pacification and coordination of Arab politics, whether on the Palestinian question or that of the Sudan. Today, local debates on the question of Middle East peace lead analysts to examine precisely the risks of the loss of Cairene centrality in relation to a resolution of the Palestinian conflict. Indeed, Cairo also capitalizes on regional instability, due to its privileged status as the country that is most sustained by the American aid that assures Egypt's key role in the pacification of the region.

Weak Commercial Integration

Despite serving as the home of the Arab League, Cairo has more political and commercial relationships with Europe and the United States than with other Arab countries. Indeed, commercial relationships between Egypt and the Arab world are quite modest. Thus, between 1992 and 1999, in the general context of export stagnation, the value of Egyptian exports to its Arab partners fell from 17.6 percent to 12.9 percent.[3] In addition, Egypt is not the premier trade partner of any Arab nation. However, the new joint-venture industry taking root around Cairo and benefiting from its fiscal facilities and especially from low-cost Egyptian labor, aims to produce for the Arab market (and the African market, if it becomes solvent). These industries also enjoy the guarantee of a teeming domestic market, insofar as Egypt is the most populous country in the region. Concerning Africa, there is a risk that the road is still long, despite the gradual progressive establishment of the Common Market for Eastern and Southern Africa (COMESA), which consists of twenty-one countries potentially comprising 385 million people. Indeed, in 1998, barely 1 percent of Egyptian exports were aimed toward these African countries, and their domestic markets are hardly comparable to that of Egypt. In 1998, the ensemble of all other COMESA countries bought fewer cars than were bought in Egypt alone—some seventy thousand units ("Round Up" 1999).

Table 6: Commercial exchanges between Egypt and countries of the Arab League in 1999

Exports			Imports		
Country	Percentage	in USD millions	Country	Percentage	in USD millions
Saudi Arabia	21.63	97.99	Saudi Arabia	69.44	699.98
Iraq	13.26	60.07	Arab Emirates	6.06	61.12
Libya	9.31	42.15	Libya	5.71	57.55
Syria	9.22	41.76	Sudan	3.66	36.86
Sudan	7.46	33.79	Syria	2.45	24.70
Arab Emirates	7.35	33.28	Jordan	2.34	23.55
Lebanon	5.12	23.17	Bahrain	2.08	20.98
Jordan	4.75	21.52	Lebanon	1.78	17.97
Tunisia	4.49	20.32	Kuwait	1.63	16.45
North Yemen	3.88	17.57	Tunisia	1.60	16.14
Kuwait	3.04	13.78	Algeria	1.45	14.61
Morocco	2.93	13.27	Qatar	0.85	8.59
Algeria	2.59	11.73	Morocco	0.66	6.70
Palestine	1.66	7.50	Palestine	0.10	0.97
Qatar	1.09	4.95	Somalia	0.08	0.79
Oman	0.91	4.14	Oman	0.04	0.43
Djibouti	0.73	3.29	Iraq	0.03	0.33
Bahrain	0.52	2.37	North Yemen	0.02	0.17
Somalia	0.05	0.25	Mauritania	0.02	0.15
Mauritania	0.02	0.10	Djibouti	0.00	0.00
Total	100.00	453.00	Total	100.00	1,008.04

Source: Egyptian Ministry of Economy and Foreign Commerce, 1990–1999. Database of Egyptian Foreign Trade (collected by L. Vignal, 2000).

Table 6 shows the weakness of exchanges between Egypt and its Arab partners. Its principal partner is Saudi Arabia, to which it exports mainly construction materials, medicines, and agricultural products, and from which it imports principally petroleum products or derivatives. There is, then, nothing comparable to the intensity of commercial flows that link Egypt to the great industrialized countries, at the head of which are the United States (12.5 percent of exports and 14.3 percent of imports in 1999) and Europe, if exchanges with the various countries are summed, with France occupying the first place among the European countries.

Over the course of the 1990s increases in direct foreign investments were linked to legislative adjustments during that time and by the guarantees of investment security that these measures offered. Attracted by the development potential of a much larger market of regional consumers, the vast majority of direct foreign investment occurs in the form of partnerships (joint ventures) that are often majority foreign-controlled. Essentially, these investments come from large countries emitting global financial flows, that is to say, from Western industrialized countries, at the head of which is the United States (Table 7). Arab countries are barely present on Egyptian soil. Their financial capacity does not, evidently, have either the amplitude or the power of the European countries or the United States. When they do possess the financial capacity, Arab investors such as the Persian Gulf monarchies often prefer to invest their wealth outside of the Arab world in markets characterized by large concentrations of global financial flows.

Table 7: The origin of FDI flows in Egypt

Investors	1997–98		1998–99	
	in USD millions	percent	in USD millions	percent
Arab countries	38.8	3.4	40.20	5.6
European Union	83.10	7.2	54.20	7.6
United States	873.6	76.0	569.1	79.5
Other countries	154.10	13.4	52.10	7.3

Source: Central Bank of Egypt 1999/2000.

In Egypt, enterprises funded with Arab capital come essentially from the Arabian Peninsula. They often serve as a relay or franchise for large international groups. Americana, for example, belongs to the Kuwaiti group Khorafi, which possesses or participates in more than seventy enterprises in Egypt, mainly in the food-product sector. Americana holds the franchise (for the Arab countries) of numerous American fast-food companies (Subway, Pizza Hut, Kentucky Fried Chicken, Baskin-Robbins, etc.), which multiplied in Cairo and in Egypt over the course of the 1990s (Pagès and Vignal 1998). For Gulf companies, Egypt represents a vast, expanding market for current consumer goods, that is to say, a potential locale for the diversification of their economies, beyond petroleum and for regional reinvestment of their income.

Principally, the enterprises taking root in Egypt are from outside the Arab/ Middle East region (Table 8). Often, they are large transnational corporations (Pepsi-Cola, Xerox, Nestlé, etc.).

Table 8: Foreign establishments in Egypt, all kinds mixed together (diffusion of brands, franchises, and establishments)

Principal countries	Number of companies	percent
United States	1,548	18.2
Germany	1,020	12.0
Italy	832	9.8
United Kingdom	818	9.6
France	646	7.6
Japan	414	4.9
Total	5,278	61.9
Others	3,244	38.1

Middle East	Number of companies	percent
Saudi Arabia	154	1.8
Kuwait	80	0.9
Lebanon	44	0.5
United Arab Emirates	32	0.4
Jordan	30	0.4
Bahrain	18	0.2
Israel	16	0.2
Syria	6	0.1
Total	380	4.5

Source: Kompass 2000.

Inversely, some large Egyptian companies are leaving to look for new markets in the Arab region and in sub-Saharan Africa. This is the case of Arab Contractors, an enterprise in the Osman Ahmad Osman Corporation that undertakes public works and projects in the countries of the Arabian Peninsula, or of Mobinil, the mobile-telephone branch of the powerful Orascom group (owned by the Sawiris family), which in 2001 won one of two RFPs to bid for the development of a mobile-phone system for Syria. The public-works branch of this group also realizes 40 percent of its activity in Persian Gulf countries, where it constructs American military bases. However, these few examples are still rare. Productive Egyptian investment remains heavily concentrated on national territory.

It is also important to note the role of bilateral aid, from the great Gulf-state families and from development banks that aim at the reconstruction of Egypt's spatial economy. If one sheikh will favor estates in the new gated cities, another will favor the redevelopment of an informal quarter, while the Arab Development Bank will loan funds for the development of infrastructure. In the background this support intends to promote greater regional integration and, as in the case of Western aid for development, prepares the ground for a deeper penetration of Arab capital.[4] Investment in the new settlements around Cairo must be understood as an alternative to Egyptian workers' migration to the Gulf. In some ways, it is about creating a productive, delocalized environment in Cairo, integrating subsidized housing and factories with Arab capital. (See Elsheshtawy, chapter 7, in this volume on investment in commercial and real estate development from the Gulf, particularly Dubai.) Like modest industrial investment by groups from the oil monarchies, the speculative drift of these projects, which are for the most part located in uninhabited areas, has not clearly strengthened Cairo's role as capital of the Middle East region.

In contrast, the redeployment of 1.9 million Egyptian workers to the Gulf countries continues to play an essential role in the socioeconomic fluidity of the Cairene metropolis. Worker remittances ($3 billion) inject income into Cairo's economy, in parity with tourism revenues ($4 billion). Certainly, these monies are not all invested in Cairo, but for the most part, they feed the growth of popular-housing settlements around the megacity. (See Ghannam in this volume for a description of Gulf influence on housing, design, and aesthetics among Cairo's returning migrants.) And for about a dozen years, with the decrease in inflation, their investment has effectively been oriented more toward productive entrepreneurial or service activities. Housing is no longer the only place to anchor and make productive the capital brought back by labor migrants. Sweatshop businesses have diversified the fabric of these quasi-legal quarters. Investment in microbuses and vans, for example, has revitalized urban sprawl and even facilitated the dispersion of old-style metropolitan patterns, since microbuses make affordable the long commutes from the capital to the 'provinces' where new manufacturing industries are located, and also make accessible the jobs that they offer. In this sense, remittance investment in the countryside or rural provinces is linked back into the cycle of capital-city urban development.

Thus, Gulf money favors a pacification of metropolitan space and the reproduction of a cheap manual-labor workforce, facilitating the expansion of the industrial economy and urban services. The network of popular housing palliates and even favors the growth of prestigious luxury housing as the informal and quasi-legal production-commerce channels assure the continuance of low salaries while furnishing current consumer products at a low price, and encouraging subcontracting circuits.

Regional Capital among Several Regional Capitals

Another common indicator of a nation's international integration is its banking sector, and the Findlay study reveals the relative financial weakness of the Egyptian banking system (1993). Indeed, it ranks only third after Kuwait and Beirut for the number of sites, and in second place for the total working population, which situates Egypt's capital at the level of Jedda, Dubai, or Baghdad before the Gulf War. During the 1990s, just as the Egyptian state was reducing its foreign debt in conformity to agreements signed with the IMF, it continued to increase its burden of domestic debt in order to finance its budgetary deficit and to promote a policy of great infrastructural works, gradually paralyzing the banking system and reducing its capacity to finance the private sector.[5]

The figures for airport-passenger traffic (Table 9) also show diverse regional polarities: Cairo's international airport is in sixth place in the Middle East for passenger traffic. To evaluate the flow of business traffic, we must subtract from this data more than two million tourists (in 1997–1998). Moreover, the volume of air freight, an excellent indicator of high value-added commercial flows, remains relatively modest when compared to that of Saudi Arabia and the United Arab Emirates.

All indicators affirm, then, the plurality of nodal points in the Arab world urban system. Egypt and its capital are rarely central from the point of view of a region that is, instead, structured around differentiated urban poles that maintain competitive relations in view of capturing the benefits of globalization, investment, stock purchases, and joint ventures.

Table 9: Airport passenger traffic and freight 1998 in the Middle East, and growth 1997–98

Country	Airport	Passengers	Growth	Freight	Growth
Saudi Arabia	Jeddah	11,661,384	-0.3	199,368	-0.1
United Arab Emirates	Dubai	9,732,202	+6.8	442,492	+4.1
Saudi Arabia	Riyad	8,308,598	0.7	161,902	+6.2
Israel	Tel Aviv	7,939,921	+2.9	286,734	+3.5
Iran	Teheran	7,887,413	+43.0	52,156	+21.0
Egypt	Cairo	7,230,103	-11.3	191,000	+13.7
Kuwait	Safat	3,704,385	-14.0	134,193	-8.8
Bahrain	Bahrain	3,434,812	-0.3	125,514	+7.7
United Arab Emirates	Abu Dhabi	3,131,283	+8.3	71,956	-11.2
Saudi Arabia	Dhahran	3,097,686	-3.4	60,076	-12.2
Qatar	Doha	2,944,895	+5.7	86,854	+60.9
Oman	Muscat	2,756,045	+7.8	53,948	+16.5
Jordan	Amman	2,138,290	+8.6	92,094	+0.8
Lebanon	Beirut	2,060,020	+2.6	57,146	-1.3
Syria	Damascus	1,666,581	+5.1	24,689	+11.3
United Arab Emirates	Sharjah	971,075	-3.9	534,899	+4.1

Source: Aéroports Magazine 1999.

However, the Egyptian capital is one of the rare regional capitals that benefits from a solid international integration, however modest it may be. Thus, while capitalizing on this relative regional void and using the new data on the global market, Cairo does assert itself as the largest metropolis in the Middle East. Persian Gulf metropolises themselves cannot compete with Cairo's centrality, which is also a reflection of an internal metropolitan diversity that is unusual. Indeed, the metropolises of the Arabian Peninsula with 'open economies' base their financial power principally on local capital. They serve more as relays in the system of franchises and licenses tied to large international groups. As production bases in a world system of duty/tax-free zones, Persian Gulf economies are destined principally for international reexportation. These are branch economies. However, in Egypt, the national economy is undergoing a deep transformation resulting from its opening to the global economic sphere. This transformation is occurring along with shifts in sources of capital, forms of production, networks of distribution, and structures of retail and marketing. Development of a new economy, carried during the 1990s by a changing private sector, turned upside down the existing modes of production while imposing the 'logic' of the market and competition. At the national level, this translates into an accrued polarization of functions and resources by the metropolis. In Cairo, pursuing an expansion dynamic, we see the juxtaposition of landscapes (industrial, residential, functional) issuing from sometimes-contradictory logics in competition with one another.

Cairo as Melting Pot and Arab World Mediator

If Egypt does not prevail as the economic and political capital of a unified Middle East, it does appear nevertheless very clearly as the most urban of the regional economies due to its diversity and by its presence in all domains. Cairo marks the region, even if the activities that are concentrated there never assert themselves at the top level. It is perhaps precisely this character that defines the undeniable centrality of Cairo: its size permits its diversity and, in a definitive way, its power. Indeed, what Arab company can neglect the Egyptian market, can afford not to have Egyptian partners, or simply deprive itself of a presence in Cairo?

Today Cairo is the theater of a cultural renewal, owing to the wide circulation of capital that it enjoys, but also to intellectual capital linked to its size. This is occurring notably in the audiovisual and musical domains. (See Sadek, Puig, and Armbrust in this volume for further discussion of Cairo's cultural role and its relationship to foreign financial and investment flows.) Despite the constraining influence of Persian Gulf investors and their conservatism in moral matters, despite the climate of censure that is increasingly forceful, Cairo's glory is being remade and may yet reaffirm the city's identity. Due to Egypt's investment in its satellite TV stations and new studios, creative activity is again finding its way to the city. Once again, the creative Cairene milieu can be deployed as an instrument of conquest for the Arab market, which counts more than two hundred million Arabic speakers.

Persian Gulf countries play a mediating role in the construction of the cultural centrality of Cairo. They bring capital and transmit transnational lifestyles like fast-food restaurant chains, but also modes of residence, like the private gated cities and deluxe desert villas (see Abaza, Denis, and Elsheshtawy, chapter 7, in this volume). Egyptian migrants working in the petroleum monarchies also play the role of ferrymen and of hybridizers of ways of consuming. The references at first glance seem American, but passage through the Gulf imprints them with specific moral and symbolic codes.

In this sense, Cairo asserts its centrality, not forcefully, as would an imperialist power, but by capitalizing on differences, as a mediating place in which a 'hybrid Arabness' is invented in accord with the global climate. The city appears as the capital of the Arab world, that is, as an undeniable passageway where contradictions and differences are visible. Numerous production and service activities that are developing in Cairo are nourished by separation, by cultural limits, and by challenges to American-style product standardization. For example, the expansion of software engineering in Cairo is much more the result of the need to 'Arabize' the programs made by large North American companies for a vast regional market, than the result of innovation or creativity on the part of this sector.

Data presented here reveal a renewed metropolis that has learned to capitalize on and exploit its position and its heritage. Clearly, this tendency is oriented toward concentrating the urban means of production and production capacities for goods that are increasingly complex, and that engage an internationalized network. This circulation and intensification of flows obliges a strengthening of the metropolitan centrality. Of course, this involves a profound transformation of relationships with the world and with the Middle East region, as the preceding observations suggest, as well as relationships relative to the articulation of capital with the provinces in Egypt.

Changing Scales

The question of a move toward reformulating the national economy, activities, finances, leadership, and competencies (such as manual labor), and to concentrate them in a metropolitan model, is not new for Egypt. It emerged clearly over the course of the twentieth century with the affirmation of an internationalized market economy, stimulated by English tutelage and oriented toward that model.

During the whole of the nineteenth century, Cairo's management role remained limited as other economic centers and foci were elaborated. From the time of the reign of Muhammad 'Ali, the map of Egypt has been enlarged, cultivated areas have been extended, the Suez Canal was dug, and new cities have been planned and inhabited. Notably, some manufacturing concerns (textiles and sugar refineries) were established in provincial cities following industrialization of the agricultural network and the expansion of large landholdings. Over more than a century, the weight of Cairo remained quite modest. In 1848, its population accounted for only 5.9 percent of the country's total and even in 1907 accounted for no more than 5.5 percent. In the next forty years it then doubled in size, and again over the following forty years, accounting for 19.3 percent of the total population in 1986, though falling to 17 percent in 1996 (the last census data available). But since 1917 Cairo, which then accounted for only 6.3 percent of all Egyptians, already accounted for 25 percent of chemical jobs, 30 percent in tanning, 24 percent in metallurgy, 34 percent in active concerns in the financial sector, and 31 percent of those in the juridical and hospitality professions (Alleaume and Denis 1998). In 1996, the Cairo agglomeration held 40 percent of industrial jobs, and 46 percent of those in the financial sector and hotel services. At the end of the twentieth century, this new metropolis must be understood as recomposing an already clearly established mode of concentration. However, it should be viewed in a renewed demographic context in accordance with the clear slowdown of population growth in the metropolis.

That which perhaps most justifies our referring to this as a 'new' kind of metropolitan structure is the increasing gap between, on one hand, a much slower pace in the rate of Cairo's demographic increase, with a population less concentrated and evenly spread out over an expanding metropolitan area and, on the other hand, the continuous, if not increased, metropolitan concentration of capital and activity (see below). This trend is confirmed by the choices of localization of investment (in production as well as in real estate) and by the implantation of innovative, high-value-added activities.

The notion of an 'inverted economy'—a misconception that imagines cities of the global South featuring populations disproportionate with economic expansion—is less pertinent than ever in the case of Cairo.[6] This productive linking of a certain type of wealth is what allows a number of metropolises of the global South to be integrated as specialized relays at the heart of a megametropolitan archipelago articulating the differentials of productivity according to a profoundly unequal schema. Informality is a functional attribute of metropolitanization at the first level, that is, of megametropolitanization or the affirmation of a very large city crushing the population hierarchy, concentrating and capitalizing on diversity. In the context of deregulation, informality is flexible capital whose expansion is not confined to countries undergoing development. The dynamic of a metropolis such as New York owes much to the exploitation of an imported subproletariat. As in Cairo, the whole laboring population creates such a system of informality, even contributing to a certain convergence making comparison of the two metropolises possible (Abu-Lughod 1990).

Slowing Demographic Increase

The last census confirmed a trend, encouraged during the 1970s, toward the reduction of Cairo's attractiveness to populations resettling within Egypt. Recently, Greater Cairo has grown less rapidly than the average for Egypt: 1.9 percent per year versus 2.1 percent for Egypt. Thus, at a constant limit, the agglomeration of Cairo grew only 18.3 percent between 1986 and 1996, versus 32.7 percent during the decade before.

Clearly, the capital no longer attracts migrants from the provinces: 35 percent of Cairo's inhabitants were not born there in 1960, and in 1996, only 12 percent were born elsewhere. But the peripheral governorates of Giza and Qalyubiya (the western and northern extensions of Greater Cairo) certainly saw the number of nonnatives growing noticeably; but more than half of these individuals are actually migrants shifting from somewhere else within the Greater Cairo agglomeration (Table 10). Nevertheless, the municipality of Cairo itself, with its downtown parks and old, degraded pericentral housing, remains the privileged welcoming place for half the migrants from the provinces. These migrants then redistribute themselves in the agglomeration while participating in a centrifugal tendency, a worldwide phenomenon. To the north of the Municipality of Cairo, Qalyubiya (a separate governorate but within the area of Greater Cairo) is beginning to play an essential role in the integration of provincial migrants vis-à-vis the megametropolitan economy. As it is in the case of Giza, it is important to understand this phenomenon as evidence of the megametropolitan sprawl of Greater Cairo. In the oldest zones (clusters of decaying neighborhoods and assimilated villages), a substitution is occurring: migrants are occupying the spaces that were formerly used by a local population that has since acquired property and better living conditions farther away, in the peripheral areas of the city.

The spread and transfer of growth is made apparent through the depopulation of an intraurban area that is increasingly extended and yet reinforced by the collapse of migration from the provinces. During the last period, 1986–96, districts in decline lost a total of five hundred thousand residents: twenty-four districts out of the thirty-eight that make up Cairo were involved, three of these were situated on the bank of the Nile in the governorate of Giza, which has been urbanizing and absorbing Cairo's spillover since the beginning of the century. The central city, which includes the old center, the business center (wust al-balad) and the decaying neighborhoods, lost more than 14 percent of its residents in ten years. At the same time, the noncentral parts of Greater Cairo have welcomed a young population and thus increased in population by more than 40 percent (newlyweds tend not to live with their families after marriage but settle in newer areas in Cairo and establish their own household). With 30 percent of this growth occurring over ten years, the increase is more clearly observed in suburban towns and villages of the provinces of Giza and Qalyubiya.

Table 10: Distribution of nonnatives in the population of Greater Cairo in 1996

	Internal	External	Inhabitants	Nonnative portion	External nonnative portion	Portion of external distribution	Portion of internal distribution
Cairo	118,714	691,048	6,675,774	12.1	10.4	50.2	14.7
Urban Giza	399,385	222,120	2,544,994	24.4	8.7	16.1	64.3
Rural Giza	192,261	67,770	2,189,172	11.9	3.1	4.9	73.9
Urban Qalyubiya	155,479	208,698	1,402,002	26.0	14.9	15.1	42.7
Rural Qalyubiya	142,118	188,215	2,095,021	15.8	9.0	13.7	43.0
Agglomeration	673,578	1,121,866	10,622,770	16.9	10.6	81.4	37.5
Extent of the Greater Cairo region	1,007,957	1,377,851	14,906,963	16.0	9.2	100.0	42.2

Source: CAPMAS 1996b.

* Nonnative refers here to Egyptians born outside Cairo.
'Internal' refers here to nonnative inhabitants from one of the areas from Greater Cairo who have moved to the interior or central area of Greater Cairo, while 'external' designates nonnative inhabitants coming from other Egyptian provinces.

Finally, in the past twenty years, migration has reversed and people have been flowing out of Cairo. At present, fewer than 10 percent of migrations are between provinces, whereas twenty years earlier, one-quarter of migrants changed province. Reflecting the same tendency, residential intervillage mobility represents, at present, 20 percent of the total number of migrations.

Graph 1: The long wave of metropolitanization (1897–1996)

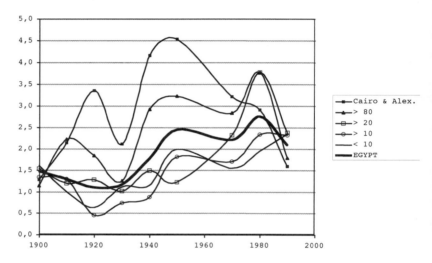

Source: GIS EGYPT CEDEJ-CAPMAS.

Morphological agglomerations are considered retrospectively in their 1996 limits. Geographic units are therefore constant during the period 1897–1996. The legend is in thousands of inhabitants.

It is not necessary to interpret this tendency as evidence of reurbanization, uniformly affecting the territory. It is, to the contrary, intimately tied to the new dynamics of all major urban poles, and in particular, the new character of the Cairene metropolis. The increasing weight of slippage toward rural zones is largely explained by the narrowness by which 'urban' is defined in Egypt. Official institutions have only designated 180 cities to be urban zones, while the entire country counts more than eight hundred actual agglomerations of more than ten thousand inhabitants. Otherwise stated, what is recorded as changes of residence in favor of rural zones is actually in large measure the overflow of city settlement into neighboring villages. This, by extension, explains why the official rate of urbanization went down from 44 percent to 43 percent between 1986 and 1996. Yet an urbanization rate on the order of 70 percent would be much more realistic if villages were counted as suburbs woven into the metropolitan fabric. It would also account for a simultaneous urban spread and in situ growth, without migration, in rural towns (Bayat and Denis 2000).

The demographic stabilization of the Egyptian territory and the uniformity of growth is the product of transformations in migratory dynamics. Egypt's internal trends of migration slide from strong growth, polarized by lengthy residential migrations to the largest metropolises, toward stabilization and decreasing migrations. Finally, and still more recently, Cairo is moving toward an explosion in the pendulum of commuter activities that support the fulfillment of matrimonial strategies, access to housing, and eventually social mobility with changes in residence. This phenomenon is completely induced by the liberal revolution of transportation routes, of microbus services particularly, which have introduced great flexibility into the accessibility of a territory that is, in the end, very cramped. Demographic growth has been able to distance or emancipate itself from the large axes of roads and railroads. On the other hand, the passage of an economy of shortages to one of consumerism has dispersed access to goods and services, reducing interest in residential migration toward the city center. However, this spatial diffusion says nothing about socioeconomic distribution. Costs of living have continued to increase, but local economic sustainability by contrast can be more easily activated at a minimal level for many, owing to the pendulum swing of migrations that allow the major urban poles easy access and low costs. It is notably easier and less costly to marry and live in a village. These patterns then take advantage of a vast field of circulatory integrations that structure Greater Cairo. Cairo combines the ability to go, temporarily, where job opportunities are concentrated and the capacity to begin social integration, networks, and the accumulation of family capital, and even to begin enhancing the value of local products. Local milieus also tend to be diverse and complex, favoring ascendant social trajectories and the emergence of urbanized towns that, according to cumulative logic, induce still more in situ stabilization. It is quite important to see the territory that is currently under construction as an interdependent whole in a state of permanent interconnection. Here the transformation of Egypt is played out with, on the one hand, tendencies toward retraditionalization linked to the reactivation of family and village structures and to the reduction of residential mobility, and, on the other hand, tendencies toward the diversification of the same village milieu, which favors the renewal of the elites. The intermixing or métissage that is occurring stimulates urban practices, owing to its indisputable modification of practices and alignments. At the same time, it fosters the reinvention of tradition combining the establishment of roots with modernity. (See Miller in this volume for a case study of the ways in which Cairene residents with Upper Egyptian identities have reimagined their ethnic and regional identity to meet the challenges of urban cultural and political life.)

This new ring of peripheral urbanization is establishing a classical model of hierarchy of cities, serviced by the still-privileged corridors of accessibility (Christaller 1933) But the new form is also metaconcentrated and structured by the increase in accessibility of the capital city from the 'country' and the reduction of distance-to-time ratios. Close to half of the Egyptian population lives within a radius of eighty to ninety kilometers of Cairo, that is to say, at a maximum travel distance of 120 kilometers, corresponding to the acceptable limit for daily commuting of 3 hours round trip. A radius of two hundred kilometers includes more than 70 percent of the population. This large-scale "third space," to borrow Giraud's and Vannier's expression (2000), also corresponds to the most densely populated *rural* districts and therefore to the greatest population densities: districts with more than three thousand inhabitants per square kilometer are not unusual there. The average population density of this largest-scale definition of Greater Cairo is established at 1,700 people per thirty-five thousand square kilometers of useable Egyptian land, already more densely populated than the North American Boston–Washington megalopolis. This third space is truly the territory of overlap and movement. We need not conceive of it only as a suburb animated by the daily work–home movement. The structure of the labor market and the weak weight of salaried workers do not favor this conception. Instead, it is a circulating territory that is also marked by transfers of merchandise, business, searches for temporary work, and by self-employment opportunities adapted to circumstances. This space is also marked by localized shortages and upswings in cities and towns—markets, religious festivals, marriages—without counting the importance of family visits that continuously reweave the contours of the social space, extending and reinforcing alliances and solidarities.

Just as concentration and reintegration of activities around Cairo does not slacken, and is even increasing, these demographic tendencies that seem contrary are in fact serving the rationalization of the metropolitan machine. They serve its center which can more easily become the object of reconstruction sites and of functional reappropriation, and reduce the high costs linked to congestion. In other words, the whole of useable space is recomposed and more largely exploited to serve the new metropolitanization. In any case, it is not about a movement toward dispersion, but much more about a hierarchical spreading of an always extremely concentrated area that is increasingly organized around the relay or circuit model. That is, circulation is organized in relation to the center, but its most intense exchanges are structured around relaying poles across flows that no longer pass by way of the center (Brown and Wardwell 1980). The third space combines classic functions of food supply for the capital, and allows the capitalization of know-how and human resources. There, a subproletariat is recreated. It bustles about, on the one hand, for its own survival while exploiting the crumbs from the metropolitan machine. On the other hand, it serves as a source of potential manual labor, in the long term guaranteeing low labor costs and an intense web of services, used as often in the heart of enterprises as by private parties in domestic settings. Thus, it also becomes a space for low-value-added activities that are linked as much to the expansion and diversification of demand at the city center and to metropolitan demands that are increasingly sophisticated. Evidently, delimiting the precise contours of this third space would be in vain. We must understand it as a zone, or rather a halo, structured by poles and corridors. In a useable space as narrow as Egypt's Nile Valley, we must also note that this megalopolis' third space may mingle with the totality, that is, the national scale as a whole. For as such, it will always serve a metropolitan machine that continues to capitalize on private incomes and surplus value, redistributing only minimally in order to reaffirm and guarantee its centrality.

An Expanded but Still-Dependent Production Model

Having taken into consideration space-time compression and the hierarchical integration of a large part of the territory of the metropolitan system, it appears that the spreading out of productive activities is linked to the capital's reconfiguration.

Thus, 85 percent of the annual industrial product is concentrated in twelve of the cities (see Table 11 below) located in the Nile Delta region (north of Cairo and south of the Mediterranean Sea). Greater Cairo always contributes more than half of the national industrial product, and, with less than three hours between Cairo and the Suez Canal, the often very specialized major poles of the Delta cities become important features. The port activities and free zones that contribute little to the export of manufactured products are especially integrated into a radial network serving the metropolitan economy of Greater Cairo. They are largely dedicated to supplying it or to the flow of its products.

The majority of the sites are in Cairo, which gives rise to a repatriation of all the revenues and does not favor the decentralization of banking activity.

Table 11: The Egyptian industrial agglomerations

Rank	Agglomeration	Industrial product 96/97*	Accumulated weight	Industrial weight	Demographic weight	Concentration index**
1	Greater Cairo Region	11,787,736	52.6	52.6	18.1	2.9
2	Alexandria	3,239,181	67.1	14.5	5.2	2.8
3	Mahalla al-Kubra	707,751	70.2	3.2	0.8	3.9
4	Damietta	618,576	73.0	2.8	0.4	6.9
5	Suez	483,966	75.1	2.2	0.6	3.6
6	Mansura	377,609	76.8	1.7	0.8	2.1
7	Port Said	374,073	78.5	1.7	0.7	2.4
8	Kafr al-Dawwar	307,908	79.9	1.4	0.4	3.4
9	Zifta Mit Ghamr	288,932	81.2	1.3	0.3	4.3
10	Tanta	284,206	82.4	1.3	0.8	1.6
11	Zaqaziq	258,054	83.6	1.2	0.7	1.6
12	Isma'iliya	190,528	84.4	0.9	0.5	1.7
	TOTAL	18,918,520	84.4	84.4	29.3	2.9

Source: CAPMAS 1996a; 1996–97.

*The number of employees is multiplied by the average productivity of each employee in the industrial establishments, according to their size and membership or nonmembership in the public sector.
** The industrial weight related to the demographic weight

In the same line, the specialized cities of the Delta, whether in textile centers like al-Mahalla al-Kubra or in furniture centers like Damietta, also enter into the commercial chains that are extremely concentrated in Cairo, or even into the production networks whose finishing activities are articulated in the industrial districts of the capital: in Shubra al-Khayma or, for trimmings, near Muhammad 'Ali Street in the downtown. The Delta region has also seen the development of a group of food-processing industries whose products respond simultaneously to attempts to get a foothold in foreign markets, notably the European Union, but especially to the sophistication of Cairo's demand where ready-to-consume articles occupy a significant place. Export markets are still confined largely to off-season agricultural products that are not only processed but entirely packaged in the Delta. The only cryogenic complex allowing export of fruits such as strawberries is in Cairo. For some time the production of strawberries intensified in the north of Cairo, in Qalyubiya, where it is closer to its consumers; the same is true for apricots. Similarly, Cairo hosts the country's only wholesale market, which plays a role in fixing export prices. Since 1996, it has been centralized on the Cairo–Isma'iliya axis. The industrialization of the network has only reinforced an old configuration, which corresponds to the classical localization scheme of garden-produce marketing at the periphery of urban soil. This scheme leads to the equilibrium of basic private income constraining urban spread. Garden-produce plots, like the nurseries, are very productive where the value of lots in the periphery is low.

The Delta's industrial cities appear to be more in a situation of hierarchical dependence with regard to Cairo insofar as they are oriented toward a single industry or at least an extremely specialized one. Consequently, they are fragile and very dependent on the conjuncture of circumstances. The population of a textile-producing city, such as al-Mahalla al-Kubra, suffers horribly from the sector's decline, increasingly subject to Asian competition against which this sector is shown not to be competitive, despite Egypt's low wages. Notably, efforts to privatize large establishments that employ more than thirty thousand salaried workers has lead to the instability of private factory orders and affects the entire local economy (Textile Holding Company 2000).

Only Cairo has at its disposition a textile industry that is sufficiently diversified, and able to adapt to circumstances. In Cairo, information is concentrated and management is relatively competent and able to react quickly to changes in demand and to modifications of the rules of commerce. Proximity to banks, government bureaucracies, and ministries is fundamental. These cumulative synergies explain why Egypt is not concerned by the deconcentration trends, except the functional ones due to the evolution of land prices. For instance, polluting steel and cement industries have, of course, moved nearer to ports and gas deposits. But if one looks at the current consumer industry, one sees that it has been reorganized in the peripheral areas of Cairo. The latter recomposition constitutes a web of industrial zones for the new satellite cities, just as the more modest sweatshops associated with food products, construction (window framing and tiles), and household equipment have flourished in the illegal quarters of the capital.

Secondary Cities in Egypt

Even Alexandria, despite its 3.5 million inhabitants and its prime Mediterranean port location, does not have at its disposal a critical mass capable of articulating a development trajectory independent of Cairo. The city lies in the wake of Cairo and submits to the evolving modalities of Egyptian integration in the world economy. With the establishment of the modern postcolonial state in Egypt after 1952, Alexandria lost its independent banking apparatus, which was folded into the nationally incorporated financial system based in Cairo. During the 1990s, Alexandria undertook embellishment and infrastructure-modernization efforts; but these are only geared toward revitalizing its façade. Backstage, the Alexandrian economy has suffered terribly from the collapse of the large industrial establishments that have marked the city's periphery since the 1960s. Alexandria is, moreover, affected by the redeployment of port activity to the banks of the Suez Canal, with the new port of Suez, and by the new port of Damietta on the Mediterranean. The port of Alexandria constitutes not more than 30 percent of Egypt's port commerce in total tons as compared to 45 percent some ten years earlier. And this percentage will again have to be lowered with the opening of the eastern port of Port Said, conceived as a Mediterranean redistribution hub for loading containers coming from Asia. Incapacity to again find an autonomous development initiative, to attract productive investment, as well as the decline of industrial activities, all combine to make the apparent renewal of Alexandria simple window-dressing for Cairo, and an extension of the capital city toward the Mediterranean. This dynamic is what inspired the Bibliotheca Alexandrina, which opened its doors in 2002 on the Corniche along the Mediterranean, with its capacity for eight million books. Nevertheless, in 2000, Alexandria lost to Cairo the unique institution of international importance that it had housed for more than fifty years; the regional headquarters of the World Health Organization, which could no longer function at such a distance from other United Nations contacts, international airport lines, and ministries and embassies.

Alexandria is not an exception among the other provincial cities. As in other cities, the elites and middle classes are not strong enough to instantiate an autonomous dynamic, political initiative, or simply to develop a 'brand' for local entrepreneurship. And undeniably, the Chamber of Commerce and Industry was politically implicated with the Governor of Alexandria in the development of illegal zones and slum settlements, through microcredit schemes. But the political integration of Alexandria's establishment with its own legal and illegal peripheries remains modest compared to its dedication to remaining in contact with the center, with Cairo, its administrations, ministries, entrepreneurs, banks, and the eyes of the Cairene media. Indeed, regional television only expresses the official point of view, full of images of progress, of national development projects or of modest attempts to create folklore from provincial identities. (See Smith in this volume on the assertion of Nubian identity and Colonna on the challenges that provincial elites and the provincial media face.)

The province is the master neither of its destiny nor of its image. The opening to foreign investment did not change this dynamic. The Cairene economic apparatus enjoyed investment almost exclusively (Table 12).

Table 12: Metropolitan weight in foreign participation, all sectors joined together (brands, franchises, and establishments)

	Participation	Percent
Total for Egypt	8,522	100
Cairo	4,961	58
Giza	2,071	24
Qalyubiya	52	1
Tenth of Ramadan	256	3
Total for Greater Cairo	7,340	86

Source: Kompass 2000.

Economic liberalization and the supply of capital are not absolutely translated into a decentralization of activity. Only the new production establishments for intermediary goods, cement and steel in particular, have moved out to new peripheral settlements. But invested markets are almost exclusively located on the perimeter of the Delta, in proximity to petroleum and natural-gas access, and near to maritime transportation. In fact, regions to the south of Cairo are excluded from redeployment of new intermediary industries. The abject marginality of Upper Egypt has been rearticulated. The poverty of the south was reduced to some extent by the industrial efforts of the 1960s, and by the expansion of international tourism. But these driving forces have largely evaporated, or been reconcentrated in Cairo. Competition with the network of major Delta cities, the new vitality of the Canal cities and ports, and the disappearance of state subsidies and development targeting under structural adjustment has encouraged the marginalization of Upper Egypt as it collides with the metropolitan dynamic.

Industrial Redeployment

The notion of redeployment, this expansion along with metropolitan reconcentration, is fundamental to understanding the dynamic effect on the city's economic base as well as on central and pericentral building projects. Industrial establishments and, more generally, production networks are restructuring themselves according to a management model that remains completely centered on Cairo's command functions. The model also articulates with provincial sites, with new perimetropolitan poles at the heart of the new cities.

Complete and rapid restructuring, in less than ten years, and the strong increase in production capacities in the steel sector, illustrate the general tendencies toward delocalizing intermediary industries. Together, these elements allow us to understand the consequences of this urban dynamic. Stimulated by the expansion of building construction around Cairo, and the megasites for

New and old industrial areas of the Cairo agglomeration (Eric Denis, SEDET-CRNS-Paris 7, 2005).

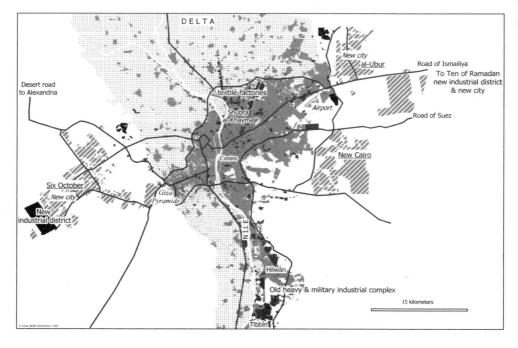

irrigation and improvement in the northern Sinai and Toshka (the desert to the west of the reservoir of the Aswan Dam, the site of a huge project to reclaim the desert), steel industrial networks were reorganized around a powerful private group, Ezz Steel Rebars, which presently controls 70 percent of the market. This occured thanks in part to the establishment of new production capacities first in the Cairo satellites of Sadat City and Tenth of Ramadan City. Soon there will be another steel-industry outpost opposite the Suez, on the banks of the Sinai, close to the first electrical center constructed along the lines of a Build-Operate-Transfer (BOT) model where a private—and often foreign—company builds the infrastructure, operates it for a certain number of years, and then transfers it to local actors. In 2000, Ezz Steel acquired 30 percent of Alexandria National Iron Steel, the most important producer of steel wire and reinforced concrete. The new alignment of the steel industry was only possible after private investors gained majority participation in the most efficient public enterprises. The public sector, which held majority shares in steel interests at the end of the 1980s, now only controls one site, Helwan Steel, to the south of Cairo, in Tibbin, at the heart of the neoindustrial complex of the 1960s, which accounts for only 5 percent of current steel production in Egypt. However, it employs twenty-three thousand salaried employees, or 26 percent of those employed by the entire sector. This site thus became the sector's least effective and most obsolete establishment; as well as a site for some of the country's most visible and effective labor organizing and protest (see Posusney 2002, 1997).

Steel, the jewel of industrialization, having at first asserted the metropolis' national independence and international stature, has since become a huge labor controversy. Its privatization is no longer reported. The cement network has been restructured according to the same scheme; the public sector now controls no more than 30 percent of this sector at the Turah site, situated to the south of Cairo. In 2000, following a privatization plan, this enterprise was bought back by another public company, Suez Cement, and appears to be doomed because of the high cost of conforming to antipollution norms. On the other hand, localized companies outside of Cairo became controlled foreign cement corporations such as Lafargue or Blue Circle. The public textile sector encountered comparable difficulties in two industrial zones of Cairo: Shubra al-Khayma and Sixth of October City.

Zoning changes away from industrial use favor reappropriation—rezoning and urban renewal. The metropolis finds itself altered little by little by the incorporation of fallow lands. Port zones on the northeastern banks of the Nile at Bulaq in central Cairo have been the object of very strong appropriation, in particular with the construction of the World Trade Center which, since then, has served as a point of departure for a total restructuring of adjacent workers' neighborhoods. (See Ghannam in this volume for a discussion of the development of this area and the forced removal of its residents.) The dynamic of rezoning and urban renewal is relatively slow, taking into account the lack of available capital. And the law always forbids the acquisition of an enterprise just for the land it is sitting on, that is to say, to use the site for an activity other than the one formerly practiced there. But many exceptions have already been promulgated, notably for vacant warehouses.

During the last ten years, the great majority of investment capacities were captured by the state. This was followed by the introduction into the market, at a very low price, of vast surfaces to be urbanized on the desert edges of Greater Cairo (about one hundred square kilometers, more than a third of the megacity's area in 1990). The abundance of the offer lead to overindebtedness to banks by the greater part of 320 companies that undertook the project to divide up and develop the desert. Indeed, the market introduction of luxury construction bids for private residences translated into diminishing investment returns. Strong price declines, increases in abandonments, and costly project revisions, as well as greater difficulty in securing investment capital, affected the sector. Since then, building construction has experienced a severe crisis that, along with the government's megaprojects, has contributed to destabilizing the entire Egyptian economy. Eighty companies have begun to implement their projects, building sixty thousand housing units, essentially stand-alone villas. A total of six hundred thousand housing units are planned equaling an estimated investment of more than $3 billion. (See Denis in this volume for further analysis of these new luxury, gated communities.)

Despite the instability and the risks of the bubble bursting, recalling the Thailand syndrome, this direction is pursued blindly. The important availability of tracts of public desert land in the hands of the state, in Cairo and at its margins, fosters this new kind of urban primacy and concentration, which has simply jumped up in scale. Even in the core of the agglomeration, the potential for reinvestment is great, if state-owned goods and housing which are 'outside' of the market, are taken into account. The various state ministries own more than half of the Cairene agglomeration's current area, while, by definition, the ability to spread onto the desert margins is almost infinite. No other Egyptian urban site offers such potential. Alexandria's coastal linearity limits its spread, the cities of the Delta are limited by the green belt of rich agricultural lands that sustain them, and the canal cities such as Port Said are constrained by the heavy investments that would be necessary in order to develop the eastern banks of the Suez Canal.

The state can play a key role by structurally lowering land prices, while introducing goods that are now in public hands and thus outside the market. Privatizing, while reducing the scarcity of land, can inject a certain kind of speculative wealth into the economy. We should note here that support of metropolitanization and privatization enters into a particular logic of the state, not the logic of any 'market' forces. The collusion of national and metropolitan interests appears clearly.

Shubra al-Khayma versus Sixth of October: A Closer Look at the Industrial Sector in the New Metropolitanization

Broken out by district, the value of industrial production represents an order of magnitude and a hierarchy of industrial concentration that indicates the modalities of redeployment and activity (Table 13). Certainly, the industrial poles of south Cairo, Tibbin and Helwan continue to appear to be dominant. But their primacy is declining, and especially, during less than fifteen years, industrial zones and the new cities of Tenth of Ramadan and Sixth of October have begun to assert themselves in relation to the traditional secondary Cairene industrial pole, Shubra al-Khayma. The new satellite cities should very rapidly occupy the highest rung of the ladder, taking into account the number of projects approaching completion and the important developing margins of already-present establishments, as the traditional industries of the public domain are very clearly declining. These displacements spatially transcribe the weakness of the public sector, whose contribution to industrial production has constantly declined, as much through obsolescence and lack of investment as through privatization. Its contribution went from 63 percent in 1983 to 24 percent in 1998, to the profit of the private sector (Soliman 1998).

The inversion of Cairo's patterns of industrial concentration—influenced by economic globalization, and by the doubling of the land area of the metropolis—are illustrated particularly in a comparative analysis of two textile centers: Shubra al-Khayma, situated to the north of Cairo and founded during the 1930s after the initial expansion of the textile industry; and the new city of Sixth of October, situated to the southwest of Greater Cairo. The latter is a result of the fruits of metropolitan planning operations launched at the end of the 1970s along with Tenth of Ramadan city. These two industrial quarters are the product of very different phases of industrialization. Shubra al-Khayma, situated in the governorate of Qalyubiya in the north of Greater Cairo, is one of the cities that have seen the most rapid growth in Egypt. The province of Qalyubiya effectively welcomed the principal centers of traditional textile production. From the 1930s, thanks to tariffs put in place for the protection of Egyptian industry, the modern textile sector began to develop, forming one of the central sectors of manufacturing production in Egypt, notably in terms of manual labor—the second sector after that of food production. Today, it still represents 24 percent of industrial employment and 25 percent of industrial production. Since the 1940s, Shubra al-Khayma has become a major textile center. The large establishments there operate to reinforce and renew a web of textile manufacturing already present in Qalyubiya. Its factories, including the largest wool mill in Egypt, Wooltex (established 1937), and the cotton mill ESCO (established 1940), were nationalized between 1961 and 1963 (Bulbul and Neguib 2000).

Shubra al-Khayma has since then been the object of an intensification project, notably around the ESCO pole which still employed twenty-six thousand workers in 1990. During the 1960s, Shubra al-Khayma was considered one of Egypt's main industrial cities in terms of the number of its factories and workers. Thus, the textile sector, the industrial base for the northern quarters of Cairo, appeared there as an integrated network, from public-sector mills to the clothing industry, which is mainly private and partially illegal/informal. During the late 1970s and early 1980s, Egypt's President Sadat launched a wave of economic liberalization (Infitah) that allowed the textile district to realize a new phase of growth, with the creation of two thousand new industrial establishments and the employment of fifty thousand workers (Bulbul and Neguib 2000).

On a quite different historical trajectory, the new city of Sixth of October was founded in 1979 within the framework of a redeployment plan for the growth of Greater Cairo. The new city waited a dozen years before experiencing even modest growth, from a demographic point of view. In 1986, it counted only 527 inhabitants, but rose to 35,477 in 1996, and more than sixty thousand in 2000. But it is not as a place to live, but as a place to work in industry, in total connection with Cairo, that the new city realizes its greatest success. The industrial zone has been functioning since 1986, during the first phase, and for the second and fourth phases since 1990, whereas the third phase was completed around 2005. Sixth of October offers prospective private enterprises the advantages of fiscal exemption formulas over a ten-year period, basic linked infrastructures, lots of space, and good deals that permit the establishment of large production units. Sixth of October is in close proximity to Cairo thanks to the new Ring Road (peripheral beltway) and to its junction with the national highway that links Upper Egypt and Alexandria. Sixth of October's ambition is of national proportions. These accumulated advantages have attracted numerous enterprises (722 in 2000, according to *Kompass 2000*). When they had the means to do so, some companies have relocated there, placing themselves near those enterprises being created (see Table 14).

Table 13: Egyptian industrial poles in 1996

Rank	Name of quarter	Profile of the place	Production Value X 1.000 LE	Accumulated weight*
1	Qism al-Tibbin	Industrial quarter, Greater Cairo	1,055,484	4.65
2	Qism Helwan	Industrial quarter, Greater Cairo	893,850	8.59
3	Tenth of Ramadan	New city, Greater Cairo	874,180	12.45
4	Shubra al-Khayma	Industrial quarter, Greater Cairo	623,074	15.20
5	Qism Sidi Gabir	Industrial quarter, Alexandria	593,849	17.81
6	Sixth of October	New city, Greater Cairo	528,631	20.15
7	Qism al-Raml	Industrial quarter, Alexandria	491,891	22.31
8	Qism Bab Sharqi	Industrial quarter, Alexandria	470,033	24.39
9	City of Damietta	City and area of Damietta	447,500	26.36
10	Qism al-Basatin	Popular quarter, Greater Cairo	407,086	28.15
11	al-Mahalla al-Kubra 2	Quarter of Mahalla	400,610	29.92
12	Markaz Imbaba	Semirural area of Greater Cairo	389,919	31.64
13	Port of Alexandria	Industrial quarter, Alexandria	344,142	33.16
14	Qism al-Gamaliya	Old city of Cairo	326,925	34.60
15	Qism al-Zaytun	Pericentral quarter, Greater Cairo	325,993	36.04
16	Qism al-Salam	Popular quarter, Greater Cairo	284,377	37.29

Source: CAPMAS 1996a;1996–97.

*The number of employees is multiplied by the average production by employee in industrial establishments, according to the establishment's size and membership or nonmembership in the public sector.

Table 14: Implantation chronology of Sixth of October enterprises

Factories	1991	1992	1993	1994	1995	1998	2000
Total	190	202	296	349	385	562	772

Sources: Dalil Madinat Sittah Uktubir 1998–99 and Kompass Egypt 2000.

The industrial makeup of the two cities presents numerous differences in nature. Shubra al-Khayma is dense and compressed, essentially composed of small industrial units. Thus, at the level of the governorate of Qalyubiya, 130 thousand people are employed by sixteen thousand enterprises: 25 percent have only one worker, and 67 percent employ from two to ten workers (that is, 92 percent of the enterprises have fewer than ten employees). The important informal sector, characterized by small-size units, is unfortunately not counted in these statistics. The enterprises present in Sixth of October are, themselves, characterized by their larger size, as shown in Tables 15 and 16.

Table 15: Size of enterprises in Sixth of October, 2000

Size	Number	percent
1–9	73	12.6
10–99	341	58.8
100–499	141	24.3
500 or more	25	4.3
Total	580	100

Source: Kompass 2000 (Only 580 enterprises participated in this inquiry).

Table 16: Size of factories in transformational industries in Sixth of October and Shubra al-Khayma in 1995

Number:	Factories	Employees	Employees per factor
Shubra al-Khayma	5,879	70,245	12
Sixth of October	385	28,415	74

Source: CAPMAS 1995.

The intensity of industrial production, measured in terms of production value, still differentiates the two industrial quarters, putting into relief the strong value-added aspect of production in the new cities. If from a national perspective Shubra al-Khayma is always placed at the fourth rank among industrial poles with a production value of LE623 million (2.75 percent of national production), Sixth of October already reaches the sixth national ranking with a rise of LE529 million produced in 1996–97 (2.34 percent of total national production, see Table 12). The same remark can be made regarding the other new and large city, Tenth of Ramadan (northeast, in Greater Cairo) which ranks third, nationally, with a production value of LE874 million (3.46 percent of total national production). In less than ten years, these new sites rank among the first industrial zones and employment sources in Egypt. However, unemployment rages in Shubra al-Khayma. The employment crisis there is in part the result of weak productivity in these enterprises. For example, the textile factory ESCO suffered from cuts in privileged sales to the public sector (large national stores such as Omar Effendi, Sednaoui, and Shamla now being overrun by global and new local competition), which sold mainly clothes fabricated by public-sector enterprises, effectively feeding an entire wing of local industry. The guarantee of these outlets, associated with low competition in a closed market, led to largely mediocre production and to little diversification of final products (in terms of style, patterns, colors, etc.). Since the 1990s, public subsidies have been cut and retail chains have been privatized, ending their market dominance. Moreover, gradual foreign-franchise implantation (Naf-Naf, Benetton, Mexx, etc.), despite the restrained social diffusion of their products, has grown to target Egyptian markets. (See Abaza and Elshestawy in this volume for a discussion of the new organization of retailing in luxury malls and the decline of older national department stores.) Large public enterprises in Shubra al-Khayma must, therefore, consider closing small enterprises, which were benefiting from the same markets thanks to the subcontracting circuit, as they are obliged to adapt their production systems and look for new outlets. Meanwhile, enterprises that engage in investment in Sixth of October are those that on the whole possess a distribution web that functions on the national level. These are, for the most part, enterprises producing strong value-added products (automobiles, for example) or those in large-scale food production for the consumer market (Chipsy, Nestlé, etc.).

Integration in the metropolitan economic sector thus comes from two different logics. From the point of view of Shubra al-Khayma, the presence of the whole production chain organized around strong textile specialization encourages clustering relationships, at the district level, among different production units. The geographic and sectorial concentration of firms with local, external economies (notably supplies of manual labor) is affirmed. This is occurring without the level of interfirm cooperation and common concerted action as the example of the clothing sector shows, in which specialization is not operating in terms of production stages (as in the network system), but more in terms of markets. Large enterprises sell on the Cairene market, whereas small firms sell on the informal and poorer markets. This distinction is important insofar as the first market consumes clothing made with high-quality cotton, while the second uses a poor-quality cotton, which is less expensive on the world market than the one produced in Egypt. Consequently, the obligation to import basic fabrics increases production costs and makes Shubra al-Khayma's industry that much more fragile when it is faced with the competition posed by inexpensive products of reasonable quality coming from foreign countries (principally from China and Pakistan). The enterprises of Sixth of October are positioned for the national, legal/formal market. They are, on the whole, enterprises at the end of the production chain (in the network system) that deliver a finished product, ready for consuming. However, in their production process, they have recourse to subcontracting with small private firms from time to time, such as those in Shubra al-Khayma.

In the end, the enterprises of Shubra al-Khayma lost the protected outlets in the markets of European socialist countries, while, on the international market, as we have seen, they must confront the competition posed by the pricing and quality levels of products coming from ready-to-wear exporting countries like China (see Bulbul and Neguib 2000 for an extensive analysis of Shubra al-Khayma; the following section relies heavily on this report). And so, despite an important increase between 1975 and 1992 (from $14,057,000 in 1975 to $70,539,000 in 1992, according to *Industrial Development Review Series* 1994), exports of ready-to-wear remain rather weak for a textile-producing country. The enterprises of Shubra al-Khayma did not profit from this growth, but the exporting enterprises did with, at times, the participation of subcontracting orders. An international presence (foreign enterprises, manufacturing under franchise or still the diffusion of foreign brands) is weak in Shubra al-Khayma. There are only twenty-six local enterprises diffusing foreign brands, generally "elements entering in the production" of other products, and only two enterprises produce under a license *(Kompass 2000)*. In Sixth of October, this presence is much more accentuated. In 1996, 10 percent of businesses there were deeply engaged with foreign enterprises. The *Kompass 2000* data show that 203 of 722 enterprises counted have some form of linkage to the international level: 168 represent foreign brands, forty-eight are franchises (manufacturing under license), and sixty have some form of foreign participation (ranging from a minority partnership to full ownership); twenty-five of them are branches of foreign companies. We note, however, that the figures do not tally perfectly as the same enterprise may be placed in different categories.

These various observations allow us to describe the relationship that is being put into place, in geographic terms, in the interior of the metropolitan region of Greater Cairo, between the local and the international level. The comparison between the textile industries of Sixth of October and Shubra al-Khayma illustrates quite well the important but often opaque rapport that is developing between the integrated and nonintegrated sectors of the 'new urban economy' issuing from the economic opening of Egypt. The old industrial fabric has become fragile because of public-sector disengagement and due to the competition posed by the new industrial zones, which attract high-return enterprises that are often international, and that have more capital and use new forms of personnel management. This situation could be illustrated in terms of a gap that is in the process of widening among the old industrial factories founded increasingly on a small, often informal private sector that suffers urban impoverishment and increases its susceptibility to poor national economic circumstances, and its dependence on relations with large enterprises. In inverse fashion, the large, privately owned new establishments control new distribution circuits in the national market, positioning themselves in relation to Middle Eastern regional, even international markets. Owing to their increasingly multinational capitalizing, they are increasing their dependence on economic circumstances, this time on a global scale.

Greater Cairo's metropolitan dynamic takes into account the following datum: the urban dynamics of Cairo no longer take place where they used to, notably in Qalyubiya and particularly in Shubra al-Khayma. Spatial increases, which are not linked to population growth, are concentrated to the southwest of Cairo, notably around the impetus given for the development of the new satellite city, Sixth of October. Inversely, one might think that it is the pericentral land value of Shubra al-Khayma that will soon constitute that neighborhood's sole and last trump card that it can play for redevelopment.

Redeployment within the large-scale urban landscape is therefore occurring under the impetus of a partial economic increase that supports and even amplifies the metropolis's control of national activity and wealth. This increase only benefits a part of the city and its inhabitants. In addition, it is giving birth to a paradoxical metropolitan countryside that is polarized and redefined. Deconcentration without decentralization created by the rapid crystallizing of industrial zones in the new cities induces a radical reinvention of intraurban topographies, values, and usages. This resonates with the processes already underway, such as demographic dedensification in the center of Cairo and the transfer of demographic pressure to the quasi-legal shantytown neighborhoods.

Recomposing the Compact City

Contributions to industrial production of many quasi-legal Cairene quarters are intertwined with those of the large industrial cities in the provinces (Table 13). For example, the industrial production of Basatin, a Cairo shantytown, rivals Egypt's second textile center, al-Mahalla al-Kubra. The six thousand microworkshops and sweatshops clustered in this extremely dense popular quarter are organized in highly diversified and flexible networks with a dominant presence of recycling and small-scale metallurgies. They rival the large and often very old establishments, yet the average size of the Basatin enterprise is four people as opposed to twenty-seven for the industrial district of al-Mahalla al-Kubra. In fact, the latter district is structured around the largest Egyptian factory, Misr Spinning and Weaving, an overindebted public establishment employing thirty-three thousand people. Meanwhile, the largest Basatin establishment is a battery-making factory that counts eight hundred employees. Whether the quarters are described as informal, illegal, slum, shantytown, or self-reliant community, they rank at the top of the most productive districts in Egypt; and this should not be surprising. These districts have indeed become at the same time the most densely populated living spaces (six hundred inhabitants per hectare, on average and locally) and the best localities in which specialized networks or 'clusters' form. These clusters very often define themselves as subcontractors for large, established companies in the new cities. These establishments are also active in small-scale metallurgy, woodworking, and ceramics, responding to an important internal demand linked to the intense construction activity that generates the informal buildings of their own neighborhood. They therefore play a double role: on the one hand, they participate in the background of the integrated assembly industry, permitting it to 'externalize' a part of its production. On the other hand, they favor the survival of a vast number of low-cost manual laborers, effectively assuring low salaries. Otherwise stated, the perimetropolitan, quasi-legal quarters are the essential engines for flexibility and are, in this sense, protoliberal. The networks of housing, services, and quasi-legal production have prepared and favored the emergence of the private sector. They have constituted, at the margins, a complement to the state's initiatives which were tied to its legitimacy, such as industrialization, its provision of housing, and other public services. This informal sector houses, at present, more than half of Cairo's residents, has satisfied for the last twenty years 80 percent of the housing needs, and has produced 40 percent of the nonagricultural jobs (Denis and Séjourné 2002).

These quarters represent, then, a fundamental 'externality' at the heart of Greater Cairo's new private-sector economies. Self-employment and self-construction, elliptical terms that would evidently merit much more in-depth analysis and critique, are based on the existence of heavy hierarchies, dominant entrepreneurs, and an exclusive mastery of the circulation of capital. These 'self-employed' are nevertheless as important to the metropolitan concentration of entrepreneurial dynamism as is their geographic proximity to power, administrations, ministries, and banks. Some quarters such as those of Basatin, Imbaba, or Dar al-Salam are, by their population, comparable to the third agglomeration of Egypt, al-Mahalla al-Kubra, and its approximately 530 thousand inhabitants. But these informal neighborhoods are characterized by participation in a much more megapolitan system. They appear very clearly as reserves of flexibility and diversity, which are missing from the provincial cities.

In the absence of innovative capacity, the informal reserve and the vast territory that it forms constitutes an important part of metropolitan wealth. Around it, or thanks to it, new production activities are entering into very competitive markets. Moreover, metropolitan society is positively awash in available domestic services. There exists an obvious synergy that, in contrast, plays out only with difficulty in the specialized and finally narrow milieu of the more provincial cities. Just as economic liberalization creates an ascendant dynamic at the heart of Greater Cairo, informality tends to converge and to be integrated into the metropolitan matrix to such a degree that, at present, its illegality is itself put into question (ECES/ILD 2000, 104). On the other hand, in the provincial cities, the already-stigmatized quasi-legal quarters are the most affected by industrial restructuring, preparing the way for privatization or the failure of networks, such as that of textiles.

For Cairene microactivities also, the logic of redeployment is in full swing. In the historic Old City, demographic decline, the seeds of which were sown some thirty years ago, has for a long time allowed residences to be replaced by a very important microworkshop sector (small-scale metallurgies, leather, wood, glass, etc.). But this sector is now experiencing a phase of decline and of redeployment on the margins of Greater Cairo. As a result of neoliberalization, the products of the small workshops, developed during a period of shortage and behind very strict tariff barriers, are now cruelly challenged by household articles from China, and even directly by new local factories built by the new private sector. Furthermore, these sweatshops are increasingly colliding with a will to reduce the nuisances associated with their establishment in the Old City (pollution, building degradation, and intense automobile traffic) and, therefore, they are also colliding with the revalorization of Islamic heritage sites for tourism. These are factors that weigh heavily on production costs and that are compensated for by lowering employee remuneration, even with that most drastic recourse, the employment of children. Depopulation, followed by the difficulties encountered by the workshops, is creating a void that is extremely favorable to transforming the Old City into a kind of museum while local opposition is henceforth reduced and dispersed. Tourism, that other vector of globalization, is in favor of this spatial redeployment. It serves to revalorize the image of a constructed metropolitan framework of Egyptian 'heritage' that becomes an economic asset participating synergistically in modernizing the apparatus of production. (See Williams, Elsheshtawy, chapter 10, and El Kadi and ElKerdany in this volume for further analysis of constructing 'heritages' in Egypt and the competing interests of local industry and residents.)

From another angle, the fragility of the informal sector appears very clear. The question that is posed asks whether this sector can adapt to the new conditions of economic opening and also whether it is capable of investing and innovating beyond the exploitation of a low-cost, available manual labor supply. If we have underlined elsewhere the positive alliances between the new industries and the quasi-legal ateliers, the model comprises some limitations and many contradictory situations. In the first place, a part of the ateliers and the floating manual labor from the quasi-legal quarters, which constitutes a system when combined with the flourishing import-substitution industry, depends on the viability of that new import-substitution industry as the tariff barriers are gradually lowered. And, notably, it also depends on conformity with the GATT accords as well as on the Association Agreement with the European Community, which is of increasing salience in Egypt. In any case, the 'normalization' of the quasi-legal quarters, their basic legalization and equipment, must be limited to the continued production of a low-cost manual labor supply and to the repressive maintenance of social peace. We must not expect a redistributive growth that would reduce intrametropolitan disparities through percolation.

Conclusion: Metropolitanization, Instability, and New Beginnings?

Neoliberalism, anchored in the notion of structural adjustment, frames a series of profound upheavals that affect metropolitan economies and, in their wake, the national economies of countries in transition which are passing from an economy of national planning, development, and social affirmation to an 'open' economy focusing on global investment, entrepreneurship, wealth concentration, informality, new industrialization, and speculation. When we think of neoliberalism and structural adjustment, we must also register the real, irremediable bifurcations that transform urban space and socioeconomic relations. Indisputably, opening, adjustment, and liberalization were implemented in Cairo with the relaunching of a process described here as "new metropolitanization." This transformation reinitiated a process of urban extension, concentration, and unequal settlement that characterized the previous 'liberal age' (1920–1950) when Egypt was under British colonial rule. There is a clear accumulation of waves of metropolitanization accompanying the modernization of industry and the state's apparatus. These waves limit and fix centralization, etching into the soil the surplus values of exploiting basic agricultural income. Each stage of metropolitanization is marked by an alteration of the urban form, a displacement of centrality, and today, by a reduction of centrality linked to demographic spread and to the devalorization of old polarities.

In this recent stage, forms of concentration have jumped scale again. The success of industrial zones in the new cities invites a brutal extension of the metropolis and the grafting of an open web adapted to the scale of the speeding automobile on the new Ring Road, as well as to a very dense tissue in which the mixed peripheral areas, called "informal," and the older city center and neighborhoods have new roles and values thrust upon them. The future will condition the form of Greater Cairo, with its inherited centralities and emerging secondary centers, with its pluri-centrality extending into New Cairo and Madinat Masr. The basic quasi-unlimited availability of space on the desert edges urges exurbanization, leaving few means for reinvesting in the old quarters and populations, or in the fallow pericentral areas. There are not any government measures or global forces encouraging one to do so. The risk of degradation by disqualification can, in these conditions, still continue, insofar as a large part of the framework is frozen by ministries and public enterprises, which reduces the potential for private reappropriation. Therefore, the present tendency is inclined toward the pursuit of redeployment and weak reappropriation of old centers, while functional centers are grouped into satellites. At this stage, the question is how Cairo's urban forms will be produced, acquired, and maintained in a context of increasing instability and insecurity of revenues, without the possibility of relying on a stable middle class that is able to acquire goods on credit. There is no doubt that the popular channels for illegal construction will continue to be the solution for the greatest number. The macroform will again depend on the capacity to invest in the fallow, pericentral areas and to create offices that are sorely missing, so that the development of a service and business sector, in Central Cairo, may be finally accomplished. Presently, 70 percent of office activity occurs in apartments (CAPMAS 1996a). Once again, the desert becomes the default answer—high-tech office complexes are already being established on the edge of the desert, alongside the great freeway axes. (See Elsheshtawy in this volume for a discussion of some new high-tech office complexes, modelled upon, and financed by, Dubai initiatives.)

The Coalescence of the Metropolitan and the National

Many have predicted the end of territory, made irrelevant at the intersections of metropolitanization and globalization. Many have identified processes of deregulation that reduce the state's power in favor of transnational networks. However, given the data on Egypt, we are instead invited to think that the state manages, exploits, and promotes metropolitanization in association with businesspeople who are the real, and only beneficiaries of the effective opening of these last ten years. Nevertheless, political power dominates and controls the margins of freedom in the business world (Kienle 2001). The alliance leads or obliges businesspeople to subscribe to a logic of 'corporate governance,' in order to assume direction of influential institutions in the new cities, even to engage in social-development projects in the quarters. Following the elections of November 2000, 9 percent of Egypt's national deputies are businesspeople. They are promoted as representing 'civil society.' In return for this submission to state power and to the ruse of national representation, the state confers privileges on these businesspeople. Meanwhile, representation, collective organization, and consultation of employees, workers, communities and citizens in general are even suppressed, as is the associative sector and the press. The Cairo metropolis is directly managed by services of the state: it has neither autonomy nor democratic representation (Denis 2000). It is in the service of a national project that acts as an interface between the exploitation of Egypt and access to world resources—to abilities, technologies, aid, markets, capital, and investments. The new kind of national, global, and regional primacy of Cairo is reinforced here by exclusive control over national construction and land allocation, dressed up in an exacerbated nationalism that seems to conjure the reality of Egyptian territory and nation from the empty desert, authorizing a strict command over the population in the name of the national interest, threatened by specters: exterior specters of the Israeli threat, and interior specters of Islamist radicalism.

Metropolitan Integration, Participation, and Liberty

Egypt, or rather, Cairo in association with Egypt, a country of weak or modest technological capacities, of course owes its integration into the archipelago of great metropolises to its abundant and cheap manual labor. Metropolitan accumulation is possible because it has learned how to make a majority of its population, living at its center, subsist at a very low cost. What is more, it is doing so while instituting illegality, notably in construction, which assures a return to dependence on the good will of the state's services and establishes the foundation for cronyism. All of the economy, from industry to households, from service sector to industry, functions on the basis of minimal salaries for work, and maximum subsidies for elite speculation. Not only is a middle class hindered from emerging, but also the exacerbation of inequality under economic neoliberalization requires the maintenance, even reinforcement of police control of public space, and repression of the population. Thus, economic liberalization without political liberalization is established, a system in which a nonrepresentative power, having a monopoly on violence, also conserves its mastery of the urban soil and its control of public space. Cairo cosmopolitan, the globalizing metropolis, will not make us free.

Works Cited

Abdel-Malek, Gamal. 2000. "Domestic Public Debt in Egypt: Structure and Consequences." *Cairo Papers in Social Science* 23: 7–62.
Abu-Lughod, Janet. 1990. "Le Caire et New York vus de la rue." *Revue internationale des sciences sociales* 42: 345–38.
Aéroports Magazine. 1999. Hors série, April.

Alleaume, Ghislaine, and Eric Denis. 1998. "Villes et campagnes d'Égypte à l'aube du XXe siècle: les temporalités divergentes des pays, des bourgs et des cités." In *Mélanges offerts à B. Lepetit*, coordinated by J. Dakhlia (EHESS), 225–56. Paris: Sindbad/Actes Sud.

Bayat, Assef, and Eric Denis. 2000. "Who is Afraid of Ashwaiyat? Urban Change and Politics in Egypt." *Environment & Urbanization* 12 (2): 185–99.

Brown, David L., and John M. Wardwell, eds. 1980. *New Directions in Urban–Rural Migration: the Population Turnaround in Rural America*. New York: Academic Press.

Bulbul, Lamia, and Sameh Neguib. 2000. "The Case of Urbanization and Industrialization in Shubra el-Khema, Egypt." Urban Partnership, Background Series 9. Washington, D.C.: World Bank.

Castells, Manuel. 1989. *The Informational City: Information Technology, Economic Restructuring, and the Urban-Regional Process*. Oxford: Blackwell.

Cairo Stock Exchange, <*http://www.egyptse.com*> (15 November 2000).

CAPMAS. 1995. "Industrial Census." Cairo.

———. 1996–1997. "Annual Industrial Survey 1996/97." Cairo.

———. 1996a. "Census of Places of Activity." Cairo.

———. 1996b. "General Census of the Population 1996." Cairo.

Christaller, Walter. 1933. *Die zentralen Orte in Süddeutschland*. Jena: Gustav Fischer.

Central Bank of Egypt. 1999–2000. "Annual Report." Cairo.

Denis, Eric. 2000. "Le Caire, quand la ville déborde son enceinte." *Villes en parallèle* 30–31: 89–116.

Denis, Eric, and Marian Séjourné. 2002. ISIS: Information System for Informal Settlement. Report. Participatory Urban Management Programme (Ministry of Planning & German Technical Co-operation) & Observatoire urbain du Caire contemporain (OUCC)—CEDEJ, Cairo.

Dalil madinat sitta Uktubar 1998–1999/Directory of Sixth-of-October City 1998–1999. 1999. Sixth-of-October Investors Association.

Egyptian Center for Economic Studies/Institute for Liberty and Democracy (ECES/ILD). 2000. *Formalization of Egypt's Urban Informal Real Estate Sector*. Cairo.

EFG-Hermes, <*http://www.efg-hermes.com*> (15 November 2000).

Findlay Allan. 1993. "Arab Cities, Arab Banking and Patterns of Global Influence." Recherches urbaines dans le monde arabo-musulman. Approches comparées des géographes allemands, britanniques et français, Fascicule de Recherches n°24, Tours, URBAMA, pp. 123–36.

"Follow-up." 1998. *Business Monthly: American Chamber of Commerce in Cairo* 15: 9.

Geographic Information System Egypt (GIS). CEDEJ-CAPMAS, Cairo, Egypt.

Gertel, Jörg. 1998. "La mondialisation du pain au Caire: profits des multinationales et insécurité locale." *Revue géographique de Lyon* 73: 219–26.

al-Ghitani, Gamal. 2001. "Interview." In *Le Caire, vu par les écrivains*. Cairo: French Cultural Centre in Cairo, 5.

Giraud, François, and Martin Vanier. 2000, "Plaidoyer pour la complexité territoriale." In *Utopie pour le territoire*, 143–72. La Tour d'Aigues: Editions de L'Aube.

Haeringer, Philippe. 1999. *L'économie invertie, mégapolisation, pauvreté majoritaire et nouvelle économie urbaine (2001 plus, Synthèses et recherches)*. Paris: Ministère de l'équipement, du transport et du logement, Centre de prospective et de veille scientifique.

Harris, Nigel. 1995. "Bombay in the Global Economy." In *Bombay: Metaphor for Modern India*, eds. Alice Thorner and Sujata Patel, 47–63. New Delhi: Oxford India Paperbacks.

International Finance Corporation (IFC). *Emerging Market Database*, <http://www.ifc.org/> (30 November 2000).

Kienle, Eberhard. 2001. *The Grand Delusion: Democracy and Economic Reform in Egypt*. London: I.B. Tauris.

Kompass 2000 Egypt. Cairo: Fiani & Partners.

Ministry of Economy and Foreign Trade. 2000. "Investing in Egypt." *Database of Egyptian Foreign Trade, 1990–1999*. Cairo: Ministry of Economy and Foreign Trade.

Moriconi-Ebrard, Francois. 2000. *De Babylone à Tokyo: les grandes agglomérations du monde*. Gap, France: Ophyris.

Moriconi-Ebrard, Francois, and Maher Rateb. 1996. "Le Caire métropole du monde arabe? Éléments de réflexion." *Lettre d'information de l'Observatoire urbain du Caire contemporain* 45: 35–45.

Pagès, Delphine, and Leïla Vignal. 1998. "Formes et espaces de la mondialisation en Égypte: une lecture spatiale des changements récents." *Géographies sociales de l'Égypte, ouverture et cloisonnements* 73: 247–58.

Posusney, Marsha Pripstein. 1997. *Labor and the State in Egypt: Workers, Unions, and Economic Restructuring*. New York: Columbia University Press.

_____. 2002. "Egyptian Labor Struggles in the Era of Privatization: the Moral Economy Thesis Revisited." In *Privatization and Labor: Responses and Consequences in Global Perspective*, eds. Linda J. Cook and Marsha Pripstein Posusney. Gloucestershire, England: Edward Elgar Publishing.

"Round Up." 1997. *Business Monthly: American Chamber of Commerce in Cairo* 11: 2.

Sassen, Saskia. 1996. *La ville globale, New-York, Londres, Tokyo.* Paris: Descartes & Cie.

Soliman, Samer. 1998. "State and Industrial Capitalism in Egypt." *Cairo Papers in Social Science* 21: 104.

Textile Holding Company. 2000. "Annual Report 2000." Egypt.

UNCTAD. 2000. *World Investment Report 2000: FDI and the Challenge of Development.* Geneva: UNCTAD.

Veltz, Pierre. 1996. *Mondialisation, villes et territoires, l'économie d'archipel.* Paris: Les presses universitaires de France.

Notes

1   The countryside is also being transformed because the quality requirements of the modernized food-produce channels create new jobs and modify the rapport between farmers and agricultural workers in production. The forms of contractualization and purchasing are also changing. The countryside, in this sense, is also coming closer to the city.

2   Besides the cost of labor, which remains very low, this authorizes the maintenance of an abundant domestic service and numerous related services.

3   During the same period, Egyptian imports from Arab countries went from 3.13 percent to 6.26 percent of the total value of imports, an increase that is linked principally to importing petroleum products from Saudi Arabia, while the total worth of imports from Arab countries doubled (to more than $16 billion) (Ministry of Economy and Foreign Trade 2000).

4   This is very clearly the case for the megasites for agricultural improvement—notably, for the Canal al-Salam in north Sinai, for which Sheikh Zayid of Abu Dhabi was the principal sponsor after Egypt's engagement in the Gulf War. In exchange, the entrepreneurs of the oil monarchies were able to acquire vast irrigated zones in these new projects. Again, we find the same faces in the management of the Toshka megaproject with its heavy ecological implications, since the princely companies are authorized unlimited extraction from the fossil layer. Opposition to this Arab appropriation of Egyptian soil begins to express itself in colonial terms and tends, perceptibly, to inhibit the debate on globalization and regional integration.

5   In 1997, public debt represented 78.2 percent of GDP or LE2,822 per inhabitant. That same year, the state's creditors were involved in 48.4 percent of the public banks and 31 percent of the joint ventures and private banks, most of them strongly participating in the public sector; in addition, they were involved in insurance and retirements funds at the level of 3.1 percent (Abdel-Malek 2000).

6   Inversion is founded on a reification of the notion of informality (Haeringer 1999). This is a refusal to consider, by classifiying formalism, the organic articulation between the expansion of legal productive activity and quasi-legal

networks that guarantee the low cost of manual labor. Additionally, periods of strong demographic growth, of metropolitanization of this demographic increase, most often occur during periods of shortage and state-run control— that is to say, during phases of nationalist affirmation in which all resources are more than ever concentrated in the capitals. Moreover, agricultural reforms accelerate productive stimulation in agriculture. This has certainly produced a surplus of manual labor, but at the same time, a greater agricultural value added that is immediately captured by metropolitan industrialization and the national administration that is being put in place. Megametropolitan activity is enriched and learns to exploit a subproletariat that is more and more numerous. This group plays the surplus role for classic manual labor, which was already present in the English industrial revolution.

4 Cairo as Global/Regional Cultural Capital?

Said Sadek

"Cairo writes, Beirut prints, Baghdad reads." Is this old saying about the cultural division of labor among the regional capitals of the Arab Middle East still true today? Cairo during the 1950s, 1960s, and 1970s was the undisputed cultural—and political, social, and religious—capital of the Arab Middle East. As the hub of President Gamal 'Abd al-Nasser's revolutionary anticolonial Arab nationalist government, and core of an industrializing outward-looking progressive metropolis, Cairo during that era produced glorious films that stirred the hearts and remade the identities of the whole Arab world, penned the novels and essays of the Arab literary renaissance, produced theatrical and singing talent that drew fanatic spectators from around the world, and cultivated the best universities and academies in the Middle East.

Today, twenty-first-century Cairo's role as undisputed cultural capital of the Arab Middle East is threatened. Beirut has emerged from times of war to rediscover its talent for writing, singing, producing, and directing. Petroleum-enriched Persian Gulf cities—Dubai, Jeddah, Doha, Kuwait—have become increasingly significant investors in culture, articulating their own creative and political visions through satellite television, journalism, film, and fashion.

And European Arab populations in Paris, London, and Amsterdam run some of the region's boldest newspapers and publishing houses, and set regional trends in music, politics, and film.

Cairo's period of overwhelming, uncontested cultural dominance is over. But this city of more than fifteen million souls remains the largest producer of film, TV shows, and the now highly popular and controversial cultural genre of the music video, or 'clip' as it is called in Europe and the Middle East.

Why, despite Cairo's high level of cultural productivity, have consumers in the Arab world come to perceive that the capital of Egypt is in sharp decline as a global/regional cultural capital? There are probably two main reasons: (1) Egypt no longer offers visionary leadership of the pan-Arab nation, neither politically, diplomatically or militarily, nor in the spheres of symbols and dreams; and (2) Egypt's cultural offerings have been swamped by edgier, less-censored, more innovative Arab cultural products that have recently become available by satellite to the whole Middle East and to the Arab diaspora worldwide. Nevertheless, when rich oil princes want to invest in culture, they still come to Cairo; when theater fans from across the Middle East want improvization and fantastic comedies on stage, they come to Cairo; when a Moroccan or Yemeni singer wants to reach a worldwide audience, s/he will come to Cairo; when investors want to open a cable station they will hire experts from Cairo. But even given these positive trends, there is no denying that Cairo's cultural capital is depleted.

One of the main reasons for this perceived decline is the absence of a charismatic political figure in Egypt who could inspire the Arab masses as did President Gamal 'Abd al-Nasser (who led the country from 1954–70). Ever since Nasser's death, Egypt's leaders have been less popular and charismatic. Whereas President Anwar Sadat (1970–81) enjoyed popularity in the West, he was ostracized in the Arab world for his peace overtures toward Israel. And Hosni Mubarak (who has been in power since 1981) seems uninspiring both at home and abroad. Demonstrators in Arab streets from Morocco to Baghdad still carry posters of Nasser to symbolize independence and challenge imperialism and never willingly carry the photos of other Egyptian leaders, except during state visits.

Cairo's perceived cultural decline is also tied to the emergence of satellite television channels in other Arab countries since the 1990s. Now able to select among the channels of all the Arab countries and a variety of international services, audiences and critics alike increasingly bemoan Egypt's supposed cultural degradation. They look back nostalgically to the earlier golden age represented by Cairo's films and music of the 1940s to 1960s. Egypt of the

1990s with its poverty, urban decline, and squatter settlements, and with its repressive, disintegrating, dependant, and hypocritical political life, bears little resemblance to the image promoted then or now by Egyptian soap operas, films, or video clips.

Satellite television news broadcasts from Arab countries in the Persian Gulf and Levant freely discuss the stagnation that characterizes Egyptian politics and the tyranny of national and international forces in the country; while the highly censored Egyptian TV channels avoid critical issues, or obsess over scapegoats and sex scandals as substitutes for genuine, more constructive forms of critique and patriotism. In Egypt, rather than back political reform and independent creativity, critics have produced conspiracy theories and paranoid visions to explain Cairo's fall from cultural hegemony. For example, in his article "The Conspiracy to Dwarf Egypt," Egyptian critic Said Al Lawindi says:

I do not deny that there is a conspiracy to dwarf Egypt's role in both the region and the whole world. Its threads have been woven since some time ago. The bloodsucking bats of darkness (from inside and outside) are also accomplices. There is talk about Arab culture seeping through the hands of Egypt like water. This follows the decline in the number of Arab students who used to come to study in its universities. They went instead to Europe and the United States. . . . The light of al-Azhar [the world center of Sunni Islamic scholarship] has also faded away. To speak of Mohammed 'Abduh, Taha Husayn, and Mohammed Hussein Heikal [leading twentieth-century critical intellectuals] is like speaking about ancient artifacts. Some even speak about the end of the Egyptian cultural era in the Arab world. Moreover, behind the wings, there are attempts to snatch the post of the secretary-general of the Arab League, thus ending Egyptian monopoly of that position. Some even claim that Egypt was not the one who had sponsored pan-Arabism but it was the Levant, with Sati' al-Husri's writings providing the clearest evidence. Even the Africans are calling for redistribution of the Nile's water. Al Lawindi 2005, 13.

It is the objective of this paper to illustrate that some aspects of Cairo's traditional cultural prominence in the Arab world have been transformed in the context of technological innovation, pan-regional diversification, and the proliferation of new forms of consumerism. This paper will also assert that Cairo's rich cultural traditions, which once dominated the Arab world, remain strong though now drained by political, social, and economic constraints at home, and by competition from emerging Arab cultural capitals. We are in the midst of a Middle-East regional redivision of cultural labor, quantitatively and qualitatively. This needs to be interpreted in Egypt not as unhealthy competition but as a source for enriching and democratizing Cairo's culture and Arab culture in general.

The transformation can be traced back to the 1967 defeat of Arab military forces by Israel. As a result of the defeat, Egypt began to preoccupy itself with internal struggles and contradictory international commitments and dependencies, losing its inspiring pan-Arab leadership role. At the same time other Arab centers of power began to grow wealthy and assertive thanks to the oil boom. What we see today is a redivision of cultural labor in the Arab world in which Egypt is the main supplier of manpower and software, while the rich Gulf states provide the finances and Beirut supplies the 'flair.' For example, many Arab satellite networks are financed by the Saudis, like the religious channel Iqra', or the ART group of stations that depend on Egyptian cultural production and professional personnel (such as Hala Sarhan, an Oprah Winfrey-style host, and 'Imad al-Din Adib, a prominent political talk-show host). Even the bold Qatari channel Al Jazeera, which dominates the news industry and is considered the number-one news channel in the Arab world, has many well-known Egyptians working for it. One of the most popular young religious preachers in the Arab world, 'Amr Khaled, is an Egyptian, whose programs are syndicated over several Arab satellite TV channels (Khaled 2005). Moreover, Egyptian shaykhs are the most popular Qur'an reciters in the Arab world. Egyptian news dominates Arab news bulletins and programming due to its regional role in politics and culture throughout the Middle East. As an Egyptian freelance writer and media consultant for several decades I have observed all the debates about the supposed cultural decline of Egypt. Using interviews and statistics, I will show, empirically, that the presumed decline of Cairo as a global/regional cultural capital is debatable.

Cairo and the Middle East

Arab culture is composed of the diverse regional cultures of twenty-two Arab countries, plus the input of significant Arabic-speaking and culture-producing populations abroad (in Paris, London, Amsterdam, Madrid, the United States, and Latin America), as well as that of several subcultures within individual Arab countries (Mediterranean, African, Upper Egyptian, Nubian, Armenian, South Asian, Berber, Bedouin, etc.). Despite the existence of political borders and dialect variation among Arab states, there appear to be no formidable cultural obstacles to the flow of electronic media and culture among the peoples of the greater pan-Arab nation. Historically speaking, the Middle East has been an arena for rival centers competing for regional hegemony like Egypt, Syria, Iraq, Turkey, and Persia/Iran. New rivals like Saudi Arabia and Israel entered the scene in the twentieth century. If we exclude the non-Arabic-speaking rivals (Israel, Iran, and Turkey) we see that the Arab cultural arena has been dominated for a large part of the twentieth century by one player: Egypt. With the oil boom in the 1970s, other Arab states began to impact the Arab media scene, particularly Saudi Arabia, Iraq, the United Arab Emirates, and Kuwait.

Culture can be seen as a kind of soft power spreading the image and influence of the state beyond its borders among the peoples of other nations. Media products, educational infrastructure, and models of economic development and modernization can be among the most important tools for spreading a country's culture. Egypt's prominent cultural influence is not a new phenomenon; as the largest and most populous Arab state with a rich political and sociocultural public life that persisted even under colonialism, Egypt had an edge over the others. The relatively tolerant atmosphere in Egypt in the late nineteenth and early twentieth centuries drew many Arab talents from more violent or repressive areas of the colonized Middle East, and made Cairo the melting pot for Arab culture.[1]

In the realm of political and sociocultural ideas, Cairo has, until recently, been Arab culture's main forum for debate and controversy. Feminism, liberalism, democracy, religious enlightenment, anti-imperialism, Arab nationalism, and curbing tyranny have been debated in Egypt, where national and Arab intellectuals like Qasim Amin, Rifa'a al-Tahtawi, Muhammad 'Abduh, and Gamal al-Din al-Afghani promoted pan-Arab culture, set its general agenda, and disseminated it through Egypt's global cultural-industrial infrastructure. Taha Husayn (1889–1973), who became the doyen of Arabic literature, preached modernization through adopting secular ways and argued in his book *The Future of Culture in Egypt* (1938) that pan-Arab identity in Egypt should reference the country's classical heritage as a Mediterranean state and culture.

Egypt had the first state-run radio service in the Middle East in 1934 (Shaheen 2002). Boasting the largest and most educated middle class in the Arab world, Egyptian centers of learning have traditionally attracted students from all over the region who later became leading politicians (e.g., the late King Husayn of Jordan graduated from Victoria College in Alexandria, and the late Palestinian leader Yasser Arafat graduated from the Faculty of Engineering at Cairo University). Moreover, Egyptian teachers, lawyers, doctors, and engineers migrated to many Arab countries and influenced their local culture, complementing the work done by Egyptian films to popularize the Egyptian dialect of the Arabic language all over the Arab and Muslim world.

Despite strong currents of Mediterranean, cosmopolitan, and Europe-inclined thinking in Egypt, the establishment of the Arab League in Cairo in

1945 meant that Egypt would identify itself as the heart of the Arab world, and relegate to second place its identity as a Mediterranean partner or rival to Rome and Athens. The Arab League headquarters, situated in central Cairo in Tahrir Square, remind the average Egyptian passer-by of the bond between Egypt and the Arab world, and assures him or her that pan-Arab issues dominate the Egyptian media. Pan-Arabism, the Arab League, Arab socialism, one-party political systems, and Islamic fundamentalism spread throughout the region from Egyptian roots. Revolutionary leader Gamal 'Abd al-Nasser was the first Arab head of state to attempt to turn Arab nationalism, postcolonial socialism, and regional unity into a political reality with the 1958–61 merger with Syria. And Anwar Sadat was one of the first postcolonial Arab leaders to ally with and promote Islamic fundamentalism as a counterweight to socialist, Third-Worldist, liberal-nationalist, and other popular Arab political trends at the time.

Culture and Political Leadership

Cairo's culture industry remains a political tool for the state and nation of Egypt, in the struggle for Middle-East regional hegemony. In fact several studies have documented and emphasized how Egypt's cultural role in the Arab world has been tied to the government's promotion of its political objectives in the region (Dawisha 1976, 173–75). During the Egyptian revolution, its leaders, the Free Officers, threw out the British colonialists in July 1952 and established the Ministry of Culture and National Guidance on 10 November of the same year. Egypt's revolutionary rulers realized that to protect Egypt from neocolonial and external ambitions, Egypt and the whole greater Arab nation needed to strengthen and unify its regional solidarity and cultural consciousness. Pan-Arabist ideas were already popular in the Levant, which had suffered division by French and British colonialists into separate states (Jordan, Lebanon, Palestine, and Syria). There was hunger in the Arab world for a strong unified Arab culture. And Egypt with its creative, educated middle classes, its well-organized and mobilized workers, cultural talent and activist farmers, provided the Arabs the new consciousness and models they needed.

Revolutionary Egypt: 1952–70

The Free Officers did not invent Arab nationalism; however they seized on the idea to promote Egyptian policies in the Arab world via culture. Egypt, with its poor natural resources and growing population, realized that good relations with its Arab neighbors were vital. Egyptian industry and the tourism sector were growing and needed a market. Promoting familiarity with Egyptian culture was an important part of promoting the broader spectrum of the country's tourism, industrial, and agricultural sectors in competition with other international and regional rivals. Egyptian cultural icons such as Umm Kulthum, 'Abd al-Halim Hafiz, and Muhammad 'Abd al-Wahab became household names in many Arab countries. Successful non-Egyptian Arab singers settled in Egypt—like Farid al-Atrash and Sabah, both from Lebanon, who came to sing in the Egyptian dialect. Ideological production flourished in Egypt and the Voice of the Arabs radio station, established in July 1953, became just as influential in its time as Qatar's Al Jazeera satellite channel is today.

To further boost the cinema industry, in 1959 the Ministry of National Guidance established the Higher Film Institute to cover all aspects of movie making. The Egyptian government also entered the field of cinema production, nationalizing the movie industry along with many other industries in the early 1960s. The state became a major producer of films although it did not ban private entrepreneurs from producing their own. Quality during this era of public ownership was high, due to revolutionary guidance, state subsidies, and the support of great Arab novelists. As stated by veteran Egyptian actor 'Izzat al-'Alayli, "In the 1960s, many classic films were produced, adapting high-quality Egyptian novels. For example, the famous trilogy of Nobel prize-winner Naguib Mahfouz, and the works of Fathi Ghanim and Tawfiq al-Hakim, among other giants of Egyptian literature, were shot on film. But once all the stock of good Egyptian novels had been exhausted, a decline in the quality of Egyptian films ensued that continues until today."[2]

Cairo's Culture Industry Under President Sadat, 1970–81

Nasser's administration made pan-Arab unity a priority in its regional policy. There were several attempts to unite with some Arab countries (e.g., the Egyptian–Syrian merger of 1958–61) and attempted mergers with Yemen and other countries. As a result Egyptian cultural production (movies, novels, media, songs, theater, and painting) experienced a boom in the Arab world. But Egypt under Sadat's administration shifted its interests radically. The experiment with a state-nourished public-sector film industry was abandoned in the early 1970s as Sadat moved toward privatization with his Open Door (Infitah) policy in 1974, defunding industries and moving to sell them to Western and Arab speculators. Under Sadat, political priorities shifted toward relations with the West, downplaying pan-Arabism. To make matters worse, many of the cultural icons of Egypt's revolutionary golden age vanished at the same time. The historic Cairo Opera House building, one of the oldest opera buildings in the world, burned to the ground during a 1972 fire. Umm Kulthum (born 1904), the diva of Arab song, died in 1975. Symbolizing the end of an era of progress and dreams, and the birth of an era of national nostalgia and dissatisfaction, Umm Kulthum's funeral was attended by more people than those who had attended Gamal 'Abd al-Nasser's funeral in 1970. And finally, 'Abd al-Halim Hafiz (born 1929), the legendary king of romantic songs and musical cinema, died in 1977.

After Sadat's Open Door policy denationalized the cinema and entertainment industry, the private sector did not fill the void. The priorities of the private sector were different from those of the public sector of Nasser's era. The public-sector movie industry had aimed at reaching political objectives, promoting social change, and spreading consciousness and ideology. In contrast the private sector's priority was short-term profit milked from commercial melodramas. Production of films in Egypt according to this new market logic, certainly did continue and was cheapened and temporarily accelerated by the introduction of video systems in the late 1980s and early 1990s (see Table 1). Maintaining its stock of seasoned directors, Egypt continued to be able to train young directors like no other Arab country, under the tutelage of, for example, the social realist Salah Abu Seif, the avant-garde Youssef Chahine, or the taboo-breaker Inas al-Daghaydi. Egyptian cinema remained the only Egyptian industry that exported 100 percent of its production. And they were also consumed locally by adoring fans.

Table 1. Egyptian film production in selected years

Year	Number of films produced	Year	Number of films produced
1945	42	1973	43
1948	49	1977	51
1950	57	1979	38
1952	59	1981	44
1955	52	1983	47
1958	58	1985	78
1961	52	1989	45
1964	44	1992	70
1966	38	1993	51
1967	34	1996	24
1970	47	2004	24

Source: al-Bindari, Qasim, and Wahbi 1994; UNESCO 2004; Nagih 2004a.

Cairo Television

Egyptian TV programs have long been popular commodities in the Arab world. When the 1979 Egyptian–Israeli Peace Treaty led to many Arab countries boycotting Egypt and its cultural production, Arab markets tried to substitute Asian products (e.g., Indian and Filipino films and music) for Egypt's TV melodramas. These appealed largely only to Asian expatriates in the Gulf and not to the average Arab who seemed addicted to Egyptian drama and films in the popular, and easily understandable, colloquial Egyptian Arabic. Other Arab cinema, such as Tunisia's, uses dialects that are not as familiar in the Arab world as the long-established Egyptian colloquial language. The cultural boycott failed quickly, however, and Egyptian culture was once again at the center of Arab culture. The social problems portrayed by Egyptian cinema were similar to those faced by other Arab nations and not explored in Asian films, and demand for Egyptian entertainment did not wane but increased with time. To protect their economic interests within the Arab market from another phase of the Arab boycott, Egyptian actors and artists have refrained from normalizing relations with Israel. Their syndicates have imposed strict sanctions against violators. Egyptian opposition media have published blacklists of those 'sinners' who collaborate with Israel, to shame them and tarnish their image. These tactics help minimalize cultural relations between Egypt and Israel. Moreover the continued Israeli military occupation of Palestinian territories has done much to maintain the negative image of Israel in the minds of average Egyptians.

Egyptian Culture under Mubarak 1981–2005

After Hosni Mubarak came to power following Anwar Sadat's assassination in 1981, the Arab world and Egypt gradually reached a rapprochement. By 1990 the Arab League headquarters, which had been moved to Tunisia in 1978 when Egyptian membership was suspended after the signing of the Camp David accords, returned to Cairo. Egypt was welcomed back, however, to a different Arab world.

The once marginal countries of the Arabian Peninsula had, thanks to the oil boom of the 1970s, begun generating a new Arab cultural scene. They had the capital to promote their own products to compete with those of the 'center' of Arab culture in Cairo. Pan-Arabist journals flourished in many areas outside of Egypt. The Kuwaiti Information Ministry, for example, had since 1959 published a strong pan-Arab cultural monthly, al-'Arabi, edited by many Arab intellectuals; and in fact, its first editors-in-chief were Egyptians such as Ahmad Zaki (1958–75) and Ahmad Baha' al-Din (1976–82). Egypt had no intellectual equivalent to this journal, or to the *Lebanese Arab Future Monthly* (1978), at the time. Strong academic and cultural journals whose main contributors were not limited to Egyptians arose in the Gulf—for example, *Dubayy al-thaqafiya* monthly, a popular cultural-literary journal that sold for only LE7, due to generous government subsidies.

In the 1980s, Egyptian universities began to face competition from other Arab universities, which were teaching their classes in foreign-language curricula to compete in the increasingly globalized economy. By contrast, Egypt's proud insistence on teaching in Arabic led to a neglect of foreign languages in the 1960s and 1970s, and many Egyptian intellectuals, editors of Egyptian newspapers and periodicals, as well as university deans, were not well versed in foreign languages.

Since the end of the last war with Israel in 1973, the subsequent Egyptian–Israeli peace treaty in 1979, combined with an avalanche of foreign aid that surpassed the Marshall Plan for reconstructing Europe after World War II, Egypt was predicted to become the economic tiger of the Middle East. However, the lack of vision on the part of the ruling elite and internal institutionalized corruption produced a lost Asian mouse, not a tiger. The Egyptian cultural elite was divided over the future course of the country with isolationists becoming stronger and more influential, especially after Egyptian–Arab diplomatic relations were cut in 1979.

Nevertheless, despite these shifts Egypt's entertainment industry (TV, cinema, video clips, and theater) remains more open to Western entertainment influences than productions coming from Persian Gulf states. With a new educated generation and the heavy presence of foreigners especially in the Persian Gulf (e.g., almost 80 per cent of the total population in some Arabian Peninsula states are foreigners) there is more demand now for diverse entertainment. Today almost 80 percent of programming on some TV channels in the Arab world, particularly specialized movie and drama channels like the Movie Channel and Showtime Network, depends on imported Western materials while only 20 percent is locally produced, usually taking the form of news programs, talk shows, soap operas, video clips, drama, and cinema (Tughan 2005). The degree of dependency differs from one channel to the next. Some specialized Arab movie, drama, and music channels depend almost totally on Egyptian production, e.g., the ART Movie Channel, ART Hekayat, or ART Variety, three different channels in the bouquet of ART. We will examine this aspect of satellite TV in greater detail in the next section.

TV and Radio News

This is the golden age of satellite TV, not radio. The days of the insurrectionary Voice of the Arabs broadcast from revolutionary Cairo are gone. In the Arab world today, where nearly seventy million out of three hundred million are illiterate, TV is indispensable. It is the primary means of entertainment and news for the average Arab citizen. The Arab consumer can chose from more than 140 channels, of which Egypt produces more than twenty-seven. Most satellite channels are available for free, some are scrambled, and some are locally transmitted on national broadcast channels. Egypt was the first Arab country to launch a satellite TV channel, the Egyptian Space Channel (ESC), on Arabsat in 1990. Eight years later, Egypt asserted its regional media hegemony by launching its own satellite, Nilesat, to support its national channels, along with regional and international channels. Unfortunately, the Egyptian government has continued to produce high-quantity, highly censored programs rather than quality, freely produced programs at a time when the consumer can flip from one foreign TV channel to the next in search of better programming, and to avoid government propaganda. Many of the soap operas are considered by viewers to be too long and in need of editing, but producers make more money when their series are long. The director of the Egyptian Radio and TV Union, Hassan Hamed, revealed that daily spending on all Egyptian channels amounts to LE3.28 million, amounting to almost LE1.197 billion a year. Meanwhile, the budget of the Nile News channel, which is supposed to compete with the Qatari Al Jazeera, is only one-tenth that of any similar specialized channel in the Arab world, and some Arab channels have an annual budget exceeding $50 million. Moreover, the twenty-seven Egyptian TV channels employ more than twenty-eight thousand employees (including clerks, managers, correspondents, etc.) compared to only eighty persons employed by the popular Lebanese channel LBC, and approximately seventy correspondents employed by the much more revolutionary, critical, and trusted Al Jazeera channel (al-Din 2004).

Al Jazeera and Abu Dhabi channels were launched in 1997. When President Mubarak visited Qatar, the base of Al Jazeera, in 2000, and peeked into one of its newsrooms, he commented, "All this noise comes from this matchbox?" (Zednick 2002). Needless to say even Egyptians began to turn away from their own news channels toward Al Jazeera and other regional channels to learn about events in their own country. The communication system in any country is dependent on the political system. Since the authoritarian Egyptian political system has refrained from developing itself and has remained slow to respond to or comprehend change, the communication system has followed suit and has remained extremely bureaucratic, heavily censored, over-cautious, and slow in covering emergencies while it awaits a 'green light' from above. This has resulted in the loss not only of Egypt's local and regional audience, but of its journalistic credibility as well. Breaking events and emergencies are covered by other Arab news channels faster than the Egyptian news channel. Competitors include the privately owned, Dubai-based Al Arabiya channel, Saudi MBC (Middle-East Broadcasting Corporation), and the Qatari Al Jazeera. Freedom is what is lacking in Egyptian channels, which, like the old Soviet channels, are silent about developments at home and simply parrot official propaganda.

According to my survey of a sample of Egyptian Internet surfers, the Lebanese currently dominate Internet news sites, with Gulf financing in news sites like Elaph.com and Metransparent.com. In radio, the Egyptian government still dominates in quantity with over fourteen radio stations. There are two private commercial FM music channels covering the Greater Cairo area so far: Nile FM for Western music, and Nugum FM for pop Arab music, both owned by the Nile Production Company of Egyptian media tycoon 'Imad al-Din Adib (Ebrahim 2004). Nugum FM earned more than LE40 million for the year 2004 compared to only LE500,000 earned by the fourteen government radio stations combined (Shuman 2005, 14). But when it comes to reliable news, the whole Arab world still turns to the round-the-clock Arabic service of the British Broadcasting Corporation (BBC).

Who Owns Arab Satellite Channels?

Arab satellite channels are owned both by governments and by private enterprises. The most popular Arab news channel, Al Jazeera, is financed by the Qatari government. Very few Arab states have specialized news channels although Egypt owns and runs Nile News and Saudi Arabia has al-Ikhbariya. Other Arab countries have TV channels with mixed programming and current affairs like the Abu Dhabi channel. Arab opposition figures have entered this field too. For example, Rif'at al-Asad, the estranged brother of the late Syrian president Hafiz al-Asad, owns the London-based news channel Arab News Network (ANN). Tunisian liberal writer, Dr. Muhammad al-Hashimi, has two news channels in London: al-Mustaqilla, which broadcasts for eighteen hours a day, and then changes on the same frequency to another channel promoting liberalism, the Democracy Channel, which broadcasts talk shows and debates about democracy in the Arab world (al-Mustaqilla 2005). A pan-Arab news channel based in London, Arabic News Broadcast (ANB), is financed by a group of Arab businesspeople and marketed to Iraq as well as the wider Arab market. It mainly concentrates on Lebanese and Iraqi news (El Ibiary 2004).

The first privately owned Arab satellite channel was the Saudi Dubai-based MBC, owned by Prince al-Walid Ibrahim in partnership with Shaykh Salih Kamil (Khayr 2005, 14). Originally a single channel broadcasting a combination of news and entertainment programs, it has now expanded to four. Egypt came late to private channels with Dream TV 1 and 2 in 2001. Egyptian businessman Ahmad Bahgat owns 80 percent of the channel's shares and, in general, the channel promotes his business. According to an article published in *al-Musawwar* (Nagih 2004a), its 2003 budget was LE35 million, with revenues of LE41 million. A third private channel, al-Mihwar, is owned by Egyptian businessman Hasan Ratib, who also controls 80 percent of its shares, while the rest is owned by other businesspeople. The Egyptian telecommunications billionaire Nagib Sawiris controls and manages a music and entertainment channel in Iraq, al-Nahrayn, to promote his business and mobile-communication services (Sadiq 2005, 50–51).

Prior to 1991 there were no subscription-TV options in the region. Egypt pioneered the phenomenon with the CNE Network that broadcast CNN plus a combination of Western entertainment channels. Three networks emerged and came to dominate the subscription-TV market. The first was the Amman-based ART, owned by Shaykh Salih Kamil, with several channels of entertainment, music, films, drama, and talk shows (Sakr 2001). The company owns the Arab Company for Media Production. The second was Showtime, a joint venture between the American-owned Viacom and Kuwait's Kipco Company, while the third, Orbit, was aimed at Westernized high-income Arabs using a selection of Western and Arab entertainment. Orbit TV and Radio Network, owned by the Mawarid Group of Saudi Arabia, was created to provide a vast selection of world-class entertainment and information in English, Arabic, and French. Saudi prince Khalid bin 'Abd Allah bin 'Abd al-Rahman 'Abd al-'Aziz, the cousin of the late King Fahd, is the owner of both Orbit and the Mawarid Group (Khayr 2005).

Thanks to advanced digital technology and piracy, many viewers enjoy Western channels including pornography which they receive free via 'descrambler' software which upgrades their receivers every month or so. Korean receivers, which upgrade their descrambling software regularly—such as Humax—are very popular for this reason. For as little as $3.50 per month, you can upgrade the software of your receiver to descramble channels worth hundreds of dollars. While I do not have exact figures about this practice, the ads published in Egyptian newspapers and visits to satellite-installation companies suggest that this is a booming business. This communication revolution in satellite media has greatly influenced Arab tastes and choices.

Egyptian TV Drama

In Egypt almost 50 percent of women are illiterate compared to 29 percent of men (CAPMAS 2003), and TV drama remains an important vehicle for communication, education, and entertainment. According to the 2002 *Arab Human Development Report*, the population of the Arab world is young, with almost 38 per cent below the age of fifteen and a median age under twenty (UNDP 2002, 2). Local demand for Egyptian drama has been on the rise to meet the needs of national and Arab channels (see Table 2). This high demand naturally affects the quality of these dramatic serials. Egypt produces, on average, almost two thousand hours of drama per year (i.e. almost one hundred TV serials and fifty drama evenings at an annual budget of LE350 million; Ramadan 2005; see Table 3 for a list of the TV drama producers in Egypt).

Table 2. Daily average TV transmission hours for eight local and central channels by drama program

Year	1995–96	1996–97	2000–01	2001–02
Length of Programming Hours	17	19.2	27.2	23.6

Source: TV & Broadcasting Union; CAPMAS 2003, 325.

Table 3. Producer and proportion of TV drama production in Egypt

Producer	Percent of the market
State TV production sector	20
Sono Cairo/Sawt al-Qahira Co.	33
Media Production City	30
Private/joint production	17

Source: Ramadan 2005, 17.

Egypt has a scrambled round-the-clock soap-opera channel—Nile Drama, established in 1996. It broadcast 8,760 hours of drama in the years 2002–03 (ERTU 2005a). The Arab TV drama market is large since the total

Arab population amounts to three hundred million, who mostly speak and understand Arabic (Higazi et al. 2005, 70). Arab immigrants all over the world demand Egyptian drama and thus Egyptian TV soap-opera exports have increased. In terms of quantity Egypt still stands as the top Arab country in this field. A quick look at the program guide to any Arab TV station will reveal the large number of Egyptian soap operas, actors, or writers involved in their daily programming. There are many reasons for this status. First, Egypt had been a pioneer in this field and had well-qualified cadres and popular stars. Secondly Egyptian drama is mainly melodramatic and often, but not always, avoids controversial subjects. Third, as in the case of the Egyptian cinema, the Egyptian dialect is more familiar in the Arab world.

Furthermore, Egyptian drama focuses upon social issues in almost 73 percent of its total production, followed by comedies (Ramadan 2005). Egypt does not import any dramas produced by other Arab countries and very few Egyptians are interested in non-Egyptian drama. Egyptian and other Arab drama, in general, lacks many common Western genres—there are no science-fiction serials like *Star Trek* or *The X-files*, and no detective stories like *Columbo* or *CSI*. Nevertheless, Egyptian TV, according to a recent feasibility study, focuses its marketing efforts on only 20 percent of what is potentially an open market by limiting itself only to the Arab world, while ignoring the wider Muslim world and the global market (Ramadan 2005). In the age of globalization where millions of Arab immigrants live all over the world, media exports cannot be limited to the regional audience. Arab satellite TV now, in theory, can reach more distant markets such as Europe and Asia.

In the Arab world, Egypt used to monopolize the production of TV dramas. More recently, Syria has begun to gain market share in the niche of high-quality historical dramas, but not in the area of more traditional soap operas and other dramatic programming. Syrian productions are coproduced with other Arab or foreign companies. On average Syria produces thirty to thirty-five dramatic works a year (Higazi 2005). Given the one hundred TV serials and fifty drama specials made in Egypt, Cairo still dominates the Arab world (Ramadan 2005). One of the most popular Syrian historical miniseries, *Saqr Quraysh* (Quraysh Falcon), aired in 2003, was the life story of the Andalusian caliph 'Abd al- Rahman al-Dakhil. Syrians have also produced other successful historical miniseries (e.g., *Salah al-Din*, *Rabi' Kordoba* ['Cordoba Spring'] and *al-Taghriba al-Filistiniya* ['The Palestinian Estrangement']). This success has introduced Syrian drama to the international markets of Europe and Latin America where Arab immigrants are settled. It has also attracted Arab investors to Syrian drama. The Egyptian minister of information, Mamduh al-Biltagi, admitted that despite weak material and technical capabilities Syrian drama enjoys a qualitative, though not quantitative, edge compared to the Egyptian genre (Higazi 2005). The success of Syrian drama has to do with its plots that deal with Syrian reality, customs, traditions, morals, fantasy, and particularly, major productions of historical drama (Higazi 2005). Meanwhile, dramatic production all over the Arab world, with the exception of Egypt and Syria, is either too parochial to be exported or uses colloquial language not easily understood in other Arab countries. According to 'Abd al-Rahman Hafiz, the chairman of the board of the Egyptian Media Production City, "Egypt is helping Syria to build a media-production city to complement, not compete with Egypt's" (Higazi 2005).

There are attempts in some Arab countries to create more media cities like the massive production site in Manama, Bahrain. Dubai, the Hong Kong of the Gulf, already features a flourishing media city. The quantity of Egyptian drama still exceeds production by emerging media capitals, which also still use Egyptian personnel in their own productions. The new media cities in the Gulf seem to be turning to producing international, South Asian, and Asian drama as much as Arabic-language content. Will Egypt's media city crumble back into the desert? No, but there is a strong need for more diversification and much higher production and talent values. The mushrooming of media-production cities in the Arab world has to do with the growing demand for programs by Arab satellite channels. The Arab TV drama market is so large that Egyptian and Syrian drama producers cannot meet demands on their own. Satellite channels try to fill the shortage with talk shows, imported documentaries, and dubbed Latin American serials, which are particularly popular in Lebanon and Syria.

Not only is Egypt the main producer of programming for Arab television, but many on-air personalities are also Egyptian and many Arab talk shows attract high ratings when dealing with Egyptian scandals and issues. For example, a case involving a paternity dispute between the young Egyptian actor Ahmad al-Fishawi and fashion designer Hind al-Hinnawi, who claimed that her daughter was the result of a secret 'urfi (unregistered common-law marriage)—not an affair as her former lover claimed—has been the main topic of many Arab satellite tabloid shows since 2004. Needless to say, neither tabloid nor revolutionary social issues will be tolerated on Saudi media, which is tightly controlled by conservative religious and political forces. But some of these issues can be raised, albeit timidly, by Egyptian shows.

One of the biggest problems facing Egyptian TV drama is the competition for popular superstars among TV-drama production companies and media-production cities. As producers compete for the limited pool of well-established TV stars, they raise the cost of production. In fact, the salaries of Egyptian TV drama stars jumped by 500 percent during the last seven years, according to a report by the state-run TV Economic Sector "Irtifaʿ ugur al-nujum . . ." ('Rise in the Salaries of Stars . . .' 2005). Some top Egyptian TV-drama superstars demand millions of Egyptian pounds. For example, some actors make millions of pounds a year, including ʿAdil Imam, the king of comedy (LE2.5 million), Husayn Fahmi (LE1.5 million), and Ilham Shahin (LE1 million). Producers now realize that any strong TV drama costs on average between LE8 million and LE12 million due to the stars' high salary demands. Therefore producers have begun turning to younger stars who do not demand such high salaries. At the same time, more viewers have begun turning to soap operas produced by the rich Arab satellite channels that can afford to pay for the expensive Egyptian stars. In this competition Egypt sustains significant though not complete losses because these stars maintain Egypt's cultural presence even on non-Egyptian channels. How does the experience of rapid transformation in the realm of satellite TV impact and compare to shifts in the cinema industry?

Egyptian Cinema

Cinema, soap operas, and music are some of the most important vehicles for Cairo's past and current dominance in the Arab world. Cairo continues to influence the region because its cinema industry is the region's strongest and oldest, and its market is not limited to a strictly local one as in the case of Israel or North Africa. In addition to linguistic factors, Middle-Eastern cinema is built on star power, and Cairo's culture and infrastructure continues to manufacture stardom like no other place. Plot and script are less important than the star factor in shaping the cinema industry, and so Egyptian actors and singer-actors remain the unofficial ambassadors of mass culture to Arab countries and the rest of the world. This explains why Egyptian rulers have always shown an interest in the welfare of Egyptian entertainers. From state-sponsored health-care programs for stars that include free treatment abroad, to special service awards, the government has lavished its attention on top Egyptian icons. In March 2005 President Mubarak showed deep concern for the dying Egyptian superstar Ahmad Zaki, who had starred in diverse roles from the comical, vulnerable Everyman, to romantic leading men, to the role of President Nasser himself. President Mubarak phoned him numerous times to cheer him up during painful chemotherapy sessions. Egyptian and Arab media allocated much print space to the coverage of Zaki's health and eventual death.

Egypt's stars may be aging and dying, but the industry is far from dead. What is the state of Egyptian cinema today? If we look at the world cinema-production-industry map devised by UNESCO, there are three main categories of film-producing countries (UNESCO 2001). The first consists of countries that produce more than two hundred feature films annually such as India (839), China and Hong Kong (469), the Philippines (456), the United States (385), and Japan (238). The second category includes countries that produce on average between nineteen to 199 films annually. Examples include Brazil (86), Argentina (47), and Nigeria (20). The Islamic Republic of Iran produces almost seventy films annually (Hadeseh.com 2005). The third category, according to UNESCO, includes countries that produce between one and nineteen films, or none at all, annually. This category includes countries like Israel.

Historically, Egypt has moved up and down inside the second category of film-producing countries. Its peak production year was 1985 with a total of seventy-eight films, while its lowest output was in 1996 and 2004 with an average of twenty-four films per year (see Table 1). The rest of the Arab world stayed mainly in the third category and so regarded Egypt as the 'Hollywood of the Middle East.' Compared to past domestic production levels, the number of Egyptian films produced annually is declining. Compared to cinema production in other Arab states, however, Egypt still leads despite the fall in numbers. Perhaps because of political instability in the Middle East produced by war, terrorism, poverty, tyranny, and religious extremism and intolerance, Arab audiences seek comedy films, and in the last few years Egyptian comedies have been the top-grossing hits in the Arab world. In 2004 the highest-grossing film was 'Aris min giha amniya ('Groom from a Security Authority') starring 'Adil Imam, which produced revenues of LE15.5 million domestically and $1 million abroad (al-Shafi'i 2005). This does not mean that other film genres are not well represented. Egypt has a variety of action, romance, and melodrama films. Nevertheless some critics and industry insiders are cynical and critical of the current state of movie production in Egypt because of low-quality plots and the fast pace of production. For example, the internationally renowned Egyptian director Youssef Chahine said he was no longer interested in watching Egyptian cinema: "If you want serious and important films, it would take years, while the currently produced films are wrapped up in three months because they are of low quality. Traders have entered the cinema business in search of material gains. They don't understand the real meaning of the cinema industry" (Mamduh 2005).

Egyptian television scriptwriter Usama Anwar 'Ukasha said that despite having a large cinema industry, Egypt does not produce films worthy of submission to competitive, international film festivals (Mamduh 2005). The reasons for the loss of quality include: the absence of a higher moral goal and ideals in the age of 'cinema to go'; producers who have become speculative profiteers; and the lack of strong scripts similar to those from the golden age of cinema, which relied on novels written by Egypt's revered literary figures such as Naguib Mahfouz, Taha Husayn, and Ihsan 'Abd al-Quddus (Mamduh 2005).

With the emergence of specialized film channels, competition erupted between their owners to monopolize control over Egyptian films, by hunting and buying the negatives of these films. Most of the competition raged between Saudi tycoons. The struggle to obtain the negatives was started by ART Film channel-owner Sheikh Salaeh Kamel ('Abd al-Hadi 2005b, 84–85). Kamel pursued production companies that owned large numbers of Egyptian film negatives, such as the the famous Egyptian star Farid Shawky's Artists Union Company, and the heirs of producers who had produced some popular films. The rationale for any specialized film TV channel is that it must have a minimum number of films—at least a thousand—to guarantee filling its air space. The Egyptian state-run TV historically paid little to rent such films for a specific period of time.

When Saudi money went after the Egyptian film negatives, buying large numbers, Egyptian film critics were shocked and began sounding alarms. They warned that once agreements between the Egyptian state-run TV and some of the producers ended, Egyptian film archives would be controlled by Saudi media moguls, not Egyptian production companies. Still, it was too late. Many Saudi media tycoons (from Orbit, Rotana, and ART) began competing and buying from one other while Egyptians looked on in vain. It seems that the rival Saudi ART and Rotana channels now own the lion's share of Egyptian film negatives.

Egypt and Saudi Arabia had been political rivals in the 1950s and 1960s, and Egyptian liberals have long been suspicious of Saudi capital because they believe it has funded the spread of fundamentalism in Egypt (see Fawda 1985). Rotana now owns three Egyptian cinema production companies that produce three to five films annually at a cost of $2 million to $4 million per film (Bakr 2005, 13). Other businesspeople have begun to enter the field of movie production to meet the expanding satellite-market demand ('Abd al-Hadi 2005b). Another giant monopolist, the Arab Holding Company for Arts and Publication, was established by Egypt's largest investment banking group, EFG-Hermes. It bought what remained of the Egyptian cinematic heritage by acquiring and merging film companies (Husni 2001).

Egypt has more than 295 first-class movie theaters and a score of medium-quality screens. (See Armbrust in this volume for a discussion of cinemas, political economy, and youth culture in Cairo.) Investment in movie theaters is attractive as the owner takes half the returns netted from any movie shown on his screen (al-Sharif 2005). The local Egyptian film market has two dominant groups. The first imports American, and to a lesser extent, Indian films. The second group produces and distributes large-scale production Egyptian films shown at popular times in several movie theaters at the same time allowing quick profits in the millions ("Cinema Market" 2005). In fact, since the late 1990s films have earned profits of almost 500 percent for their producers (Husni 2001, 62–64). The average film costs between LE4 million and LE5 million, and lower-budget films between LE1 million and LE3 million. The number one box-office hit for the year 2004 was the slapstick comedy 'Ukal, which grossed LE19.7 million (al-Samahi 2005b). The financing of Egyptian films comes from three main sources: the local market, foreign distribution (including Arab states, Europe, and the United States where there are more than five million Arab-Americans), and Arab satellite TV channels (Nagih 2004a).

However, relatively speaking, the Egyptian cinema industry is weak compared to Indian cinema. In the year 2004, for instance, Egypt produced twenty-four films, but their total cost combined with their box-office returns did not exceed LE120 million (the average cost of producing a film in Europe is almost $20 million and $3–4 million in India) (Sadek 2005). The most expensive film to date cost LE10 million, but new giant production companies like Good News For Me is planning to invest LE18 million in the film 'Imarat Ya'qubiyan ('The Yacoubian Building'), based on the bestselling novel by Alaa Al Aswany (Nagih 2004a).

There are many film-producing companies operating in Egypt, like the giant Rotana, the Arab Company for Sound, headed by Muhsin Gabir, and the Arab Company for Publishing, headed by the director of Dar al-Shuruq and chairman of both the Egyptian and the Arab Publishers' Union, Ibrahim al-Mu'allim (Rakha 2001).

Egyptian producers began employing actresses from other Arab countries to sell films to the Arab satellite audience. For example, al-Bahithat 'an al-huriya ('The Liberty Seekers') (2004), by Egyptian director Inas al-Daghaydi, employed in the leading roles an Egyptian, a Moroccan, and a Lebanese actress. The script and novel were written by Syrians Rafiq al-Sabban and Huda al-Zayn (Nagih 2004b). So like the video clip, Egyptian cinema combines many Arab talents for a wider audience than the local Egyptian market. Despite all the criticisms that can be leveled against Egyptian cinema, Egypt still has the most popular Arab cinema stars and professionals. The most respected and popular belly dancers in the Arab world are still Egyptians: Fifi 'Abduh, Dina, and Lucy. Fifi 'Abduh publicizes herself by claiming, "Tourists come to Egypt to see the Pyramids and Fifi 'Abduh." Attempts to establish media cities in other Arab countries like Dubai would succeed if the objective were to reach the international market where producers seek audiences with Arab backgrounds. However if the target market is the Arab world, such media-production cities would require Arab stars, scripts, producers, and themes. In such a situation some Arab countries, including Syria, Lebanon and Egypt, are better providers of manpower. Why? These countries have a larger number of superstars, while in the Gulf, with its small population and conservatism, show business is still not regarded as an attractive career.

Egyptian Music: Age of the 'Porno-Clip'?

Music, like movies, is easy to export in the form of video clips, cassettes, CDs, MP3s, live concerts, and private recitals. Many Arab heads of state, princes, and notables still invite prominent Egyptian and other artists for live recitals and concerts in their palaces on various personal occasions. The late King Hassan II of Morocco, for example, hosted private recitals for 'Abd al-Wahhab and 'Abd al-Halim Hafiz in his palaces on many occasions.

The deaths of Umm Kulthum and Hafiz in the 1970s represent irreparable losses to Egypt; to some extent, their style of singing also faded as new cadres of singers and music arose, reflecting larger societal changes. Instead of singers standing still behind microphone and orchestra, performing traditional long, repetitive songs, Arab youth wanted short, five-minute, fast-paced songs with dancing, scantily clad, beautiful models surrounding a jumping singer. The tempo, technology, and the cultural stakes changed as pop music became more identified with elites, and high fashion and consumerism on the one hand, and pop music reflected, or became challenged by, new controversies about morality, gender roles, and religio-nationalist politics on the other. In new music-video forms, singers dance and seduce, engaging the audience to participate in the frenzy.

The history of the so-called 'youth song' started in Egypt after 1967 but it took some time to find its place in Egyptian music. Some of the first songs of this new genre appeared in 1972 with artists such as Hani Shakir who at first tried to emulate Hafiz's traditional style, but in 1980 switched to the new youth style. Cassette companies also switched to the changing style and many new singers became popular, like Muhammad al-Hilw and Hamid al-Sha'iri ('Ukasha 1999). This genre became dominant in Egyptian radio and TV.

However it was not until the age of satellite and the video clip that the real boom in this genre began to take hold and stir controversy with specialized channels airing such songs. As Egypt no longer has a charismatic political leader like Nasser, a diva like Umm Kulthum or a superstar like Hafiz, it has ceased to dominate the music world. Stars from various Arab countries are now popular, yet Egyptian stars are still important and considered the richest and most successful of all Arab stars. A recent survey of the richest Arab music stars, in terms of cassette sales and commercials, listed the Egyptian Amr Diab at the top with $37 million in sales and commercials. Second was the Lebanese Fayruz with $34 million, and third was Egyptian Hani Shakir with $32 million ("Amr Diab . . ." 2005). Among the ten-richest living Arab singers, two Egyptians top the list, while the rest are mainly Lebanese, and one is Iraqi.

In terms of singing and dancing, the Lebanese appear to have taken the Arab world video-clip industry by storm. Lebanese female singers are the most provocative, stylish, and innovative. Feeling the heat of the competition, the moralistic Egyptian press launched a campaign against video clips accusing them of exploiting the sexuality of female singers and the chorus. They derogated such clips as "porno-clips," with "undressed singers" and "video-clip nudes" (al-Samahi 2005a; Fuad 2005). Lebanese female singers were the subject of more attacks than others. One prominent Egyptian journalist questioned the virginity of famous Lebanese singer, Nansi 'Ajram, because of her suggestive singing style. According to the Egyptian opposition daily al-Wafd another Lebanese singer, Hayfa Wahbi (whose mother is Egyptian) insulted the Egyptian press by claiming in an interview with the Lebanese TV channel, LBC that they (the Egyptian media) had attacked her because Lebanese singers are prettier and more fashionable than their Egyptian counterparts (Mustafa 2005). The paper said that the Egyptian Musicians' Union was considering banning Hayfa from singing in Egypt. Foreign singers planning to perform public concerts in Egypt need an entry visa approved by the Ministry of Interior and permission from the Musicians' Union. In practice these potential hurdles are not so difficult to overcome. In fact, intimations of a ban against a singer are sometimes merely a publicity stunt designed to promote that singer and attract an audience. Even if there is a ban, good connections and contacts subvert it. Another controversial singer, the Tunisian Najla, was actually banned from entering Egypt to shoot a video clip in which she was to appear in her underwear trying to excite a horse ('Abd al-Rahman 2005). Egyptian responses to challenges by their Lebanese counterparts came with the Egyptian singer, Rubi. Like her Lebanese counterparts, Rubi tried to stir a similar controversy by dancing suggestively in tight jeans in her video clips.

Nevertheless, this Egyptian counteroffensive seems to have had no effect. According to an Egyptian weekly, "Rubi may be voice-wise superior to singers like Najla and Poussi Amir but they surpass her in terms of sex appeal and seduction" (Fuad 2005).

In March 2005, almost three thousand students at Alexandria University of all political stripes, not limited to the Islamic current, demonstrated against nudity in video clips. The campaign was organized by the circulation of a leaflet among humanities and social sciences students, which argued that students had "had enough." They condemned the music channels and described video-clip singers as waging a war against youth. Their banners carried slogans like "No to stimulating the desires of the youth," and "*Kifaya* (enough) to Rotana and Melody." They also twisted Rotana's slogan, "You won't be able to shut your eyes," into "We can shut our eyes." As an alternative, the students also circulated free counter-video clips for singers like Iman al-Bahr Darwish and Hani Shakir in which no nudity appears (Muhammad 2005). They also performed a drama entitled *Yawmiyat sha'b ta'ban* ('Diary of a Tired Young Youth') reflecting the suffering of young men who are excited and frustrated by watching these video clips. They also issued a newsletter, *al-Makshuf* ('Bluntly'), in which students condemned the stations that promoted video clips and asserted that their stars, like Maria and Hayfa Wahbi, were waging a war to destroy youth (Muhammad 2005).

Both cassettes and CDs are common in Egypt and the Arab world. Cassettes are still the most common music format, due to their low price and the high taxes on imported CDs. However, music sites on the Internet and MP3s are gaining in popularity. The Egyptian cassette industry is declining rapidly from an investment worth LE250 million to LE60 million now (Tayib 2005). Egypt has more than thirteen hundred cassette-producing companies (see Table 4). Sawt al-Fann is the largest of the private music-producing companies in Egypt. It was founded by Hafiz and 'Abd al-Wahhab in 1960 as a joint stock company producing music and films. The company controlled the distribution of works by Hafiz and 'Abd al-Wahab, and in doing so, made a fortune. It is now owned by the Egyptian EFG-Hermes company (Essam El Din 2000). The major public company under the control of the Ministry of Information is Sono Cairo (Sawt al-Qahira). Sono Cairo in 2002–03 produced cassettes worth LE11.7 million (ERTU 2004, 266).

The World of Arab Video-clip Production

On Egyptian satellite television, NileSat, there are more than fifteen unscrambled free-to-air music channels in Arabic, or that mix international with Arab video hits (Melody, Melody Arabia, Melody Hits, Strike, Rotana, Rotana Tarab, Rotana Clip, al-Shababiya, Mazzika, Nujum al-Khalij, Nurmina, al-Khalijiya, and Music Plus). There are others that are scrambled, including ART Tarab (variety), and Western channels like MTV and VH-1. NileSat is the major music satellite for all Arabs because it has far more music channels than are provided on Arab satellite. All of these round-the-clock channels thrive on video clips, commercials, and mobile-phone advertisements.

Table 4. Egyptian audio production 2001 sanctioned by the Censorship Department

Category	Number of recordings
Recorded Egyptian songs on cassettes (Egyptian production)	2,431
Arabic Songs (non-Egyptian singers) produced by Arab countries on cassettes	1,070
Foreign songs on cassettes	5,332
Arab songs (non-Egyptian singers) recorded on Egyptian records	795
Arab songs (non-Egyptian singers) produced by Arab countries	357
Foreign songs on CD	114
Imported CDs for sale	17,746
Exported cassettes	119,368
Imported cassettes	428

Source: Egyptian Ministry of Culture 2001, 105–106.

Singing success is today no longer dependent on the possession of a good voice, it also requires good looks and exciting dance, fashion, and sets. Also, globalization, hybridization, and Arabization of Western music-TV techniques have occurred rapidly in the Middle East. Arab singers are no longer conservative in either their performance or in the way they dress. With competition sharpening to feed mushrooming Arab satellite channels, singers vie for public attention by offering more and more taboo-breaking performances. The old-style Arabic songs, such as those perfomed by Umm Kulthum, used to last for more than an hour, with the diva poised with dignity before a large, formally dressed orchestra. By contrast, today's Egyptian and Arab video clips adopt the short format of less than five minutes, with provocative singing and dancing.

Who is producing this entertainment that is in such high demand? The answer is complicated by the merging and splitting of many of the companies involved. Some producers work for several companies at the same time, and one gets the impression of a thick jungle of interconnected relations. For example, the Mazzika channel is owned by Sawt al-Fann, and Rotana owns 60 percent of its shares.Muhsin Gabir, chairman of the board for Mazzika, also owns a company called Digital Sound that produces video clips (al-Saghir 2005). Mazzika has plans for two more channels, Mazzika 2 and 3 ("Mazzika 2 . . . " 2005). Satellite music channels, plus independent producers and directors, have their own specialized studios for producing these video clips. An average Egyptian video clip may cost between LE40,000 to LE60,000 to produce. Each channel plays videos of its own production, usually cheaply produced. If the video clip becomes a hit, they produce it as a cassette recording for the singer (Mursi 2005). Egypt has the first Arab video-clip magazine, *Majallat vidiyu klib*, produced by the Arbtonality Company for Artistic Production, Circulation, and Services.

The largest number of Arab video clips is produced in Egypt. An article published in *al-Musawwar* in 31 December 2004 quoted industry officials, who claim that on average, four are produced per day (Nagih 2004a). This number may increase as more Arab music channels enter the market. Egypt remains an attractive and cheap place for their production. Technically and artistically, there is stiff competition between Egyptian and Lebanese video-clip directors. Egyptian video-clip director Muhsin Ahmad told *al-Ahram al-'Arabi*, "Only famous and rich Egyptian superstars like Amr Diab and Hani Shakir resort to Lebanese directors, while new singers turn to Egyptian directors. The Lebanese directors are advanced in makeup and costume design, but when it comes to ideas we are better." ("al-Mukhrij al-libnani yaghzou al-saha al-ghina'i" 2004). The average cost of a video clip produced in Lebanon amounts to $100,000; in Egypt the cost of production is much less. High fees allow Lebanese directors to employ expensive models, sets, and costumes.

The Rotana Channel Network monopolizes the music of more than 120 singers from Egypt, Lebanon, and other parts of the Arab world. Among those on its payroll is Amr Diab, who has a five-million-dollar contract with Rotana ('Abd al-Hadi 2005a). Rotana has produced 2,439 video clips, seven musical programs, three variety and four entertainment programs, 4,576 live songs in concerts and music festivals, and 724 program songs, according to their website (Rotana 2005). The cost of producing one cassette album is almost LE500,000 (Muhsin 2005). In the year 2004, approximately 150 cassette albums were produced in Egypt (al-Samahi 2005b).

Today's Middle-Eastern video clip is a product of cooperation among investors, talent, and media from a variety of Arab countries. The video-clip singer can be Lebanese, and the director Egyptian, while the music, setting, and may originate in the Gulf. The Arab world in the twenty-first century has witnessed intensive interaction among its citizens through labor migration, tourism, and investor and consumer flows back and forth throughout the region. Millions of workers from poor Arab countries like Egypt, Sudan, and Yemen traveled in search of higher salaries in oil-rich countries like Libya, Iraq, and the Gulf states. When workers return home, they may feel nostalgic for the music of the country where they had worked. On the other hand, millions of tourists from the oil-rich states spend their holidays in the oil-poor countries—particularly in the hotels, theaters, cinemas, and nightclubs of Cairo. Arab–Arab intermarriage rates jumped due to this strong and historically unprecedented level of sociocultural and economic interraction. Arabs have experienced first-hand the subcultures of other Arab states. So it is no surprise that it is now common for modern Arab songs to be made up of a mixture of Gulf music and Lebanese melodies or lyrics—listen to the songs of Lebanese singer Diana Haddad, who is married to a Gulf citizen, and you will notice a new fusion of both musical cultures.

Many singers purposely use a number of different dialects and melodies from the Arab world to win satellite audiences, for example, the famous Iraqi singer Kazim al-Sahir uses a mixture of Iraqi, Lebanese, Gulf, and Egyptian tones and lyrics in his songs. In Cairo, one can see many billboards promoting the new albums of Lebanese, Iraqi, Tunisian, and Moroccan singers, who flock to the city to become stars. Such a sight was unprecedented in Cairo, even in the heyday of the pan-Arabism of the 1950s and 1960s. Today, thanks to labor migration and the communications revolution, a cultural pan-Arab union has been achieved on the streets, websites, and billboards of Cairo and other Middle Eastern metropolises, if not in the political and institutional sphere.

Away from the sultry Lebanese singers, and neotraditional folk-protest singers like Sha'ban 'Abd al-Rahim, many Egyptian rap-music bands and singers have appeared under the influence of Western TV video hits from MTV-style channels. However, their singing is far less violent, vulgar, and politically rebellious than mainstream U.S. hip-hop, and more playful and seductive. For instance, the Egyptian band MTM produced the successful hit "My mom is traveling so I will throw a party" ("Ummi misafira, w-ha'mil hafla"). The song celebrates freedom from authority, represented by the mother figure who is away at a funeral. The young man in the clip celebrates her departure and calls his friends for a big party. Also, the famous Egyptian laundry-man-turned-rap-singer, Sha'ban 'Abd al-Rahim, has become notorious and hugely popular in Egypt and the Arab world for his nationalist anthem "Bakrah Isra'il" ('I hate Israel,') and in a later verse adding, "and I love 'Amr Musa" (the Egyptian secretary-general of the Arab League, and a relatively young Arab nationalist leader), and for his antiwar song, "al-Darb fi al-'Iraq" ('Hitting Iraq'). (See Nicolas Puig in this volume for further discussion of the influence of singers and music from the working classes.)

The State of Egyptian Theater

With the Free Officers coup in 1952 that ended the monarchy, established the republic, and sought to revolutionize Egyptian culture, the state began to support the theater sector along with the movie industry. The theater was considered a better revolutionary tool because it permits more direct interaction between the audience and the actors. New theatrical companies, playwrights, and artists were supported with state subsidies. This theatrical movement of the 1960s resulted in what has been branded by Egyptian critics as the golden age of Egyptian theater. Many successful plays were produced and stars were born. This boom can be attributed to several factors. First of all, the state sent educational missions to top specialized drama centers in Europe. The Egyptian dramatists who returned from Russia, Germany, and other European countries rejuvenated Egyptian theater. Many became top stars like Karam Mutawi', Sa'd Ardash, Ahmad Zaki, Hamdi Ghayth, Zaki Tulaymat, and Faruq al-Dimirdash. They experimented with new forms such as realism, melodrama, and the absurd. Secondly, the state supported the theater arts at several universities, creating new, talented cadres over time. The academies of arts at Helwan University and Alexandria University have departments that teach drama, acting, directing, and related subjects. Many superstars first emerged during the golden age of Egyptian theater, and urban audiences were enthusiastic about the new art. Some attended theater for the first time in their lives and loved it. Third, the Egyptian government's enthusiasm to create a new socialist world gave a boost to Egyptian theater by providing subsidies, technologies, and training. Fourth, Egypt had a strong, politically engaged critical movement of artists and intellectuals (*muthaqqafin*, 'the cultured ones') that boosted the theatrical movement.

The 1960s witnessed many powerful political events: the end of the Egyptian–Syrian merger, the nationalization of the Egyptian press in 1962 and its subsequent adoption of a revolutionary ideology that supported liberation movements all over the world, the emergence of the Palestinian resistance movement Fatah in 1965, the 1962 revolution in Yemen supported by Egypt, the 1967 war in which Egypt, Syria, and Jordan were defeated, and the death of Che Guevara in 1967 who had earlier visited Egypt and met with its intellectuals. This political climate left Egyptian theater boiling with revolutionary ideas and inspiration.

From a regional perspective, the 1960s created a class of Cairo-based theater professionals who would later help in establishing theater in other Arab countries. In Kuwait, the efforts of Egyptian dramatist Zaki Tulaymat to develop Kuwaiti theater are well known and publicly acknowledged (Shaheen 2002). Egypt was also among those Arab countries, such as Iraq, Algeria, and Syria that pioneered the development of children's theater (Nigm 2003) through the establishment of the first official Egyptian children's theater in 1968 (Sulayman 2004). The ministries of education, culture, and youth are active in schools to develop the cultural participation of pupils in children's theater (Atallah 2004).

Egypt and Tunisia host the biggest annual international theatrical festivals in the Middle East. Since 1988, Cairo has also hosted an international experimental theater festival. The demand for theater in Cairo is such that it annually hosts seventy to eighty different theatrical troupes from all over the world. Egypt now has 185 theatrical troupes in the governorates supervised by the Ministry of Culture and Mass Culture Palaces.[3] There are theatrical clubs that hold annual festivals in the provinces (Husayni 2004). For ten days in September 2004, the fourteenth annual festival for theatrical clubs took place in the city of Zagazig. It costs no more than LE1,000 (about $166) to produce each play, and the provincial troupes, for some reason, are able to work with greater freedom of expression than their urban counterparts (Husayni 2004). The shows are free to the public. They are usually hosted by local cultural palaces, run by the national Ministry of Culture, which are typically historic public cultural buildings renovated for seminars, art exhibitions, cinema, and plays.

The collapse of the golden age of theater in Egypt began in 1970 when the new President, Anwar Sadat, began withdrawing State financial backing of the theater, leaving funding to the private sector. By 2004, the state theater only produced LE2.2 million in earnings, according to Usama Abu Talib, head of the Technical House of Theater ('Abd al-Hamid 2004a). The veteran playwright Sa'd Ardash dates the collapse of the Egyptian theater to late 1970, when

President Sadat conveyed to him a message that revolutionary plays should be replaced by light and farcical entertainment. The subsequent deterioration of Egyptian theater was associated by many people with the increasing ruralization of Egyptian tastes and urban life ('Abd al-Hamid 2004a).

In fact, theater, with its limited audience, scared the government more than cinema, with its wider exposure. Why? Theater is more realistic than cinema as the audience sees the drama unfolding live before their eyes. The actors on stage can be spontaneous, and improvise and interact with the audience to comment on current events. By contrast movies are censored before screening to ensure that lines and scenes conform to state policy and social norms. Everything in a movie is predictable, whereas surprises are inevitable in a theater, whether they are intended or not.

Unfortunately, Cairene audiences did not rise up and defend their theater. Instead, they turned to comic and superficial plays produced by the private sector. The crisis in Egyptian theater can be attributed to two fundamental causes, as analyzed by veteran Egyptian playwright Saad Ardash (Ardash 2004). First, the private sector has come to dominate the stage with long plays that run for years and which are commercially driven by foreign, wealthy audiences, with prurient tastes, not by Cairene artistic or public tastes. The audience for contemporary theater in Cairo consists mainly of Saudi, Kuwaiti, and other Persian-Gulf-based tourists who want to see a vaudeville format, enjoy sexual insinuations, and laugh at semiclad voluptuous actresses.

Despite these constraints, however, some names stand out and have become renowned despite the limitations of this genre of comedy—e.g., director Galal al-Sharqawi, comic actor 'Adil Imam, and actor-director Muhammad Subhi. The private sector is quite conservative, and does not produce experimental theater in the that public sector did in the 1960s.

The second reason for the deterioration in theater quality in Egypt is the absence of strong scripts dealing with real, socially relevant issues (Ardash 2004). In terms of quantity, the public sector dominates. Al-Hanagir Arts Center, a publicly subsidized stage, is the most active in Egypt, producing several successful new plays every year and bringing Arab artists to its productions (see Table 5). By contrast, the private sector may invest in one play only and run it for years to recoup the investments. One of the most successful plays at al-Hanagir Theater in 2004 was "al-Li'b fi-l-dimagh" ('Messing with the Mind') which was sold out for three consecutive months (Samir 2004). It was played by a revolutionary theatrical troupe, the Movement, founded in 1989 (Fathi 2004). This group believes in independence from commercial theater and the adoption of a revolutionary approach (Fathi 2004). The play dealt with the U.S. invasion of Iraq and the media's manipulation of the news to justify the war in order to spread democracy. The play substituted humorous names for those of the top U.S. figures who waged the war against Iraq, e.g., "Colin Power," "Condoleezza Margarine," and the "General Tommy Fox" (for Tommy Franks, the head of the U.S. Central Command, who led the invasions of both Afghanistan and Iraq). In the play General Fox is interviewed by an Arab TV station about the reasons for the invasion of Iraq. He responds by saying that he wanted to liberate the Arab citizen and make the marriage wishes of frustrated Arab youngsters come true with Barbie dolls as gifts from the United States. He tells the Arab youth, "We love you and we want you to relax instead of waiting in line in front of the U.S. Embassy for immigration visas. Stay put, don't come to us, we will come to you" (Fathi 2004).

The international media gave broad attention to the play. Writing for the *New York Times* on 19 March 2004 under the title "Who Messes with Egyptian Minds? Satirist Points at U.S.," Neil MacFarquhar attributed the success of the play to its harshly anti-American thrust and fiercely satirical wit, describing the opening scene in which the actors storm into the cafeteria of al-Hanagir in American military uniforms, waving guns and ordering people about, as "intended to mimic the jolt felt across the Arab world when the United States army stormed into Iraq" (MacFarquhar 2004). The play also depicts a suicide-bomb attempt against General Fox, at which the audience applauds (Samir 2004).

Busloads of youth from various governorates came to Cairo to watch this play, which became even more controversial and popular after it was claimed that the U.S. Embassy in Cairo had objected to the play and demanded its suspension (Samir 2004). How do we explain the success and popularity of this play? First of all, culture and politics are inseparable. In 1965 Egypt banned the film *Dr. Zhivago* because it attacked a state friendly to Egypt, the Soviet Union. In 1975, with Egyptian–Soviet relations deteriorating as Egypt began shifting toward the Western bloc, Egyptian state censorship permitted the film to be broadcast on TV. The Mubarak regime, though it has a close relationship with the United States, believes in channeling internal opposition and grievances toward that country as well as Israel. Consequently Egypt is full of anti-American and anti-Israeli cultural works like "Messing with the Mind" as a means of diffusing domestic criticism of local corruption and tyranny. Whether the U.S. Embassy did complain about it to the Egyptian censorship department, or whether the story was just part of the publicity campaign for the play, the fact remains that it was very popular. Theater critic Sharif Samir also believed that the timing of the play was ideal when emotions in the area were running high because of the war in

Iraq, and that the play dealt directly with issues instead of adopting a symbolic approach. Finally, the official sponsorship of the play by al-Hanagir Center, the Egyptian media, and the Ministry of Culture seemed to demonstrate that Egypt's cultural institutions are independent of American policies nationally and internationally (Samir 2004).

Because they recognize Cairo's central role as the political and infrastructural hub of Arab culture, the United States and Israel intervene regularly in the politics of culture in Egypt. In 2003 U.S. President George W. Bush reiterated his call for liberalization saying, "The great and proud nation of Egypt, which showed the way toward peace in the Middle East, can now show the way toward democracy in the Middle East" (El Amrani 2005). Israel tries every now and again to participate unofficially in the Egyptian cultural scene through international cultural events such as the sixteenth Cairo International Experimental Theater Festival in 2004, where Israel was accused of 'sneaking' participants into the American play, A Generous City. It was officially performed by an American troupe, the Golden Thread, with Israeli actors as members ('Abd al-Hamid 2004b). In the past Israel has attempted to attend the annual Cairo International Book Fair, but threats of boycott by Arab publishers have forced Egypt to decline granting Israel a pavilion. Israel has not yet been successful in normalizing its relations with the Arab world on the cultural front and has yet to weaken the resistance of anti-Israeli forces in Egypt.

In 2004, after a twenty-year absence, the state-run TV theater was revived and produced eight plays (al-Samahi 2005a). However the private sector has continued to dominate the theatrical scene, producing mostly comedies with superstars such as 'Adil Imam, Samir Ghanim, and Muhammad Subhi. Less famous stars open new farcical plays full of semiclad women and vulgar language in the summer season to cater to Gulf Arab tourists. On average, the private sector comes up with five to six new plays a year, mostly very weak, commercial comedies. Generally speaking, according to my observations and the views of Egyptian critics, Egyptian theater no longer attracts Egyptian audiences because of the private sector's steep ticket prices (over LE200) and overcommercialization, with exceptions for certain actors such as 'Adil Imam. Moreover, as satellite channels proliferate, it seems that the audience for serious theater is declining.

Regardless, Egyptian theater remains the only theater in the Arab world that can be exported with any degree of success. Many Egyptian theatrical troupes visit Arab countries for performances and Arab summer visitors to Egypt do not miss theatrical performances in Egypt as part of their tour. By contrast, North African theatrical troupes with their unfamiliar accents cannot successfully do the same. Moreover, North African theater is strongly affected by French trends. Gulf theater has been developed by Egyptians but still remains too parochial for export. However, because of generous funding, Gulf theater is becoming more advanced in techniques and equipment than Egypt,while the annual Cairo International Experimental Theater and Arab Theater festivals permit more Arab–Arab interaction than before.

The general state of the Egyptian theater is not a happy one, when you discuss it with Egyptian critics. Its financial problems and vague objectives are most prominent. Theater is supposed to reflect the real problems of society and must enjoy freedom of expression. However, as Egyptian society swings between authoritarianism, fundamentalism, and liberalism, theater avoids controversial social problems and issues of democratization. It engrosses itself with reproducing world classics like *Hamlet* and *King Lear* but avoids any script that tackles current domestic issues like political succession, religious revival, and the status of women. Theater is not only an entertainment but also a force for social change, if the public sphere wills it.

Table 5. Plays produced by the public-sector theater and al-Hanagir Center for Arts, 2001

Name of the theater	Number of plays
National Theater	11
Children's Theater	2
Puppet Theater	2
Modern Theater	6
al-Tali'a Theater	6
Comedy Theater	4
al-Hanagir Center for the Arts	19

Source: Ministry of Culture 2004, 150–52, 184–46.

Conclusion

For several decades, the dominant pattern of cultural interaction between Egypt and the rest of the Arab world was defined hierarchically, with Cairo as the center and the rest of the Arab world as the periphery. But in the age of globalization, cultural conflict, war, regional shifts, and urban transitions, many gains have been made by cultural sites once considered peripheral in the Arab world. The success of a small Persian Gulf country, Qatar, with its tiny population of about 860 thousand, is illustrative. Qatar has exploited the technology offered by globalization and has been politically bold, giving freedom and autonomy to its journalistic media. The result was Al Jazeera channel, which has overtaken the old established media of overpopulated countries like Egypt with its population of almost 75 million, and frequently out-scooped CNN and the world's dominant media entities.

In the past, size mattered. Today it is quality and boldness, not quantity, that counts. Egypt's cultural role changed from being the main producer of all cultural forms in the Middle East to being a coproducer, as in the production of Arab video clips, for example. In cinema and soap opera, Egypt still dominates despite some advancement in particular genres by Syria. In theater, Egyptian plays still attract regional and international attention, but struggle not to become overwhelmed by tourist cabarets.

Is Cairo finished as *the* creative and entertainment capital of the Arab world? In this chapter we have explored assertions that new flows of investment and the reemergence of new centers of cultural production in the Middle East have made Cairo into a backwater. But data on music production, the star industry, video and satellite ventures, and even popular theater and literary productivity reveal that Cairo's central role as cultural mediator, broker, and disseminator has not diminished, quantitatively. But there is no denying that its power to exert a deeper influence on the broader Arab nation, to promote a role for culture through means other than fleeting headlines and obeisance to consumer trends, has come to an end. Former golden-age levels of quality and productivity, as well as political and social inspiration, have collapsed.

Nevertheless, Egypt's culture industries today do seem to be reemerging in new venues, via new transnational technologies, and in new pan-Arab partnership forms. But Cairo will have to work very hard—and with high levels of public, artistic, and popular mobilization—to better use its human, material, and creative resources, to make the most of its legacies and opportunities, and to become a more free, creative, socially relevant, cosmopolitan center for Arab-regional and global culture.

Works Cited

'Abd al-Hadi, Husam. 2005a. "Khitat tagmid al-mutribin al-misryin fi rutana." *Ruz al-Yusuf Weekly*, 15 January, 78–79.

'Abd al-Hadi, Husam. 2005b. "Malayin al-fada'iyat al-'arabiya fi studiyu al-Qahira." *Ruz al-Yusuf Weekly*, 7 January, 84–85.

'Abd al-Hamid, Amani. 2004a. "Masrah al-dawla yaftah abwab li-l-shabab wa-l-shuyukh aydan." *al-Musawwar*, 31 December, 45.

'Abd al-Hamid, Amani. 2004b. "al-Masrahiyun al-isra'iliyun yatasalalun li-mahragan al-masrah al-tagribi." *al-Musawwar*, 24 September, 42.

'Abd al-Rahman, Muhammad. 2005. "Nagla talga' li-l-sahafa al-safra'," 25 March, <*http://www.Elaph.com/music/2005/3/50524.htm*> (14 April 2005).

"Amr Diab = $37 Million." 2005. *al-Misri al-Yawm*, 24 March, 16.

El Amrani, Issandr. 2005. "Egypt: Opening Up the Constitutional Debate." *Arab Reform Bulletin*, 3 March, <*http://carnegieendowment.org/publications/ index.cfm?fa=view&id=16643*> (27 May 2005).

Ardash, Sa'd. 2004. "Hala min al-khuf wa-l-gubn ta'tari 'ala al-masrah al-'arabi." *Masrahiyun* (September), <*http://www.masraheon.com/372.htm*> (9 April 2005).

Atallah, Ikhlas. 2004. "Future Perception of Children Theater." *al-Masrah*, October, 168–71

Bakr, Muhammad. 2005. "Akhbar mukhatat khaligi li-tadmir al-sinima al-misriya." *al-Anba' al-Dawliya*, 1 March, 13.

al-Bindari, Muna, Mahmud Qasim, and Ya'qub Wahbi. 1994. *Mawsu'at al-aflam al-'arabiya*. Cairo: Bayt al-Ma'rifa.

Central Agency for Public Mobilization and Statistics (CAPMAS). 2003. *The Statistical Yearbook 1995–2002*. Cairo: CAPMAS.

"Cinema Market." 2005. *Al-Ahram Weekly*, 23 March, 25.

Dawisha, A. I. 1976. *Egypt in the Arab World: The Elements of Foreign Policy*. London: Macmillan Press.

al-Din, Sa'd Tariq. 2004. "Hasan Hamid, ra'is ittihad al-iza'a wa-l-tilvizyun yakshif al-haqiqa." *al-Musawwar*, 24 September, 40–41.

Ebrahim, Raafat M. 2004. "Private Sector Jumps into Mass Media." *Business Monthly*, 4 April. <*http://www.amcham.org.eg/Publications/BusinessMonthly/ April%2004/reports(privatesectorjumpsintomassmedia).asp*> (2 February 2005).

Egyptian Ministry of Culture. 2004. *Culture Registry 2001*. Cairo: Egyptian Ministry of Culture.

Egyptian Radio and Television Union (ERTU). 2004. *Annual Book*. Cairo: ERTU.

———. 2005a. "Qanat al-Nil li-l-qanawat al-mutakhassisa." *ERTU*, <*http:// www.ertu.org/Nile_Chan/nhome.html*> (5 June 2005).

———. 2005b. "Qanat al-Nil li-l-dirama," ERTU, <*http://www.ertu.org/nile-chan/NL-drama.html*> (13 April 2005).

Essam El-Din, Gamal. 2000. "The Business of Culture." *Al-Ahram Weekly*. 502 (5 October), <*http://weekly.ahram.org.eg/2000/502/ec2.htm*>

Fathi, Du'a'. 2004. "al-Li'b fi-l-dimagh tatanabba' bi-intifada sha'biya li-l-
taghyir." *al-'Arabi*, 15 Feburary, <*http://al-araby.com/articles/896/040215-11-
896-art04.htm*> (3 June 2005).

Fawda, Farag. 1985. *Qabl al-suqut*. Cairo: al-Hay'a al-Misriya al-'Amma li-l-Kitab.

Fu'ad, Khalid. 2005. "Rubi la ta'raf al-'ib." *al-Khamis*, 17 March, 11.

Hadeseh.com. 2005. "UK gets set for Iranian Film Bonanza, January 21,
2005." Hadeseh.com, <*http://hadeseh.com/english/archives/004828.php*>
(3 June 2005).

"Hasad al-sinima al-misriya fi 'am 2004." 2004. *al-Funun* 88 (Summer): 34–39.

Higazi, Muhammad, et al. 2005. "Fawda dramiya tagtah al-fann al-'arabi."
al-Shuruq, 21 February, 66–77.

Husayn, Taha. 1938. *Mustaqbal al-thaqafa fi Misr*. Cairo: Matba'at al-Ma'arif.

Husayni, Ibrahim. 2004. "Shabab masrah al-aqalim yasrukh la li-l-harb."
al-Masrah quarterly, October, 119–20.

Husni, Diya'. 2001. "al-Sinima al-misriya wa ihtikar al-masalih fi muwaghit
al-kayanat al-kabira." *Ahwal Misriya*, 12 (Spring): 64.

El Ibiary, Rasha. 2004. "Arab Businessmen Target Iraq with a New News
Channel." *Transnational Broadcasting Studies* 12 (Spring–Summer), <*http://
www.tbsjournal.com/ibiary.htm*> (13 April 2005).

"Irtifa' ugur al-nugum." 2005. *al-Ahram al-'Arabi* (TV Supplement), 29
January, 6.

Khalid, 'Amr. 2005. "'Amr Khalid Official Website," <*http://www.amrkhaled.
net*> (14 April 2005).

Khayr, Fatima. 2005. "Sa'wadat al-fada' al-'arabi." *al-Ahali*, 9 February, 14.

al-Lawindi, Sa'id. 2005. "Mu'amarat taqzim Misr." *al-Jamaheer*, 23 March, 13.

Macfarquhar, Neil. 2004. "Who Messes With Egyptian Minds? Satirist
Points at U.S." *New York Times*, 18 March, <*http://nytimes.com/2004/03/18/
international/middleeast/18CAIR.html?ex=1394946000&en=4957d89eaaf43b
e6&ei=5007&partner=USERLAND*>.

Mamduh, Ahmad. 2005. "Inhiyar sina'at al-sinima." *Sayyidati al-Jamila*,
16 March, 16.

"Mazzika 2 for Programs and Mazzika 3 a Surprise." 2005. *Mazzika Monthly*,
5 April, 5.

Muhammad, Usama. 2005. "Muzaharat tulabiya didd al-klibbat al-'arya."
Mazzika Monthly, (8 April): 8.

Muhsin, Mahmud. 2005. "Singers Raising the Slogan, the Single is the
Solution." *al-Misri al-Yawm*, 22 March, 15.

"al-Mukhrig al-libnani yaghzu al-saha al-ghina'ia." 2004. *al-Ahram al-'Arabi*
(TV Supplement), 4 December, 12–13.

Mursi, Tariq. 2005. "Wirash bir al-silim li-intag mutribat al-vidyu klib."
Ruz al-Yusuf, 21 January, 82–83.

Mustafa, Amgad. 2005. "Niqabat al-musiqiyin tadrus man' Hayfa min
al-ghina' fi Misr." *al-Wafd,* 13 March, 10.

al-Mustaqilla. 2005. Homepage. *<http://www.almustakillah.com/>*
(14 April 2005).

Nagih, Khalid. 2004a. "Nugum bi-l-malayin wa aflam miqawlat."
al-Musawwar, 31 December, 46–47.

――――. 2004b. "Kuktayl nisa' 'arabiyat fi film Inas al-Daghidi." *al-Musawwar,*
10 December, 38–40.

Nigm, al-Sayyid. 2003. "Masrah al-atfal fi-l-'alam al-'arabi" Middle East
Online, 2 January, < *http://www.middle-east-online.com/?id=11036>*
(9 April 2005).

'Okaska, Sa'id. 1999. "Su'ud al-aghani al-shababiya." *Ahwal Misisriya* 3 (Fall),
209–14

Rakha, Youssef. 2001. "No Business like Show Business." *Al Ahram Weekly*
524, 8–14 March, *<http://weekly.ahram.org.eg/2001/524/fe3.htm>*
(9 April 2005).

Ramadan, Tariq. 2005. "Dirasa 'ilmiya li-islah ahwal al-dirama al-misriya."
Nahdit Masr, 24 March, 17.

Rotana. 2005. Homepage, *<http//www.rotana.net>* (14 April 2005).

Sadik, Samya. 2005. "Malayin wizarat al-thaqafa fi sharayin al-sinima."
Ruz al-Yusuf, (21 January), 84–85.

Sadiq, Ashraf. 2005. "Limadha bada' Nagib marhalit al-istithmar al-'ilmi?"
al-Ahram al-'Arabi, 1 January, 50–51.

al-Saghir, Mamduh. 2005. "Mufag'at li Muhsin Gagir." *Elaph, <http://www.*
elaph.com/elaphweb/Music/2005/2/41668.htm> (14 April 2005).

Sakr, Naomi. 2001. " Whys and Wherefores of Satellite Channel
Ownership." In *Satellite Realms: Transnational Television, Globalization
and the Middle East.* London: I.B.Tauris. *<http:// arabworld.nitle.org/texts.*
php?module_id=13&reading_id=1029&print=1> (6 June 2005).

al-Samahi, Ahmad. 2005a. "Mazzika 2004: kathir min al-'ari qalil min al-
ghina'" *al-Ahram al-'Arabi,* 1 January, 68–69.

――――. 2005b. "Hasad al-sinima al-misriya fi 'am 2004." *al-Ahram al-'Arabi,*
1 January, 66–67.

Samir, Sherif. 2004. "al-Li'b fi-l-dimagh: 'ard masrahi yasrukh fi wagh al-
gami'." *al-Masrah,* October, 56–58.

Seliha, Nehad. 2004. "Bright spots . . . Bleak Breaches." *Al Ahram Weekly,* 30
December, *<http://weekly.ahram.org.eg/2004/723/cu2.htm>* (6 June 2005).

al-Shafi'i, 'Ula. 2005. "Mi'at milyun ginih iradat al-sinima al-misriya fi 'am 2004." *al-Ahram al-'Arabi*, 1 January, 63.

Shaheen, Heba. 2002. "The Development of New Media in Egypt and its Effects on Local Realities." Mafhoum.com, <*http://mafhoum.com/press4/125C31.htm*> (28 May 2005).

al-Sharif, Amina. 2005. "Sira' al-'ashara al-kibar 'ala suq dur al-'ard al-sinima'i." *al-Musawwar*, 11 March, 42.

Shuman, Hanan. 2005. "Nugum FM afdal 40 milyun marra min al-iza'a al-hukumiya al-misriya." *Sawt al-Umma*, 28 March, 13.

"Sina'at al-sinima al-misriya." 2005. *Ruz al-Yusuf*, 15 January, 84.

Srivastava, Sanjeev. 2001. "Cash Boost for Bollywood." BBC News, 25 July. <*http://news.bbc.co.uk/1/hi/entertainment/film/1456962.stm*> (20 February 2006).

Sulayman, Fawzi. 2004. "Masrah al-tifl al-'arabi: iftikar li-l-ma'na wa-l-dalala." *Masrahiyun*, 18 June, <*http://www.masraheon.com/383.htm*> (9 April 2005).

Tayib, Magdi. 2005. "Azmat suq al-kasat." *Nahdit Misr*, 19 April, 11.

Tughan, Walid. 2005. "al-Fada'iyat wa-l-haqiqa al-day'a." *Sabah al-Khayr*, 29 March, 13–14.

'Ukasha, Sa'id. 1999. "Rise of Youth Songs." *Ahwal Misriya* 3 (Fall): 209–14.

United Nations Development Program. 2002. *Arab Human Development Report*, "Executive Summary," <*http://rbas.undp.org/ahdr/press_kits2002/PRExecSummary.pdf*> (27 May 2005).

United Nations Educational, Scientific, and Cultural Organization (UNESCO). 2001. "Survey on National Cinematography: Summary," <*http://unesco.org/culture/industries/cinema/html_eng/survey.shtml*> (1 June 2005).

Zednick, Rick. 2002. "Perspectives on War: Inside Al Jazeerah." *Columbia Journalism Review*, 2 (March/April) <*http://www.cjr.org/issues/2002/2/war-zednik.asp*> (29 September 2005).

Notes

1   For instance, although pharaonic Egypt staged the world's first plays—religious dramas about Isis and Osiris—modern Arab theater began in the nineteenth century with the translation of French plays by Syro-Lebanese dramatists. Among the first was a Maronite Christian in Beirut, Marun al-Naqqash, who translated works by Molière in 1848. Ottoman persecution of Lebanese and Syrian Christians produced waves of immigration to Egypt around 1860; and the contributions of these resettled artists enhanced Arab theater in general. The first known stage drama officially opened in Egypt in 1870 when Egyptian Jewish writer Ya'qub Sannu', commonly known as Abu Naddara, staged an Arabic play also inspired

by the French satirist Molière. Many Egyptian and Arab talents subsequently enriched Egyptian theater, including Salama Higazi, 'Ali al-Kassar, Nagib al-Rihani, Jurj Abyad, Yusuf Wahbi, Mahmud Taymur, Tawfiq al-Hakim, and Nagib Surur. In the realm of print media, Egypt was the site for pioneering creativity and cross-cultural exchanges in the Middle East. The oldest Arabic-language newspaper in the Arab world was the Egyptian government-produced *al-Waqa'i' al-misriya* in 1828. The leading newspaper in the Arab world today is the Egyptian daily *al-Ahram*, founded in 1876 by Lebanese immigrants Salim and Bishara Taqla.

Egypt also pioneered in the development of the Arab film industry. In 1927 'Aziza Amir, a well-known Egyptian stage actress, became the world's first female film producer when she financed and played the leading role in *Layla*, Egypt's first full-length feature film. Egyptian cinema success drew the support of Egyptian entrepreneurs. In 1935 Bank Misr financed the building of a major modern studio, Studio Misr, as the basis for a major professional cinema industry. Experts were sent to Europe for training and foreign specialists were imported to give the nascent industry a strong boost. These movies conveyed colloquial Egyptian Arabic to the rest of the Arab world whose cinema industries were either nonexistent at the time or too weak to compete on this grand scale of huge musical productions and glamorous stars. Cairo boasted the first opera house in the Arab world, opened in 1869 to celebrate the inauguration of the Suez Canal with the opera, *Rigoletto*, by the great Italian master Verdi. By contrast, Lebanon's opera house opened in 1924; and Syria opened one in 2004. Other Arab countries are following, particularly in the Persian Gulf states. Nevertheless, the most active opera house in the Arab world is still the Cairo Opera, now housed in its beautiful new multibuilding Arabesque-modern campus on an island in the Nile.

2   Interview with the author, 26 March, 2005.
3   Personal interview with Mohamed Ghounim, former Undersecretary, Ministry of Culture. "The Theatre of the Sixtieth: Positive and Negative" seminar, Supreme Council of Culture, 27 March 2005, Cairo.

Cairo

Consumer and Investor Geographies

Egyptianizing the American Dream

Nasr City's Shopping Malls, Public Order, and the Privatized Military

Mona Abaza

An Introduction You Can Suck or Shove

She wasn't a corpse yet.

Hind doesn't like wasting time because she's never been like other girls.

Place: Geneina Mall, the ladies' toilet.

Hind writes the mobile phone number on the insides of the doors of the toilets with a waterproof lipstick, then passes a Kleenex soaked in soda water over it, 'cos that way, cupcake, it can't be wiped off!

I told her to write it at the eye level of a person sitting on the toilet seat.

Above it two words: CALL ME

Why?

Because these things happen.

The woman goes into the toilet to relieve herself.

The woman goes into the toilet to use something that emerges, from her handbag, to protect her.

Her sin, of which she is guiltless.

A naked fragile butterfly—and
Enter the terrible number.
The number gazes at her weakness.
The number *permits itself* to intervene instantaneously.
The number asks no permission and has no supernumeraries.
This is the number...
Zero-one-zero, six, forty, ninety, thirty.
CALL ME
010 6 40 90 30

Arkadia Mall:
CALL ME
010 6 40 90 30

Ramses Hilton Mall:
CALL ME
010 6 40 90 30

The World Trade Center:
Accept no imitations.
Zero-one-zero, six, forty, ninety, thirty.
CALL ME

There's a thing I like to get up to from time to time.
As though I was living like any other lunatic.
As though I was myself, with all the little stupidities I like to commit.
And with all the stupidities that have become—by now—part of my make-
up, it was obvious I'd ask her to push it.
How far?
You guess.

This is the opening page of the much-celebrated short novel written by Ahmed
Alaidy, *Being Abbas El Abd.*[1] The novel sold out its first publication run within
three months after its appearance in Arabic in 2004. The writer, born in 1977
and barely in his late twenties, is representative of the younger generation of
Egyptian writers. When reviewing the book, Yusif Rakha identified the work as
defying any type of categorization, which was certainly accurate (2003). It is hard
to follow the outline of the story. The technique is postmodern; there is in fact no
consistent story, no beginning, no real end, and plenty of comical hallucinations

and obsessions. What interests us in this emerging genre among the younger generation of Egyptian writers is that most of these incomprehensible human encounters happen in toilets of shopping malls. It is in the mall where the main character simultaneously dates two young women. Both young women are waiting for him there, but one waits in a café upstairs while he first meets the other woman downstairs. Both girls are named Hind, but one is a working-class prostitute who uses very common Arabic and the other is an upper-class American University in Cairo student who fills her speech with English words. Both are comical characters and the communication is Kafkaesque. He dates them instead of, or being mistaken for, his friend 'Abbas al-'Abd, his supposed alter ego, who is a working-class street fighter.

This style of writing has caught the attention of the critics through the amalgamation of multiple levels of language. Rakha says:

Al-Aidi is conscious of living in the electronic age and he invests the surface of his text with the omnipresent symbols of the internet and the mobile phone: clip art, English words like 'cut' and 'paste' and a constantly flickering visual plane of communication make an unusually disorienting . . . reading experience. . . .

The text is written in a hybrid language mixing colloquial street talk with different layers of more classical Arabic.

Al-Aidi benefits from the irony inherent in a linguistic orientation that combines the latest Egyptian Arabic slang with standard Arabic, the traditional language of literary prose, and predominantly English expressions that, due to the spread of the implements of the electronic age, have been incorporated into everyday speech. Rakha, 2003.

The starting point of my interest in the new consumer culture in Egypt includes questions about how alienation and meaninglessness are experienced by youth in these empires of consumption and how the shopping mall has become the locus of alienated encounters.[2] This novel explores the emerging lifestyles and the growing feeling of uprootedness and alienation among youth. But before looking at today's youth and consumer lifestyles, it is first important to understand the recent urban transformations of the city of Cairo.

Greater Cairo

How can we read the consumer culture of a Third-World city like Cairo? A leisure and consumer city is mushrooming even as the huge slums alongside it continue to grow into an ever-expanding nightmare. By reading cities as texts where their topographies reveal the social stratification of urban life, previous studies have pointed to the reading of the mall as a city. For instance, Nancy Backes argues that, more than the city, the mall "with its recombinant properties, its reduction to basic forms not unlike those of abstract art, offers a more democratic hope and possibility, despite its connection to private enterprise" (Backes 1997, 1). Already at the turn of the century, urban futurists like H.G. Wells, who predicted the diffusion of great cities into a series of villages connected by high-speed transportation, have imagined the utopian city as a huge shopping mall. For H.G. Wells the posturban city will be "essentially a bazaar, a great gallery of shops and places of concourse and rendezvous, a pedestrian place, its pathways reinforced by lifts and moving platforms, and shielded from the weather, and altogether very spacious, brilliant, and entertaining agglomeration" (Fishman 1996, 79). In other words, the city shopping mall will end up pushing away productive activities to the fringes and the decentralized urban areas.

American shopping malls have kept sociologists busy since the mid-1980s. Many might argue that the topic has become old fashioned, especially as American shopping malls are suffering a significant decline. Dead shopping malls are described today as littering the American landscape; nearly one out of every five malls standing in the 1990s will be out of business by the end of next year. An article in the *International Herald Tribune* (3 January 2000) noted that while in 1960 there were three thousand shopping centers in the United States, now there are nearly forty thousand. As Meaghan Morris noted in her study on Australian shopping malls, it is change in the city, the management of change itself, and the changing role of shopping centers that is worth attention (1993). But the question remains: why is it that Egyptians want to multiply a borrowed experience that has proven to be a failure elsewhere?

For example, shopping centers have increased in Brazil from one in 1980 to nineteen in 1995 as a way of providing nonviolent monitored space as a response to the rise of violence in Brazil over the last two decades. In Rio, Barrashopping (73,906 square meters), the largest shopping center in Latin America, has been described as a place associated with "humanizing" space against violence (Freitas 1996, 95). Zygmunt Bauman reminds us that it was Walter Benjamin who invented the *flâneur* or stroller as the symbolic figure of the modern city. Through associating the new space of the malls with flâneurie, Bauman tells us that shopping malls make the world "carefully walled-off, electronically monitored and closely guarded" and "safe for life-as-strolling" (1996, 95). The names of Walter Benjamin and Georg Simmel constantly reappear in the literature of the city, emphasizing the stranger and loneliness as the inspiration for the reinvention of spaces; they initiated discussion of wandering in modern cathedrals and empires of consumption. Mike Featherstone reworks Benjamin's concept of *flâneurie* through its multifarious dimensions and argues that the *flâneur* is not just a stroller in the city, rather his or her *flâneurie* is also a "method of reading texts" and "for reading the traces of the city" (1998, 910). How far are Bauman's observations appropriate for understanding the changes taking place in the Third World? Could unexpected uses of spaces in the Third World by youth and women be a new field for social investigation?

In their 1998 study of British shopping malls, Miller et al. argue that shopping does not merely reproduce identities, but provides an active and independent component of identity construction. The study provides new insights about how to theorize and link ethnicity and consumption through the different use of public space. It points to the fact that consumption has become a world of its own, and highlights the importance of space and place for consumer identities as well as the cultural practices of shopping. It also emphasizes the need to look at shopping malls from the perspective of shop workers and how shopping influences sexuality and social relations (Morris 1993). Inspired by the works of the French sociologist Michel Maffesoli, Ricardo Ferreira Freitas produced a monograph in which he compared various shopping centers in Brazil with the Parisian Forum des Halles (1996). Freitas often uses the notion of *imaginaire* about the internal reshaping of the space. The shopping center, according to Freitas, symbolizes the ideal city. This space is protected from pollution and nature.

The atrium of the Yamama Center, the first mall in Cairo, 2003 (photograph by Mona Abaza).

In 2003 there were already twenty-four of these empires of consumption in Cairo, according to the survey I conducted. In the Nasr City district there were the Tiba Mall, al-'Aqqad Mall, the Geneina Mall, the Wonderland Mall, al-Sirag Mall, the City Center, the Group Center, and al-Hurriya Mall (Heliopolis); downtown in Cairo one can shop at the Tal'at Harb Mall and the Bustan

Center. Along the Nile Corniche is the Arkadia Mall, the malls of the Ramses and Nile Hilton hotels, as well as that of the World Trade Center in Bulaq. Farther away from central Cairo, in Ma'adi one can find the Ma'adi Grand Mall, the Bandar Mall, and the Town Center. Finally, the Yamama Center in Zamalek, the Cairo Mall near the Pyramids, the Mustafa Center, the Florida Mall in Masakin Shiratun, the First Mall in Giza, the Amir Mall in Shubra and the Binyan Mall in Zaytun quarter comprise the remaining malls in the Greater Cairo area.

I started to undertake research on the malls of Cairo in 1999, first through participant observation. At a later period I conducted interviews with several managers of malls. I taught a class on consumer culture at the American University in Cairo (AUC) and together with the students conducted several studies in various malls based on participant observation and interviews with managers, shopkeepers, and the public. During the year 2002–03, I supervised a research project undertaken in eighteen shopping malls where managers, workers, salesmen, and the public were interviewed by a research team, with support from AUC. Together with the team we conducted open-ended interviews that were tape-recorded. We encountered the following problems: not all managers wanted to be interviewed by my research assistants, who were sociologists trained at Cairo University. The fear of industrial and security leakages is strongly felt and more generally, a certain bias and suspicion against research is strongly persistent in Egypt due to the concentration of authority in the executive branch and the military. In several cases, I had previously interviewed the same managers before sending my assistants. My position as a female professor at the American University in Cairo, and perhaps my privileged class background, very much facilitated the task.

The construction of malls is not an isolated phenomenon, but it has developed side-by-side with the proliferation of ever-larger hyper- and supermarkets like Alfa Market, Metro Market, and the famous Carrefour centers, which recently opened in two locations (at the fringes of the suburban district of Ma'adi and in Alexandria). The French chain Carrefour became the newest tourist and leisure-time attraction for middle-class Egyptians. Carrefour is among the first hypermarkets opened in Egypt by the Majid Al-Futtaim group of Dubai (MAF), after Sainsbury's pulled out of Egypt after being attacked as pro-Israeli.[3] (See also Elsheshtawy, chapter 7, in this volume for further analysis of the influence of consumer models and financing from Dubai on Cairo.) Carrefour has an incredible capacity to both cater to local tastes and mold new desires for consumption and new tastes, but this is a research topic beyond the bounds of this chapter. The most striking thing about these malls is how new they are (most were erected during the last two decades). For example, the Yamama Center, erected in the residential island of Zamalek in 1989, was the first mall ever built in Cairo.

This chapter attempts to explain the sudden expansion of malls despite the fact that these enterprises are not as successful as one might think (many of them have only a brief life span of eighteen to twenty-four months). Less than 20 percent of all Egyptians can actually afford to shop in malls, and as a result many of the upscale malls today are described as "ghost towns" (Mostafa 2003). Recession and the devaluation of the Egyptian pound have been indicators that Egypt is facing an economic downturn. Social scientists specializing in Egypt, like Assef Bayat and Timothy Mitchell, provide a pessimistic view of growing rural and urban poverty and the unbearable urban density which has been exacerbated in the last decade, increasing the deplorable living conditions of the silent majority (Bayat 1977, 2–8; Mitchell 1999, 28–33). As Mitchell argues, in the 1990s Egypt witnessed the consolidation of neoliberal ideology between the state and international actors after Mubarak's government accepted the conditions set by an IMF austerity program. The economy experienced at that time a 5 percent growth rate (Mitchell 1999, 272), but growth was short lived and led to trends that were opposite to what had been expected by the architects of structural adjustment. Egypt's exports collapsed from 88 percent in 1985 to 47 percent in 1996–97 (Mitchell 1999, 275). Mitchell's analysis of the last decade's economic performance predicts a gloomy future. The figures reveal a sharp decline in real per-capita consumption, a drop in real wages, and an increase of the numbers of those below poverty line (Mitchell 1999, 286).

Is gentrified Cairo going to become one huge shopping mall nestled next to rampant slums? The lovers of the city of a thousand minarets have long been aware of the last decade's dramatic urban transformations which have led to the aggressive reshaping of the cityscape (see Denis, and Vignal and Denis, in this volume). The forces driving them are obvious: land speculation from about twenty major family capitalists and their cronies has led to slum clearance to make way for high-rise buildings and hotels, towers, cineplexes, restaurants, malls, and other leisure spaces. A forcible gentrification has been taking place, while urban poverty is simply concealed, not addressed. Any urban sociologist would immediately conclude that this also occurred in most nineteenth-century European towns. Such towns witnessed the systematic pushing away of the poor to the fringes of the city. In today's Cairo, gentrification is taking place as large consumer spaces are created. This is most drastically felt in two areas which this chapter will discuss: the historical quarter of Bulaq facing the upscale residential island of Zamalek, and the newly constructed satellite Nasr City at the fringes of Heliopolis.

Bulaq Old and New

I start with Bulaq, which is famous for its eighteenth-century houses of urban notables; its vanishing historical *hammams* (public bathhouses) and mosques; its remarkably beautiful late nineteenth-century European architecture; and its famed printing house.[4] Bulaq is famous for being the home of Egypt's oldest school of maritime training, a highly populated informal, second-hand clothing market, a car retail and repair district, and particular markets for cloth and fabric, secondhand military items, and scrap metal and iron. All these have been slowly disappearing. In short, modernization has led to the death of one of the most important popular quarters of Cairo. With it, a *baladi* way of life and culture is quickly erased to cater to the new Cairene yuppies. *Baladi* literally means 'country' or 'local.' It is a designation for everything that is popular. Yet, for many decades the middle and upper classes have used the word to show their contempt for the vulgar taste of inferior classes.

These new large spaces, of course, imply a new lifestyle and norms of public behavior. While old Bulaq is vanishing, all along the boulevard lining the Nile an agglomeration of towers and skyscrapers hosting international hotels and empires of consumption are conquering the space. Near the Ministry of Foreign Affairs, the twin towers of the World Trade Center (WTC) have been erected to include the Hilton, then the tower of the Conrad hotel. The WTC hosted Mobinil, another successful enterprise of Orascom, the company owned by the Sawiris family. I have written earlier about the WTC during its successful days (Abaza 2001). When I returned to Cairo in November 2004, I discovered that the WTC was completely dead, left with only three open shops. Many offices had closed down or moved elsewhere, the cafeteria was shuttered, and there were practically no visitors. Was it the effect of economic recession or had the *baladi* lifestyle triumphed over aggressive modernization? No one knows, but the people of Bulaq felt and continue to feel great pressure from the government's constant 'strangling' of their markets and neighborhood. Egyptian officials restricted vehicles transporting goods and material for the markets from entering the quarter and failed to restore the crumbling buildings. In other words, high government officials were content to let the buildings of the popular area collapse so that they could grab the land. It is odd then, that despite the failure of many of these initial malls like the World Trade Center and consumer-oriented projects, land speculation continued. I have no explanation for that.

A little bit further down the Corniche, two new gigantic, futuristic-looking towers, called Nile City, have been erected by Orascom Enterprises, which was also heavily involved in the Bulaq malls. The Nile City towers are a $200 million project, designed to include a 552-room international hotel of the Fairmont chain, whose recent success in Dubai has inspired them to replicate their model in Cairo. The Nile City complex consists of two twenty-four-floor towers with one hundred thousand square meters of office space and eleven thousand square meters of retail space, restaurants and cinemas. A huge shopping mall will open in the complex by 2005.

View of the "New Bulaq" and the World Trade Center towers from Zamalek (photograph by Mona Abaza).

Just beyond this new construction is the Arkadia Mall, which opened a few years ago. It is considered a success because of its multipurpose design, combining fancy stylish shopping with leisure. The Arkadia architects created an interior space of terraces bordered with plants. Huge screens constantly play music videos and children's games, and cafeterias and coffee shops in the mall have contributed to its success.

Soon this new landscaping will reach the nearby quarter of Shubra, one of the oldest popular quarters of Cairo. Shubra was not spared from change, since a quasi-mall called al-Amir (consisting of crammed shops) was opened in 2002. As old Bulaq vanishes, a new Bulaq has been born out of its ashes. The aggressive process of 'cleaning up' and consequently modernizing the area started late in the Sadat era (1970–1981) when the government decided to relocate five thousand working-class families from Bulaq to the public-housing area of al-Zawya al-Hamra. Farha Ghannam argues that the state justified its forced removals by articulating an image of a civilized, modern, and contemporary new Bulaq versus the criminal, traditional riffraff of old Bulaq (2002, 2). Sadat was portrayed as the hero of modernization and spiritual renewal (Ghannem 2002, 35; see also Ghannam in this volume).

Nasr City, Shopping City

For those interested in consumerism in Egypt, the example of Nasr City raises many questions. This neighborhood has seen a dramatic proliferation of shopping malls, which for some reason, generally seem to be more successful than in other parts of town. Most of these malls opened in the late 1990s. With eight malls, Nasr City has the largest number of these huge enterprises, if al-Hurriya Mall of nearby Heliopolis is included. This said, Nasr City also has the largest concentration of military institutions and military subsidized housing. It hosts the main central headquarters of the army (al-Qiyada al-Markaziya), the Military Academy (al-Fanniya al-'Askariya), the Ministry of Defense, various officers' clubs, the Internal Security Apparatus, or secret police (Mabahith Amn al-Dawla), which moved recently from Lazughli Square, and the Military Industries complex (al-Masani' al-Harbiya). The Military Museum, a military hospital, and various housing complexes for the military are located there. The military also owns a few hotels in the area.

The military gradually sold off its sizable camps and bases, located at the fringe of the desert, to civilians, until Nasr City became the quarter it is today. The main road of Nasr City, which leads to the airport, has a large complex of high-rise buildings called al-'Ubur (the crossing), constructed after the 1973 victory to house army officers (the term has wide symbolic meaning since it celebrates the Egyptian military's ability to surprise the Israeli army and cross the Suez Canal to launch the 1973 War). These flats were then sold privately.

The concentration of military installations in the area explains why a strong feeling of suspicion and resistance was often expressed when I undertook fieldwork with my assistants. Several managers and retired army officers reported that "Israeli intelligence" had been using the shopping malls to "spy." Until today, it is practically impossible to obtain a map of Nasr City that shows the location of all the existing military institutions. To undertake research on Cairo's malls, as several managers told me, is an extremely politically sensitive issue. But I continue to wonder whether there is an indirect link between the army's extended occupation of the space of Nasr City and consumer culture—is the rise in consumerism in this area sheer coincidence, or does the military play a concurrent role?

The Army Going Private

In recent years much has been said about the privatization of the army, or rather the army 'going civil' by penetrating the business and financial world. Since Egypt signed the Camp David peace treaty in 1978, many expected that the military role of the army would shrink. In the early 1980s, as conflicts declined, many retired army officers were recruited to work in food-security projects (*gama'iyas*) and other businesses (some located in Nasr City's Military Industries area) that had been launched by the government. Today many retired army officers have turned today into successful businesspeople. Anouar 'Abd al-Malek (1971) has brilliantly explained the continuity and the swelling of the army in civil and cultural life and public-sector companies after the revolution of 1952. This pattern continues because the presence of the military is still felt in Egypt's civil administration and government today. For instance, Eric Denis argues that since 1952 the administrative framework of the city of Cairo has remained controlled by the army. Three of Cairo and Giza governorates' recent governors have been retired, high-ranking army officials (Denis 1998).

Al-'Aqqad Mall in Nasr City is a good example of how the army has managed to go civilian. This mall was constructed by the association of officers of the Republican Guards (an elite group that guards the president of Egypt) who sold it later to a group of individuals. The person who constructed it was a retired general and the mall opened in 1999. However the land for the complex of six buildings, consisting of numerous flats, still belongs to the Republican Guards, and the flats are themselves occupied by Republican Guard families. Al-'Aqqad Mall is thirty thousand square meters in size and it includes 250 shops, ranging from fifteen to 220 square meters. There are three entrances with electronic doors and escalators, and a garage of ten thousand square meters. It was constructed after, and in reaction to, the entertainment-laden Tiba Mall. The manager explained that the owners consciously excluded a billiards room, game arcade, cinemas, and restaurants from its design so that the mall had no space for *flâneurie*. The planners of this mall, we were told, were mainly targeting families attracted by the shopping. At first the shops were offered for sale but prices rose so much that two-thirds of them are rented instead.

Whether or not the military's dominance of Egypt's government continues after the end of the Mubarak regime, the public visibility of the 'retired army' staff is still felt everywhere. For example, many retired army officers have opened private security companies and today, practically all the malls employ them. It is not uncommon to see retired generals sitting in atriums observing passersby and supervising the private security guards. This is logical since these retired army functionaries would be the best candidates to enforce law and order. Some see the business of private security companies as an American phenomenon that Egyptians have adopted. Apart from the security companies, some malls are managed by retired army officers. Tiba Mall in Nasr City, for instance, is managed by a retired colonel as is Cairo Center, even though the owners of the latter are civilian businesspeople, entrepreneurs, and engineers. These private security companies need to recruit guards, and a mall the size of al-'Aqqad in Nasr City requires approximately 150 security guards. The salary of the guards is rather modest, ranging from LE250 to LE300 per month.[5] They are responsible for curbing sexual harassment, a routine complaint in all malls, and shoplifting. In spite of the constant camera surveillance and the monitoring of space by retired army officers, shoplifting is a vexing and common problem. In Tiba Mall, most of the security guards originate from Upper Egypt. They sleep in the garage of the mall to return only once a month to their village. Some of the young guards have even graduated from university, but with very high youth unemployment, particularly among the educated in Egypt, they are desperate for any job.

Nasr City and Mall Culture

Many attribute the success of these commercial centers to the simplistic grid environment of this comparatively newly constructed satellite city on the edge of the desert. Nasr City could easily be described as a geometrical arrangement of cement matchboxes lining the longest streets in Cairo, such as Mustafa al-Nahhas, al-Tayaran, and 'Abbas al-'Aqqad streets. These consist of kilometers-long, wide streets, cut with roundabouts and perpendicular streets. Nasr City grew as the military and their private-sector partners developed new quarters, expanding one after another into the desert. The city has no heart, or rather, no center, but this obvious flaw does not seem to bother anyone. As a result, the streets are wider and the size of the average flats are larger than elsewhere while real estate is definitely cheaper than in such sought-after comparable middle- and upper-class areas, closer to the city center, as Muhandisin or Zamalek. Moreover, the designers of Nasr City included green spaces and parks, such as the International Garden (al-Hadiqa al-dawliya).

Yet, for most Cairenes, Nasr City is best known today for its endless variety of shops, spaces for leisure, restaurants, coffee shops, and cinemas. For many, its newness and its ambiguous shape symbolize the tastes of the returning middle-class professionals who spent the last two decades, if not more, as migrant workers in the Gulf oil-producing countries. These former migrant workers purchased property in Nasr City as they prospered, and many view

Nasr City as a place that 'smells of new money.' It symbolizes Cairo's nouveau-riche suburban culture that has been influenced by the Gulf lifestyle. Still, why are the malls of Nasr City more successful than others? On holidays or during hot summer nights, they are very popular. The coffee shops, fast-food restaurants, and atriums seem to be bursting until late at night. The cinemas and children's arcades are packed on Thursdays and Fridays.

One interpretation one hears is that the mall culture has been imported into Cairo from the United States via the oil-producing countries, since the mall is originally an American invention. Others view the Cairene version of malls as a consequence of Saudi influence on Egyptian customs and tastes and the new 'public' that former migrant workers have created in Egypt. In fact, some Egyptians refer to the people who have returned from working or living in oil-producing countries and seem particularly drawn to the malls as *nafti* (oil). These returnees were accustomed to spending their leisure time in closed, walled-off, air-conditioned spaces to escape the harsh weather of the Arabian Peninsula. During summers the malls are frequented by Arabs from the oil-producing countries. Women in long black robes are often seen smoking water pipes in upscale cafes. The First Mall in Giza, considered to be one of the most expensive shopping places in Cairo, caters mainly to Persian Gulf Arab customers. In relation to emulating Saudi Arabian or Gulf affluence, in Nasr City on *Ard al-Ma'arid* (the international fairgrounds) a 'snow city' was constructed, imitating what my informants tell me is an infatuation among Gulf Arabs with building snow games and ice-skating rinks in the middle of the burning desert. The visiting public in Snow City rents heavy winter clothes to ice skate in the middle of wintry ice sculptures of the Eiffel Tower, White House, Kremlin, Pyramids, the Sphinx, and Abu Simbel.

If the birth of the mall in America was closely related to a suburban lifestyle that arose with the automobile age and 'drive-in' culture, Nasr City would be the next best example of emulating such a concept (Jackson 2000). In fact, Nasr City is a suburb *par excellence* and the economic status of its residents allows many of them to own cars. The big Nasr City malls such as Geneina, Tiba, and al-Sirag have large parking garages and parking lots, which many see as a great advantage. Even for Muhandisin residents who live relatively close to downtown Cairo, it is easier to shop in Nasr City than to drive downtown where parking is an ordeal.

A huge mall, catering to Egyptians with cars, opened in Nasr City in 2005 when the commercial development company Golden Pyramids Plaza, controlled by the Sharbatli and Shubukshi Saudi Arabian families, purchased 115 thousand square meters of land at the junction of Nasr City and Heliopolis to open City Stars (Mitchell 2002; Mostafa 2003, 61).[6] One of the motivations behind the design of this new mall is to keep luxury shoppers satisfied in Cairo, so they won't fly to Dubai for their shopping (Mitchell 2002). The press defines the new project in the district of Nasr City as a city within a city, which also includes an international conference center, and large retail spaces for international retail outlets. It is advertised as follows:

The project's blueprints envision a complex housing three five-star hotels, 70,000 square meters of office space and 266 luxury apartments, all centered on a 550-shop mall. It's a retail center larger than any in the Middle East or Europe— slightly bigger, in fact, than the gargantuan Mall of America in Minnesota. City Stars' backers have so far sunk some $750 million (LE4.27 billion) into the ground in Nasr City and are looking forward to a partial opening in November. Mostafa 2003, 61.

Even before the official opening of the City Stars Mall in 2005, thousands of people started to flock there every evening simply to roam around. Marveling at the grandeur of this empire of consumption, they wandered aimlessly. The cafeterias, fast-food restaurants and food stalls were packed. The gigantic children's arcade was already fully operational with frightening success. Another huge section of the mall was designed as a simulation of the Khan al-Khalili Bazaar displaying the same jewelry, handicrafts, and other items that are sold there—only it is cleaner, newer, and cooler than the centuries-old, dusty bazaar. Definitely, for middle- to upper-class uptight Egyptians, and in-transit Gulf and foreign customers (the mall is located some twenty minutes from the airport), it will be faster and more comfortable to shop there. The complex, which includes the adjacent Intercontinental Hotel, is an amazing remake of kitsch façades guarded by huge pharaonic statues. City Stars is certainly inspired by a pharaonic temple, except that one is immediately reminded that this temple of consumption has tight security measures, like checking all the trunks of the cars when parking in the underground garage.

Among business circles, many gossiped that constructing shopping malls is the other side of the money-laundering coin. Malls and megaprojects have been used to obtain huge bank loans that were then smuggled out of the country, resulting in a series of scandals and arrests of businesspeople. This might explain why in spite of the short lifespan of malls, they continue to multiply. But how will such a gargantuan project survive with the frightening current recession? Certainly no one can answer that question yet.

The Sirag Mall in Nasr City, owned by an engineer, is managed by a civilian who holds a B.A. in literature but has been working in mall administration for seventeen years. He started at the Yamama Center in Zamalek. The Sirag Mall opened in 1999 and the shopping area consists of three complexes joined together by passages, three floors of shops topped by ten more floors of apartments. Each complex is a separate building joined by a passage to the next building, and each has around one hundred shops. The mall has three cinemas, six coffee shops, escalators and elevators, enough parking space for two hundred cars, bowling and billiards rooms, video and laser games, a gym, megascreens, and children's arcades. Since there is no real center, the mall gives the impression of being a crammed space containing one shop after the other. Shops are both rented and sold to individuals and companies. Here again there are cameras all over the mall and videotaping is constant.

Geneina Mall in 'Abbas al-'Aqqad Street was constructed in 1998 by five principals and supported by various banks. It seems to be the most popular mall in Nasr City. The director of the company, and its largest shareholder, is Muhammad Ginayna, and the mall has 718 shops, ranging from six to eight square meters to 350 square meters. The mall includes six cinemas, five coffee shops, one billiard room, a skating rink, a beauty center, and a playground and game arcade.

City Center, on the Autostrade, opened in 2002 and was constructed by the Afaq Company, which owns the mall. It is an entrepreneurial company that specializes in building high-rise towers. There are more than one hundred shops, all rented, with an average of one to three employees for each shop. Including the restaurants and other coffee shops, the mall employs around five hundred workers. The underground floor is where most international franchises, like Nike and Adidas, are to be found. The City Center opens at ten AM and families seem to be the first customers, followed by elderly people, then students and young people. In the summer, European and Arab foreigners also frequent the mall.

Tiba Mall was constructed in 1995. It is one of the smaller malls with only fifty shops and fewer employees and, unlike other malls, its managers supervise the aesthetics and focus of the shopping experience. For instance, they limit the number of shoe stores in their mall because there are so many elsewhere (downtown Cairo is dominated by hundreds of shoe shops).

Wonderland Mall is a good example of a dying mall. Many of the shops there have gone bankrupt and closed down. It includes thirty-one stores, two coffee shops, two restaurants (including a Kentucky Fried Chicken), one discotheque, three cinemas, an internet café, and a computer shop. The mall was successful for only one year and it has declined in the last few years, as rents reached LE3,000, skyrocketing to LE6,000 in some cases.

The shopkeepers said that the economic crisis had been felt strongly and even the number of customers in the mall's arcade and amusement park declined. Meanwhile, this mall became known for being a place where young men and women tried to meet one another and date, which many Egyptians find illicit or inappropriate. It is open from 11 AM until 2 AM. The public is mainly attracted by the cinema and the discotheque, whose clients are typically between fourteen and eighteen years of age. Several shopkeepers blamed the bad reputation of the mall on its petty crime and sexual harassment. Not infrequently, security guards themselves were said to be the source of some of the harassment.

Downtown Malls and Shopping in Suburban Malls via the New Ring Road

From the architectural point of view, the malls of Nasr City are the largest and most spacious in town, qualifying them as 'proper' malls. Alternatively, many of the malls in dense downtown commercial areas, such as Shubra and Bulaq, are too small to qualify, in popular terms, as malls. Shemla, for example, an established old *grand magasin* (department store), has been transformed into a depressing mall by simply partitioning the main hall and cramming shops into every inch of space, so that there is practically no room left for rest and recreation. The same mechanism has also been employed in the old Omar Effendi *grand magasin* in 'Abd al-'Aziz Street near 'Abdin Square in Cairo's older downtown *(wust al-balad)*.

The architecture, the décor, and façades of the new malls are often marked by their attempt to emulate buildings seen elsewhere. Some of these influences may well have come from the both the Gulf and Southeast Asia. In fact, the manager of the Ma'adi Grand Mall stated that its owners traveled to Southeast Asia and were inspired by the architecture there. The Ma'adi Grand Mall consists of six floors, with 410 shops and around 140 or 150 employees, excluding maintenance. The developers even watched videos about foreign malls and were inspired to emulate the idea of atrium fountains from the Far East. The architecture of the Wonderland Mall evokes a Hollywood vision of the Orient. Wonderland's kitschy style is described by managers and shop owners as *tiraz al-Sindibad*, the Sindbad style. The mall is just beside an Egyptianized Disneyland *mol tarfihi*, or *malahi* (amusement park).

Some of the façades, like the Geneina Mall's, with its transparent glass elevators, remind me of Southeast Asian malls in Kuala Lumpur, Singapore, and Jakarta. The malls' proximity to one another is what makes them intriguing and apparently meaningful. Most of the directors of these malls maintain that they are not in competition with each other because of the diverse customers frequenting each mall and the difference in goods and prices from one mall to another. Tiba Mall, for instance, is "a family mall" according to its manager; whereas Geneina Mall, with its huge skating rink, bowling alley, billiard center, and computer games, attracts the younger generation. Wonderland Mall has a "bad reputation," because it caters to flirtatious youngsters who are trying to pick each other up and to those who frequent the discotheque. The Sirag Mall, with its fourteen thousand square meters, competes in size with the second-largest mall in Nasr City,

The Ma'adi Grand Mall, inspired by Southeast Asian models (photograph by Mona Abaza).

the Geneina Mall, although its manager insists that it is really the largest mall in Cairo. The Geneina Mall consists of twelve thousand square meters, integrating a huge ice rink and parking for eight hundred cars. The designs of the Sirag, the Geneina, City Center, and the 'Aqqad malls also included associate housing, largely apartments above the shopping spaces.

These new malls not only have introduced new designs for commercial space but also often demand a specific behavior and dress code from their customers. When this research began in 1999 some malls, like the World Trade Center and al-Hurriya Mall, put restrictions on those wearing *gallabiyya*s, long robes that are mostly worn by peasants and the lower classes. This restriction was probably lifted later, because of the influx of Gulf visitors who also commonly wear white traditional *gallabiyya*s whether they are conducting business or shopping.[7] The general manager of the Arkadia Mall stated that he gave instructions to security guards at the doors to filter the public simply through appearance (*bi-l-shakl*). *Gallabiyya*s, flip-flops, and *baladi*-looking attire are good enough reasons to stop what he thought to be the 'invading' public from the popular neighborhood of Sabtiya who, he claims, cause serious problems to the mall's maintenance. This public, according to the manager, often steals electric bulbs and supplies from the public toilets. They are the undesired "class D" while the mall only wants to "attract classes A and B."[8] The Nasr City malls are, however, not as posh as the Four Seasons' lavish mall, where few *flâneurs* would be found and where riffraff and groups of youngsters would clearly be unwelcome. But with time, some malls, like the Tal'at Harb and Bustan malls of downtown, have become largely *baladi* by attracting masses of night strollers.

The Atrium of the Tal'at Harb Mall (photograph by Mona Abaza).

Most if not all malls only rent their space to individual shops, with the exception of the Arkadia Mall where 90 percent of the shops are owned. The rent differs from one mall to another, because there are differences between *baladi* and chic malls (see Abaza 2001). While the World Trade Center has become a 'ghost mall,' the First Mall attached to the Four Seasons luxury hotel complex is today one of the poshest malls in town. However, with economic recession and the devaluation of the pound since January 2003, the purchasing power of many Egyptians has also declined and Egyptians can no longer shop there. However, they can certainly window-shop, which is free. These new spaces offer good ways for groups of friends to spend time, stroll in cool air in hot summers, ride up and down the escalators, and enjoy a sandwich of *ful* (broad beans) or chicken. The Tal'at Harb Mall, for example, is successful because it is filled with people until very late at night and its atrium has a mix of fast-food restaurants—such as the popular chain restaurant al-Tab'i that sells the best *ful* and *ta'miya* (falafel, the food of the poor) at a slightly inflated but still affordable price.

How to Spend Time in Polluted Cairo

The mall is much cleaner than the street . . . to a certain extent the client is finer than the one of the street. Manager of a shop in al-'Aqqad Mall.

Strolling, shopping, and hanging out at the Tal'at Harb Mall (photograph by Mona Abaza).

The client likes imported items—even if good-quality Egyptian items are available, the client prefers imported ones. Silvie, a shopkeeper in the City Center Mall.

The mall is controlled . . . but the street is not. . . . You find harag wa-marag *(noisy and frenetic, chaotic behavior) in the street.* Shopkeeper, al-'Aqqad Mall.

The street is always busy . . . it takes a lot of time to enter any shop . . . while here in the malls it is an agglomeration of varied shops. A forty-two-year-old engineer interviewed in al-'Aqqad Mall.

Outside the mall there are very popular shops and it is zahma *(packed with people) . . . but the mall is better and more secure than outside . . . the place is more refined . . . the people here have 'style.' . . . They are guaranteed clients.* Shopkeeper, al-'Aqqad Mall.

The mall is a good thing. It is a great place for youngsters. It is ordered. Ahmad 'Ali, nineteen years old, medical student from Tanta and frequent visitor to the Cairo Mall and Cairo Mall Giza.

The mall is secure. It offers work opportunities to young people, and it is better than the street. 'Ali al-Sayyed, engineer, Cairo Mall.

The mall is more refined and cleaner (arqa wa andaf) *than the street, even though the prices might be higher.* Muhammad 'Abdallah, a shopkeeper, Gregor, Cairo Mall Giza.

Most of the public's views about visiting and shopping at malls were astonishingly optimistic and positive. Many of them expressed satisfaction with the malls' tight security measures. In fact, security guards were appreciated and few people worried that these low-paid workers might be restricting their freedom or controlling them. Cairo is generally a safe town and one is secure whether walking in the streets or in a mall. But nobody seems to be bothered by the fact that in some malls the public is under twenty-four-hour video surveillance. The malls are popular, according to my informants, because they are more pleasant and cleaner than the chaotic street. The mall provides a feeling of 'elevation,' of being modern and protected from the outside world. For example, the Geneina Mall has become a tourist attraction for rural Egyptians. Ahmad 'Ali, one of the informants quoted above, told me that buses filled with visitors from the countryside often tour the mall and if one lives in Tanta, it is possible to come spend the day touring the malls and return in the evening.[9] Al-'Aqqad Mall organizes well-attended yearly fashion shows, and films and *musalsalat* (TV serials) are often filmed in this mall as if it was the best place to be in town. However, a paradox arises—on the one hand, almost all informants say that the mall is cleaner and protects strollers from the riffraff in the streets, that order and security prevail there, and that the mall is definitely more pleasant, even though expensive. On the other hand, they all also made statements like "The mall incorporates all levels and classes," or "The mall includes everything and is less exclusive and certainly cheaper than the club."[10] It is thus a restricted space, where if one comes from a popular background, a disguise is desired; but being less restrictive and controlled than private clubs, malls are attractive to youngsters. Once 'riffraff' or lower-class people are spotted by the security guards, however, they are in trouble.

Interviews revealed that although shops in all the malls in Cairo are failing financially due to high rents and the economic recession, many sales assistants insisted that it was better to work in a mall than elsewhere. What has to be taken into consideration is that the salaries of the sales staff in these malls start at LE150 and reach a maximum of LE450, certainly not even half of what a foreign domestic servant would earn. Although some of the sales assistants earn commissions as high as LE750, their salaries would be no higher if they were to work in shops outside of malls. Nevertheless, they seem to prefer working in the malls, despite their relatively modest wages, because their workplaces are cleaner than the street and more protected. They argue the public is better behaved since cameras are watching and security is all over, while the street is 'vulgar,' the air is polluted, and people are constantly rushing around and have bad manners. It was clear that even the higher prices in malls did not stop people from shopping, or at least browsing, since it was still a more 'civilized' and pleasant place.

For many, Cairo's pollution has become a major hindrance to window-shopping and strolling in the streets. The chaos of traffic makes it really difficult to walk. One salesman said, "The weather in Egypt has become very hot and humid and there is dust in the air—the weather is not consistent or predictable in Egypt." Thus, the financial success of a mall has much to do with the fact that many customers today prefer to shop in air conditioning, especially in the hot summers. To a European or an American, it seems odd that the malls' peak hours begin around 10 PM. Shops do not typically close before one or two o'clock in the morning. Coffeehouses are full of *shisha*-smoking patrons until long after midnight. Especially in summer, Egyptians turn into night owls. Most of the malls do not even open until late in the morning, around 11 AM. No one is astonished that beauty salons and hairdressers work until midnight in Geneina Mall.

The most fascinating point in the interviews, which were conducted in Arabic, is the overpowering intrusion of the English language to describe the malls, often accompanied by Arabic slang. Whether managers, the public, or shopkeepers, many answered our questions in Arabic but used English words. Many Egyptians today constantly insert English words into their speech (and this is evident in films, television serials, and talk shows). First of all, the word 'mall' has been Arabicized to *al-mol*, plural *al-molat*. The shops selling casual clothes, the most popular among youngsters, are called *mahallat kazual* (casual shops). In fact the word 'casual,' or *kajwal*, is used in Egyptian Arabic to mean informal dress or an informal situation. For example, one shopkeeper in the Cairo Mall describes the set of shops on his floor as specialized in *kajwal* dresses. Words such as 'shopping,' 'internet café,' 'coffee shop,' 'bowling,' 'billiards' (*bilyardu*), 'disco,' 'the underground,' 'sound systems,' 'décor,' and 'modern' have all intruded into the Egyptian dialect. The term 'all in one' was used in English to include leisure, shopping, walking, cinemas, and children's arcades by one manager in Nasr City when he was asked to describe what the concept of 'the mall' meant. Some informants often used the word 'style' in their descriptions of malls, which has been Arabicized also. Others speak of *istayl gidid* (new style), and *hay kilas* (high class), to describe the wealthier public that frequents malls compared to the street 'riffraff.' The names of shops are also frequently westernized, sometimes with incorrect spelling. While one can still find many Arabic names in malls and franchised brands like Lapidus, Adidas, or Mövenpick, one also finds foreign names like Bellini (men's wear), Dandy (men's wear), Wild (casual dresses), Sky Class (women's clothes), Fablos (women's clothes), La Reine (patisserie), Twiti Shoes, Diamond Canary (children's wear), Dream Café (coffeehouse), Lisa House (women's shoes and handbags), New Brand (casual clothes), Crazy House, Ted Lamond, Mix, Haidy, Fantasia, Frutti, Chance, Cadre (for picture frames), Western, BabyWorld (maternity clothes), Champion Women's Clothes, and Chico (children's toys). One interesting point to be made from my interviews is that the public was divided on the choice of Western or Arabic names. Some said that the name of the shop did not really matter, although there was a tendency among younger men to think that Western names were 'cool' and would attract more people (*al-asma' al-riwsha*, derived from *riwish*, a newly introduced word in Arabic, to define cool-looking, fashionable youngsters).

One can see that a new culture related to these spaces is emerging. It is not new to argue that the usage of foreign languages is a clear class marker but increasingly English words are becoming part of the Arabic Cairene dialect.[11] A broader population, across classes, is intermingling foreign words with Arabic.

Conclusion

It is obvious that there is an ambitious, brave new world in the development of new public spaces of consumption in and around Cairo. Many individuals from across Cairo and Egyptian society interact in these new malls, whether they are the maintenance workers and cleaners, the growing numbers of (often female) shoplifters, or the army of security guards.[12] Many of them have university degrees and/or migrate from the countryside. These basically low-income and poor young men and women are forced to work in sanitized dream spaces where they can only participate through 'voyeurism' and window-shopping. These spaces seem to raise expectations as well as to increase frustrations. Cairo is suffocating from cars, pollution, and chaotic planning. The few newly created gardens are walled off and inaccessible to the public under the excuse that Egyptians do not know how to keep public spaces clean. It is evident that public space is scarce in Cairo, while the American import—the mall—carries with it a fascination for those who embrace the new consumerist culture. Jean Baudrillard's analysis of consumption as collective, institutional behavior, and his critique of affluent society, aptly applies to the Egyptian case (Baudrillard 1998). Baudrillard argues that consumer culture ultimately leads to growth that produces both wealth and poverty at a parallel pace (Baudrillard 1998, 2). He further argues that waste is functional and provides short-term elusive satisfaction (Baudrillard 1998, 5). The inherent logic of consumption implies unequal abundance because "some have rightful access to the miracle, while others end up with the by-products of the miracle" (Baudrillard 1998, 60). Most importantly, it is the unlimited character of consumption, the infinite activated desires and the uncontrolled aspects, inherently contradictory to the notion of satisfaction, which are worth addressing (Baudrillard 1998, 61–62). In a society where 65 percent of the population is under the age of thirty, the public visibility of youth and youth culture has become obvious (CAPMAS 1996). However, young people's prospects are becoming increasingly restricted. Other than migrating, galvanizing desires without fulfillment will lead to an unhappy end. It is clear that social life in malls invites new reflection about 'socializing' and gendering space in Cairo. (See de Koning in this volume for an analysis of new gendered middle-class spaces in new coffeehouses designed along the Starbucks model.) It is most interesting to observe flirting youngsters strolling in groups, extended families going to cafés (the male family members sipping coffee while their wives are shopping), outings at McDonald's, or movie-going in these empires of consumption. Both 'nature' and 'the street' have been alienated if not destroyed. It appears that few Egyptians are conscious of the negative health effects of air conditioning and walled-off, monitored spaces. A critique of consumer culture among middle-class Egyptians is far from taking place.

Yet it is astonishing how quickly the recent phenomenon of 'dead malls,' common also in the United States, has spread. The World Trade Center, Wonderland, and the Bustan Center seem to belong to that category. Some malls, like the Tal'at Harb Mall, have been seized by banks after their owners failed to repay their loans. Nevertheless, why is it that more and more malls are still constructed? One explanation, rumored among the financial and real-estate community, is that mall construction is an excuse to launder money, but this is speculation and I have no concrete evidence to support it.

Semipublic spaces, such as the many new coffeehouses and shopping malls, are clearly outlets for youth. These are clean spaces where youth can socialize and simply circulate. The young men and women may still live in 'ashwa'iyat (slums, informal housing areas) but once in these walled-off, exclusive spaces, they can imitate a higher social status through their dress and mere presence in a mall. The spaces might encourage a feeling that one can participate in a better world, even if merely by window-shopping. These spaces of eternal leisure are meant to give citizens the illusory and ephemeral feeling that poverty can be erased.

Although malls seem to democratize public spaces through the fantasy that we can all mix together and be equals, malls are still exclusive and closely monitored spaces, from whence security guards frequently eject 'undesirables.' Today in Cairo the gated communities and the exclusive condominiums in Qattamiya Heights, Dreamland, Gardenia, or Beverly Hills, meant for the richest of the rich in Egypt, are similarly isolated, walled-off communities constructed in the desert. (See Denis in this volume for further details of these new luxury communities and the way in which they have changed Cairo's spatial and political geography.)

These malls symbolize the growing alliance between foreign capital, foreign expertise, imports, technology, and Egyptian capitalists. For instance, the World Trade Center was founded in 1990 through a joint venture supervised by the architectural firm Owings, Merrill & Skidmore from Chicago and Ali Nour el Din from Egypt. Orascom, one of the Sawiris family's most successful companies, has been associated with the construction of many malls. The

Yamama Center in Zamalek was built with Saudi funding, more precisely by Prince Bandar, much like the Ma'adi City Center—a large shopping complex including Carrefour and created by MAF, which also operates a series of malls in Dubai, Abu Dhabi, and Oman. (See Elsheshtawy, chapter 7, in this volume for further analysis of the Gulf influence on Cairo's commercial and residential development.) The Ma'adi Grand Mall was constructed by the Bitter Lakes for Habitation and Development Company, and was meant to be the largest center in the Middle East. The chief architect is Ahmad 'Azmi whose brother, Nabil 'Azmi, is a previous deputy chairman of both Osman Ahmad Osman (a huge construction firm) and the Suez Canal Bank, and is currently chief executive officer of Suez Insurance. The project's top eight investors represent 90 percent of its capital, and they are all members of the 'Azmi family (Rafaat 1998).

The recent flotation of the Egyptian pound during the month of January 2003 caused a decrease in the real consumption power of most Egyptians. Economic recession has led to job cuts for thousands in various sectors of the economy. In such a gloomy atmosphere, one wonders how the opening of the Carrefour mall, with a pompous celebration and masses of cars packed in the parking lot, could still occur. How far can we rely on window-shopping to appease unrealized dreams? Again, I have no answer.

Works Cited

Abaza, Mona. 2001. "Shopping Malls, Consumer Culture and the Reshaping of Public Space in Egypt." *Theory, Culture and Society* 18: 97–122.

_____. 2004a. "Advertising History." *Al-Ahram Weekly Online*, 1–7 July, <http://weekly.ahram.org.eg/2004/697/feature.htm> (30 July 2004).

_____. 2004b. "Brave New Mall." *Al-Ahram Weekly Online*, 16–22 September, <http://weekly.ahram.org.eg/2004/708/feature.htm> (2 October 2004).

'Abd al-Malek, Anouar. 1971. *Ägypten: Militärgesellschaft: das Armeeregime, die Linke und der Soziale Wandel unter Nasser.* Frankfurt: Suhrkamp Verlag.

Alaidy, Ahmed. 2006. *Being Abbas El Abd.* Translated by Humphrey Davies. Cairo: The American University in Cairo Press.

Ambriere, Francis. 1932. *La vie secrète des grands magasins.* Paris: Flammarion.

Backes, Nancy. 1997. "Reading the Shopping Mall City" *Journal of Popular Culture* 31 (3): 1–17.

Bauman, Zygmunt. "From Pilgrim to Tourist—or a Short History of Identity." In *Questions of Cultural Identity*, eds. S. Hall and P. Du Gay, 18–36. London: Sage.

Baudrillard, Jean. 1998. *The Consumer Society.* London: Sage.

Bayat, Assef. 1977. "Cairo's Poor: Dilemmas of survival and Solidarity." *Middle East Report* 202 (Winter): 2–8.

Bontemps, Maurice. 1894. *Du vol, les grands magasins et du vol a l'étalage, étude medico-légale.* Thesis, Faculté de medicine et de pharmacie de Lyon.

Central Agency for Public Mobilization and Statistics (CAPMAS). 1996. *The Egyptian Census.* Cairo: CAPMAS.

Denis, Eric. 1998. "*al-Takhtit al-hadari wa-al-numuw fi al-Qahira.*" In *al-Qahira fi lahzat tahawwul*, eds. Mustafa Kamel al-Sayyed and Assef Bayat, 61–72. Cairo: Center for the Study of Developing Countries, Cairo University.

"Dubai's Great Shopping Mall Race: The Majid al-Futtaim Group and Emaar Properties are Competing to Build Dubai's Best and Biggest Shopping Mall." *AME Info*, 12 February 2004, <*http://www.ameinfo.com/news/Detailed/34732.html*> (29 July 2004).

Featherstone, Mike. 1998. "The *Flaneur*, the City and the Virtual Public Life." *Urban Studies* 5 (5–6): 909–25.

Fishman, Robert. 1996. "Beyond Suburbia: The Rise of the Technoburb." In *The City Reader*, eds. Richard T. LeGates and Fredric Stout, 79. New York: Routledge.

Freitas, Ricardo Ferreira. 1996. *Centres commerciaux: îles urbaines de la post-modernité.* Paris: l' Harmattan.

Ghannam, Farha. 2002. *Remaking the Modern: Space, Relocation and the Politics of Identity.* Berkeley: University of California Press.

Jackson, Kenneth T. 2000. "The Drive-in Culture of Contemporary America." In *The City Reader*, eds. Richard T. LeGates and Frederic Stout, 67–76. New York: Routledge.

Miller, Daniel, Peter Jackson, Nigel Trift, Beverley Holbrook, and Michael Rowlands. 1998. *Shopping, Place and Identity.* London: Routledge.

Mitchell, Donna. 2002. "Cairo's Wealthy Won't Need to Leave the City to Shop," *Shopping Centers Today*, May, <*http://www.icsc.org/srch/sct/sct0502/page160.html*> (29 July 2004).

Mitchell, Timothy. 1999. "Dreamland: The Neolibralism of Your Desire." *Middle East Report* 210 (Spring): 28–33.

Morris, Meaghan. 1993. "Things to Do with Shopping Centers." In *The Cultural Studies Reader*, ed. S. During, 391–409. London and New York: Routledge.

Mostafa, Hadia. 2003. "Retail goes Wild." *Business Today*, June: 61.

Rakha, Yusif. 2003. "On Alternative Tracks," *Al Ahram Weekly Online*, 18–24 December, <*http://weekly.ahram.org.eg/2003/669/bo21.htm*> (27 July 2004).

Rafaat, Samir. 1998. "Ma'adi Grand Mall." *Egy.com*, 19 February, <*http://www.egy.com/landmarks/98-02-19.shtml*> (27 July 2004).

United Nations Development Program (UNDP). 2003. *Taqrir al-tanmiya al-insaniya al-ʿArabiya lil-ʿam*. New York: United Nations Development Program.

Notes

1   Ahmed Alaidy. 2006. *Being Abbas El Abd*. Translated by Humphrey Davies. Cairo: The American University in Cairo Press.

2   I wish to thank Ahmad Yusif and Ahmad al-Shirbini for being part of the research team. This article should be read as an extension to my previous articles (Abaza 2001; 2004a; 2004b).

3   The Egyptian subsidiary MAF Misr intends to invest $440 million in Egypt by the year 2011. MAF has so far allocated one billion Egyptian pounds to Carrefour (Rashdan 2003). MAF has experienced amazing growth in recent years through retail and shopping-center activity which began with opening the largest mall in Dubai, Deira City. They also have the exclusive franchise for Carrefour in the Gulf. The group owns malls in the neighboring emirates of ʿAjman and Sharjah, and in Muscat (see "Dubai's Great Shopping Mall Race . . ." 2004).

4   The printing house vanished due to a fire that was possibly arson. Many public-sector factories and companies that were no longer the key motor of Egyptian development in the 1970s were similarly torched. Arson was one excuse to declare such companies bankrupt and sell them to the private sector, from which high-level government officials profited.

5   In al-Bustan Mall, for example, an ad hung saying: "Wanted: security guards, to be paid LE120 per month."

6   According to John Sfakianakis, a specialist on business elites in the Middle East, in the post–11 September world many Saudi millionaires have encountered tighter controls on their business activities in the United States and Europe. These businesspeople had to redirect their investments to the Arab countries like Egypt, where they evidently have more freedom of action. Personal communication with John Sfakianakis. 20 March 2005.

7   In spite of the fact that Gulf Arabs, like Egyptian *baladi* people, wear long robes or *gallabiyyas*, no security guards would stop them from entering a mall because this social class is immediately spotted.

8   Interview with the general manager of Arkadia, 19 February 2005.

9   In fact Ahmad himself comes frequently to Cairo from Tanta just to shop and wander around, his favorite pastime. Thus, he had broad knowledge about the price differentials among the various Cairene malls.

10   Many people eat or socialize in Cairo's private country clubs, sports clubs, or clubs for people in a profession or government service (these latter are partially subsidized by the state).

11   The Arab Human Development Report of 2003 mentioned that the Arabic language is facing a serious crisis due to its mediocre pedagogy in the schools. Classical Arabic is facing a serious threat since many government officials give priority to foreign private schools, which concentrate on teaching foreign

languages at the expense of Arabic. The result is that many young students end up with a very low level of Arabic, which seems to be no longer in demand in modern sectors of the economy like banking, advertising, management, and business. The report also mentions that there are few published works translated from English into Arabic (UNDP 2003, 120–25).

12 Shoplifting was a frequent phenomenon in the nineteenth-century *grands magasins*. It led to a prolific literature about the psychic and neurotic effects of kleptomania and shoplifting on women (Bontemps 1894; Ambriere 1932).

6 Café Latte and Caesar Salad

Cosmopolitan Belonging in Cairo's Coffee Shops[1]

Anouk de Koning

On an ordinary weekday in summer 2004, I am meeting Dina and Maysa at the Retro Café in Muhandisin for an interview about coffee shops.[2] In the course of my research, I had become thoroughly familiar with up-market coffee shops like Retro, which have become an essential part of the daily routines of almost all my upper-middle-class friends and acquaintances.[3] Upscale coffee shops like Retro have changed the urban fabric of affluent neighborhoods; enjoying a café latte or a ceasar salad in one of these coffee shops has become part of the semidaily routine of many young and relatively affluent Cairenes. These are 'coffee shops,' always referred to in English, never to be confused with *ahawi baladi*, the male-dominated sidewalk cafés for which Cairo is famous. The diverse coffee shops have become spatial orientation points, as well as social markers of a certain belonging and self-evident normality. A new and distinctive leisure culture has emerged in and around these coffee shops, centered around, but not exclusive to, young single affluent professionals like Dina and Maysa. Yet, coffee shops are a relatively recent phenomenon. They started appearing in the late 1990s in central affluent districts like Zamalek and Muhandisin, as well as in the outlying Heliopolis and Ma'adi. New coffee shops open regularly, crowding certain streets and turning formerly residential areas into lively downtown hot spots.

I find Dina sharing a table with our mutual friend, Maysa. These single women in their early thirties, primarily employed in the upper echelons of the economy, are part of a new professional upper middle class that is marked by its global connections and aspirations. Like the other women at Retro, they wear tight cotton pants or jeans, and equally tight shirts, which nonetheless do heed the bottom line of public decency, covering everything but the arms. The small café, with its art, earth tones, and modern wooden furniture, is designed to give a contemporary, yet warm sense of comfort and home. Jazzy music, including global hits by the Buena Vista Social Club and Norah Jones, provide the finishing touch.

Beano's Café, Zamalek (left), and Trianon, Muhandisin (right) (photographs by Anouk de Koning).

Before we launch into our discussion, we choose some salads and sandwiches from Retro's extensive offer of "creative food" (Dina's term) and place our order with one of the young waiters dressed in the Retro uniform: black jeans and a blue polo shirt that carries the name of the café. Our discussion soon converges on the extent to which coffee shops provide new public spaces, especially for women. "Coffee shops were able to gather girls from their houses and the club," they say. "Before, we did not have places where we could spend time after work." The overwhelming presence of women in most upscale coffee shops is one of the striking features of the social life that unfolds in them. Unchaperoned mixed-gender socializing and the presence of single women in leisure venues are issues generally surrounded by suspicions and restrictions. Yet in these upscale coffee shops, veiled and nonveiled women often constitute more than half of the customers. Many single professional women like Dina and Maysa have taken to spending much of their time in coffee shops like Retro.

Half an hour after we start, our interview is interrupted when two other friends join our table, and a constant stream of other friends and acquaintances arrive and are enthusiastically greeted. Retro's social life has swung into full gear now that the workday has ended. Our conversation veers to the playful mix of tall tales and entertaining news typical of coffee-shop socializing. The relatively small Retro Café has a large number of regular visitors, like Maysa's *shilla* (group of friends, pl. *shilal*), who come to the coffee shop on a semidaily basis to meet up with friends and acquaintances. Dina, who knows the names of all the waiters and is friendly with the owner of the coffee shop, explains that Retro is much like her second home.

Spectra Café is another popular venue, located only a few streets away, behind the popular Mustafa Mahmud Mosque in the heart of Muhandisin. It is stylishly decorated with simple, modern wooden furniture and is divided into two parts. The quiet front part offers seating to small groups; the back room offers space to larger groups in American diner style, with wooden benches that seat six people around a table. A number of television sets soundlessly screen the music videos featured on one of the new Arabic music channels, Melody Hits or Lebanese MTV, while similar Arabic and Western pop hits provide the musical background.

One evening I had an appointment with Ahmad, a professional in his mid-twenties, to talk about coffee shops. When I arrived, he had already occupied a table in the back room, with his sister, a female friend and his two cousins. The space was packed with mixed-gender *shilal* of young people. When I sat down next to one of Ahmad's cousins, everybody turned silent. Ahmad's sister came to me and asked me to move further away from my neighbor. He is a very religious person, she said, and did not feel comfortable with me sitting next to him.

When I was alone with Ahmad and his female friend, we had the chance to talk about coffee shops. He explained that he liked Spectra because of the level of its clientele, "clean, respectable people," its classy style, and the high quality of its food and service. Ahmad said that it used to be shameful for young people to hang out in cafés. Now, even if their dress had become more modest, there is more freedom.[4] The public at Spectra seemed to confirm his observations. Spectra differed from the Retro Café because it attracted a relatively large number of veiled patrons. Ahmad's female friend, who covered her hair with a scarf, gaily told me that the *higab* was simply obligatory for Muslims. Yet that did not mean that her lifestyle had to be that different from her female peers who did not wear it. Later on, she drew my attention to a music video that zoomed in on three long-legged, sexily clad girls dancing seductively to please their viewing audiences. "My favorite," she said.

The transnational formula of the coffee shop inserts itself in locally significant and often highly contested domains of leisure and sociability, urban public life, and public space. In Cairo, familiarity with the significant outside *(barra)* and the adoption of explicitly cosmopolitan styles has long been a marker of elite status. Mixed-gender socializing in leisure venues is one of the hallmarks of such distinctive cosmopolitan lifestyles (Armbrust 1999). However, it is also the source of anxiety and contestation. In this chapter, I explore the way in which these upscale coffee shops create spaces of cosmopolitan belonging. These spaces reflect class distinctions in modern Cairo and are illustrative of the way mixed-gender sociability norms, particularly in the upper middle class, begun to change.

Segmented Landscapes

At the beginning of this new century, Cairo is marked by a high degree of segmentation in the spheres of both production and consumption. Most Cairenes must consume the products and services provided by informal markets of consumption and leisure that accommodate their limited buying power. At a time of rising market costs, decreasing social benefits, high levels of unemployment, and sustained periods of economic recession, average Cairenes must either seek out what social benefits are available from the subsidized system or purchase goods on the informal market, often inexpensive Chinese imports. Simultaneously, however, the urban landscape speaks of the existence of an 'other' Cairo that began its boom under the Infitah (the open-door economic policy initiated in the mid-1970s), which encouraged foreign imports and foreign investment in Egypt. This 'other' Cairo grew significantly during the 1990s period of structural adjustment, neoliberal policies, and the search for integration into global markets (Mitchell 2002). While most Cairenes have been confronted with steadily declining real wages and the withdrawal of a whole range of government subsidies and services making life increasingly expensive, Cairo has also seen the rise of a new bourgeoisie, a relatively affluent professional upper-middle class. Amidst rampant youth unemployment among university graduates and extremely low starting wages, young professionals like Dina and Maysa find work in a small, yet significant internationally oriented top segment of the labor market (Amer 2002; Tourné 2003). In this niche of the labor market, wages tend to be three to five times higher than those paid in similar occupations in the 'less-modern' sectors of the formal economy, including the large public sector and civil service.

The signs of a turn to neoliberalism and the global market are inscribed in the landscape of Cairo. Five-star hotels and shiny office buildings rise up in new business districts. Condominiums are built in the desert around Cairo, the Cairene streets are filled with luxury cars, and the upscale area of Muhandisin is steadily replacing Wust al-Balad (literally: center of town) as the city center for those who can afford it (cf. Armbrust 1998, 417–20; Kuppinger 2004; Denis 1997; and all three in this volume). Affluent districts like Zamalek, Muhandisin, Heliopolis, and Ma'adi cater to Cairo's economically comfortable groups. An ever-growing number of private schools, institutes, and universities, as well as private hospitals, cater to families that can afford to leave the increasingly decrepit government services behind. In these same districts, spotlessly clean supermarkets like Metro and Alfa Market offer the commodities necessary for an upscale lifestyle. (See Mona Abaza's chapter in this volume for a discussion of the upscale malls in Nasr City.) Here one can find fancy clothing shops that are not stuffed full to economize space, as is common in the no-longer-fashionable downtown shops. Rather, the newer, upscale shops present their products as pieces of art that exude a promise of cosmopolitan elegance. All these upscale venues are marked by the cosmopolitan references of the products and services on offer—from café latte to Italian furniture and American diplomas—as well as their comparatively steep prices. Coffee shops that cater to an upper-middle-class public will charge over LE5 per drink (excluding 5 percent taxes and 12 percent service charges) and most require a minimum purchase. Compare these prices with the LE0.50 to LE1 for a Turkish coffee or a soft drink in an 'ahwa baladi (the Egyptian pound was officially equivalent to $0.25 at the start of 2002 and $0.20 at its end).

Transnational Landscapes of Leisure

Coffee shops have taken up new positions within a multitude of local geographies of leisure all over the world. The taste for cappuccino has become a potent global sign, signifying gentrified tastes in highly diverse local taxonomies of cultural distinction. While the kind of spaces coffee shops constitute within local geographies of leisure, and the kind of distinction conferred by the taste for café latte, are eminently local matters, they lend much of their signifying potential, prestige, and distinctiveness to their embeddedness in global flows (Appadurai 1990; Guano 2002).

Though most coffee shops have local owners, they are clearly modelled on American counterparts, including their food and beverages.[5] Several interviews with owners and staff suggest that initially, coffee shops were set up by relatively young Cairenes with significant experience in the West. As I was told, coffee shops represent relatively cheap, yet highly lucrative projects, an analysis that seems to be confirmed by the rapid spread of coffee shops in recent years. Through trial and error, the formulas of the two biggest coffee-shop chains, Roastery and Cilantro, changed from small outlets specializing respectively in luxury coffee and delicatessen to their present format, with more comfortable and luxurious seating and a broader menu of dishes and nonalcoholic drinks to meet local conceptions of an outing. (See Battesti in this volume for further understanding of Egyptian outings among the popular classes at the Giza Zoo and other public spaces.)

Some people liked the homey, but slightly kitschy interior of the different Roastery branches. Others preferred the fresh modernism of Cilantro, all stainless steel and metallic shine, with cubistic leather pillows in primary colours; or the stylish and hip, but warm earthy coziness of Retro Café. Despite differences in style, menu, and public, upscale coffee shops form a clearly recognizable segment of leisure venues that are set apart from other establishments also offering food and beverages. There seem to be implicit laws and minimum standards that must be observed in order to attract a certain clientele and maintain an upscale status. Well-trained, polite, young, and fashionable staff and waiters are of prime importance, as are style and suggestions of First-World belonging. These spaces are unmistakably set apart and distanced from other venues and the immediate surroundings by their Western style, immaculate cleanliness, and the strikingly perfect maintenance of the interior, as well as the air conditioning that generates a constant comfortable climate. They have become part of detailed, but shifting mappings of places and people. Some cater to the hip in-crowd, others to a younger public. Some are considered proper, whereas others are reputed to host a somewhat more risqué public. As I will argue below, such mappings reflect not only preferences for this or that style or a differentiation along age lines, but also significant concerns over gendered notions of propriety, principally female respectability.

Most coffee shops carry English names, invariably written in Latin letters. English is prominent on the menus, ranging from a simple English list (with typos) to an exclusively English menu that describes the food in baroque terms. These choices point to the exclusive clientele coffee-shop owners wish to reach. The use of English and the claim of direct or indirect links to North American counterparts bestow a sense of cosmopolitanism and exclusivity on the place, its food and beverages, and its clientele. Smith argues that a taste for the specialty coffees in U.S. coffee shops constitutes a new form of easily accessible cultural capital (1996). In Cairo, coffee shops introduce a major contradiction between foreign food and drink and local ones. The person who has developed a taste for anything from a cappuccino to a double espresso stands in contrast to those people who keep to their *ahwa mazbuut* or *ziyada* (Turkish coffee with medium or extra sugar). Distinction lies in this case not in the knowledge of, and taste for, the specifics of specialty coffees, but in the cosmopolitan referents of food and drinks, the venue and its clientele. In line with the menu, the common language used in coffee shops is the hybrid Arabic-English argot that is characteristic of young upper-middle-class professionals (see Abaza in this volume for additional discussion of this phenomenon). It blends in nicely with the globally inspired decoration and menu.

The Mint Café in Muhandisin (photograph by Anouk de Koning).

The American referents of coffee shops and restaurants indicate the extent to which these spaces are tied into larger transnational geographies of power. Local configurations of cosmopolitan belonging have a long history in Cairo. In earlier times, Europe, and particularly France, was the measure of all things elegant, and many of the shops catering to the upper-middle classes of the time carried French names and sold the latest French products and fashions (Abaza 2001). Then-exclusive establishments like Groppi or À l'Américain similarly conveyed a sense of cosmopolitan belonging and local distinction with Paris as their golden standard. France has ceased to be the measure of sophistication and cosmopolitanism. "Nowadays," as one coffee-shop manager says, "Middle-Eastern youth want an American style."

The use of English in names and menus, as well as in social interaction, signals that coffee shops do not only create new commonalities, they also divide. While creating a sense of cosmopolitan belonging, they simultaneously distance themselves from the surrounding spaces and the majority of the Cairenes who "don't have a language" *(ma-'andahumsh lugha)*, i.e., do not speak a European language. In present-day Cairo, the 'possession' of foreign languages, particularly English, has come to denote a major split within society. It divides the educated middle class between those 'with' and those 'without' language. Those who have attended *madaris lughat* (language schools) and speak their languages fluently are generally born and bred in the 'better' families and can look forward to working in the upper segments of the labour market (De Koning 2005; Haeri 1997). These divisions are reproduced in the urban landscape through spaces like the coffee shop.

"It is as if you are not in Egypt," said a woman in her thirties when she enthusiastically recommended a bar in Muhandisin. She frequently visits Europe, so she knew what she was talking about. The bar could indeed have been situated in hip London, Paris, or New York, with its minimal interior design, blue leather benches, soft lights, and range of cocktails on offer. While the occasional bar or café still arouses such feelings of surprise and delight at the presence of a hip and First-World establishment in all-too-familiar Cairo, the opposite has actually become commonplace. Spaces like the coffee shop, the upscale supermarkets that offer all products for cosmopolitan preferences, or the exclusive malls hardly ever elicited awe or excited comments from the young upper-middle-class Cairenes I encountered in the course of my research. In the span of a few years, these have become the self-evident spaces where upper-middle-class public life unfolds. Coffee shops like Retro, Beano's, and Tabasco suggest membership in an imaginary cosmopolitan space that is local, Cairene, and Egyptian, yet part of wider First-World circuits and publics. At the same time, they are the venues for local class projects, in which conspicuously cosmopolitan references indicate belonging in Cairo's upscale circuits of production and consumption.

New Spaces, New Sociabilities

The mixed-gender sociabilities and performances of professional upper-middle-class identities that are at home in Cairo's coffee shops appear effortless and self-evident. Yet these privileged sociabilities—the mixing of young single men and women—do not present an uncontested norm. Leisure practices of the elite have served as some of the most evocative symbols of both modernity *and* depravity, depending on the convictions of the commentator. The central contentious issue with respect to such elite leisure practices is their mixed-gender character: the mingling of women and men in public spaces (Armbrust 1999). Coffee shops have been able to attract a wider, and slightly less exclusive, mixed-gender public. These mixed-gender sociabilities are remarkable, given the problematic nature of mixed-gender socializing outside of the purview of the family and the usual restrictions that surround the presence of single women in public leisure venues without the functional rationale of study and work. (See Armbrust in this volume for descriptions of gender norms, young people, and the popular activity of film spectatorship.)

In comparison to coffee shops in Western settings that are marked for limited activities and times of the day, Cairene coffee shops host an encompassing leisure culture comparable to night-time leisure culture in Western cities. These are *the* spaces, and for many upper-middle-class women, the only spaces, where social life outside of the family takes place. On Thursday night some coffee shops become as crowded as popular bars in Western cities on Saturday night. *Shilal* of young people meet, show off the latest fashions, and engage in a low-key flirting. Within upper-middle-class circles, coffee shops have by and large succeeded in introducing a First-World feel, while avoiding more damning associations with immoral Western night-time leisure. The absence of alcohol and the specific class and gender markers inherent in the transnational formula help define the coffee shop as a civilized and distinctive space that is marked as safe for women and decent mixed-gender sociability.

These gatherings usually last until 10 o'clock or 11 o'clock at night, the time when many single women are expected at home. As I was jokingly told,

Woman in a Nasr City café (photograph by Jean Pierre Ribière).

"We all have *shibshib* [slippers] at home." This common expression conjures up an image of angry parents waiting for their child to come home, slippers in hand, ready to beat the transgressor for disregarding her curfew. Familial supervision is an important feature in the lives of single upper-middle-class women who, almost without exception, live with their families. Familial responsibility and accountability for a single woman's behavior does not cease when she becomes adult or financially independent. Many young women told me that nighttime deadlines are enforced in order to protect the reputation of the family in front of the neighbors. More generally, such censorship is generally taken to be a fundamental part of familial responsibility to keep a daughter from going astray, thereby protecting her reputation and future (Macleod 1991; Abaza 2001; Ghannam 2002).

Whereas men have somewhat more manoeuvring space in choosing the places where they spend their leisure time, this is not the case for young women. The presence of women in both professional and social public life has become critical to upper-middle-class lifestyles, yet it is a fragile one, lived out in closed class-homogeneous spaces, with respectability and protection being the *sine qua non* of their ventures into public space. The trajectories of the young upper-middle-class women I came to know in Cairo were invariably based on class maps; places that are safe for women are classy places. It is only in these places that these women can be *bi-rahithum* (at ease), dress and socialize as they like, without being annoyed or being seen as disreputable.

In coffee shops, high prices and/or a minimum charge keep out those who do not belong to the 'comfortable' class. Such social selectiveness is crucial to the image of a coffee shop. All guests are assumed to be of a similar 'cultural level,' observing a shared code of sociability and decency. Many visitors would not want to sit in and be seen in a place populated by *bi'a*, a derogatory term for those of a 'lower social level' with their unfashionable, cheap taste. Economic controls are often augmented by an entry policy. One coffee-shop manager clearly considered such selectivity of utmost importance when he stated, "We have a door policy because we don't want *unqualified guests*." He explained that by "unqualified" he meant young people who were poorly dressed or appeared to be flirtatious or noisy "troublemakers." The constant fear of attracting those of a lower social level is not only based on the importance of guarding the class markers of a place, but is also stirred by the conviction that the riffraff might not abide by the implicit rules of gendered sociability. Young men, overwhelmed by the availability of young women, might flirt or harass customers, and some young women might come to pick up wealthy regulars. These fears echo assumptions about other, less-elitist leisure spaces with a mixed-gender public, which are commonly thought to be marketplaces for easy relationships involving some kind of exchange of money. The social exclusivity of coffee shops creates a semblance of community and creates hegemony of an upscale normality, comprised of particular class codes of sociability and intergender behavior. In such a venue, one is afraid to overstep the boundary of hegemonic sociality that is associated with upscale publics. The class markers of the venue and its clientele in turn define these mixed-gender sociabilities, the presence of young single women, as well as the relatively 'naked' outfits—a *mini-jib* (short skirt), *budi* (body-tight shirt), or *cut* (sleeveless shirt)—as part of a class normality and therefore respectable.

Yet even within the spaces of the coffee shop, the intermingling of single young men and women—and concomitant modes of femininity—are not as normal or uncontested as they appear to be on first glance. Reading between the lines of chatter and normative performances in coffee shops, one notices a constant concern and anxiety over propriety and respectability. Whereas the female coffee-shop patrons I know condone most coffee shops that are clearly upscale and classy, they do monitor these spaces for possible breaches of propriety and respectability. During spring 2002, the recently opened Retro Café was the talk of the town in the different upper-middle-class circles in which I moved. Whereas other coffee shops and restaurants created islands of privacy where already existing *shilal* could socialize, the design of the Retro Café, with a long table and a comfortable common sitting area, allowed for more chance encounters. After a few visits, Hala, a single woman in her late twenties and an avid coffee-shop patron, told me that she stopped visiting this specific coffee shop. As she said, "This place attracts girls looking for relationships. Did you see how they crawl up to each other?" Continuing to frequent this place would put her in an awkward situation. What about the others who might see her there? Would they think she is also *that* outgoing, "easy," and, by implication, less than respectable?

Hala shared these concerns about respectability with many other young single women. The sexual reputation of a young woman is of vital importance for her position in society and her chances of future marriage, as well as her family's reputation. These reputations are the stock subject of whispered gossip and constant concern. Coffee-shop discussions often playfully touch on issues of respectability and virtue, especially in mixed-gender groups. The frequency of comments about the morality and codes implied in meetings with male friends, or, for example, swimming in a bathing suit, are striking, as is their intentionally public character. These topics are brought up in the presence of male friends and acquaintances to publicly illustrate concern over respectability, in case these men might think that by virtue of being present in the mixed-gender leisure space of a coffee shop, the women might be just a little too *available.*

Configurations of Closeness and Distance

The constitution of a local cosmopolitan community of coffee-shop-going young professionals redraws maps of familiarity and belonging. Cosmopolitan capital is highly valued cultural capital that opens doors to the best professional jobs and social circles and confirms that one belongs to a Cairo of relative affluence, ease, and cosmopolitan elegance. Coffee shops are part of larger upscale circuits of products, services, and venues that have become seemingly autarkic realities within the city. While those immediately below in terms of cultural and economic capital provide the most concrete points of contrast, Cairo's other spaces and people become a lurking unknown and almost unreal constitutive outside. Fear, avoidance, concern, and compassion can all be part of attitudes toward this 'outside.' Whether positive or negative, such attitudes invariably imply a momentous unfamiliarity and distance. The fellow Cairene who is watching your car parked next door to that nice restaurant seems far removed from your cappuccino enjoyment, an experience you, in contrast, share with millions of other people all over the world. Communalities of cosmopolitan belonging come with their counterparts of distance, and increasingly they reconstitute all other spaces of the urban landscape into a lurking unfamiliar unreal.

Works Cited

Abaza, Mona. 2001. "Shopping Malls, Consumer Culture and the Reshaping of Public Space in Egypt." *Theory, Culture & Society* 18 (5): 97–122.

Amer, Mona. 2002. "Youth Labor Market Trajectories: A Comparison of the 1980s and 1990s." In *The Egyptian Labor Market in an Era of Reform*, ed. Ragui Assaad, 233–57. Cairo and New York: The American University in Cairo Press.

Appadurai, Arjun. 1990. "Disjuncture and Difference in the Global Cultural Economy." *Public Culture* 2 (2): 244–55.

Armbrust, Walter. 1998. "When the Lights Go Down in Cairo: Cinema as Secular Ritual." *Visual Anthropology* 10 (2–4): 413–42.

———. 1999. "Bourgeois Leisure and Egyptian Media Fantasies." In *New Media in the Muslim World: the Emerging Public Sphere*, eds. Dale F. Eickelman and Jon W. Anderson, 106–32. Bloomington: Indiana University Press.

Denis, Eric. 1997. "Urban Planning and Growth in Cairo." *Middle East Report* (Winter): 7–12.

Ghannam, Farha. 2002. *Remaking the Modern in a Global Cairo: Space, Relocation, and the Politics of Identity.* Berkeley: University of California Press.

Guano, Emanuela. 2002. "Spectacles of Modernity: Transnational Imagination and Local Hegemonies, Neoliberal Buenos Aires." *Cultural Anthropology* 17 (2), 181–209.

Haeri, Niloofar. 1997. "The Reproduction of Symbolic Capital: Language, State and Class in Egypt." *Current Anthropology* 38 (5): 795–816.

de Koning, Anouk. 2005. *Global Dreams: Space, Class and Gender in Middle-Class Cairo.* Ph.D. thesis, University of Amsterdam.

Kuppinger, Petra. 2004. "Exclusive Greenery: New Gated Communities in Cairo." *City & Society* 16 (2): 35–61.

MacLeod, Arlene Elowe. 1991. *Accommodating Protest: Working Women, the New Veiling, and Change in Cairo.* New York: Columbia University Press.

Mitchell, Timothy. 2002. *The Rule of Experts: Egypt, Techno-Politics, Modernity.* Berkeley: University of California Press.

Smith, Michael D. 1996. "The Empire Filters Back: Consumption, Production and the Politics of Starbucks Coffee." *Urban Geography* 17 (6): 502–25.

Tourné, Karine. 2003. "Figures of Youth in Egypt: The Young Graduates Between Visibility and Illegitimacy." Paper presented at the Fourth Mediterranean Social and Political Research Meeting, 19–23 March.

Notes

1   This contribution is an abridged version of a longer chapter of my dissertation on the changing sociocultural landscape of middle-class Cairo under conditions of neoliberal policies and a search for global inclusion (see de Koning 2005). This article has profited much from a follow-up research trip in 2004 that was financially supported by the Netherlands Organization for Scientific Research (NWO). I am indebted to Yatun Sastramidjaja and the editors for their insightful comments on earlier versions of this chapter.

2   I have changed the names of the people who appear in this chapter.

3   Research for my Ph.D. thesis was carried out from September 2001 through February 2003, complemented by a shorter stay in 2004.

4   In her discussion of malls, Mona Abaza similarly observes that the "Islamization of public space in the 1990s coincides with survival strategies taking the form of a 'relaxation of norms' among youth, within an Islamic frame of reference" (2001, 118).

5   In contrast, a number of restaurants that cater to the same young, affluent public, like T.G.I. Friday's and Chili's, are franchises of North American chains.

7

From Dubai to Cairo

Competing Global Cities, Models, and Shifting Centers of Influence?

Yasser Elsheshtawy

For decades it was the big, central Arab powers that set the tone for the Arab world and led innovation. But today the region is being led from the outer edges. It's the little guys that are doing the most interesting stuff, and it's the big guys that will be left behind if they don't wake up.

Thomas Friedman, "The Fast Eat the Slow" (*New York Times*, 2 February 2001)

A prominent *New York Times* journalist recently argued that the direction of influence in the Arab world has shifted from the traditional centers of Cairo, Baghdad, and Damascus to states in the periphery. According to the author these states—those in the Arab Gulf among them—are the most innovative and forward looking. A variety of events and projects are cited as evidence. While the political motives behind such proclamations are questionable it nevertheless raises interesting questions: do these new 'post-traditional' environments exert an influence on the traditional centers of the Middle East? What are the urban and spatial manifestations of such an influence (if they exists)? Should this influence be construed as one-sided or is it part of a larger global network in which influences occur on multiple levels and display numerous directions (rather than the naïve one-sided direction emphasized by the journalist)?

Using this argument as a starting point, this chapter sets out to investigate the influence of the glittering United Arab Emirates city of Dubai, an emerging global player, on Cairo. Traditionally, Cairo had a strong cultural, social, and architectural influence on the Arab world, yet this influence is now diminishing. A series of projects have emerged that respond to Dubai's new prominence. They include: the Smart Village Project (a copy of Dubai Internet City); Ma'adi City Center (a replica of Dubai City Center, a retail chain); and the various gated communities emerging in New Cairo, which are an echo of similar ventures in Dubai. These parallels do exist and in many instances references are made directly to Dubai.

While these projects and events do 'work' in places like Dubai that are not restrained or restricted—in essence a *tabula rasa* allowing for experimentation and a response to global conditions—their appropriateness in a 'traditional' city such as Cairo is questionable. These new projects are created at the periphery and seem to be detached and disconnected from any surrounding reality. While characteristic of all global cities, they are acquiring acute (and some might say amusing) dimensions in Cairo. It is interesting to observe however, that Cairo in its drive to become a global city is apparently drawing inspiration and precedents from a post-traditional center such as Dubai, which in turn is responding to, and is influenced by, larger global conditions and other global cities. This raises the issue of identity. This chapter hopes to tackle this by arguing that in a post-global world the concept of identity has been challenged; it is a changing, fluid, and ambiguous construct. Examining these projects would throw some light on changing notions of Egyptian identity in which its own heritage (in its Muslim and pharaonic incarnations) as well as those of others (Dubai's, for example) are used as 'branding' devices to attract multinationals and in turn 'globalize.' It is assumed that this will be followed by prosperity and happiness (questionable as that may be). In discussing these influences, this chapter will first explore the construct of the global city and the emergence of a network of cities. This will then be followed by an analysis of the case studies noted above, as an example of a perceived reversal of influence which will entail an inquiry into their compatibility (or lack thereof) within an Egyptian context. The relevance of such comparative studies in the context of the post-global/tradition discourse, using the framework outlined in this abstract, will conclude the chapter.

Theoretical Framework: Global Cities and Networks

As a result of globalizing processes many scholars have coined the term "global city" to indicate the emergence of a new type of city with certain distinctive characteristics that can be found throughout the world. In particular the relevancy of the nation-state is questioned—in that respect city governments are emerging as the centers of the new global economy. Transactions occur between multinational corporations, financial centers, and cities. However, it is noted that the nation-state still has a role to play, albeit through a restructuring process involving a move into supranational levels (the European Union or the Gulf Cooperative Council, for example). But cities are assuming a powerful role, and as a result of such processes they are increasingly being viewed as a product that needs to be marketed. These marketing efforts involve attracting headquarters or regional branches of international companies and the staging of 'mega-events.' Other projects include luxury housing, dining establishments, and entertainment amenities to attract the professional personnel required to operate these global activities. Urban projects, such as trade centers, conference centers, and hotels, provide a catalyst for further encouraging investment and tourism. Architecture in many instances is used to create eye-catching impressions—the Guggenheim museum in Bilbao is an example (UN-Habitat 2001). Such projects are the means to revitalize an otherwise stagnant city—a process sometimes called "the Bilbao effect."

As a result of all this some have noted that a dual city is emerging in which social polarization is becoming a dominant feature. The work of Saskia Sassen, is perhaps representative of such a viewpoint (2001). Due to the presence of these high-profile projects there is an influx of a highly skilled, and highly paid, workforce. To maintain and service such activities, however, low-wage employees are needed who form the backbone of corporate and financial activities. Thus, a geographical/spatial division occurs in which there are areas with a high concentration of the poor in contrast to enclaves housing the very rich. Furthermore, whether or not there is a rub-off effect on local industries has been questioned by research. Needless to say such disparities provoke "resentment, social instability and conflict" (UN-Habitat 2001, 30). In other words these megaprojects do not necessarily benefit most of the cities' residents since they are geared to a certain class (for further analysis of these debates, see Vignal and Denis in this volume).

One of the most visible aspects of globalizing cities is what has been sometimes described as the "quartering of urban space" due to a sharper division between rich and poor. This quartering manifests itself in the presence of residential cities—the most distinctive of these is the enclave or 'citadel.'

These are "areas that can be considered as protected enclaves of the rich, the representatives of an extremely mobile top, operating at a more global level than ever before . . . [they] generally consist of expensive apartments in favorable locations" (Marcuse and van Kempen 2000). Examples of these citadels are gated communities and private, high-rise condominiums with heavy security. In simple terms it is an effort to "wall some in and keep others out" (Marcuse and van Kempen 2000, 30).

These developments have prompted some such as Castells to note that there is a new spatial logic in these global cities called "space of flows" contrasted with traditional forms of urbanism termed "space of places" (1997). Concentration of high-level services occurs in a few nodal centers. He notes that "it is a process that connects advanced services, producer centers, and markets in a global network with different intensity . . . depending upon the relative importance of the activities located in each area vis-à-vis the global network" (Castells 1997, 380). Furthermore, "territories surrounding these nodes play an increasingly subordinate function sometimes becoming irrelevant" (Castells 1997, 380). A major characteristic of these metropolitan centers is that services disperse and decentralize to the periphery (e.g., La Défense in Paris, or Canary Wharf in London). Thus, Castells argues that the global city is primarily a "process by which centers of production and consumption of advanced services, and their ancillary local societies, are connected in a global network, while simultaneously downplaying the linkages with their hinterlands, on the basis of information flows" (Castells 1997, 386). What characterizes these mega- or global cities? Again, Castells (and others) suggests that a distinctive feature is that they are "globally connected and locally disconnected, physically and socially" (Castells 1997, 404). They are "discontinuous constellations of spatial fragments, functional pieces, and social segments" (Castells 1997, 407). He then goes on to list some of the common characteristics of these global centers: secluded communities, airport VIP lounges, etc., which all cater to an "international culture" whose identity is linked to multinational corporations. Sassen, in an edited collection, examines what she terms the emergence of a "network of cities" whereby cities in regions begin to form networks, creating a global city web whose constituent cities become global through the networks they participate in. Emphasis is placed on emerging global cities such as São Paulo, Shanghai, Hong Kong, Mexico City, Beirut, and Dubai. Of interest is how these globalizing zones are replicating many features of global cities (Sassen 2002).

What emerges from these readings is that if one were to examine the construct of 'influence' it is far too simplistic to talk of one 'center' or city influencing another. If one conceptualizes these centers as lying on a network their influence becomes multidimensional, exerted in multiple directions. Thus, using the notion of 'flows,' images and ideas move from one part of the world to another instantaneously, and from particular cities to this wider network. The question then is not so much who influenced whom, but to what extent do local conditions allow for the unfolding of global processes? Examining both Dubai and Cairo is particularly illuminating since both are attempting to become global cities—but the results have been quite different.

In looking at the directionality of influence in Cairo there are two possible areas of investigation: state-sponsored projects which more or less adopt an idea without directly copying its form (such projects are modeled on similar ventures throughout the world); direct investment from Dubai-based companies, directly installing a successful Dubai formula. Thus influence can be connected to either idea (lending itself to multiple sources) or form. The first category in Cairo includes the Smart Village project; the second category includes the Ma'adi City Center shopping mall, based on a concept introduced by Dubai's Al-Futtaim group. Both of these are apparently distinctive Dubai-influenced ideas. But they are not unique to the city and occur in other centers throughout the world in different forms. Internet City, for example, is modeled after California's Silicon Valley and technology parks in Southeast Asia. The concept of the hypermarket is not a Dubai invention but one that occurs throughout the developed world. However, the singularity of these projects within an Egyptian context—occurring after their success in Dubai—does of course suggest a strong influence, particularly with regard to the Ma'adi City Center project. The following two sections will explore the extent to which these two projects deviate from, and approximate, the Dubai model.

The IT Link

In 1999 Dubai's de facto ruler Shaykh Muhammad bin Rashid announced the creation of an IT (information technology) center called Dubai Internet City (DIC). One year later the center was complete, in landscaping elements and the presence of office buildings, and has since then become an unqualified success. Occupied by big names in the IT industry it has made Dubai the IT hub of the region. Comprised of a series of buildings overlooking an artificial lake and lush gardens, the city is located adjacent to Shaykh Zayed Highway, a newly formed corridor along which the city is currently expanding. Entry is through a gate designed in the form of a traditional wind tower with a series of screens containing a set of 'Islamic' motifs. This gate leads to a series of glass buildings such as one may find in any high-tech park in Malaysia or Silicon Valley.

The entire project is protected by a fence although entry is free to anyone (provided they have a car). Located nearby is Media City, a similar arrangement to Internet City, although in this case related to the media industry. This city is also comprised of office blocks within an artificial landscape. It houses studios and newsrooms and has become a regional center for many media companies such as Reuters, CNN, MBC, and others. The anonymity of the office blocks in either of these two cities, distinguished only by their tenants' logos, highlights the fact that they operate primarily on a global level, in some way disconnected from the surrounding reality.

The Smart Village Project in Cairo is Egypt's attempt to claim the title of the region's IT hub and also to integrate with the burgeoning global economy, with its emphasis on IT and communication-related services. The project is a technology park designed to cater to the IT industry, and represents an attempt by Egypt to enter this market as a service-driven economy. Officials claim that it is modeled after Ireland and India, who have successfully integrated into the global IT service sector. Located along the Cairo–Alexandria desert highway the three-hundred-acre park will eventually house more than fifty office buildings accommodating between twenty thousand and thirty thousand employees. Plots of land are offered to companies, which can then build their own office space. As of now, only three companies have signed up for the project: Microsoft, Vodafone, and Alcatel. A recent visit to the project showed the Microsoft building, in an isolated area, and a call center to be

Smart Village project, Cairo–Alexandria highway (photograph by Yasser Elsheshtawy).

the only buildings actually operating according to plan. A building was being constructed for the Ministry of Communications. The entire park, however, with its various futuristic buildings, had not yet been built. These buildings are to include a pyramid-shaped think-tank café, as well as a main conference and meeting center with a shape reminiscent of communication satellites. An architectural competition in Egypt was the source of these forms.

The project has its skeptics, of course. Many question its relevance in an Egyptian context. A business publication notes, "The Pyramids Smart Village, Egypt's new technology oasis, is everything that isn't associated with Cairo: spacious, pristine, ultramodern and green" (Hassan 2004). It is always compared to Dubai's, and here the responses vary. On the one hand officials like to argue that the relationship is symbiotic: both projects complement each other—Dubai offers marketing whereas Cairo's focus is on development. Also, great emphasis is placed here on the notion that Cairo is more suitable for an Arab market (Mostafa 2003). Another view suggests that Cairo has more to offer culturally and that Dubai's "antiseptic" living is not suitable for the "taste of the restless adventurers of the new economy" (Thornton 2003). Both of these views are of course misguided, and do in fact play into a few cultural stereotypes: Cairo has the human resources and the brains, but lacks Dubai's money; and the notion that Dubai is located in the middle of the desert ruled by fundamentalists (some sort of Saudi Arabia).

The differences between these two ventures are striking. With regard to location, DIC is located outside the traditional city on a highway leading to Abu Dhabi. Nevertheless, it is located on a growth corridor and will eventually become the center of a new Dubai which is currently being constructed (nearby projects include luxury resorts, the ruler's palace, various gated communities, and of course the Palm Islands [Palm Jumayra and Palm Jebel 'Ali, two reclaimed palm-shaped islands housing a mixed-use development]). Driving to DIC one does not have the feeling of 'leaving' Dubai. Yet this is not the feeling in Cairo. Smart Village is located along the Cairo–Alexandria highway, next to a toll station. The sense of leaving Cairo and embarking on a long journey is strong. Also the architecture of the park is insightful. In Dubai, the office blocks are generic buildings that can be found anywhere in the world. In Cairo, however, an attempt was made to make a compelling architectural statement by proposing buildings with a strong symbolic content (a pyramid-shaped café suspended in the middle of a lake, supposedly to encourage creativity) or a building whose shape is suggestive of communication satellites (expressed by a series of curves). While DIC has added a few vernacular elements (wind towers and ornaments), the Cairo village has a more neutral look—although the main mosque has for some reason been designed with pharaonic imagery. Running the risk of being interpreted as cheap gimmicks, none of these structures have actually been built—but their designs are nevertheless displayed prominently in the local media as a sign of Egypt's entry into the twenty-first century as an IT center.

Another difference relates to accessibility. In Dubai anyone with a car can enter and walk into the project without interference from anyone. The food court is a common meeting place containing a variety of shops and restaurants. It thus integrates strongly with the city. The situation in Cairo is quite different. Here entry is through a guarded gate and subsequent movement within the grounds is closely observed. In both cities photography is only allowed after securing permission from the authorities.

The City Center Idea

The retail sector is one segment where the 'Dubai idea' is directly transplanted into an Egyptian context, as evidenced in the Ma'adi City Center. In mid-November 2001 the Majid Al-Futtaim (MAF) Group of Dubai broke ground in the desert outside Cairo for a 22,500-square-meter shopping mall to be anchored by the French food retailer Carrefour. (See Abaza in this volume for further discussion of this and other luxury malls in Cairo.) The project, Egypt's first hypermarket, is one of three developments planned in the country in the next two to three years by the MAF Group and Carrefour.

Ma'adi City Center, constructed by the Majid Al-Futtaim Group of Dubai, where Carrefour is located (photograph by Yasser Elsheshtawy).

Long-term plans suggest that twenty centers will be constructed throughout Egypt, according to an interview with the regional director of Carrefour Egypt (al-Saddiq 2005). The Ma'adi City Center is modeled after similar MAF Group and Carrefour projects in the United Arab Emirates, Oman, and Qatar. The partners started the concept in Dubai in 1995 with the Deira City Center, which now gets fifty thousand visitors per day and includes such retailers as U.S. department-store chain J.C. Penney, Swedish furniture maker Ikea, and British chains Woolworth's and Marks & Spencer (Postlewaite 2001). In addition to the French hypermarket the mall includes more than forty shops, several restaurants, and a family-entertainment center.

Official accounts suggest the positive impact on Egypt by pointing out that the market will "feature a large range of top quality Egyptian products and international brands targeted to meet the increasing demands of Egyptian consumers" ("Majid Al-Futaim . . . 2001). In addition officials view such a development as a way to modernize Egyptian shopping behavior, as argued by the minister of internal trade: "A new and civilised (sic) marketing approach . . . will be introduced to peripheral areas outside of the capital, supplying commodities to small traders seven days a week, 365 days a year. It will supplant the traditional weekly *suq* (market) held in villages throughout the countryside" (Sami 2001a). Such efforts are, however, greeted with skepticism in the local media, particularly in light of the failure of a similar venture by the British conglomerate Sainsbury. This particular case is interesting since it prompted many to call for a radical reorganization of the Egyptian retail sector, after it was described by Sainsbury's chairman as "hostile" (Sami 2001b). One retail consultant suggests the possibility of a negative impact on Cairo's small grocery stores: "They've been the staple and the backbone of society for so long they'll never totally disappear, but I think you'll see a lot of them downsizing . . . if you can downsize from 75 square meters" (Hinde 2003).

Aside from these economic arguments one particular area of concern is the cultural acceptance of such a project within an Egyptian context. While the concept of hypermarkets has been successful outside Egypt in terms of social approval, some would argue that the Egyptian culture may take time to follow the trend (Rashdan 2003). Essential to society's acceptance of Carrefour is an appreciation for its concept, and what it has to offer. For Egyptians, this means making an effort to spend their free time shopping at Carrefour rather than at smaller, perhaps more conveniently located, neighborhood supermarkets. In a culture that highly values a family-oriented and neighborhood-friendly environment, it is not clear whether Egypt is a place conducive to hypermarket success. While the market caters to the nearby upper-middle-class suburb of Ma'adi, it is aimed at Greater Cairo as well; however large distances and endemic traffic jams may preclude such an orientation. The center's management, however, argues that the mall caters to middle income families: "People coming to us must have a car, so we only cater to a very small percentage of the population. We are here to complement, not compete" (Hinde 2003). At present, the center is successfully attracting a large number of visitors. It should be noted however that for the most part these visitors represent a certain segment of Egyptian society which has the necessary purchasing power, i.e., Egyptians residing in the Gulf, or expatriates. A common denominator is mobility since the center is only accessible by car. Ordinary Egyptians are thus excluded from this setting.

This raises the issue of location. The center is located in an area of Cairo known as Qattamiya at the foot of the Muqattam mountain, near the suburb of Ma'adi. It is located along a highway leading to a new development appropriately styled New Cairo. The site is surrounded by empty tracts of land, undeveloped areas, and a large public-housing project. The location was chosen specifically to "develop new residential zones" according to the developer (Rashdan 2003). An "example of the type of undeveloped area targeted by the group's development scheme," it thus ties in with what is termed "Carrefour's vision" for Egypt (Rashdan 2003). "France-based Carrefour's vision for Egypt entails a series of 'city centers,' large shopping complexes located on the outskirts of the city that serve not only as places to buy food, but as entertainment and retail destinations, often complete with countless stores, cinemas, restaurants and other activities, with Carrefour as the anchor" (Hinde 2003).

This vision entails, in addition to location, a provision of land large enough to accommodate such a complex; the presence of extensive areas for parking. Thus the Maʿadi City Center stands on a 69,000-square-meter parcel of land, of which 3,500 square meters is taken up by Carrefour (Hinde 2003).

Surroundings of Carrefour/Maʾadi City Center (photograph by Yasser Elsheshtawy).

It is interesting to observe that the Egyptian local press largely downplays the Dubai connection and the fact that the entire center is based on a Dubai model. In fact, more emphasis is placed on the French connection, in a sense suggesting that Egypt will become Western by constructing centers such as these. It is suggested that this is a universal or global setting, not tied to a particular culture or region. According to one consultant, "From a shopper's point of view, the shopping center in Qattamia is perfect. Once you walk inside, you could be anywhere in the world" (Hinde 2003). This of course stands in contrast to accounts in the local Gulf press which note with constrained glee that Dubai-based businesses are making inroads into Cairo (and other cities as well).[1]

The similarities between them are quite striking. For one thing, the logo is prominently displayed in Cairo on the mall's entrance but also in advertisements throughout the city. Entering the mall one is struck by the neat detailing of the parking lot with traffic signs pointing out that traffic rules "still" apply in the area (see image, page 243). The atmosphere stands in strong contrast to the stark, and somewhat shabby, surroundings.[2]

The same applies to the interior, which is well decorated to a high standard and enjoys a level of cleanliness not found in other Egyptian malls. The Dubai connection becomes even more apparent due to the presence of a UAE-based bank branch. There are some differences but the most obvious of them is size. Deira City Center is a large center comprised of multiple levels and several buildings. It occupies a space equivalent to several city blocks. In Cairo, however, the City Center is spread out on one level and is dominated by Carrefour. Another difference pertains to location. In Cairo the center is located at the edge of the city making it difficult to reach, unlike Dubai where it is located in the heart of Deira and is a major hangout and meeting place for city residents. The place is notorious for always being crowded, catering to a cash-rich clientele comprised of Arab and Western expatriates in addition to locals from Dubai and other emirates as well. In Egypt the targeted population seems to be the nearby Ma'adi suburb but other segments are also targeted. Its location however precludes the center from becoming a major meeting place—it has more the feel of a curiosity. While this still holds at the time of writing (2005) the center is viewed as a catalyst spurring urban growth. It remains to be seen if this will actually happen. While it is part of New Cairo which is currently being built, and which may (or may not) become a new center of Cairo, it nevertheless remains an isolated structure along a highway.

The Jumayra Mosque in Bur Dubai (photograph by Yasser Elsheshtawy).

Dubai Parallels: Constructing an Identity

The previous section showed that Dubai does indeed exert a strong influence in Egypt. The remainder of this chapter is devoted to examining the influence of Cairo on Dubai—and if in fact such an influence does exist in the first place. In examining these influences it must first be noted that multiple influences operate in Dubai. For example, the DIC concept is based on various models from around the world, as has already been described. Hardly a revolutionary idea, Dubai simply adopted this model. Here the attempt by Dubai to become a global city is apparent—its adoption of Western models and symbols should be understood in that context. Yet it also is looking toward the Middle East's traditional cities in its effort to become the new center of the Arab world. Here the influence is primarily at the level of historical imagery.

This manifests itself at a number of levels. For example, in advertising for the Palm Islands the image of Egypt's pyramids is prominently displayed, suggesting that a new landmark is in the making. Advertisements for the opening of stores in the new extension to the Burjuman Shopping Mall includes images relating to old Arab souks, traditional elements such as *mashrabiya* (latticed wooden windows), etc. Again, the use of historical imagery indicates that officials are trying to ascertain the emergence of Dubai as the new center, replacing the traditional cities of the Middle East. At another level, the Jumayra Mosque in Bur Dubai is built according to a Cairene Mamluk style.

The mosque seems to have been transported from Cairo to Dubai. The significance behind this is that the mosque represents an itinerary on the tourist trail—shown by Dubai officials as an example of its 'Arab-Islamic' architecture. It is a common sight to see tourists having their pictures taken alongside the mosque—usually in a hurry while the bus is waiting. Aware of the perceived absence of history and cultural roots in Dubai, such adaptations become ways to ascertain rootedness.

This whole notion of appropriating cultural elements, in a sense positioning itself as the region's cultural hub, has been the source of a recent newspaper article in the English language *Al-Ahram Weekly*. Here the writer argues that while Beirut is the "cultural capital" of the Arab world and Cairo its "political and historical" center, Dubai is attempting to take that title away. Noting that Dubai has a "newfound image" the writer argues (with a certain sense of alarm) that Dubai is "emerging as the region's Mecca of business, culture and the arts" (Howeida 2002). This occurs at a number of levels as noted above: establishing international linkages and also making connections to regional and historical elements. The name of its major landmark—the Burj Al-Arab Hotel—suggests that the city is indeed the center of the Arab world. New developments such as Madinat Jumayra are designed to reflect 'traditional' Arabian souks—their audience in both cases are primarily Western tourists and multinationals. But in adapting these elements they show that if one wants to seek an Arabian experience it is sufficient to visit Dubai (Elsheshtawy 2004).

Conclusion

The flight from Cairo or Beirut to the Gulf states takes only a couple of hours, and in that time the traveler is transported to what might as well be a different planet. He leaves behind a world of decay and dulled tones and steps into one of glitter and dazzle. Lamb 2002, 34.

Has Dubai been successful in positioning itself as the region's center? A number of events suggest a positive answer. For example, the relocation of businesses from Cairo to Dubai, visits by Egyptian delegations to learn from Dubai, and articles in international business publications heralding the arrival of an Arabian tiger, a place of "new Pharaohs," are all supportive of this viewpoint.[3] Other cities are influenced as well. In the case of Beirut some observers have noted that Dubai has in effect become a "gateway to the East." "The legend of the Lebanese gateway to the Middle East, if it were ever based on anything solid, has now attained the status of myth. Economically, at least, the gateway is lying in ruins" (Champion 2004). Qatar is at the present constructing an island named the Pearl, modeled after the Palm Islands in Dubai. Dubai thus has become, for better or worse, a model for cities throughout the Arab world. Its traditional centers have tried to catch up with these developments but have been unable to do so, and in fact some indications seem to suggest that they have failed. A failed infrastructure and dilapidated housing, some quite near to the new luxury malls, are just some of the urgent issues in Cairo that need to be resolved first.

The whole notion of a global world in which its cities are linked in a network and where images circulate freely challenging traditional notions of identity, place, and heritage does seem to be supported by examining cities such as Dubai. Here the city has been successful in appropriating imagery from the region's traditional centers, in effect replacing them. It is aided by a cash-rich economy (partially relying on oil, even though Dubai is not a major oil producer) and a centralized government facilitating various decision-making processes. Its various 'cities' are indicative of a new form of urbanism in which fragmentation figures highly, and where the built environment is geared to, and becomes supportive of, the new global economy. The impact of such developments on the cities' social structure—the "quartering effect" discussed earlier—has to be further examined and studied. Otherwise, as is the case in Cairo which has explosive sociopolitical issues, such developments could be counteractive and may in fact contribute to the persistent state of underdevelopment present in the region.

Works Cited

"Allahs blutiges Land—Politik und Kultur." 2003. *Spiegel Special. Das Gold der neuen Pharaonen* (February): 126–29.

Castells, Manuel. 1997. *The Rise of the Network Society*. Oxford: Blackwell.

Champion, Daryl. 2004. "Does the Gateway to the Middle East lie in Ruins? Golden Days Seem Far Away." *The Daily Star Online*, 10 February, <*http://www.dailystar.com.lb/article.asp?edition_ID=1&article_ID=4238&categ_id=13*> (21 September 2005).

"Dubai: Arabia's Field of Dreams." 2004. *The Economist*, 29 May, 61–62.

"Egyptian Delegation Visits Dubai." 2004. *Gulf News*, 4 January.

Elsheshtawy, Yasser. 2004. "Redrawing Boundaries: Dubai, the Emergence of a Global City." In *Planning the Middle East City: An Urban Kaleidoscope in a Globalizing World*, ed. Yasser Elsheshtawy, 169–99. New York: Routledge.

"GM Relocates Regional Office from Cairo to Dubai." 2004. *Gulf News*, 2 April.

Hassan, Abdalla. 2004. "It Takes a Village." *Arabies Trends*, January, 10.

Hinde, Tim. 2003. "Interview." *Business Today Online*, February, <*http://www.businesstodayegypt.com/default.aspx?issueID=116*> (July 2003).

Howeida, Amira. 2002. "Metamorphoses on the Gulf." *Al-Ahram Weekly Online*, 9–15 May, <*http://weekly.ahram.org.eg/2002/585/fe3.htm*> (23 September 2005).

Lamb, David. 2002. *The Arabs: Journeys Beyond the Mirage*. New York: Vintage Books.

"Majid Al-Futaim Starts Egypt Project." 2001. *Gulf News Online Edition*, 30 November, <*http://www.gulf-news.com/articles/news.asp?ArticleID=34053*> (21 September 2005).

Marcuse, Peter, and Robert van Kempen. 2000. *Globalizing Cities: A New Spatial Order?* Oxford: Blackwell.

Mostafa, Hadia. 2003. "Towering Technology." *Business Today Online*, <*http://www.businesstodayegypt.com/default.aspx?issueID=116*> (July 2003).

Nair, Manoj. 2004. "Retail Giant MAF Plans New Egypt Mall." *Gulf News*, 28 January.

Postlewaite, Susan. 2001. "FDI Still Apparent: Gulf Investors Stay Despite Capital Flight." *Business Monthly Online*, November, <*http://www.amcham.*

org.eg/Publications/BusinessMonthly/December%2001/Followup(InvestmentG oesOn).asp> (23 September 2005).

Rashdan, Hannah. 2003. "Egypt Gets Hyper." *Al-Ahram Weekly Online*, 30 January–5 February, *<http://weekly.ahram.org.eg/2003/623/li1.htm>* (23 September 2005).

al-Saddiq, Muhammad. 2005. "Rasadat milyaray dolar li-khitattha al-istismariya fi Masr khilal ashr sanawat." *Al-Ahram*, 15 May.

Sami, Aziza. 2001a. "Supermarketing Hysterics." *Al-Ahram Weekly Online*, 19–25 April, *<http://weekly.ahram.org.eg/2001/530/ec1.htm>* (23 September 2005).

_____. 2001b. "A New Saga." *Al-Ahram Weekly Online*, 18–24 January, *<http:// weekly.ahram.org.eg/2001/517/ec1.htm>* (23 September 2005).

Sassen, Saskia. 2001. *The Global City.* Princeton, N.J.: Princeton University Press.

_____, ed. 2002. *Global Networks, Linked Cities.* New York: Routledge.

Thornton, Jasper. 2003. "Utopia in a Village." *Al-Ahram Weekly Online*, 4–10 October, *<http://weekly.ahram.org.eg/2001/554/it2.htm>* (23 September 2005).

UN-Habitat. 2001. *Cities in a Globalizing World: Global Report on Human Settlements.* London: Earthscan Publications Ltd.

Watson, Geoffrey. 2004. "Dubai is the Best Place for Regional Business." *Gulf News*, 4 April.

Notes

1   Countless articles and news items make this observation, for example Nair 2004.

2   As one interesting account noted: "Some other City Centre visitors find the mall's crowd to be overwhelming; but they seem to acknowledge some of its perks. Among these is a very large car park providing free parking directly at the mall's entrance, and the convenience of a variety of stores and products. And while free parking may seem to be a plus for some, Sherif Salama, 39, complained, 'The lagna (traffic inspection) as you enter Carrefour's parking lot is terribly misplaced. How can anyone walk into Carrefour and spend money after receiving a mokhalfa (ticket)?'" (Rashdan 2003).

3   See, for example, "Dubai . . ." 2004; "GM Relocates . . ." 2004; "Egyptian Delegation . . ." 2004; Watson 2004. In addition the last few years have witnessed a plethora of newspaper articles, attempting to describe and analyze this newly emerging city. For example, a recent edition of Der Spiegel on political Islam included an article titled "The Gold of the New Pharaohs." In that article the new developments were being described and it was noted—with alarm—that Dubai would like to become the most modern city in the world, a metropolis which will merge East with West—Dubai as a mixture of Singapore, Seattle, and Saint Tropez ("Allah blutiges Land" 2003, 126–29).

Keeping Him Connected

Globalization and the Production of Locality in Urban Egypt

Farha Ghannam

In the early 1990s, while working on my dissertation, I came to know a family in al-Zawya al-Hamra well. Yet, despite the central role of one of the sons in this family's life, I never met Magdi until years after concluding my fieldwork. A young man in his late twenties, Magdi had been working in Kuwait since 1992 and had only visited Cairo twice over the period of six years. Still, I felt that I knew him despite our lack of face-to-face contact. He was often the subject of discussions between his family members and their neighbors. His mother always talked about him with affection and described his achievements with pride. His sisters and brothers always recalled his jokes, retold his stories, and remembered his tenderness and sensitivity. Magdi's fiancée and her family also described his good manners and hard work to secure his future home. I also felt that I knew Magdi through reading some of the letters and hearing some of the tapes that he sent to his family. Occasionally his mother had asked me to write to him on her behalf. When the family gathered, often with some of Magdi's close friends, to record audiotapes for him, I also greeted him and mentioned a few things about myself and his family.

But most importantly, I knew Madgi because, in spite of his long absence, he played a significant role in al-Zawya al-Hamra, a low-income neighborhood in northern Cairo, where his family lives. Through tapes, phone calls, letters, occasional visits, and financial support, Magdi maintained connections that allowed him to participate actively in decisions related to his family and to the formation of his neighborhood. Since my research started in 1993, I have followed and captured some of Magdi's dreams, preferences, and aspirations through the efforts of his family and fiancée to remodel his apartment, which he bought in 1994.

In this paper, I focus on Magdi's case to highlight three theoretical and methodological issues related to current discussions of globalization: First, there is a need to go beyond the current explicit or implicit division of the globe into the West and the Rest. There is much talk about "compression of the world" (Robertson 1995), "time-space compression" (Harvey 1989; Massey 1994), transnational connections (Hannerz 1996), and global flows (Appadurai 1996). In spite of this, however, globalization is still viewed as essentially flows between the West (or the rich North) and the Rest (or the poor South). This view has been taken for granted in previous attempts that aimed to show that the globe is being 'homogenized' or 'Westernized' and is still largely present in recent studies that aim to show the complexity of the articulation between global forces and local contexts (Hall 1991; Hannerz 1996; Featherstone 1995; Sassen 1996). Such a view excludes a major part of the complex flows that are central to the growing connectedness between different parts of the world and weakens the analytical potentials of the concept of 'globalization.' The problems with such a view are clearly seen in how globalization is frequently reduced into notions such as 'neocolonialism,' 'cultural imperialism,' 'Americanization,' 'clash of civilizations,' or even 'Jihad versus McWorld' (Benjamin Barber's famous phrase).

My aim here is not to deny the significance of flows from the United States and Europe. In fact, these flows shape Cairo's landscape in powerful ways and especially inform the life of upper- and upper-middle-class Egyptians. What I want to emphasize is the need to broaden the concept of globalization to account for the multiplicity of flows that shape cultural identities and practices. In a working class neighborhood such as al-Zawya al-Hamra, social imagination is not only, or primarily, shaped by American movies (such as *Terminator* and *Hercules*) and TV programs. It is also and perhaps more strongly shaped by Indian films, Lebanese singers, Brazilian soccer players, and Algerian *rai* music. As will become clear later in this chapter, oil-producing countries in particular have a major role in stimulating desires and fulfilling dreams of Magdi's siblings and neighbors.

Second, my paper addresses part of the new boundaries, differentiations, and social inequalities that are being produced, reinforced, and challenged by global flows. One of the interesting things about Magdi's case is that it directs our attention to other emerging hierarchies and power relationships that regulate interactions between cities other than New York, Los Angeles, and London. It also directs attention to new forms of inequality produced by global processes within the same city, the same neighborhood, and even the same family. In addition, Magdi's case conveys how access to and appropriation of global discourses and images are structured along national, class, and gender lines. Class in particular has been significant in regulating Magdi's travel plans, work in Kuwait, and transnational connections. While upper-class Egyptians travel to and from the United States and Europe (for education, vacation, and treatment) with ease, cities such as Paris and New York are largely off limits to young men like Magdi. In short, global flows are not only structured but they also structure. The question thus becomes: Which groups are being empowered by having access to oil-producing countries and Indian movies? And which groups are being strengthened by access to e-mail, satellite dishes, and strong connections with Western cities?

The third point I address is linked to agency and the production of urban locality. While earlier writers claim that space was going to be obliterated by the increasing movement of images, commodities, and peoples (i.e., a different version of the global-village argument), in recent years there has been a shift toward emphasizing the significance of place and locality in the articulation, appropriation, and transformation of global flows (Sassen 1996; Featherstone 1995; Massey 1994; Hannerz 1996; Appadurai 1996). Rather than stable, changeless, and spatially bounded, locality, as Arjun Appadurai reminds us, "is an inherently fragile social achievement" (1996, 179). As a structure of feeling, a material reality, and an attachment to a particular community, locality has to be continuously recreated and reinforced. This process, as well as the task of studying it, is especially challenging with the increasing movement of peoples, goods, and discourses between different parts of the globe. How can we conceptualize the attachment of feelings to specific spaces while accounting for movement, fluidity, and travel? (Malkki 1997; Gupta and Ferguson 1997). How can we study the role of Magdi in his neighborhood without immobilizing him or depriving him of agency? One strategy, which I am using here, is to trace the logic of flows through precise enactments. This strategy allows us to grasp how locality is produced through the interplay between dwelling and traveling, presence and absence, and roots and routes. It also enables us to follow individual and collective trajectories (which may take us to Kuwait, New York, or Sarajevo) and to analyze how global flows are articulated, transformed, and resisted in different contexts and by various social groups.

During the rest of this paper, I share with the reader how I got to 'know' Magdi through the flows that let him stay connected with his family and neighborhood. I analyze Magdi's apartment and the tapes circulated between him and his family as powerful techniques for the production of locality. These techniques kept Magdi part of the lives of his siblings and friends, provided him with moral support, and reinforced his attachment to his neighborhood in Cairo. Magdi's apartment, in particular, became a visible sign that objectified and reinforced his active role in the making of al-Zawya al-Hamra and the production of locality.

Globalizing Cairo

Magdi is one of eight children. He was born and raised in Bulaq, a working-class neighborhood, in central Cairo. The most dramatic encounter between Magdi and the forces of globalization took place when he was thirteen years old. His family was one of five thousand Egyptian working-class families who, between 1979 and 1981, were moved from Bulaq and relocated to public housing in two low-income neighborhoods on the outskirts of the city. This relocation was part of President Sadat's attempts to promote his open-door policy (Infitah) and to construct a 'modern' capital (Ghannam 2002). Sadat's policies aimed to "open the universe . . . open the door for fresh air and remove all the barriers *(hawajiz)* and walls that we built around us to suffocate ourselves by our own hands" (Sadat 1981, 12). For Sadat, the development of Egypt was linked to opening its boundaries to the West, especially the United States. He believed that the United States "is bound in duty, even naturally expected, to assist all those striving for a better future alike for themselves and for the whole world" (Sadat 1978, 328). His policies aimed at modernizing the country by accelerating economic growth, promoting private investment, and attracting foreign and Arab capital (Ikram 1980). (See Abaza, and Elshestawy's "From Dubai to Cairo," in this volume to examine the ways in which the creation of luxury malls is still redrawing commercial centers like Bulaq.)

Many changes were needed to facilitate the operation of capital and to meet the demands of the new users of the city, especially tourists and investors. Sadat wanted Cairo, especially its center, to be reorganized in line with Western standards (Ibrahim 1987). He hoped to remake Cairo along the lines of his favorite American cities, Los Angeles and Houston. Magdi's family and their neighbors were occupying a piece of land in downtown Cairo close to the Nile. This land became valuable and central to the state's attempts to modernize Cairo and to secure space for luxury housing, five-star hotels, and fancy offices. The state's public discourse urged Magdi's family and their neighbors to sacrifice for 'the good of the nation' and to accept to be modernized by moving into public housing on the outskirts of the city (Ghannam 2002).

Magdi's family was relocated to al-Zawya al-Hamra, an agricultural settlement during the 1940s that started growing rapidly during the 1960s, when a massive public-housing project was built under Nasser to house government officials and low-income families. In addition to this project, thousands of families moved to this area from villages, other cities, and different parts of Cairo over the past fifty years. They built new homes or rented rooms or apartments in privately constructed houses. Another public-housing project was built during the late 1970s to house families displaced from other parts of Cairo. Magdi's family was one of them. His mother and siblings consider themselves lucky. Instead of the single big room that they all (eleven members at the time) had to share, they were allocated a two-bedroom apartment, with their own separate kitchen and bathroom, in al-Zawya al-Hamra. While most families welcomed the new housing units and saw them as an improvement over their older houses, the project physically and socially segregated them from the rest of the neighborhood (Ghannam 2002). Relocation also distanced the community from the city center and rearranged their relationships with their neighbors and Cairo at large. Since then, many families have transformed the housing units themselves to reflect their material and symbolic capital.

The Road to Prosperity

When Sadat started his open-door policy, he also relaxed the constraints previously imposed by President Nasser on migration from Egypt to other countries (LaTowsky 1984). However, while Sadat saw the road to development and modernization as going through the West, Arab countries such as Libya, Iraq, and Saudi Arabia became the sources of financial prosperity for many skilled and unskilled Egyptian workers. Since the mid 1970s, these countries have continued to inform the imagination of young men and to promise to fulfill their dreams of accumulating the funds needed for marriage, housing, and investment. Over the years, millions of Egyptians have worked abroad and sent money back home. In 1994–95, the number of Egyptian labor migrants was almost three million and their remittances were estimated at more than $3 billion (EIU 1996, 25, 52). Like these millions, Magdi saw work in an Arab country as his main road to prosperity.

In the late 1980s, Jordan and Iraq were the first countries that attracted Magdi, who after nine years of education quit school to work in a printing company in Cairo. In his early twenties, Magdi traveled with one of his friends to Iraq and Jordan hoping to find good jobs and reasonable incomes. During this trip, Magdi failed to secure the money that he desired. According to his sister, Magdi and his friend suffered considerably because they did not manage to find suitable jobs. They had to work as street peddlers to secure enough money to be able to return with some gifts for their families. Magdi's next destination was Kuwait. Through an employment agency in Cairo, he managed to find a job as a security guard in Kuwait in 1992. He was hired for one year, but while there, he took an additional part-time job with a printing company to supplement his income. Before the end of the year, he secured another contract that enabled him to stay in Kuwait as a full-time worker in the printing company. He worked there during the following six years.

It is worth noting here that national boundaries are important in regulating Magdi's movement and participation in the social, economic, and political domains in Kuwait. Citizenship rights, social-security benefits, and residency are still largely determined on the basis of nationality. Labor migrants (from India, Pakistan, and other parts of the Middle East) are usually excluded from many aspects of life in oil-producing countries. They are often clearly segregated from the native inhabitants and they cannot attain citizenship no matter how long they work and live in these countries (Nagy 1998). Given these exclusionary practices, it was not strange that Magdi maintained strong connections with his neighborhood in Cairo and sent a major part of his income back to his family.

Since he started working in Kuwait, Magdi had financed major reconstruction of his family's apartment, which was allocated to them by the state. He continued to send monthly remittances to his mother and covered extra expenses during Ramadan, the Feast of Sacrifice, and other social occasions. When Magdi sent money, he usually included specific instructions on how it should be spent. Once he asked his mother to buy a new gas stove, a new carpet, and a wardrobe. Another time, he asked her to buy a table and some extra chairs.

Like many other migrants, Magdi came back to Cairo loaded with gifts for his family and close neighbors. He brought soap, shampoo, hair oil, whitening creams, clothes, fancy blankets, and electric appliances (such as tape recorders and food processors). These gifts were highly regarded and were displayed to visitors and relatives to communicate to them Magdi's success and commitment to his family. Some utilized their gifts in ways that Magdi did not intend. The Atari game that he brought as a gift for his young nephew, for instance, became part of his older brother's business. Magdi's brother attached the game to a small TV set and placed it in the small shop run by his wife. This game became the attraction of many children who come to play for a nominal fee.

With this flow of money and goods from Kuwait to Cairo and meager wages at home, it is not surprising that many young men and their families view work in an oil-producing country as the only way to save enough money to secure an apartment and get married. Young men and their families dream and try hard to travel (often unsuccessfully) to one of these countries. The migration of young men, however, is surrounded by uncertainty and raises many questions: Would he succeed in finding or maintaining a good job? Would he remember his family and commitment at home? Would he come back prosperous and safe? These fears and questions are justified since, unlike Magdi, several young men fail to make the expected income or do not send their families substantial amounts of money. In fact, one of Magdi's older brothers, who worked in Iraq and Libya, exemplifies how young men may not only fail to save money but may also acquire 'bad' habits such as drinking and frequenting nightclubs. Thus, many parents try to ensure that their children do well in their work and save as much money as possible. In this regard, ensuring continuous communication with young men and encouraging them to buy housing units or remodel existing apartments are important techniques that secure the flow of currency and reinforce the attachment of labor migrants to their families and neighborhoods in Cairo.

Tapes: The Art of Hearing

Besides the flow of money and goods from Magdi, there was also a continuous flow of ideas, news, and information that enabled him to participate effectively in making decisions related to the daily life of his family and friends. Letters, phone calls, photos, and tapes were significant in overcoming the physical distance that separated Magdi from his mother, siblings, and fiancée. One of his sisters, Nisma, who is very close to Magdi, was the main letter reader and writer. She was more educated than her other siblings and had better handwriting. While his other siblings could read his letters, they either did not know how to write or thought that their handwriting was illegible. Sometimes, when Nisma was not available or when she refused to write to ask for more money, Magdi's mother asked me to write letters on her behalf.

In addition to letters, phone calls and audiotapes also facilitated the flow of information between migrants and their families. A phone call is a very fast way of communicating that allows direct discussion of pressing issues. Although the number of phones was limited in al-Zawya al-Hamra during the 1990s, a migrant could always talk to his family by calling a neighbor who had a phone. Phone calls, however, were very expensive and used infrequently. Tapes were another important alternative for effective communication. Unlike fax and e-mail that are available to upper-class Egyptians, both of which can escape the censorship of the nation-state, tapes have to go through the state apparatus. When Magdi's sister took a tape to the post office, she also needed her identity card. Her name and address have to be clearly printed on the envelope and the employee in the post office kept track of her identity card number. Each tape, it was explained, was monitored for religious materia or attacks against the government.

Even though a tape sent via mail was more costly, was monitored by the state, and required coordination between family members, it was usually preferred to letters for various reasons. First, a tape enabled illiterate parents and relatives to communicate with their loved ones without a mediator (i.e., writer/reader of the letter). Most parents in al-Zawya al-Hamra are illiterate and even some siblings who went to school for six years (and sometimes even for nine) cannot write. Thus, with the help of a tape, Magdi's illiterate mother could communicate with him directly. The sincerity and warmth of her prayers were almost impossible to express in writing. Her expressions of affection often turned into cold words when inscribed in a letter written by a daughter or a neighbor. When she recorded for Magdi, her soft deep voice reflected her strong emotions and her words express her longing for him. She also could communicate to him her pride in his achievements, retell her expectations, and repeat her advice. As a letter writer, Nisma was always selective. She sometimes dismissed her mother's requests for money or refused to write about some problems in the family. No one, however, could stop his mother from saying what she wanted when recording for Magdi. They might comment on what she taped but still she had the chance to express her ideas without the mediation of a third party. At the same time, a tape from Magdi allowed her to hear his voice repeatedly, especially when she missed him. I often saw her happy face and big smile while she replayed one of Magdi's tapes, heard his tender words addressed directly to her, or listened to one of his jokes or funny stories.

In addition, a tape provided flexibility to discuss in detail various issues and to include the voices of several relatives and friends. A tape allowed Magdi to address all of his family members and to discuss different topics such as the health of his mother, the future career of his younger brother, and the weight of his younger sister. Tapes also enabled Magdi to transmit the latest songs from Kuwait to Cairo and allowed his brothers and sisters to provide him with the latest Egyptian songs and jokes. Some sing for him to express how much they missed him while others, less confident of the beauty of their voices, recorded a song from the radio. A tape also brought together all his siblings and some of Magdi's close friends. Taping often becomes a session for telling stories and jokes. Such tapes gave Magdi a feeling for his neighborhood, reminded him of the days when they used to be together, and provided him with assurances of his family's well being.

At the same time, a tape was expected to provide more 'spontaneous' communication than a letter, enabling the migrant to analyze the tone and quality of the voice on the tape and to conclude things that their relatives do not verbally mention. Nadya, for instance, asked me to write to her husband in detail about issues such as the relatives who visited her after she delivered her baby, the length of their visits, and how much money they gave as gifts to the baby. Despite this, her husband asked her to send him a tape that would inform him about all of this in even greater detail. Nadya's husband not only wanted to read her words, mediated by writers such as Nisma or me, but he also wanted to monitor the voice of his wife to figure out how she really felt about the visits of his family. Similarly, Magdi realized when his mother is sick or in distress even though she tried to cover that up while recording for him. When he felt that her "voice was different," as he stated in one of his letters, he wrote or called to ask for explanations and assurances from his siblings regarding his mother's health.

But above all, a tape could and was often used as a 'document' that was circulated between family members and close friends and that could be replayed several times for literate and illiterate members. While they could save a phone call and a letter is only accessible to those who could read, Magdi's family and future in-laws saved the tapes that clearly expressed his preferences and reactions. These tapes were consulted when disagreements emerged regarding any proposed changes to his apartment.

These tapes, therefore, keep the migrant informed of what happens in his neighborhood and ensure his emotional and material connectedness with his family. They often aim to remind the young man of his obligations, encourage him to save more, and persuade him to invest his money in durable items. Investment in material objects, and particularly in an apartment, becomes a powerful tool that ensures the continuous flow of cash and information from the migrant and that includes him in the production of locality.

Building Modern Dreams: Magdi's Apartment

The apartment, the organization of its space, and the quality of its furniture are all central to the representation of the self in daily life in al-Zawya al-Hamra. The housing unit is a material manifestation of the man's ability to earn money and the woman's skill in cleaning and beautifying their home. It is a visible and privileged site for expressing the identity and status of the family. This is clearly manifested in the various changes that people have introduced to the housing units (which were identical in shape, color, and organization of space) allocated to them by the state. Many of these changes are signs of distinction and manifestations of the material and symbolic capital of the inhabitants (Ghannam 2002). Many families invested money and labor in transforming their housing units to express their financial status and social distinction. As previously mentioned, one of the first things that Magdi financed was major remodeling of his family's unit. For instance, they installed a water heater, remodeled the kitchen and bathroom, installed expensive glass shutters on their balcony, and repainted the apartment with costly oil paint.

The role of the apartment, which is a central social requirement for the consummation of marriage, gains considerable significance for young unmarried migrants, who are encouraged by their families to invest a major part of their income in restructuring, furnishing, and decorating their housing units, where they will eventually live after they return from abroad. The apartment shows that the migrant 'did something.' It signifies not only his success and distinction but also symbolizes and reinforces his rootedness and attachment to his neighborhood.

As soon as he started working in Kuwait, Magdi's family started pressuring him to secure enough money to buy an apartment in al-Zawya al-Hamra. Their letters and tapes encouraged him to save money and included estimations of the cost of housing units in their neighborhood. Even before the search began, it was clear to everyone that Magdi's apartment, its location and size, would reflect his income and status. His younger brothers are forced to consider renting or buying one-bedroom units in satellite cities outside Cairo, an option that they do not like but still may be the only one available given their low incomes. But from the beginning, his family took it for granted that Magdi could afford to buy at least a two-bedroom apartment near them in al-Zawya al-Hamra. And this is exactly what happened after Magdi's engagement to a young woman called Layla, who also lives in al-Zawya al-Hamra. The details of Magdi's engagement and buying the unit are very interesting topics but are beyond the scope of this paper (see Ghannam 2002). Here it is sufficient to say that Nisma (Magdi's sister) searched for an apartment and with the help of her brothers finalized the purchase of a two-bedroom unit very close to their family's apartment.

The original structure of Magdi's apartment consisted of two bedrooms, a living space, a bathroom, and a relatively spacious separate kitchen. This apartment is identical to his family's apartment, where, until recently, ten to twelve individuals lived. Meanwhile, his older brother Fahmi, a driver for a rich family in another neighborhood, lives with his wife and an eight-year-old son in a one-bedroom apartment. Although Fahmi and his wife were lucky to find this unit ten years ago, since it was close to both of their families, the apartment is currently very small for them. In addition to the bedroom, there is a small hallway but there is no separate living space that can be used to receive guests. A couch, placed in the hallway next to the entrance, is used to seat visitors. This area is so small that if two or three people visit simultaneously, the place becomes uncomfortably crowded. Fahmi's wife is especially unhappy with the fact that her 'kitchen,' which consists of a sink and a gas stove occupying the corner of the hallway, is exposed to visitors who are seated on the couch in the opposite side of the hallway. Since I met her in 1993, she has been dreaming of saving enough money to install a metal balcony, part of which she can use as a kitchen.

The changes that Magdi was introducing to his unoccupied apartment increased the differences even more between him and his siblings. These changes were encouraged by his family and future in-laws, who often drew on modern images and ideas to motivate Magdi to invest in expanding the apartment, organizing its space, and buying fancy furniture. A few months after buying his unit, four families in the building decided to expand their apartments by building new structures attached to the units allocated to them by the state. Despite the fact that Magdi's new two-bedroom apartment was considered spacious and few young men of his age can afford to acquire such a unit; his family and fiancée thought that expanding his apartment would be a good investment that could save him money in the future. Building with the neighbors was not only important because they would collectively share the high cost of the foundation of the new additions. It was also crucial to avoid the state's attempts to remove the new unlicensed structures. Neighbors cooperate to collect money to pay off government employees to overlook such changes. At the same time, conducting the additions as a group makes it harder for government officials to demolish the new expansions (for more on these processes, see Ghannam 2002).

Magdi's family and his future in-laws collectively produced a tape that explained to him in detail the plan and the money needed. Magdi approved of the proposal and sent the required money to his family. His siblings, his fiancée, her father, and some of Magdi's close friends supervised the implementation of the expansion. Currently, Magdi's apartment has two bedrooms, one living room, a dining room, a spacious kitchen, two bathrooms, and a large balcony. Communication with Magdi had continued through tapes, letters, photos, and phone calls to discuss further developments related to the shape and structure of the additions.

It is interesting to notice here that Magdi's migration brought his family closer to his friends and future in-laws. In his absence, his mother and siblings were expected to visit Layla during major religious holidays and to offer her gifts on special occasions. The apartment created another need to communicate with her on a regular basis. Eventually, the unit represented the articulation between Magdi's ideas, the expectations of his family and friends, and the opinions of his fiancée and her family. They all generate new 'needs' they communicated to him and at the same time, they all contributed in one way or another to the renovation of the apartment. Layla shopped with two of Magdi's sisters for the ceramic tiles to be installed in the kitchen and bathrooms. One of his close friends helped in transporting the tiles from the market to the apartment. Layla's father contacted the workers and supervised the installation of the tiles. One of Magdi's brothers found the technicians who installed the electrical and water connections needed for the automatic washing machine that Magdi was expected to buy. During all of this, there was clear supervision of the money and how it was spent. Each time Layla went to buy something, she took one of Magdi's sisters with her to witness the transaction and the amount of money she spent. One of his sisters keeps a written account of the various expenses to report to Magdi on regular basis. In short, the apartment became a project that united all of them in their attempts to help Magdi in materializing his and their dreams.

Magdi's travel allowed his fiancée more freedom in shaping their future home. Despite the fact that women are active in organizing, cleaning, and decorating their apartments, they usually assume this role after marriage. A woman who is only engaged to be married is rarely involved in preparing her future home until the final stage, when she and her sisters (or female friends) arrange the furniture that she buys (normally for the living room and the kitchen) and organize her belongings in the bedroom. Unlike this general tendency, the role of Layla and her family was central to the changes introduced to Magdi's apartment from the beginning.

Layla decided on various issues related to the unit such as the color of the ceramic tiles, the kind of bathtub, and the color of the paint. She was also taking initiatives in the organization of the unit. For example, she insisted on a large kitchen. Unlike other brides, Layla also participated in decisions related to their future bedroom. While a bride participates in the selection of the furniture of the living room and kitchen, the furniture of the bedroom, which is closely linked with sexuality, is the responsibility of the groom and his family (Ghannam 2002). In Magdi and Layla's case, she was the one who was deciding on these issues. To be able to select the most fashionable and beautiful furniture, Layla watched TV, looked through magazines, and visited various newly married women to see their bedrooms. After deciding on a style, she sent a picture of the furniture she liked to Magdi to solicit his opinion. She said that Magdi liked the design of the room and suggested a white color. Layla, however, preferred black and wine-red colors. According to her, the white was very common and dated while the black and the wine-red were newer and more fashionable. After discussing her preferences with Magdi over the phone, he told her to choose the color that she prefered.

Another thing to notice was how the manner and style in which Magdi had chosen to remodel and furnish his housing unit also reflected part of his experience outside Egypt. Items such as the water filter, the kitchen fan, and the vacuum cleaner, which he bought in Kuwait, were not common in al-Zawya al-Hamra. He also decided to invest money in building both a full bathroom and a separate guest restroom. Among the many apartments that I visited in the neighborhood, Magdi's unit was the only one that had two bathrooms and the only one that had a bathtub.

Through his apartment, Magdi was not only participating in the material production of his neighborhood but he was also presenting new forms and ideas to the people around him. His ideas and housing unit joined the global flow of images and discourses in stimulating new desires and in presenting new physical realities that were evaluated and admired by his family and neighbors. For many people, his unit became a signifier of the modern, the new, the beautiful, and the desired. Thus, through materializing his modern dreams, Magdi was actively contributing to the formation and transformation of his neighborhood and the making of Cairo at large.

Afterword: Cracks in the Ideal

In 2000, Magdi went back to Cairo. He found a job in a printing company, got married, and moved with Layla to their new apartment. In the summer of 2001, I had the chance to meet Magdi for the first time. He was as thoughtful and delightful as described by his mother and siblings. His apartment was beautifully furnished. Layla (who was pregnant with their first child) and one of

Magdi's sisters took me on a tour to see the different rooms and new furniture. The automatic washing machine was nicely covered and so was the dining room set. The formal living room was furnished with a fancy sofa set with matching armchairs but almost never used; the family's living room had a TV set and two big sofas seating three to four. The kitchen was nicely organized, and the bathrooms were spic-and-span. It was clear that everyone was very proud. Magdi and his family see the signs of his success from working abroad and Layla and her family know that she has a beautiful home that few of her peers could afford.

Still, I noticed some cracks in the ideal image that his family and fiancée had of him while he was abroad. Financially, he was not able to offer his mother the same type of support he secured while in Kuwait. In addition, his new home and job were absorbing much of his attention and some family members complained that he did not visit as often as expected. His wife also complained that he was not as "respectful" as he used to be while in Kuwait. One of the most significant points of contention between the new couple was Layla's work. While she saw this as part of her identity and focused on the benefits of her job, Magdi only highlighted the negative aspects of her absence from home. He had asked her to quit her job but she convinced him that her work would not interfere with her responsibilities for their home. He was waiting, as he said in front of Layla and me, for her to utter any complaints about the amount of work she had to juggle to force her to stay at home. So far, Layla has been supported by her family. They verbally sided with her and offered her help with the housework on a regular basis. After giving birth, Layla took unpaid leave for one year and when she resumed her work, her mother looked after the baby boy. Last time I saw her in the summer of 2003, Layla was pregnant again and later gave birth to a baby girl.

In al-Zawya al-Hamra, the apparent success of Magdi and other migrants stimulates more desires for consumer goods and ideal homes. Its inhabitants work as vendors, plumbers, craftsmen, mechanics, drivers, waiters, petty traders, metal and construction workers, shoemakers, factory laborers, low-level government employees, teachers, and managers of small businesses. Many men have more than one job to meet the needs of their families. Yet, it is oil-producing countries like Kuwait that capture the attention of most young men and their families, stimulating their desires for more income and new consumer goods. Dreams, aspirations, and consumption styles are shaped in powerful ways by ideas, money, and products brought from these countries. The growing shortage of housing, the rising level of unemployment, and the increasing emphasis on consumption promoted by the media all intensify the pressure on young men to seek jobs abroad.

In fact, two of Magdi's brothers are currently working abroad. One of them, Ahmad, who is five years older than Magdi, is married and has three daughters. When he got married, Ahmad and his wife rented an apartment near his family. After a couple of years, they had to leave that unit due to conflicts between his wife and the neighbors. At the time, he could only afford to rent an apartment in another neighborhood, an arrangement that everyone viewed as temporary. The hope was that he would eventually buy a unit in al-Zawya al-Hamra or a nearby area. With the help of his sister-in-law, who had married a much older Saudi man and had been living in Saudi Arabia for over twenty years, Ahmad managed to find a job in an auto-repair shop in that country. He has been working there for the past five years. Magdi's younger brother, 'Imad, was literally forced by his mother to find a job abroad. She was distressed because 'Imad had reached thirty years of age without having any savings that would allow him to secure an apartment and a wife. Despite the fact that he worked in a local auto-body shop six days of the week (for ten to twelve hours a day), he managed to spend all the little money he earned on his friends and "bad habits," as described by his mother. Traveling abroad, she argued, would not only allow him to earn more money but would also force him to be more responsible and save most of his income. She and her sons tried several times to find a way for him to travel to Kuwait or Saudi Arabia, and when they could not, 'Imad managed to find a job in Libya two years ago. It remains to be seen how long it will take them to accumulate the money needed to materialize their dreams and the expectations of their extended families and communities.

Works Cited

Appadurai, Arjun. 1996. *Modernity at Large: Cultural Dimensions of Globalization*. Minneapolis and London: University of Minnesota Press.

Barber, Benjamin. 1996. *Jihad vs. McWorld: How Globalism and Tribalism Are Reshaping the World*. New York: Ballantine Books.

EIU (The Economist Intelligence Unit). 1996. *Egypt: Country Profile, 1996–1997*. London: The Economist Intelligence Unit Limited.

Ghannam, Farha. 2002. *Remaking the Modern: Space, Relocation, and the Politics of Identity in a Global Cairo*. Berkeley: University of California Press.

Gupta, Akhil, and James Ferguson, eds. 1997. *Anthropological Locations: Boundaries and Grounds of a Field Science*. Berkeley: University of California Press.

Featherstone, Mike. 1995. *Undoing Culture: Globalization, Postmodernism, and Identity*. London: Sage Publications.

Hall, Stuart. 1991. "The Local and the Global: Globalization and Ethnicity." In *Culture, Globalization and the World-System*, ed. Anthony D. King, 19–39. Binghamton: State University of New York Press.

Hannerz, Ulf. 1996. *Transnational Connections: Culture, People, Places.* London and New York: Routledge.

Harvey, David. 1989. *The Condition of Postmodernity.* Cambridge: Blackwell.

Ibrahim, Saad Eddin. 1987. "Cairo: A Sociological Profile." In *Urban Crisis and Social Movements*, eds. Salim Nasr and Theodor Hanf, 87–99. Beirut: The Euro-Arab Social Research Group.

Ikram, Khalid. 1980. *Egypt: Economic Management in a Period of Transition.* Baltimore: The Johns Hopkins University Press.

LaTowsky, Robert J. 1984. "Egyptian Labor Abroad: Mass Participation and Modest Returns." *MERIP* (Middle East Report) 14 (4): 11–18.

Malkki, Liisa. 1997. "New and Culture: Transitory Phenomena and the Field Tradition." In *Anthropological Locations: Boundaries and Grounds of a Field Science*, eds. Akhil Gupta and James Ferguson, 86–101. Berkeley: University of California Press.

Massey, Doren. 1994. *Space, Place and Gender.* Minneapolis: University of Minnesota Press.

Nagy, Sharon. 1998. "'This Time I Think I'll Try a Filipina': Global and Local Influences on Relationships between Foreign Household Workers and their Employers in Doha, Qatar." *City and Society* 19:1, 83–104.

Robertson, Roland. 1995. "Glocalization: Time-Space and Homogeneity-Heterogeneity." In *Global Modernities*, eds. Mike Featherstone, Scott Lash, and Roland Robertson, 25–44. London: Sage Publications.

Sadat, Anwar. 1978. *In Search of Identity.* Great Britain: Collins.

———. 1981. *al-'Alaqat al-asasiya i-l-insan: al-'alaqa bi-Allah, 'alaqatuhu ma'a nafsihi, al-'alaqa bi-l-nas, al-'alaqa bi-l-kawn wa-l-ashya'.* Cairo: al-Hay'a al-'Amma li-l-Isti'lamat.

Sassen, Saskia. 1996. "Whose City Is It? Globalization and the Formation of New Claims." *Public Culture* 8: 205–23.

Cairo
Heritage and Touristic Globalization

9

Reconstructing Islamic Cairo

Forces at Work

Caroline Williams

Cairo's historic and architectural center—its Islamic heart and soul—is currently the target of the Egyptian government's reconstruction and transformation. Manifestly this rehabilitation is an update to bring this historic area of traditional values into the global cosmopolitan track that is the itinerary of the modern tourist. In the larger context, however, the rapid timeline of this venture (combined with questionable conservation practices), and the threat posed to the fabric of society, engender a debate as to how to use this initiative as an economic transfusion for an ailing national economy, how to conserve a valuable cultural heritage, and how to integrate the people who live in the area in its revival. This chapter sketches the way in which these questions have become focused in the Historic Cairo Restoration Project (HCRP) established by Decree No. 1352 of May 1998.

The traditional, medieval, Islamic part of Cairo, long ignored in the twentieth century is, in the twenty-first century, the focus of new government attention. In the mid-1960s, during the Nasserist era of go-it-alone socialism, when I was a student of Islamic art and architecture at the American University in Cairo, the medieval area of al-Qahira was virtually uncharted territory.

There were few maps or portable books to guide one around its streets and alleys. The only map had been published in 1948 by the Ministry of Awqaf (Religious Endowments) for its two-volume book, *The Monuments of Cairo*, and only the Arabic version was available. In order to accommodate the six hundred monuments of historic Cairo, the map was in two pages, each 110 by 80 centimeters. As students we would stand in narrow streets with the huge sheets flapping around us as we deciphered the small print of the Arabic letters. Neither the people of the quarter, nor our friends in Zamalek or Garden City, seemed to have heard of any of the mosques or buildings for which we were looking. Individually and actively we were forced to find our own way to the monuments we wanted to study. In this way we became intimate with the old city, its fascinating architectural heritage, and its welcoming inhabitants.

Forty years later it is this area of Cairo that is being subjected to a massive intervention designed not only to restore 150 of its ancient and important monuments, but also to refashion the historic city itself. Decree No. 1352 of May 1998 launching the HCRP, which emanates from President Husni Mubarak himself, will cost much more than LE1 billion, and involves the largest number of officials, supervisors, planners and workers ever engaged in a comparable restoration project for Islamic Egypt. The government is evacuating many of the merchants, artisans, and residents who live in—and give life to—this nucleus of Cairo so that large groups of tourists, directed by signs and guides, will be able to traverse it along designated paths as quickly and summarily as possible. This massive reconstruction of the oldest parts of Cairo has received very little public attention or discussion, even though the number of surviving monuments concentrated there is the greatest in the Islamic world. However, details pieced together from observation and various press stories suggest that this heritage of Islamic Cairo is now a new 'development industry' and point to an alarming future for this old and interesting area.

President Mubarak has blamed runaway population growth as the cause of many of Egypt's problems. In March 2004 the Egyptian population was announced as 70.5 million, of whom 68.5 million live in the country ("Population passes . . ." 2004). This is an increase of ten million over the January 1993 figure of 58.98 million. Meanwhile, however, the value of the Egyptian pound has declined since 1991 (El-Rashidi 2003b). Cairo, a megalopolis of 17 million people sprawled over an area of 450 square kilometers, suffers many problems of unsustainable urban growth: economic and infrastructure developments have not kept up with need, and 80 percent of the housing built between 1966 and 1986 is substandard, and violates the building code (Farag 2003). Additionally, the increase in population has not been accompanied by the necessary increase in land designated for housing, and the result is the growth of slums (Farag 2003). To solve, or at least mitigate its economic woes, therefore, the government is turning to tourism.

The Middle East is one of the world's fastest-growing tourist markets (second only to Southeast Asia) and Egypt is its gateway ("Special Report . . ." 2003). Tourism is now Egypt's number-one foreign-currency earner. Growing at 7 percent per annum (Wells 2004), tourism accounts for 30 percent of foreign-exchange receipts and the industry provides employment to nearly 30 percent of the country's labor force ("Egypt Country Profile" 2003). The figures have jumped from one million tourists in 1982, just after the country was opened up to outside visitors, to six million tourists in 2003 ("Tourism to Egypt" 2004). In 2000, 5.5 million foreign tourists spent $4.3 billion (Saad 2002) and currently, despite the nullifying effects of 11 September 2001 and the Iraq War, tourist figures and the money received have bounced back to the 2000 level ("Special Report" 2003). Gulf Arabs, seeking Nile breezes and unrestrained night life, have filled in the gap left by Europeans and Americans and have kept Egypt's tourist figures high. Egypt has seven thousand licensed guides for its multiple archaeological, historic, and natural attractions. In addition to its pharaonic, classical, Coptic, biblical, and colonial historic sites, Nile cruises, Red Sea diving, ecotourism, desert oases, and village scenes, the Ministry of Culture has embarked on the creation of an ambitious series of new museums. In Alexandria, the Bibliotheca Alexandrina (which cost $225 million) opened in October of 2002; the National Museum (LE39 million) opened in September 2003 in the old residence of the U.S. Consulate. The new Grand Egyptian Museum (GEM) will open in 2010 (Ionides 2004) on approximately fifty acres of the Giza plateau. It is a cultural and economic investment that will cost $350 million for an estimated three million visitors annually (Marei 2003). Thirteen other national museums across Egypt are part of a program to focus on a variety of new and different themes, such as the Mosaic Museum in Alexandria, and a museum in Damietta dedicated to the development of furniture from the pharaonic period to modern times. In Cairo, the Bayt al-Umma, the house of Sa'd Zaghlul, the hero of the 1919 Revolution against British rule, opened in February 2003 (El-Aref 2003a). Of the new cultural tourist offerings, however, the most spectacular and far reaching, and the one that best exemplifies the government's new economic drive, is the initiative to restore the monuments and rehabilitate the area of historic Islamic Cairo. This initiative, while spotlighting the span and beauty of Cairo's unequaled urban architectural Islamic legacy, also subjects it to exploitation.

The Area: Physically and Historically Defined

So far there has been no precise definition of the physical boundaries of the HCRP (see map).

The area is made up of various parts, and is referred to by three names: Fatimid, Islamic, and Historic Cairo. Fatimid Cairo delineates the central area in which there is the heaviest concentration of monuments, and corresponds with al-Qahira, the palace-city founded by the Shi'i Fatimid Dynasty in the tenth century. The Fatimid city was also a base upon which subsequent rulers left their mark. The Mamluk sultans (1250–1517) embellished it and made it the center of the Islamic world, while as part of the Ottoman Empire (1517–1798) Cairo maintained its commercial preeminence. Al-Qahira lies three miles due west of Midan al-Tahrir. Its parameters are one kilometer square, bounded on the north and south by the eleventh-century gates and walls and on the east and west by major arteries, Port Said and Salah Salim Streets. Islamic Cairo is another name used by the HCRP. It adds the neighborhoods south of al-Qahira around the ninth-century Mosque of Ahmad ibn Tulun and the twelfth-century Citadel to the Fatimid area. This area also includes the southern and eastern cemeteries whose burials range from the ninth to the twentieth centuries and include saints, sultans, Sufis, and singers. Finally, a third designation, Historic Cairo, adds two outposts lying along the Nile: to the south, Misr al-Qadima (Old Cairo) with its Roman fortress, Christian churches, and Jewish synagogue, and Fustat, with its early Islamic remains; and to the north Bulaq, the port area developed in the seventeenth and eighteenth centuries from fifteenth-century beginnings.

An appreciation of this area also includes an understanding of its historic and its spiritual relevance. In the fourteenth century it was in Cairo, a city of 250 thousand inhabitants, that the final version of *The Thousand and One Nights* was compiled. Ibn Battuta, pilgrim and world traveler, described medieval Cairo in 1325 as "mother of cities . . . boundless in multitude of buildings, peerless in beauty and splendor" (Gibb 1956), and Ibn Khaldun, the fourteenth-century polymath who lectured in Cairo in 1384, wrote, "He who has not seen Cairo does not know the grandeur of Islam . . . the thronging-place of nations and the anthill of the human race." Between 1415 and 1437, Ahmad al-Maqrizi wrote his *Khitat*, a topographical/historical/urban study of medieval Cairo that is still its single most important and influential source (Rabbat 2000). For al-Maqrizi, Cairo was both the visible architectural and urban spaces he described, and the images and evocations of the past with which he animated his descriptions (Jarrar 2000). His work was an original contribution to Islamic historical writing, a creative interpretation not duplicated until centuries later (Rabbat 2000).

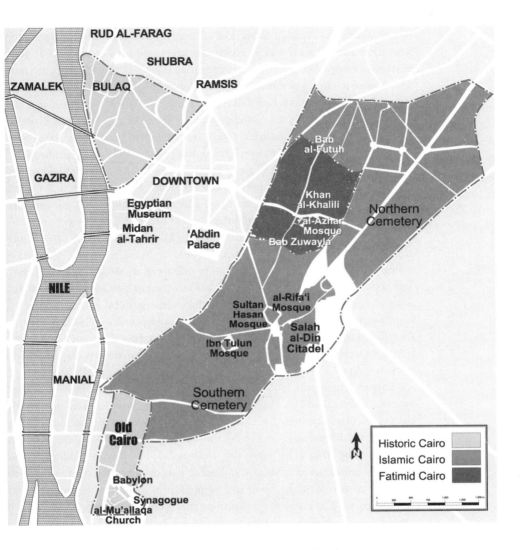

More than four hundred years later it was essentially the constituent parts of Historic Cairo that Napoleon's expedition mapped and depicted in the *Description de l'Égypte: l'état moderne.* Later in the nineteenth century it was to this part of Cairo—described by the French as *le grand Caire*—that Western visitors, scholars, authors, painters, and photographers, gave visual and literary shape. Among them was Pascal Coste who spent the years 1817–1827 as Muhammad 'Ali Pasha's chief architect, during which time he studied and drew the architecture of Cairo (Coste 1837). Coste was the first European

Fatimid–Islamic–Historic Cairo (map by Moody M. Youssef).

to appreciate that Cairo's collection of Arab monuments running unbroken from the seventh to the eighteenth centuries endowed it with an Islamic heritage unsurpassed by other Islamic cities (Coste 1878, 125). Another man who played an important role in the development of the nineteenth-century portrait of Cairo was Edward William Lane. His book, *An Account of the Manners and Customs of the Modern Egyptians* (Lane 1836), described Cairo as a medieval city untouched by Western influence and provided visitors with an authoritative aide-mémoire. David Roberts was the first professional artist to come to Egypt. He spent seven weeks in Cairo in 1838, sketching the Islamic monuments as part of the urban landscape. Roberts' legacy is the best visual record of the medieval Cairene cityscape. His paintings of noteworthy structures and animated traffic breathe atmosphere into the city's past. A hundred years later Naguib Mahfouz used the streets and alleys of historic Cairo as the backdrop for his socialist-realist novels. He won the Nobel Prize for his trilogy of novels *Bayn al-qasrayn*, *Qasr al-shawq*, and *al-Sukkariya*. In 1979, UNESCO acknowledged this medieval, historic, Islamic core as one of the world's historic and cultural assets by placing it on its newly established list of world heritage centers (UNESCO 2002). (See El Kadi and ElKerdany in this volume for further discussion of Cairo's heritages and the complex system of registering monuments and historical sites in Egypt.)

Egypt's nineteenth-century rulers spared medieval Cairo intensive development. Muhammad 'Ali, the new pasha, was more interested in Alexandria than in Cairo, although he maintained the Citadel as his administrative center, and built a palace on the Nile at Shubra. Building along the Nile was accelerated by Isma'il, his grandson. He was fascinated with modernity, and laid out a new quarter, western and secular in orientation, stretching from the Nile to the Western boundary of al-Qahira. The new foundation was juxtaposed with the old Arab, Muslim, and medieval center. When Isma'il moved from Gamaliya in Fatimid Cairo where he had been born to the newly finished palace of 'Abdin, the rich and the elite followed him. The old city was spared an over-layer of new buildings, but its monuments and spaces were left in the care of the poor.

In 1881, alarmed by the wholesale destruction of medieval monuments involved in creating new roads, and in order to safeguard them from total deterioration, a distinguished group of architects, primarily European, created the Committee for the Preservation of Monuments of Arab Arts (referred to by its French name: the Comité). The first such body in the Middle East, the Comité's operating policy, as defined by Max Herz, its first real head, was to study all available documentation, historians' accounts (such as what al-Maqrizi had to say about topography and architectural history), chronicles by travelers and journalists, paintings, and photographs, so that its efforts would be as faithful to the original as possible (Ormos 2002, 129). From 1881 until 1961, when its functions were taken over after the Nasserist revolution by what is now the Supreme Council of Antiquities (SCA) under the Ministry of Culture, the Comité did a great deal to preserve, restore, and maintain Cairo's remarkable Islamic heritage.

The years since 1952 were not kind to the monuments or the medieval city. Many factors have contributed to the structural and urban decay of the area. Population pressures, especially by refugees from the Suez area after the 1973 war, placed a strain on housing and sanitary services, causing a rise in the subsurface water level. The economic liberalism and capitalist orientation of Anwar Sadat's 1974 Open Door policy (Infitah) added vehicular congestion and pollution to the increased commercialization of the area, while the lack of communication, cooperation, and coordination among the main government bureaucratic agencies led to a confusion of mandates, gray areas, and wide gaps in responsibility (Williams 1985, 2001–2002, 2002a, 2002b, 2002c; Rodenbeck 2000). The neglect, dilapidation, and abuse suffered by the heritage monuments were exacerbated by the earthquake of October 1992, which registered 5.9 on the Richter scale. At least 125 historic buildings were badly damaged and many others were weakened. The recent growth of tourism, however, has provided the incentive and financing to do something about this area of the city. The Egyptian government has been galvanized into action, but its approach and methods have raised grave doubts about the future of the area and its cultural heritage.

The Historic Cairo Restoration Project (HCRP)

There are two parts to the HCRP: the remaking of the historic area and the restoration of its monuments. For the first time in the history of conservation in Cairo, the area is being considered as a unit rather than as individual or clusters of monuments. At present the government is concentrating on al-Qahira or Fatimid Cairo. As part of the HCRP, the Ministry of Culture intends "to transform the whole area into an open-air museum" (Hassan 1999). It is preparing the area to be part of the European Union-sponsored Museum With No Frontiers and its Euromed Heritage program "Islamic Art in the Mediterranean" (Farouk 2001).

The program is inspired by the simple idea that with catalogs and on-site information, the historic and archaeological sites will themselves become the

The "Museum with No Frontiers" sign sits in place although the complex of Sultan Barsbay and other buildings around it are still being reconstructed (photograph by Caroline Williams).

prime exhibition spaces (Euromed Heritage Programme and Ministry of Culture, Egypt, 2001). Visitors to Egypt can travel to the country and experience art and architecture as a living illustration of history (Bakr 1998; Hassan 1999). For this, there are plans to pave Shari' al-Mu'izz li-Din Allah, the main ceremonial artery of al-Qahira, along which stands a veritable chronology of architectural history, and line it with trees. Furthermore, the Ministry of Culture plans to establish green areas around several monuments, notably the complex of Sultan Qalawun and the Mosque of al-Hakim ("Travel News" 2004). This vision, however, does serious harm to the original medieval layout and purpose of the architecture. Buildings of single and multiple functions were deliberately set next to each other so as to demonstrate the prestige and station of the patron. The resulting canyon-like façade and clusters of monuments on main streets show power expressed through architecture. It was a monument's juxtaposition and contextual relationship to the other buildings in the ceremonial center that indicated the patron's status and position, not its isolation. Furthermore, in the medieval city, it was the internal courtyards that provided the open, breathing spaces within the buildings; there were never open spaces around the monuments.

The Egyptian government, has kept its pronouncements about the HRCP vague and ill-defined, and has deflected debate and discussion about its course of action. Even so there are warnings and criticisms about what is occurring. UNESCO, thirty years after the adoption of the World Heritage Convention, cautioned that unchecked tourist development is among the threats to world heritage (Tresilian 2002). Inclusion on the World Heritage list as one of the world's significant cultural sites can significantly enhance a site's tourism potential, but it can also be abused by tasteless exploitation. Gamal al-Ghitani, an activist and historical novelist who grew up in the Gamaliya district of al-Qahira and has campaigned to save Islamic Cairo, denounces the government's intention in the HCRP: "The vision in this project is commercial and not cultural" (Drummond 2003).

Peter Sheehan, directing activities designed to lower groundwater levels around the monuments in Old Cairo, is more damning. "Historic Cairo has taken on a momentum of its own. For the sake of tourism, the nation has opted to perfectly reconstruct its past. The shape and spirit of the ancient city has been irrevocably lost" (El-Rashidi 2003a). He disapproves of the restoration work currently in progress, and cites as its aim the attraction of tourists to a spruced-up "outdoor museum," not a respect for authentic conservation techniques and materials, or for the

Street scene in the Gamaliya quarter with restoration activity to the Mosque of Mahmud Muharram (photograph by Caroline Williams).

communities that live in them. (See Kuppinger in this volume for a discussion of recent plans to build the Grand Egyptian Museum, a mega-museum at the foot of the Pyramids that will cost $350 million, at least.) This is also the position of a concerned Egyptian historian/architect who feels that the exorbitant sums spent on 'cosmetic veneer' would be much better spent on upgrading and maintaining the city's infrastructure. These issues, the restoration of the monuments, and the prospects for the people who work and live around them, also concern other critics.

Monuments

The HCRP announced in 1998 that by 2006 it would restore 149 listed historic monuments, for which LE250 million had been allocated. In addition, forty-eight buildings not now on the Monuments List would be listed and preserved (Williams 2002b, 462). The restorations were tendered to general contracting companies which had little experience or expertise in historic restoration: Ruba'iya, Samkrit, Hassan 'Alam Sons, Orascom, the Arab Contractors, Wadi al-Nil and Aswan (Williams 2002b, 461–62). Since these companies were dealing with unique monuments of major cultural significance, international experts and historians of Islamic architectural history and urban conservation voiced their concerns to UNESCO and to the Egyptian government in the form of a letter to First Lady Suzanne Mubarak, dated 8 June 2001. (See appendix 1 for text and signatories.) For these professionals—Egyptian, Arab, European, and American—the areas of greatest concern were: the rise of the water table; the fact that there was no adherence to the basic international principals of minimal intervention, reversibility, compatibility, and documentation; the use of Portland Cement, damaging to limestone structures; engagement of contracting companies that were not specialists in the delicate work of conservation; and finally, that the work was apparently being done more to stimulate the Egyptian economy than to benefit its cultural heritage (Williams 2002b, 463). The response from the Ministry of Culture was defensive, but it agreed to discuss the matter in the International Symposium on the Restoration and Conservation of Islamic Cairo held in 2003, which UNESCO's World Heritage Center cosponsored (Williams 2002b, 465). Since then it has been almost impossible to get an accurate assessment of what is happening. The Ministry of Culture, sensitive to criticism, has not cooperated with the press

Madrasa of Sarghatmish (1356) the interior courtyard, with new marble contrasting with original marble floors and walls (photograph by Caroline Williams).

Looking down into the interior courtyard of the mosque of al-Muayyad Shaykh where the Wadi al-Nil Construction Co. is completely reconstructing the courtyard and side colonnades (photograph by Caroline Williams).

and forbids access to the buildings, which remain swathed in green netting and scaffolding while under restoration, with armed policemen to prevent entry or investigation. Photography is strictly forbidden in all monuments where restoration is in progress, a worrying sign that the authorities are not confident that the methods being employed are in accordance with internationally agreed guidelines for the conservation of historic buildings in a World Heritage site. The Mosque of Sarghatmish, recently reopened and unveiled (El-Aref 2004b), is an example of work condemned by UNESCO architects and conservators (Williams 2002b, 460, 462). For example, abrasive sand blasting under high pressure destroyed delicate details of the façade; new marble paneling was added around the courtyard despite the fact that no original marble remained to guide such a replacement; and externally, a new, unwarranted plaza-staircase connects the mosque to its neighbor, the Mosque of Ahmad ibn Tulun. A Canadian conservator observed that in the restoration of the Mosque of al-Muayyad Shaykh "all historic elements are being removed for bright new ones."

The Egyptian authorities in promoting restored buildings full of new marble and landscaped surrounds are expressing an idea of restoration that values the new and the shiny. This approach runs counter to that practiced by international conservators which aims to preserve what is authentic about the structure by using materials that are compatible, in a manner that is recognizable and reversible (Stille 2002, 53). Most Egyptians tend to esteem a site for its religious and associative values rather than for the artistic

or historic value of a particular structure (Reid 2000). The same Canadian conservator noted with surprise that it was more the spirit of the place than the historic fabric of the building that interested her Egyptian coworkers. Thus in 1999, when the Ministry of Housing and the Arab Contractors put on view their finished work at the Mosque of al-Azhar (cost: LE50 million), the many faults of its restoration (the loss of details on its façade due to sandblasting; the acrylic repainting of the original stucco; the relaid and polished marble floors, etc.) caused hardly a public murmur, since its value as a living center of worship and study continued (Williams 2002b, 461, fn.20). However, Muhammad al-Kahlawi, professor of Islamic

Bayn al-Qasrayn. On left complex of Sultan Qalawun under gray wraps, with a view of the complex Sultan Barquq, rear. The dark stain to the first window level of the façade is due to water damage (photograph by Caroline Willams).

architecture and antiquities at Cairo University, admits, "Al-Azhar, in my opinion as a specialist, does not have any archeological value after the renewal work" (Blair 2004).

The rising water table is not being dealt with and continues to have a disastrous effect on the foundations of many buildings. This water accrues from the sewage of a dense population, as well as from subterranean seepage from the higher water table following the construction of the Aswan High Dam. Water is pumped out of the foundations of an individual monument, but there is no overall strategy to deal with the larger problem of subsurface accumulation. Waterlogged foundations and crumbling walls will thus continue to threaten the monuments.

In a letter to the author dated 30 July 2003, Peter Draper, the president of the Architectural Historians of Great Britain, returning from a teaching trip to al-Qahira, expressed his horror at what he saw in the restoration of a number of major monuments. Instead of "careful and sensitive conservation of priceless monuments," he saw a "wholesale renewal of historic features." At the Mosque of Ahmad ibn Tulun, Draper witnessed the original ninth-century stucco being scraped away and replaced with modern plaster.

Mosque of Ibn Tulun, sanctuary arcade. Pier, on left, with original stucco and ninth-century foundation tablet. Piers, behind yellow tape, showing bare brick after removal of stucco (photograph by Caroline Williams).

"In a city where there are so many important monuments crumbling away and in dire need of attention," he wrote, "what worries me particularly is the unnecessary extent of the restoration in the high-profile monuments in the Bayn al-Qasrayn, well beyond any necessary consolidation of the structure."

In many of the cases, he further observed, "quite modest expenditure would be sufficient to consolidate the structure and halt the dilapidation until money can be found for the painstaking conservation of the decorative elements." An Egyptian conservation architect, in speaking of the work the contracting companies are doing on the monuments along Bayn al-Qasrayn, agrees: "The international conventions talk about using traditional techniques and using new materials only if they fail. That is not happening in Egypt. When contractors do the work, they estimate costs based on the square meter and they try to finish it in the shortest possible time."

Of the forty-seven monuments restored in Phase One, twelve were

Mosque of Ibn Tulun, side arcade. Pier, on left, covered with new plaster undercoat; pier, on right, covered with final coat of twentieth-century stucco (photograph by Caroline Willams).

*sabil*s or water dispensers. The Minister of Culture's plan for them is that of adaptive reuse as small museums. "They will be cultural centers in neighborhoods which don't have any. They will thus serve a new function and fill a void. They will become new tourist sites" (Samir 2003; MacDonald 1999). One of them will become a library for Islamic and Coptic studies; another a museum of Islamic textiles and rugs; a third, an information center for the students of al-Azhar and the inhabitants of the region; a fourth will be transformed into a club where writers can meet, and where the cultural elites can come in contact with ordinary people; others will become centers for the teaching of the *'ud* (lute), flute, or drawing (Samir 2003). Restored buildings should not stand empty, and a use for them should be found, but to dot the area with mini-museums is a Western intrusion on the form of an Islamic city and of little practical value to its inhabitants whose main focus is often just economic survival. Planned reuse must include the participation of people of the neighborhood. "If changes are not integrated . . . alienation ensues" (Ibrahim 2001, 190).

Other adaptive uses for these buildings are as spectacular party venues in which the Islamic monuments join pharaonic sites as colorful backdrops for the festivities of the rich (El-Aref 2004a). A justification for such use is that fees will help maintain the archaeological heritage, but they will also go into the coffers of the government. A permit for up to two hundred guests costs LE15,000 plus LE500 for security and supervision. For foreign companies the price can be $500 per guest, with numbers ranging from twenty to 1,500 predominantly American and European guests. This is comparable to what a five-star hotel would charge without the 'magnificent backdrop.' In the Islamic quarters it is the newly restored residences of the Ottoman seventeenth and eighteenth centuries, such as Bayt al-Sihaymi and Bayt al-Harrawi, that are being used. Luxury celebrations catering to pleasure-seeking travelers and big business produce an inevitable jab at the traditional and conservative sensibilities of the inhabitants. It is ironic that al-Maqrizi's motivation to write his famous *Khitat* was the imminent destruction of the medieval monuments of Cairo. He blamed their deterioration on the mismanagement and greed of the ruling Mamluk class (Rabbat 2000, 23, 29).

People

The HCRP pays little attention to the people who live in the area. Successful conservation programs must involve local residents since, unlike museums where glass protects the exhibitions, historic cities and cultural centers are places where the heritage is part of a living, working community. The preservation practices of the international community are moving away from the single-monument approach to area conservation. Contemporary thinking integrates monuments and people and sees them as interrelated and interdependent. Current initiatives in other parts of the world include multidimensional, integrated layers of action that link cultural-heritage management with socioeconomic sustainable development (H. Williams 2001). Just as the object of focus has expanded from historic monument to historic city, so has the base of its support also widened and broadened: from the advocacy of art specialists and cognoscenti to a global recognition that the heritage of the world is finite. The Egyptian government, however, is still pursuing a policy acceptable a century ago when the work of the Comité focused on the single monument, not its context. Merchants' booths attached to the facades of buildings were considered parasitic, disfiguring, and damaging, not only in their appearance, but as organic clutter that blocked narrow streets, impeded traffic, and made it impossible to view the façades of monuments to their full effect (Ormos 2002, 143). The Comité thus removed them. It is this approach that the Egyptian government continues.

The Egyptian authorities (primarily the Ministry of Culture, the Ministry of Housing, and the governorate of Cairo as the main administrators of the HCRP) pay little attention to the local communities, and by ignoring them distort the nature of Islamic urban society. The debate between preserving the past (monuments) at the expense of the future (people) goes on. While it is true that a nation without a past can have no future, a past without a future is also unsustainable. Cairo's historical areas pulsate with the activities of everyday life. They are also deep-rooted communities. Dina Shehayeb of Cairo's Housing and Building Research Center, speaking of the Darb al-Ahmar area (just south of al-Qahira's Bab Zuwayla), noted that 89 percent of the people were born there, a social cohesion not characteristic of newer suburbs of the city. She further explained that foreigners or nonresidents cannot appreciate the binding forces of the community. "Our tendency in looking at the crumbly walls and overflow street water," she said, "is to wonder how the residents can stand it. We do not understand the strength of community ties, the convenience value of neighboring shops and needs, and the economic benefits from the concentration of complimentary uses and functions" (Fernea 2001).

Cultural heritage sites are especially at risk from uncontrolled development and environmental degradation in urban areas. Mohammad Ibrahim Suliman, Minister of Housing and Population, has acknowledged that the strategy for dealing with slums since 1994 has been either upgrading or eviction (Farag 2003). Upgrading is expensive, and it is easier for the government to evict. The restored Bab Zuwayla, in al-Qahira's southern wall, was opened in September 2003, after five years of work by the American Research Center in Egypt in partnership with the SCA. At the ceremony, Faruq Husni, the Minister of Culture, announced that the whole area would be transformed into an open-air museum as part of the HCRP (El-Aref 2003b). This would entail the removal of "slums" and workshops from the neighborhood (El-Aref 2003b). "Slums" are the Minister's designation, but in fact various socioeconomic groups that include merchants, traders, and craftsmen live in this area by choice as well as need (Fernea 2001). Husni indicated the removal would take place in cooperation with the inhabitants, and compensation would be provided for every family and trader because "we do care about people and not just monuments" (El-Aref 2003b). The experience of the residents in the Gamaliya area outside the city walls to the north would suggest otherwise. When Shari' Galal was turned into an east–west expressway linking Shari' Port Said and Shari' Salah Salim in 2001 it was necessary to dismantle sections of the Bab al-Nasr cemetery. One hundred and nine families were summarily relocated to suburb-cities to the northeast. Their complaints have been ignored: "All our interests—work, school, family, contacts—are based in Gamaliya. What will we do in a new area where we have no ties?" (Halawi 2001).

Another plan to move people is the Cairo governorate's project to forcibly move thousands of fabric merchants out of the textile stalls in the center of al-Qahira (Nafie 2003; Samir 2004).

HCRP model of the twin complex of Sultan al-Ghuri, with new plazas and walkways to replace the old textile stalls (photograph by Caroline Williams).

There are nearly 1,200 fabric merchants in the area, but the governor wants to move them to a new mall in al-'Abbasiya, near the police station, because it is alleged that the noise, crowds, and pollution affect tourists negatively. The details of how the shops will be compensated in this move are not clear. This relocation will also affect affiliated industries, such as tailoring, which will not move. The government gave the merchants no direct information; they heard about the move only by word of mouth. One of the merchants said, "If they move us, it's over for our business" (Nafie 2003). The commerce in textiles is far from negligible, since it is a prime sales area for the inhabitants of Egypt, as well as Cairo. It is also part of the authenticity of the environment, and of the history of the place. Al-Maqrizi mentions the textile trade there in the fifteenth century. In the sixteenth century, when Sultan al-Ghuri built his twin complex at the corner of what is now Shari' al-Azhar and the main north–south street of al-Qahira, the rent from these shops helped to finance the different activities and maintenance of his establishment. Laila Mahmud, an expert on Islamic art, has said, "There is no good done to historical areas by restoring monuments and evacuating the inhabitants. The charm of this place does not come uniquely from venerable walls, but derives also and above all from the activities of the artisans and merchants, and of the life which surrounds it" (Samir 2004).

The notion of evacuating the shops, which are the property of the Ministry of Religious Endowments, also represents a grave violation of the idea of *waqf* as one of the most important bases of Islamic civic and spatial organization. The importance of cultural meaning is often overlooked by urban-conservation projects in Cairo (Sedky 2001). The dynamic between building and context has always been part of the Islamic system known as *waqf* (pl. *awqaf*), or endowment, a system whereby wealthy patrons deeded the profits from various urban and rural properties they owned to provide for the building, staffing, and maintenance of religious and civic foundations which became part of the public–municipal domain. The building was thus actively integrated into the community in both a spiritual and secular way, and *waqf* established a balance between private and public property in an equilibrium that generated a socioeconomic mode of life marking the Islamic city. There are, thus, at least three inconsistencies in the government's relocation of the textile merchants and their shops. The first is its violation of the current view of conservation, which sees as one of its goals the preservation of the nonmaterial authenticity of urban life. The second is that tourists will not come to admire a phantom village. Thirdly, the transfer of the textile shops is harmful to the economic activities which form part of Islamic urban life;

an infraction of one of the region's most characteristic traits (Samir 2004). These are points that residents also appreciate. One shopkeeper whose small stall fronts the tentmakers' market outside Bab Zuwayla remarked: "Move the people of the area and it becomes a museum, beautiful but empty. Tourists don't want to see just antiquities, they want to see people also" (Fernea 2001). The people and their activities (including shopping, crafting, baking, selling, and praying) provide life to the historic districts. There is a symbiotic relationship between the monuments and the people.

One of the ongoing problems in dealing with the material upgrade of the environment for Historic Cairo is that its areas along the Nile (Bulaq and Old Cairo) and its acreage (al-Qahira and its extensions) next to Isma'il's business-governmental-residential-tourist center make these historic quarters prime real estate. The authentic area of Bulaq is being utterly overwhelmed by new investment ventures on its Nile-side premium location (Schemm 2003; Ghannam 2002). The Saudi Egypt Tourism Development Company has just opened its $380 million Park Hyatt Hotel in Bulaq. The Nile shore here—with the Park Hyatt Cairo Mall, the Misr Bank Tower, and Nile City, whose towers are the tallest in Cairo—deliberately excludes the dense community of a million people in the streets behind them. To make room for these new buildings, hotels, and malls, the residents are being moved to new desert suburbs, like Madinat al-Salam, far away from families and friends. (See Farha Ghannam's chapter in this volume about the relocation of residents from Bulaq to construct 'modern' luxury hotels and government buildings.) One resident admitted, "I went to live in Madinat al-Salam. But I came back to where I was born. It's my neighborhood, my people—everyone is here" (Fernea 2001). One sociologist explained that in Madinat al-Salam "they all come from different areas and do not know each other, and there is no spirit of solidarity." Dr. Ahmed Sedky, an Egyptian architectural historian, provides an insight into the government's attitude toward traditional areas. The Minister of Culture heads an organization called *al-Tansiq al-Hadari* ('civilized management') (Farag 2000). In this title the use of *hadari* (civilized) instead of *hadri* (urban) is no mistake. Sedky contends that the minister's use of *hadari* is a deliberate reflection of the government's concern to update the city in a 'civilized/modern' way through the management of its spaces (Sedky 2005).

While the government is working hard to attract more tourists to the country and to increase its revenues, the record numbers of tourists expected seem to be bad news for its monuments and their preservation. What is happening to the Giza Plateau is a prospect for Islamic Cairo that gives great pause (Cunningham 2003; Abdel-Latif 2001). Zahi Hawass, secretary general of the SCA and director general of excavations at Giza, has said, "To preserve the Pyramids we must isolate them." To do so a chain-link fence with a foundation two meters deep will encircle the plateau and protect it from exposure to the village of Nazlat al-Simman and its rising water table, the traffic of mass tourism, and 'undesirable' cameleers, horsemen, and touts. While the village's growth and water consumption does provide an environmental threat to the plateau, its dancing horses and festivals also provide a lot of local color. There is also fear that if the town is moved, the valuable site adjacent to the Giza Plateau will be turned into a five-star hotel. The plateau is where the Grand Egyptian Museum, referred to as the "fourth pyramid," will be located. Visitors will enter from one of two gates: one at Mena House for official and VIP visitors, and the other for tourists and Egyptians. The exit will be near the Sphinx. The plateau will be provided with modern lighting, an electronic security and surveillance system to screen for weapons and to ban illegitimate entries, and electric carts to protect the area from pollution. The cost of this change to the plateau will be LE50 million (apart from the $350 million for the new museum). (See Petra Kuppinger in this volume for further analysis of the history and tourist industry surrounding the Pyramids.)

The United Nations Development Program's Human Development Index for 2003 ranks Egypt 120th out of 162 countries (UNDP 2003). Since the latest devaluation of the Egyptian pound in 2003, the cost of daily staples has increased by 70 percent. A common coffeehouse complaint is that the government is wasting billions of pounds on extravagant projects of little concern or use to most Egyptians (El-Rashidi 2003b).

For Historic Cairo the issue remains the scale, speed, and insensitivity of the renovation work, the lack of transparency in the government plans, and the disregard for the role of the local inhabitants in this city. Still unresolved is an agreement on a real vision for the historic zone. Once restored, how will these buildings be adapted for reuse? Who primarily is to benefit from this 'massive intervention' and museumization: world citizens who value historic and cultural variety? Cairenes who live in the historic area? Contracting companies who are doing the work? Or tourists, whether foreign or Arab, who visit Cairo? The preservation problems that face Cairo are immense, and far surpass those being confronted by any other Arab city. Still, selling the nation's authentic heritage for the short-term rewards of capital gain does not seem a good bargain. Perhaps here the cautionary wisdom of an Arab proverb is appropriate: "He tried to beautify her with *kuhl* [dark eyeliner], but blinded her instead."

Appendix

Caroline Williams
June 8, 2001

Mrs. Suzanne Mubarak
Qubba Palace
Heliopolis, Cairo

Dear Mrs. Mubarak:

May we enlist your help? Cairo is a remarkable treasure house of Islamic architecture dating from the earliest days of the Arab conquest. Its monuments are an irreplaceable historical record, an architectural legacy without equal in the entire Islamic world. There has long been a need for significant steps to be taken to protect the monuments from the perils of ground water, atmospheric pollution, neglect and urban encroachment and we are grateful that the Ministry of Culture has now found the financial resources to permit substantial restoration projects to be undertaken. We are concerned, however, at the methods and materials being used in some cases and believe these are posing a new threat to the safety of the monuments.

Briefly, instead of pumps and drains being installed, synthetic damp-proofing materials are being applied. They have a cosmetic effect but do not solve the water table problem. Instead of painstaking repair and documentation of architectural features that are original, authentic and significant, they are being discarded and replaced by replicas. Most alarming, walls are being injected with Portland cement, the use of which for preservation purposes has been opposed by UNESCO for years because it adds intrusive and damaging chemical mixtures to the natural materials of the original structure. A more detailed description of specific problems is attached.

We hope that we are not, as one author recently predicted, "the last generation to experience the joy and wonder of the Mother of the World; for neither memory nor legend will ever take the place of the real thing." As members of the international community we join with our Egyptian colleagues and associates to call on the Egyptian government to oversee more closely the work being done on these remarkable monuments. There are many praiseworthy restoration projects that the Arab contracting companies need to be aware of, such as the work at the Darb al-Qirmiz, the Bab Zuwayla, the Bayts al-Sihaymi, al-Harrawi and al-Sinnari. As a reference point, the Supreme Council of Antiquities might refer the Arab Contracting companies to these standards.

Cairo has been placed on the world cultural heritage list. The preservation of this unique and still living city, its rich historical dynasties, its chronology of styles, its variety of architectural types, is thus of international as well as national concern.

Respectfully yours,
Committee for the Preservation of Islamic Monuments in Cairo,
(List of Signers Attached)

Caroline Williams, Corresponding Secretary
(List of signers attached)

SOME CURRENT THREATS TO CAIRO MONUMENTS

At least thirty-one prime monuments are being overhauled by nine different contracting companies. For example, the Mosque of 'Amr ibn al-'As which was restored 20 years ago by the Arab Contractors is now being totally redone by the Wadi al-Nil Co. Many of these companies have little experience with the fine art of restoration.

Resolutions from the Venice Charter of 1964, and recommendations set forth by the Egyptian Society of Friends of Antiquities (al-Jam'iya al-Misriya li-Muhibbi al-Athar) in 1980 are ignored. Both charters *ban the use of Portland Cement*, which is currently being used in the restoration of the Mosques of Ahmad ibn Tulun, of Qanibay al-Muhammad, of Mahmud al-Kurdi, as well as in the Khanqah of the Amir Shaykhu, the complexes of Sultans Qalawun, and of Qaytbay and Qurqumas in the Northern Desert, to name a few.

The Venice Charter and the Egyptian Society of Friends of Antiquity both subscribe to the basic principles of minimal intervention, reversibility, compatibility and documentation. Yet a look into the interiors of the Mosques of Mahmud al-Kurdi, of Muayyad Shaykh, and Shaykhu reveals chaotic scenes of scaffolding, cement, asphalt, debris, destruction. The men in charge are engineers. They admit knowing nothing about Mamluk history or architectural principles.

In many cases the original, authentic fabric of the building, the patina of time, is being discarded and replaced with replicas. Whole areas of the Mosque of Mu'ayyad Shaykh were stripped of the original marble. Old columns in many mosques are now replaced by generic concrete replicas.

It is widely recognized that the major problem attacking these buildings is the rise of the water table. Before long term intervention can take place the rising ground water must be solved. Yet this is slow to happen, and valuable monuments such as the Mosque of Ulmas al-Hajib in Hilmiya, Fatma Khatun in the Qarafa, and Sitt Hadaq off Sharia Port Said, continue to stand deep in water as they have for the past twenty years.

Al-Qahira is envisioned as an open-air museum, and yet no zoning safeguards seem to ensure this prospect. All over the medieval city new building initiatives, of concrete buildings, disfigure the cityscape at both pedestrian and aerial levels.

The view, once famous for its thousand minarets, is being overtaken by new multi-storied square intrusions.

Much of Cairo's unique historical and architectural legacy has recently been lost. The earthquake of 1992 damaged one hundred and twenty-five buildings, many of them still under repair. The Fatimid heritage was handed over to the Bohra Shi'i subsect, who without any research or documentation, engaged not in restorations, but in historically unauthentic and culturally self-serving recreations. In November 1998 the Musafirkhana Palace was gutted by fire. Some of these unfortunate events could not have been anticipated, but others could have, and hence our appeal for your support.

SIGNATORIES TO THE LETTER TO MRS. MUBARAK:

H.R.H. Princess Dr. Wijdan Ali, President of the Royal Society of Fine Arts, Jordan, & Dean of Research at the Jordan Institute of Diplomacy

Dr. James Allan, Prof. Islamic Art & Keeper, Eastern Art, Ashmolean Museum, Oxford

Mr. Jeff Allen, Aga Khan Cultural Services, Egypt

Mr. Colin Amery, Director, World Monuments Fund, United Kingdom

Dr. Doris Behrens-Abouseif, Khalili Prof. of Islamic Art & Archaeology, SOAS, London University

Dr. Jonathan Bloom, Norma Jean Calderwood Prof. of Islamic and Asian Art, Boston College

Dr. Sheila Blair, Norma Jean Calderwood Prof. of Islamic and Asian Art, Boston College

Ambassador Hermann Eilts, Member, Board of Trustees, American University in Cairo

Dr. Eleonora Fernandez, Prof. Islamic History, Center Arabic Studies, American University in Cairo

Mr. Finbarr Flood, Center for Advanced Study in the Visual Arts, National Gallery of Art, Washington, D.C.

Dr. Oleg Grabar, Aga Khan Professor of Islamic Art & Architect, Emeritus, Harvard University

Ms. Raymonda Guirguis, freelance photographer, Islamic Cairo

Dr. Nelly Hanna, Director & Prof., Center for Arabic Studies, American University in Cairo

Ms. Nawal Hassan, President, Association for the Urban Development of Islamic Cairo; Founder, Center for Egyptian Civilization Studies

Dr. Robert Hillenbrand, Prof. Islamic Art and Architecture, University of Edinburgh

Dr. Renata Holod, Prof. & Chair, History of Art Dept., University of Pennsylvania

Mr. Sabri Jarrar, doctoral candidate, Islamic Architecture, Oxford University

Mme. Chahinda Karim, Prof., Islamic Architecture of Cairo, Center for Arabic Studies, American University in Cairo

Dr. Nuha Khoury, Prof., Islamic Art and Archaeology, University of California, Santa Barbara, & President, Historians of Islamic Art (HIA)

Dr. Günter Meyer, Director, Center for Research on the Arab World, University of Mainz

Dr. William Quandt, Member, Board of Trustees, American University in Cairo

Ambassador Richard Parker, author of *A Practical Guide to Islamic Monuments in Cairo*, and past editor of the *Middle East Journal*

Dr. Jerry Podany, President, American Institute for Conservation of Historic and Artistic Works (AIC), Washington, D.C.

Dr. Nasser Rabbat, Prof., Islamic Architecture, Aga Khan Program, Massachusetts Institute of Technology

Dr. André Raymond, Prof. Emeritus, Université de Provence; past director, Institute for Research And Study on the Arab and Islamic World

Dr. John Rodenbeck, Founder, Society for Preservation of Architectural Resources of Egypt (SPARE)

Dr. Nezar al-Sayyad, Chairman, Center for Middle East Studies, University of California, Berkeley

Ms. Sarah Searight, Islamic art specialist, and author/speaker

Mme. Samia Serageldin, author of *The Cairo House*

Mrs. Janet Starkey, Center for Middle East Studies, University of Durham, England

Hilary Weir, member of SPARE, author of *Medieval Cairo: a Visitor's Guide*, former director, Architectural Heritage Fund, United Kingdom

Ms. Caroline Williams, author of *The Islamic Monuments of Cairo: The Practical Guide*

Works cited

Abdel-Latif, Omayma. 2001. "A Long and Winding Road." *Al-Ahram Weekly*, 4–10 January.

El-Aref, Nevine. 2003a. "House of the Nation." *Al-Ahram Weekly*, 27 February–5 March.

———. 2003b. "Young Elegance Restored." *Al-Ahram Weekly*, 18–24 September.

———. 2004a. "Party in History." *Al-Ahram Weekly*, 1–7 January.

———. 2004b. "Medieval Mosques Re-Open." *Al-Ahram Weekly*, 15–22 May.

Bakr, Mahmoud. 1998. "Pulling and Pushing." *Al-Ahram Weekly*, 7–13 May.

Blair, E. 2004. "Islamic Cairo Grapples with Restoring its Treasures." Reuters, 21 June. <*http://news.yahoo.com*> (28 June 2004).

Coste, Pascal-Xavier. 1837. *Architecture arabe ou monuments du Kaire: mésurés et dessinés de 1818 à 1825*. Paris: Firman Didot.

———. 1878. *Mémoires d'un artiste: notes et souvenirs de voyages, 1817–1877*. Marsaille: Cayer, 2 vols.

Cunningham, Joanne. 2003. "Walled Off." *Cairo Times*, 17–23 July.

Drummond, James. 2003. "Special Report from Egypt: The Great Conservation Debate, and the Enemy of Archaeology." *Financial Times*, 22 October.

"Egypt Country Profile." 2003. *Africa Review*, 23 September, 6. *Janet Matthews Information Services*, Lexis-Nexis (15 March 2004).

Euromed Heritage Programme and Ministry of Culture, Egypt. 2001. *Mamluk Art: The Splendour and Magic of the Sultans*. Cairo: MEDA-Euromed Heritage Programme and Ministry of Culture, Egypt.

Farag, Fatemah. 2000. "Mission Impossible?" *Al-Ahram Weekly*, 500, 21–27 September. <*http://weekly.ahram.org.eg/2000/500/eg8.htm*> (7 July 2004).

———. 2003. "Urban Matters." *Al-Ahram Weekly*, 2–8 October.

Farouk, Dalia. 2001. "L'art mamelouk en 8 étapes." *Al-Ahram Hebdo*, 31 October.

Fernea, Elizabeth W. 2001. *Living with the Past*. First Run/Icarus Films.

Ghannam, Farha. 2002. *Remaking the Modern: Space, Relocation and the Politics of Identity*. Berkeley: University of California Press.

Gibb, H.A.R., trans. 1956. *The Travels of Ibn Battuta, A.D. 1315–1354*. Cambridge: Hakluyt Society at the University Press.

Halawi, Jailan. 2001. "A Breath of Dust." *Al-Ahram Weekly*, 30 August–5 September.

Hassan, Fayza. 1999. "Down the Yellow Brick Road." *Al-Ahram Weekly*, 22–28 July.

Ibrahim, Saad Eddin. 2001. "Addressing the Social Context in Cultural Heritage Management: Historic Cairo." In *Historic Cities and Sacred Sites*, eds. I. Serageldin, E. Schluger, J. Martin-Brown, 186–92. Washington, D.C.: World Bank.

Ionides, Alex. 2004. "Digging In." *Egypt Today*, July. <*http://www.egypttoday. com*> (7 July 2004).

Jarrar, Sabri. 2000. "Al-Makrizi's Reinvention of Egyptian Historiography through Architectural History." In *The Cairo Heritage: Essays in Honor of Laila Ali Ibrahim*, ed. Doris Behrens-Abouseif, 31–53. Cairo: The American University in Cairo Press.

Lane, Edward William. 1836. *An Account of the Manners and Customs of the Modern Egytians*. London: John Murray.

MacDonald, Neil. 1999. "Put Those Sabils to Work." *Cairo Times*, 15–28 April.

Marei, Jehan. 2003. "The Grand Scheme." April 20. <*http://www.artarabia. com/artman/publish/printer_67.shtml*> (2 January 2006).

Ionides, Alex. 2004. "Digging In." *Egypt Today*, July. <*http://www.egypttoday. com/article.aspx?ArticleID=1785*> (7 July 2004).

Nafie, Reem. 2003. "History versus People." *Al-Ahram Weekly*, 23–29 October.

Ormos, István. 2002. "Preservation and Restoration: The Methods of Max Herz Pasha, Chief Architect of the Comité de conservation des monuments de l'art arabe, 1890–1914." In *Historians in Cairo*, ed. Jill Edwards, 123–53. Cairo: The American University in Cairo Press.

"Population Passes 70mn mark." 2004. *Middle East Times*, 5 March. <*http:// www.metimes.com/articles/normal.php?StoryID=20040305-042723-9123r*> (24 August 2005).

Rabbat, Nasser. 2000. "Al-Maqrizi's *Khitat*, an Egyptian *Lieu de mémoire*." In *The Cairo Heritage: Essays in Honor of Laila Ali Ibrahim*, ed. Doris Behrens-Abouseif, 17–30. Cairo: The American University in Cairo Press.

El-Rashidi, Yasmine. 2003a. "Reconstructing the Past." *Al-Ahram Weekly*, 14–20 August.

———. 2003b. "Dollar-denominated Depression." *Al-Ahram Weekly*, 6–12 November.

Raymond, André, ed. 2002. *The Glory of Cairo: An Illustrated History*. Cairo: The American University in Cairo Press.

Reid, Donald Malcolm. 2000. *Whose Pharaohs?: Archaeology, Museums, and Egyptian National Identity from Napoleon to World War I*. Berkeley, Calif.: University of California Press.

Rodenbeck, John. 2000. "The Present Situation of the Historic City: A Road Not Taken." In *The Cairo Heritage: Essays in Honor of Laila Ali Ibrahim*, ed. Doris Behrens-Abouseif, 327–40. Cairo: The American University in Cairo Press.

Saad, Rehab. 2002. "At the Tip of a Knife." *Al-Ahram Weekly*, 28 November–4 December.

Samir, Amira. 2003. "La deuxième vie des sabils." *Al-Ahram Hebdo*, 28 May.

_____. 2004. "Une commerce traditionnelle menacé." *Al-Ahram Hebdo*, 14 January.

Schemm, Paul. 2003. "Cairo's Port (Bulaq)." *Cairo Times*, 1 January. *<http://www.cairotimes.com/>* (1 July 2004).

Sedky, Ahmed. 2001. "The Living Past." *Al-Ahram Weekly*, 558: 1–7 November. *<http://weekly.ahram.org.eg/2001/558/li1.htm>* (2 July 2004).

_____. 2005. "The Politics of Area Conservation in Cairo." *International Journal of Heritage Studies* 112 (May): 113–30.

Stille, Alexander. 2002. *The Future of the Past*. New York: Farrar, Straus and Giroux.

"Special Report: Egyptian Tourism Bounces Back." 2003. *Middle East* 338 (October): 52.

"Tourism to Egypt." 2004. *Business Today*, 15 January. *<www.businesstodayegypt.com>*.

"Travel News." 2004. *Egypt On-Line*, 12 January. *<http://www.sis.gov.eg>* (25 June 2004).

Tresilian, David. 2002. "World Heritage at Risk." *Al-Ahram Weekly*, 6–11 December.

UNDP. 2003. *Human Development Report 2003*. *<http://hdr.undp.org/reports/global/2003>* (28 June 2003).

UNESCO. 2002. *World Heritage: Archaeological Sites and Urban Cities, Muslim Cairo*, 254–261. Paris: UNESCO.

Wells, Rhona. 2004. "Special Report on Middle East Tourism." *Middle East* 341 (January): 45–47.

Williams, Caroline. 1985. "Islamic Cairo: Endangered Legacy." *Middle East Journal* 39 (Summer): 231–246.

_____. 2002a. *The Islamic Monuments of Cairo: the Practical Guide*. Cairo: The American University in Cairo Press.

_____. 2002b. "Transforming the Old: Cairo's New Medieval City." *Middle East Journal* 56 (Summer): 457–75.

_____. 2002c. "Islamic Cairo: a Past Imperiled." *Massachusetts Review* 42 (Winter): 591–608.

Williams, Harold. 2001. "Historic Cities: The Sense of Place, Sacred and Secular." In *Historic Cities and Sacred Sites*, eds. I. Serageldin, E. Schluger, and J. Martin-Brown, 401–05. Washington, D.C.: World Bank.

10

Urban Transformations

Social Control at al-Rifa'i Mosque and Sultan Hasan Square

Yasser Elsheshtawy

Prologue

In 1984 an area located between the Sultan Hasan Madrasa (a fourteenth-century religious school) and al-Rifa'i Mosque (dating from the nineteenth century) was closed to traffic and converted to pedestrian use. The subsequent use of the space (and its apparent success) by neighborhood residents was unusual for Cairo, where such projects are rare. Is it really possible for the government to forsake commercial and political interests and create a setting aimed at Cairo's poor within a prime tourist site? I decided to investigate this further and in 1994 began a one-year research study aimed at studying this space. One of my first tasks was to find the architect who designed it. This turned out to be quite an undertaking, leading me from the headquarters of the Supreme Council of Antiquities (SCA) in Zamalek to their offices in the Citadel, from an obscure office in downtown Cairo back again to their headquarters in Zamalek, where I finally found him. Details of that encounter are described in this chapter. During this search I met an official at the SCA who offered a fascinating inside glimpse of the motivations behind the closure and foretelling many of the changes which would occur in the space leading to its current state. This official was based in the Citadel in an office located next to the military museum. Housed in a historic building, he occupied the position of general manager (*mudir*—no further details were offered to me at that time!). Entering his office I was struck by its immense size and by the fact that it contained only a single desk. Sitting opposite the manager I began by describing my study and enquiring about the architect. After verifying my credentials (and motives) and exchanging the usual pleasantries and how nice the space has become after closing the street, he articulated a rather disturbing (to me) vision of the space. In particular he argued that the street closure has been in response to various "threats" in the form of drug use in the vicinity of the buildings in addition to the forming of various "fundamentalist" cells in the area. However, he was particularly disturbed by the increasingly visible presence of neighborhood residents (working class, or *baladi* people) who according to him were "bothering" tourists. To counteract these "subversions" he noted that plans were in the works for surrounding the area with a fence and controlling access through two gates. A cafeteria operating in the area would be accessible from outside, and as such this closure would not pose a problem for anybody (except of course for the *baladi* people). Here for the first time it became apparent to me that residents in this area were looked at as a 'threat' that needed to be contained and removed so that tourists would be able to enjoy a sanitized space (i.e., one without Egyptians). The fulfillment of this vision took some time to materialize but in 2003, on a visit to the space, I found that it had turned into reality. The conversion of this space into a neighborhood setting was an accident, a sideshow which, according to SCA officials, had to be 'returned' to its original purpose—a tourist site where the display of 'Egyptianness' is done according to a carefully crafted script.

Introduction

The privatization of public space, or what some have called the "quartering of urban space," is a phenomenon afflicting cities throughout the world (Marcuse and van Kempen 2000). City officials, in their drive to make money, are reserving large areas of urban space to attract tourists, investors, and in general those with superfluous financial resources. As a result, a sharper division between the rich and poor has become one of the most visible phenomena in 'global' cities (Sassen 2001). Cities in developing countries are not immune from such developments. Cairo in particular has been suffering from explosive population growth which, in turn, has resulted in high densities and a lack of appropriate public spaces. There are, however, some 'success stories' which illustrate that even with difficult conditions architects can create settings which are responsive to the needs of Cairenes. Unfortunately, such stories often do not have happy endings. By examining the transformations that have occurred in such spaces one can read sociopolitical factors operating within Cairo and its response to global conditions. Such projects reveal the extent to which these factors transform public space to conform with an 'elite' vision on what constitutes the 'public.'

This chapter tells the story of the al-Rifaʻi/Sultan Hasan Square located in an area of Cairo known as al-Khalifa at the foot of the Citadel. The space has undergone extensive transformations that are symptomatic of changing circumstances within Cairo, and were in turn a response to various globalizing tendencies, particularly the privatization of public space and the exclusion of certain undesired segments of the population. While this pedestrianization effort was done primarily to cater to tourism, the space was nevertheless 'taken over' by people from the surrounding community. (See Williams in this volume for further analysis of the place of tourism in the Egyptian economy.) It became a popular hangout for the elderly and the retired, teenagers, women and children—it truly became a people's space. SCA authorities—as I have noted above—grew alarmed by this and surrounded the entire area with a fence and two gates. These gates were kept open however, so it was still accessible for passersby and tourists who continued to visit it as well. Within the last few years one gate (bordering Muhammad ʻAli Street) has been closed and the entire area declared a 'tourist site,' thus effectively creating a private space for tourists and eliminating its function as a community gathering space. By the time of this writing in 2003, it was empty and desolate, quite a contrast to the lively and diverse activities that used to take place there.

My main argument in this chapter is that for cities in developing countries, in this case the Middle East, the danger is not from external forces (also known as orientalists, colonialists, imperialists, etc.) but from the inside, since local decision-makers view the general public as a threat that has to be dealt with and contained. In doing that a large segment of the population is precluded from certain rights (such as enjoyment of outdoor activities and socializing in urban historic areas) which become symptomatic of more serious infringements leading to their disenfranchisement, with its potentially dangerous drawbacks (e.g., fundamentalism).

The main crux of the study relied on interviews, observation, and photography done over a six-month period in 1994 (see Elsheshtawy 1996). In subsequent years I regularly visited to observe the changes taking place, and I worked on situating the space within a larger historical context by studying the history of the surrounding area as well.

The following is an account of the initial success of al-Rifa'i/Sultan Hasan square and its subsequent evolution into its current state. Images throughout the chapter are meant to complement, and add to, the narrative. I first begin by providing a historical context.

Al-Rifa'i and Sultan Hasan Square: History and Evolution

The square is an extension of a major boulevard known as Muhammad 'Ali Street. It is located between two religious buildings: a fourteenth-century *madrasa* (religious school) named after its founder Sultan Hasan, a Mamluk ruler, and al-Rifa'i Mosque containing the tomb of the saint al-Rifa'i, in addition to those of members of the Egyptian royal family and the late Shah of Iran. The *madrasa* was initially part of a tight urban fabric as it was located at the conclusion of Suq al-Silah Street. At the turn of the twentieth century Cairo underwent a series of dramatic changes manifested in numerous construction projects that aimed to open up the medieval city and connect it to the modern metropolis. In the process, wide thoroughfares were drawn through and wide *midan*s (squares) superimposed on the old city. The area surrounding the Sultan Hasan Madrasa located at the end of one of these boulevards received special attention as it connected the old center of power (the Citadel) with its contemporary counterpart (Azbakiya Square).

A monumental mosque (al-Rifa'i) was constructed opposite the Sultan Hasan Madrasa, the two buildings set within a large open area (Al-Harithy 1996). Removing the *madrasa* from its surroundings (i.e., disconnecting it from the urban fabric) was a radical departure, unprecedented in 'Islamic' cities, which established the building as an object whose primary value lies in its aesthetic appeal as opposed to its integral role and place in the community. In other words, the value of the mosque became established *visually* rather than socially, by providing a large open area allowing for a comprehensive perception of its physical structure. This was not typically the case in Cairo. Small vistas and squares occasionally opened up in front of important buildings but never at such a large scale, which is more typical of European medieval cities, and quite in line with the modernization efforts undertaken at that time (Elsheshtawy 2000).

The square prior to its closing was a main passage for cars and buses on their way to, or leaving, Muhammad 'Ali Street. Only a narrow walkway was provided for pedestrians. Although a small park area located at the rear of al-Rifa'i Mosque was occasionally used, it appears from pre-pedestrianization photographs to have been severely neglected. SCA officials suggested to me

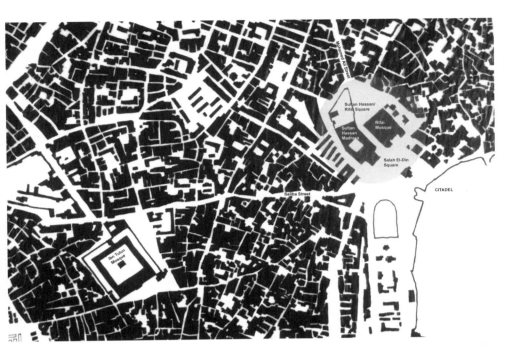

that this area was known for the presence of illegal activities such as drug use—
a common accusation in this area, due to the proximity of various drug centers
such as the neighborhood of Batniya. Such claims were difficult to verify,
however, and seem highly improbable given the high visibility of the space.
It seems more likely that this was merely an excuse for subsequently closing
off the square. In 1985 the SCA began a large effort to restore the monuments
located around Salah al-Din's Citadel, including the Sultan Hasan Madrasa.
Parallel to these developments, plans were made by its chief architect, Nabil
'Abd al-Sami', to close the space to car traffic and convert it to an area for
pedestrian use. Inspired by 'traditional' streets from Islamic Cairo, as well as
a visit to Italian cities, the architect divided the space into various sections to
accommodate the natural incline in its topography through the provision of
steps. Also, a gate was built near Muhammad 'Ali Street to mark the entry into
the square. In an extensive interview with the author in 1995, he noted that
one of his main objectives was the social component of the project, striving to
integrate with the surrounding neighborhood, which he viewed as vital to the
success of any preservation project. He voiced his opposition to any closure of
the street to pedestrian traffic, and noted his awareness of these plans by SCA
organization officials.

Map showing al-
Rifa'i/Sultan Hasan
Square in relation
to the Citadel and
Ibn Tulun Mosque
(Figure-ground
drawing by Yasser
Elsheshtawy,
based on a map
of Cairo from Dar
Al-Misaha, Cairo,
1994).

The square is marked by a number of features. Most notable is its overall structure consisting of two parts: the section located between the mosque and *madrasa*, characterized by a strong sense of enclosure, and an open area bordering the park. Additional interesting features include a ramp defined by a continuing ledge passing through the entire length with occasional interruptions, the previously mentioned gate, and the Islamic-patterned pavement. The space is located in the midst of a district which is poor but not considered a slum. Described as "traditional" and "urban," it is a vital mix of work and residence, sales, and consumption (Abu-Lughod 1971; Singerman 1995).

Observing the Square: A Behavioral Portrait

My observations show that in terms of numbers and types of people using the square, it was frequented by a large number distributed throughout the day in a way that reflected the daily rhythm of the city. Use was not restricted to a particular season or occasion but was consistent throughout the summer and winter months, as well as weekdays and weekends. A variety of activities occurred among a range of visitors: teenagers playing chess, children playing and fighting, and many others.

Women also use the square on a regular basis. An important measure of its success is the presence of regular users who can be seen on any given day such as the elderly, retirees, etc. For many of them this space has become an integral part of their daily activities acquiring almost a mystical dimension due to its location next to a mosque: "[Pedestrianizing] this street is something

Children playing soccer with tourists (photograph by Yasser Elsheshtawy).

natural . . . we were born and we found those mosques. . . . This is proof that they should have done this a long time ago. . . . After they pray they come and sit here under God's protection" (an elderly informant).

It has become a place where the presence of friends is expected as one of my informants suggested.

A handicapped person with crutches stopped and asked two elderly people sitting on one of the ledges: "Good morning, Hagg [title for elderly people signifying respect] . . . is no one sitting here today?" One of them responded by saying, "They are sitting on the stairs, there. . . ." [pointing with his hands].

Street vendors are present as well, thus adding another component to the vitality of the space. Therefore, from a strictly quantitative as well as qualitative standpoint, closing the square to traffic could be considered a success.

I then tried to understand the reason(s) behind this success. My argument at that time was that this could be directly attributed to the fact that it was able to accommodate change while at the same time responding to deeply rooted (core) cultural traditions. This was based on a particular definition of 'culture' articulated by Amos Rapoport. He argues that culture can be defined as a way of life typical of a group, a particular way of doing things (Rapoport 1989). I used this definition as an appropriate starting point in examining the construct of culture and identifying several elements of Cairo's traditional urban subculture which I felt were responsible for the use of al-Rifa'i/Sultan Hasan Square. They are (1) the concept of *fusha*; and (2) outdoor celebration. In addition to these, three more components—while not unique to this subculture—were considered as well: (3) the *'ahwa* custom; (4) the changing role of women and gender relationships; and (5) the dramaturgical aspect of street life. In Cairo the ability of this space to cater to all these components through its unique physical structure resulted in its heavy use, hence its success. In the following sections I define and explore each of these constructs.

The *Fusha* Concept

Examining the etymology of the word *fusha*, an Egyptian derivation from an Arabic verb meaning 'to go out for recreation,' shows that it is a very unique cultural construct with very specific architectural implications that are all present in the square, thus contributing significantly to its success. According to classic Arabic dictionaries, the word *fasaha* is defined as a wide place; its usage is in such sentences as 'people widened the place for him so he could sit.' It is also associated with the meaning that someone felt depressed but then

A couple from rural Egypt visiting the square (photograph by Yasser Elsheshtawy).

became relieved, i.e. "his spirit was widened." In Egyptian colloquial Arabic this word was developed into *yitfassah* and *fusha*. These words are used when someone is going out for leisure activities, to have fun, or simply to hang out. Thus, in the past tense someone *'itfassah*, or "he went out on a *fusha*." Also, in traditional urban areas the reception area in an apartment is called a *fasaha*, a direct derivation from the original word.

The use of this term is significant and has strong architectural and urban implications particularly since it has no equivalent in the English language. The significance stems from the association between enjoying oneself and being in a wide, open place. While this is probably a common feature among most cultures, it is notable that there is a special term devoted to this purpose in Arabic. Moreover, the word indirectly suggests that this wide place is not attached to one's place of residence but that one must go out and seek it.

The square could be examined from the perspective of *fusha*. It was a perfect urban manifestation of this idea. It fulfilled the two criteria which make a space suitable for a *fusha*: presence of open, wide areas; and distinction from residential use. Therefore, it was an appropriate space for an outing. Its successful use could thus be directly attributed to the extent to which it accommodates a highly specific cultural concept of the Egyptian people.

Outdoor-Event Celebrations

Two events are typically celebrated outdoors: weddings/engagements and feast ceremonies. The former is increasingly being performed in indoor

Retirees enjoying
the square
(photograph
by Yasser
Elsheshtawy).

spaces; whereas the latter is synonymous with going out and engaging in some outdoor activity. The square accommodates both, thus adding another measure to its success.

Katb al-kitab ceremonies (when couples and their families celebrate the signing of the marriage contract) are ordinarily preceded by a procession accompanied by music and dancers, as well as relatives who gather around the bride and groom. Usually, this procession would occur in the street leading to the apartment, house, or tent where the formal wedding ceremonies are performed. It is also worthy of note that this is typically associated with poorer areas. Middle- and upper-middle-class segments of society perform all of these events indoors in hotels. Increasingly, the occurrence of an outdoor procession is diminishing in traditional areas due to various societal changes such as the desire to emulate the rich and also the unsuitability of the street as a space for such activities (e.g., the crowded and unsanitary conditions in many working-class *sha'bi* areas preclude the performance of such important events).

I frequently observed outdoor celebrations of *katb al-kitab*. Through its location, physical structure, and the presence of a major mosque where such events could be formally performed, the space was conducive to this type of activity. The central location of the space accounted for its visibility and its perception as an important gathering place, a setting known by everyone. Frequently, respondents would tell me that it was used as a meeting place for neighborhood residents, which explained the occurrence of weddings and

A marriage
ceremony
(photograph
by Yasser
Elsheshtawy).

engagements. The physical structure manifested in the ledges where people
could sit, the presence of zones allowing for a spatial separation between
participants in the ceremonies and the rest of the users, and the gates conveying
an image of a protected space shielded from any outside interference; all are
supportive of the *katb al-kitab* ceremony.

In sum, events that are increasingly diminishing in traditional Cairo had been relocated to the square. People were taking advantage of its unique physical characteristics and used it as a way to revive a deep-rooted tradition, an important component of their lifestyle, or their culture. In that way continuity is established between 'tradition' and 'history' while at the same time recognizing societal change. The square also offered a useful precedent to be applied in other areas of traditional Cairo, relieving some of the financial pressure which newlyweds face since the ceremony is performed outdoors for free, in contrast to the expensive fees for renting indoor reception halls at hotels.

The second important event catering to a larger audience is the celebration of the feast or 'id, which is done on two occasions: one following the fasting month of Ramadan, also known as the 'small feast' (al-'id al-sughayyar) and the other during the pilgrimage to Mecca, the 'big feast' (al-'id al-kabir, or Feast of Sacrifice). During celebrations children are dressed up in new clothes and their parents take them out to a park, or any outdoor area which has a wide expanse of green space. In Cairo, for example, people usually go to the Zoological Garden, or the river walk along the Nile. (See Battesti in this volume for a discussion of holiday visits and the use of public space at the Giza Zoo.) In many poor neighborhoods special rides are set up for children. This particular square, on both occasions, was filled with an immense number of people no doubt encouraged by the rides bordering Salah al-Din Square located immediately next to the southern entrance, in addition to the park-like atmosphere in the street itself.

Similar to the wedding ceremonies, the 'id celebrations were performed in the square, thus showing the extent to which it catered to people's lifestyle by providing an alternative setting where such activities can be performed. To further illustrate this point, one of Cairo's main newspapers, in an issue following al-'id al-sughayyar, discussed in an article the enthusiastic response by Cairo's residents to the celebrations; the article was accompanied by a picture of the rides around the square with al-Rifa'i Mosque in the background ("al-'Id . . ." 1995). While this could be construed as anecdotal evidence, it nevertheless illustrates the extent to which the space had become expressive of an important component of Cairo's culture.

The 'Ahwa Factor: A Changing Tradition
In Cairo the 'ahwa (a traditional coffeehouse) is considered to be the primary meeting and gathering place for male residents in lower-income (sha'bi) neighborhoods. Recently, however, changes have taken place. (See de Koning

for further discussion of the changes in coffeehouse culture in Cairo.) Many people are shunning the *'ahwa* for a number of reasons such as economics, the increasingly negative connotations derived from being in an *'ahwa* (among traditional Cairene the expression 'sitting in an *'ahwa*' is synonymous with having nothing to do and wasting one's time), and the simple desire to be away from others.

Al-Rifa'i/Sultan Hasan Square has replaced the traditional *'ahwa* for those who do not wish to use it for all the above reasons, according to my informants. Many noted that the space is much better than the *'ahwa* since entry/use is free, they are not forced to partake in any interaction, and it is not as noisy. One informant told me that many people who used to sit in the *'ahwa* are not doing so anymore and have in fact substituted it for the square. The most frequently mentioned reason is that they are left alone and are not bothered by anyone. In other words they are still able to observe the social life surrounding them, but from a safe distance, without being forced to participate. The following account is particularly illustrative:

Elderly informant: Yeah, this [street] made a difference. . . . People used to sit in the 'ahwa [coffeshop]. . . . I am not a fan of 'ahwa-sitting, but most of the youths who sat in the 'ahwas now come to the street. . . . So there is a small number who spoil the place . . . the youths who have bad morals.
Author: They make a lot of noise and so on?
Elderly informant: Yeah, and bothering people and talking [loudly].

While it would be an exaggeration to argue that the *'ahwa* has disappeared, for some people the square has become a reasonable alternative for a meeting and gathering place that accommodates the changes in their lives.

The Role of Women: Changing Gender Relationships

Traditional Arab-Islamic societies were characterized by gender segregation (public places were reserved for male use, whereas women were restricted to the home). Recognizing that such practices are not based on religious principles but inherited traditions, Islamic societies underwent many changes and the liberation of women was one outcome of these. In the same vein gender relationships underwent many changes. Whereas in the past it was unthinkable for an unmarried couple to appear in public, this has become a usual sight, at least in Cairo. The square reflected these changes. It became a place for unmarried individuals to meet, socialize, flirt, and exchange glances. The following event was quite typical:

Four male and four female teenagers were sitting opposite each other. The male kids were talking loudly trying to attract the girls' attention ... an 'ar' sus (liquorice-drink) vendor passed by and they ordered from him, then the girls also ordered. The male kids saw this as a chance for some attention so they threw around various comments: "Hey, that drink tastes really bad," or yelling at the vendor, "Don't forget to take your money." It never went beyond these exchanges of words.

It was not a domain exclusively reserved for men, as is the *'ahwa*, but rather both genders were among its users. While the numbers suggested a majority of males, I discovered that for adults both men and women were almost equally represented. In addition the spatial structure of the square allowed for certain sections to be occupied exclusively by women, families, or couples, without feeling that they were being observed or watched. It also became an 'acceptable' setting for couples to meet since they were in the middle of a busy, public place (for more on acceptable social settings where couples can meet, see Armbrust's chapter on the Egyptian cinema in this volume and de Koning on upscale coffeehouses). In this way persisting cultural and religious sensibilities were respected and honored. Thus, the participation of women in public life found an appropriate outlet in the square by providing a setting in which both genders could safely interact.

Performing and Watching: The Theatrical Component

Classic urban-studies literature (e.g., Alexander et al. 1977; Jacobs 1961) suggests that one of the critical ingredients of any successful public-space design is the ability to see others and to be seen (distinct from the previously discussed concept of *fusha*, which indicates a desire to go out, whereas here it suggests what one does). While the concept itself has global dimensions shared by many cultures, it is how this activity is carried out, where it is done, and how it is done, that imbues it with a unique characteristic making it an integral component of individual subcultures, as was the case in the square. The separation of actors and spectators was achieved since the street was wide enough to allow for people to distance themselves from each other and watch what was going on without appearing to be too intrusive. The ledges acted as excellent seating, and the performance tended to occur in the middle of the street. Sometimes, as in modern theater, the spectators were immersed in the middle of the play and could actually become part of the play itself. Thus the role of actor and spectator became interchangeable, however, no one was forced to participate. It is interesting to note, though, that the external events that were being watched provided an incentive for people to talk, as they provided a context, an excuse, for the start of a conversation. In many instances conflicts, stereotypes, perceptions were projected upon what was being observed:

Informant A: The youths and the kids are spoiling it [the street]. . . . This is a place for tourism but these youths are making noise and other nonsense . . . this isn't right. . . . It is not right that these kid things should happen there . . . there should be order."
Informant B: These are the youths who are trying to show off . . . they like to fight and so on. . . . This is happening in the area and the street as well.
Researcher: This is a common phenomenon?
Several informants at once: A common phenomenon in all of Egypt . . . especially in al-Khalifa [the nearby neighborhood}, here it is very common. . . . This is what is dislikeable.

The success of this pedestrian space was thus dependent upon the extent to which it catered to an important cultural component among Cairo's residents, namely the desire to watch and to be seen, which is one of the critical ingredients in any public-space design. In all of these instances mentioned above, change is an important element, whether it is in the changed physical setting in which an old tradition is performed or a changed tradition which found its expression in the square.

Transformations: Privatizing the Square

During my research I met a high-ranking official at the SCA who expressed his dismay at what he termed the "unruly" behavior of neighborhood residents. He told me that plans were in the making to close off the space to regular pedestrian traffic, by utilizing the newly constructed gates. Al-Rifa'i Mosque, still a functioning building, would be accessed from an external street. His main argument revolved around a mixture of "protecting tourists" and "preserving the monuments" (for further discussion of the Egyptian government's plans for Fatimid, Islamic, and historic Cairo, see Williams in this volume). It was not clear to me at that time, and still is not, how the presence of residents could be in any way harmful for either tourists or buildings. A few years later, this 'inspired vision' turned into reality.

As I have noted above the space was initially a traffic thoroughfare. In 1984 it was converted to pedestrian use. At that time there was no fence and no closable gate. It was quite a remarkable setting—a public, open, and accessible space located next to one of the most significant monuments in Islamic history. This was simply too good to be true. Officials, somehow perceiving residents as a 'threat,' constructed a fence with gates which surrounded the entire site in the

1990s. However, the gates were left open, thus enabling people to use the space as a pedestrian thoroughfare and for it to be used as a 'public park' as described above. In 2000, however, the transformation was eventually completed by closing the southern gate situated next to Muhammad 'Ali Street, and placing a ticket booth at the northern entrance. Signs were placed around the site announcing that this was a "historic area." Security officers were placed visibly at the entrance. Thus what once was an accessible urban space became, through these 'inhibiting' symbols, a "museum." While Egyptians could enter without paying a fee, the closing of one gate effectively removed the thoroughfare function, which was one of the key components of making this street a success. The signs of power—the gate, security officers, signs proclaiming a historic/tourist area—also inhibited people from entering and sitting in the street.

Tourists entering the square from the only available entrance (photograph by Yasser Elsheshtawy).

During a recent visit in 2003, I was stopped by a security guard who thought I was a foreigner (I was carrying expensive camera equipment). Once I convinced him that I am, in fact, an Egyptian, I was allowed to enter without paying an entrance fee. Inside I was in a supposedly sanitized area—achieved by removing *sha'bi* or *baladi* Egyptians. It was lacking life, however. What once was a thriving site, a place in which tourists interacted with locals, where arguments were carried out, couples met, and many other activities occurred, had become an alienating space. In its present state it is a stage for tourists to take pictures and to visit the Sultan Hasan Madrasa, an open-air museum isolated from the rest of Cairo and geared toward the global trade of tourism.

Conclusion

I began this study with simple observations about the use of a popular urban space in Cairo. In the process of uncovering the reasons behind the success of this space, I discovered that people appreciated this setting because it responded to [or accommodated] changing cultural traditions, via its physical structure. Rather than providing stereotypical 'Islamic' and 'Arabic' design patterns, the architect opted for a more subtle and indirect approach, inspired in part by European urban patterns (street use in Italian cities), which caters primarily to people's needs and desires, thus responding to changing needs as well as deeply rooted cultural traditions. At the same time, during subsequent visits I found out that the changes occurring within the space are nothing but a reflection of the sociopolitical conditions in Cairo. What initially began as a 'social experiment' quickly degenerated into a typical reaction in which the 'poor' public is viewed as a threat that needs to be contained and overcome. The closure of the space was conceived in the early 1980s—a time following the opening of Egyptian society to the West during Anwar Sadat's rule. A peace treaty was signed with Israel and there was in general a great sense of optimism that the country was finally embarking on a path of reform and modernity. Sadat's assassination in 1981 briefly clouded this atmosphere, yet Mubarak's regime quickly established a sense of stability and continuity. The street's closure to car traffic and its initial opening to neighborhood residents could be a reflection of this optimism. It symbolizes a desire for coexistence in which the public is part of any development effort. However, things quickly deteriorated—the 1980s and 1990s saw the rise of terrorism with Egypt—and Cairo—the object of relentless attack by fundamentalists. In their desire to protect tourists from any threat, real or perceived, officials quickly began a series of security measures. This included of course the complete closure of al-Rifaʻi/Sultan Hasan Square and the elimination of its function as a thoroughfare and hangout for residents. This is, however, only one explanation.

Changes in this square are also a response to global conditions and trends in which various attractive spaces within the city are turning into gated communities whether through the erection of fences, presence of 'inhibiting' symbols, or distant locations, as indicated in the introduction to this paper. According to a recent UN report on globalization, it is an effort to "wall some in and keep others out" (UN-Habitat 2001, 30 and for further elaboration see Elsheshtawy 2004).

New developments in Cairo seem to be following this trend—Sixth of October City and the Qattamiya developments, also termed "New Cairo," which include a series of gated communities catering to the rich (see Denis and Vignal/Denis in this volume for further analysis). Of more relevance to this paper is the development of al-Azhar Park, located at the edge of Old

Cairo next to al-Azhar Mosque. Previously a garbage dump, the area has been converted into a park, carefully designed and landscaped. Funded by the Aga Khan Development Corporation, the project is meant to be a green oasis not only for Cairenes in general, but also for the residents of the nearby Darb al-Ahmar area (a low-income community). The park is—no surprise here—surrounded by a fence and guarded by security officers. The authorities plan to charge a symbolic entrance fee at entrances located on the Darb al-Ahmar side, whereas those entering from Salah Salem Street will pay a higher fee (Krauss 2004). Recent events in Cairo, such as developments in al-Rifaʿi/ Sultan Hasan Square, do not suggest that such crude egalitarian measures will prevail—and that in effect the gating and closing of Cairo's public spaces will continue.

Works Cited

Abu-Lughod, Janet. 1971. *Cairo: 1001 Years of the City Victorious*. Princeton: Princeton University Press.

Alexander, Christopher, Sara Ishikawa, Murray Silverstein, Max Jacobson, Ingrid Fiksdahl-King, Shlomo Angel. 1977. *A Pattern Language*. New York: Oxford University Press.

Elsheshtawy, Yasser. 1996. "Tradition, Change and Street Encounters: The Case of Two Pedestrian Streets in Cairo, Egypt." Ph.D. dissertation, University of Wisconsin-Milwaukee.

_____. 2000. "Nineteenth-century Globalization: Tansforming the Historic Center of Cairo." *IASTE: Working Paper Series, Volume 125. Preservation, Transformation and the Making of Place*. Berkeley: University of California, Berkeley.

_____. ed. 2004. *Planning the Middle East City: An Urban Kaleidoscope in a Globalizing World*. London: Routledge.

Al-Harithy, Howyda N. 1996. "The Complex of Sultan Hasan in Cairo: Reading between the Lines." In *Muqarnas: an Annual on the Visual Culture of the Islamic World*, vol. 13, ed. Gülru Necipoglu, 68–79. Leiden: E.J. Brill.

"al-ʿId: intilaq wa-bahga." 1995. *al-Ahram*, 7 March.

Jacobs, Jane. 1961. *The Death and Life of Great American Cities*. New York: Random House.

Krauss, Joseph. 2004. "Green Acres: In a Concrete Heavy City, Landscapers Hope Al-Azhar Park will Help Unearth a Greener Cairo." *Business Today*, August, 36–38.

Marcuse, Peter, and Robert van Kempen. 2000. *Globalizing Cities: A New Spatial Order?* Massachusetts: Blackwell Publishers.

Rapoport, Amos. 1989. "On the Attributes of Tradition." In *Dwellings, Settlements and Traditions: Cross-cultural Perspectives*, eds. Jean Paul Bourdier and Nezar AlSayyad, 77–105. Lanham, Md.: University Press of America.

Sassen, Saskia. 2001. *The Global City*. Princeton: Princeton University Press.

Singerman, Diane. 1995. *Avenues of Participation: Family, Politics, and Networks in Urban Quarters of Cairo*. Princeton: Princeton University Press.

UN-Habitat. 2001. *Cities in a Globalizing World: Global Report on Human Settlements*. London: Earthscan Publications Ltd.

11 Pyramids and Alleys

Global Dynamics and Local Strategies in Giza

Petra Kuppinger

Giza is a vibrant city with more than two million residents. This is no news to insiders, yet seen from the international scale Giza is all too frequently reduced to the few square kilometers surrounding the Pyramids. No similar discrepancy in perception exists with regard to Giza's larger sister across the Nile, Cairo. Insiders and outsiders alike recognize Cairo as a prominent global center of the twenty-first century, as much as it has been a world and regional center for a millennium. Giza exists in the shadow of Cairo. Indeed, Giza, on the west bank of the Nile just across the river from the core of Egypt's capital, has now been fully absorbed into the body of the Greater Cairo metropolis. Little has been written about the specificity and complexity of Giza's global and urban modernity, which dates to the late nineteenth century when new bridge-construction technologies allowed for better connection of the two banks of the Nile. In the early years of the twentieth century, Cairo's urban growth gained unprecedented momentum and the city spilled over the Nile onto Giza territory. The old country town of Giza, located in an agricultural zone across the Nile slightly south of modern Cairo's downtown, could have easily shared the fate of many of its counterparts across the world: swallowed and surrounded by a metropolis and her name reduced to that of a mere urban quarter. But Giza survived as center of the governorate of Giza, the seat of local administration. Located a few miles west of central Giza are the famous Pyramids. Historically they have little to do with the contemporary town of Giza and of course predate it. But they remain known as the "Pyramids of Giza," not ". . . of Cairo."[1] This linguistic detail in itself is not very relevant, yet it has left traces in the making of modern Giza, and continues to influence the construction and negotiation of Giza spaces. Cairo's rapid expansion over the last 150 years and the gravitational pull of the Pyramids are central to the history of modern Giza. The Pyramids have constituted a dramatic point of interest for colonial and postcolonial tourism, Western cultural imaginations, national-development and state-promotion projects, as well as global financial interests. The two stories—the first of the town of Giza and its surrounding villages' integration into a global metropolis, and the second of the Pyramids as an icon of colonialism and then global tourism—structure this chapter's exploration of the Giza cityscape.

In this chapter I introduce two Giza spaces—the Pyramids Plateau, and the small lower-class urban quarter of al-Tayyibin—to illustrate local and global spatial dynamics.[2] Juxtaposing the two spaces, I aim to show how spatial transformations and everyday practices rooted in disparate local and global historical, political, and social agendas and trajectories differently shaped two spaces. While the larger historical and spatial dynamics are similar for both places, what accounts for the resulting different spatialities is the relative weight of particular political and economic interests and forces. With the reorganization of global capitalism, and specifically the extension of the global tourism industry, sites like the Giza Pyramids increasingly eluded merely local control and came to cater to global politics and financial interests. Rationales of tourism became central for spatial policies and decisions. Subsequently, such spaces become economically and culturally removed from their territories and displaced into global realms. Such globalized spaces have been turned into global symbols that are mined for various economic and political purposes. Decisions about their futures are increasingly made in a global sphere by globally oriented actors and institutions, with national and local actors positioning themselves for maximum advantage within this context. The Pyramids and their environs are the focus of outside interest and are hyper-responsive to global transformations.

In contrast, spaces that are not visible to a global audience, even if located in close proximity to the tourist sites, do not partake in many of these transformations. But these 'irrelevant' spaces are exposed to global dynamics and respond to these in their own manner. Residents' rationales and ideas structure this place-making process. Analyzing al-Tayyibin, located a few kilometers from the Pyramids, I maintain that global dynamics define the broader outlines of the stage on which local residents construct lives and places. The global and the local are no easy opposites; they are intricately linked, and indeed each forms a fundamental part of the other (AlSayyad 2001).

The Pyramids and the Logic of Tourism

Questions of ownership and control of particular tourist sites become relevant due to the tremendous cultural and economic impact of modern Pyramids tourism. Concepts such as 'world heritage' or 'wonders of the world' or 'world civilization' symbolically transfer ownership of monuments from their specific geographical environment, from the respective city or nation-state, to the 'world' (Lowenthal 1988; Nuryanti 1996). The Pyramids were designated a World Heritage site by UNESCO in 1979. This identification represents the concerns of a specific modern global secular community. Because representatives of this community hold considerable global political and economic power, the fact that they do not represent humanity as a whole in any direct or accountable way often goes unchallenged.[3]

A lone rider near the Pyramids in the early morning (photograph by Jean Pierre Ribière).

The modern Western fascination with the Pyramids is rooted in the European Enlightenment. Starting in the eighteenth century, thinkers formu-lated a new model of history, a unilinear progress of civilization, culminating in modern European civilization. Ancient civilizations became the ancestors and transmitters of a single human civilization; and pharaonic Egypt was assigned the honorable role of civilization's cradle. This new historical understanding in Europe combined with the availability of financial means and possibilities for travel accounted for the surge in travel to Egypt, and to the Pyramids in particular (Kuppinger 1998, 107). As the Pyramids were slowly inscribed into the minds of the elite and in the minds of the popular classes in Europe, they were remapped into the territory of 'world heritage.' They entered a long process of deterritorialization as the place became increasingly dependent on and responsive to dynamics that originated beyond its physical territory, and was less responsive to locally based encounters and transactions.[4] This symbolic sense of European ownership intensified with reports from nineteenth-century travelers and scholars describing how contemporary Egyptians had little understanding or respect for the masterworks of their ancestors. This ignorance, it was and is still frequently suggested, will harm the monuments. It implied that control of the monuments should not be left to Egyptians.[5] The advent of modern transportation, communication and media starting in the nineteenth century allowed wealthy Europeans (and later Americans) to explore the world by boat, train, print media and later also film. Subsequently, a new sense of ownership was no longer solely based on immediate spatial relations, but aspects of symbolic ownership entered the picture.[6]

This shifting sense of place and belonging played a role in the colonial project, which underwrote new possibilities of travel and claims of ownership. As scholars dreamed of symbolically mastering the Pyramids, colonial armies and administrators made this a brutal reality. When Egypt came under British control in 1882, the Pyramids became more than a colonial possession, they "were appropriated as an imaginary ex-territorial extension of Europe" (Kuppinger 1998, 107). The Pyramids had 'returned' to their true owners. The armies of colonial (and postcolonial) tourists with their footsteps did the important additional work of inscribing quasi-physical ownership into the Pyramids. They strengthened and continue to strengthen the claim to symbolic possession.

The realization of projects, however, was and is tied to the local contexts of workers, residential communities, and to the structures, interests, and political dynamics. These elements tie the Pyramids to other parts of Giza and its historical, cultural, and political structures and legacies. These ties ground the Pyramids in local specificity, and complicate the seemingly 'deterritorialized' or internationalized qualities of the site.

Al-Tayyibin and the Logic of Everyday Life

Al-Tayyibin is a small community in central Giza. It is not 'traditional,' nor pristine, nor timeless. From its inception, al-Tayyibin was deeply rooted in the universe of emerging Egyptian modernity. Built by a wealthy landlady around 1915, the older parts of the community were conceived as a model village. Little evidence of the early years of the community and the actual planning process are available, but we know that the community was constructed as an innovative solution by an individual invested in ideas of Egyptian nationalism and modernity (Kuppinger 2000, 116; Reid 1991, 31). The landlady wanted to settle her estate workers in a clean and orderly manner, as many landlords were doing at the time, influenced by ideas of rural reform, modern nation building and rational spatial planning (Mosséri and Audebeau 1921; Lozach and Hug 1930). Thus, the community was established as a modernist entity and continues to be fundamentally 'modern' in the sense of embodying ideas conceived in the context of national and global innovation (see further details below).

This new model community became the home of peasants and workers who negotiated their use of space on terms different from those who had originally planned their community. Drawing on local traditions and wisdom, they remade the community to serve their needs, culturally reappropriating the planned community. How precisely this came about is not central here; what matters is that multiple, often contradictory forces have been at work in al-Tayyibin from the beginning. With the death of their landlady, modernist planning and outside control of the community largely ceased. Residents were left to remake the community as they saw fit, yet tightly framed by the emerging larger cityscape.

In the 1920s, as the result of rising real-estate prices and the scramble for prime Nile-front land that accompanied Cairo's expansion into Giza, a village that had been situated on the Nile not far from al-Tayyibin was resettled next to the model community. al-Tayyibin grew by several times its size. As agricultural land began to disappear, the newly enlarged community slowly transformed over the next decades into a working-class quarter. Many men started to work in the new factories on the urban fringes, for example in Imbaba. Others turned to service jobs such as selling newspapers, or more recently, driving taxis and fixing cars. Life as it unfolded in al-Tayyibin over the last ninety years represents a complex interaction between urban, national, and global forces, and residents' responses conceived in the context of local tradition and wisdom.

Separate and Interwoven Trajectories: The Pyramids and al-Tayyibin

The Pyramids have stood for almost five thousand years. Al-Tayyibin is less than one hundred years old. There was an earlier informal community on the estate, but even that earlier community did not date back further than the 1870s. While al-Tayyibin does not have a long history, the Giza countryside does, with its old villages and peasant populations. Influences on the changes of the space of El Tayyibin are rooted in the transformation of the Giza countryside, and its present fate is tied to other working-class quarters of Greater Cairo. Despite their age difference, the comparison between the Pyramids and al-Tayyibin can provide insights into the making of Giza and Greater Cairo. The rest of this chapter will shuttle back and forth between the two places and illustrate seemingly unrelated events and transformations, illustrating interactions between global, national, and local forces in Giza.

The Pyramids: European interest in Egypt predates the modern era. There are records of travelers, merchants, and scholars who ventured from Europe to Egypt in the Middle Ages. In 1175 Gerard Burchard from Strasbourg was impressed with the size, markets, and cosmopolitan products of Babylon, the name of the old Roman port city on the Nile adjacent to where Arab conquerors founded Cairo (Dopp 1950, 123). Numerous accounts by medieval Europeans speak with admiration of the splendor of Babylon/Cairo, its diverse populations, buildings, markets, products, and army. These travellers wrote about churches, feasts, agriculture, commercial, and cultural issues, and were intrigued by the city and its vibrant life (Dopp 1950, 1951, 1953). Some medieval visitors who crossed the river to visit the Pyramids were less impressed. Roberto da Sanseverino mentioned his visit to the Pyramids in 1458 only in passing. He noted that they resembled the tomb of Romulus in Rome, but much larger (Dopp 1953, 97). These men did not identify the Pyramids with universal civilization nor ascribe a particular historical significance to them. This fact was to change over the next centuries.

Beginning in the eighteenth century, leisure travelers arrived with the agenda of exploring ancient grandeur. They had increasingly read about pharaonic Egypt and they thought in civilizational terms conceived by Enlightenment thinkers. The Pyramids had been reconceived as an object of European fascination. Egypt became identified as the origin of European civilization, now claiming to constitute 'the' civilization, and the apex of human progress. Politically, European civilizationism aspired to global reach and transcontinental colonial domination. Unwittingly, the new travelers played a role within the broader project of strengthening Europe's quest for political, cultural and economic power. The earlier admiration for Cairo as an important center of human commerce, urban development, and civilization became displaced by a new language consonant with Europe's colonizing mission that appropriated Egypt's meaning within it.

The Giza villages: By the late eighteenth century, the ups and downs of dynasties and governments had marked the lives of Giza villagers for centuries. Villages, built and deserted depending largely on political circumstances, were sustained and administered by a complex and shifting mix of tax farming, state ownership, religious endowment and quasi-private holdings (Cuno 1994; Al-Damurdashi 1991). In 1798, the French invasion brought more ruin and despair to these villages, which had already suffered considerably under Mamluk strife in the late eighteenth century. When Napoleon's armies defeated the Mamluk forces outside Imbaba, a few kilometers north of the town of Giza, the surrounding villages entered the global struggle for the extension of imperial power. For the next few years competing armies looted villages and carried away crops and livestock (Al-Jabarti 1994).

The Pyramids: Napoleon, as he saw it, was not simply invading Egypt, but was on a civilizational mission. To carry out this mission, his forces included an entire academy of scholars who set out to record, measure, and classify every millimeter of Egypt, its population, culture, architecture, agriculture, flora, and fauna. The mapping of Ancient Egypt was central to this project. Napoleon's scholars flocked to the pharaonic monuments to describe, decipher, and measure, and to take cultural ownership of tombs, temples, and other achievements, literally, as they often looted and shipped away massive quantities of artifacts.[7] Although the French were defeated, and left after only a few years of occupation, the question of cultural ownership of the Pyramids persisted. While Egypt was under the control of the dynasty of Muhammad 'Ali, the Pyramids entered their own historical trajectory as an increasing flow of travelers visited Egypt and the Pyramids (Legh 1816, 22; Wiemken 1963, 213).

German Egyptologist Richard Lepsius camped at the Pyramids from October 1842 until January 1843. He studied the Pyramids and surrounding tombs while on a three-year expedition to Egypt (Scurla 1961, 340, 353). At the Pyramids, he had forty to sixty workers with him (Lepsius 1961, 363, 365). It is not clear whether Lepsius had permission for his work; he only noted that he saw the Pasha several times and that he "found him always in a favorable mood for our expedition" (Lepsius 1961, 353).[8] Whether this was 'the' Pasha, meaning the ruler Muhammed 'Ali, remains unclear. As a spectacle for Christmas, Lepsius had a huge fire lit on top of Great Pyramid "to surprise his fellows" (Lepsius 1961, 367). Lepsius took a curious form of ownership of the Pyramids that seemed natural to him. In 1853, another German Egyptologist, Heinrich Brugsch, made a similar expedition to study the tombs surrounding the Pyramids. Together with his French colleague, Mariette, he camped at the Pyramids "with the necessary servants" (Brugsch 1961, 507–8). Brugsch used Lepsius's maps for a quicker entry to the tombs. As the body of knowledge about ancient Egypt grew, claims to ownership and the right to free access to the site became more pronounced.

Giza Villages: Imbaba, Bulaq al-Dakrur, Mit 'Uqba, and Duqqi—some of the older Giza villages—strengthened their collective positions (although not necessarily those of individual households) in the nineteenth century as their proximity to Cairo allowed them to consolidate their roles as suppliers of produce to the city's expanding markets. The increase in private and quasi-private landownership, the emergence of large landholdings in the hands of the ruling family, and the related advent of capitalist agriculture produced a growing number of large estates where landowners settled their workers in special communities, called *'izab* (sing. *'izba*).[9] Al-Tayyibin was one of them.

Photograph (by Petra Kuppinger) of postcard from the early twentieth century, n.d.

The Pyramids: From the late nineteenth century, when most of the central Giza landscape was agricultural, the Pyramids and their surroundings experienced changes that symbolically removed them from their immediate environs, and increasingly established their presence on a European mental map. An early outpost of European control was the Mena House Hotel.[10] Built as a hunting lodge by Khedive Isma'il, the original building was later enlarged to accommodate visitors for the festivities marking the opening of the Suez Canal in 1869 (Nelson 1997, 7). At the turn of the twentieth century, the Mena House was bought by the Egyptian Hotels Company, run by George Nungovich, the self-made magnate of the Egyptian hotel industry (Nelson 1997, 7; Kuppinger 2000, 161). Already the owner of the Savoy, Continental, and Helwan Hotels, he added the Mena House to his group of Cairo's best hotels.

Photograph (by Petra Kuppinger) of postcard from the early twentieth century.

CAIRO. - A wiew in Guizeh during the flood.

Al-Tayyibin: Around 1915, a landlady in central Giza decided to have her workers live in a more orderly environment. These workers had been living in housing most likely built by themselves outside the estate gates. This old *'izba* was torn down, and forty of the families were each assigned a house in the new *'izba.* The new community with its straight alleys and right angles reflected ideas of social engineering and supervision. Only one family was allowed per unit. No tenants were allowed to mingle with family members. Expressing their modernist, disciplinary design, the units were given to nuclear families instead of extended families. The layout of houses afforded distinct spaces for livestock, storage, tools, and living quarters (for slightly later and more elaborate models, see Lozach and Hug 1930, 129). Straight alleys allowed for supervision of residents. However, unlike other model villages that had gates and one central supervised point of entry (Lozach and Hug 1930, 51), al-Tayyibin had a supervisor's unit at a central location, but no gates or guards.

The physical and social plan of the *'izba* was rooted in the ideological framework of emerging nationalism, which saw the peasants as the wealth and soul of Egypt.[11] If these peasants were settled in rational contexts of healthy lives and productive work, Egypt's strength and independence would be guaranteed. The construction of al-Tayyibin was not merely the isolated idea of a benevolent landlady, but reflected broader nationalist ideas. The death of the landlady in 1920 meant the end of immediate supervision. In response to pressures on existing land, as reflected in the addition of a second and larger part in the 1920s, al-Tayyibin underwent transformations that were largely of its own residents' design. The original forty families started to take in tenants, subdivide spaces, and enclose space originally reserved for animals and agricultural appliances, in order to create more living space.

The Pyramids: In the first years of the twentieth century, the Mena House was frequently described as an elegant hotel with classy entertainment and superior amenities. Its dances and teas were discussed on the social pages of the *Egyptian Gazette (EG)*, the colonial newspaper. The Mena House's unique attraction was its location just below the Pyramids. On 19 February 1900, one observer noted:

It would be difficult to find a more delightful place to be idle in than the Mena. Those majestic masses that tower like mountains nearby seem to induce disinclination to movement. Then, too, sitting down on the desert, with the Pyramids for companions, it would be impossible for any creature of average sensitiveness not to be conscious of the atmosphere of bygone ages which perennially abides about them.

The years before World War I, despite the economic crisis of 1907, were glamorous for colonial elites, upscale travelers, and tourists (Margoliuth 1907; Loti 1909). Elite social life was vibrant, and demanded ever-better amenities (Kuppinger, forthcoming). In August of 1900, the Pyramid tram (trolley) line was inaugurated, which connected the Pyramids to Cairo by way of the Qasr al-Nil Bridge (*EG* 2 August 1900). This allowed for fast travel to the Pyramids and made the Mena House an easy destination for afternoon visitors. Demand increased and by 1908 (during the winter season) it was announced that the tram would leave the Gazira terminal every ten minutes on Sunday afternoons versus every half hour or hour on other days (*EG* 4 December 1908). Other amenities followed. In 1904, "a swimming bath" was added to the hotel's facilities (*EG* 18 April 1904).[12]

The improved infrastructure facilitated the opening of additional leisure establishments. In November of 1904, a bar and restaurant opened at the Pyramids (*EG* 3 November 1904). In 1906, credits were approved of "4000 Egyptian Pounds (LE) for water mains along the avenue to the Pyramids" (*EG* 2 August 1906). Real estate along the Pyramid Road became increasingly attractive. Also in 1906, the Building Lands of Egypt owned property on the Pyramid Road valued at LE16,000. Giza, and the Pyramid Road, in particular, became part of the construction mania underway in Cairo in the early twentieth century (*EG* 3 October 1906; 14 December 1906).[13]

Improvements continued to be made to add to the exclusive pleasures of colonial residents and tourists. In 1914, for instance, new streetcars were added and existing first-class cars were improved (*EG* 13 January 1914). In 1930, bank credit for the widening of Pyramid Road was increased to LE140,000. The road was planned to "be divided in four divisions. One will be for cars going toward the Pyramids, one for cars returning, one for trams and the other for animals (*EG* 8 February 1930).[14]

Al-Tayyibin: While al-Tayyibin had no fancy balls, it did not lack in entertainment. For example, a few older residents remembered that for some years after the death of the landlady in 1920, her family provided meat for residents on religious feasts. Religious festivals, engagements, and weddings were celebrated in the community's alleys. Residents also participated in larger public spectacles such as the wedding of King Farouk in 1939 (Sabet and Farag 1993). One woman recalled that her mother waited for hours by the side of a street to see the motorcade with the splendid cars and the magnificently decked-out couple. Another woman remembered enjoying watching King Farouk in later years approaching the Royal Shooting Club in Duqqi, Giza. "He had many cars, and they were all red," she remembered. "We used to sit in the grass and watch them go by," she added. With Farouk's passion for hunting, the Shooting Club was one of his favored locations. Some al-Tayyibin residents worked in the restaurant and elsewhere in the club.

The Pyramids: The Pyramids fascinated Europeans for different reasons. There was the dream of combining the ancient with cutting-edge technologies, or to use the Pyramids as a place for scientific experiments where technological advances could be presented as even more impressive with ancient glory as a backdrop. In 1906 "Mr. Jacques Foa, a well-known engineer, applied to the Government for permission to construct an aerial cablecar from the Mena House to the top of the Cheops Pyramid" (*EG* 28 November 1906). While Mr. Foa's project never materialized, it is interesting to note that the project combined technological experiments with a vision for future profits, a combination that is central to much tourist investment.

More successful in their realization of Pyramid fantasies were some pioneers of modern aviation. In January of 1914, several 'airmen' came with their airplanes to Egypt. After some spectacular landings in towns like Zagazig and Kafr al-Zayyat, one pilot "flew to Mena from Heliopolis. . . . After lunch at the hotel he flew around the British camp at Mena and also around the Pyramids" (*EG* 13 January 1914). Another pilot arrived later. As the highlight of the day, "at 3:30 PM. both airmen were circling around the Pyramids simultaneously" (*EG* 13 January1914).[15]

Al-Tayyibin: While the colonial elite and foreign tourists enjoyed new technologies like electric lights, telephones, and the pool, al-Tayyibin and other communities did not get serviced by water mains, electricity, or telephone lines. Access to transportation, communication, and conveniences was structured by differences in race, class, and location. The Pyramids became globally connected in the most literal sense. Yet al-Tayyibin did not become disconnected although it was less intensely connected and denied privileged linkages. Residents of al-Tayyibin were aware of the services and conveniences available to their new neighbors, partly because some individuals worked in the new tourist sites. Like Mr. Foa at the Pyramids, people in al-Tayyibin did not lack in technological ingenuity and creative ideas. Sometime in the 1930s or 1940s a clever and handy resident built an (illegal) extension from a public water pipe outside the community to his house, to install his private tap. This was a well-received new service and the family made a little money on the side selling tap water to neighbors. Eventually they were caught and the tap was removed by the authorities.

Photograph (by Petra Kuppinger) of postcard from the early twentieth century.

CAIRO - Dates palmers at Gizeh   LE CAIRE - Dattiers á Gizeh

The Pyramids: With the 1942 battle in al-'Alamayn, Egypt's Western Desert became a theater of battle in World War II. In November 1943, one year after the German defeat in Egypt's northwest, international attention turned once more to Egypt, as Churchill, Roosevelt, and Chiang Kai-Shek met "under the shadow of the Pyramids" (*New York Times* 1 December 1943, 29). Almost overnight the Mena House Hotel was cleared of its guests to serve as the headquarters of the British and U.S. staff (Nelson 1997, 66). "The three great present enemies of Japan" had come together there to discuss "the strategy of war and peace in the Pacific" (Nelson 1997, 66), and "settle the German fate" (*New York Times* 6 December 1943, 7). From the Mena House, Churchill and Roosevelt continued their journey to Tehran to meet Stalin. While the three leaders stayed in private villas in the vicinity of the Pyramids, meetings were held in the hotel.[16] The Mena House had turned into a first-rate global location that provided all the necessary aspects of transportation, communication, and security to accommodate world leaders in the most difficult times.

Al-Tayyibin: Soon, al-Tayyibin became integrated into the British war efforts. A large army camp was situated at a short distance to the community and attracted workers from the community and beyond. This brought a wave of new tenants to al-Tayyibin that was not altogether well received by the older residents. The community grew in numbers and density as housing in the modern quarters of al-'Aguza, Duqqi, and Giza was too expensive for ordinary workers.

Workers at the military camp learned valuable new skills like bicycle repair which some residents later drew upon to set up workshops in the postwar period. One family, in which a younger member was running a bicycle shop until the 1990s, traced their expertise in the bicycle sector back to one ancestor who had worked in this army camp. With the large numbers of soldiers and workers traveling to and from the camp, some women realized the economic potential of selling cooked and other foods to passers-by. Some of the same women had set up similar food businesses already in 1928–29 when the main building of the Ministry of Agriculture was under construction in the vicinity. Residents of al-Tayyibin were well informed about urban possibilities and quick to exploit them.

The Pyramids: The 1950s and 1960s witnessed the slow but steadfast expansion of the tourism industry. For example, the Nile Hilton was built in 1958 (Gray 1998, 91). In the Nasserist era, Egyptian agencies and individuals lead efforts to transform the Pyramids into a global tourist site. In 1954, Egyptian archaeologist Kamal al-Mallakh discovered the famous solar boat next to the Great Pyramid, which was eventually surrounded by its own museum (Hawass 2001b; Nelson 1997, 119). In the 1960s Ahmed As'ad became the first Egyptian to be manager of the Mena House (Nelson 1997, 111). And adored Egyptian singer and national(ist) icon Umm Kulthum frequently dined at the hotel in the 1960s.[17]

On 13 April 1961 "President Nasser, H.R.H. Prince Constantine, the former king of Greece, and some two thousand distinguished guests" witnessed the first Sound and Light Show at the Sphinx (Nelson 1997, 126). That night and countless times ever since, hundreds of thousand-watt lamps have illuminated the Sphinx and the Pyramids, as the Sphinx set out to tell his story. Since then this show has been a major attraction, bringing tourists back to the area at night, after their daytime visits. Tourism became an important feature of the Nasserist economy (Gray 1998).

Al-Tayyibin: The years after World War II and Egypt's independence brought new challenges and opportunities to al-Tayyibin. In the 1950s and 1960s the remaining peasants had to give up farming as urbanization swallowed their last fields. Some held on to larger livestock, like water buffaloes or cows. Soon even this became impossible as it was no longer profitable for their suppliers to carry large quantities of fodder into the city. By the late 1960s the local animal population was reduced to smaller 'urban' species such as goats, geese, ducks, and chickens. State-run industrialization and the expansion of the government bureaucracy made up for the lost agricultural jobs. One man, for example, moved from agriculture to work in a plant nursery maintained by the Ministry of Agriculture. Others worked as helpers *(farrash)* or guards *(bawwab)* in public institutions, private businesses, and households. Public education allowed younger individuals to enter the bureaucracy and even the professions. Some looked for opportunities beyond the community. One family ran an appliance store in downtown Cairo. Another opened a bicycle-repair shop in the wealthy quarter of Zamalek. One man established a newspaper stand at a popular corner in downtown Cairo. The more successful left the community and moved elsewhere in the city.

By the 1960s, Greater Cairo had engulfed the community and residents were completely integrated into urban life and economy. Yet the city and state administration had not embraced the community as an integral part of urban modernity. Houses remained without electricity, piped water, and telephones throughout the 1960s. While there is no clear evidence as to why the community was not evenly integrated into the urban infrastructure, one can speculate that the general attitude prevailed in municipal quarters that al-Tayyibin and similar quarters were not here to stay, and therefore not worth the long-term investment of modern services. In this context the sense of 'otherness,' of being out of place in the city, emerged. For those outside the confines of the community, al-Tayyibin became a 'slum' and an 'eyesore,' and later an 'informal community,' depending on the dominant idiom and discourse (Al-Wali 1993). For its residents the community was an ordinary urban quarter. Only the absence of urban services was an ever-present reminder of al-Tayyibin's precarious situation. Residents witnessed how similar communities were bulldozed to make room for institutions of the modern state and new residential quarters.[18]

By the late 1970s, al-Tayyibin was surrounded by public buildings and private residences. Whereas in the past residents had been able to stroll out of the community in all directions into the fields, they were now enclosed by walls erected by their various neighbors. Entry to the community was reduced to three alleyways.[19]

The Pyramids: The 1970s under the leadership of President Sadat marked Egypt's economic liberalization and entry into the global capitalist economy.[20] Dramatic expansion of tourism was paramount to boost and globalize Egypt's economy (Gray 1998). From the early 1980s, under President Mubarak, considerable public and private resources were invested in rapid improvement of the tourist sector.[21] Pharaonic Egypt and its magnificent monuments became the single most important marketing elements for Egypt's mass tourism industry (Beirman 2001, 69). The Pyramids were *the* symbol for Egypt that guaranteed instant product recognition.[22] The arrival of thousands of tour groups necessitated further changes in the local tourist infrastructure. New hotels were opened on the Alexandria Desert Road at a short distance north of the Pyramids.

Al-Tayyibin: Egypt's new orientation toward global capitalism initiated new projects and produced new urban visions. Lack of space in Cairo and Giza pushed real-estate prices to unprecedentedly high levels. Older villas and smaller apartment buildings gave way to highrises on the Nile riverfront and in upscale quarters like Zamalek, Ma'adi, and Muhandisin. (See Denis, and

Central Giza from Zamalek (photograph by Petra Kuppinger).

Vignal and Denis, in this volume for more detailed analysis of the changing dynamics of real estate, the economy, and space in Cairo.) Squeezed into an increasingly dense cityscape, al-Tayyibin looked ever smaller and more out of place. Threats and rumors about the community's impending removal became a recurrent aspect of residents' lives. Abu Rashad, an elderly resident, remembered one occasion, very likely in the 1970s, when demolition was threatened and residents were upset. People felt unfairly targeted and marched to the Ministry of Agriculture to protest. When I asked Abu Rashad why they marched to this ministry, as it had nothing to do with urban planning, he said, "Of course not, but it is the one closest to al-Tayyibin." The mass of protesting residents gained the attention of officials at the ministry who then called the bureaucrats in charge to withdraw the demolition order. Aspects of this event might have been exaggerated in popular lore; but the residents did secure their settlement's survival. Umm Ibrahim recounted another removal story. One day the government was already sending bulldozers to start the removal when residents—many of them women, as many of the men had gone to work—engaged the workers and police officers in physical battles. Some women were said to have hit the latter with broomsticks. Again, details might be embellished, but the point remains that residents experienced several threats of removal, and stood together, men and women, to face down authorities. When discussing past and present threats of removal, one of the key terms of discussion frequently is *istismar* (investment). On numerous occasions individuals noted that the community would be removed to make way for investment projects. A rumor circulated that a hotel would replace al-Tayyibin.

Greater Cairo's rapid transformation into a global metropolis made al-Tayyibin's situation more precarious. The community was out of place. Almost completely walled in, except for the three alleyway entries, al-Tayyibin by the 1980s had become visibly different and cut off from its neighbors, comparative latecomers to the scene. But long-term tenure did not count. With the new state-articulated urban-renewal discourse on informality, al-Tayyibin became assigned to the 'informal' category since it was not a recent and appropriately scaled community (Al-Wali 1993). The fact had long been forgotten that an 'enlightened' landlady had originally built its core forty houses as an innovative modernist and progressive nationalistic experiment in urban hygiene and social engineering.

The Pyramids: Some of the hotels that were built in the early 1980s soon fell victim to newly emerging political tensions in Egypt. In February 1986, conscripted police soldiers violently protested upon hearing rumors that their time of mandatory service would be extended. These paramilitary police units poured out of their barracks and rioted, targeting and burning down those nearby hotels (Jolie Ville and Holiday Inn) that represented the wealth and power they lacked. In the same riots, religious currents became apparent as some soldiers headed for the nightclubs and similar establishments along the Pyramid Road. While the riots took their starting point at the Pyramids largely because the army barracks were near by, this spatial aspect nonetheless is important. The Pyramids and their environs (hotels and nightclubs) were viewed by at least some groups as foreign, and symbols of wealth and outside power. The quick end of the riots did not diminish these sentiments which were to emerge time and again in the future (*Al-Ahram Weekly* 23–29 September 1999; *New York Times* 26 February 1986).

Al-Tayyibin: On Monday, 12 October 1992, at 3:15 PM, the earth shook violently in Cairo. More than five hundred people were killed in the metropolitan area (*al-Akhbar* 18 October 1992). Al-Tayyibin had no casualties. But, the earthquake caused considerable political upheaval, as a large number of Cairo's victims were children killed in stampedes in what turned out to be substandard school buildings (*al-Ahkbar* 26 October 1992; *Al-Ahram Weekly* 5–11 November 1992). Seventy individuals died in the collapse of a highrise in upscale Heliopolis where a landlady had violated building codes (*EG* 22 October 1992; 3 November 1992).[23] In al-Tayyibin some houses were damaged, but none were destroyed.

Incidents of corruption and building-code violations led to public outrage immediately after the earthquake. Combined with ongoing political struggles with Islamic militants, this constituted a dangerous political moment. It was paramount for the government to devise quick solutions. Within a few weeks, debates were shifted from corrupt contractors, state and municipal responsibility, and greedy landlords to the identification of 'ashwa'i (the informal, self-constructed, improperly constructed) and 'ashwa'iyat (informal neighborhoods) as the main culprit for the city's problems (Kuppinger 2001, 197). The new discourse proposed that 'ashwa'iyat were the root of urban problems, because they were informal and did not follow official building codes, and in their unplanned physical environments they sheltered social chaos and criminal activities.[24] The logic was that if the city could rid itself of these 'urban sores,' life could return to normal.[25]

Political controversies fired up by these debates were fought out on a metropolitan and national level and directly affected al-Tayyibin. Long seen as out of place and repeatedly threatened with removal, many residents were sure that this would spell the community's end. The days and weeks after the earthquake were marked by fear and insecurity. Heated debates took place among residents whether one should or should not register damages. Discussions were driven by rumors that the community would be bulldozed in a matter of weeks, and by tempting TV images of earthquake victims moving into new beautiful apartments. Soon it became clear to residents that registrations for earthquake damages were accepted and processed with little concern for actual physical damages. One resident reported that a clerk at the office where he registered his damages remarked to him: "See, what we have not managed to do in years—that is, to remove you people—the earthquake managed so easily" (Kuppinger 2001, 192). The more people left al-Tayyibin, the better it was for the urban authorities. Starting by late October 1992, families were relocated to housing projects elsewhere in Cairo and Giza. A long exodus followed which abruptly stopped in spring 1993. Those who had registered damages late never received apartments as the authorities ran out of housing.

While the earthquake had terrified residents, many of whom slept outside for days afterwards, the political aftershocks hurt al-Tayyibin more. Labelled as an 'ashwa'iya, al-Tayyibin became stigmatized once more as a potential problem and a detriment to urban and national harmony. Suddenly, its out-of-place nature was a concern not only for its immediate neighbors, but also for the entire city and nation.

The Pyramids: Political turmoil shook Egypt in the early to mid-1990s. Militant Islamic groups engaged the police and army in battles, and they targeted tourists and tourist sites to hurt the economy and government. When an alleged bombing occurred in spring of 1993 inside the Chephren Pyramid, authorities were quick to insist that the 'explosion/noise' was caused by renovation work (*Al-Ahram Weekly* 18–24 March 1993). Starting from 1992, militants and the government played a bloody game of attack and counterattack. Matthew Gray estimated that from 1992–95 alone, Egypt lost tourist revenues of about $1 billion because of militant attacks (1998). Since that time, every so often officials announce that they have finally eliminated all militants. No sooner have they done this, another militant attack follows. In 1996, armed militants attacked a group of Greek tourists outside the Europa Hotel on the Pyramid Road, killing eighteen and wounding fourteen individuals (Moussa 2001).

Al-Tayyibin: The mid-1990s in al-Tayyibin were marked by transformations of the physical and social community. A few thousand residents left for resettlement communities after the earthquake. Discussions of whether going or staying had been the best options were endless. Younger people had left with great hopes, older people had left with sadness, and indeed numerous older individuals returned to move back into their old rooms. The new communities were too alien and lonely for them. A few absentee owners tore down their buildings to prevent squatters from taking over. Most residents simply waited to see how the situation would develop. In the months and years

Wedding celebration in an al-Tayyibin alley (photograph by Petra Kuppinger).

that followed, no statement was ever issued with regard to the concrete future of al-Tayyibin, no official ever announced that al-Tayyibin had been deleted from the lists of communities (published right after the earthquake) targeted for possible removal. Nonetheless, informed by their keen observation of local politics and sharpened by lengthy discussions of current events, news, and local experiences, by this time residents al-Tayyibin had come to the conclusion that the community was no longer in danger of immediate removal. A number of owners thus felt sufficiently reassured to start renovating old houses, or even building new ones. Cracked walls were fixed and soon a vibrant market in rental property developed. New tenants moved in. One young man who originally was from al-Tayyibin moved his family back to a small two-room arrangement, giving up an apartment in a more distant neighborhood where he had never felt at home. Two other local couples in quick succession rented the remaining upstairs rooms in the same building (not apartments—the three families shared one bathroom and water tap) when they married in 1994. Children once more filled alleys that had temporarily been empty. In the late 1990s, one woman noted that the community *itmalah 'ala 'aynuh* (filled up despite itself).

The Pyramids: In recent decades the Pyramids frequently served as the location of glamorous globalized events that played on the juxtaposition of timeless beauty and the glitter of technologically underwritten spectacles. In 1977 the U.S. band The Grateful Dead spent $500,000 to ship 23 tons of equipment to play in front of the Sphinx ("Grateful Dead" 2005). Not everybody was happy. Zahi Hawass, secretary general of the Supreme Council of Antiquities and director of the Giza Pyramids excavation, remembers the occasion:

I was a young archaeologist and I attended a Grateful Dead concert in front of the Sphinx. There was a huge crowd of 10,000 young people standing, shouting, screaming, drinking beer and I even saw foreigners smoking. The sound of their music was so loud that I could feel the stones of the pyramids trembling with vibration, and the delicate rock of the Sphinx crumbling. Hawass 2001a.

Hawass voiced similar concerns about a Sting concert two decades later: "The concert was oversold and too loud, causing fears for the preservation of the monuments," and "The sound reverberated and every stone of the pyramids, not to mention the Sphinx, suffered" (Hawass 2005). Tickets in the cheapest category had been sold for LE65, yet at that price "you could not see the stage" (Farag 2001).

Another interesting event that thrives on the Pyramids as an attraction is the Pharaos Rally. In 1993, "five hundred drivers from Egypt, Belgium, German, Italy and Spain, as well as a number of Middle Eastern countries" were expected to race a distance of "3307 kilometers stretching form Giza to Abu Simbel and then back to Giza" to mark the twentieth anniversary of the rally, which starts at the Sphinx and ends in the vicinity of the Pyramids (*Al-Ahram Weekly* 28 August–3 September 2003).

On several occasions Verdi's *Aida* has been performed in front of the Sphinx, using the Pyramids as a monumental background and as a target for colored, programmed laser and floodlighting effects. For the 2002 performance, Nabila Erian notes, "the breathtaking and unique site used for the production, together with the cool breeze off the desert in the October air, made this *Aida* one of the greatest of all artistic spectacles" (2002). Erian situates the performance of *Aida* in a global political context and notes that this was more than an artistic spectacle:

Not only is this year's Aida *at the Pyramids a* tour de force *due to its being staged at all in the light of the world political situation, but mainly in its triumph in its response to the world in its light-heartedness and courage. This is the first time since the production was staged at Luxor some years ago that so many foreign faces were to be seen in the audience, many of whom had come to Egypt specially for the event* (2002).

Erian noted that Egyptians were sparse in the audience and speculated that this might be the result of high ticket prices. Organizers seem to have aimed at attracting foreigners, more likely to be able to pay. It was a global and not a local spectacle.[26]

The most spectacular globalized event in recent years at the Pyramids probably was the Millennium celebration, once more combining cutting-edge technologies and ancient glory.

Lasers, floodlights, and fireworks lit up the ancient Pyramids at Giza at midnight as Egypt greeted the new millennium with a lavish electronic bash that officials said drew more than 120 thousand people. French composer Jean-Michel Jarre laid on an extravaganza of song, dance, and music featuring one thousand performers, entitled "The Twelve Dreams of the Sun" (Reuters 2000).

Among the visitors was President Mubarak, whose government saw this extravaganza as an attempt to boost Egypt's image as a safe tourist destination (as the country still suffered from the aftermath of the 1997 Luxor massacre when fifty-eight tourists had been killed). While the majority of the visitors stood at the foot of the Pyramids, "some 8,500 wealthier people were wined and dined in luxury tents at $400 a head (Reuters 2000). Rajiv Kaul, vice president of Oberoi Hotels of Egypt (which runs the Mena House), proudly noted, "Egypt has become one of the top three destinations for the Millennium" (Reuters 1999). Moreover he predicted that Egypt would once more become an upscale tourist destination. For the Millennium the Mena House catered to "moneyed tourists," as it had raised its prices to $350–$3,000 per night (from the regular $150–$1,450) for the glitzy spectacle (Reuters 1999).

Meanwhile on regular days, the rich and famous often visit the Pyramids. Queen Sofia of Spain dropped in at the Pyramids in 2002 after she attended the opening of the Bibliotheca Alexandrina (*Al-Ahram Weekly* 24–30 October 2002). Tony Blair took his family to the Pyramids to "celebrate New Year in the land of the Pharaohs" (*Al-Ahram Weekly* 3–9 January 2002). Such unofficial visits are relevant (the Blairs' picture outside the Pyramids was published widely in newspapers) because at a moment of political (and tourist) crisis this "could boost Egypt's tourist industry and show that Egypt is still a safe tourist destination" (*Al-Ahram Weekly* 3–9 Janurary 2002).

Al-Tayyibin: In the mid-1990s al-Tayyibin received its first streetlights. This is interesting for two reasons. First, because it was almost a century after the wealthier quarters of Cairo received such services. Second, the fact that the municipality put in streetlights indicated to residents that their 'removal' was certainly not on the immediate agenda. Some families received new telephone lines, which was similarly interpreted. Despite these indications of at least momentary and partial recognition of the community as some part of the modern city, al-Tayyibin was given no news on its future at large. One might ask why such a precarious situation has persisted for so long? I can only speculate when I say that modernist urban planning and politics in Cairo have always contained a number of contradictions and oversights. This phenomenon is a blessing for al-Tayyibin in some respects, but it also makes its residents' lives unpredictable and never quite safe.

As the twentieth century came to a close and laser shows caressed ancient monuments, some women in al-Tayyibin were far removed from such technologies as they continued to carry large containers of water home from the public taps or squatted next to the tap rinsing large piles of washed laundry or dishes.

The Pyramids: The Pyramids' twenty-first-century existence will be marked by the gigantic project of the Grand Egyptian Museum (GEM). Planned at a cost of $350 million, this megaproject is "located at the first plateau between the great Pyramids of Giza [representing] not only . . . the largest museum of Egyptian artifacts in the world, but also one of the largest museums in the world" (Ionides 2004). Minister of Culture Faruq Hosni even stated that the project represents "the biggest museum in the world" (ESIS 2003). The project covers an area of 117 feddans (*Al-Ahram Weekly* 7–13 February 2002). Conceived of in superlatives, the new complex seeks comparison with similar institutions on a global scale. In February 2002 President Mubarak laid the foundation stone for the new

Alley scene
in al-Tayyibin
(photograph by
Petra Kuppinger).

museum (ArabicNews.com 2002). Shortly thereafter a large international contest was announced, which eventually attracted 1557 designs from eighty-three countries. A jury consisting of Italian, French, British, Korean, Romanian, and Egyptian experts awarded the first prize to a relatively unknown firm from Ireland, Heneghan Peng Architects (International Union of Architects 2003). First Lady Suzanne Mubarak handed the two architects their $250,000 prize in a ceremony at the old Egyptian Museum (ESIS 2003). Not everybody was happy with the selection process or the committee (three Egyptians and six foreigners), or the fact that only one Egyptian proposal made it to the final twenty (Elgendy 2003; Asfour 2003). Although Egypt submitted 126 entries, no Egyptian national received even an honorary mention (Asfour 2003).[27]

The character of the built form also sets it apart from local realities. One observer argued that it was "unjustified to have a concrete building that is almost fully air-conditioned" in particular in a city "where power cuts are common place" (Elgendy 2003). Another noted that the museum should really be located in downtown Cairo to "bring new life to deteriorated areas" (Al-Naim 2003). The latter remark is interesting because it situates the project in an Egyptian cultural and social context, where the museum, beyond the immediate charge of housing antiquities, is assigned the social task of urban revival from which local residents could benefit. Yet, this is not its task as envisioned by planners. To them, the museum is an isolated project devoid of direct spatial and social links to its environment. Focused inwardly, the new museum aims for different horizons.

With extensive conference, library, and multimedia provisions, the building is intended to be more than a mere container of Egyptological artifacts, becoming instead an international center of culture, and a spectacular landscape of features (Gregory 2003). It is planned to "serve as a fully computerized information center for Egyptologists" (El-Aref 2003). It will also include "extensive restaurant and shopping facilities" and a "publication center for books, CDs, videotapes, . . . etc." (El Zahlawi 2000). Moreover, the project will include "proper laboratories for scientific research, conservation, restoration and photography according to the latest technology" (El-Aref 2002). The museum is planned to accommodate an estimated fifteen thousand visitors per day. Reaching out globally, the "museum will contribute to the development of tourism in Egypt and meet the varied tastes and needs of visitors from around the world to promote learning about Ancient Egypt" (El-Aref 2003). Once more, the tastes and needs of global tourists take precedence.

The frequently voiced claim that the GEM "will be one of the largest museums in the world" clearly moves its point of reference beyond Egypt's boundaries (El-Aref 2003). It vies with its counterparts across the globe and not with local competitors. A project of these outlines cannot be realized by one nation. In 2003, Faruq Hosni "announced the establishment of a coordinating committee made up of Egyptian and international figures," including the president of the World Bank, James Wolfensohn (*Al-Ahram Weekly* 24–30 October 2002). This committee moved control and authority at least partly to the global sphere. Similarly, the financing of the costly project is shared between local and global interests, including the Egyptian government, international institutions, transnational investment companies, a big-budget state-run exclusive tour of King Tut's treasures throughout the world, and "donations and grants from within Egypt and abroad" (ArabicNews 1997; Ryan and Elbendary 2002).

The new museum is not the only project that seeks recognition and competition outside its immediate geographical context. The Mena House Hotel—run by the Indian global Oberoi Company (motto: "Luxury. Redefined") with five-star hotels in India, Indonesia, and Australia—similarly looks for global points of reference (Oberoi Hotels 2005). The Mena House Oberoi website proudly lists the hotel's awards and rankings. In 2002 and 2003, the hotel was listed among "The Most Exclusive Hotels in the World," "The Best 500 Hotels in the World" and among the "Top Ten Hotels-World's Best Service." Moreover it was "Ranked Eighth Best Leisure Hotel in Africa, Indian Ocean and the Middle East" (Oberoi Hotels 2005). Only two of the twelve awards listed (Best Landscaped Garden in Egypt; Highest Guest Service Standards amongst all Hotels in Egypt) situate the hotel in an Egyptian context.

Al-Tayyibin: In January 2005 I talked by phone with Umm Zaki in al-Tayyibin. After exchanging other news, she told me that Umm Hani, her cousin who had moved away with her husband after the earthquake, was back in al-Tayyibin. When I asked how that had happened, she explained that Umm Hani's husband had died and his relatives had taken away the apartment given to the couple after the earthquake.[28] So Umm Hani returned home once more. Things worked out well as the other cousin who had taken over Umm Hani's room after she had left in 1993 had recently moved in with her daughter elsewhere. Al-Tayyibin accommodates lives and sometimes alleviates miseries, if circumstances allow. While constantly on the lookout for opportunities and improvements, the community does not compete with high-flung outside standards, awards, and globally competitive solutions, but instead provides practical support when needed and available. The emphasis is on what is locally possible and what can feasibly be offered to those in need.

The community provides local and individualized solutions to problems that sometimes are the result of larger urban, national, and global dynamics. Yet, in their everyday lives, residents first and foremost interact with their immediate social, economic, and spatial environment.

The Pyramids: Dynamics at the Pyramids are different. They offer leisure, entertainment, and with the new museum, knowledge to a global audience. The Pyramids and their vicinity are first and foremost a place of financial investment and service. This provides jobs for numerous people, but little social ties to the surrounding cityscape. As noted above the Pyramids are responsive to the needs and demands of global financial and cultural circuits and subsequently they become deterritorialized and delinked from the social fabric of Giza and the needs of most of her residents. One issue probably most characterizes the Pyramids' entry into the twenty-first century: the fear of more tourist crises, even those which have little to do with Egypt such as 11 September 2001, the Iraq War, or even the tsunami of 2004. For example, the Mena House, which largely depends on U.S. tourists (unlike Egyptian tourism generally) "suffered a 90 percent drop in bookings compared to last year" after 11 September (Saad 2001). With the ups and downs of global tourism, Egyptian authorities and entrepreneurs are constantly searching for new and hopefully less crisis-sensitive investments and projects in order to safeguard against future uncertainty, such as convention tourism (Samy 2001). In order to attract customers in the competitive global tourist market, the attraction of eternal beauty is not enough. As global tourism continues its mad race, the Pyramids will have to contend with ever-new and different competitors. Even virtual reality and fake monuments enter the contest. One such new competitor is the Luxor Las Vegas, a hotel built in Nevada in a pyramid shape that houses an illustrious remake of pharaonic artifacts, where historical accuracy is no longer a guiding principle. "Egypt on steroids," as one author called this postmodern orientalist monstrosity, offers security, year-round air-conditioning, and no interference from locals, militants, or others who might detract from the pleasures of consuming history (Cass 2004). Only one piece in the hotel is 'real.' "Encased in hard plastic" there is a piece of the Cheops Pyramid, "donated by the Tourism Sector of Egypt" (Cass 2004, 252). Does this legitimize the rest of this incredible spectacle, or hint at a possible future for the Pyramids? If the Pyramids want to stay in the game, beauty needs to be boosted by cutting-edge facilities, utmost convenience, and the occasional grand spectacle for added appeal. And even then, crises might hit. Such are the demands of global competition.

Works Cited

AlSayyad, Nezar, ed. 2001. *Consuming Tradition, Manufacturing Heritage.* London: Routledge.

ArabicNews.com. 2002. "Mubarak Lays Foundation Stone of Grand Egyptian Museum." 5 February. *<http://www.arabicnews.com/ansub/Dail/ Day/020205/2002020532.html>* (29 August 2004).

_____. 1997. "American Donations to Build the New Egyptian Museum." 6 October. *<http://www.arabicnews.com/ansub/Daily/ Day/971006/1997100625.html>* (15 June 2004).

ArchNet.org. 2003. "The New Egyptian Museum." 7 November. *<http:// www.archnet.org/forum/view.tcl?message_id=16616>* (29 August 2004).

El-Aref, Nevine. 2001. "Browsing through Documented History." *Al-Ahram Weekly,* 22–28 March.

_____. 2002. "Final Home for Tutankhamun's Treasure." *Al-Ahram Weekly,* 24–30 January.

_____. 2003. "Museum of the Millennium." *Al-Ahram Weekly,* 12–18 June.

Asfour, Khalid. 2003. "The GEM and the Egyptian Architects—Bad Luck?" *The Architectural Review.* October. *<http://www.findarticles.com/p/articles/ mi_m3575/is_1280–213/ai_111030372>* (9 December, 2005).

Baedeker, Karl. 1906. *Aegypten und der Sudan. Hanbuch fuer Reisende.* Leipzing: Verlag von Karl Baedeker.

Beirman, David. 2003. *Restoring Tourism Destinations in Crisis.* Oxon: CABI Publishing.

Brugsch, Heinrich. 1961 [1855]. "Reiseberichte aus Aegypten." In *Reisen im Orient,* ed. Herbert Scurla, 483–614. Berlin/DDR: Verlag der Nation.

Cass, Jeffrey. 2004. "Egypt on Steroids: Luxor Las Vegas and Postmodernist Orientalism." In *Architecture and Tourism: Perception, Performance and Place,* eds. D. Medina Lasansky and Brian McLaren, 241–63. Oxford: Berg.

Cuno, Kenneth. 1994. *The Pasha's Peasants: Land, Society, and Economy in Lower Egypt 1740-1858.* Cambridge: Cambridge University Press.

al-Damurdashi, Ahmed. 1991. *Al-Damurdashi's Chronicle of Egypt, 1688-1755.* Leiden: E.J. Brill.

Description de l'Égypte. 1809–1813. Paris: Imprimerie Impériale.

Dopp, P.H. 1950. "Le Caire vu par les voyageurs occidentaux du Moyen Age." *Bulletin de la Société Royale de Géographie d'Égypte* 23 (34): 117–49.

_____. 1951. "Le Caire vu par les voyageurs occidentaux du Moyen Age." *Bulletin de la Société Royale de Géographie d'Égypte* 24 (November): 115–62.

_____. 1953. "Le Caire vu par les voyageurs occidentaux du Moyen Age." *Bulletin de la Société Royale de Géographie d'Égypte* 26 (August): 87–118.

Egyptian State Information Service (ESIS). 2003. "Mrs. Mubarak
   Distributes Egyptian Grand Museum Awards." 9 June. <*http://www.sis.
   gov.eg/online/html9/o090623c.htm*> (29 August 2004).
Elgendy, Karim. 2003. "The New Egyptian Museum." 28 June. <*http://www.
   archnet.org/forum/view.tcl?message_id=16616*>. (29 August 2004).
Erian, Nabila. 2002. "Celeste Aida." *Al-Ahram Weekly,* 17–23 October.
Farag, Fatemah. 2001. "Mad About Sting." *Al-Ahram Weekly,* 3 September.
"Giza, Pyramids." 2005. *Encyclopaedia Britannica Online* (23 February 2005).
"The Grateful Dead." 2005. *MusicWeb Encyclopedia of Popular Music.* <*http://
   www.musicwebinternational.com/encyclopaedi/g/G88.HTM*> (19 January 2005).
Gray, Matthew. 1998. "Economic Reform, Privatization and Tourism in
   Egypt." *Middle Eastern Studies England* (April): 91–112.
Gregory, Rob. 2003. "Grand Project: By Occupying Sight Lines Drawn
   between Cairo and the Pyramids, Heneghan Peng Architects'
   Competition-Winning Scheme for the Grand Museum of Egypt uses
   Light to Span between Ancient Culture and Modern Complexity." *The
   Architectural Review.* August: <*http://www/findarticles.com/p/articles/mi_
   m3575/is_1278_213/ai_1111105880*> (29 August 2004).
Haikal, Mohammed Hussein. 1989. *Zainab.* Translated by John Mohammed
   Grinsted. London: Darf Publishers. (Orig. pub. 1913.)
Hawass, Zahi. 2001a. "The Sphinx Cried Twice." *Al-Ahram Weekly* 24–30 May.
_____. 2001b. "The Man Who Found the Solar Boat." *Al-Ahram Weekly* 15–21
   November.
_____. 2002. "Dancing with Tomb Robbers." *Al-Ahram Weekly* 7–13 March.
_____. 2005. "Sting and the Pyramids." <*http://www.guardians.net/hawass/
   Sting_and_the_Pyramids.htm*> (19 January 2005).
Hazbun, Waleed. 2002. *Between Global Flows and Territorial Control: The State,
   Tourism Development, and the Politics of Reterritorialization in the Middle
   East.* Ph.D. diss., Massachusetts Institute of Technology.
International Union of Architects. 2003. "International Project Competition
   in Two Stages for the Design of the Grand Egyptian Museum, Cairo." 9
   June: <*http:// www.uia-architects.org/texte/england/Cairo2003/2results.html*>
   (29 August 2004).
Ionides, Alex. 2004. "Digging In." *Egypt Today* 25 (8). July: *http://www.
   egypttoday.com/article.aspx?ArticleID=1785* (19 December 2005).
al-Jabarti, Abd al-Rahman. 1994. *Abd al-Rahman al-Jabarti's History of Egypt.*
   Stuttgart: Franz Steiner Verlag.
Kuppinger, Petra. 1998. "The Giza Pyramids: Accommodating Tourism,
   Leisure and Consumption." *City and Society, Annual Review:* 105–19.

_____. 2000. *Giza: Enframed and Lived Spatialities.* Ph.D. diss., New School for Social Research.

_____. 2001. "Cracks in the Cityscape: Traditional Spatial Practices and the Official Discourse on 'Informality' and *irhab* (Islamic Terrorism)." In *Muslim Traditions and Modern Techniques of Power*, ed. A.Salvatore, 185–207. Muenster: LIT Verlag.

_____. Forthcoming. "Entertainment and Control: Social Life in Colonial Cairo." In *The Discipline of Leisure: Embodying Cultures of Recreation*, eds. Simon Coleman and Tamara Kohn. New York: Berghahn Books.

Lasansky, D. Medina, and Brian McLaren. 2004. *Architecture and Tourism: Perception, Performance and Place.* Oxford: Berg.

Legh, Thomas. 1816. *Narrative of a Journey to Egypt.* London: John Murray.

Lepsius, Richard. 1961 [1852]. "Briefe aus Aegypten, Aethiopien under der Halbinsel Sinai." In *Reisen im Orient*, ed. Herbert Scurla, 353–482. Berlin/DDR: Verlag der Nation.

Loti, Pierre. 1909. *Egypt.* London: T.W. Laurie.

Lowenthal, David. 1988. "Classical Antiquities as National and Global Heritage." *Antiquity* 62: 726–35.

_____. 1996. *Possessed by the Past.* New York: The Free Press.

Lozach, J. and G. Hug. 1930. *L'habitat rural en Égypte.* Cairo: L'Institut Français d'Archéologie Orientale du Caire, pour La Société Royale de Géographie d'Égypte.

Margoliouth, D.S. 1907. *Cairo, Jerusalem, and Damascus.* London: Chatto & Windus.

Meskell, Lynn. 2002. "Negative Heritage and Past Mastering in Archaeology." *Anthropological Quarterly* 75 (3): 557–74.

Mosséri, V. M., and Ch. Audebeau Bey. 1921. "Quelques mots sur l'histoire de l'ezbeh égyptienne." *Bulletin d'Institut d'Égypte* 3: 27–48.

Moussa, Ahmed. 2001. "Uprooting Terrorism." *Al-Ahram Weekly*, 11–17 October.

Al-Naim, Mashary. 2003. "The New Egyptian Museum." 18 August. <http://www/archnet.org/forum/view.tcl?message_id=166167> (29 August 2004).

Nelson, Nina. 1997. *Mena House.* Cairo: The Palm Press.

Nuryanti, Wiendu. 1996. "Heritage and Postmodern Tourism." *Annals of Tourism Research* 23 (2): 249–60.

Oberoi Hotels. 2005. *Mena House Oberoi: Cairo, Egypt.* <http://www.oberoihotels.com> and <http://www.oberoimenahouse.com> (13 January 2005).

Rafaat, Samir. 1995 "When Doctor Goebbels Came to Cairo." *Egyptian Mail* 30 September.

Reid, Donald Malcolm. 1991. *Cairo University and the Making of Modern Egypt.* Cairo: The American University in Cairo Press.

Reuters. 1999. "Egypt Hotels Set for Millennium Bonanza." 2 December.

_____. 2000. "Pyramids Pulsate as Egypt Greets New Millenium." 3 January.

Ryan, Nigel, and Amina Elbendary. 2002. "Without a Scratch." *Al-Ahram Weekly*, 6–12 June.

Saad, Rehab. 2001. "Preparing for a Harsh Winter." *Al-Ahram Weekly*, 4–10 October.

Sabet, Adel M., and Maged Farag. 1993. *1939: The Imperial Wedding.* Cairo: Max Group.

Samy, Ahmed. 2001. "Budding Industry of Conference Tourism." *Al-Ahram Weekly*, 8–14 March.

Scurla, Herbert. 1961. *Reisen im Orient.* Berlin/DDR: Verlag der Nation.

Seton-Williams, Veronica, and Peter Stocks. 1993. *Blue Guide: Egypt.* London: A & C Black.

Al-Wali, M. 1993. *Sakan al-'ishash wa-l-'ashwa'iyat.* Cairo: Engineers' Syndicate.

Wiemken, Helmut, ed. 1963. *Fuerst Puecklers Orientalische Reisen.* Hamburg: Hoffmann und Campe.

El Zahlawi, Naglaa. 2000. "The New Egyptian Museum to be Erected Soon in a Newly Arranged Area." Paper Presented at the Eighth International Congress of Egyptology, <*http://www.guardians.net/sca/congress2000/congress_2000_pt2.htm*> (29 August 2004).

(Newspapers: *Al-Akhbar, Al-Ahram, Al-Ahram Weekly, Egyptian Gazette, New York Times*)

Notes

1   See, e.g., the entry "Giza, Pyramids" in the *Encyclopaedia Britannica* (2005), or the chapter heading "The Pyramids of Giza" in the *Blue Guide: Egypt* (Seton-Williams and Stocks 1993).

2   Al-Tayyibin is a pseudonym, as are all names of individuals quoted in the text. My narratives about al-Tayyibin are based on several years of anthropological fieldwork in the community between 1989 and 1997. I returned to al-Tayyibin for a short stay in 2003.

3   Lynn Meskell provides an interesting critique on the concept of "global world heritage." She notes that the "very concept of world heritage is flawed by the fact that it privileges an idea originating in the West and requires an attitude toward material culture that is also distinctly European in origin" (2002, 567).

4   Waleed Hazbun offers a good definition in this context: "The process of *deterritorialization* refers to the condition of economic activity becoming less

dependent on resources and markets which are place specific, or in the language of institutional economics when spatially dependent transaction costs are decreased" (2002, 54). I would add that the process of deterritorialization transcends the economic realm and includes cultural, social, and spatial features.

5   One example here would be the ongoing debate about how the village of Nazlat al-Simman is accused of endangering the Sphinx with its leaking sewage, which raised the groundwater level (El-Aref 2001). There is also the issue of robberies of antiquities (Hawass 2002).

6   David Lowenthal quite aptly observes about this shift of "ownership" with regard to ancient monuments: "The 'rightful inheritors' [...] were in London, Paris and Berlin. They were the truer heirs not only because they cared and knew about it, but because in their hands it became truly universal—a legacy inspiring philosophers and states men, poets and architects everywhere." (1996, 243)

7   For a description of the town of Giza and the environs of the Pyramids, see *Description de l'Égypte*, v. 2, 747.

8   The translations from German are mine.

9   New *ezba*s were established, as the following note from the *Egyptian Gazette* states: "The Ministry of the Interior has been asked to consent to the creation of two ezbehs at a distance of two kilometers from Aboukir. One is to be called Ezbet-el-Kasir, near Kharaba, and the other, Ezbet-Aly-Hussein" (17 June 1902). *Ezba*s along with their respective estates could also be sold. For example, Youssef Pasha Talaat bought Ezbet Zohra and its estate of 2150 feddan for the price of LE150,000 in Spring of 1906 (*EG* 20 March 1906).

10 For a more detailed version of this account see Kuppinger 2000, 161.

11 Mohammed Hussein Haikal's novel *Zainab*, first published in 1913, is a literary example of these ideas (1989).

12 The Baedeker travel guide described the Mena House in 1906 as follows: "A splendid hotel complex with 180 rooms, baths and a swimming pool, play/sports and riding grounds" (1906, 29).

13 "Interest in land speculation in Cairo centres just at present around the Pyramids road [sic]. . . . Here land may be bought at from 10s. to £6 the square meter, and as all this part will be drained off and lighted within the next few years the price is reasonable for the most select quarter of the city. The news that the Tramway Company has applied to the Public Works Department for the right to lay a double track on this portion of their line will give an additional flip to values" (*EG* 10 November 1906).

14 As one of Cairo's prominent 'promenades' the Pyramid Road early on had seen its share of car accidents as drivers raced on this straight road (see a report in the *Egyptian Gazette* about a car going "at a good speed" which then "hit against one of the tramway poles," 30 August 1907).

15 Lepsius' large Christmas fire on top of the Great Pyramid comes to mind here (see above). It seems that the Pyramids inspire Westerners to set up spectacles of glitter and grandeur.

16 Among the era's less-illustrious guests at the Mena House was Joseph Goebbels, the Nazi minister of propaganda. In April 1939, he lunched and stayed there. Samir Rafaat notes that Goebbels "was so taken in by the Giza

pyramids that he opted for a moonlit camel ride before tucking in at the Mena House" (1995).

17 Nina Nelson tells her readers that Umm Kulthum loved "lentil soup, fish, a whole baby lamb . . . surrounded by mounds of spiced oriental rice and small grapes. The pigeon split down in the middle and grilled, served with eggplant mixed together with spices and pureed tomatoes" prepared by a Swiss cook by the name of Hans (1997, 13).

18 One small community in the vicinity was bulldozed for the National Research Center on Shari' al-Tahrir, another (the southern part of the older 'Aguza village) was removed to make room for the Sixth of October Bridge (on Shari' al-Mathaf al-Zira'i).

19 One older woman remembered that as children they would just run out of the community, across the small irrigation canal to its north, and then run all the way to Mit 'Uqba to visit relatives.

20 Law 43 of 1974 formed the basis for Sadat's Infitah policies of economic liberalization (Gray 1998).

21 In a 1998 interview, Minister of Tourism Mamduh al-Biltagi noted about these initiatives: "After having passed through a successful period of economic reform, incentives, guarantees, and legal administration, investors from Egypt and abroad have been encouraged to take part in the tourism development process. As a result, lodging capacity was raised from 18,000 in 1982 to 75,000 in 1997. And we now have 603 projects under construction." As the same time, he noted, "Egypt has invested more than $50 billion . . . to improve the infrastructure and public utilities" (Al-Ahram Weekly 21–25 May 1998; Gray 1998).

22 In an interesting twist of consumerist representations and cultural reduction, in a recent edition of a Barbie coloring book, in which she travels the world, Barbie is depicted in front of the Pyramids on her stop in Egypt. Egypt has become the Pyramids, as much as France has become the Eiffel Tower in Barbie's stereotyped world. One author claims that indeed, "the Great Pyramids of Giza and the Sphinx are the unofficial emblems of world tourism" (Beirman 2003, 69).

23 The following section is largely based on a much more detailed earlier analysis of the political aftermath of the earthquake (Kuppinger 2001).

24 President Mubarak's speech on 5 January 1993 further elaborated on the dangers of informal neighborhoods, while also outlining a program of how the government was going to solve the problem (al-Ahram 2 and 3 May 1993).

25 For a detailed treatment of informality as an aesthetic and social sore in the Egyptian context, see Al-Wali 1993.

26 It is interesting to note that the tradition of staging Aida in front of the Pyramids goes as far back as the early twentieth century (Nelson 1997, 28).

27 The internet discussion forum ArchNet records an interesting exchange of Egyptian architects about this project (Archnet.org 2003). Khalid 'Asfur, an Egyptian architectural critic, took the GEM competition as an opportunity to discuss the weaknesses of Egyptian university programs in architecture (2003).

28 The damaged room in question was not in al-Tayyibin as Umm Hani's husband had kept a second residence from his previous marriage elsewhere in the city.

12

Belle-époque Cairo

The Politics of Refurbishing the Downtown Business District

Galila El Kadi and Dalila ElKerdany

Introduction

It may seem surprising the degree to which a proudly nationalistic Arab state like Egypt takes interest in and dedicates scarce resources to architectural and urban legacies inside its territory which date back to an era of foreign hegemony—of British colonialism and Turko-Circassian monarchy. Nevertheless, in Egypt since the 1980s and more urgently since the 1992 earthquake, state officials and assertive home-grown intellectuals have expanded efforts to conserve threatened late nineteenth- and early twentieth-century buildings and sites. They have articulated and marketed a wholly new kind of heritage campaign aiming at the local and global media, and publicizing the effort at scientific, cultural, legal, and urban-planning conferences.

Rather than focus on Egypt's extensive and better-known pharaonic, Coptic, or Islamic heritages, this new coalition of Egyptian cultural elites and state actors has generated a new idea of heritage aiming to restore certain aspects of Cairo's urban landscape and rewrite the historical narrative of its pre-revolutionary, colonial-monarchical epoch. A new coalition of preservationists has manufactured a resurgent, generalized nostalgia for a previously unvalued period—now relabeled 'Cairo's belle époque.' This campaign selectively ignores the foreign hegemony of the period 1870–1952 and, instead, reidentifies this time as a golden age of urbane, liberal, cosmopolitan Arab creativity, grounded in the art deco, art nouveau, French Empire, Arabesque modern, and neo-Orientalist structures of Cairo's downtown villas, theaters, cafés, shops, and institutions. These rediscoverers of Cairo's belle-époque heritage consist of a class of well-connected professional, financial, commercial, and creative elites in today's Egypt who look back to this era not as one of colonial-monarchical decline but as a proud moment of Egypt's urban rebirth, when liberal nationalist movements emerged and important modernist, secular, literary, social, and cultural experiments were generated.

This urban-preservation movement has been preceded and accompanied by TV serials, films, gallery openings, and literary events that have glorified the 'good old' social life in central districts that emerged in the last years of Turko-Circassian (Khedival Ottoman) dominance and during the British Protectorate. These districts include the once-bohemian art-nouveau enclave of Garden

Prominent buildings in Cairo's city center built during the belle époque (photographs by Alain Bonnamy).

City, the villas of al-Hilmiya al-gadida, and the boulevards of the nineteenth-century downtown areas. This label of 'belle époque' resurrects the memory of Cairo as a world-class, cosmopolitan capital, dreamed up and built by some of the best global and local architectural talent of that era. While viewing the past with nostalgia, this neoliberal coalition of heritage preservers sees the present moment as a time of great risk and urban decline. Cairo is portrayed as the decaying, overcrowded victim of haphazard state planning efforts and natural disasters. This nostalgia for belle-époque Cairo is articulated during a time of economic and political decay, which these preservationists consider worse than the now-mythic era of the colonial monarchy.

Photographic essays and coffee-table books on the villas and apartment buildings from these glory years have become very popular (Ra'fat 2003; Myntti 1999). The ministries of culture, information technology, and housing have responded to this trend toward recapturing the belle époque by mobilizing to revalue and protect Cairo's architecture of this modern era.

Local communities, university research centers, consultants, businesspeople, and stockbrokers have come together in a preservation movement. Their campaign strives to promote this era's legacy so that the belle époque becomes a part of Egypt's heritage, equivalent to and more chic than Cairo's original millennium-old, architecturally magnificent medieval core.

It has taken great effort and planning to solidify the new meaning of the belle époque's legacy. The state began by banning the destruction of palaces and houses linked to key events or personalities from this modernist period of Egyptian history in a series of decrees between 1993 and 1998. The last decree ordered the selection of any architecturally outstanding palace, house, or building used for administrative, educational, or any other activities, and prohibited alterations of these selected buildings, in accordance with the new decrees. Government agencies surveyed and inventoried nineteenth- and early twentieth-century sites and city districts to identify buildings in need of protection. Among those, more than sixty buildings in Cairo alone have been included in the national list of historical monuments. There is a difference between a listed and a registered building: a listed building is considered a monument, but a registered one is just of value.

The governorate of Cairo has also launched projects specifically focused on rehabilitating Cairo's central downtown area (wust al-balad). From the late nineteenth through the early twentieth century, Cairo's urban center of government, culture and banking was located in the 'Islamic' city, elevated above the floodplain on the eastern side of the Nile Valley. In the nineteenth century, as dams were erected to control flooding and the Nile's wetlands were drained, a new city center was built on the eastern riverbank, adjacent to the old squares, palaces, mosques, and Citadel of Cairo proper. This new nineteenth-century downtown was constructed according to the Parisian Haussmannian model, featuring broad boulevards, shopping arcades, and uniform bourgeois residential apartment blocks constructed for emergent Egyptian landlord and merchant classes dominant during the reign of Khedive Isma'il in addition to European and Syrio-Lebanese immigrants. Since the 1990s, Cairo's governors have come to invest this nineteenth-century downtown with great national value as a potential hub for a municipal renaissance, encouraging the restoration of about sixteen buildings by private and public actors.

The Ministry of Culture has pursued a policy of converting houses and palaces to new cultural, educational, and recreational uses since the early 1980s. This ministry is now a key actor in managing and safeguarding the heritage of the belle époque. Egyptian businesspeople, entrepreneurs, and shopkeepers have now joined in and have begun investing their financial and political support to restore and rehabilitate this area. As the private sector has increased its partnerships with government agencies that have a stake in this campaign (the ministries of tourism, culture, housing, and *awqaf* [religious endowments]), the visibility and popularity of these projects have steadily increased.

University studies, academic and historical surveys, websites, and publicity campaigns have educated the public about the importance of these little-known sites and objects. Although efforts to foster awareness of the need to safeguard late nineteenth- and early twentieth-century edifices have largely been led by intellectuals, architects, and urban planners, other high-profile agencies have been active as well. For example, in 1997 the U.S. Fulbright Commission, *Al-Ahram Weekly* newspaper, and the Mubarak Public Library under the patronage of Egypt's first lady, Suzanne Mubarak, launched the high-profile and elite-supported National Campaign for the Preservation of the Architectural Heritage of Modern Egypt.

The proliferation of state decrees, administrative policies, and private- and public-sector enthusiasm has resulted in a paradoxical situation. On one hand, the inadequacies of urban planning in general, and of national-heritage management in particular, have deepened with each day and given rise to controversy in both local and international arenas. And on the other hand, the rediscovery of a once-stigmatized era of Western hegemony-modernity and liberal nationalism has mobilized the public to defend the capital city's modern legacy. For example, the destruction of Mattatia's Café in downtown Cairo in 1999—the meeting place for the leaders of the 'Urabi Rebellion, Egypt's first nationalist uprising, against the British in 1882—caused a public outcry and called attention to the emerging importance of nineteenth-century sites and their symbolical value (Hassan 1999). The renewal of the public's relationship with places deserted for decades by the intelligentsia and the middle class illustrates the emergence of a new cultural identity amongst the neoliberal elites, certain state authorities, and Egyptian businesspeople.

How did this process of cultural heritization emerge? What is the real nature and significance of these sites and objects? How have actors' strategies developed and to what degree have they been articulated? What impact have these initiatives had on society, and what are their limits? Do these actions follow a coherent pattern? Is cultural heritization a sustainable movement or a passing trend? To answer these questions we first describe the heritization process in Egypt by placing each step into its sociocultural and political context, measure successes and failures, and assess the trajectory of this process.

The Process of Heritization in Egypt

Heritization is the ranked valuation of historical buildings and sites as patrimony and as the essential property and collective meaning-repository of a nation, city, or of humanity. Heritization is a process articulated differently in its political, administrative, legislative, cultural, and application dimensions. This process may be a relatively new (and wide-ranging) concept, but the word 'heritage' is historically rooted and has accumulated a wealth of different connotations over time. (See Williams, Elsheshtawy, chapter 7, Smith, and Kuppinger in this volume for other analyses of the politics of historical renovation in Cairo and its role in economic development, national identity, and tourism promotion.) In its original legal sense, heritage refers to inherited property. Each generation inherits goods, takes stock of them in a notarized inventory, assesses their value and decides whether to keep or destroy them. These actions amount to an act that is both cultural and economic in nature: cultural because it enables people to relate to a collective past, and to memory via symbolic and material goods; economic because it involves value in use, exchange, and class entitlement. As far as we are concerned, the term 'heritage' relates to architectural objects and urban sites that have been, or are in the process of being, recognized as a tangible vestige of a bygone age. Heritization, then, is a process geared to converting exchange value into cultural value by enhancing objects and sites with new functions so that they might serve as a means to transmit knowledge and construct culture and identities; as places where people (or certain classes of people) can spend their leisure time and contemplate aesthetic beauty; as driving forces for local and regional development that draw in tourists, stimulate consumption, and generate income and profit on national and global scales.

The heritization process comprises a range of successive and/or concomitant stages: study, appraisal, documentation, selection, classification, enacting protective laws, creating special institutions to manage safeguarding efforts, deploying the tools, making the renovations, raising public awareness, training consumers, and ensuring ongoing maintenance.

The Egyptian state's interest in heritization has triggered an enlargement of heritage as a concept, expanding typologically and chronologically to integrate more historical epochs and more diverse objects and sites into its matrix. The state follows an evolutionary process, developing the legal framework, and progressively strengthening legislation for more effective protection.

Nevertheless this process has an exogenous origin; the local Egyptian elite throughout history did not initiate it. This mismatch between external and internal has produced a clash between two goals: one, to broaden the coverage of types of heritage goods and eras and, two, the goal of Egypt's local elites, which is to make their society collectively aware of the importance of protecting and celebrating this heritage. In other words, one may admit that heritage could function as a unifying element between members of an urban-scaled or national community who recognize that they all stem from the same corpus of objects and inherited values worthy of transmission. This heritization process, however, has always been politicized and controversial in Egypt. Within the elite, the content and notion of 'heritage' is not agreed upon or consensually shared. Accordingly, we can talk of 'heritages' in the plural, with each faction of the elite defining heritage one way or another. The popular classes also identify with other heritages. For some it is a sheikh's grave, for others, a relic in a church. Very few in Egypt seem to have pluralistic commitment to embrace the totality of heritages and to draw meaning from a variety of legacies.

Heritage Management in Egypt

Heritization, in the first instance, is managed by the Supreme Council of Antiquities (SCA) according to Law 400 of 1983 for the protection of antiquities, which defines heritage in the following manner:

Any building or movable object produced by the arts, sciences, literature, religions, morals, etc., since the prehistoric era and up to 1883 is considered a heritage. And also: any building or movable object discovered on Egyptian territory and produced by a foreign civilization having had relations with Egypt in one of the above mentioned periods. EAO 1985.

This new law expanded the power of the SCA, now the central institution in charge of managing conservation, restoration and rehabilitation of Egypt's immense cache of universal, religious, and national patrimony. The law allows the SCA to expropriate property, to issue demolition and construction licenses, and to protect monuments and their surroundings. Due to the affiliation between the SCA and the Ministry of Culture, the law confirms the supremacy of central national-level authorities to the detriment of local municipal or provincial authorities. Therefore, the SCA is the sovereign body in heritization; all other state agencies in charge of regional, national, and urban planning must receive approval from the SCA in protected or classified areas, or in areas which contain heritage sites and objects. The SCA is comprised of six sections: one responsible for the management of prehistoric sites, pharaonic wonders, and objects up to the end of the Arab epoch; a second section for managing Coptic and Islamic monuments; a third runs museums; a fourth draws up and seeks contractor bids for projects;

a fifth operates a financing fund for antiquities; and the sixth represents the oversight organ, the General Council.

The SCA is caught between two systems of heritage classification. International bodies have sought to protect global cultural legacies and those in Egypt. UNESCO has designated five archaeological sites—the Giza Pyramids, Abu Simbel Temple and Philae Island, Fatimid Cairo, the monastery of Saint Catherine, and the Abu Mina monastery—as part of its World Heritage list. Secondly, the Egyptian state has designated, or requested to be registered, fifteen archaeological sites containing about 3,200 monuments, three nature preserves as part of its official and state-protected national heritage (according to an interview with Fikri Hassan, a consultant for the SCA), and 821 Coptic, Islamic, and Jewish monuments (*Dalil al-athar . . .* 2000, 11). The SCA or any other institution or individual can seek official classification to protect a site or monument; but this official status is only conferred by a decree from the prime minister's office. The official list of protected sites and objects expands every year according to new archaeological discoveries, inventories compiled by the SCA, or requests for protected status submitted by other parties. Yet, only sites more than one hundred years old can be protected by this legislation, which includes objects and sites of unique esthetical and historical value.

Exceptional measures must be taken for the classification of objects less than one hundred years old that otherwise meet the above-mentioned criteria. Since 1982, scores of belle-époque buildings of various typologies have been classified on the heritage list. Among them are buildings that constitute important landmarks of early twentieth-century Cairo, such as Misr Bank (1926), the Arab Music Institute (1928), and the Hindu-style palace of Baron Empain (1907–1911).[1] This new interest does not lead to an efficient management system.

Egypt's efforts to manage its national heritage in the Nile Valley is regularly disparaged by international bodies and local experts. It seems only those sites of major interest to international tourism are well managed, for two reasons: first, income generation, second, the Egyptian government's desire to promote Egypt's image as a modern state. Even those sometimes do not escape the adverse effects of faulty management. We still remember the momentary withdrawal of the Pyramids site from the World Heritage list at the beginning of 1990.[2] The Islamic monuments, which are the glory of the city of a thousand minarets, are targeted for restoration and, oftentimes, badly repaired, without respect for the Venice Charter.[3] (See Williams in this volume for further analysis of the suspect restoration efforts of national monuments of Islamic-Fatimid

Cairo.) Monuments open to the public in this category represent only 6 percent of those included on the national list of protected sites (*Dalil al-athar . . .* 2000, 3). We might ask, if the management and restoration of Egypt's already-protected pharaonic, Coptic, and Islamic heritage falls drastically short, why have the relevant authorities embarked on expanding their responsibilities and manufacturing an entirely new form of heritage?

The Nature of the Resource

Cities and districts constructed in the nineteenth century and at the beginning of the twentieth are characterized by wide-ranging geographical, urban, architectural, and historical diversity. They include new towns created *ex nihilo* since 1858, such as Port Said, Bur Tawfiq, and Isma'iliya along the Suez Canal; a satellite town (Heliopolis) east of Cairo; new districts on the east bank of the Nile in Cairo, luxury residential suburbs, public-housing compounds, and workers' cities. As for the architecture, it exhibits diverse typologies: large monolithic modernist residential buildings, ornate villas, more modest buildings for the middle class, commercial structures (cinemas, theaters, banks, general stores, and hotels), and impressive public architecture (ministries, universities and schools, and industrial buildings).

A local Egyptian and Turko-Circassian elite, prior to and during the British Protectorate (1882–1922) envisioned and constructed the majority of these sites and objects. European architects introduced urban models, 'exogenous' or cosmopolitan architectural styles that were commissioned by this local elite who embraced these new styles, which were later diffused throughout the middle class. This explains why in Egypt, unlike other countries in the Arab world, districts have rarely been identified as purely 'colonial.' Cairo's belle-époque spaces have been identified with colonizers, but also with the agency, presence, and identification of Egyptian elites, middle classes and popular classes, before, during, and after the colonial period (Arnaud 1993, 352–57). Egypt is not like Algeria or Morocco, where French cities or European zones were maintained in isolation from local-national frequentation and reappropriation patterns. This factor facilitates and legitimizes recent campaigns to equate and incorporate the belle époque into Egypt's national heritage. Let us study more thoroughly the steps that have led to these demands.

The Return of the Hybrid *Moderne*

In 1984, the Agha Khan Foundation organized an international symposium on Cairo.[4] One of the major contributions focused on the suburb of Heliopolis, a satellite town constructed in the eastern desert of Cairo at the start of the

Two famous department stores built during the belle époque: Sednaoui (left), designed by Georges Parcq in 1913; Omar Effendi (right), designed by Raul Bandan in 1923. Both stores were nationalized under Nasser (photographs by Alain Bonnamy.

twentieth century by the Belgian Baron Empain (Ilbert 1984, 36-42). It noted the eclectic character of its architecture, which had subtly integrated certain characteristics of Cairo's architecture from that era. Participants talked about a "happy marriage between East and West" that deserved to be safeguarded and even recognized as part of Egypt's national heritage. This first attempt to culturally rehabilitate a site envisioned and constructed during the British Protectorate was not followed up by effective measures. Nevertheless, some preservation initiatives emerged and were led by private individuals, educational institutions, and cultural-management and -preservation institutions. These institutions mainly focused on relatively obscure, minor edifices ignored by prevailing heritage lists.

Cairo's al-Azhar University was a pioneer in the field and its students surveyed twenty to thirty houses each year, to prepare the initial research for further preservation efforts. Following a series of workshops co-organized by the Helwan College of Fine Arts and Germany's Goethe Institute in 1992 and 1993, Salah Zaki, a prominent architecture professor, founded the new Association of Egyptians Graduated from German Universities for the protection of the old town in order to restore old houses, working in tandem with the support of local residents (Goethe Institute Cairo 1997). It targeted one house and an unused school for restoration, while local residents agreed to finance a project to renovate their basic infrastructure, carry out structural reinforcement work, and clean up façades. The association drafted an action

plan that envisioned establishing a head office in the neighborhood, organizing restoration-training courses, creating a database, sensitizing residents to the importance of this work, and raising funds for restoration and rehabilitation. Although none of this actually came to fruition, Helwan students nonetheless managed to survey nine houses and their reports were later collated and published in Arabic, German, and English.

Despite the limited scope of these initiatives in terms of time and space, they are illustrative of an emerging interest in vernacular architecture of another kind that was never taken into consideration by the process of heritization. When the 1992 earthquake struck Egypt, Cairo's interest in the belle époque accelerated at an urgent pace.

The Catalytic Effect of the 1992 Earthquake

In 1992, an earthquake of medium magnitude (5.6 on the Richter scale) struck Cairo. The tremor wrought considerable material damage and hundreds of lives were lost as well. Ancient structures suffered the most damage, and nearly two hundred historic monuments were damaged, the majority of which were situated in the old city of Cairo. In fact, many of these monuments had only been recently restored before the earthquake struck and they were only opened to the public again around 2004. Schools were the second hardest hit by the earthquake, as nearly three thousand of them suffered structural damage and some were completely destroyed. Many of these schools were located in palaces and villas confiscated from the deposed aristocracy after the 1952 Revolution, which the nationalist authorities then rededicated to education. Historic monuments classified on the list of national heritage were earmarked for restoration. However, the Ministry of Education decided that palaces and villas hit by the earthquake would be demolished. In response, the press launched a debate on heritage that ran for several months. The prior awareness of the vulnerability of Cairo's architectural and urban heritage was accentuated by the earthquake, which engendered a sweeping consensus in favor of more efficient management to safeguard the glorious legacy of medieval Arab-Islamic civilization. Over and above the mobilization of the cultural elite, the earthquake's destructive power sparked a new discourse no less consensual in favor of protecting the villas and palaces of the nineteenth and twentieth centuries, which the Minister of Education initially had sought to raze to the ground. The earthquake highlighted and brought to life a new category of Egypt's heritage, hitherto neglected, unknown and déclassé: the modern belle époque.

At first, intellectuals, architects, and urban planners spearheaded the campaign to safeguard these sites and objects. The first lady of Egypt, Mrs. Suzanne Mubarak, nationalized the campaign by sponsoring a committee that signaled to those in power that the initiative would henceforth proceed at a higher level of legitimacy and authority. This committee was composed of representatives from the Fulbright Foundation, the Mubarak Public Library (a government agency operated by a nongovernmental organization, The Society of Comprehensive Care [al-Ri'aya al-mutakamila]) and Al-Ahram Weekly. They launched a campaign to safeguard these sites and objects in 1997. Parallel to this campaign, the weekly Akhbar al-adab ('Literary News') was the first to publish a special edition in 1996 on the evolution of the modern city center, which included compilation of important sites and their significance. The special edition also noted the obvious decay of Cairo's modern city center and called for its revival.

Both the national and opposition press consequently began to play an unprecedented role by denouncing the abuse of the buildings, and reviving public memory through well-documented feature articles on period buildings. They publicized any development projects that might endanger heritage sites. Thanks to this press campaign, the authorities issued decrees banning the demolition of palaces and villas as well as modern buildings of "great value."

However, things did not proceed according to standard rules, that is to say, by following a rational chronology: inventory, definition of selection criteria, classification, and elaborating new regulatory mechanisms. The new heritage conservation initiative, built upon private and public initiatives, lacked coordination on the one hand and a coherent strategy on the other.

Pointless Legislation

In 1993 the governor of Cairo issued Decree 300 for that year, banning the destruction of palaces and houses linked to any key events or personalities from Egyptian history. In 1994, the governor declared a twelve-month moratorium on all demolition work (Decree 244). But the most explicit and wide-ranging measures came in 1996 with Decree 238. Superseding Decree 300, it ruled that applications for permits to demolish any residential building "of outstanding architectural style" were to be rejected. It furthermore ordered the registration of any architecturally outstanding palace, house, or building being used for administrative, educational, or any other activities with the appropriate authorities, and prohibited alterations in accordance with the law for the protection of historic monuments. Finally, it recommended ongoing restoration of such edifices, without detriment to their characteristic architectural style, under the aegis of the competent authorities.

Thus, the governorate of Cairo had implicitly granted the heritage of this period the status of historic monuments, thus taking a significant step toward its protection. However, these objects had not yet to be defined in number, geographic location and typology, etc. What was lacking at the time was a general inventory and consensual selection criteria based on architectural, urban, structural, and historic analyses. The term "buildings of great value" remained vague as long as a competent authority did not spell out their worth. Moreover, the impact of the three decrees was virtually insignificant since modification and demolition of ancient buildings continued. Power and capital were the main obstacles.

Despite these official rulings, attempts to demolish buildings or flout height restrictions continued. In 1997 when a heritage-protection association managed to block the demolition of a Zamalek villa housing the headquarters of the Dutch Embassy, the governor of Cairo issued a further decree reinforcing the powers of those already in place (Decree 118). In 1998 the prime minister introduced a range of penalties for failure to comply with the law (Decree 463). Article One of this legislation specified that when a building is demolished, any new building constructed in its place must be of exactly the same height (same number of stories) as the old one. This additional dissuasive measure applied to the whole of Egypt.

The 1998 decree reinforced Military Order 2 of 1998 that ended the regulatory mechanism for managing the conservation of buildings of "great value." Despite these multiple shortcomings and continued deterioration of older buildings as highlighted in the press, these decrees contributed to slowing down the destruction of villas and palaces while waiting for a proper inventory of modern urban heritage to be prepared.

Inventories and Classifications

The first inventory covering houses and palaces in every town and city in Egypt was carried out by the Historic Buildings Authority (HBA), a body set up in 1996 by the Supreme Council of Antiquities (SCA) and headquartered in the Citadel of Cairo. A tripartite committee determined three specific selection criteria: architectural style, ornamentation of frontages, and historical value (linked to a key figure or event).

Several dozen Cairo buildings were inventoried and presented in a table detailing their addresses and ascribed values. But the HBA was dismantled after three years, largely because it lacked the authority to handle disputes arising between its members and the owners of inventoried properties.

The second inventory was carried out by the governorate of Cairo, or to be more precise, the Committee for the Safeguarding of Architectural Heritage, which had been set up in 1998 under the chairmanship of the head of the Department of Housing and Infrastructure. It covered more than four thousand Cairo buildings and was presented by the governor at a seminar in September of that year. Selection criteria were by and large the same as in the above case. Findings were entered into building-specific forms indicating the location, number of stories, condition (good, bad, average), and year of construction (if known), accompanied by a photograph of the façade. Each building was allocated a registration number, which amounted to formal registration, and prohibited the demolition, change of use, and any form of alteration without authorization from the governorate.

The third inventory, commissioned by the General Organization for Physical Planning (GOPP), was launched in 1997 by a number of consulting firms and covered eleven late nineteenth- and early twentieth-century sections of Greater Cairo. Ultimately, it aimed to serve as a basis upon which to draft detailed sector-specific urban-development plans specifying construction norms, density levels, and measurement mechanisms, and defining the means to ensure that future urban-development efforts would suit the nature, characteristics, and potentialities of each sector.

Selection criteria in the GOPP effort were by far the most comprehensive to date (GOPP 1997). They revolved around historical, aesthetic and architectural values, including:

- Age and inclusion on the register of listed monuments;
- Whether the building had been the site of an important event;
- Whether it had been inhabited by important people;
- Architectural style: neoclassical, neo-Renaissance, art deco, art nouveau, Arab revivalist, etc.;
- Whether its style matched that of other local buildings;
- Whether it had been designed by eminent Egyptian architects or foreign architects with other outstanding works in Egypt to their credit.

The scope of this inventory extended beyond the mere listing of valuable buildings; it sought to diagnose environmental and proximate threats and, hence, scientifically gauge the degree of degradation. It was unfortunate that the results have never been implemented or distributed to the public, as is usual for these types of institutions.

Regardless of their rudimentary character, these two inventories did establish an initial documentation of built forms that had been previously unidentified by the state. Field surveys—identifying, listing, and registering sites with the relevant government authorities—constituted the basis for a nationwide scientific method. This key survey stage of the conservation program worked to gradually build up a wealth of historical and iconographical documentation on modern buildings, monuments and sites.

With these inventories, the meaning of 'heritage' in Egypt became extended to embrace residential/commercial architecture and the entire urban fabric of Cairo's belle-époque downtown, thus paving the way for new analytic assessments and mandatory preliminary stocktaking. Typomorphological studies, which have acquired a following in France, Italy, Great Britain, and Switzerland, offer a fresh way of looking at the architectural design of the city as a whole, taking account of its clusters of built forms, and classifying its constituent parts. These studies aim at settling a method of analyzing and categorizing the urban spaces and architectural forms. Some of the most telling examples include the work of the Italian school's Carlo Aymonino (1985), Aldo Rossi (1981), and Aymonino and Rossi et al. (1970), Saverio Muratori (1959), the Anglo-Saxon school under the leadership of Ben Hillier (1996; Hillier and Hanson 1984), the Swiss research projects involving Roderick J. Lawrence and Albert Lawrence, and France's Syntaxe group under whose auspices Philippe Panerai has joined forces with Jean Castex (1983). In France, Marcel Poëte (2000), Pierre Lavedan (1974, 1982), Georges Chabot and Jean-Pierre Tricard—despite not working solely on historic old-town conservation alone—began treating the city as an organic whole and, hence, laying the theoretical foundations for the acceptance of urban morphology as a science of urban phenomena. Their work has gone beyond the original visual analyses of Camillo Sitte (1980) and Kevin Lynch (1977) with their inclination toward the picturesque rather than theorizing or building a descriptive model of the city designed to enable its analysis in terms of both its spatial and temporal materiality. In Egypt, the result of these methodological debates has been the development of a three-pronged scientific approach that takes account of architectural typology, urban morphology, and urban history to generate an all-embracing study of human settlements.

Thanks to these recent research efforts and the debates surrounding them, there has been considerable progress in inventory methods. Egypt's criteria now take greater account of basic *urban values* such as silhouette, street networks, structure and homogeneity of urban fabrics, and how the constituent parts interrelate; and *environmental values* such as the presence of green spaces, the quality of public places, and local inhabitants' perspectives.

The social value of a city's heritage first gained recognition through Italy's Bologna experiment, ratified at the world level by the so-called Nairobi Recommendation on "the protection of traditional historic groupings and their role in contemporary life," in turn adopted by the UNESCO general conference of 1976.

Until recently, the criterion used to designate cultural objects in Cairo was based exclusively on visible markers of historic value, producing listings of built forms analyzed solely from the point of view of their outstanding surface features. Current work on the city and its architecture increasingly calls for selection criteria which take account of the urban context of a body of objects as well as their various characteristics: design, structure, style, etc.

In view of the lacunae in the inventory process carried out by Egyptian organs, a Franco-Egyptian team, Heritage Conservation and Management in Egypt and Syria (HERCOMANES), financed by the European Union, undertook research to further elaborate and develop conceptual and methodological instruments in order to safeguard sites.[5] The inventory method indicated in this research has since been applied at the national level in Egypt for some other projects undertaken by HERCOMANES team members.

Dissemination of Information Management

The publication of Muhammad Sharabi's encyclopedic work on the architecture of Cairo's modern city center in 1987 marked a breakthrough. But it took another few years before other titles began to appear on the shelves (Sakr 1993; Tamraz 1994; Myntti 1999; Morgan 1999). Two other publications have been issued in 2002. The first one, in the monthly journal *Misr al-mahrusa* ('Egypt Preserved') has focused on efforts to upgrade the quality of life in downtown Cairo (El Kadi and Atia 2002). The second, a more specialized publication by Sohair Hawas, is a nearly complete architectural guide to the belle-époque area. As for periodicals, the bimonthly *al-Madina* (The City) is developing a regular section on late nineteenth- and early twentieth-century architecture, and *Misr al-mahrusa* is campaigning to safeguard the memory of this period's sites and edifices.

Heritage information is also diffused through two new websites. The oldest and best-documented one is permanently animated by the input of its correspondents and carries the very attractive title "La belle époque" (*http://www.egy.com/people/98-10-01.shtml*; *www.egy.com/landmarks/gardencity/gdncity01.html*) and then there was the HERCOMANES website (*http://www.hercomanes.com* only operable through 2004). In Egypt this information has been managed and maintained by CULTNAT (the National Center for the Documentation of Cultural and Natural Heritage). This body was created in 2000 by the Ministry of Communication and Information Technology to document the entire cultural heritage of Egypt. Within a few years CULTNAT disseminated a number of CD-ROMs on music and folklore, along with inventories and maps of all existing archaeological sites in Egyptian territory, and launched a website on pharaonic heritage (*http://www.eternalegypt.org*). In 2003, CULTNAT became affiliated with the new Bibliotheca Alexandrina. It works in association with Egyptian and French groups to prepare an inventory of objects and sites of the nineteenth and twentieth centuries in Egypt. The CULTNAT database continuously enriches itself with new data and has now become the most important source of information on Egypt's heritage. Moreover, CULTNAT actually plays a triple role—coordinating, formalizing, and publicizing, Egypt's patrimony.

Due to all the efforts that were mentioned above, after a period of trial and error and disparate beginnings, matters have been organized in a rational manner. Finally, the initial links in the chain of heritage management are beginning to be formalized: to know, spread, and diffuse knowledge, in conformity with the requirements of organization and articulation.

Reuse of Old Buildings

HCA and the Ministry of Culture have been pursuing a policy of adapting restored buildings for cultural and tourism-related activities since the 1980s. Two types of reuse have been identified: permanent and occasional. First, registered palaces and houses dating back to the late nineteenth and early twentieth centuries have been permanently converted into hotels, museums, libraries, etc. The best-known example is that of Khedive Isma'il's palace, built in 1863 during the festivities to mark the opening of the Suez Canal. Designed by Julius Franz (otherwise known as Franz Bey) and decorated by another German architect, Carl Wilhelm Von Diebitsch, the palace was sold to the Behler Society in 1879 and became the exclusive Gezira Palace Hotel. In 1919, it was bought by a prince, who turned it back into a private residence. In 1962, following the revolution, the authorities impounded the building and converted it back into a hotel—the 'Umar al-Khayyam—which was subsequently purchased and restored in 1982 by the current owners, the Marriot chain (Schmid 1990).

Another former royal residence built at around the same period, the 'Abdin Palace (designed by De Curel Del Rosso), has been partly converted into a museum within the framework of what remains a relatively new approach to conservation strategy on the part of the Ministry of Culture. Houses once occupied by major artists and poets have also been turned into museums under the scheme, one in particular at the initiative of—and financed by—the artist's family, the Nagy Museum.

Secondly, palaces and houses from the belle époque have also served as temporary venues for concerts, plays, exhibitions, or even banquets. A recent round table organized by the Centre Culturel Français with Egyptian Ministry of Culture officials (during the festivities of "les Français aiment le Caire," May 2001) explored the possibilities for eventually transforming the temporary reuse of newly restored palaces and houses in the old town into permanent facilities.

Meanwhile, in the modern downtown, whole floors of old buildings have been converted into art galleries, such as Town House, and Om El Donia, thus drawing fashionable classes back into parts of the city that they had long since deserted (HERCOMANES Report Phase III Dec. 2003). (See Denis and

Vignal in this volume for a discussion of the desertion of Cairo's downtown area by the middle and upper classes.)

The conservation movement was accelerated by the creation of three libraries: the Library of Greater Cairo on the island of Zamalek, the Mubarak Public Library in Giza, and the National Archives in Bab al-Khalk. At the same time, nine museums were installed in period villas and palaces linked to prominent personalities in the arts, literature, and poetry as well as former aristocrats (HERCOMANES 2000–2004). In certain cases, the latters' heirs donated these historic properties to the Ministry of Culture. In others, it was the Ministry of Culture that took over the buildings.

Attributing new functions to old buildings in Egypt today constitutes a new approach to conservation management. Although reused buildings were few in number, their transformation represented a milestone with each inauguration. State officials and private sector advocates hope that this heritization process will transmit knowledge, enhance culture and identity, open areas for aesthetic contemplation and recreation, ignite local and regional development, and finally, attract touristic and profit-generating activity.

Operational Interventions

Restoring public edifices and rehabilitating two downtown belle-époque areas brought together a number of actors: the governorate of Cairo, the Ministry of Culture, diplomatic missions, private proprietors, conservation societies, and merchants. A new category of actors also stepped in—businesspeople. Although a sum total of just fifteen edifices in downtown Cairo (wust al-balad) restored over the past ten years may seem somewhat paltry, it does nonetheless attest to a growing commitment and will to safeguard Cairo's colonial-modern and liberal-nationalist heritage. The restoration work in question involved large-scale projects to reinforce the structure of a varied range of edifices: cafés (Café Riche and the Groppi tearoom); public buildings (the Misr Bank, Institute of Arab Music, Club des Diplomates, and the Stock Exchange); department stores (Sednawi and Omar Effendi), chancelleries (the Swiss Embassy and the Italian and German arts centers); investment properties, insurance company headquarters, a hotel, and a hospital (ElKerdany 2004).

There was significant participation by the private sector in financing restoration activities. As for urban rehabilitation, the first test case was initiated and carried out by the governorate of Cairo in 1997. The district in question covered some twenty-three thousand square meters centering on 'Imad al-Din Street. The zone contained three main roads and residential and commercial buildings—housing, restaurants, cafés and a cinema—dating back to the 1920s and 1930s. Initially, the project aimed at converting several downtown streets into pedestrian areas. Its scope subsequently narrowed to this particular district, however, with the intention to serve as a pilot project that would, if successful, be transposed to other parts of town. By renovating infrastructure networks, paving over roads, installing basic street furniture and cleaning up frontages, it transformed the urban and social landscape completely. Saray al-Azbakiya Street used to be awash with wastewater spilling over from the sewer system, a repellent place by its garbage and hazards. Now people come to meet friends and relax in a pleasant environment, a pedestrian zone buzzing with lights and activity late into the night, equipped with brand-new cafés and restaurants.

Strolling on the pedestrian mall created in 1997 on Saray al-Azbakiya Street (photograph by Alain Bonnamy).

The second operation was three times the scale of the first, covering a district of sixty thousand square meters. This included four financial buildings (the Stock Exchange, the Central Bank, the National Bank, and the Suez Canal Bank), the Cosmopolitan Hotel (built in 1903), the national radio station, as well as a good number of commercial and residential buildings largely dating back to the 1920s and 1930s. There were many architectural styles among the buildings in this area, including baroque, rococo, neoclassical, and art nouveau. But the focal point was the Stock Exchange, designed in 1928 by the architect Georges Parcq, creator of numerous other elegant edifices built in Cairo during the interwar period. The project to rehabilitate the district was initiated in 1999 by the secretary of state for governmental affairs, Tal'at Hammad. Its original objective was simply to save one building—the Stock Exchange, since its basement had been flooded with rising groundwater for years. But planners soon realized that the entire district (the capital's financial center par excellence) would need to be taken into consideration as well. It has been rehabilitated thanks to private-sector funding supplied by consulting firms, entrepreneurs, and businesspeople. Roads were paved over, green space created, palm trees planted, urban furniture installed (e.g., lampposts in the style of the buildings), and frontages cleaned up and color-coordinated. With the infrastructure now renovated and the Stock Exchange fully restored, a special committee, Friends of the Bourse (or 'stock exchange' in French, which was the popular foreign language of the belle époque), was set up to take charge of maintenance.

The pedestrian mall and renovations surrounding the Bourse and other financial buildings in wust al-balad. The Bourse was designed by Georges Parcq in 1928 (photograph by Alain Bonnamy).

These two projects highlight new ways to manage city-center redevelopment work. Indeed, the latter increasingly hinges on seeking partnerships between the private sector, municipal services, and public agencies within a context where public-sector urban action is becoming more extensive and diversified: going beyond spatial planning, housing, and amenities to embrace the preservation and enhancement of the urban environment. These projects had a very positive impact on residents and users, according to a social study of community satisfaction that the HERCOMANES project team conducted. Their effect is undeniable. The downtown district can be transformed if car traffic can be banned or restricted, roads pedestrianized, and tree-lined zones created. The area could become an oasis of tranquility where people could stroll at leisure, sit in a terrace café, discover the wealth, beauty, and diversity of the architecture around, pose questions about the history of sites, and thirst for more information and knowledge. Such projects would allow the people to experience the site so that they appreciate, love, and perhaps even defend it one day. Safeguarding Cairo's heritage and improving the quality of life can also be an issue of public concern. Finally these operations ensure accessibility and enjoyment of sites and objects that we currently look at but do not truly see.

The partnership established between the private sector, municipal officials, and public bodies also reflects a new orientation in the domain of protecting and ameliorating the urban environment in general and heritage in particular. In fact, it is thanks to these two operations that cultural reinvestment in sites has been realized. These projects have sensitized the public to the value of its heritage in recent years, and for two consecutive years (2000–2001), artists, painters, and sculptors organized exhibitions, round tables, and concerts downtown in restaurants, cafés, art galleries, and passages. Cairo's downtown has been revived and is recovering its long-lost ambiance under the sign of *Nitaq* (an ambiguous term referring to Orion's Belt, which also was the name of a dynamic arts festival held in 2000 and 2001 organized by three independent downtown galleries; it drew large crowds within a triangular area bounded by three major boulevards in *wust al-balad* [see Elmessiri and Rakha 2001a; 2001b; Issa 2000]).

Conclusion

Let us return to the question posed at the beginning of this article, namely: are we witnessing a new system for managing Egypt's heritage from the nineteenth and early twentieth centuries? If we first consider the process of creating a heritage, that is to say how heritage is manufactured, then we can affirm that steps have indeed been taken in this domain. First, the Egyptian state, private-sector elites, and foreign advocates have rediscovered the modern-colonial, cosmopolitan, and liberal-nationalist legacies of Cairo and recognized the different values these heritages propagate. Second, efforts to foster awareness of these values have animated the contemporary media. Third, inventories have been compiled to designate buildings and sites, including modern vernacular, commercial, and public locations. And finally, the organization, documentation, and dissemination of such information has produced new legal and state mechanisms for managing and making decisions about built heritages.

Many lacunae obviously exist in the field of management. For management per se is understood as the definition and establishment of a judicial and institutional framework as well as financial measures capable of ensuring restoration and the protection and maintenance of heritage. Moreover, the issuing of six decrees, as previously mentioned, constituted a response to an exceptional situation. Certainly, these decrees succeeded in averting the destruction of numerous architectural edifices that were doomed to disappear. However, these decrees were not subsequently supplemented by regulatory measures and institutions to safeguard listed buildings and their environment. Nor did the public and private sectors provide the necessary funds to restore buildings and rehabilitate public space. Fifteen buildings in downtown were restored, but the two rehabilitation operations were not inscribed within a framework of a coherent policy of safeguard management. Even if the restoration of a group of buildings produced a demonstrable effect, efforts remain unfinished. They were limited to planning a public road without taking into account the need to restore or protect the buildings bordering its two sides from continuous modification. To this one can add the lack of coordination between the different actors who intervened during the past fifteen years in a bid to safeguard "buildings of great value." Clearly it is the Ministry of Culture that should ensure such coordination. However, the ministry already has difficulty in managing Egypt's immense pharaonic, Islamic, and Coptic patrimony and does not have at its disposal the financial means or required expertise to manage Egypt's modern heritage as well. Who then should manage this modern heritage? The answer may be local communities or private-sector driven initiatives. But the management of architectural and urban heritage cannot be separated from overall urban management, including issues such as maintaining public space, building new parks, fighting pollution, mitigating traffic congestion and transportation problems, etc. In spite of the high stakes of urbanization, local groupings in Cairo and elsewhere have maintained a low profile. Since community-driven efforts in the past have not been able to ensure respect for the most basic laws related to the traffic rules, zoning laws, or construction permits, it is difficult to speak of a new management system. It suffices to stroll through the center of modern downtown Cairo to witness the shortcomings of this system. There are a number of hazards that threaten buildings of great value, buildings that were inventoried and classified in the governorate's list, buildings that continue to deteriorate and are subjected to irreversible modifications. For example, in downtown Cairo, ground-floor shops in large impressive buildings commonly break open walls or rebuild storefronts on street level with hardly a thought for the stylistic authenticity of the façade of the larger building in which they occupy one part. The result is often disfigurement of the buildings through demolishing or concealing moldings, arcades, cornices, and decorations, replacing them with ugly window displays. Also we can even see in 2005 an ominous reversal in the recent annulment by the Counsel of State of the prime minister's decree of 1998 banning the demolition of palaces and villas and any change in use permits for ground floors.

Were all efforts exerted during the past fifteen years, whether to promote the concept of national heritage or reap the fruits of establishing a management framework, however modest, a mere temporary deviation from a broader tradition of neglect and disparagement of modern urban heritage? We, the authors of this chapter, hope not, since local awareness of the need to safeguard this heritage has deepened day by day. This awareness is not dictated by an international organization but emanates from national and Cairo-based sentiment that Egypt cannot afford to lose its connection to its modern belle-époque heritage (UNESCO 1993). This awareness is enriched continuously by new discoveries: One learns that the surrealist art movement was born in Café Groppi (Karnouk 1995); that leaders of the 1919 Revolution met in Café Riche; that the first demonstration demanding freedom of the press was launched from the modern center of the city; that parliamentary deputies met on the terrace of the Continental Hotel following the dissolution of Parliament by King Fouad in 1924, etc. Another corpus of information has also been building around residential areas linked to key personalities who played a prominent role in political and cultural life.

Egypt's belle époque, a remarkable phase of innovation, struggle, and creativity, was not 'rediscovered' by European architectural historians or international institutions. Rather, new awareness evolved as the fruit of local initiatives lead by Egyptians, reviving our national pride, remembering the birth of our own kind of urban modernity, and commemorating a time of flourishing liberal, revolutionary, cosmopolitan urban life. This particularly Cairene form of heritization keeps alive the essential esprit of our Egyptian modern, urban past—and our future.

Works Cited

Aymonino, Carlo. 1985. "Typology." *Architectural Design* 5: 49–51.
Aymonino, Carlo, Aldo Rossi, F. Brusatin and L. Lovero. 1970. *La Littàdi Padova*. Saggiodi Analisi Urbana, Roma, Officina edizioni.
Arnaud, Jean Luc. 1993. *Le Caire—mise en place d'une ville moderne, 1867–1907: des intérêtes khédiviaux aux sociétés privées*. Ph.D. diss., Aix-en-Provence.
Castex, Jean, J. Charles Depaule, and Philippe Panerai. 1983. *Formes urbaines: de l'îlot à la barre. Collection Aspects de l'urbanisme*. Dunod (October).

CULTNAT. 2004. "Eternal Egypt." <*http://www.eternalegypt.org*> (20 February 2004).

Dalil al-athar al-Islamiyah bi-Madinat al-Qahira. 2000. Cairo: Ministry of Culture and Information Center.

Egyptian Antiquities Organization (EAO). 1985. "Law no. 117 of 1983 concerning the issuance of Antiquities with a preface by Dr. Ahmed Kadry." Cairo.

ElKerdany, Dalila. 2004. "The Rehabilitation of Cairo Modern Heritage: Conservation Management and Design Decisions." Paper presented at the third International Conference on Science and Technology in Archaeology and Conservation in Zarqa, Jordan, 7–11 December.

Elmessiri, Nur, and Youssef Rakha. 2001a. "To Wake Up in the City." *Al-Ahram Weekly,* 8–14 March.

_____. 2001b. "It's Your Life Charlie Brown: The Nitaq Festival in Downtown Cairo Opened Last Week, *Al-Ahram Weekly* Takes a Look." *Al-Ahram Weekly* 22–28 March.

Goethe Institute Cairo. 1997. "Citizens' Participation in the Renovation of the Old Town." Cairo: Goethe Institute Cairo, Faculty of Fine Arts.

General Organization for Physical Planning (GOPP). 1997. Project for the Upgrading of Urban Environments of Historic Districts, Terms of Refrence.

_____. 1997. "The Upgrading of Valuable Districts in Greater Cairo." Unpublished report for the Project for the Upgrading of Urban Environments of Historic Districts, Terms of Reference.

Hassan, Fayza. 1999. "Well May They Weep." *Al-Ahram Weekly* 29 April–5 May.

Hawas, Soheir. 2002. "Al Kahira al Kediweyyah: Rasd wa Tawthik Emarat wa Omran al Kahira wasat al Medina." Cairo: Center for Architecture Design.

Heritage Conservation and Management in Egypt and Syria (HERCOMANES). 2000–04. *HERCOMANES Programme Website.* <*http://www.hercomanes.com*>. (1 June 2004).

Hillier, Bill. 1996. *Space is the Machine.* Cambridge: Cambridge University Press.

Hillier, Bill and J. Hanson. 1984. *The Social Logic of Space.* Cambridge: Cambridge University Press.

Ilbert, Robert. 1984. "Heliopolis: Colonial Enterprise and Town Planning Success." In *The Agha Khan Award for Architecture: Acts from the Seminar on the Expanding Metropolis, Coping with the Urban Growth of Cairo,* 36–42. Singapore: Concept Media Pte Ltd for the Aga Khan Award for Architecture.

Issa, Iman. 2000. "Cairo's First Arts Festival—Al Nitaq." In *Medina* 12: *Architecture, Interiors & Fine Arts*, ed. Yasmeen M. Siddiqui, 84–87.

El Kadi, Galila, and Sahar Atia, eds. 2002. "Special Issue on Restoring Cairo 17." *Misr al-mahrusa* (February).

Karnouk, Liliane. 1995. *Contemporary Egyptian Art*. Cairo: The American University in Cairo Press.

Lavedan, Pierre. 1974. *L'urbanisme au Moyene Age*. Genèves: Droz.

⸻. 1982. *L'urbanisme à l'époque moderne*. Genèves: Droz.

Lynch, Kevin. 1977. *L'image de la cité, collection aspects de l'urbanisme*. Dunod: Poitiers.

Morgan, Ihab. 1999. *Kairo: die Entwicklung des modernen Stadtzentrums im 19. und frühen 20. Jahrhundert*. Bern: Peter Lang Publishing Group.

Muratori, Saverio. 1959. *Studi per una Operante Sturia Urbana di Venezia*. Instituto Poligrafico dello stato. Roma.

Myntti, Cynthia. 1999. *Paris Along the Nile*. Cairo: The American University in Cairo Press.

Panerai, Philippe, J. Castex, and J. Charles Depaule. 1978. *Formes urbaines: de l'îlot à la barre*. Paris: Dunod.

Poëte, Marcel. 2000. *Introduction à l'urbanisme, Sens et Tonka*. Paris: Sens et Tonka.

Raafat, Samir. 2003. *Cairo the Glory Days: Who Built What, When, Why and for Whom*. Alexandria: Harpocrates.

Rossi, Aldo. 1981. *Formes urbaines*. Paris: Edit de l'Espace.

Sakr, Tarek. 1993. *Early Twentieth Century Islamic Architecture in Cairo*. Cairo: The American University in Cairo Press.

Schmid, Anne M. 1990. *International Hotel Redesign*. New York, N.Y.: PBC International.

Sitte, Camillo. 1980. *L'art de bâtir les villes*. éd L'Equerre. Paris. Vienne: Der Statebau.

Tamraz, Nihal. 1994. *Nineteenth-century Cairene Houses and Palaces*. Cairo: The American University in Cairo Press.

UNESCO. 1993. *World Heritage Papers: Identification and Documentation of Modern Heritage*. Paris: UNESCO.

Notes

1   Misr Bank was built in the days following the 1919 Revolution, which resulted in the declaration of Egypt's independence in 1923. It is the first Egyptian bank established by decision of the Wafd Party, which negotiated the country's independence and was entirely financed by Egyptian funds. The bank's

headquarters were designed by architect Antonio Lasciac in a neo-Arabic style. The Arab Music Institute was designed by architects Verucci, Pasteur, and Farag Amin in the neo-Arabic style much in fashion at the time. It was inaugurated by King Fouad I in 1926 and was considered one of the most elegant buildings of the capital at that time. It was restored by the Ministry of Culture in 1997 and now houses the museum of the late renowned singer Muhammed 'Abd al-Wahab. The palace of the Belgian Baron Eduoard Empain was designed by the architect Alexandre Marcel and is located in the eastern suburb of Heliopolis, the first satellite town of Cairo founded at the beginning of the last century by the Baron and his investors.

2   The Master Plan for Greater Cairo, approved in 1984, provided for the passage of the Ring Road (a highway surrounding Cairo that was designed to ease its notorious traffic and connect the exurbs and suburbs with the city center) through the Giza Pyramids site. The Pyramids were then removed from the World Heritage list, pressuring the Egyptian government and its international consultants and builders to change the Ring Road's final route.

3   The second International Congress of Architects and Technicians of Historic Monuments, which met in Venice from 25–31 May 1964, put forth new rules that had the intention of conserving and restoring monuments in order to safeguard them no less as works of art than as historical evidence.

4   Seminar organized in Cairo by the Agha Khan Award for Architecture within the framework of a seminar series on *Architectural Transformations in the Islamic World,* 11–15 November 1984.

5   This program concentrated on the city centers of Cairo and Aleppo and had the objective of upgrading the conservation-management system of sites and objects of the late nineteenth and early twentieth centuries.

Cairo Subcultures and Media
Contestation

13

Upper Egyptian Regionally Based Communities in Cairo
Traditional or Modern Forms of Urbanization?

Catherine Miller

Migration and Affiliation

Chasing Away Upper Egyptians from Cairo Streets. al-Kadiri 2002.

Upper Egyptians are Indignant at the Governor's Plan to Forbid Them from Entering Cairo. 'Abd al-Jawad and Sha'ira 2002.

Does the Governor Plot to Expel the Shaykh of al-Azhar and Pope Shenouda? al-Salimi 2002.

During a three-week period in July 2002 these headlines, among many others, filled some Egyptian newspapers. They were part of a media campaign involving mainly opposition newspapers against the alleged decision of the governor of Cairo to regulate and limit rural migration to Cairo to preserve urban stability. From what was reported in the press, the governor had stated that he wanted to study "a project which could forbid rural people to settle in Cairo." Apparently, no one from Lower Egypt dared to react to the governor's statement while

375

eminent Upper Egyptians, including national deputies, reacted violently to this declaration and threatened to open a lawsuit against him. Upper Egyptian politicians believed that the governor's declaration exclusively targeted Upper Egyptian migrants. The event was interpreted as a confrontation between the governor, a state actor, and members of the Upper Egyptian population in Cairo. The same governor had been previously suspected by some Upper Egyptian journalists of being "anti-Sa'idi" (*al-Usbu'* 27 April 1998). In contrast some other newspapers denounced the presence of a Sa'idi lobby ("*Lubi Sa'idi* . . ." 2002). Sa'idi is the Arabic term for someone from southern, i.e. 'upper' Egypt—'upper' because the Nile flows down toward the Mediterranean sea from these elevated lands that stretch toward Sudan and into Ethiopia. This press campaign was one of these usual 'tempests in a teapot' by which a number of small opposition newspapers tend to criticize the government. But it was also one of the many manifestations of the tension between the state apparatus and some segments of the Cairene Upper Egyptian population.

The perception that massive migration, either internal (i.e. from rural/ provincial areas) or external (from other countries), is a destabilizing factor for urban development is a kind of universal public metanarrative. The migrants who come to join the low-income urban classes have always been perceived as different and potentially dangerous for the social order (Wacquant 1997). In the Middle East, the old urban elite has always considered rural migrants as threats to the 'refined civilization' of the city. This has also been the case in Cairo, since the famous historian al-Jabarti and the urban elite pejoratively described the inhabitants of the sixteenth–nineteenth century popular peripheries of Cairo as *fallahin*, or peasants (Raymond 1987). In a similar fashion, early twentieth-century Egyptian intellectual reformists such as Muhammad 'Abd al-Karim also considered poor migrants a threat to urban stability (Rousillon 1996).[1] By the second half of the twentieth century, the early pejorative perception that the dominant Cairo elite had of the traditional popular urban districts had been transferred to the new urban informal settlements (*al-'ashawa'iyat*). A number of academic works and institutional reports did not hesitate to stress the anarchic "ruralization" of Cairo's peripheries, describing them as places of serious sociocultural problems characterized by their "disruption of social organization" (Egypt Human Development Report, UNDP 1996).

The debate around the ruralization of the urban periphery raises the issue of the migrants' cultural and social integration within the city. How and when does a migrant become an established urban citizen? What is the impact of urbanization upon the migrant communities? Upper Egyptians in Cairo represent an interesting case here. They do not constitute a local religious, non-Arab minority, or a foreign community. Like the majority of Cairenes, they are Egyptian, Muslim, and Arabic-speaking. However, there is evidence that Upper Egyptians are often perceived in the public discourse as being more 'particular' than the other Egyptian regional migrants and less prone to integration. Conversely, it appears that migration and urbanization have effectively reinforced identification with a collective Sa'idi grouping.

In this chapter I analyze why Upper Egyptians residing in Cairo appear so often as the 'internal Other' in the Egyptian media and in the various public narratives. Why is their integration in the urban setting conceived as 'more problematic' than other groups, on the eve of the twenty-first century, at a time when internal migration to Cairo has considerably slowed down (Denis and Bayat 1999)? Drawing from the Upper Egyptian case, I investigate the relevance and the strength of regional-based communal networks in the social structuring of premodern and contemporary Cairo. Are communal networks/communities the expression of traditional local types of organization or are they the expression of new social constructs, induced by urbanization and migration? These questions raise the issue of identity construction in a modern urban context (i.e., 'otherness and boundaries') and echo a long-standing debate concerning the status of 'communities' within Middle Eastern cities. Communities, like families, have often been conceived as rather static and specific entities. However, a more fluid and contextual conception of identity indicates that communal/regional affiliations are not fixed and can express new forms of grouping. Like kinship, a regional sense of identity, sometimes known as 'asabiya in the Middle East can be a modern urban social construct (Bocco 1995, Eickelman 2002, Salibi 1992, Seurat 1985). In this paper I pay particular attention to the interlocking between past and present social urban constructions in order to analyze continuity and changes and to avoid an essentialist vision of identity construction.

Upper Egyptians in Cairo: Intruders or Urbanites?

Many factors have contributed to the present perception that Upper Egyptians form a distinct group among the Cairene population (for more details see Miller 2004). The interlocking of three main factors has crystallized a contemporary stigmatized vision of Upper Egyptians. These include: the historical divide between Upper and Northern Egypt; the economic underdevelopment of Upper Egypt; and the recent political instability of Upper Egypt. A rapid historical overview indicates that the economic and social status of Upper Egypt vis-à-vis Northern Egypt deteriorated considerably in the last two centuries and that this unequal relationship was progressively justified or explained by reference to a supposed different cultural background.

For many centuries the links between Cairo and Upper Egypt had been rather limited (Garcin 1987). In the fifteenth and sixteenth centuries, Upper Egyptians represented only 30 percent of the Egyptian internal migrant population and were less numerous than the Syrian population. Few Upper Egyptians were recorded among the Cairene religious or merchant elite (Petry 1981, 41–48). Conversely, the presence of religious notables from the Nile Delta region in Nothern Egypt reinforced the cultural and social relationship between Cairo and its northern hinterland and facilitated the integration of the migrants from this area (Garcin 1969). The presence of Upper Egyptian religious authorities (*'ulama'*) became more important in the second half of the eighteenth century, as attested to by the creation of a Sa'idi *riwaq* (Upper Egyptian section) in al-Azhar. In the second half of the nineteenth century, a number of Upper Egyptians joined the new academic and scientific institutes created by Muhammad 'Ali forming a new group of reformist elites. Some of them became famous national figures, such as Rifa'a al-Tahtawi. A few other intellectual figures, like Shaykh al-Marari, promoted a kind of cultural revalorization of Upper Egypt. However, the population size and the social weight of Upper Egyptians in Cairo never reached the level of the Lower Egyptians coming from the neighboring Delta. Therefore, the sociocultural distance between Upper (southern) and Lower (northern) Egypt has remained significant even until now.

The economic gulf between Lower and Upper Egypt goes back to the eighteenth and nineteenth centuries when the development of a market economy in the irrigated Delta led to the economic marginalization of Upper Egypt (Baer 1967; Gran 1998; Holt 1967). The status of Upper-Egyptian migrants reflects this ongoing economic marginalization. Beginning in the late nineteenth century many Upper Egyptians started to migrate to the North, working as seasonal daily laborers (Abu-Lughod 1961; Baer 1967; El Messiri 1983). Until the early 1970s, four-fifths of the Upper Egyptian migrants in Cairo were male, while migrants from the Delta were already established with families in the region (Ireton 1997). This discrepancy indicates that many Upper Egyptian migrants were still seasonal or very low-paid migrants living at the margin of the society and not yet well integrated within the city. Upper Egyptians still represent an important percentage of low-paid Cairene daily laborers, who can be seen waiting for employment in the Cairo streets (Zohry 2002). In the 1990s, Egyptian political experts considered Upper Egypt to be the most "neglected impoverished region" of the country and asserted that this underdevelopment was one of the main factors contributing to political violence (Abu al-ʿIzz 1994; Shafiq 1994).[2] As one account argued, "The north neglected the impoverished south and then made jokes about it. Militant Islamist violence was one way in which Upper Egypt told the rest of the country that the joke has soured" ("The South Recalled" 1996).

In the 1990s, many kinds of armed as well as peaceful Islamic revivalist movements were particularly active in Upper Egypt and also in the Cairene popular informal housing settlements known as *al-askan al-ʿashwaʾiya*. (See Denis in this volume for additional information on informal housing areas.) Although Upper Egyptian migrants represent only a small percentage of the inhabitants of these settlements, many political analysts, government officials, and journalists described them as demographically dominant and particularly drawn to Islamist activism as a result of their alleged culture of 'violence' symbolized by a vendetta (Haenni 2001). The political and media discourses of the 1990s reinforced the stereotyped perception of Upper Egypt (so prevalent in movies, TV series, novels, and jokes) and contributed to the notion that Upper Egypt was indeed a specific area, characterized by its cultural conservatism, its resistance to modernity, and even its violence. Moreover these media discourses spread the idea that the presence of large segments of "poor Egyptian migrants" was one of the main causes of urban political violence and destabilization (Subhi 1999).

As a result of the general historical and socioeconomic context described above, Upper Egyptians in Cairo, who belong to all social classes and who have occasionally become top public figures, tend nevertheless to be collectively identified with poor unskilled migrants and with the stigmatized perception of the *ʿashwaʾiyat* (informal housing settlements) as the locus of extremism, crime and poverty (Denis 1994; Haenni 2001; Singerman 1999). Nevertheless, a number of Cairene Upper Egyptians have been reacting to these stereotypes and have developed their own discourse praising the pride and purity of their 'genealogical origin' *(asl)*, their supposed specific Upper Egyptian ethos, and their refusal to assimilate to the dominant Cairene urban culture, described as decadent and Westernized.

The tensions between the migrants and the ruling urban groups are rarely described in socioeconomic terms (poor migrants versus well-off urbanites), but are often interpreted, by both Saʿidis and non-Saʿidis as the result of a deep cultural and communal difference symbolized by the dichotomous relationship between Modernity (Cairo) and Tradition (Upper Egypt). This cultural and essentialist vision has helped to reinforce processes of ethnicization (the 'we' group versus the 'they' group) and the strengthening of social boundaries (Miller 2004).

Processes of Affiliation among Upper Egyptian Migrants

Behind stereotypes and discourses, what has been the practical social/cultural impact of migration upon the migrant groups and upon the social structuring of the city? Investigating Upper Egyptian migrants' personal networks in Cairo between 1994 and 1998 in various informal settlements of Giza (the southern governorate of Greater Cairo), I came across two main findings. The first was the relative importance of region-based, village-based, or kin-based networks among the migrants and the importance of the ethic of *qaraba* (closeness) which symbolically divides the society between 'kin' and 'foreigners' (Miller 2000). The second was the development of a strong Upper Egyptian identity *(al-Sa'idiya)* (Miller 2004). This identification with a collective Upper Egyptian grouping transcends social classes and can be found among both the lower classes of the migrant Cairene population and the Upper Egyptian intellectual and political circles. The well-known poet al-Abnudi as well as the newspaper *al-Usbu'* are good examples of this Upper Egyptian intellectual trend. In the Cairene popular settlement, this Upper Egyptian identity described in terms of adherence to a genealogical origin *(asl)* that transcends residential location, was claimed by many young educated Upper Egyptian males, even those born in Cairo and belonging to the second or third generation:

We are born in Cairo but our brains, our heads are Sa'idi. We kept our principles, our Sa'idi values, we have been raised like Sa'idis. We don't like concessions (tanazulat), *we don't like to bow our heads.* 'Ishmat, 22 years old, Abu 'Atata, Bulaq al-Dakrur village.

We came here; we were raised here, but we kept our tradition because we are linked to our asl. *My father and my paternal uncle are in Cairo, another is in Alexandria but for all of us, our* mansha', *our place is in Sa'id. The basis is the* 'a'ila *(family), the* asl. *I know all the jokes about the Sa'idi. But the one for whom asl does not matter, where does he come from? I am born in Cairo. Does it mean that I am cut from the Sa'id? Is it a shame to originate from the Sa'id? It is not the place I am raised in, but my asl which is important. Some others say no, I am raised in Muhandisin, I am from Muhandisin. They are ignorant.* Ahmed, 23 years old, Ard al-Liwa.

My findings concerning the strength of this regional affiliation were rather different from what had been previously observed. Many urban and historical studies on Cairo have indicated that 1) communal networks and organizations were premodern phenomena, which disappeared following the urban transformation of the second part of the twentieth century; and that 2) communal/regional solidarity among migrants characterized the first phase of settlement and shifted progressively to new forms of solidarity and new social links based primarily on neighborhood associations (Deboulet 1994, 1996; Ghannam 2002; Hoodfar 1997; Oldham et al. 1987). This apparent contradiction led me to investigate the evolution of Cairo's social organization, and more particularly the role of communal/regional networks in both the past and present, in order to analyze their roots and contemporary relevance. A review of existing literature reveals that very little is known about regional networks and regional identification in Cairo. The lack of literature on this topic raises another problem: is it due to the fact that regional networks have never been *de facto* an important component of the Cairene social structure, or is it a result of the fact that social scientists neglected this field? Although I do not yet have a definite answer to this question, I would think that many social scientists have disregarded communal networks because they implicitly assume that communal networks are traditional forms of organization that do not function in a modern city like Cairo. Unlike many other Middle Eastern countries, Egypt is known for its strong political centralism and its rather nationalist ideology. Since the Nasserist revolution, nationalist ideology has prohibited public expression and political expression of any kind of communalism, either based on religion (the Copts for example) or ethnicity (non-Arab Nubians). (See Elizabeth Smith in this volume on Nubian identity.) Moreover, the settlement of the former bedouin groups had been achieved in the nineteenth century and since then few consider tribal or clan affiliation in Egypt to be an important means of contemporary social identification, except in the margins of the Egyptian desert (Baer 1967). Therefore, it is assumed by most social scientists that communalism/sectarianism does not shape the spatial and social distribution of contemporary Cairene society. A closer look at the status of regional communities in Cairo reveals that, in fact, communal networks may have always functioned as rather important means of urban organization, even when they do not appear as institutionalized organizations.

The City and Its Communities: a Historical and Contemporary Overview

Communities *(tawa'if)* represented an important social, spatial, and juridical reality of Ottoman Cairo, particularly within the *hara* (pl. *harat*), the old established popular districts of Cairo (Abu-Lughod 1971; Al-Messiri Nadim

1979; Lapidus 1984; Raymond 1994). Popular quarters are described as forming homogeneous social units in terms of occupations or ethnic or religious origins and as having a strong local identity. However, the basis of this homogeneity is not detailed and is still problematic. The most precisely identified Ottoman Cairene *tawa'if* have been the 'ethnic' or 'national foreign' communities like those of the North Africans *(magharba)*, the Palestinians, the Syrians, the Turks, the Armenians, or the Greeks, as well as the religious minorities like the Jews and the Christians. All these communities have been characterized by various degrees of spatial segregation and professional specialization and have had their own juridical and confessional representation (Raymond 1983, 1988, 1990, 1994).

Conversely, little is known about a gradual regional-based specialization and spatial distribution of the Egyptian Cairene population. Egyptians, who belonged to the two main social categories, the populace *('amma)*, and the elite *(khassa)*, have been identified by opposition to the other communities; i.e. as 'natives' vis-à-vis 'foreigners' and as 'Muslims' vis-à-vis 'non-Muslims.' The little available historical information concerns the spatial distribution of the religious and civilian elite, the origin of the *'ulama'* and the distribution of the regional sections in al-Azhar (Garcin 1969; Petry 1981; Raymond 1987; 1994). From this, we know that in the past students coming to study at al-Azhar University from within Egypt were organized like the 'foreigners' and that each had their own section *(riwaq)*: the *Sa'ayda* (Upper Egyptians), the *Sharaqwa* (from the north-

Upper Egyptian men congregating at a Cairo café. (photograph by Jean Pierre Ribière).

east Delta), the *Fayyumiya* (from the Fayyum), and the *Baharwa* (from the north-west Delta). Members of each section clustered around their local *zawya* (mosque), *khandaq* (hostel), and *wikala* (caravansary) and had little contact with outsiders (Raymond 1987). Unlike many other Middle Eastern cities, there are no details of specific regional spatial clustering within the city, or of quarters inhabited by a specific tribal group.

Social and political transformations of the late nineteenth and early twentieth centuries disrupted the social organization of religious/ethnic communities and the social unit of the quarters (Baer 1967). The assimilation of the former national Muslim communities (North Africans, Palestinians, Turks) within the Egyptian population was achieved in the latter half of the nineteenth century. The administrative and juridical dissolution of the other religious and national communities began in the early twentieth century and culminated in the dissolution of the confessional jurisdictions in 1955 after the Nasserist revolution (Abecassis and Kazazian 1992). The architectural transformation of the old quarters, the extension of Cairo, the creation of new quarters and the movement of population, have all led to the transformation and renewal of the *hara* population.

Today the spatial distribution of the population is divided by social levels with rich *(raqi)* and popular *(baladi/sha'bi)* neighborhoods. Among the popular areas however, a distinction must be drawn between the old established neighborhoods and the new ones. Old popular quarters benefit from a historical legitimacy and are perceived as the locus of popular ethnic identity (i.e., the *baladi* identification). Their inhabitants are said to share a strong feeling of solidarity and identification to their quarters (El-Messiri 1978; Ghannam 2002; Singerman 1995). This common identification to the neighborhood does not however totally eradicate other in-group identification like affiliation to kin group or to a village group (Al-Messiri Nadim 1979). But the new popular districts established since the 1960s–1970s do not benefit from this historical legitimacy and still lack a recognized identity (Ghannam 2002, and in this volume). They are not perceived any more as *baladi* but at best as *sha'bi* 'popular' (in the socioeconomic sense, without the ethical-cultural connotation of *baladi*) if not *'ashwa'i* (illegal and unplanned) due to the fact that most of the popular neighborhoods built in the 1970s and 1980s were constructed illegally (for further analysis of these neighborhoods see Denis in this volume). It is mainly within these areas that the importance of communal/regional affiliation and networks has been recorded and often discussed in order to evaluate the degree of social cohesion and urbanization of these areas. Many urban studies tend to consider that the presence of

Children walking to school in an informal housing area where Upper Egyptians have settled (photograph by Jean Pierre Ribière).

strong regional networks restrains urban integration and identification to a common local space, the urban district. In agreement with the development paradigm and modernization theories, these urban studies describe regional networks/affiliation as transitional phenomena that will disappear following the migrants' integration. On the contrary, my research on Upper Egyptian migrants indicates that regional affiliation is reprocessed in the urban context and can become a powerful means of political and social mobilization.

Regional-Based Affiliation and Networks

The paucity of research on Cairene contemporary regional networks makes it difficult to assess whether regional networks represent a marginal/transitional phenomenon or, on the contrary, if they constitute an important socioeconomic feature of the city. Concerning professional networks, it is commonly asserted that at the beginning of the twentieth century "natives of a specific village or district migrated to a specific town and specialized in a particular occupation" (Baer 1967; Abu-Lughod 1961). But most of the recorded examples refer to rather limited economic networks: the porters from Muha village (Asyut) and the water carriers from Dar al-Baqar (Gharbiya) recorded by Baer for the early twentieth century; the sellers of *ful* in Fatimid Cairo originating from the oases (Al Messiri Nadim 1979); the bread-makers in downtown originating from a village near Asyut (Meyer 1988); the vegetable sellers of Dar al-Salam and Rod al-Farag originating from the Suhaj region (Kharoufi 1991; 1995); the clothes-sellers of Wikalat al-Balah

(Bulaq Abu al-ʿIla) originating from the village of al-Ighana in the Asyut area (Usama and Subhi 1996); etc. It is difficult to assess whether these regional specializations constitute an important pattern of what is usually labeled the 'informal economic sector.' There are indications, for example, that the fruit-and-vegetable-selling sector is highly organized along regional networks, and there is a probability that the same occurs in the building sectors of Giza, where contractors from Upper Egypt tend to play an important role.

Regional-based, village-based, and extended family clustering have been found in a number of informal settlements or former villages around Cairo (Deboulet 1994; El Kadi 1988; Fakhouri 1987; Florin 1999; Miller 2000; Oldham et al. 1987; Taher 1986; Tekçe et al. 1994). Regional or kin clustering appears to be very important to the Upper Egyptian migrant ethos. This does not mean that kin clustering is solely the function of Upper Egyptians. In fact it concerns almost every Cairene, whatever his/her origin. Like in all of the Middle East, kinship and family ties are the bases of social life (Hopkins 2001, Rugh 1985, Singerman 1995). However, in Cairo family is referred to as *ahl* or *usra*, i.e. the closed family which will not extend further than the immediate relatives in a nuclear family. In Upper Egypt and among Upper Egyptian migrants, family is referred to as *'a'ila* or *badan* and includes all the members of the extended lineage.

Living among kin *(qarib)* is perceived as a social ideal, because it provides individuals with a sense of comfort and security. Therefore people tend, if they have the financial means, to cluster in the same area. Family or regional clustering is not restricted to the first migrant generation. Sometimes groups of relatives who are living in the same area manage to move together to a new area and attract relatives from their original region. Migration to the Gulf countries has helped members of extended families to buy land, to build houses, and sometimes to invest in real estate and the construction industry. Settlers' narratives tell how a group from the same extended family, village, or 'tribe' came to occupy empty land or gathered to buy land for construction. In many instances a group of related families were the 'heart' of the historical settlement. In the new areas they constituted what they called an *'izwa* (support group) which enabled them to survive through hardship and still to play a social or political role in their area. Many places are still commonly identified as the "area of the sons *(awlad)* of region X or the hamlet *('izba)* of region Y":

My grandfather came from Girga and settled in Misr al-Qadima in the 1940s. Many people from Girga came to Misr al-Qadima. We bought three houses there. Then we came to al-Andalus and we bought land here. We own three buildings. Most of the Saʿidi like to cluster together. If I want to buy somewhere, I speak to my kin in order that they buy land near me and we constitute an 'izwa. *We were the first ones of the family to come to the Pyramids district and then many relatives joined us. We became an* 'izwa, *shoulder against shoulder. Here most of the owners are from Asyut or Suhaj. The street there is almost Asyuti from Dayrut. On the other side, there are many Fayyumis. There is a street called "the sons of Fayyum," they are all Fayyumis.* Hamdi, 42 years old, born in Misr al-Qadima.

Through these residential strategies, the settlers developed a particular vision of urban spaces and considered that some areas 'belong to them,' even if they now represent a demographic minority. Most stories, however, often refer to a 'heroic past,' when the people struggle to move to the unplanned areas of Greater Cairo in order to establish a living:

The family grouping occurred at the beginning, when my father and my uncle settled here and brought their close relatives. This is the tagammu' *system. We say that "the numbers win over courage"* (al-kutra tighlib al-shuga'a). *Even if we are weak we can defend ourselves, because there were many thefts and the area was an agricultural one. Therefore the* 'izwa *system goes back to the time of the fields.* Usama, 30 years old, Imbaba.

Today all these areas have grown tremendously and their population has diversified, attracting new segments of the Cairene population fleeing the deterioration of the old Cairo districts (Deboulet 1995). Interestingly, the old 'pioneers' who were former squatters often complain that their areas, which before were controlled by well-known families, have now been invaded (*itlamm*) by 'foreigners' and 'intruders' (*dukhala*) (Miller 2000). As stated by a number of settlers:

Before there were only families from Qina here. But then, in the 1980s, newcomers (dukhala) *came—Cairenes* (masarwa), *whose houses had collapsed, arrived in Imbaba. And because of this, the relationship between the people deteriorated. Our fathers from Sa'id keep strong relationships between them; the families know their origin. But the* dukhala, *they brought problems. They scattered all around, they don't know each other . . . they don't have asala.* Muhammad, 25 years old, 'Izbat al-Sa'id, Imbaba.

At the same time, educated children of the original 'pioneer' families established in the 1960s have now moved to middle-class districts in order to find better accommodation.

Regional-based residential clustering and regional professional networks appear closely linked to the first phase of migration and there is a probability that residential clustering will not resist the ongoing urban transformation. However, for the time being, regional or family networks still play a very important social role as a powerful means of social and political organization. The relevance of regional networks/affiliation should not be restricted to the analysis of residential distribution or professional networks. Regional affiliation can develop through more sophisticated or symbolic tools, as I demonstrate below.

From *rawabit* to *'asabiyat* in Cairo

Regional networks are active at three sociopolitical levels in Cairo. First, regional-based associations (*rawabit*, sg. *rabta*) are among the major type of officially registered associations in Cairo (together with the Islamic Associations) although it is difficult to assess their actual vitality because a number of them are still recorded but may not really function (Ben Nefissa and Qandil 1994). These associations encompass migrants from various socioeconomic backgrounds and districts of Cairo, who share a common regional origin. They can be village-based or regional-based and their size varies greatly. A *rabta* is usually headed by a wealthy 'notable' and receives donations from its richest members. Their main activities involve helping poor migrants, particularly with funeral arrangements, one of the most important Egyptian social duties (either by sending the corpse to the home region or by buying tombs in the vicinity of Cairo). *Rawabit* also provide occasional help for needy families and function as mediators in cases of family or neighborhood disputes. They further help maintain relationships between the members by organizing feasts or meetings. Such regional associations played an important role in the 1960s and 1970s, helping poor rural migrants to integrate and to keep links with their home region (Ben Nefissa 1994). Their social activities weakened in the 1990s because many former migrants had enough financial means and did not need to rely anymore on the *rawabit*, particularly for funeral arrangements. *Rawabit* now appear to be less publicly active than other associations such as Islamic welfare associations. They do not play a prominent political role. Even so, regional-based associations still maintain a link between the Cairene migrants and their original region, especially in the case of village-based associations, and a number of them are active both in Cairo and in the home region (Ben Nefissa 1994).

Second, the *majalis 'urfiya* (ad-hoc customary councils or reconciliation assemblies) that encompass local personalities (political figures or notables) as well as representatives of big families, village groups, and regional groups in the districts, are an important means of social control and conflict regulation in case of serious neighborhood conflicts and sometimes political or religious conflicts. These *majalis 'urfiya* are informal noninstitutional bodies whose composition varies according to the conflict. They can take place in various places (in a house, an office, an association, a coffee-shop, etc.) and their main goal is to mediate between the contending parties and to reach an agreement that will avoid judicial sanctions such as jail. They do not have official status but nevertheless they often work in close collaboration with state institutions like the police and the judicial authorities. In case of serious conflicts, their decisions can be officially recorded in the police or in the state court (Ben Nefissa et al 2000, Haenni 2001). In case of minor conflicts within a neighborhood, informal reconciliation meetings bring together the head of each family *(kabir al-'a'ila)* in order to solve the problem without the intervention of the police. In any case, the persons who act as mediators in these *majalis 'urfiya* must have a strong network and support group *('izwa)* as well as political connections. Rawabit, *majalis 'urfiya*, and informal councils testify that family/village/regional solidarities are an active means of urban social control and urban solidarity and are *de facto* recognized as such by state institutions.

Third, the weight of regional lobby or regional networks has become more salient during recent Cairene local and national elections (Ben Nefissa 2004, Longuenesse 1997; Mursi 1988). In a number of districts, known for their important migrant population, political parties have to look for a 'regional' candidate in order to attract the vote of his fellow migrants and to win the election. A number of newspapers complain that the Upper Egyptian *'asabiyat* dominate the elections in some districts of Cairo and Alexandria. Originally, the term *'asabiya* referred to the feeling of solidarity or belonging which joined together the members of a group, who supposedly share a common origin, such as a clan or a tribe (Seurat 1985). As such, an *'asabiya* reflects a primary type of affiliation, and most political experts consider that *'asabiyat* in Cairo reflect traditional forms of organization because they are a result of rural migration (Ben Nefissa 2004).

However, if the urban *'asabiyat* reproduce traditional discursive devices (family ethos, nobility of origin), they, in fact, represent new forms of affiliation and organization. At the political level, urban *'asabiyat* activate links and networks far wider than the original kin or lineage networks. In the case of Upper Egyptians, the potential political instrumentalization of regional *'asabiyat* in Cairo relies partly on the emergence of a common Upper Egyptian identity/affiliation *(al-Sa'idiya)*. An important dimension of the *Sa'idiya*, in the context of Cairo, is the fact that it overpasses the traditional divisions of the Upper Egyptian society and enables the grouping of all Upper Egyptians on the basis of a common regional and cultural origin (Miller 2004). Therefore, individuals who, because of their family status, would have little or no chance to play a political role in their home region, have the opportunity to participate and can potentially become a type of political 'leader' in Cairo. For this, they resort to many means of mobilization like creating or participating in welfare associations, creating their own newspapers, developing wide client networks, becoming members of local political assemblies, etc. This political and social activity is relayed by a strong cultural discourse, which mobilizes references to tradition, culture, and religion in order to criticize the Westernized Cairene elite and to legitimize the growing influence of the Upper Egyptian networks. These 'new leaders' try to attract all of their *baladiya* (i.e. people from the same regional origin). It may be noted here that regional origin is a very fluid device without fixed geographical boundaries that enables these 'new leaders' to attract more people on the base of a common cultural/religious ethics.

The expanding regional networks do not represent the former members of the small Upper Egyptian elite/aristocracy, which has been established in Cairo for more than a century. Rather, these networks represent an emerging class of people linked to the economic changes of the Infitah period. Many members of this new class worked in the Gulf countries and then settled in Cairo and developed their own businesses. According to their individual history, they can be very rich, living in upper-class neighborhoods like Muhandisin, or they can be small contractors living in the *'ashwa'iyat*. Whatever the case, they help to construct mosques, schools, etc., in the low-income neighborhoods, and they can be identified as *ahl al-khayr* (people of good) or as *kubar al-mantiqa* (big men of the area). They are able to weave regional affiliations with urban activities and moral ethos.

A New Urban Vision?

Through their action and discourse, these Upper Egyptian local 'leaders' participate in developing another vision of urban spaces. This vision reproduces elements of traditional popular discourse, which contrasts the strong solidarity of the popular districts to the individualism of the well-off ones (cf. the *baladi* ethics described in El Messiri 1978 and Singerman 1995). However, the typical *ibn al-balad*—'the son of the country' (the typical urban popular figure)—is supposed to be proud of his/her urban identity and rather disdainful toward the rural migrants. In contrast, the *Sa'idiya* discourse

assumes the superiority of Upper Egyptian moral values (like the sense of honor and solidarity, respect for elders, kin solidarity, piety, and respect for religious duties). Moreover, this discourse preaches the need to transplant *(istaqlam)* Upper Egyptian tradition and culture into the urban districts. Therefore, people who stick to their regional culture and ethics are more able than others to behave well in their neighborhood and to protect the social cohesion of their area. As stated by a young educated man from Bulaq al-Dakrur:

Here, everybody is from the Sa'id, we share the same traditions. It is like a part of our home region. Here the social ties between the people are strong. If we quarrel, an elder will come and solve the problems. We organize a majlis *(council) and we solve the problems. He is from Suhaj, I am Asyuti, but our habits are close. . . . We brought here the traditions of the Sa'id and we try to adapt them to the area. We are the majority and you find other peoples who embrace the Sa'idi habits because our social features are in agreement with the religion, with tradition. So they are stable. And the newcomers have to adapt to us. And sometimes we are the newcomers but they (non-Sa'idi) are still the ones who have to adapt to us. Ties are stronger among us than among those from the Delta or Cairo. Our traditions form an entity and this comes from their similarity to religion. They are semi-sacred.*
Ustaz Jamal, 27 years old, born in Cairo, holder of a commercial diploma, al-Nahya district.

To what extent do these segments of the Cairene population develop or contribute to a new vision of urban life? It is not easy to answer this question. On the one hand, the *Sa'idiya* discourse reproduces well-known rhetorical figures, like the representation of Upper Egypt as the locus of resistance and authenticity *(asala)* against colonization and Westernization. This rhetorical figure has been part of the national discourse since at least the early 1900s (see the figure of Husayn Mu'nis in Roussillon 1992). On the other hand, the *Sa'idiya* discourse reintroduces the notion of clan *('a'ila)*, lineage *(bayt* or *badan)*, origin *(asl)*, and blood *(damm)* as central values and pillars of the society, urban or not. These values are not antagonistic with the family ethos of the Cairene society but the *Sa'idiya* discourse as well as the Islamic discourse reinforces the legitimacy of 'non-Western' types of grouping (family/ clan/tribe) upon individuals or other type of networks (trade union, political parties, neighborhood, etc.). For example, many Upper Egyptians tended to reject the well-known proverb, "The Prophet recommended taking care of neighbors within a range of seven neighbors" *(al-Nabi wassa 'ala saba' jar)*, which stresses the importance of solidarity among neighbors. Instead they always insist on the importance of a 'blood link.' Hearing a woman saying that neighbors and foreigners (i.e. like social workers for NGOs) were often more helpful than kin, a young man promptly reacted:

The sister said that the gharib *(outsider) is becoming better than the* qarib *(kin), but this is a particular situation. She cannot do without her brother. She is his honor and his flesh. She will come back to her family. The* gharib *does not fit in at the end. He can be a dear neighbor, faithful and dedicated, but your kin is your kin. Blood does not change into water.* Ustaz Jamal, 27 years old, al-Nahya.

Upper Egyptian man in Cairo (photograph by Jean Pierre Ribière).

In this respect, the Sa'idiya urban ethos seems very similar to the Gulf urban model which is spreading as the 'ideal model' in many Middle Eastern cities (Beyhum 1997). It is also very close to the Jordanian Bedouin popular nationalist genealogist dis-course (Shryock 1997). Both models value the 'tribe' as one of the most authentic and legitimate types of social organization. Regional/communal solidarity and networks are by no means the monopoly of Upper Egyptians in Cairo. The ethics of the *Sa'idiya* discourse is shared by large segments of the Cairene population.

Conclusion

The case of Upper Egyptians in Cairo shows that identification processes have always had deep historical roots. The rather antagonistic relationship between Lower and Upper Egypt goes back to centuries of unequal development and partly explains the present strength of identity boundaries. These historical roots do not mean, however, that collective identies such as national, ethnic, or regional groupings are fixed entities. Regionally based identities, or *'asabiyat*, are a contextual process of construction, which like other types of emerging collective identity may make reference to tradition in order to adapt to changes (Hobsbawn 1993).

Communal and regional networks have existed in Cairo for a long time in various forms and have played different roles. Today regional networks need to be investigated through 'objective facts' (like spatial clustering or professional networks), but they also need to be investigated at a more symbolic level. Regional networks enable Upper Egyptian migrants who have lived in stigmatized districts to build their own vision and discourses regarding urban citizenship. Regional affiliation also gives Upper Egyptians new social and political weight. Therefore regional networks play an important role in the representation of the city and in its transformation.

The fact that *'asabiyat* are an affirmation of modernity, and not a manifestation of tradition, has been mainly advanced in multiconfessional countries like Lebanon and in societies known for their clan/tribal organizations like Yemen, Oman, and Jordan (Bocco 1995). The presence of *'asabiyat* in a modern global city like Cairo challenges our vision of modernity, which supposedly has no more room for ethnicity. The social reforms of Egypt during the nineteenth and twentieth centuries were supposed to have broken down the former 'tribal' affiliations of the Egyptian provincial population. It therefore sounds strange that a tribal rhetoric (the importance of blood origin and genealogy) works in a city like Cairo. But different factors explain this apparently strange phenomenon. First, if the rhetoric refers to the importance of origin and kinship ties, it appears that in Cairo the regional networks go far further than kin or clan networks. Hence, the tribal reference is more metaphorical than real. Second, many Cairene Upper Egyptians have lived and worked in the Gulf countries and have found there an ideology that values their 'pure' tribal Arab origin and helps them to contest the legitimacy of the more open and Western-oriented Cairene upper-class culture. Third, this Arab tribal ideology converges partly with the Islamist ideology in that it contests the supremacy of Western culture. For all these reasons, regional affiliation among Upper Egyptian migrants appears to be drawn as much by internal factors (the North/South relationship) as by more global factors.

Works Cited

Abecassis, Frédéric, and Anne Kazazian. 1992. "L'identité au miroir du droit—le statut des personnes en Egypte (fin XIX, début XXe siècle)." *Égypte/Monde Arabe*: 11: 11–38.

'Abd al-Jawad, 'Isam, and Wafa' Sha'ira. 2002. "Al-Sa'ayida yahtajjuna 'ala khittat al-muhafiz bi-man'ihim min dukhul al-Qahira." *Ruz al-Yusif*, 13 July, 37–39.

Abu al-'Izz, Sami. 1994. "Al-Sa'id saqata min dhakirat al-hukuma." *al-Wafd*, 5 May, 8.

Abu-Lughod, Janet. 1961. "Migrant Adjustment to City Life: The Egyptian Case." *American Journal of Sociology* 67: 22–33.

———. 1971. *Cairo: 1001 Years of the City Victorious*. Princeton, N.J.: Princeton University Press.

Baer, Gabriel. 1967. "Social Change in Egypt 1800-1914." In *Political and Social Changes in Modern Egypt*, ed. Peter Holt, 135–61. London: Oxford University Press.

Ben Nefissa, Sarah. 1994. "Deux formes de regroupement à vocation sociale et caritative en Egypte: les ligues régionales et les associations islamiques." *Cahiers du Gemdev* 21: 163–83.

———. 2004. "Asabiets et élections: les égyptiens sont-ils démocrates." In *Dispositifs de démocratisation dans le nord de l'Afrique*, ed. Jean Noel Ferrié and Jean Claude Santucci. Paris: CNRS Editions.

Ben Nefissa, Sarah and Amani Qandil. 1994. *al-Jama'iyat al-ahliya fi Misr*. Cairo: Al-Ahram Strategic Center.

Ben Nefissa, Sarah, Sameh Eid, and Patrick Haenni. 2000. "Réglements des conflits et ordre politique urbain au Caire: les faux semblants des Jalassats Orfia." In *Un passeur entre les mondes, le livre des Anthropologues du Droit, disciples et amis du Recteur Michel Alliot*, ed. J. Le Roy, 207–26. Paris: Publications de la Sorbonne.

Beyhum, Nabil. 1997. "De la ville Ottomane chargée d'histoire à une ville du Golfe partagée entre tribalisme et modernité, l'économie politique du changement à Beyrouth." In *Sciences sociales et phénomènes urbains dans le monde arabe*, ed. Muhammad Naciri and André Raymond, 233–48. Casablanca: Fondation du Roi Abdul-Aziz Al Saoud.

Bocco, Ricardo. 1995. "'Asabiyât tribales et Etats au Moyen Orient: confrontations et connivences." *Maghreb-Mashrek* 147: 3–12.

Deboulet, Agnès. 1994. *Vers un urbanisme d'émanation populaire. Compétences et réalisations des citadins, l'exemple du Caire*. Ph.D. diss., Université Paris XII, Créteil.

_____. 1995. "Des quartiers centraux vers les périphéries spontanées. Eléments sur la mobilité résidentielle dans la région du Grand Caire." In *Les nouvelles formes de la mobilité dans le monde arabe*, ed. Robert Escallier and Pierre Signoles, 433–62. Tours: Urbama.

_____. 1996. "Devenir citadin . . . ou partir à la conquête de droits urbains élémentaires: exemples tirés de faubours récents du Caire." In *La citadinité en questions*, ed. Michel Lussault and Pierre Signoles, 141–57. Tours: Urbama.

Denis, Eric. 1994. "La mise en scène des 'Ashwa'iyat." *Egypte/Monde Arabe* 20: 117–32.

Denis, Eric and Assef Bayat. 1999. "Urban Egypt: Towards a Post Metropolization Era?" *Cairo Papers in Social Science* 21: 48–27.

Eickelman, Dale F. 2002. *The Middle East and Central Asia. An Anthropological Approach*. Upper Saddle River, N.J.: Prentice-Hall.

El-Kadi, Galila. 1988. *L'urbanisation spontanée au Caire*. Tours, Urbama: Fascicule de Recherche.

al-Khadiri, Muhsin. 2002. "Mutaradat al-Sa'ayda fi shawari' al-Qahira." *al-Ahrar*, 19 July, 3.

El-Messiri, Sawsan. 1978. *Ibn Al-Balad: A Concept of Egyptian Identity*. Leiden: E.J. Brill.

_____. 1983. "Tarahil Laborers in Egypt." In *Migration, Mechanization and Agricultural Labor Market in Egypt*, ed. L. Philip Martin and Alan Richards, 79–100. Boulder, CO: Westview Press.

Al-Messiri Nadim, Nawal. 1979. "The Concept of the Hâra: A Historical and Sociological Study of Al-Sukkariya." *Annales Islamologiques* 153: 13–48.

Fakhouri, Hani. 1987. *Kafr El-Elow: Continuity and Change in an Egyptian Community*. Prospects Heights, IL.: Waveland Press.

Florin, Benedicte. 1999. *Itinéraires citadins au Caire: mobilités et territorialités dans une métropole du monde arabe*. Ph.D. diss., Université François-Rabelais, Tours.

Garcin, Jean Claude. 1969. "L'insertion sociale de Sha'râni dans le milieu cairote." In *Colloque internationale sur l'histoire du Caire*, 15: 9–67. Paris: CNRS éditions.

_____. 1987. "Pour un recours à l'histoire de l'espace vécu dans l'étude de l'Egypte Arabe." In *Espaces, pouvoirs et idéologies de l'Egypte médiévale*, ed. Jean Claude Garcin, 436–51. London: Variorum Reprints.

Ghannam, Farha. 2002. *Remaking the Modern: Space, Relocation and the Politics of Identity in a Global Cairo.* Berkeley: University of California Press.

Gran, Peter. 1998. *Islamic Roots of Capitalism: Egypt 1760–1840.* New York: Syracuse University Press.

Haenni, Patrick. 2001. *Banlieues indociles? Sur la politisation des quartiers péri-urbains du Caire.* Ph.D. diss., Institut d'Études Politiques, Paris.

Hobsbawn, Eric John, and T. Ranger, eds. 1983. *The Invention of Tradition.* Cambridge: Cambridge University Press.

Hoodfar, Homa. 1997. *Between Marriage and the Market: Intimate Politics and Survival in Cairo.* Berkeley: University of California Press.

Holt, Peter, ed. 1967. *Political and Social Changes in Modern Egypt.* London: Oxford University Press.

Hopkins, Nicholas, ed. 2001. "Special Edition on the New Arab Family." *Cairo Papers in Social Science* 24 (Spring).

Ireton, François. 1997. "Les migrations vers cinq grandes villes d'Egypte (Le Caire, Alexandrie et les trois villes du Canal), 1907-1986." *Egypte/Monde arabe* 32 (4): 81–96.

Kharoufi, Mostafa. 1991. "Du petit au grand espace urbain: le commerce des fruits et légumes à Dâr al Salâm." *Egypte/Monde arabe* 5: 81–96.

_____. 1995. "Société et Espace dans un quartier du Caire (Dâr al Salâm): secteur informel et intégration urbaine." *Les Cahiers d'Urbama* 1: 57–91.

Lapidus, Ira M. 1984. *Muslim Cities in the Late Middle Ages.* Cambridge: Cambridge University Press.

Longuenesse, Elisabeth. 1997. "Logiques d'appartenance et dynamique électorale dans une banlieue ouvrière: le cas de la circonscription 25 à Helwân." In *Contours et détours du politique en Egypte. les élections legislatives de 1995*, ed. Sandrine Gamblin, 199–228. Paris: Harmattan-Cedej.

"Lubi Sa'idi yadummu wuzara' wa-a'da' Majlis al-Sha'b didda muhafiz al-Qahira." 2002. *al-Jil*, 17 July.

Meyer, Gunter. 1988. "Manufacturing in Old Quarters of Central Cairo." *Eléments sur les centres villes dans le monde arabe.* Tour: Urbama.

Miller, Catherine. 2000. "Réseaux et territoires migrants de haute Égypte à Guizah (Le Caire)." In *Les Compétences des citadins dans le monde arabe*, ed.

Isabelle Berry-Chikhaoui and Agnès Deboulet, 221–46. Paris-Tour-Tunis: Karthala-Urbama-IRMC.

———. 2004 " Between Myth and Reality: The Construction of a Saidi Identity." In *Social and Cultural Processes in Upper Egypt*, eds. Nicholas Hopkins and Reem Saad. Cairo: The American University in Cairo Press.

Mursi, Fouad, ed. 1988. *al-Intikhabat al-barlamaniya fi Misr, dirasat intikhabat 1986.* Cairo: Sina li-al-Nashr.

Oldham, Linda, Aguer El-Hadidi, and Hussein Tamaa. 1987. "Informal Communities in Cairo: the Basis of a Typology." *Cairo Papers in Social Science* 10 (4): 110.

Petry, Carl F. 1981. *The Civilian Elite of Cairo in the Later Middle Ages.* Princeton, N.J.: Princeton University Press.

Raymond, André. 1983. "Les quartiers de résidence des commerçants et artisans maghrebins au Caire au XVIIᵉ et XVIIIᵉ siècles." *Revue d'histoire maghrébine* 31–32: 355–64.

———. 1987. "Les rapports villes–campagnes dans les pays arabes à l'époque ottomane (16ème–18ème)." In *Terroirs et sociétés au Maghreb et moyen orient*, ed. B. Cannon and F. Metral, 19–58. Lyon: CNRS.

———. 1988. "Les résidences des artisans et commerçants turcs au Caire au XVIIIᵉ siècle." In *Mélanges Professeur Robert Mantran*, ed. Abdeljelil Temimi, 209–19. Zaghouan: Publication du Centre d'Études et de Recherches Ottomanes (Ceromde).

———. 1990. "Palestiniens au Caire au XVIIIe siècle." *Revue d'Études Palestiniennes* 36: 57–66.

———. 1994. "Le Caire traditionnel: une ville administrée par ses communautés?" *Maghreb-Mashrek* 14 (3): 9–16.

Roussillon, Alain. 1992. "Egyptianité, arabité, islamité: la recomposition des référents identitaires." *Egypte/Monde Arabe* 11: 77–132.

———. ed. 1995. *Entre réforme sociale et mouvement national: identité et modernisation en Egypte (1882–1962).* Cairo: CEDEJ.

———. 1996. "Comme si la ville était divisée en deux: un regard réformiste sur l'urbain en Egypte au tournant des années 1940." *Genèses* 22: 18–39.

Rugh, Andrea. 1985. *Family in Contemporary Egypt.* Cairo: The American University in Cairo Press.

Salibi, K.S. 1992. "Community, State and Nation in the Arab Mashriq." *The Beirut Review:* 339–51.

al-Salimi, Bahir. 2002. "Hal yu'amir muhafiz al-Qahira bi-tarhil Shaykh al-Azhar wa-al-Baba Shenuda?" *al-Midan*, 22 July.

Seurat, Michel. 1985. "Le quartier de Bâb Tebbâne à Tripoli (Liban): étude d'une 'assabiya urbaine." In *Mouvements communautaires et espaces urbains au Mashreq*, 45–86. Beyrouth: Cermoc.

Shafiq, Amina. 1994. "Kasr 'uzlat al-Sa'id." *al-Ahram*, 10 October, 3.

Shryock, Andrew. 1997. *Nationalism and the Genealogical Imagination: Oral History and Textual Authority in Tribal Jordan*. Berkeley: University of California Press.

Singerman, Diane. 1995. *Avenues of Participation: Family, Politics and Networks in Urban Quarters of Cairo*. Princeton, N.J.: Princeton University Press.

_____. 1999. "The Construction of Political Spectacle: The Siege of Imbaba or Egypt's Internal Other." Paper presented in the conference *La Naissance du Citoyen*, 3–5 November. Cairo: CEDEJ.

"The South Recalled." 1996. *Al-Ahram Weekly*. 29 August–5 September.

Subhi, Karim. 1999. "Imbaba qunbulat al-Sa'ayda." *Ruz al-Yusif*, 15 February, 32–36.

Taher, Nadia. 1986. "Social Identity and Class in a Cairo Neighborhood." *Cairo Papers in Social Science* 9 (4): 110.

Tekçe, Belgin, Linda Oldham, and Frederic Shorter. 1994. *A Place to Live: Families and Child Health in a Cairo Neighborhood*. Cairo: The American University in Cairo Press.

Usama, Salama and Karim Subhi. 1996. "Hadm Wikalat al-Balah bi-al-ikrah." *Ruz al-Yusif*, 11 November, 36–38.

Wacquant, Loïc. 1997. "L'underclass urbaine dans l'imaginaire social et scientifique américain." In *L'exclusion, l'état des savoirs*, ed. Serge Paugam, 248–63. Paris: La Découverte.

Zohry, Ayman Gaafar. 2002. *Rural to Urban Labor Migration: A Study of Upper Egyptian Laborers in Cairo*. Ph.D. diss., University of Sussex, Brighton.

Notes

1   The term 'reformists' is used to describe those members of the Egyptian elite who, since the mid-nineteenth century, had been calling for the modernization and social transformation of Egypt. This movement, initiated partly by the rulers of the state (e.g., Muhammad 'Ali), is known in Arabic as *al-Islah al-ijtima'i* (social reform), and includes numerous trends and leading intellectual figures such as Rifa'a al-Tahtawi, Muhammad 'Abduh, Lutfi al-Sayyid, Taha Husayn, etc. (Rousillon 1995).

14

Place, Class, and Race in the Barabra Café

Nubians in Egyptian Media

Elizabeth A. Smith

At the Arminna Village Association in the 'Abdin neighborhood of Cairo, Mr. 'Ali Salim, a retired accountant nearing eighty who spoke Greek, French, and English, in addition to Arabic and his native Fadicca language, presided over the Fadicca language class to teach native speakers of the oral language to write using the medieval Nubian alphabet.[1] When I arrived at the association for class one evening about a week before the end of Ramadan in December 2001, Mr. 'Ali was asking Fu'ad, also a retired accountant and student in the Fadicca class, if he could open the office of the Nubian Heritage Association in the neighboring flat the following Wednesday night for a special meeting. Mr. 'Ali had invited the prominent Egyptian writer and intellectual Khayri Shalabi and four Nubian novelists to the association for a friendly meeting to resolve their differences.

What had happened that called for such a reconciliation *(sulh)* in an intimate gathering *(wanasa)* among intellectual colleagues and friends to resolve conflict over tea? Mr. 'Ali related how a few weeks previously, Shalabi had written a newspaper column on terrorism in Egypt in *al-Usbu'* newspaper, mentioning the 1993 bombing of a café in Cairo's nearby central square,

Tahrir Square. In the article, Shalabi referred to the café, named *Qahwat Wadi al-Nil* ('Nile Valley Café'), by its nickname *Qahwat al-Barabra*, or the *Barabra* Café. "And so it happened that our Mr. Khayri Shalabi's pen slipped and wrote 'Barabra Café,'" said Nubian novelist Haggag Oddoul in a response to Shalabi, continuing, "Many Nubians became angry, and well they should have" (Oddoul 2001).

Shalabi's public use of this appellation, *al-barabra*, had ignited an exchange of angry replies from several Nubian writers opposed to use of the word, apologetic explanations by Shalabi, and a final call for reconciliation by Oddoul ending at the meeting at the Nubian Heritage Association. The Nubian writers, originally from the region of Nubia spanning southern Egypt and northern Sudan, framed their objections to the term *al-barabra* (singular *barbari*) in a language of racism, color, rights, and citizenship that often attends controversies over public representations of Nubians. *Barbari* is a pejorative term used and understood as an insult in reference to color, but it can also be applied to anyone—Nubian or not—as a reference to brutishness or idiocy. Historically, *al-barabra* was the blanket term used to refer to Nubian and Sudanese male migrant laborers in metropolitan Egypt as a group.

Nubians, who are darker-skinned than most Egyptians and may call one of the two dialects of the Nubian language their mother tongue, have been migrating from Nubia to Egypt's northern cities for work primarily in domestic service for centuries while women maintained their southern village homes (Geiser 1986). However, during the construction of the Aswan High Dam, the government relocated all forty-four villages in Egyptian Nubia to new villages just north of the city of Aswan in 1963–64. Throughout the twentieth century, Nubians gained economic and educational advantages from both urban migration and the relocation, while at the same time suffering from decreased agricultural viability in Nubia and the final devastating loss of their homes and villages due to flooding from the High Dam.

In situating the debate over the Barabra Café, and other debates like it, within the context of citizenship and rights, certain male urban Nubian intellectuals oppose conflations of color, class, and geographic origins and relocations that effect a dual exclusion and inclusion of Nubians vis-à-vis dominant discourses of what it means to be Egyptian. On one hand, prevalent stereotypes of Nubians situate them in a subordinate urban class position within the nation as servants, chiefly doormen. On the other hand, as I will go on to suggest, other racialized stereotypes also exclude Nubians from dominant concepts of Egyptian identity by associating them with either a *past* slave origin in sub-Saharan Africa, or a *contemporary* African origin. Egypt is popularly understood by Egyptians to be culturally and civilizationally distinct from sub-Saharan Africa, notwithstanding its geographical location in the continent. Discourses that link contemporary Nubians with their former servant status, blackness, slavery, and Africanness, simultaneously include Nubians within the nation and locate them in a subordinate position.

In two years of ethnographic fieldwork on the representation of Nubians in the Nubia Museum and in tourism between 1997 and 2002, I often encountered such debates. Here I will examine several racialized representations of Nubians in media and museums in order to suggest a way to understand such debates on their own terms without stopping at assertions for or against the existence of racism. Dominant discourses about national unity appearing daily in the semiofficial press assert that Egypt does not 'have' racism, ethnicities, or minorities in such terms, formulated in reference to a global discourses about race, ethnicity, and minorities and democratic ideals of equality among citizens. Such discourses differentiate Egypt from nations with, for example, a history of institutionalized racism (the United States and South Africa), the danger of ethnonationalist separatist movements (Kurdish resistance in multiple states), or actual civil war (Sudan). However these kinds of assertions obscure the operation of racialist discourses that are both applied to and mobilized by Nubians in Egypt. Rather, I wish to consider here the complexities and historical development of how such racialist discourses—based on the social-historical association between phenotype, language, and culture—do operate in convergence with class and gender.

To be clear, color in Egypt does not form the basis for collective identities such as 'black' or 'white,' or any other color. More significant are class, most importantly, region, religion, and family. The population with origins in the region of Nubia contains a wide variation in skin color and features, much as the rest of the population of Egypt, from very light, to medium brown (wheat-colored or *qamhi*), to brown and black. Because of this variation, many Nubians resent being stereotyped only as black rather than brown or any other color. Nubians in both Cairo and Aswan view the representation of Nubians as black in color, and with what are called *zanji* or African features, as inaccurate, exaggerated stereotypes that imply non-Egyptian Africanness and perpetuate ignorance of Nubian origins and appearance. They reject the assumption that dark color indicates being 'from' Africa, here understood as sub-Saharan Africa, not Egypt.

A Slip of the Pen

The central Cairo neighborhood of 'Abdin is a socializing hub for an older generation of Nubian men like Mr. 'Ali, born and raised in the villages of Old Nubia before the 1960s relocation. Many have lived in Cairo since the first half of the twentieth century when their fathers and grandfathers migrated from Nubia to the cities of the north. The earlier migrants usually worked as servants, doormen, and cooks in the neighborhood's palaces, apartment buildings, and hotels in the city's then-center of political power. Today, Nubians often gather in 'Abdin at the dozens of Nubian cultural and village associations (gama'iyat) which had originated in the principle of self-help by providing assistance for funerals, educational and recreational activities, Arabic and English lessons, and a place to congregate socially. Along with mutual aid, the associations have also long been the locus for Nubian collective political action vis-à-vis the state, pressing for proper compensation from the flooding, and provision of services like schools in Nubia since at least the 1920s (Salih 2000, 259–60). Established as independent organizations before the current Ministry of Social Affairs existed, all associations are now registered with, monitored by, and in receipt of minor financial support from the ministry (Geiser 1986, 199–209; Poeschke 1996, 68–82 for more details on the associations). On one block between the two major streets linking Khedive Isma'il's nineteenth-century 'Abdin Palace and downtown Tahrir Square, the Arminna Village Association, the Nubian Heritage Association, and the Abu Simbel Association are all located in an apartment building next to busy cafés, stores, and a mosque.

The meeting called by Mr. 'Ali inviting the sparring parties to reconcile at the Nubian Heritage Association included Haggag Oddoul, novelist and association member who had apologized personally to Khayri Shalabi in his article "A message of love to the great writer Khayri ashri . . . maas kagna!" (Fadicca for "beautiful Khayri . . . greetings!") (Oddoul 2001). Oddoul defended Shalabi as one of the few Egyptian intellectuals who had shown respect for Nubians when in the early 1990s, novelists like himself began applying the term 'Nubian literature' to their work and Egyptian literary critics hostilely called their work and the term itself 'racist' and 'separatist' (Oddoul 1993). He excused Shalabi's recent use of the name Barabra Café as a thoughtless mistake or "slip of the pen," maintaining that unlike others, Shalabi himself was *not* "a racist (*'unsuri*) who purposefully intends to hurt the Nubians."

While exonerating Shalabi however, Oddoul used the opportunity of the debate to draw attention to three ongoing issues of concern for Nubians. First, he decried the exclusion of any dark-skinned people ("of brown or black color") from the media. Second, he argued against accusing Nubians of separatism because they speak and wish to revive the Nubian language. And third, he criticized the government's failure to compensate urban Nubians who had lost village homes in the 1960s relocation. Oddoul framed all three issues in a language of the rights of citizens: the right to be represented equally on state-controlled television regardless of skin color, the right for the Nubian language to be recognized as part of the national heritage, and urban Nubians' right to monetary or other compensation from the government for the loss of their homes. First, his article pointed out that since its inception in 1960, Egyptian television, under the Ministry of Information, "has not accepted any black-skinned people to work as a program host or hostess . . . as if the color black is a deficiency that brings shame upon Egypt and exposes its Africanness" (Oddoul 2001). He argued against considering black skin color, with its implied Africanness, to be shameful and a defect, asking:

Should we be silent as if we were not Egyptian citizens? We have only to sacrifice for the sake of the greater nation Egypt and bear our responsibilities, but we are not entitled to claim our rights? Or are we not of the same level as those who are wheat-colored [qamhi] or closer to white? Oddoul 2001.

Next, he claimed that concern for preserving the Nubian language should not be interpreted as separatist tendencies leading to "an attack on the Arabic language, the partition and isolation of Nubia, and then its independence!" but rather as a kind of "freedom of speech." Finally, he stressed that the government should live up to its forty-year-old promise to compensate those victims of the High Dam relocation from Nubia with homes in the flooded areas who were not residing there at the time. They are known as the *mughtaribin*, or migrant households, who never received new homes in relocated New Nubia despite the state's initial promises. Oddoul's response to the use of the name Barabra Café thus linked prejudice against representation of color in the media to both the rights of citizenship, and the patriotism of Nubians who sacrificed their homes and homeland for the sake of the nation, against accusations of separatism.

The café in question in Shalabi's article was located on Tahrir Square, close to 'Abdin and the central neighborhoods of Qasr al-Nil, al-Azbakiya, and Bulaq where Nubian migrants had historically worked and resided (Geiser 1986, 100). It was commonly called the Barabra Café because of the Nubian and Sudanese laborers who had frequented it, as it was close to their places of employment and residence. However, using the name 'Barabra Café' *in print* located Nubians as a group spatially and racially in ways that today certain actors publicly contest and seek to transcend. Although male Nubian migrants had been working as paid laborers in urban Egypt for centuries, after slavery was outlawed at the end of the nineteenth century they replaced slaves in paid servant positions, which maintained the prestige of the aristocratic former slave owners. Because of their occupation and appearance resembling slaves, Nubians therefore became "associated with slavery and servitude in the public mind and were considered particularly suitable for this work" (Fernea and Gerster 1973, 36–37). The name 'al-barabra' links Nubians in urban geographies such as Cairo, but also Alexandria and the Suez towns, to their former lower-class position as servants to the rich, the aristocracy, and foreign occupiers.

The images of Nubians I discuss in what follows—as barabra, slaves, 'African,' or black—are produced overwhelmingly in the metropolitan center of Cairo, in television, state publications and museums, and the press, and debated in the mainly male space of the urban village and cultural associations. However, as I will show, Nubians articulate with and against their racialized positionings differentially based on place of residence, class, and gender.

No Nubian Theme Song for Slavery

The Nubian language with its two dialects Kanzi and Fadicca is the most significant marker of difference for Nubians in Egypt, in addition to their darker skin color and the shared experience of migration and relocation. The size of Egypt's population with origins in Old Nubia is difficult to estimate today. No category designated 'Nubian' has been counted in the Egyptian census since before the 1952 revolution. Constituting less than half a percent of the total population of Egypt in 1960, Geiser estimated Egyptian Nubians to number approximately 150 thousand in 1970 (1986, 59–86), while in 1993, Poeschke estimated a figure of three hundred thousand (1996, 45).

Because they are unwritten, Kanzi and Fadicca (the two variants of the Nubian language spoken in Egypt) are devalued by Nubians and non-Nubians alike as primitive lahjat (dialects) without grammar or history, as opposed to a formal lugha (language) such as Arabic. Nubian is still spoken today, although during the Islamization of Nubia from the thirteenth through the fifteenth centuries C.E., the Nubian alphabet was replaced with the Arabic script. In the 1980s, although anthropologist Aleya Rouchdy found the majority of Nubian speakers to be bilingual in Nubian and Arabic, she noted a strong shift toward Arabic, the official state language (Rouchdy 1991). Those who attended the Fadicca and Kanzi Nubian language literacy classes offered in Cairo in 2001 were older members of the associations who had spent their early childhood in Old Nubia and were fluent speakers of their native language. Most of these men—who included accountants, businesspeople, and a novelist—had come to Cairo for primary, secondary, or university education usually before or around the time of the 1963–64 relocation, married Nubian women, and settled to raise their families in Cairo. They were concerned that the oral language might disappear because it was only being used in the home, and younger generations were not learning it. For them, learning to write in Nubian would not only preserve it, but prove it was a language, not a mere dialect.

These classes—the first of their kind in Egypt—were the culmination of a five-year-long project by twelve speakers from Egypt and Sudan to revive use of the medieval Nubian script based on Coptic and Greek. The book that this collective finished in 1999, called *Learn the Nubian Language* in Fadicca and Kanzi respectively, was based on the Ph.D. work of Dr. Mukhtar Khalil Kubbara. Kubbara's Ph.D. dissertation in Egyptology from Bonn, Germany, used Christian medieval manuscripts written in the Nubian script to demonstrate that the alphabet could be revived to write all of the contemporary oral dialects.

After the language classes, Bahgat Yusif, an accountant, and Bashir 'Abd al-Ghani, a retired civil servant, often invited me upstairs to the Abu Simbel Association for tea and conversation. Covering the wall in the main room was a giant mural depicting Pharaoh Ramesses II's two temples at Abu Simbel. In the 1960s UNESCO had relocated the temples above the rising waters behind the Aswan High Dam, at the same time that Egyptian Nubians were relocated to new villages north of Aswan. Under Ramesses' gaze at the Abu Simbel Association, members and friends played backgammon while smoking and watching a wall-mounted television.

One December night during Ramadan of 2001, after retiring from the meeting room to the office to enjoy our tea, Bahgat, Bashir, and I were explaining my research to an association member who had come in to say hello. In response, the man mentioned that another Nubian association had recently sent a letter of complaint to Egyptian state television Channel 1 about a Ramadan drama series. The series was an adaptation of a novel by Nobel prize-winning author Naguib Mahfouz, called *Conversations of the Morning and the Evening*. Set in the nineteenth century, one of the male protagonists of the series was a dissolute aristocrat who married his black female slave, named Jawhar, late in his life, abandoning his aristocratic wife and children. Apparently, a Nubian club had protested to the television channel because whenever the slave character Jawhar appeared on screen, Nubian music played in the background. The nature of the association's objection was that Nubians had not been enslaved as a people. The character of Jawhar was not Nubian, therefore the creators of the series should not have implied that she was by using Nubian music to accompany her on-screen presence.

Like Haggag Oddoul, other urban Nubian intellectuals in the associations were concerned with broadening their media image beyond the occupational niches of doormen and servants to reflect the educated white-collar professionals many had become. Having achieved a degree of class mobility like many rural migrants, and through education entered white-collar professions of all kinds, they seek to correct the erroneous identification of Nubians as sub-Saharan African and/or slave origin, rather than indigenous to the Egyptian Nile Valley. Along with their objection to the term *barabra* itself, they also seek to dismantle the omnipresent media stereotypes repeated in the classic Egyptian films of the pre-1952 Revolution period, continuously replayed on state and satellite television. These films invoke the Nubians' history of lower status, portraying images of domestic service in the urban context.

Being linked to slavery *as slaves* themselves could be understood as objectionable on several levels. While as mentioned above, Nubians were considered 'suitable' for domestic service due to the historical conjunction of abolition and the professions they took up in the cities, Nubians themselves also participated in the slave trade both as merchants and slave owners in Old Nubia until abolition in the late nineteenth century. For example, according to court documents from the mid-nineteenth century, two *barabra* from Ibrim in Nubia were the heads of the Cairo and Alexandria slave merchant's guilds (Walz 1978, 247). Nubians owned slaves particularly in the southern region of Nubia among the Kushaf, landowning tribes whose origins date to the Ottoman rulers posted to Nubia in the sixteenth century who intermarried with the local population (Fernea and Gerster 1973, 11–12). Slave families and their descendants formed a part of the landless agricultural workers (Hamid 1994, 45). Up until the relocation in the 1960s, the urban Nubian associations were perceived to represent the interests of these landowning families in the cities (Hamid 1994, 139). Thus this former slave-owning society had its own deep historical prejudices that located former domestic and agricultural slaves of African origin within the lowest social status (on slavery in Nubia also see Fernea and Gerster 1973, 36; al-Katsha 1978; Kennedy 1977, 1978; Walz 1978). The protest over the Ramadan series objected to the inaccurate implication that Nubians themselves had been enslaved as a people. The use of Nubian music, recognizable to the audience as such, had effected this misrepresentation.

Nubians attribute perpetuation of the servant stereotype to classic films, and view media as significant and influential for shaping the image of Nubians in Egyptian society. The urban associations devote a great deal of time and effort to managing media representations. They are all located a short distance from the Egyptian Radio and Television headquarters in downtown Cairo, and those of several major newspapers. Media consultation, production, and debate over Nubian representation all take place at the associations. A small number of association members may either appear in or contribute to television and radio shows. They give media producers contacts with family and friends in Aswan and their home villages; conduct interviews; act as consultants on Nubian language and traditions; and arrange home visits and performances. Members constantly debate the results, not only of their own efforts, but of media produced without their involvement. In meetings I attended over the period of two summers in 1997 and 1999, and during 2001–02, members debated on a nearly weekly basis both the authenticity and accuracy of radio programs, novels, films, folkdance performances, theater, and numerous newspaper articles featuring Nubians or Nubian themes. Though they often complain about the process of media production and its eventual products, association members urge each other to live up to the responsibility of representing Nubian heritage accurately to media producers, "or else they'll go looking for any old brown guy sitting in a café!" said one novelist.

Effective Misrecognition: "They Put Africans on Television!"

The aesthetics of color also influences not only views of attractiveness and marriageability among Nubians themselves, but also their perceived citizenship within Egypt. Urban Nubian associations are an almost exclusively male social space and place of action. Women sometimes attend the meetings, but membership is mainly counted by male heads of households (Geiser 1986). However in the regular meetings of the Nubian Heritage Association and the Nubian language classes, male participants frequently referred both to female family members, mostly wives or mothers, and to 'village girls' in general from New Nubia and the Nubian villages in and around Aswan City, as sources of authentic Nubian customs and traditions that needed to be preserved. In the absence of a geographical focus (since authentic Old Nubia no longer exists as a place), nostalgia for a rural Nubian authenticity is trained on 'village women' themselves. Women are seen to embody the traditions, language, and way of life from Old Nubia. Men in the metropolitan center express a gendered nostalgia for a rural Nubian authenticity located in village women themselves.

Zayna was not one of these authentic sources of tradition about which the Cairo association members spoke both fondly and urgently. A smart and thoughtful young woman in her early twenties from the city of Aswan, Zayna attended university in the southern provincial capital of Asyut, about halfway between Cairo and Aswan. With both Kanzi and Fadicca parents, which is rare, Zayna was raised in Aswan City and had never lived in a Nubian village, nor had she ever learned either dialect of the language.

At the 'Id al-Adha in February 2002, which came two months after Ramadan, I told Zayna about the protest against using Nubian music with the slave character Jawhar in the Ramadan serial. I traveled to Aswan from Cairo to spend the holidays with Zayna and her family. While we were relaxing and watching television on the second day of the holiday, a new commercial for Ariel detergent came on, depicting a Nubian woman working as a waitress in an Aswan tourist hotel. Multinational corporations such as Proctor and Gamble (which makes both Ariel and the more familiar Tide detergent) and Toshiba electronics indigenize their television advertisements using local stereotypes immediately recognizable as representing different regions of Egypt. In the Ariel commercial, the Nubian waitress kept her uniform and her family's clothes spotless with Ariel brand. As she says in Nubian, "Totally *ashri*!" (totally beautiful).

When the Ariel commercial came on, Zayna asked if I had seen the other commercial. I said, "The one for Rawabi clarified butter, with the Nubian women singing and dancing on a boat talking about cooking with Rawabi?" "No," she said; she was referring to the Toshiba television commercial. In the Toshiba commercial, a Nubian man dressed in a typical Nubian folkloric dance outfit is playing a drum called the *duff* and saying "*Aika dolli!*," meaning "I love you" in Nubian. Zayna said that back at school in Asyut, she and some roommates and friends, all non-Nubians from Upper Egypt, had been watching TV in their student housing. When the Toshiba commercial came on, she said:

They kept saying, "They put Africans on television! They put Africans on television!" They don't understand anything; they're completely ignorant. I have to tell them where we're from, and that we're Kenuz and Kushaf. They don't even know where Aswan and Nubia are on the map, that they're part of Egypt. This is supposed to be the next generation of college-educated youth!

Zayna sighed while telling me the story. The indigenization of multinational corporate advertising and the use of Nubian language in this case signals 'Africanness' to Zayna's peers, who misrecognize Nubian language as something non-Egyptian.

Continuing, Zayna went on to relate that during Ramadan one of her dormitory flatmates teased her by calling her by the name Gawhar (the Cairene pronunciation of Jawhar), for no reason she could fathom. Zayna did not have a television in her room and was too busy studying to watch the many television series all night during Ramadan. Partway through the month, she said:

I found this girl calling me "Gawhar" and I didn't know why. I thought, "What's she talking about? Maybe she means Jawahir [a popular Sudanese pop singer who is not Nubian], but even so . . . she's Sudanese, and there's a difference." So finally I asked her, "Who's this 'Gawhar'?" She said, "Haven't you seen the television series? She's the servant who married the aristocrat." The girl has this thing where because she's white she thinks she's so beautiful, but because I'm brown, I'm not.

When directly confronted, the roommate adjusts the identification of Gawhar from *gariya* (slave) in the TV show to *khaddama* (servant). Through multiple media, Zayna experiences misidentification by her fellow students as being alternately African, of slave origin, or just plain ugly because of her darker color. She explains these everyday misidentifications in terms of their ignorance of history and language, and color prejudice in beauty standards. In her retelling to me, Zayna expressed both disgust with her fellow students' ignorance of Nubian origins, and indignation at her roommate's evaluation of her own whiteness as beauty. Zayna took the joke as an insult to her appearance based on an evaluation of her color, and the assumption that anyone dark-skinned was, like Gawhar, linked to a history of slavery, or generically 'African.' Yet she was also troubled by her peers' lack of knowledge of Nubia's location geographically in Egypt, and the details of its history, not even knowing where Nubia was on the map, and that it formed part of Egypt. Just as Haggag Oddoul frames his argument about the *Barabra* Café in terms of citizenship and rights, Zayna links her concern to youth as fellow Egyptian citizens.

Embodied Misrepresentation: Not 'African,' but Nubian

Nubians themselves may also share the negative assessment of very dark color common among Egyptians in general. During the biweekly Fadicca class I attended that year, novelist Yahya Mukhtar gave me a copy of his 2001 novel *Jibal al-kuhl* (Mountains of Kohl), which had just been published. The motivation driving his writing of this and other works, he told me, was to document the relocation and life in pre-Aswan Dam Old Nubia for future generations before his own generation, raised in Old Nubia, disappeared. Mukhtar's *Mountains of Kohl* is critical of the government's handling of the relocation, including the imagery used to depict Nubian faces in official publications. The novel depicts the relocation through the character of a

Nubian schoolteacher, 'Ali Mahmud, in a diary chronicling his education in Cairo and years teaching at the government secondary school at 'Aniba in Old Nubia. The character of 'Ali's uncle gives him a booklet called *Relocation of the Inhabitants of Nubia*, published before the relocation from October 1963 to June 1964 by the Egyptian Ministry of Social Affairs. The cover of the ministry's booklet depicted three heads in profile in Nubian dress—a man, a woman, and a young boy—looking toward icons of a modern socialist future. The booklet was issued by the public relations administration for the Ministry of Social Affairs. The cover, in three colors, black, brown, and green, carried the symbol of the falcon and the Socialist Union. The title was written in large type: "The time has come to go to New Nubia."

I recalled . . . "The time has come for Revolutionary work." Beneath the title was a drawing of a man, a woman, and their son—a symbol of the Nubian family—all three smiling. The faces were not Nubian, but had African features, purely Negro [zanji] with thick lips and flat noses. The rest of the cover was drawings of new model Nubian homes in Kom Ombo, the image of an ideal modern Nubian village, a school and a factory, a mosque and a hospital, surrounded by a field of green. Mukhtar 2001, 65.

The government booklet was issued to prepare Nubians to look forward to the relocation within the framework of Nasser's new revolutionary society. Mukhtar criticizes the three faces on the cover as having *zanji*, or African, Negro features—wide lips and broad noses—and black skin color, which he understands as *not* Nubian. For Mukhtar, this image exemplifies the ignorance of the government authorities who produced the booklet and executed the relocation, who considered Nubians to be African and primitive, therefore somehow foreign and un-Egyptian.

In West Aswan when Nura's first granddaughter was six months old, I heard her lament, "The baby is black! *Blaaack!*" drawing out the word for emphasis. Another woman in Nura's home at the time remarked, "Well, what were you expecting? Look at her two parents," referring to Nura's dark-colored oldest daughter and her son-in-law. Nura's evaluation of her beloved first grandchild is a common, negative evaluation of very dark skin color. Being described as black *(aswad)* rather than brown *(asmar)* is essentially an insult to one's attractiveness, for women more than men. It was the girl's projected fate of being considered an unattractive marriage prospect in this sense that Nura lamented.

Women in West Aswan also objected to state representations of Nubians as inaccurately 'black' *(zanji)*, or African, in Aswan's Nubia Museum. West

Aswan, a village across the Nile from the Aswan City train station, was located above both dams and therefore had never been relocated. No women I knew in West Aswan had heard of Yahya Mukhtar, and few would have the inclination or the time to read a novel, if they knew how to read. But all had heard of, and some had visited, the Nubia Museum up on the hill across the Nile in Aswan. Built by UNESCO and the Egyptian Supreme Council of Antiquities over a period of ten years before its opening in late 1997, the national museum houses archaeological artifacts from Nubia and an ethnographic exhibit depicting dioramas of life in Old Nubia. A committee of Nubians, including members of the Cairo Nubian Heritage Association, had been formed to consult on the design of the museum's ethnographic exhibit. Government officials, said one committee member in a 2001 Nubian Heritage Association meeting, "didn't listen to a thing we said," expressing his frustration and disgust with the state and UNESCO.

Most married women I knew there were housewives who did not work outside the home, but a number of them, such as Nura and her cousin Zuba, did work at home hosting large tourist groups visiting the village as part of a day-long tour of Aswan. During a visit to West Aswan in 1998 after the museum had opened, one woman at Zuba's criticized the mannequins in the ethnographic display of old women making baskets, saying that Nubian women were much more 'beautiful' than those mannequins. She claimed the museum had made the models too dark, because "they think Nubians are black *(aswad)*." Others present all agreed that they were ugly. The wax models for the exhibits had been based on photographs of local Aswan Nubians but manufactured by a company in England, then clothed by the museum's staff. These women and other Nubians who live in Aswan and West Aswan tended to view the $21 million museum as providing a newly positive focus on Nubian history and culture that has been absent in wider Egyptian society. However they viewed the representation of Nubians as black as insulting and as reinforcing Egyptian perceptions about Nubians as African, not Egyptian.

While some women in West Aswan criticized the mannequins' appearance, a group of young Cairene Nubian women visiting the museum appreciated the high-civilization connotations of the archaeological artifacts from prehistory to the early Christian period. They appreciated the parallels between Egyptian pharaonic history, familiar to educated visitors from schoolbooks, and the Nubian history of the corresponding eras. During an *'Id al Adha* visit to the museum in March 2001, some visitors whose families were originally from the Nubian village of Kalabsha stated that the museum's benefit to society was that historically locating Nubia firmly within the framework of Egyptian history helped distinguish Nubians "from Africans." One young woman said, "People other than those from Aswan . . . those who are not Nubian in general, the rest of Egyptians, . . . they deal with us like we're from Africa, not like we're Egyptians like them." The museum, they felt, "will make them know that Nubians are originally Egyptian, and that civilization began here from Nubian civilization." These girls appreciated the museum's assertions that Nubians are and always have been Egyptian as a force to counter negative perceptions of Nubians as 'uncivilized' Africans. In this sense, the museum bestows civilizational equivalence on Egyptians and Nubians against a generalized African other.

For some educated urban Nubians the term for 'servant,' *barbari*, in referencing their fathers' and grandfathers' occupations rather than their own generation's achievements, represents a too public association with their lower-status past. But others contend that 'everybody' uses the word casually, even to refer to themselves. In the spring of 2002 Zayna, her mother, and her sister visited Cairo for medical care. I could not convince their mother to accept my invitation for them to stay with me rather than in a hotel. Firmly refusing while repeatedly thanking me, Zayna's mother said, "I'm a stubborn *barbari* woman, you can't change my mind," using the contentious term to refer to herself.

Zayna and her family, Nura and her family in West Aswan, Mr. 'Ali, Yahya Mukhtar, and Haggag Oddoul in Cairo all experience the complicated conflations of color with social and spatial relocations, from Africa to Egypt, and from the villages of the south to the cities of the north. Frequent assertions to the contrary notwithstanding, my examination of debates about media shows that color is not only evaluated aesthetically, that is, in terms of individual attractiveness (Fernea and Rouchdy 1991, 200). Color also serves as a marker of former or assumed current class status, or origin in servant occupation. At times, it can assign a former or current African origin, whether from a historical black slave population or from contemporary sub-Saharan Africa and *not* indigenous to Egypt and the Nile Valley. The conflation of color, slavery, or presumed African ancestry on one hand, with Nubianness on the other, is experienced and contested differently by those whose families migrated to Cairo from Nubia in the first half of the twentieth century, those whose villages were never relocated, and generations of young urbanized Nubians who may not have ever known Old Nubia or a Nubian language.

Works Cited

Fernea, Robert A., and Georg Gerster. 1973. *Nubians in Egypt: A Peaceful People*. Austin: University of Texas Press.

Fernea, Robert A., and Aleya Rouchdy. 1991. "Contemporary Egyptian Nubians." In *Nubian Ethnographies*, ed. Elizabeth Warnock Fernea and Robert A. Fernea, 183–202.

Geiser, Peter. 1986. *The Egyptian Nubian: a Study in Social Symbiosis*. Cairo: The American University in Cairo Press.

Hamid, al-Sayyid. 1994. *al-Nuba al-jadida: dirasa anthrubulujiya fi al-mujtama' al-Misri*. Cairo: Ein for Human and Social Studies.

al-Katsha, Samiha. 1978. "Changes in Nubian Wedding Ceremonies." In *Nubian Ceremonial Life: Studies in Islamic Syncretism and Cultural Change*, ed. John G. Kennedy, 171–202. Berkeley: University of California Press.

Kennedy, John G. 1977. *Struggle for Change in a Nubian Community: an Individual in Society and History*. Palo Alto: Mayfield.

———. 1978. "Zar Ceremonies as Psychotherapy." In *Nubian Ceremonial Life: Studies in Islamic Syncretism and Cultural Change*, ed. John G. Kennedy, 203–23. Berkeley: University of California Press.

Mukhtar, Yahya. 2001. *Jibal al-kuhl: riwaya min al-Nuba*. Cairo: Dar al-Hilal.

NSDC. 1999. *Ta'allum al-lugha al-Nubiyya*. Cairo: Nubian Studies and Documentation Center.

Oddoul, Haggag. 1993. "Hawla mustalah 'al-adab al-Nubi.'" *Majallat al-Qahira*, November.

———. 2001. "Risalat hubb ila al-adib al-kabir Khayri al-jamil [ashri] . . . Mas-Kagna!" *al-Usbu'*, December.

Poeschke, Roman. 1996. *Nubians in Egypt and Sudan: Constraints and Coping Strategies*. Saarbrücken, Germany: Verlag für Entwicklungs-politik Saarbrücken.

Rouchdy, Aleya. 1991. *Nubians and the Nubian Language in Contemporary Egypt: A Case of Cultural and Linguistic Contact*. Leiden: E.J. Brill.

Salih, Mohy al-Din. 2000. *Min a'lam al-Nuba fi al-qarn al-'ishrin, al-juz' al-awwal*. Cairo: al-Nisr al-Dhahabi lil-Tiba'a.

Walz, Terence. 1978. *Trade between Egypt and Bilad as-Sudan (1700–1820)*. Cairo: Institut Français d'Archéologie Orientale.

Notes

1   In this chapter, I use a mix of pseudonyms and real names. I use the real names of public figures and authors of published works I cite, but pseudonyms when quoting from private interviews with them. Individuals who chose to use their real names, either here or in previous publications by this or other authors, are identified accordingly.

15

When the Lights Go Down in Cairo
Cinema as Global Crossroads and Space of Playful Resistance

Walter Armbrust

The image of teenagers necking in the back row of a dark movie theater is a staple for Americans. For them, making out in theaters is semisanctioned behavior that occurs in the margin of privacy created by darkness, which enables the audience to cross over into the world on the screen. This basic 'stage' on which film spectatorship occurs can be found throughout much of the world. But the dark semiprivate space created everywhere by the technical demands of film exhibition to mass audiences is also structured by specific social and political geographies. Filmgoing in downtown Cairo—the subject of this chapter—had long taken place in the gap between official hopes for cinema as a vehicle for socially edifying purposes, and the unpredictable reality of audiences in movie theaters. Certainly by the late 1980s movie theaters had lost favor in the eyes of cultural gatekeepers. Male youth had taken them over. Elites willfully mischaracterized these young men as a barbarian invasion of lower-class "tradesmen," thereby obfuscating a phenomenon that was, in reality, connected to a broad downgrading of middle-class fortunes in the post-Nasser era. As open-market economies inexorably became the only policy choice on offer, promises made in an earlier era of social advancement through education began to ring hollow. The life stage of 'student' began to look like a prison sentence as it elongated into eternity, while marriage—traditionally the boundary between childhood and adulthood—receded into the distance.

A declining middle class, combined with young men unauthorized to deal with the opposite sex outside of a marriage that now primarily occurs after the age of thirty, is a recipe for disaster for any state. One might say that the rise in Islamist radicalism in the 1970s and 1980s was a symptom of such a disaster. But not all politics are so straightforward. In downtown Cairo the liminality of the movie-theater space between audience and screen was expanded to encompass the entire district. The theater district *itself* became like a theater where, once the lights went down, behavior unsanctioned by the authority structures governing the lives of youth—a modernizing state, parents (especially fathers), or moralizing Islamists—could be indulged. However, the triumph of (male) youth in the downtown movie theaters appears temporary. Youth with little disposable income make a poor economic basis for a film industry. Consequently the Egyptian film industry, long the dominant 'content provider' for downtown theaters, has declined, and newer theaters exhibiting a higher proportion of foreign (mostly Hollywood) films have sprung up in neighborhoods accessible only to those with access to the global economy, most often people from the Arab Gulf states, or with connections to their economies. As new theaters geared to this transnational economy open, many of the older theaters have closed. Downtown lives on as an entertainment district, but for middle-class youth the diminishment of moviegoing palpably narrows the range of feasible leisure activities in the area. Cafés and window-shopping remain, but these are generic activities, whereas the movie theaters were unique to downtown. The diminishment of movie theaters is part of a seismic shift in the economic and political center of gravity in Cairo. Cairo is 'globalized' for all of its citizens, but what this means is less a democratization of cosmopolitanism than the hardening of a new hierarchy of access to certain kinds of activities. The rituals of moviegoing, dominated in downtown Cairo for a few brief decades by downwardly-mobile middle-class male youth, are gradually being set aside for a more fortunate class defined by their access to Gulf or European economic standards. The fate of the downtown movie audience therefore is a microcosm for broader processes that marginalize everyone restricted to the national public sphere.

Work and Leisure: the Two Faces of Downtown

Most of my filmgoing experience in Egypt took place in a wedge-shaped part of central Cairo—the colonial center of town from the mid-nineteenth century to roughly the mid-twentieth century—that could be described as a theater district.[1] The area is referred to as *wust al-balad*, literally 'the center of town,' or downtown. Most of Cairo's old theaters are on three streets within this downtown area. Several of the theaters not located directly on these streets are still physically very close to them. Although there are theaters in Cairo outside the area which might be described as basically still middle-of-the-road (such as the Roxy in Heliopolis), many of the theaters falling significantly outside this area are at the economic margins of the theater business: either very expensive or very cheap. There has been quite a bit of new theater construction since the mid-1990s. Virtually all of the new theaters are at the high end of the price spectrum, located either in new luxury hotels, or in new shopping malls, both of which are built substantially by Gulf money, and which to a substantial degree cater to Gulf visitors, who now easily outnumber Western tourists in the urban parts of the country. The new theaters are points in the urban landscape increasingly accessible only by car. Downtown is the only part of Cairo in which several theaters are located within easy walking distance of one another, and which is, by the same token, easily accessible by several means of public transportation. (See El Kadi and ElKerdany in this volume for further detail on the history and architectural heritage of downtown Cairo and recent renovations of the area.) In the mid-1990s there were ten movie theaters (plus several live theaters) on the three main avenues of the theater district, plus a few more scattered in other parts of downtown Cairo. The streets upon which most theaters are situated are also lined with numerous restaurants serving inexpensive food such as *ful* and *ta'miya* (both dishes made from beans), and a few that serve more expensive fare such as kabob and roast chicken. A few streets in this area have been pedestrianized and turned into open-air food and café malls catering to an Egyptian middle- to lower-middle-class clientele, few of whom can afford the amenities offered by the newest malls. The downtown theater and entertainment district is compact. To walk the entire district from Midan Ramsis to Midan Tal'at Harb takes approximately fifteen minutes at a brisk pace.

The theater district—indeed, all of downtown—is run-down today. In colonial days, downtown was a more high-powered place where various types of foreigners rubbed shoulders with Egyptians of various classes. This social mixing is described by both foreigners and Egyptians as having taken place in downtown's many small Greek- and Armenian-owned businesses, the most famous of which was Groppi's.[2] Other establishments, such as Shepeard's Hotel, were exclusively for foreigners.

Although as a whole *wust al-balad* might have been considerably more fashionable than it is today, the theater district always had a touch of carnival.

Actor/director Yusuf Wahbi describes his childhood memories of the area as a series of encounters with the movers and shakers of the theater world (circa World War I):

I used to loiter about 'Imad al-Din Street . . . Once in front of the 'Abbas Theater [now the Cosmos] we saw the streets filled with grand carriages pulled by beautiful horses. In each carriage there were seated two uniformed men, brass buttons shining, and tarbushes brilliantly red. . . . Suddenly the onlookers were flooded by people from the theater, but many of them stood their ground, and both 'Imad al-Din and Qantarat al-Dikka (now Nagib al-Rihani) streets were jammed with crowds. We heard yelling. For the first time my ears heard the name "Sara Bernar [the actress Sarah Bernhardt], Sara Bernar." . . . Most of the onlookers were speaking French. A fabulous carriage pulled by four horses approached . . . I heard one of the crowd say, "She is the greatest actress in the world!" . . . With great effort they reached the carriage and helped pull it along. The short man was yelling in French, "Vive Sara Bernar". Wahbi 1973, 9.[3]

Later Wahbi describes meeting his friend Istefan Rusti, an actor/director of Turkish descent:

Istefan was a member of Nagib al-Rihani's troupe, which was working at the time in the Abbé des Roses Theater. This was when he created the character Kishkish Bey, a wealthy 'umda [village headman] dissipating himself in women, lavishing money on dancers and "artistes" who were common in the theater of the time. Kishkish was followed by "Franco-Arab" [dance] shows, which were popular with the audience, especially the rich awlad al-dhawat [sons of aristocracy] who competed in trying to befriend the foreign actresses. Among these audiences there were also futuwwat [tough guys], most of whom were vagabonds brought by their patrons. Fights often broke out in the course of this competition. No night was without gunfire and stabbings. Wahbi 1973, 51–52.

Wahbi's description of rich men backed by bands of ruffians competing for the favors of foreign women may have been a bit fanciful, and was in any case recalling a period eight decades ago. But even allowing for some exaggeration on his part, it would be a mistake to regard downtown Cairo as having been, in some golden age, either unambiguously chic or homogeneous in terms of class. But neither should the likelihood that downtown always had a dark side be allowed to obscure the general fact of the area's decline. Today one hears people refer to downtown as *baladi*, which means, in this context, low-class.

The Metro Theater, on Tal'at Harb Street, circa 1950s. (Postcard from Kofler Studio, photograph by Walter Armbrust).

This would not have been said before the area went into a slow but inexorable decline, starting in the 1970s. For some time there has been no question that the economic center of gravity in Cairo is no longer *wust al-balad*.[4]

Films themselves reflect the change in the fortunes of downtown. From the 1930s to the 1960s film images of the area showed downtown alternately as the center of modern life or else as a dangerously Westernized place. Downtown was either where people worked in offices or where the elite partied until dawn. Areas labeled *baladi* in films of this period were distinctly and spatially separate from downtown, where uneducated and generally unsophisticated people lived. Since the 1970s, however, films have tended to show downtown office workers not as the end product of modernity, but as economically marginalized and corrupt in a seedy way. Even in corruption, the high rollers have left the area, at least in cinema.

In real life the daily rhythm of downtown revolves around two extended periods of each day: daylight work hours and nighttime leisure hours (from about 7:00 PM until well past midnight). During working hours most of the downtown crowd are office employees, whereas the nighttime leisure crowd is predominantly *shabab* (youth) in their late teens or early twenties. Intellectuals also occupy a niche in the night world of downtown, because the decline in the economic fortunes of downtown has made it a quasi-bohemian district.[5] But the majority of the leisure crowd consists of friends from school or from neighborhoods.

In the leisure mode there is a tendency for people to socialize with members of the same sex or, in the case of women and girls, with their families. This tendency follows Egyptian society's dominant pattern of gender relations, but with the important difference that in the downtown area both men and women are present in public. The more common pattern is that women stay primarily (but by no means exclusively) in the domestic sphere during both work and leisure activities, while men occupy public space.

In the downtown area we can also observe 'dating' of male-female couples. Some of these are brother-sister couples, but many are unmarried single men and women on an outing. Dating goes against the grain of the conservatism that many assume to be the prevailing cultural trend. There is no socially sanctioned custom of single males and females socializing in an unchaperoned setting. Consequently dates are talked about (and represented in films) more as an element of a marriage that will take place than as a courtship ritual practiced by two individuals who might decide to get married.

Consequently, many of the couples regularly seen in the area are nominally engaged, and hence refer to one another as *khatibi* or *khatibti* (fiancé, male or female). They might use these terms among themselves, in the company of close friends, and sometimes with parental consent even when there are actually no concrete plans for a formal engagement. The English terms 'girlfriend' or 'boyfriend' are sometimes used by Egyptians derisively to refer to an illicit, possibly sexual, relationship assumed to be outside the bounds of potential or planned marriage.[6]

A date need not entail attending a film, but going to a film is nonetheless a potential date activity. Many couples simply window-shop and perhaps sit in cafés or restaurants. Some of the cafés suitable for mixed couples are run-down but still expensive relics from downtown's earlier more glamorous days.[7] Most of these establishments are in or near the theater district. The downtown area also has a number of rooftop restaurants and bars, which are popular with couples because of their secluded locations. The basic pattern of women attending films as part of a post-engagement outing is sometimes represented in films, such as the cinematic version of the Naguib Mahfouz novel *Bidaya wa nihaya (A Beginning and an End)* (Abu Sayf 1960).[8] In this story a young girl will not willingly speak to a man who wants to marry her until after her father has accepted his proposal. Then she eagerly accompanies him to the cinema where we see them stiffly watching a 'Popeye the Sailor' cartoon.

Art does seem to imitate life. Once I attended a film with a young middle-class man and his fiancée. When asked how many times she had been to a movie theater, she replied, "This is the second time. The first time was years ago when my father took the entire family to a film." I expressed surprise, and she added matter-of-factly, "Who would I go with?"[9]

Some women go to the cinema more frequently. A woman in her fifties reported having gone "ten or eleven times." Her oldest daughter, she said, "used to go every week with friends from the university." For her part, the daughter scoffed at the idea that she used to go every week, saying that she only went a few times. The same woman reported that her younger daughter, a teenager, had only been to the cinema once or twice. The most recent visit any of them had made was two years ago when the older daughter got engaged and her fiancé

Couple window-shopping on Tal'at Harb Street, fall 2004 (photograph by Lucie Ryzova).

took them all to a film. Thus, while the frequency of cinema going varied for the women I knew, it was not unusual for them to answer with little hesitation with a specific number of occasions. Men, however, tend to reply to questions about the frequency of their visits to cinemas less precisely: "I go frequently" or "I go rarely," but not often, "I have been X number of times."

In its leisure mode downtown is also a place where one can be anonymous. Few of the people who go downtown for leisure purposes actually live there. Downtown at night is neutral territory removed from the eyes of elders, and out of the grasp of social institutions. This means that social norms are at least partially relaxed, and that the young people who frequent the area can engage in a certain amount of experimental behavior that may conflict with the social patterns of everyday life.

Theater Hierarchy

Within the downtown theater district's general atmosphere of ambiguity regarding social norms, theaters are yet another step toward anonymity. Naturally, theaters in Cairo fit into a hierarchy of social status according to the condition of the theater and the price charged for admission. In the mid-1990s average ticket prices for a first-run theater were between LE3.50 and LE7, depending on the seat (an Egyptian pound in 1993, when I initially drafted this paper, was worth approximately $0.30, thus the cheapest seat in an average theater cost a little more than a dollar). The cheapest seats are in what is called the *sala* (hall—the main floor of the theater), the most expensive seats are in the *loj* (loge—usually the first few rows of the balcony), and sometimes there is a two-tiered balcony arrangement in which an intermediate price is charged for the *balakon* (balcony—seats above the *loj*). Seats in second-run theaters cost between LE2.50 and LE3.50. At the very bottom of the pricing scale are the 'third-rate cinemas,' which (again, in the 1990s) cost between LE2 to LE2.50 for a seat. These theaters, however, were actually far cheaper than all the others because they showed four films for the price of one. At the high end of the scale tickets in theaters such as that of the Ramsis Hilton, located at the top of a shopping-mall annex of the Ramsis Hilton hotel, cost between LE7.50 and LE20.

Most people consider average ticket prices in middle-range theaters to be on the high side, and each time a theater is renovated the price inevitably rises. As recently as four years ago the price range was from LE2.50 to LE5, as opposed to LE3.50 to LE7.00 today, and prices continue to rise. The rise in ticket prices is part of general inflationary trends. Salaries, especially for middle-class office jobs, have not kept pace. Often salaried workers make LE200 per month or less.[10] Many of these workers must hold second and third jobs, and even more simply cannot make ends meet.

The most popular venues for dates are probably the middle-range theaters—or more precisely, the most expensive theater that the man can

The Opera Theater was originally a first-run theater that grew increasingly dilapadated. It was recently torn down and replaced by an extremely seedy shopping mall (photograph by Walter Armbrust, ca. 1990).

afford. Dates are expensive because, regardless of the price range, couples sit in the more expensive seats in the balcony and loge. Although many audiences at films I attended were overwhelmingly male, I could discern no gender-based pattern of attendance at particular types of film. Violent karate films seemed to be as popular a place to take a date as Egyptian films.

Women do not attend theaters at the very bottom of the hierarchy—the 'third-class theaters' (al-Royal al-Jadid and al-Kursal al-Jadid). At these theaters the audience was entirely male when I attended. The Royal and the Kursal are both on the edge of the neighborhood of Bulaq, which is given over to car repair and other small-scale industries, and is not a place where both men and women spend their leisure time in public.

In all the downtown theaters where there is a noticeable proportion of women in the audience, a substantial majority of them wear *hijab*, the neo-Islamic style of dress pioneered in universities in the 1970s, but now widespread.[11] The wearing of the *hijab* is an ambivalent statement, signalling both a woman's intention to enter the public sphere, as well as her acknowledgement of patriarchal social norms that work against allowing women access to that sphere. This bears mentioning because there is a striking disjunction between the way women in the audience dress, and the way women dress in films. In most parts of Cairo, 80 to 90 percent of women wear *hijab*. In films the proportions are roughly reversed, and it is uncommon for the few *muhaggabat* in films to have speaking roles.[12]

The *hijab* is at least nominally about modesty, but modesty enters into the dynamics of film spectatorship for women in other ways. One of the difficulties faced by couples on a date is that the starting times of films are not strictly adhered to, which means the couple must wait in the street with the crowd before the theater opens. One can enter the theater earlier than the scheduled time and wait in the lobby, but anyone who does this will be asked to buy refreshments at hugely inflated prices. Couples almost always sit in the expensive seats, raising the cost even more. This means that in order to avoid having to enter early and buy refreshments a couple must arrive late, which may mean that all the seats will be taken if the film is popular. The alternative, loitering in the streets waiting for films to begin, is problematic for women, even when accompanied by men. Most of the crowd outside a theater consists of young single men who often behave boisterously. In practice almost all who submit to the added expense of entering early and buying refreshments are couples. There are cafés near many of the theaters, but these also tend to charge high prices.[13]

Cheap Theaters

At the bottom end of the theater hierarchy it is possible that more foreign films are shown than Egyptian films. The dominant genres are karate films, Western 'action' films, horror films, Indian films, and (in the 1990s) a few Western 'teen' films meant to be titillating to a youthful audience.

The lowest tier of cheap theaters, which featured four films for LE2, often showed Indian films. In the 1980s and 1990s the government also broadcast one or two Indian films a year on television, and these were much anticipated by some of the people I knew. Contrary to a widespread assumption that Indian films appeal mainly to the uneducated lower classes, all the Indian film fans I knew had middle-class aspirations. Indian films raise the issue of the horizontal foreign relations of modern Egypt—relations not conceived 'vertically' with respect to a 'high' European or Western center, but 'horizontally' with respect to the formerly colonized world. Of course Egypt's relations to Europe over the past two centuries were more important than Egypt's relations to India. The point is that contemporary historiography tends to reflect both Egypt and India only in relation to Europe (or, more broadly, 'the West'). This tendency affects attitudes toward Egyptian cinema, which is thought of in one of two ways. First, it is seen as a national film tradition developing out of the internal dynamic of Egyptian society.[14] Secondly, Egyptian cinema is seen as a national tradition corrupted by European and Hollywood cinema.[15] In writing, and often in casual conversation, the typical assumption, sometimes made implicitly and at other times more openly, is that there is, or should be, an essentially Egyptian character to the Egyptian cinema. Often negative views of Egyptian cinema—the opinion that Egyptian films are nothing but bad copies of Hollywood models—take for granted the domination of the Egyptian periphery by a Western metropole. Therefore the only influence allowed on Egyptian cinema is a 'vertical' influence insofar as the dominant metropole is imagined to be 'higher' in a hierarchy of political and economic power than the local, or peripheral, film industry. The center-periphery relation between Europe and its colonies is indeed an important aspect of the historical development of Egyptian media. Unfortunately, in the case of the cinema and other forms of popular culture, European hegemony has served as a point of analytical closure rather than as one element, albeit a crucial one, in a larger picture that takes into account other transregional influences. Such influences are not evident in the content of films—Egyptian cinema has never been directly influenced by Indian cinema. But at the level of audiences, and in any analysis of film spectatorship, India is a palpable presence. In the 1990s the name Amitab Bachchan was widely known in Egypt. Bachchan is a world-famous megastar of the Hindi cinema, but his popularity in Egypt was not at all apparent on the official level, where Indian cinema is usually treated with scornful silence. Newspapers, for the most part, do not publish articles about him, or about any Indian films. The Egyptian public was sufficiently enamored of Bachchan that the issue of whether or not to put his films on the state-run television program was discussed. But it was his cinema following that generated demand for his presence on whatever screen would carry him. Before 1993 an inexpensive clothes market on Twenty-Sixth of July Street (just on the edge of the downtown theater district) sold T-shirts with Bachchan's face on them. A poster of Amitab Bachchan was also the prize of a game of skill set up on the fringes of a *mulid* (saint's festival) I once attended.[16] One urban legend circulating in the early 1990s was that a plane carrying the Hindi film superstar Amitab Bachchan touched down briefly in the Cairo airport for refueling. Word got out about Bachchan's presence, and tens of thousands of people allegedly came to the airport hoping to catch a glimpse of him.

Arabic-Hindi poster for Amitab Bachchan's film, *The Greatest Challenge* (photograph by Walter Armbrust).

In 'legitimate language,' to be Indian was to be quite 'other' in Egypt. All the same, Bachchan was popular with millions of Egyptians.

Currently Egyptian filmmakers and most elites are happy to disparage the Indian cinema. On the surface this appears to conform to highbrow attitudes about things Indian. And indeed, despite the demonstrable popularity of Indian film stars, in everyday language *Hindi* (Indian) is synonymous with 'melodramatic.' European attitudes about melodrama have been neatly transferred abroad, hence an association with melodrama implies silliness, stupidity, or strangeness. "*Fakirni Hindi?*" means "You think I'm an Indian?" More precisely, it means "You think I'm completely stupid?" or simply "I wasn't born yesterday" (I'm not so alien as to be clueless). But whatever the nature of Egypt's actual relations with Indians, it is Indian cinema that colors vernacular usage of the term 'Indian.' *Film hindi* means 'an Indian film,' but is also synonymous with the received wisdom about melodrama. Melodrama is 'a silly thing'; melodrama is Indian. Therefore *film hindi* is a derogatory label. The derogatory use of 'Indian' is also an index of the presence of Indian cinema.

The subterranean presence of Indian films suggests that Egyptian cinema can be looked at outside the imperative to develop a national film tradition, and beyond anxieties about the degree to which the national cinema has been polluted by Western influences. India is a ubiquitous official nonpresence in recent decades.[17] It was a young Cairene woman who first made me think about Indian films. She was more or less middle class, and therefore undoubtedly fully complicit in the sentiment that a *film hindi* is laughably melodramatic and hence synonymous with silliness. But she was also capable of talking about Indian films with completely unselfconscious enthusiasm. Just before Ramadan in 1990 she told me with great excitement that the state-run television was going to give them a treat for the holiday: an Indian film broadcast on television every evening of the month. "*Film hindi kull yom. Kull yom.*" She could barely contain herself. Unfortunately either her information was wrong or the state lied: in the end only one Indian film was broadcast.

Lower-class people probably do express a liking for Indian films more readily than those who consider themselves middle class. Nonetheless, the young woman's enthusiasm for Indian films on television was not anomalous. A number of college students I met in the early 1990s confessed to liking Indian films. One young man explained his attitude by saying, "Indian films are more Islamic than Egyptian films—they don't show as much sex, and you can easily tell good from evil." By contrast, I have never met an upper-class Egyptian who hesitated to call Indian films vulgar. Employees of the shop where I bought my videos reported a brisk trade in Indian films but at the same time they kept the Indian films hidden in the back (along with the Chinese karate films), whereas all manner of Western films, including poorly-made low-budget action films as well as sexually provocative films were displayed prominently.

The majority of films shown in second-run cinemas were action films (mostly from the United States) or karate films. One might assume that the primary consumers of such films are male but in my experience there are as likely to be significant numbers of women at karate films as at Egyptian films. I attended one action film at the Radio (a nearly inoperative theater that was closed for renovation shortly after I went there) that had an all-male audience. This was *Stone Cold*, starring American football dropout Brian Bosworth.

The film was so violent it was censored down to a length of less than an hour. There were, however, only three people in this all-male audience. I later discovered that the film had been shown recently several times, thus the lack of interest may have been due more to overexposure than to the unpopularity of the film. In the same week down the street at the Metro a large audience including many women was attending the newer (but equally violent and much-censored) *Hard Target*.

Another phenomenon of second-run theaters is that some of the films shown in these venues have achieved a cult status reminiscent of midnight showings of *The Rocky Horror Picture Show*, at least in the sense that the audience engages in a dialogue with the film (I have seen nothing so elaborate in an Egyptian theater as *Rocky Horror* rituals involving water, toilet paper, and dressing in drag). A prominent example is *Abi fawq al-shajara* ('My Father is up the Tree,' Kamal 1969). The lasting appeal of *My Father is up the Tree* has no single explanation. It was (and is) regarded as rather sexy by its fans. Although the film starred an extremely popular singer, it is one of a handful of popular films that were regularly described to me as "bad." But it was 'bad' not so much in the sense of 'awful' as in that of 'naughty.'

Poster for the film *My Father is up the Tree* (photograph by Walter Armbrust).

That the film was showing was first brought to my attention when I was walking down 'Imad al-Din Street with an Egyptian friend and his fiancée. Both knew I was interested in seeing films, and started kidding me about going to see it. I said I would certainly go, and asked if they would join me. They then affected an attitude of mock moral outrage. My friend's fiancée threatened him with violence if he set foot in the theater. The young woman still let it be known that at least in theory proper girls did not go to see such films.

My Father is up the Tree tells the story of a young man (played by the late singing superstar 'Abd al-Halim Hafiz) from a wealthy family who spends his summer vacation on the beach in Alexandria, where his fiancée from the university is also vacationing. He wants to spend time alone with her away from their *shilla* (their group of regular friends). But she is too modest and insists they stay safely within the group. He gets frustrated and ends up having a wild escapade with a prostitute, including hashish-smoking sessions with her pimp and a 'road trip' to Lebanon. His clean-living *shilla* is shocked at his debauchery and shuns him. Finally the boy's father comes looking for him, but finds the prostitutes first and ends up carrying on with them just as uncontrollably as his son had. The two men encounter each other in a seedy nightclub and each realizes that they have both gone morally astray. Since the father has proved no better than the son they make up. Their reconciliation also brings the boy back into the bosom of his *shilla* and his shy girlfriend accepts him back with no recriminations.

The friend whose fiancée half seriously threatened him if he went to see this film later told me a joke about the film that neatly echoes the plot: "A young man goes to see *My Father is up the Tree*, and later his father finds out about it. The father then storms into his son's room yelling, 'How dare you go to a film with a hundred and twenty-three kisses!'" (i.e. the man obviously saw the film himself, and apparently for the same reason as his son: for the steamy sex scenes, which he watched so avidly he was counting the kisses).

The continuing popularity of *My Father is up the Tree* is often attributed to the fact that it was singer 'Abd al-Halim Hafiz's last film. 'Abd al-Halim was far too old for the role of a teenaged boy, but he was a legendary singer, one of the 'giants' of modern Arabic music, and the film was a smash hit rumored to have been the most lucrative film in Egyptian cinema up to that time. In the official media 'Abd al-Halim is one of the holiest of sacred cows. In public one only praises him. The attitude of the audience at the showing I attended, however, was not one of reverence. They treated *My Father is up the Tree* almost as camp. Given the hallowed status of 'Abd al-Halim Hafiz in the media, the irreverence of these young men qualified as slightly subversive. It might be going too far to say that they were laughing at 'Abd al-Halim, though it might not be far wrong to say that they were laughing at their parents (after all, 'Abd al-Halim is of their parents' generation). His songs remain genuinely loved, and many people know the words by memory. 'Abd al-Halim is an icon of the

Nasser era, for which some are nostalgic and others disdainful. But mostly the 'misuse' of 'Abd al-Halim by these youth is the product of a sharp disjunction between official culture's heavy-handed obligatory reverence toward him and their own circumstances. Popular culture is full of fantasies about running off with beautiful women, but powerful cultural institutions do not, for the most part, insist that they be respected as art.

The film was playing at a small run-down venue on 'Imad al-Din Street which often shows karate films. I attended a 3:30 PM weekday showing, usually a slow time in a first-run theater, and sat in the *sala* (the main hall). A fairly large audience of nearly two hundred was in attendance. The *sala* was populated entirely by young males. Given the reputation of the film, I was surprised to see that there were some women in the audience, and that they appeared to be mothers with children. One would not normally take one's ten year-old daughter to a 'bad' film, so I can only surmise that some people did take the film seriously as a either a cultural icon or an object of nostalgia—the adored 'Abd al-Halim's last film rather than "the film of a thousand kisses." Indeed, 'Abd al-Halim has a strong romantic appeal to girls and young women. The first time I asked for an 'Abd al-Halim tape in a cassette shop the owner grinned and asked, "Are you in love?" Later I was told that 'Abd al-Halim was particularly popular with women. In this case, as usual, all the women and their children were seated in the expensive seats, which were, however, barely marked off from the cheap seats in this cheap theater.

In the cheap seats young men were smoking something that looked like cigarettes obviously laced with marijuana. As the film progressed the young men seated around me grew sillier and more relaxed. They gleefully spoke the actors' lines before they were said on the screen, and made wry comments to each other at various points in the film. 'Abd al-Halim's plunge into debauchery was accompanied by a noticeable rise in the gleeful commentary from the *sala*. When the prostitute's effeminate pimp started plying the protagonist with liquor and hashish, cries of "Get him high!" rang out from several young men in the cheap seats who were, by my estimation, following their own advice. Well before the licentious 'road trip' with the prostitute began the audience was advising the protagonist to "go to Lebanon," which was considered a libertine place.

The irreverent young men watching *My Father is up the Tree* in some ways recalled a stereotype of cheap films, which is that the audiences, like some of the films, are 'bad' in a moral sense. For example, some theaters are said to function as homosexual pick-up spots. The theater-as-site-of-debauchery stereotype was represented in a recent film called *Mirsidis* (*Mercedes*, Nasrallah

1993).[18] *Mercedes* described the life of the illegitimate son of a rich woman. Throughout most of the film the boy searches for his half brother who, he is told, "is a fan of third-rate cinema." When he goes to such a venue, he finds a fantastic world of rival gangs, homosexuality, drug abuse, and robbery in the theater's bathroom. In the background of the "third-rate theater" scene another film plays: *Bi'r al-hurman* ('Insatiable,' al-Shaykh 1969)— a vintage film about a girl with a split personality, prostitute by night and good girl by day. At one point in *Mercedes* one of the homosexual gangs improbably descends through the ceiling of the theater on ropes, Batman style. As this happens both the real audience and the diegetic "third-rate theater" audience see the heroine of *Insatiable* projected in the background as she puts on makeup and a wig (rather like a man putting on drag) in preparation for a night of whoring. When the protagonist of *Mercedes* ventures into the bathroom looking for his brother, his brother's homosexual lover beats him up and robs him.

If anything remotely like this was happening in the theater showing *My Father is up the Tree*, it was not obvious to an outsider. Some of the young men seemed to be getting high, and the members of the various *shilal* seemed quite intimate, but no more so than any typical group of friends common almost anywhere in Cairo. The venue, however, is far from the lowest of the low where theaters are concerned. After seeing *Mercedes* I decided to see a film at the al-Royal al-Jadid theater on Twenty-Sixth of July Street. This theater is located outside the middle-class theater district—though still within walking distance of it—and is much cheaper than even the second-run theaters located within the downtown area. My experience was not like that depicted in *Mercedes*. Everybody I told that I was planning to go to the theater suggested that I not bring very much cash and that I not go alone. So with nearly empty pockets and a friend in tow I attended a four-film session that began at 10 AM during a weekday. Two of the four films were Egyptian products that promised to be of similar quality to *Insatiable*, the film featured in *Mercedes*. The film playing when we arrived was *al-Mar'a hiya al-mar'a* ('Woman is woman,' Barakat 1978)—a farce about marital infidelity featuring two fleshy actresses.

Having attended morning showings in middle-class theaters, I expected to find a nearly empty house, but we were surprised to find ourselves tripping over men who had arrived before us. When our eyes became accustomed to the dim light we found that there was a fairly large crowd already in the theater. Like the audience in *Mercedes*, the people watching the film were all men, but that was where the resemblance to *Mercedes* ended. The average age of the men in the al-Royal al-Jadid appeared to be much higher than either the gangs depicted in *Mercedes* or, for that matter, a typical audience in a middle-class theater. Most of the audience here were in their thirties or even older. There were a few men accompanied by their sons, but most appeared to be by themselves or in pairs. The audience was *less* vocal than at most theaters, and there was no ironic commentary. Indeed, this was one of the most attentive audiences I saw in any Egyptian theater. Although there were more vendors hawking tea and sandwiches than in middle-class theaters, there wasn't much conversation. The men were actually watching the film, old and beat up as it was (it broke several times during the performance and had to be spliced together). During the course of the film more men continued to come into the theater until by the end of the first feature it was three-quarters full. The most remarkable (and depressing) thing about this "third-rate cinema," as *Mercedes* described such venues, was that it was full of adult men with no better place to go at midmorning on a weekday.[19]

Expensive Theaters

In the early 1990s audiences in expensive theaters tended to bear a closer resemblance to the sort of people most often represented in films than did those of middle-class theaters. This was especially true in terms of the way women in the expensive theaters were dressed (not in *hijab*). In effect the theater itself functioned as a kind of class-*hijab*, which excluded the eyes of people outside a particular class-community. Since the mid-1990s the situation has changed considerably. The number of expensive and relatively inaccessible theaters has increased, while many theaters at the bottom end of the business have been closed. Many of the people in the expensive new theaters would describe themselves as "middle class," but they are middle class in global terms.[20] In material terms this puts them in a completely different position than vast numbers of people who have an image of middle-class life, but not the means to fulfill the image. More women in the expensive theaters wear *hijab* now than did in the 1990s, but many do so nominally, in ensembles that include everything from blue jeans to quite form-fitting dresses and suits.[21]

Another very significant change over the past decade has been the influx of visitors from the Gulf, who form a significant portion of film audiences in the new theaters, particularly during the summer months. (See Abaza and Elsheshtawy in this volume for a discussion of the ways in which Cairene malls are influenced by investment and consumer models from Dubai.) Although visitors to Egypt from the Gulf are often described as 'tourists,' this misleading label suggests a false equivalence to Western tourists. Many visitors from the Gulf spend far more time in Egypt than almost all Western tourists.[22] They spend their money differently—not at antiquities sites or in tourist bazaars, but on such things as domestic labor, apartments, and, of course, leisure, including going to the cinema. Gulf Arab visitors to Egypt were certainly present in the 1990s, but on nothing like the scale of the 2000s. No doubt the visa restrictions imposed by Europe and the United States after the 11 September 2001 attacks played a role in the rise of long-term Gulf tourism. The result is a remarkable boom in luxury hotels and shopping malls. Egyptians benefit in terms of employment, but at the consumer end most of these new establishments are far beyond the means of most people.

In the mid-1990s one of the pioneers in the new theater boom was the theater at the top of the Ramsis Hilton shopping-mall annex. This is located on the edge of the downtown area I am discussing here, in Bulaq. The Ramsis Hilton Theater was constructed and priced so as to exclude all but the wealthiest. (See Ghannam in this volume for a discussion of President Sadat's plans to transfer residents from this old neighborhood, to make room for the construction of luxury hotels and new government buildings.) In the 1990s, at LE7.50 to LE20 for a ticket (the prices have gone up since), the theater is too expensive for most people to attend. It is located at the top of a parking garage, thus one can go to the theater by car, reach the top floor by elevator, then leave by the same route without ever being exposed to the street.

Most of the audience in the expensive theaters is Arabic-speaking. Even in the 1990s a substantial number of them were from the Gulf countries or Egyptians who had worked in the Gulf. This tendency is more marked during the summer months when many Gulf Arabs are visiting. The presence of large numbers of non-Egyptians at the most expensive theaters (and best in terms of sound and picture quality) fits with a widespread notion that all the first-rate goods and services in the country are earmarked for foreigners.

Like the really cheap theaters, the expensive theaters are spatially marginal to the downtown theater district. Also like the cheap theaters, the expensive theaters tend to show mostly foreign (Western) films. In the case of expensive theaters, however, the foreign films shown are generally first-run, or at least first-run for Egypt.

Newsreels

In the 1990s one element of a middle-class theater performance not found in the marginal theaters, either at the cheap end of the economic spectrum or the expensive end, was the newsreel (by the 2000s this custom seems to have been dropped). The newsreel was an excellent vehicle for illustrating how a middle-class audience could indulge in subversive behavior reminiscent of the stereotype of 'indecent' film audiences previously mentioned, while at the same time watching a film that is inherently conservative.

I only observed newsreels in the downtown theater district. They almost always focused on the activities of the president—sometimes lesser officials or government-sponsored conferences—and were made in a predictable, plodding, positively primitive, documentary style. Usually they displayed Hosni Mubarak surrounded by the trappings of power and conferring with various important dignitaries. Television, which reaches far more people, often broadcasts (and continues to broadcast) the same footage on the evening news. Nonetheless, in the 1990s the government continued the newsreel tradition in theaters.

To me, one of the most memorable of these was aired before a film called *Tiyatru al-Basha* ('The Pasha Nightclub,' 'Iryan 1994). The film was rumored to be sexy, therefore the theater (a 9:30 PM showing on a Thursday—the night before the weekend in Egypt) was sold out to a 90 percent male and youthful audience (I would estimate on average about seventeen years old). The crowd was rowdy. There was much yelling across the theater, and much gleeful smoking despite the prominently displayed 'no smoking' signs. But before *The Pasha Nightclub* could begin we were treated to a newsreel showing President Mubarak's trip to the United States and France. It was so badly done that one had to entertain the unlikely thought that the government had conducted an exhaustive search to discover the nation's worst filmmakers, and then assign them the task of presenting the Egyptian president to the people. Although the trip had occurred that week, the film appeared to have been shot on worn-out stock so that it already looked red and grainy, as if it had long been decaying in some badly maintained archive.

On the Washington segment of the newsreel the background music was a Muzak version of the Bee Gees' "How Deep Is Your Love." My field notes, written the evening of the performance while the event was still fresh in my mind, described it as "bad squared: the *Bee Gees?* and in Muzak style? played while the president is busy meeting Lloyd Bentsen and [Senator] Paul Simon (complete with bow tie)?"[23] Each time Hosni Mubarak met a different official the camera would shift for an instant to either a gas lamp or to a badly photographed building with an Egyptian flag flying from it, presumably the Egyptian embassy. The French segment was slightly better: it featured the Muzak version of Louis Armstrong's "What a Wonderful World." The camera's 'resting place' between the appearance of one official and another was either flowers or the face of an ugly French soldier dressed in a quasi-eighteenth-century uniform.

The striking thing about this newsreel was not the incompetence of the film itself but the decision to play it in a theater full of hormonally charged teenagers. Similar propaganda played every day on the television. I had often sat in peoples' homes while the evening news churned out identical footage of the president shaking hands with officials. On television such stuff was generally ignored, or the channel changed. But when this incompetent footage of the Egyptian president meeting American congressmen and French officials was played prior to the screening of *The Pasha Nightclub*—a film that the audience had chosen and paid to see—the newsreel was not ignored. Instead four hundred teenaged boys in the audience hooted in derision for a good ten minutes. Only when the film began did the noise subside. Whether or not by design, the newsreel functioned as catharsis, a chance for the young men in the audience to 'get it out of their systems' for ten minutes so that they could keep a properly respectful demeanor when it really counted.

Spy Films

In an analysis of spectatorship, a film's content matters. People choose to see it, unlike television, in which the element of choice is blurred by virtue of the constant flow of imagery. Consequently, the reception of a pair of spy films in the summer of 1994 was revealing. Whereas the newsreel shows a clear disjunction between the state's attempts to legitimize itself through propaganda and the audience's way of receiving the message, the reaction to the spy films was more ambiguous. Their titles were *Kashf al-mastur* ('Exposing the Hidden,' al-Tayyib 1994) and *Hikmat Fahmi* (Mustafa 1994). Both were about female spies, and the actresses featured in both were known for playing sexually provocative roles.[24] Both were nationalistic. Their depictions of the state, however, were diametrically opposed. The films were about sexual espionage, but *Exposing the Hidden* depicted a deceitful Egyptian government, whereas *Hikmat Fahmi* featured heroic struggle against foreign occupiers.

Exposing the Hidden portrayed a continuous thread of corruption through successive Egyptian governments, which the film alleges recruit women to spy on Egypt's enemies by sleeping with foreign diplomats. The means are dirty, but the women are constantly told by their male handlers that the ends are noble. Despite the alleged worthiness of the cause, the women are blackmailed into governmental service by having their bedroom espionage recorded on videotape: as long as the tapes exist the women are forced to keep working.

Still, the threat posed to Egypt by foreigners is portrayed as quite real. The governments upon which the women are made to spy are *Arab*, not Western. This resonated with local criticism of Gulf Arab influence, and contrasts markedly with the increase in Gulf presence from that time to the present. Much of the public holds beliefs about the immoral behavior of Gulf Arabs in Egypt.[25] The film also portrays nests of fundamentalists in league with international capitalism. *Exposing the Hidden* is antigovernment, antifundamentalist, and yet nationalistic at the same time. It was easily the longest-running film of the summer of 1994. It was hard to know whether this was because of the antifundamentalism, the antigovernmentalism, the nationalism, or the allure of the sexy female star of the film. A leftist told me that the film was interesting, but that its message had been destroyed by crude censorship. Others snickered at the nonevent of crowds flocking to see a buxom sex kitten playing a government prostitute. And yet both times I attended the film the audience contained a much higher than usual proportion of women and families, which tends to undercut the assumption that the film's appeal was based entirely on the sexiness of the protagonist.[26]

Hikmat Fahmi is a cruder film about the attempts of Egyptian nationalists, including former president Anwar al-Sadat, to spy on the occupying British for the Nazis during World War II. Again, the protagonist is a woman who spies on the enemy through her sexual exploits.[27] The enemy (the British this time) is thoroughly corrupt. Unlike *Exposing the Hidden*, this film did not criticize the Egyptian government, even though many in the government cooperated with the British occupation. The film portrays Sadat as a prudish nationalist who initially opposes using a woman being kept by a British general as a spy. Later he warms to her and she to him. She even flirts with him:

Hikmat: Are you married, Anwar?
Anwar: Yes.
Hikmat: And you love your wife?
Anwar: Yes, and if only she loved me as much as I love her. Do you know who she is, Hikmat? Egypt.

A reviewer noted that Sadat's lines elicited peals of laughter from the audience (Amin 1994, 134). This was true at the showing I attended. Laughter at *Hikmat Fahmi* was consistent with the audience's reaction to the newsreel, and to the general spirit of *Exposing the Hidden*. However, *Hikmat Fahmi* ends with the spy getting caught and tortured by the British. She refuses to reveal that Sadat had been involved. Egyptian commandos led by Sadat attack a squad of British soldiers about to execute Hikmat.[28]

Although the film was historical nonsense, and starred an actress widely ridiculed for her poor acting abilities, and regardless of its leaden propagandistic dialogue, openly scorned by the audience, when the Egyptian commandos rescued Hikmat and cast the British flag into the sand, the audience at the showing I attended cheered lustily. *Hikmat Fahmi* was the only film I have ever attended, Egyptian or otherwise, in which the audience left the theater literally humming the national anthem.

Conclusion

Establishment culture has ponderously proclaimed the civilizing influence of 'the seventh art' for quite some time. In 1940 the Egyptian variety magazine *al-Ithnayn* detailed the process in the context of teaching young people how to watch films:

The Ministry of Social Affairs granted an opportunity for our children to increase their "cinematic culture," with which European countries are very concerned. The first of these events took place in the Diana Theater last week. A large number of children from kindergarten, primary, and secondary school attended, the youngest of whom were accompanied by their fathers and mothers. The camera of al-Ithnayn *came with them to record these exquisite pictures of them as they watched the program of cinematic culture.* "Atfaluna fi-l-sinima" 1940, 22.

The 'exquisite pictures' documented the event. One, captioned "What is the reason?," showed a mother with four children, two of whom were sitting in one chair on top of one another. An accompanying paragraph explained: "This sedate mother accompanied her four daughters to the event. One of

"Our children at the cinema," from *al-Ithnayn* (8 January 1940, 22–23.)

them sat to her left and the others on her right, except that one has sat on top of her sister in a single seat. One wonders whether this was for economy or because there wasn't a fourth empty chair" ("Atfaluna fi-l-sinima" 1940, 22). The didactic lens of al-Ithnayn zeroed in on a transgression of order, albeit an adorably cute one. On the whole, the article promoted order. Another photograph depicted the right way to watch a film, showing a group of children (one to a seat) watching intently. The caption proclaimed, "As if they are one family" and the explanatory paragraph noted that "The theater was crowded with thousands of children and their parents. Adults explained what they were watching to the extent they were able. Among the grownups were some servants who came in the place of mothers who did not know that the films were not subtitled in Arabic" ("Atfaluna fi-l-sinima" 1940, 23).

The modernizer's goal of sober, ordered spectatorship lives on, usually in irate denunciations of the domination of theaters by lower-class audiences (Farid 1988, 13). But what the audience does 'when the lights go down' rarely conforms to official prescriptions. Semi-licit dates, open mocking of official imagery, the frank admiration of 'vulgar' Indian films, homosexual liaisons, and deliberate misreadings of the older generation's sacred cows are all contraventions of order. Each of these acts is a small rebellion, but in total they constitute an appropriation of public space by a liminal group, namely male youth. The creation of youth as a liminal category is quintessentially modern. In premodern society the boundary between childhood and adulthood was marriage, but mass education created the necessity for the intermediate category of youth. As a social category, youth is symbiotically related to school. When school ends, youth should be ending also. School is what structures youth as a modern category. However, school only structures part of the day. Non-school time is 'free' for leisure, but 'free time' is potentially dangerous. There are all sorts of social strategies for filling free time with productive activities. In Egypt film and television were always seen as potentially edifying activities, though not many journalists, educators, or social reformers have ever expressed satisfaction that these media are doing 'their job' properly.

But the problem of leisure takes on greater importance in the context of an endlessly prolonged stage of youth. Youth should end with marriage, but for most of the young men in Cairo's downtown movie theaters marriage is a distant dream. In the 1980s and 1990s one frequently heard the complaint that uncouth 'tradesmen' had driven polite society (including, it must be said, women) from the movie theaters. But the 'tradesmen' in almost all the theaters I have entered in the downtown area always looked suspiciously like students. The increasing youthfulness of cinema audiences is a global phenomenon, but in Egypt it has a unique resonance. Since the 1970s Egyptian males have been twice marginalized: first structurally, by virtue of their position between childhood and adulthood; and secondly, by the indefinite prolongation of their youth due to the economic impossibility of entering married life. Many of the young men in the theaters have no realistic chance of marriage before they are in their thirties. This fact creates obvious tension when there are few socially sanctioned rituals for interacting with the opposite sex. The appropriation of movie theaters by marginalized youth has to be seen in this context. Taking over movie theaters in the 1990s constituted an *intisar shabab*—a 'victory of youth.' In an earlier age this was a hopeful slogan.[29] But in the 1990s it was a Pyrrhic victory. Increasingly the theaters themselves are being closed, and the new theaters opening in malls and hotels are not for the downtown male youth. They are rather for Gulf Arab visitors, and the stratum of society that has access to a global standard of living. Youth will undoubtedly find some new space to call their own, but it seems to be increasingly difficult for them to appropriate spaces that can be equally inhabited by male and female youth. An imagined world of free interaction on the screen is now pushed increasingly onto the small television screen, where images of unlicensed interaction between young men and women multiply in music videos and advertisements. But they do so under the watchful eyes of adults rather than in the dark semiprivacy of the movie theater.

Works Cited

Amin, Nura. 1994. "Hikmat wa-Anwar." *Adab wa-naqd* 109. September: 131–34.

Armbrust, Walter. 1994a. "Plastic and Vinyl." *Al-Ahram Weekly*, 15–21 September: 9.

_____. 1994b. "Take One, Take Two." *Al-Ahram Weekly*, 30 June–6 July: 8.

"Atfaluna fi-l-sinima." 1940. *al-Ithnayn* 291. January 8: 22–23.

Cooper, Artemis. 1989. *Cairo during the War: 1939–1945*. London: Hamish Hamilton.

Farid, Samir. 1988. *Huwiyat al-sinima al-'Arabiya*. Cairo: Dar al-Farabi.

El Guindi, Fadwa. 1999. *Veil: Modesty, Privacy and Resistance*. Oxford: Berg.

Ghosh, Amitav. 1993. *In an Antique Land*. New York: A.A. Knopf.

Husayn, Nasir. 1992. "Haribat min gannat Salah Nasr." *Ruz al-Yusuf* 3348. August 8: 47–49.

"Isma' ya bey, isma'i ya hanim." 1934. *al-Ithnayn* 1: 38.

Macleod, Arlene. 1991. *Accommodating Protest: Working Women, the New Veiling, and Change in Cairo*. New York: Columbia University Press.

Mahfouz, Naguib. 1956. *Bidaya wa-nihaya*. Cairo: Dar Ruz al-Yusuf.

Muhammad, Muhammad 'Ali. 1981. *Waqt al-faragh fi al-mujtama al-hadith*. Cairo: Dar al-Ma'rifa al-Jami'iya.

Al-Sadat, Anwar. 1978. *In Search of Identity: An Autobiography*. New York: Harper Colophon Books.

Wahbi, Yusuf. 1973. *'Ishtu alf 'amm*. Cairo: Dar al-Ma'arif.

Wynn, Lisa. 2003. *From the Pyramids to Pyramids Road: An Ethnography of the Idea of Egypt*. Ph.D. diss., Princeton University.

Filmography

Abi fawq al-shajara ('My Father is up the Tree'). 1969. Husayn Kamal. Cairo: Sawt al-Fann.

Bi'r al-hurman ('Insatiable'). 1969. Kamal al-Shaykh. Cairo: Ramsis Nagib.

Bidaya wa-nihaya ('A Beginning and an End'). 1960. Salah Abu Sayf. Cairo: Dinar Film.

Hikmat Fahmi. 1994. Husam al-Din Mustafa. Cairo: Amandinku.

Intisar al-shabab ('Victory of Youth'). 1941. Ahmad Badr Khan. Cairo: Studio Misr.

Kashf al-mastur ('Exposing the Hidden'). 1994. Atif al-Tayyib. Cairo: Osiris Film.

al-Mar'ah hiya al-mar'ah ('Woman is Woman'). 1978. Henri Barakat. Cairo: Aflam Barakat.

Mirsidis ('Mercedes'). 1993. Yusri Nasrallah. Cairo: Aflam Misr al-'Alamiya.

Tiyatru al-Basha ('The Pasha Nightclub'). 1994. Tariq al-'Iryan. Cairo: Aflam Riyad al-'Iryan.

Notes

1   My analysis is based on films I have watched from the early to mid-1990s in theaters, in the company of Egyptian friends, occasionally with other foreigners, and sometimes by myself. Since then some of the dynamics of film spectatorship, and of leisure more generally, have changed. I will address some of these changes, but the historical center of gravity in this analysis remains the early to mid-1990s.

2   This is the impression given by Artemis Cooper, who says, "Groppi's was one of the few smart places open to everyone [British officers, enlisted men, and Egyptians]—although it was not cheap, and the clientele therefore tended to be officers" (Cooper 1989, 120–21). Another image of Groppi's can be found in the Egyptian magazine *al-Ithnayn*, in which a tongue-in-cheek 'advice' column tells a husband:

   a   If you take 'the lady' to the cinema . . . don't pay any attention to her.

   b   If you bring guests with you . . . stop in at Groppi's. ("Isma' ya bey, isma'i ya hanim" 1934).

3   'Aziz 'Id and Nagib al-Rihani both became prominent actors and directors, the
    former on the stage and the latter both on stage and in the cinema.
4   To some extent downtown is still a political center of gravity. A number of important
    ministries are located there, and downtown is also adjacent to the Parliament and
    quite a few embassies. But this might change too. In 2007 the American University
    in Cairo—an institution increasingly patronized by the political elite in favor of the
    national universities—will move to a new location on the suburban periphery of
    Cairo. This is partly in response to the distaste of the student body for downtown
    Cairo. Furthermore, the decentralization of government functions has long been a
    goal, albeit one that has seen little progress. The departure of AUC might well be a
    harbinger of the accelerated political decline of downtown.
5   The cultural energy of urban bohemians often attracts capital, which paradoxically
    raises prices and drives out the energy that made the district attractive in the
    first place. Thus far downtown has attracted scrutiny, and at least one speculative
    investment. This is the Townhouse Art Gallery, just to the northwest of Midan
    Tal'at Harb. Townhouse is backed by NGOs rather than by private capital, but
    the standard of success for the gallery will be the same: namely to attract paying
    customers who may not mix well with the intellectuals who frequent nearby bars
    and cafes. However, it is likely that Townhouse would not survive without NGO
    backing, and on the whole it seems unlikely that the area will attract the sort of
    investment that would raise prices to the point that the quasi-bohemian character
    of the area would be dissipated.
6   The literal Arabic equivalents—*sahbi* said by a woman, or *sahbiti* said by a man—
    can of course be used casually and innocently, but in this sense the terms are more
    like the unmarked English word—'friend'—applied to either sex. The social sense
    of the English "girlfriend"/"boyfriend" would be closer to the Arabic *'ashiqi/'ashiqti*,
    i.e. 'lover,' which is a status outside social sanction.
7   There are, for example, two dilapidated Groppi's cafés, two Cafés Americaines,
    the Excelsior, and the Kursal. All of them are relatively very expensive—LE1 or
    more for tea, for example—but safe for middle-class women accompanied by men.
    Women do not go to regular cafés (*'ahwa*s), which serve primarily tea and coffee
    for around 50 piasters. (See de Koning in this volume for a discussion of newly
    proliferating 'coffee houses' in Cairo, which attract middle-class women.)
8   The novel was published in 1950 and made into a film in 1960. It was the first
    Mahfuz novel turned into a film (Mahfuz 1956; as distinct from the many
    screenplays he had already written by 1960).
9   There are few statistics indicating actual theater attendance. However, a survey
    of student preferences in leisure activities published in 1981 gave the following
    results: 64.63 percent went to the cinema "sometimes"; those who went "often"
    were 24.33 percent, 11.04 percent responded that they "never" went to the cinema;
    45.74 percent said they went once a month; 31.45 percent went twice a month;
    22.81 percent went three times a month (Muhammad 1981, 306). These figures did
    not distinguish between male and female respondents. The size of the sample was
    3,793, 67.45 percent of whom were male; the average age was almost 22 years old;
    90.36 percent were Muslim (the rest were Coptic Christian); 84.17 percent were
    resident in urban areas, 9.29 percent rural, and 6.54 percent semi-urban; their

family income level was estimated to be "middle working class," averaging LE84.27 per month (Muhammad 1981, 32–33).

10 Since the original draft of this chapter the public-sector wage may have risen a bit. But a steep devaluation of the Egyptian pound in 2003 instantly erased any gains that public-sector salaries might have made. It should be noted that many private-sector salaries are in the same low range as public-sector salaries.

11 As is by now very well known, the neo-Islamic *hijab* was initially a middle-class phenomenon (Macleod 1991; El Guindi 1999). It is now worn also by many elite women. *What* is worn, however, has also diversified, often in directions far removed from the original ideological purpose of the new style of veiling. In a nutshell, the *hijab* is now as much subject to the dictates of fashion as any other article of clothing. As such the point of wearing 'modest clothing' is as much to reveal as to conceal.

12 It must be said that the visual politics of *hijab* on the screen are far more complex in 2005 than they were in 1994. Satellite television has changed the media landscape enormously. In the new landscape Arab (as opposed to strictly Egyptian) media still portray most women as un-*hijabed*, but in genres as diverse as music videos to religious discourse the *hijab* is discernable in ways that simply didn't exist in the mid-1990s, when satellite broadcasting to the Arab world was still very new and relatively undeveloped. Egyptian cinema has been slowly pulled into the orbit of these new politics of representation, not to the point that the *hijab* is 'normalized,' but certainly to the extent that one can no longer flatly say that it is excluded.

13 I discovered this on a number of occasions when I went to films with my wife. Marked by our evident foreignness, we were ostentatiously ushered into the theater before the film began, only to discover that on many occasions we were the *only* couple on the inside. Everyone else waited outside until the general admission began.

14 In this sense Egyptian cinema has 'horizontal' economic and cultural relations, but only to the Arabic-speaking world, and only as a provider of media content rather than as a consumer of non-Egyptian Arabic-language content. It should be noted, however, that the influence of Egyptian cinema within the Arab world might be seen from non-Egyptian perspectives as a form of cultural imperialism rather than as a 'horizontal' relation. Historically films have flowed only from Egypt to other Arab countries, never to Egypt from the Arab world. Aside from cinema, the advent of satellite broadcasting since the mid-1990s has greatly reduced Egyptian dominance of audiovisual media.

15 Amitav Ghosh, a Cambridge-trained Indian anthropologist who did his fieldwork in Egypt, developed the same dynamic in his book, *In an Antique Land* (1993). In this work he alludes to "partitioning"—a word often used in the context of the division of Pakistan from India in 1948. Ghosh's book is an antinationalist reflexive meditation on nationalism in postcolonial societies. He applies the notion of "partitioning" as a nearly generic characteristic of nationalism.

16 *Mulid*s in Egypt are essentially carnivals held in honor of charistmatic religious figures, and celebrated by Sufi orders. The focus of the celebrations is the tomb of the saint. In Egypt the larger *mulid*s, particularly those of Husayn, Sayyida Zaynab (in Cairo), and Sidi Badawi (in the Delta city of Tanta) attract

hundreds of thousands of followers. Official religious authorities generally frown on *mulids*, though some of the Sufi orders that celebrate at *mulids* have adopted more austere attitudes toward religion that are more in sync with state-sponsored Islamic authority. (See Madoeuf in this volume for further analysis of Cairene *mulids*.)

17 This was not always the case. Indian cinema was sometimes openly admired in the Egyptian press during the 1950s. The importation of Indian films began some time after World War II, and during the 1960s there was a great deal of official contact with India in the context of the importance of both countries to the nonaligned movement. There was even a rather expensively produced Egyptian magazine, *Sawt al-sharq*, which promoted Indian-Egyptian relations.

18 The film was controversial on moral grounds, but was attacked largely on the basis of its link to French funding. It was shown at the Fourth National Film Festival (June 1994). After each film was shown the audience was given a chance to ask questions of people involved in the production (usually the director, producer, or writer with a handful of actors, generally 'new faces' who had played secondary roles in the film). Almost the entire session on *Mercedes* was taken up by angry protests against Egyptian filmmakers who seek financing from Europeans. The questioners all believed that the French would only finance films that 'slandered Egypt.' The director's response was that most Egyptian films are financed indirectly by foreign capital from the Arab Gulf video market. In his view the strings attached by Gulf financing are far more inhibiting than any conditions stipulated by French television.

19 I do not discount the possibility that the homosexual dynamics depicted in *Mercedes* convey an element of truth. I did not go to the 'third-rate' theaters more than the one time described here. Indeed the idea of writing about film spectatorship was not a fieldwork project, but an afterthought; hence this entire analysis is based on memory rather than on systematic purposeful experience. It is entirely reasonable that the homosexual activity described in the film might be more evident at some times of day than at others (i.e. possibly not at the time or the day of the week that I went to the theater), and possibly affected by seasonal factors as well (e.g., the school year, religious holidays, etc.). It is also not unreasonable that such activities would take place within communities of trust, which is to say that a one-time visitor to the theater would, as a matter of course, have been excluded from acts which are far more socially disapproved even than the unsanctioned practice of heterosexual dating. And finally, I am not gay, and hence would have been unlikely to discern subtle forms of communication between men, had any such communication taken place on the day I was in the theater.

20 Egypt has several economies, including the informal economy, the public-sector economy, the local private-sector economy (for example, the shop that may sell imported goods that are, however, obtained entirely through local distributors), and the global economy. Of course there are a variety of paths to the final category (e.g., political connections, employment in foreign-aid institutions which pay at far higher levels than local institutions, and access to the higher levels of importation and distribution; of course none of these paths to the global economy are mutually exclusive).

21 In some ways wearing the *hijab* has become for women like wearing pants for men: one does it as a matter of course, and the most socially important thing about it in both cases is what the clothes say about the wearer in terms of class and individual choice. In this sense a display of piety by the *hijab* wearer is only one in a spectrum of personal choices.

22 See Lisa Wynn (2003) for one of the few in-depth analyses of Gulf tourism in Egypt.

23 Bentsen had been Michael Dukakis's vice-presidential nominee in the 1988 election. Paul Simon, a senator from Illinois, had also been a presidential candidate that year. He had won only the primary in his home state, and had distinguished himself mainly by his custom of wearing a bow tie.

24 Nabila 'Ibayd in *Exposing the Hidden* and Nadya al-Gindi in *Hikmat Fahmi*. Neither woman garners much respect from critics, but both are reliable box-office draws.

25 Filmmakers also oppose Gulf influence. For one thing, they object to a *de facto* censorship of their films by the requirements of the Gulf video market. Public mythology is more about the immorality of Gulf men and their potential corruption of Egyptian women. As in the case of the gay scenes in *Mercedes*, I do not necessarily deny an element of truth to the mythology. But neither have I directly observed the behavior in question. For a fuller account of both the mythology and the actual practice, see Wynn 2003.

26 The first time I viewed *Exposing the Hidden* was in May 1994 in at the fourth annual Egyptian National Film Festival, a screening of the best Egyptian films from the previous year together with a few premiers of yet-to-be-released films. *Exposing the Hidden* was one of the films premiered, and the version shown at the festival was uncut. The second time I saw the film was in July 1994, by which time the censored version of the film had been released to the general public (see also Armbrust 1994b).

27 For reviews of *Hikmat Fahmi* see Amin (1994), and Armbrust (1994a). Both *Hikmat Fahmi* and *Exposing the Hidden* were loosely based on history. The real Hikmat Fahmi was a dancer during World War II who was involved in a plot to spy on the British. *Exposing the Hidden* bears a certain resemblance to allegations made about a secret police chief from the Nasser regime named Salah Nasr, who was disgraced and imprisoned after Egypt's total defeat by Israel in 1967. Nasr, it has been claimed, used actresses and media personalities to spy on foreign politicians (Husayn 1992).

28 This was historically inaccurate: Sadat's own memoirs mention that his role in the plot to spy for the Germans landed him in prison, where he was treated well, studied English, and for a time occupied the cell next to Hikmat's (el-Sadat 1978, 43).

29 *Intisar al-shabab* ('Victory of Youth,' Badr Khan 1941) was the title of a film in which youth triumphs over adversity.

16

A Round Trip to Isma'iliya

Cairo's Media Exiles, Television Innovation, and Provincial Citizenship

Fanny Colonna

The aim of this chapter is to explore a new trend in the Arab world—provincial intellectuals abandoning the capital city to return to their rural origins (see Colonna 2004). Why are media innovators and cultural elites now striving to exercise certain professional and social roles 'at home' that previous generations would have cultivated only in the capital? Does this trend signal the emergence of a decentralization dynamic that will forever alter Cairo's metropolitan role? Does the emergence of alternative provincial cultural nodes indicate a liberalization or pluralization of cultural production, or merely a phase of exile and marginalization? How does this process relate to shifts and surges in national(ist) identities tied tightly to Cairo?

The focal point for this exploration will be an in-depth profile of an important Egyptian television pioneer, set in the context of Egypt's controversial, strategic frontier region of the Suez Canal Zone.

In the late 1990s, our research team wrapped up our tour of Egypt's provinces and finalized our interviews with Egyptian intellectuals and cultural figures who had resisted the call of Cairo, the capital city, and had instead based themselves, and invested their efforts, in provincial capitals.[1] Kamel Chachoua,

445

an Algerian sociologist, Patrick Godeau, a French photographer, and myself, an Algerian-French sociologist, closed our study with a mission through the three towns of the Suez Canal in November 1997. Our larger study had begun the year before, at the opposite, southern end of the country, with a set of interviews with university-diploma holders living in the provinces of Aswan and Luxor, and the surrounding areas. Looking back toward the northeast corner of the country, the Suez Canal Zone seemed a particularly important region to examine because of its contested, changing, strategic value, and because of the 'modern' (post-nineteenth-century) history of its cities.

The Canal Zone seems even to Egyptians to be promiscuously connected to alien lands and contexts. After the Suez Canal had been dug by European investors and colonial strategists in 1869 the area around it remained an empty stretch of desert neither documented by social scientists nor treated by national artists, until this generation. The zone is poor in writers; as a result, few narratives have been spun to capture the life of this province. Only the charming social-realist, bucolic novels of Mohammed El-Bisatie (Sounds in the Night, Houses Behind the Trees, Clamor of the Lake) help us understand the immense contrasts that define the region. The landscape varies between the beautiful towns that sprang up after the canal opened (Port Said, Isma'iliya, Suez) and the desolate shores of the haunting Lake Manzala. Successive wars in neighboring areas from 1948 to 1973 ravaged this small peninsula and identified it with danger. Conflicts, commercial penetrations, military occupations, and 'peace processes' have displaced city dwellers and villagers, often forcing them into traumatic mass exodus. But the Canal Zone is not only a space of retreat, but also of victory. On 26 July 1956, Egyptian President Gamal 'Abd al-Nasser nationalized the Suez Canal (then British-controlled, French-owned). This bold nationalization was the crowning act of the Egyptian revolution that began in 1952 with a military coup against British troops that had enforced colonial power in the country. The revolution achieved full national independence for Egypt with the Suez War of 1956. In an attempt to retake the canal, British, French, and Israeli forces launched an invasion of Egypt which was pushed back by Egyptian force and American diplomatic pressure—a moment still widely debated and celebrated in the region.

Culturally and socially the Canal Zone nurtures a cosmopolitan and multilingual atmosphere influenced by the legacies of the Canal as a multinational corporation and world crossroads of commerce. This history gives the area a particular rapport with Europe, the Arabian Peninsula, India, and the rest of the world. The Canal Zone cultivates a characteristic harbor culture—of militant dock workers, soldiers, and sailors—that has fostered a tradition of strong labor unions and military protests which still make waves felt by the Egyptian Parliament down in Cairo. The Canal Zone has also led the trend, now felt increasingly in Cairo, to engage culturally and economically with the Arabian Peninsula (Saudi Arabia, Dubai, Kuwait, etc.) rather than looking primarily toward the Mediterranean and Levant as trendsetters. The *simsimiya* (the lyre-shaped string instrument identified with the locality) has come to articulate the melodies that reflect this new level of Egyptian–Arabian cultural dialogue.

Nevertheless, cultural and commercial vibrancy have not eliminated the militaristic ambiance of the zone, as continuing struggle and tension with Israel has infused the area. For six decades this area has remained a battlefront or a barely pacified military zone, unchanged by the passing of thirty years since the Camp David Accords.

This geopolitics of war and commerce, as well as new institutions such as the large university founded at Bur Fuad, have woven stronger ties between the capital and coast of this strategic territory. Immense contractor projects, free-trade zones, and industrial parks have irrevocably changed the region's character, adding to its national and international visibility. In the context of these changes, reflecting the visibility as well as the strategic value of the area, Egypt launched its first provincial (i.e. non-Cairo-based) television station in the Canal Zone in Isma'iliya in 1987. Since we are interested in understanding this flourishing of Egyptian media cultures in tension with, but outside of the overwhelming dominance of Cairo; and since we are interested in the social

Tariq (right), Kamel (left) and the author in Isma'iliya (photograph by Patrick Godeau).

geography of cultural elites, we sought out key figures associated with these pioneering regional television stations.

Tariq, age 35, met us in a small shaded plaza in Isma'iliya. He was working as a local newscaster on the regional Suez Canal TV station, Channel 4. Wearing a blazer and a pair of jeans, he exuded calm. He did not seem bothered by having to accommodate us into his hectic schedule. Tariq proposed going to his house for our meeting and ushered us into his small well-used red car. He took us on a long ride toward the poorer periphery of the city, which bore no resemblance to the belle-époque downtown area where we had been strolling while we awaited him. The periphery did not maintain the late nineteenth-century French style of the old colonial downtown. We turned down a street lined with modern buildings, with no niceties or boutiques, where Tariq lives. We ascended with him to the second story and as we crossed the landing he peeked through a curtain and gave a friendly greeting to unseen family members in the apartment that his mother occupies. We then went up one more story to where Tariq lives with his wife and two children. A third child was on the way; he told us in passing that he would like many children.

Reflexivity and Citizen Engagement

Our intention was to allow a spontaneous dialogue to evolve in which Tariq would guide us and by which we would draw our essential conclusions and 'theories' by following his leads (Colonna 2004, 449–69). Our goal was to explore relations of domination between the capital and provinces in Egypt and more precisely, new kinds of resistance to, or disidentification with, the capital city, as articulated by television elites in the provices. We wanted to explore this matter from the inside. Tariq's point of view featured ambiguity as well as complexity, as he strongly articulated a notion of the local not as a periphery, but as a particular set of limitations, in relation to national patterns of distribution and global flows of influence and access. We found nothing like the "rural Mideastern provinces" depicted in the chauvinist stereotypes of Cairo's contemporary cultural elites, or in the prejudices of orientalist Westerners, who see the countryside as backward, cut-off, overwhelmed by Islamic traditionalism "pulling the country toward the archaic" (Colonna 2003). In fact, local actors are becoming politically and socially more innovative and engaged, and are utilizing imaginative resources in the process. Egypt has witnessed a process of demographic deconcentration where population flows between the smaller towns and huge cities have stabilized (Denis 1998). Similarly, the national government's efforts to decentralize the country's university system since the 1980s has encouraged cultural and intellectual stimulation in provincial public spheres and encouraged the emergence of locally based intelligentsia. Moreover, disseminators of new cultural messages, engaging concrete social changes and diverse provincial realities, have begun to tap into a reservoir of talents and public demands that had been previously neglected.

In this atmosphere of shifting currents and opportunities, Tariq found himself moving into a career in television. His career, his vision, and the ideas and forces that underlie them, are a window into the changes affecting Egypt and more specifically the nature of this more assertive, innovative, and broadly dispersed generation of media and cultural actors. Our interviews revealed that Tariq and his generation see attachment to and engagement with the provincial scale and local specificity as a necessary part of a broader sense of belonging and citizen empowerment. This project not only addresses the locality or the province/region, but also is aimed at transforming the whole of Egyptian society, to give it new voices and new groundings for the realities of its popular and provincial classes. This project of "provincial grounding" expressed insistence on claims to participatory citizenship and participatory culture formation, imagining simultaneously a national reimagined street-level utopia, as well as desires for real transformative action (Rancière 1999). Describing the creation of local television stations, Tariq let us glimpse this geography of citizen opportunity, political participation, and risk. It was a unique moment, as he describes, "It was, in the beginning, a nice idea. We chose to establish the [first regional TV station] in this zone of high sensitivity to the nation."

One of Tariq's goals for founding the local TV station was to challenge stereotypes about the provinces; but he also avoided the idealizing image of a "fertile, healthy, and joyful periphery" and the demonizing image of the countryside as hopelessly riddled with corruption. Local stations appeared during a moment in which Cairo expressed "good will" toward the provinces. But sustaining the stations has proven very difficult as this moment of "good will" passed. Despite the limitations, Tariq and many media pioneers of his generation did build their experience into a broader claim for participatory democratic engagement and civil-mindedness. After a decade of struggles to build provincial media outlets, Tariq remained hopeful.

'Ascending to Cairo': The Discovery of Another Egypt

As for me, I wanted to go to Cairo to see what was happening there. The important thing for me was to be present at Cairo University in particular because it has a history. It possesses different kinds of cultural traditions and ways of thinking. It is a world altogether different from the one that I had experienced until that point. The first thing that we felt on arriving in Cairo was a shock. A social-class shock. There, elite, important people lived a lifestyle that we had only seen in films. We were astounded, because we had come from a more modest society in Isma'iliya! Even our rich people have limited riches and their appearance reflects these limits. In Cairo, there was another class that lived a life completely different, that we didn't know. That was our first impression of Cairo.

This confession made me think of a hugely popular Egyptian movie musical, *Isma'iliya rayih gayy* ('A Round Trip to Isma'iliya'), all the rage in Cairo and in the provinces in 1998. The film, directed by Karim Dia' al-Din recounts the story of the rise of a charming local singer (played by Egyptian pop star Muhammad Fuad) and his adventure with a band of friends from Isma'iliya (portrayed by a band of vaudeville-type comedic character actors including the break-out star Muhammad Hinidi, who stole the show). The plot weaves around the history of Egyptian national struggles, but grounds it in the efforts of youth to defend their freedom of thought, and the pleasures of friendship, sex, music, and romance under the strict limits of economic austerity, looming warfare, and political repression. The film was a record-breaking success in Egypt's theaters—and in the towns of the Canal Zone in particular. The film

Isma'iliya Rayih Gayy, Karim Dia' al-Din (photograph by Jean Marc Lamour).

portrayed the culture shock and amazement that this group of provincial youths felt, from their first contact with a surly Cairo-based music producer (who served as the source of multiple gags and jokes). The film also presented many revealing contradictions that define identity and nostalgia in contemporary Egypt: province versus capital, elite versus popular, revolutionary-era pride versus neoliberal era malaise, etc. *A Round Trip to Isma'iliya* seemed to tell a musical version of Tariq's generation's collective biography:

[In the 1970s we came from the province to the capital.] We met intellectuals from other regions and we became Cairo's intellectuals, although we knew very well that most of us come from the provinces! It is our simple presence in the capital, our love of study, our desire to deepen our knowledge of philosophy, politics, and many other things that gave us an intellectual presence in Cairo.

There are people who stayed in Cairo and managed to survive there some way or another. Many others like me came back to their region and adapted to the limitations of their local realities. What motivated me to come back was that I simply couldn't afford the cost of Cairo; I was still financially dependent on my father. There was no way for me to live in an autonomous way, to make ends meet there.

Kamel (my Algerian research partner), speaking frankly, intervened: *And if you had found a way to make ends meet in Cairo, would you have ever come back to Isma'iliya?*

Tariq: *No, we wouldn't have come back. You could say that that at that time to come back would have seemed like a failure! Nevertheless, when we created the television station here in 1987, the ways of defining success versus failure changed completely for me.*

In short, he began to realize his dream—to have the status equal to a 'Cairo intellectual,' but to be based in and identified with his own hometown.

Tariq: *And now you want me to talk about how I adapted here and if I am happy or not? We came back here to the family house. We came back to our home; we looked for work; we lived here. There wasn't a way to make a living over there [in Cairo].*

There was bitterness in his voice.

Kamel: *Have you thought that learning languages would have allowed you to go abroad for work?*

Tariq: *Of course, speaking a foreign language is a prerequisite to being accepted as a speaker or presenter anywhere, at least. But I don't think about this much. I like to be here and I think that my personal success would not happen anywhere else; I have to be in Egypt. I don't know exactly why, I couldn't adapt outside of Egypt.*

Kamel: *Outside of Egypt . . . or outside of Isma'iliya?*

Tariq: *In Egypt generally speaking, in Cairo or Isma'iliya or anywhere else in Egypt.*

Kamel: *Me too. I graduated from the University of Algiers in 1987 and I think that I felt the same way then.*

Tariq, speaking over Kamel: *I think that it is a common problem to all Arabs. They all want to go abroad. Because the problem is that 'over there,' you see civilization, science, and modern technology. As to people's attitudes, the way people treat each other, it is better overseas. That is what people think; we are told to think in that way—'we go abroad to advance ourselves, we Arabs.' The films that we see, the American films, only show us the well educated who mutually treat each other extremely well, very chic.*

Kamel: *For money . . . lifestyle. . . .*

Tariq, at the same time: *For money . . . a certain lifestyle.*

Kamel: *And freedom?*

Tariq: *And freedom. That drives the typical dream of each young Arab.*

Channel 4 Invents Reporting

Tariq: *In Egypt, there are eight stations, plus the satellite stations and the new private stations—reflecting some achievements and some ambitious projects. Unfortunately, today, no one cares about the regional stations any more that were once the product of avant-garde initiatives in the Arab world. The great interest in satellite [private, elite-targeting stations] made people forget about the regional state-run TV stations.*

Successively created between 1987 and 1995 in the north of the country (the Canal Zone, Alexandria, and the Nile Delta region), and in the south of Egypt (Asyut, Aswan, etc.), these regional TV stations oriented themselves toward children and young people, students in particular, even if their mission envisioned a wide expression of regional particularities as well as social, cultural, and intellectual commitments. These stations were given a vocational, pedagogical mission like the national stations, Channels One and Two, created in 1960. Within this didactic framework these new 'provincial' channels were subject to the absolute monopoly of the state, supervised through the hegemony of its organizational director, the Egyptian Radio and Television Union (ERTU) which controlled the structure, financing, and content of the provincial channels' messages. As a researcher at the Al-Ahram Center for Strategic Studies stated in an interview in 1997, "Television is traditionally an instrument (in the hands of the state) to mobilize public support in relation to foreign policy, domestic politics, and social policy. That is why the predominance of state ideology is clearly transmitted by television" (Guaaybess 2003).

At the same time, these innovative stations were influenced in turn by the trends and ambitions of the state struggling to adapt to the "communications revolution" (a term that one hears repeatedly in all the media) that began to sweep through Egypt in the 1990s (El-Khawaga 2003b). In 1991, Egypt launched its first satellite station oriented to the non-Arabic speaking public, to tourists, and also targeting Middle-Eastern diasporas in the West and in the Persian Gulf. (See Sadek in this volume for further detail about the "communications revolution" in Egypt and across the Middle East.) From there, the "communications revolution" snowballed. The state's new objective was to become competitive with two international groups of Saudi-funded private satellite companies, ART and Orbit, who broadcast 'Western'-style programming from Rome and London. In 1995, Egypt purchased from France a Mideast regional satellite, NileSat 101, to receive Gulf Arab, Levantine, and Mediterranean stations, encrypted or not. In 1998, Egypt struggled to maintain its media edge by launching CNE, a semipublic, investor-friendly satellite company that grouped together eight themed stations (news, culture, variety, sports, etc.). Most importantly, in 2000, Egypt launched a second satellite commissioned to feed the programming generated by the new Media City constructed with state subsidies and public-private partnerships in the desert on the outskirts of Cairo. (See Elsheshtawy in this volume for greater detail on the creation of Media City and its Gulf investment partners.)

Kamel: *Why the change in priorities?*

Tariq: *We are not a rich country. It is a national problem. To put in place six regional stations and two national ones from Cairo, in addition to the satellite stations, with all of the necessary equipment and technology, requires large amounts of funds. But that doesn't stop the regional stations from having a large role, each in its own region. Each station operated to explore its surrounding environment. For example, when I was growing up in Isma'iliya, I didn't know what was happening in the next street over. I didn't know what the government was doing, what the problems were. By tuning into the station, locals now can learn everything.*

These costly television innovations marked the entrance of Egypt into the international media market and generated much investor activity in the national stock market. This satellite dynamic expressed the new global but elitist state-subsidized market logic behind the new stations and the constraints among the more modest public broadcast provincial stations that threatened to downsize the 'democratic' dreams of the provincial innovators. The ERTU continues to preserve the power of the capital city and governs the ensemble of messages reaching the public.

Kamel: *What do you do on this regional station in your specific programs to distinguish yourself from Cairo?*

Tariq: *At first we were very close to the region, very tied, but now we have distanced ourselves. From its creation, the station made some completely unprecedented shows. We went into the street to interact with and film the public and built this interaction into programming. It was the regional stations that were the first to highlight people in the street in programming. Before, all the programming of Channel One was done in the studio, saturated with sweetness and traditionalism. We, the young regional stations, we wanted to reflect something new. And we did it!*

Urban services for example—the cleanliness of the streets—we went down into the streets and we filmed them. This place isn't clean, why? Where is the head of the block, the administrator of the city, the governor? We insisted on seeing the people in charge of the problem. We were the first to do that. That was never seen either on Channel One or Two [the national channels]! It's us, Channels Four and Five, who went into the streets, camera in hand, and we filmed the people—we were the first ones. When Channel Four started, the people switched from Channels One and Two to watch us. . . . Today, our notoriety has diminished. The national stations took our ideas and surpassed us, because they have the resources and the means. Shortly after this, they went into the streets filming, and made programs on hot topics.

Kamel: *What brought about this choice to go into the streets, locally?*

Tariq: *We are a region. We are local. The al-Salam neighborhood is my own. I went back to where I grew up and I realized that no one was receiving their entitled government services. I have the means to say important things in front of people through my camera and television, my presence in this place influences my neighbors, and I show the problem to the viewers. Regional TV stations brought to Cairo something that has existed for a long time in other countries—the reporter or on-site journalist. Channels One and Two only had an anchor, the one who was sitting behind a desk, reading the news. Or the one who stayed in the studio, the* one who invited people onto his show and then interviewed them while seated on a chair—chic, still, and very formal. By contrast, we went down and presented the news from the streets.

It is one of the advantages, by the way, of regional TV, because at any other channel, I couldn't have done but one job. Here we can present the news, produce programming for children, and create new programs. I can, from time to time, be a producer, but in an unofficial way. I define my work myself.

Kamel: *Does that mean that these 'street-reportage' programs and their concepts were 'by the people, for the people'?*

Tariq: *Well, they weren't revolutionary, of course. More importantly they were symbolically attuned to their environment, their surrounding social world. Nevertheless, these experiments were terminated. The 'idea people' started to push other types of programs: game shows, variety shows, singing shows, and things like that. It wasn't like it had been at the beginning anymore. Channel Four became like Channels One and Two.*

Kamel: *How did it stray?*

Tariq: *I'll tell you how it strayed (he pauses for a long moment). . . . Maybe through deception or thwarting. You know what ihbat means? Thwarting, or intentional frustration of an effort.*

The Capital and the Political Monopoly

Kamel: *If there were no financial limits, what would you do, professionally, if you had the chance now?*

Tariq: *Oh, I would like to do many things! I would like to be more in touch with reality, with the reality in which I live. This region isn't detached at all from the national reality. What we suffer from here is the same as in Cairo, Alexandria, Aswan. The same problems are found all over Egypt. I would discuss these problems on a regional level and discuss them on a national level. But give me the means. Give me a camera for five hours instead of two. Give me a cameraman who is happy to work and who isn't here against his will.*

And this thwarting isn't only a regional problem but clearly a national one. The problems of the provinces are certainly the same as the national ones, but there is a difference: the political dimension. If I want to speak about politics in the provincial context, what am I going to say? When in Cairo and on the national stations, they are talking about politics. Me, I want to do a show about politics, for example. But I can't do it here because you are a regional station. There are limitations/boundaries that you can't cross. You can, for example, talk about what happened in Luxor, about "the attack" (in 1997, many tourists were brutally killed by Islamist extremists) in a limited way. But I can't invite a politician or an economist on the air; and I don't know how to organize a meeting and discuss the affair. That isn't part of who we are.

Kamel: *In fact, the regional problems are national problems, but the national problems are not regional problems. . . .*

Tariq: *In fact, the connections are not apparent at first glance. And yet, what is pertinent to the citizen of Cairo about tourism, for example, is also pertinent to the provincial region. The terrorist attack on tourist sites at Luxor had repercussions on the people called bambutiya [the merchants working in train stations and stops] in Port Said. Port Said is far from Luxor, but the attack's impact still greatly affected us, as it touched the people of Cairo, and Aswan as well. But here, in Isma'iliya, that state says that I don't have the right to talk about it.*

One would think that paradoxically, it is the success of these same regional television stations to the north—the first ones created—that brought them trouble. Their interface with the state remains, for historical reasons, very close to the Soviet model. In this highly limited, censored, centralized, nationally centralized command structure, what is a local public space? Is this a contradiction in terms? Regional stations 'invented' the concept of street-level reporting, and investigative journalism, and public-opinion reporting in Egypt. They developed these tools for public accountability and local citizenship activation. But can these practices survive in the context of the elite, private-sector, state-favored globalizing dynamic of the new satellite stations that have effected radical change in the Egyptian audiovisual landscape (El-Khawaga 2003a)? Can we really be as naïve as some U.S.-based analysts (Eickelman and Anderson 2003) who assume that the recent proliferation of high-quality Persian Gulf–based Arab satellite television journalists will foreshadow the emergence of an 'Arab public space' of the Habermassian type, where free debate is engaged in order to deliberate and articulate independent, rational public opinion and civic norms? This Habermassian model recognizes the importance of television as a deliberative space, unfortunately only in a highly mediated, televisual sense. Tariq argues that his creative imagination and deliberative model of reporter-citizen dynamics can only exist in the context of local, autonomous, publicly supported television stations, not centralized satellite or national forms.

Kamel: *If you had to change jobs, would you think of contacting, for example, Channel One?*

Tariq, laughing: *Contact Channel One? I can work for Channel One, but where would I live [in Cairo]? The problem would be where and how would I live? I have a family. Where could I find housing? For how much? It might have been possible to work in Cairo if I didn't have a family.*

Kamel: *In your opinion, and if we take you for example, you and your fellow intellectuals in the provinces work here because you are forced economically and politically to do so and you can't leave?*

Tariq: *Not exactly, on a personal level, I am very happy.*

Kamel: *If there were a chance to leave?*

Tariq, with a trace of impatience: *I tell you that I could indeed work for Channel One, but I'm doing well here, and over there [Cairo], I wouldn't be. I'm happy to live here with my family, my work is here and I can do things that are satisfying to me. Furthermore, in Cairo there would be problems at work as well. Just like if someone was new here, it would be difficult for him to do what I do. I am known, I have a history from years of work, I have a career and things that I have accomplished. I have a place here [one understands that by this, it is not merely a job]. But, if I live over there, I'm going to find myself a newcomer, without history, without. . . .*

Kamel, in a somber tone: *Without hope?*

Tariq: *Yes, without hope. We have a colleague, he was with us at Cairo University and later he worked for Channel One, in programming and sports, for three years. I only saw him on screen two times . . . two times! In Cairo, you have to find people who let you work there. If only I could count on certain people.*

Kamel: *But here you have regional notoriety? When you walk down the street, people recognize you?*

Tariq: *Yes, they say, "Ah! It's the guy that works for Channel Four." If we go out to a café together, they tell me: "Thank you Mister Ibrahim!" They know me from TV.*

We then began to discuss the question of censorship. As Tariq said, "we started off with more liberty and finished with less liberty." For example, Tariq produced a documentary on street children, as part of a regular program on sensitive social problems. According to him, such work could not have been produced anywhere else other than Channel Four. This program ran for some time and elicited diverse reactions up until there was a call to have the minister of information intervene, who at the time, according to Tariq, was "a very tolerant, very open, and very flexible man [who] didn't say anything about the program and allowed it to be shown normally!"

Tariq: *And yet, suddenly and without warning, censorship appeared among us. [In fact, Tariq's regular program was banned following his broadcast about homeless children—the straw, he believes, that broke the camel's back.] And I don't know what triggered it. We didn't have censorship and suddenly, we did. Before that, we had acted as our own censors. If you could see that we were going a bit too far, we would bring it up for discussion. If you were afraid about something, you could ask the president of the station for advice. We were comrades! Today there is censorship! On channels Six, Seven, and Eight since 1995 [that is to say the sensitive zones of Middle Egypt and of Upper Egypt], censors preview all of the tapes before they are put on the air. Ironically, I notice that today, channels One and Two [the national, state-controlled channels] have more liberty than we do. I don't know why.*

"Young People Here Live in a Dream"

Our discussion of Tariq's controversial documentary on homeless children brought us then to discuss questions of the identity of Egypt's younger generations.

Kamel: *They are in a dream world?*

Tariq: *Yes, like the one that we lived in, in our time. The dream changes but it is still a dream! My own dream was to go to Cairo. The dream of young people today is to leave for London or the United States. And now everyone has a satellite dish. The majority of young people watch it to see things that they won't find on Egyptian stations. Not important things, but 'shameless' things.*

Kamel: *It is like in Algeria. The regional stations have two enemies: the satellites and the Cairo stations. Qahiriya, the conqueror, let your vanquished free! [A play on the word for which Cairo was derived, qahara: to conquer, dominate, or to force submission.]*

Tariq: *Domination of the enemy. Cairo, the conqueror, treats us like punished children. We would be very happy first to get a new camera. Like little kids, we wait for a long time. Regional stations—if they are treated with care and attention and remain true to their message—will be very strong stations. They will have an important role to play.*

Kamel: *Are there any young people who work for the station?*

Tariq: *The majority of them are young. I am maybe the oldest, apart from the president who is fifty-seven years old. In the beginning we didn't have scope or direction and there was a huge age gap between the president and the rest of the staff who were in their twenties.*

Kamel: *And you, how do you surmount these problems? What are your plans for the future?*

Tariq, fiercely: *In the future, we need financial means and resources.*

Kamel: *And if the means don't come?*

Tariq: *We are going to work; we will not stop working. But we will produce great things. God only knows.*

Kamel: *And have your friends who have left for Germany and Switzerland found work?*

Tariq, laughing: *They don't do anything. They don't do anything. They feel oppressed over there.*

In the bedroom where the VCR is located, Tariq plays a tape and gives us commentary on his film about the street children. On the screen, he is surrounded by a diverse group of children ranging from ten to seventeen years old who were abandoned and living in the street in Isma'iliya. One of them killed one of his unfortunate companions. In the course of the film, Tariq and his journalist team investigate the event and question the police commissioner in charge of the case at length and the children themselves that were filmed in a shelter under a bridge. The film is shot is such as way as to highlight darkness, visually, to match the grim subject matter, no doubt.

Committed to the Province, Committed to the People

Before we left, Tariq told us that he had decided to commute back to study in Cairo for a few hours a week. His life had begun to resemble the film narratives of a new wave of popular Egyptian cinema, which features creative, tormented

Viewing Tariq's documentary on homeless children at his home (photograph by Patrick Godeau).

youth, circulating through Cairo and referencing Egyptian nationalism, but longing for another place in the provinces to call home.

In the last shots of the movie *A Round Trip to Isma'iliya* a group of girls and boys plunge into the sea fully clothed, in a sort of exuberant ballet. They leap into the waters of the Canal and Red Sea that border Isma'iliya, not into the rivers of the Nile in Cairo that serve as the traditional symbolic baptismal site for national identity. For this generation, the Red Sea and Canal Zone represent an alternative national heart, a meeting place and frontier for Egypt, even for those stuck on a never-ending round trip between the provinces and the capital.

Tariq's ambitions are simultaneously enormous and modest. Symbolic relations between the provinces and the capital, from the perspective of the engaged cultural/media actor, are enormous because of the radical difference in prerogatives and resources between the center and regions, but also modest because Tariq became acutely aware of the real limitations of provincial initiatives during his ten years of effort. But within these limits he has come to realize the provincial-local as a place whose value can be constituted autonomously, a universe on its own to know and to make known. This awareness of rare and neglected provincial forms of value is one of the common characteristics remarked in all our interviews with provincial intellectuals throughout Egypt. These 'virtues' do not fall from the sky nor from a particular ideology, but from the intersection of new demographic realities (the deconcentration of populations) and the postrevolutionary or neoliberal political-economic context (in which decentralization of education and activation of liberal citizenship is initiated, at least experimentally). What is fascinating is how attachments to families, regions, 'the people,' and certain sentimentalities become preserved by these professionals who stay linked to the smaller towns, never renouncing their origins to adopt a professionalized, individualized Cairo-centric identity. Nevertheless, the assertiveness and innovativeness of this alternative provincial intellectual culture has been neglected by those who assumed 'backwardness' or 'fundamentalism' was all there was to find in the provinces. Similarly, the intelligentsia of Cairo and the Arab world has also ignored this alternative provincial intellectual culture.

During the era of Egypt's high-tech, highly exclusive communications revolution, the voices of a new provincial Arab cultural-media class had appeared on screen, if briefly, in a momentarily open and decentralized public sphere.

Works Cited

Colonna, Fanny. 2003. "How the Center Sees the Muhajirin of Knowledge: Normative Processes vs. Demographic Evidence." In *Politics from*

Above, Politics from Below: The Middle East in the Age of Economic Reform,
Eberhard Kienle, ed., 284–303. London: Saqi Press.

_____. 2004. *Récits de la province égyptienne: une ethnographie Sud/Sud.* Arles:
Sindbad/Actes Sud.

Denis, Eric. 1998. "Lettre de l'OUCC." No. 48, June, Le Caire: CEDEJ.

Eickelman, Dale, and Jon Anderson. 2003. *New Media in the Muslim World:
The Emerging Public Sphere.* Bloomington: Indiana University Press.

Guaaybess, Thourya. 2003. "De l'état-émetteur à l'émetteur état dans le
champ télévisuel égyptien." In *Mondialisation et nouveaux médias dans
l'espace arabe,* ed. F. Mermier, 103–123. Paris: Maisonneuve et Larose.

El-Khawaga, Dina. 2003a. " Le journalisme télévisuel dans le monde arabe."
In *Mondialisation et nouveaux médias dans l'espace arabe,* ed. F. Mermier,
17–42. Paris: Maisonneuve et Larose.

_____. 2003b. "La restructuration de l'audiovisuel en Égypte." In
Mondialisation et nouveaux médias dans l'espace arabe, ed. F. Mermier,
91–101. Paris: Maisonneuve et Larose.

Rancière, Jacques. 1999. "Les hommes comme animaux littéraires."
Mouvements 3: 133–44. Paris: La Découverte.

Notes

1   I would like to thank Paul Amar and Diane Singerman for their very useful
suggestions and editing work, Ugo Colonna for his help in translating and editing
this chapter, and Patrick Godeau for his wonderful photography. This chapter
is revised and translated from a much longer discussion of provincial elites in
Colonna 2004.

Cairo

Celebratory Spaces and Vernacular World-Crossing

17 Mulids of Cairo

Sufi Guilds, Popular Celebrations, and the 'Roller-Coaster Landscape' of the Resignified City

Anna Madoeuf

In Cairo as the month of Rabiʿ al-Thani begins, each person knows that the *mulid* or festival of Husayn is imminent.[1] This *mulid* commemorates the birthday of Husayn, the grandson of the Prophet Muhammad. Fixed on the Islamic lunar calendar, the date of the celebration moves forward approximately ten days each year within the global solar calendar. Organized around the Cairo mosque that is dedicated to the man who is considered a saint by Sufis, this festive celebration brings together residents and pilgrims from the entire country, animating the whole quarter that bears Husayn's name according to rituals of the *mulid*, recodifying and rhythmically reordering the space.[2] In the context of increasingly heavy-handed attempts by Cairo city police and the national government to close down public space to hugely popular Sufi festivals as a way to repress any large-scale public gathering (particularly after large public protests in Cairo after the 2003 U.S. invasion of Iraq), this chapter sets out to map out the special meanings, practices, and pleasures of the Cairo *mulid*. Although not expressly political, the *mulid* does continue to articulate alternative collective urban identities and solidarities, and to overpower conceptual, geographic, and religious attempts to contain it.

This chapter offers a reading of ways in which public space in Cairo is created, or at least expressively resignified, during the special circumstances created by these festivals or *mulids*.[3] These events constitute particular, circumscribed, holy space-time occurrences because they are at once popular festivals and devout pilgrimages. In search of possible ways to interpret the nature of public space, I shall turn to Hannah Arendt's laconic but allusive definition of public space as "the appearance of potential space between acting and speaking people," while specifying that in the context of these festivals, language is not only that of the word, but is also composed of gestures, attitudes, codes, and staging (Arendt 1972, 57). In addition, these *mulid* spaces are characterized not only through dialog and contact, but also through the remixing of categories, social types, spatial codes, and norms. Certain modalities of co-presence—juxtapositions, situations, confrontations—are constructed only in *mulids* in the context of surging, celebrating crowds.

As far as the analytic side of our approach is concerned, we need to state the fundamental premises of this research project and underline certain cautions. We will neither, on the pretext of dealing with an exotic domain, track and highlight changeless and permanent features and relics, nor will we overemphasize the purely theological aspects of these collective, public practices. In this light, it would be illusory to try to sift what falls under 'established religion' from what is considered 'popular belief.' We prefer to consider this field as one with intersecting and dovetailing aspects.

Similarly, it would be futile to strive to formally classify what is religious and sacred, and what is festive; to establish a dichotomy 'disentangling' the elements of this composite set of inseparable situations and scenes. There is no *mulid* without a Sufi guild, just as there is no *mulid* without a fairground, attractions, and trade stalls. Furthermore, rather than attempt to separate the two aspects of the feast, we will view them as merged into one whole. True, there is a logic behind the spatial distribution of these two traits, and not every participant necessarily partakes of all dimensions of the festival. But the feast is a space, a system where no holds are absolutely barred and where flexible, shifting combinations are plotted by a variety of individuals and actors. We will deal with aspects of the festive and the sacred by presenting several different temporal and spatial sequences, drawing upon observations made mainly in the two largest *mulids* of Cairo—those of Husayn and Zaynab.

We will view the sacred place as a spatial structure built around the imagination of those who participate in the *mulid*—as a real place constituted by a collective process of active 'imaginary' territorialization. We should stress the fact that the *mulid* does not come 'from out of the blue,' but is an event woven into neighborhood inhabitants' knowledge and practice of the territory. When the *mulid* celebrates a very important saint, such as Husayn or Zaynab or 'Aysha, the knowledge and practices and participation of devotees from throughout the country stream into Cairo and come to bear on the constitution of the space. Residents, particularly women, know the saints or holy men and women of these neighborhoods and mark their feast days on the calendar. For example, in her study of the alleyways of al-Sukkariya, Nawal al-Messiri Nadim notes that the tombs of saints stand as some of the most significant elements that structure the feminine geography of Cairo (1979). If we view *mulid*s as the space-time of vivid memory, it is necessary to recall that memory is a perpetually current phenomenon, a living link to the eternal present.

Egypt's Festivals

Festivals are cyclical celebrations that determine the rhythm of the year for many tied to agriculture, for those among Cairo's popular classes, and for the extensive and critically important 'popular-class civil society actors' cum political-machine organizations, the Sufi brotherhoods of Egypt. At these sacred interactions, publics come together to celebrate the festival of the Prophet Muhammad and of the members of his family *(ahl al-bayt)*, as well as the birthdays of other Muslim, Christian, and (in the recent past) Jewish saints or holy men. Attendance levels at these all-important festivals vary from tens to many hundreds of thousands of people. The most important festivals, besides those in the Delta region of Egypt (Sayyid al-Badawi at Tanta and Ibrahim al-Disuqi at Disuq), take place in Cairo. In Egypt, according to the minister of *awqaf* (Islamic charities), there are more than forty commemorations of saints and, according to the Sufi Counsil, at least eighty festivals for founders of brotherhoods. And tens of small festivals should be added to these census figures. The practice and the continuity of the festivals are evidently linked to the prominent popularity and social relevance of brotherhoods. At least six million men are members of Sufi orders in Egypt, distributed throughout more than 120 brotherhoods, of which seventy-three are officially recognized. The brotherhoods are clustered within and affiliated with various orders, of which the principal ones are the Khalwatiya, the Ahmadiya, the Burhamiya, the Shadhiliya, the Rifa'iya and the Qadiriya (Luizard 1990).

Egypt's press estimates that a million visitors participate in the great festivals of Husayn and his sister Zaynab, a figure which is as aleatory as it is symbolic. Cairo residents come in great numbers to these festivals, but visitors also come *en masse* from all over Egypt, under the banners of the many

Sufi brotherhoods. As objects of study, historians are especially interested in the festivals, principally in the interest of studying Sufism, the organization of confraternal groups, their social, political and cultural functions, and the mysteries of Sufi ecstasy and sanctity (Chich 2000, Luizard 1993, Mayeur-

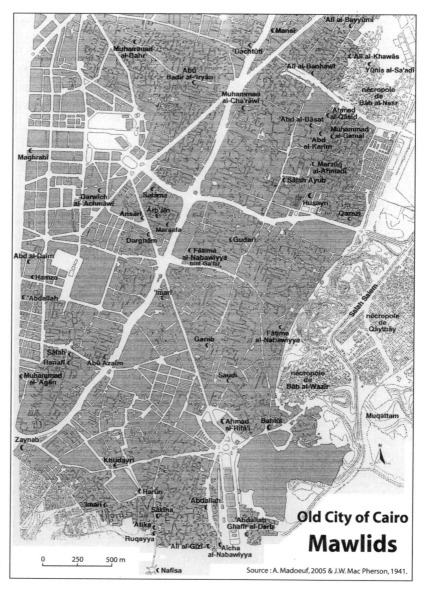

Map of *mulids* in Cairo.

Jaouen 1995). Here we focus on urban geographic and semiotic functions as crucial, neglected dimensions.

The modern literature on the *mulid* festivals may have begun with the *Khitat* by 'Ali Pasha Mubarak compiled at the end of the nineteenth century, or MacPherson's descriptive festival census (1941). The book of photographs commented upon by Biegman provides a variety of perspectives on the ensemble of Egyptian festivals (1990). Travelers' narratives sometimes include information on the development of certain celebrations in specific locales (Lane 1989, de Nerval 1980). Finally, contemporary Egyptian literature—in novels (Haqqi, Mahfouz, Qasim), and particularly in autobiographies (Husayn, 'Iways)—brings out the meaning and intensity of the social, personal, urban, and spatial bonds knit together within the *mulid* context.

However, an 'urban geographic' reading of these events is lacking. Although in other countries, notably in the Maghrib under other forms and appellations *(musims)*, these festivals receive much attention, particularly in anthropological and sociological research. It should be noted that Sufism and its modes of mystical, celebratory, ecstatic exteriorization have been the object of virulent criticism by state, religious, and middle-class authorities since before the modern period. To be sure, since the arrival of Islamic reformism, this entire culture has been accused of obscurantism and a number of social practices have been represented as archaic, and therefore, in the process of disappearing. The festivals can be considered as forms of expression of a 'traditional,' popular, syncretic, and perhaps antiorthodox Islam, ignored or sidelined as more researchers focus attention and concern on the more doctrinaire, middle-class and militant voices of 'puritanical' political Islam. A paradox posed by the urban *mulid* festivals is that they are noisy, public, and religiously identified but relatively discrete, nonpuritanical, and apolitical events. In this chapter I argue that *mulid*s, until recently, have been considered by the state to be neither a form of political resistance nor a public menace. Perhaps this is because they are contained within marginalized areas of Cairo's Old City and necropolises, and because they occur during an ephemeral and explicitly 'counter-realistic' temporal framework. On the surface, they may not have impacted political agendas directly, yet they teem with potential inversions, solidarities, and subversions.

An Aesthetic and Practical System

A *mulid* emerges and evolves in dialogue with the overall spatial, cultural, and contested character of its quarter. It reconfigures the space and takes on the form of a veritable stylistic exercise, based on eurhythmics: importing, arranging, and composing decorative and meaning-making elements. This staging, although often realized with a notable economy of means, nevertheless produces an arresting effect. The framework of the décor throbs with life, plugged into a recurring, polyvalent use of vivid wall-coverings and colored lighting. This repetitive web spans the ensemble. Houses and stalls complete and complement the ambiance with matching colors and patterns, creating a harmonious whole. The tall minaret-spires of the saint's mosque-mausoleum are garlanded with strings of colored blinking lights, and the dressed-up mosque takes on the name of the 'bride' ('arusa) of the festival. The strings of lights stream off the mosque and zigzag over the streets and alleys and frame the geometries of neighboring buildings, creating a vibrating canopy of angular illuminations. Rectangular tents, draped over wooden frames, are made of thick fabrics whose reddish coloring is punctuated by geometric figures and interlacing designs. These occupy all possible spaces, from the eastern flank of the al-Husayn mosque or the square of the Zaynab mosque to the alleyways and courtyards of the surrounding residential areas. The large and beautiful tents, with internal suspended lights and floors covered by oriental rugs, belong to the brotherhoods themselves. Members of the brotherhoods find lodging inside these tents, and this is where the music and ceremonies take place. The tents are topped by banderoles whose color signifies, simultaneously, the affiliation of a confraternal Sufi order (black: Rifa'iya; red: Ahmadiya; green: Burhamiya) and the geographic origin of the pilgrims within Egypt. As such, they attest to the presence of the rural provinces in the heart of the capital city: "Burhamiya from Disuq," "Ahmadiya from Minya," etc. Also deployed are shelters made of raw canvas, for lodging other pilgrims, celebrants, entourages, and extended families. These groups camp in the middle of the streets, principally those around the mosque, or in stairwells, doorways, rooftops, sidewalks, or in virtually any place where a temporary installation is possible. Decorated stands offer pyramids of sweets and of dried chickpeas; ambulant carts carry pointed hats, masks, skirts, ornaments, jewelry, and good-luck charms. Other street stalls cater exclusively to children and include all kinds of toys and carnival games such as rifle shooting, but also offer dance, music, and puppet-show performances. On occasion, small playgrounds with Ferris wheels and bumper cars complete the ensemble of amusements.

The noise and intensity of the festival varies by the day (increasing toward the last day of the festival period), hour (peaking around 11 PM or midnight), and by location within the sprawling space. The *mulid* is an auditory as well as luminary roller coaster: The crack of toy-rifle fire aiming for prizes, the squeak of swing-sets being carted in, the clash of cymbals and drums accompanying merry-go-rounds, the calls of merchants competing for customers, the sounds of whistles from bands of children, the cry of battling marionettes in shows, the steady chant of Qur'an recitations, and the bouncing lyrics of

Mulid night in Sayyida Zaynab (photograph by Jean Pierre Ribière).

Children riding bumper cars during the Sayyida Zaynab *mulid* (photograph by Jean Pierre Ribière).

popular secular music, all mingle together with the rhythmic chanting of the Sufi *dhikr*s that flow from the tents and loudspeakers. One also hears the sound of swarms of mini pick-up trucks invading the quarter, loaded with material for setting up the tents, with carpets and chairs, generators, electric installations, sound equipment, as well as those necessary effects of daily life (food, table and bed coverings, kitchen utensils, etc.). The raising of tents, placement of equipment, and set-up of the fairgrounds lasts several days. The quarters hosting the *mulid*s seem to almost disassociate themselves from the city and become a busy world unto themselves while settling into the rhythm of the festival.

When restaged and decorated for the *mulid*, that part of the city becomes less defined by its permanent built horizontal and vertical surfaces. The distinction between these two dimensions are suspended, producing a visual continuum, like a roller-coaster landscape of flows and flashes. A temporal continuum is also established: night and day are tied together by the delights and noise and flow of life. The *mulid* is inscribed as a nocturnal celebration and its date next year is proclaimed on the last night of the previous year's festival. Nights and days, although contrasted and differing rhythmically, invested and animated by different protagonists, are both equally dense. Seen from this angle, the *mulid* appears as a hybrid festival where one cannot formally isolate the sacred from the mundane. The general atmosphere of joy is created as much by fervor as by delight and playful exaltation. In this sense, the *mulid* does not appear as a confused assemblage. The spatial

A member of a Sufi brotherhood performing in a tent at the Sayyida Zaynab *mulid* (photograph by Jean Pierre Ribière).

distribution of the elements that compose the *mulid*, as a function of their affiliation to sacred and profane registers, corresponds to the alternative coherant spatial and urban logic of the *mulid*. These are identifiable in the details and readable by all participants. In the same way, *mulid*s are composed of ambivalences, of closed and open places, of zones of noise and meditation, of expansion and of concentration. The *mulid* forms a territory. It has an epicenter and defines exposition places, which are well lit, noisy, and tidy, as well as side aisles, corners and nooks, cul-de-sacs, and lit and shadowy zones. Its edges melt into vagueness, in frayed spaces where only the halos (of sounds and lights) are prolonged as the *mulid* transitions into the ordinarily structured city.

Each *mulid* is unique, but they do have many common features. They are superimposed on a preexisting space, while absorbing it and partially blurring it. They present a range of dominant characteristics that create a climate that is at once unique and banal, a landscape as original as it is familiar. In this sense, when locals or pilgrims go to a *mulid* they may feel they are embarking on an ideal voyage toward a place that disconcerts and reassures simultaneously, is spatially and temporally predictable, but with possibilities for discontinuity and surprise built in. The possible modulations of the parameters of the landscape and festival arrangements remain infinite and subtly nuanced.

To promote disinhibition and a sacred ambiance, one may expect *mulid*s to have a lighting scheme emphasizing shadows and muted illumination. However, the opposite effect prevails. Lighting is extremely intense: the light of multicolored bulbs, and above all, of neon lights, is both violent and raw. Light and noise seem to compete with each other to the point of finding a shared register and mingling in a paroxysmal fusion. Here, night is not a time that would be qualitatively opposed to an urban day. Rather, it reveals itself, by its amplitude, as an elaboration of the day: there are more people, more activities, more noise, and more lights than one finds during the daytime.

Who frequents the *mulids*? Evidently all kinds of people, especially those belonging to social categories that might be qualified as among the popular classes.[4] The festival throws together provincial Egyptians and Cairene residents, hedonists and the pious, and provokes other possibilities for social mixing. However, the most manifest mixing, and the most evident in its nonevidence, is that of men and women. In this context, men and women find themselves side by side in a public space where, generally, the distance between the sexes is maintained, where physical contact and touching between men and women are minimized, and where the presence of women, particularly of young women, is tightly controlled.

A scene observed during the last night of the *mulid* of Fatima al-Nabawiya, around ten o'clock at night, serves as an example: on a busy street, a mother who is seated in a chair at the doorstep of her apartment building and her daughter (about twenty years old) are arguing. The young woman, who is dressed up and made up with dyed-blond hair, is manifestly disposed to go out, and her mother is not allowing it. The mother, who is shouting, addresses those who observe the scene (neighbors and passers-by) rather than her daughter, who cries and protests. In fact, the mother is raising her daughter alone and cannot accompany her this evening; therefore, she prefers that her daughter does not go far. Then some neighbors intervene: "But we are all there, all of the quarter is there, let her go out this evening for the *mulid*," they say. Despite the shouts, tears, and negotiations the scene remains relatively calm. After some reticence, the mother gives in; the young woman, accompanied by a friend, goes off; the mother will await, from the doorstep, her daughter's return. Thus, the neighborhood is witness to the mother's firm attitude, to the daughter's obedience, to the display of principles regulating the mobility and freedom of young women. But it will also act to caution this outing, which is rendered possible—even imposed—by the evocation-invocation of confidence, the transfer of responsibility, and by the exception that this festival day represents. The return, like the permission and departure, will also be effected in public and in the same place, in front of the apartment building.

The *Mulid*: A Festival and an Object

How does one apprehend a *mulid* as a geographic object? How does one capture and analyze the perpetual movement contained in a finite space-time configuration? Festivals only a few days in duration offer the researcher little real time to construct an analysis. The evanescent character of the festival drives a researcher's quest for fragments. During a festival, everyone seems to live and act in an accelerated way and it is impossible to grasp the simultaneity of situations and scenes. Thus we have experimented with adapting sociogeographic methodologies to the roller-coaster landscape of the *mulid*, instantaneously capturing data created during aleatory, virtiginous peregrinations. We have chosen to accept the immediacy of the *mulid* and adapt research tactics—impressionistic, sampling—to its constraints. However, a broader field of more empirical analysis is also open to the researcher, because the festival is also a long-term product of less-ephemeral social, state, and urban organizing patterns, and cultural-political contestations; a *mulid* is debated, decided upon, struggled over, programmed, permitted, policed, and organized. Although the analysis we offer in this chapter does not take these aspects into account, we recognize that future research on these phenomena would complement this chapter's semiotic and sociogeographic accounts. By choosing the ephemeral, we have been quite selective, serendipitously isolating the *mulid*s.

Here, then, are exposed and transcribed some scenes captured by chance on the occasion of erratic journeys taken during the *mulid*s, sketches presented like unframed images, which, owing to this fact, may appear as *happenings* (actions deliberately produced with the immediacy of the moment). These allow us to envision the ways in which microambiances are created, and to peel away the outer shell of large-scale events. This style of reading the city can lend to these event-moments a 'performance' character, selectively taking into account the most recurrent situations and locating them in their meaningful context.

The City during the *Mulid*: Forms, Situations, and Labile Practices

The space of a city neighborhood during the *mulid*'s implantation appears to be full of possibilities, interpretations, and multiple microterritorializations. It is constituted as an infinity of 'little corners,' occupied and signified through labile practices—i.e. adaptable, recombinable, and mutating. During the *mulid*, the presence of visitors materializes through a deployment of objects placed in the streets, against walls, on the curbs of the sidewalks, etc. In observing, in detail, exposed places as well as hidden recesses, one notes a multitude of objects and effects. If al-Husayn square (situated in front of the great mosque) is not accessible to people, it is quite open to things. Inside the inaccessible perimeter, along the low wall surmounted by the grates that delimit it, there appears a veritable deposit area for baggage: a line of suitcases, sacks, shopping bags, bundles, and packages, left there and taken in passing, simply by reaching over the enclosure. Even the central (dry) fountain is filled with visitors' effects. The spikes on the gates to the al-Husayn mosque are used as coat hangers, each one piled with clothes and suspended bags. The base of the gates serves as a sideboard for teapots, glasses, plates, goblets, etc. The windowsills of the same mosque are stacked with scaffoldings made of many layers of packaging, bags, and bundles. The few trees of the quarter are also used as supports and their branches are covered with bundles. Around the feet of the streetlamps, bags are also placed. The sidewalks and edges of the streets, delimited on the ground by mats and occupied by distinct groups, are covered by gear used for eating and sleeping. In the same way, the corridors and hallways of apartment buildings serve as lodging and storage areas.

Public and private distractions are partially blurred and blended and the functions of places are redefined. The quarter is encumbered, but things are organized, and people specifically placed. Other forms of signposting include banners stretched on the façades of religious or residential buildings where confraternal Sufi groups reside or hang from windows and balconies, or dangle across streets behind loudspeakers—these banners function as visual and sonorous markers, bearing witness to the location of diverse brotherhoods. To this are also added advertising banners for businesses and businesspeople from the quarter.

All surfaces are exploited, thanks to the many practical gimmicks employed by necessity, but also according to unbridled inventiveness and imagination as urban space is appropriated in its multiple dimensions, volumes, and structures. These appropriations draw from the city's resources, but also imagine new ones, making the space more dense, refashioning it and creating new perspectives. Also, a multitude of minute urban objects (windowsills, various corners, sidewalk steps, etc.) are restyled and individualized, becoming signifiers and other supports for the *mulid*. These objects, which are 'nothing' during ordinary times, when one does not even notice them, are diverted from their usual function by the festival. Thus, a thousand and one ways of being positioned, placed in a niche, and blended with surroundings are tested. Of all the possible uses of the city, all the outlined and realized gestures, let us concentrate on one of the most common—the staking of a small claim to a corner of a sidewalk: When a person unfolds a square of fabric, lays it open,

Banners outside of Sayyida Zaynab Mosque during the *mulid* (photograph by Jean Pierre Ribière).

and places it on a sidewalk, it may not seem like a very impressive trick. But the cloth must conjure some magical power, for a family of six people will spend the length of a week (days and nights) reinventing their gender/urban/class/spiritual identities, eating, drinking and sleeping, maintaining dignity and renegotiating boundaries, and experiencing the *mulid* as the year's greatest pleasure, all while occupying a square of fabric on the concrete sidewalk!

Tightrope Walkers Here and There: Movements, Installations, and Stabilizations

During the days of the *mulid*, Cairo's urban life does not stop. People come, go, attend to their own affairs, and work, passing through and beside the space of the festival. This space is not absolute, but a watchful presence, suggested or traced here and there by décor, sceneries, and attitudes that are deliberately inscribed in the festive register. As Pierre Sansot recalls, "The public space hesitates between the daily and the festive" (2003, 41). This hesitation is translated by the porous quality of this urban universe and of *mulid* attitudes. People walk, but others sit or lie down; some talk, sleep, eat, and drink; others laugh, watch, or do nothing; but all are there together, tied to the *mulid* world-making process of the city. How can one be connected to one scene or to one action, and then disconnect from it in order to involve oneself in another story that is unfolding in parallel? Simply by turning from one place, either by looking elsewhere or by leaving it physically. In this way, many levels of integration are combined in one or many scenes, simultaneously or not, from exclusive to disparate, from subjugation to indifference, from intense to the dilettante experience.

One afternoon during the *mulid* of Husayn (June 2003) on the eastern edge of the mosque, an open café welcomed an orchestra. Seated on chairs with velour cushions, the first row of clients (who seem to be habitués of the establishment) reward the orchestra with ten-pound notes; the singer thanks them returning the compliment, to which the café-owner adds his voice. All around, there are other consumers, seated on wooden seats. Behind are rows of standing spectators, interested as much by the music as by the distribution of people, who excite commentary among them. Beyond the café is the encumbered street where, from time to time, vehicles pass by. Each car that expertly manages to pass through captures the attention of some of the spectators, certain customers get involved, guiding the car. It is often the intermezzo created by a vehicle that will eclipse or determine the retreat of certain participants who, after the distraction, leave to pursue or to take up their own way again. In the same manner, during the *mulid* a number of audiocassette vendors settle in and diffuse music. There are many people who, while crossing these spheres, will manifest their passage by whistling, dancing a step, or snapping their fingers. In this way, many individual peregrinations are constituted, woven together or swept clear by an infinitely variable succession of facts, scenes, and ambiances that take on meaning over the trajectory of each person, according to the intensity of the solicitation, but especially according to the receptivity and time afforded by those who participate in these travels. Thus, sequences in the city are developed that are at once oriented and disoriented. During a *mulid*, modulations are produced by the jostling and aspirations of perpetual unpredictability.

The *mulid* crowd is a specific social formation distinct from the 'mobs' of old sociology, or the 'collectives' of social-movement studies. The *mulid* crowd joins anonymity with identity, and allows for simultaneous exhibition and the dissimulation of participants. It also allows one to visit and socialize intensely or, just as intensely, to completely forget about the presence of other people. The 'sleepwalker,' a certain kind of *flâneur* (one who strolls) character interpreted by Isaac Joseph in *Le passant considérable*, is constructed as a social individual who nourishes his urban identity and longings by immersing himself or herself in public space and the crowd (1984). (See also Battesti in this volume for his discussion of the ways in which the crowds that visit the Giza Zoo celebrate its density, arguing that "people give the breath of life [a soul] to the place.") From inside the *mulid*s, another recurring, metaphoric figure emerges, which is that of the 'tightrope walker': s/he enters into universes according to a halting trajectory marked by hesitation, solicitation, and risky choice-making. The tightrope walker is also a balancing specialist whose progress is often aided by a balancing pole, parasol, or some other object that helps him or her maintain the necessary movement and define unfolding action. The objects that *mulid* participants carry help them in their balancing acts immersed in these crowds; these objects act as reminders or evocations of a certain role, attitude, or process of social, spiritual, sexual, or spatial articulation, as we shall see later in this chapter.

Effects and Facts of the Crowd: The Last Evening of the *Mulid*

It seems that in the case of the *mulid*s, when one fills up a densely shared space, some may feel latent apprehension. Each individual confronts a situation that does not always depend on him or herself, but that, instead, depends on who and what one is—a woman, or, perhaps, a vulnerable person. During that last night of any *mulid*, particularly in the great squares of Husayn and Zaynab, the hesitations and reticence of some (men and women) are obvious, while the delectation of others is just as evident. In this way, actions and figures crush together with an almost systematic character, fusing 'complementary' roles—those who touch and the touched, jostlers and the jostled. These instantaneous forms of contact are consented to or imposed, accepted or not, but they serve to determine the circulating fluctuations that delimit relatively stable groups (families, young men, groups of pilgrims, etc.). It seems that each one makes an intuitive reading of the crowd, of its composition, and of the stratifications that flow from it—a rather immediate interpretation that results in individuals placing themselves in passageways and directing themselves according to these logics, and not according to their estimation of the shortest distance between one point and the other. In the crowd, levels of depth, immersion, and orientation, are measured and distinguished according to concrete points of reference (distance or proximity of walls, sidewalks, etc.).

Despite the press and the crush, this distribution functions relatively well and everyone seems to adapt to it. However, certain narrow places or passages blur this order and generate confusion: the bottlenecks are, from this point of view, chaotic places where everyone mixes in confusion, as they leave or enter the square. At these obligatory, difficult passages, police are placed. They try to manage the flow and even deliver some baton blows, not at random but in a way that tends to target young men, obliging them to advance and pass quickly, using their arms as protection, in order to dodge the blows. The object of this violence is to temper their vague desires to touch and dissuades those who attempt to linger there. At these places, young men, who act as a particular kind of lookout, effectively wait for the passage of young girls in order to rush after them. The girls hesitate, laugh, shout, go there, do not go there; the jostle intensifies.

During other important *mulid*s, in similar topographic contexts, the role played here by the police may be filled by civilians, who act according to the same procedures. During the last night of the Sayyida Zaynab *mulid*, ambulant merchants keep their carts at the edges of the crowd and stand on crates, scrutinizing the movements of the crowd and intervening, coming to the aid of women who are being bothered. Drawing water from their jars with goblets, they spray the culprits (with generally good aim), while shouting to those men and women who were attempting to leave the crush, suggesting to them the path to take to reach the edges of the square and the easiest points of passage.

Another manner of maintaining or creating distance is enacted during the last night of the Fatima al-Nabawiya *mulid*, toward eleven o'clock at night. Around an orchestra, comfortably placed on the platform of an open-air café, some fifty people are dancing. It is difficult to be precise about the exact nature of this dance; the songs are by reference religious, the music is by those who accompany the *dhikr*. But the *dhikr* is, in principle, a collective, codified exercise. Movements of the body, men and women together, ample and supple, are essentially created by lateral swaying in a *dhikr*; legs are straight, arms swinging, as the head moves from side to side. Other masses of people outside the carpeted open-air dance zone are dancing in more individual ways, without worrying about the others, while keeping themselves in harmony with the shared rhythm. Even if their movements are clearly related to another register of expression, their gestures and attitudes are impregnated with the *dhikr*. Among the participants, many are women, of which some are young. Around them, spectators press to watch and many men direct their gaze at feminine anatomies exposed and animated by dance movements. But these women, certain ones of whom have strained faces and others, expressions of ecstatic delight, all have their eyes closed. Whether real or feigned, their indifference appears to be absolute: there is not any coquettishness in their gestures, nor any deliberate suggestiveness in their postures, nor exhibitionism. This scene, evolving with a partial and continuous renewal of protagonists, will last for hours. Although this situation is out of the ordinary, since women dance without restraint in the street all night long, there may not be any exchange of glances. The context is that of the *mulid*, and the music that provokes the dance is of religious inspiration. It is also true that exposed feminine bodies are not objects of indifference, so much more so because they are at once static—in place and observable at one's leisure—and animated—visible from various angles and in various positions. These women move their bodies, but do not show themselves off; they do not permit any possible hold on their bodies, defusing as such any possible contact.

Reading these *mulid*s may contribute to thinking about the city as an animated space, a place notably invested spiritually and symbolically, but also full of a material and tangible presence, those of décors, bodies, and objects. Cairo's *mulid* space-times are intermediary zones where contacts are made and practiced between people, but also between objects and positions. Because of this fact, it is appropriate to extend one's attention to places and individuals, toward objects, whether fixed or tended. Objects in these festival urban contexts are active, they move people, provide impulses to action. Innumerable worry beads wrapped around wrists are ceaselessly caressed; handles of teapots are gripped by men and women ceaselessly serving and offering tea to friends and passers-by; sides of women's dresses or headscarves are clutched by children who are either carried or walking on their own. In terms of the density of the crowd, imposed proximity is intense. But it is the consensus of those at the *mulid* to further intensify this density by holding each other close—arm-in-arm, or hand-in-hand, or embracing a comrade around the shoulder as they move around in groups of two, three, or in lines. Is contact with others reduced, attenuated, or enabled when one is submersed within this gender-mixed crowd? Squeezing the arm of one's family member or companion, is it a show for the others, against the vertigo experienced by the individual in the middle of the crowd? Or is this a paradoxical attempt to escape, by a demonstration of linkage, from the non-sense of being alone among a multitude of other beings? Or is this a way of integrating oneself into this collective gathering of bodies while affirming oneself through a concrete touching gesture?

"It Was the Festival and Now It's Over! That's Life! What Did You Think It Was?"[5]

The extraordinary festive time is a period when control of the family/society and one's surroundings abates, and full rein can be given to attitudes that would be castigated or concealed outside the *mulid* context. The mingling, the crowd, and the exceptional circumstances confer some degree of anonymity. Such moments when one is more prone to mind one's own business lead to variations in behavior. Many deeds perpetrated in public remain unknown or are tolerated: they become acceptable under such fleeting moments and within this closed space, the ideal and arguably necessary place for transgression, exception, and deregulation, under cover of religious celebration. Thus, it is possible to directly accost young girls who may on such occasions be strolling unaccompanied, a daring act that goes unnoticed under anonymous circumstances but which would be hard to accomplish in surroundings where she is known. The same goes for carnal contact and dance, consumption of alcohol and drugs, choosing fancy dress, and the parody and derision of 'institutions' such as marriage, class and state icons, and normative sexual identity. At Sayyida 'Aysha, the local young men organize a cart procession on the afternoon of the last day. On these carts, they act out various scenes featuring the café waiter, the police officer, the thief, and men disguised as women, some mimicking and parodying marriage, and suggesting illicit forms of sexual intercourse.

Young men dress up as women during a procession of carts in the Sayyida 'Aysha *mulid* (photograph by Jean Pierre Ribière).

We should however point out that such entertainment is neither systematic nor is it present in all *mulid*s. Each generates its own mood. Such peculiarities are determined solely by spontaneous local initiatives. The *mulid*, an occasion for exteriorization, is an important moment in the life of the neighborhood, enabling various social groups to express and assert themselves. The young men in drag and in costumes of different 'types' who file past in the cart procession unquestionably display provocation. Café waiters (the real ones, along the parade route) seize free-speech rights by grabbing loudspeakers and bark out commentaries on costumes and on the street show while also vaunting their businesses. Children, in the spotlight, become temperamental and are spoiled. Families, in their full numbers, come on an outing while young girls turn on their seductive powers and spend lavishly on hairdressing and makeup, highlighting and displaying their strong points.

*Mulid*s are important moments in the life of Sufi guilds. The ecstatic rituals that they foster strengthen the cohesion of disciples and encourage people to join the brotherhood. Major celebrations serve—at various levels—as public forums and representatives. In tents privileged to be mounted on the square itself, official representations, the Sufi Council and the prestigious Sufi guilds—those with the most charismatic and influential sheikhs—are very conspicuous.

Politicization of *Mulid*s in Today's Egypt: Will That Stop Them?

Unable to ban and much less organize such gatherings, the authorities may try to use them for political ends. In December 1994, the *mulid* of Sayyida Zaynab was used as an electoral campaign platform. Its distinguishing feature was the great number and lavish display of lights and perpetual fireworks, attributed to the extravagance of Fathi Surur, the local district's member of Parliament. The portraits and banners in his name at the festival signaled his intention to run in the forthcoming legislative elections billed for autumn 1995. It further affirmed the state's presence and involvement in the neighborhood, since Fathi Surur was also president of the People's Assembly.

During a clash with the police, three Islamists had been killed in the same Sayyida Zaynab neighborhood in February 1994. But the politician's contacts and his political base in Sayyida Zaynab assured that the 'show went on' despite insistence from elsewhere within the state that the district be put on lockdown. A luminous and more-splendid-than-ever *mulid* followed a year later (December 1995), proving Surur's success in the earlier elections. Further proof was the banner, heartily congratulating Surur, hoisted by local traders and notables who gave the neighborhood a treat by financing the lighting. Such patronage obviously translated into their increased personal prestige and publicity for themselves and their businesses. As interface between public and private feast, the *mulid* not only benefits many protagonists through interactive links, but also offers them potential profits, and a degree of protection that sometimes, if not always, assures the public celebration's survival.

After the repression in Cairo of large protests against the American invasion of Iraq in the spring of 2003, the government asserted a much greater degree of control over the great square in front of the al-Husayn mosque. The square was permanently occupied by police battalions. During the *mulid* that followed (June 2003), the large open public space in front of the mosque was confiscated. Not a single tent, attraction, cart, or café-restaurant terrace was tolerated there. One could no longer settle in the space for rest or prayer; one could only pass straight through. Owing to the closing of the great open space that the al-Husayn square had been, and on which the most visible confraternal groups used to gather, the *mulid* had to sprawl out, snaking through the streets and alleyways—dispersing not disappearing.

This eviction from the center toward the peripheral areas, from opulent to cramped space, gave the *mulid* a more confused, less coherent aspect. The *mulid* seemed deconstructed. Exiled to decorated alleyways, Sufi orders' installations were rendered nearly invisible. But they insistently proclaimed their presence through their audibility, by means of the installation of loudspeakers oriented toward the square. Over the duration of the *mulid*, the forces of order (approximately twenty policemen permanently present in a constant ring) did not cease to dissuade those people attempting to sit down or to lean against the grates of the square, who were relieved during the afternoons by a water cart spreading water on the hot sidewalks. In the same way, the police prohibited people from parking their cars there. Tables,

Tables set up for meals in Husayn Square during the *mulid* of Husayn, before the government declared the square off-limits to *mulid* activities in 2003 (photograph by Jean Pierre Ribière).

chairs, tablecloths, and dishes from cafés and restaurants that were set up in violation of the new rules were confiscated and thrown together in trucks. Owners had to pay a fine to retrieve them. However, each day, as the evening gradually advanced, and the *mulid* neared the last night, these restrictions and repressive actions became more difficult to apply and less and less firm. During the last night, despite police reinforcements, the people overcame the prohibitions, with the exception of the one concerning access to the central square during prayers, which was maintained by a police cordon.

By the call to evening prayer, on the Friday preceding the last night of the Husayn *mulid* (19 June 2003), the mosque was filling. The overflowing crowd settled in front of the southern entrance alongside the mosque. The lack of space pushed some men to climb the grates of the square and to take off their shoes to pray on the lawn. The first groups of them were stopped by the dozen police who stood guard. They attempted to push the men back, then gave up as they noticed the increasing numbers of arrivals. Many rows of people praying were forming. Some of the police then joined the prayer, which, finally, took place in the public square, which filled up despite the fact that the state had ordered it closed and evacuated. After the prayer, everyone left, except for the police. The same scene was reproduced the following days, until the last evening.

Conclusion

Big *mulid*s provide the necessary forum for the rural, urban, provincial, Cairene and other communities to meet around shared representations and pleasures that strengthen the cohesion and identity of the social groups present. They also help to create occasions for affirming the feeling of belonging to layers of communities (Sufi brotherhood, village, Cairo neighborhood, business network, etc.), and occasions for suspending norms of social control, and for perpetuating spiritual, spatial, and friendship rites. *Mulid*s stand as essential periods for the individual and the community. The *mulid* is also a space-time with boundless opportunities for spiritual intercession *(madad)*, and to articulate new wishes, desires, and hopes. It is presupposed that the Prophet is present and mention is made of his diverse miracles. Contrary to many recurring events whose past is often steeped in nostalgia, *mulid*s are seen by their practitioners as perpetuated in a continuity that precludes any comparative description. Thus, by definition, a *mulid* is always a success and is generally always appraised as "very good this year, as always."

Will Cairo's *mulid* publics—tightrope walkers in a roller-coaster landscape— survive the new waves of repression and policing? Popular classes' insistence in the *mulid*'s continuity, their growing investment in the power of celebration, festival, and prayer, and their adaptive world-making practices offer proof that the *mulid* is perhaps irrepressable.

Works Cited

Arendt, Hannah. 1972. *La crise de la culture.* Paris: Gallimard.

Biegman, Nicolaas-H. 1990. *Egypt: Moulids, Saints, Sufis.* La Haye: Gary Schwartz-SDU.

Chich, Rachida. 2000. *Le soufisme au quotidien: confréries d'Égypte au XXᵉ siècle.* Paris: Sinbad, Actes Sud.

Haqqi, Yahia. 1991. *Choc.* trad. par Charles Vial et Sayyed Abul Naga. Paris: Denoël–Alif.

Hussein, Taha. 1947. *Le livre des jours.* Paris: Gallimard.

'Iways, Sayyid. 1989. *L'histoire que je porte sur mon dos.* Le Caire: CEDEJ.

Joseph, Isaac. 1984. *Le passant considérable: essai sur la dispersion de l'espace public.* Paris: Librairie des Méridiens.

Lane, Edward. W. 1989. *Manners and Customs of the Modern Egyptians.* London: East-West Publications.

Luizard, Pierre-Jean. 1990. "Le soufisme égyptien contemporain." *Égypte/ Monde Arabe* 2: 35–94.

———. 1993. "Un *mawlid* particulier." *Égypte/Monde Arabe* 14: 79–102.

MacPherson, John W. 1941. *The Moulids of Egypt: Egyptian Saints' Days.* Cairo: Nile Mission Press.

Mahfouz, Nagib. 1989. *Trilogie: Impasse des Deux-Palais, Le Jardin du passé, Le Palais du désir.* Paris: J.C. Lattès.

Mayeur-Jaouen, Catherine. 1995. "Gens de la maison et *mulid*s d'Égypte." In *La religion civique à l'époque médiévale et moderne (chrétienté et Islam),* ed. André Vauchez, 309–22. Rome: École française de Rome.

Al-Messiri Nadim, Nawal. 1979. "The Concept of the Hara: A Historical and Sociological Study of Al-Sukkariya." *Annales Islamologiques* (15): 313–48. Le Caire: IFAO.

Mubarak Pasha, 'Ali. 1888. *al-Khitat al-Tawfiqiya al-Jadida.* Cairo: Bulaq Press.

de Nerval, Gérard. 1980. *Voyage en Orient.* Paris: GF-Flammarion.

Qasim, 'Abd al-Hakim. 1998. *Les sept jours de l'homme.* Paris: Sindbad, Actes Sud.

Sansot, Pierre. 2003. *Jardins publics.* Paris: Petite Bibliothèque Payot.

Schielke, Samuli. 2003. "On Snacks and Saints: When Discourses of Rationality and Order Enter the Egyptian Mawlid." Paper presented at the Netherlands-Flemish Institute of Cairo, 23 January.

Woolf, Virginia. 2000. *Mrs. Dalloway.* Paris: Gallimard-Folio.

Notes

1 This festival is known as a *mulid* in Egypt (*mawlid* [birthday]; in the plural, *mawalid*). But beyond marking the anniversary of a precise event—birth or disappearance (both cases exist)—the *mulid* simply marks the day that is consecrated to the saint.

2 The literature in French and English on the veneration of holy women and men and descendants of prophets in Sufi Islam and parallel Jewish practices often refers to these figures as 'saints' (see Beigman 1990; Schielke 2003; MacPherson 1941). This term offends some orthodox sensibilities, since neither Judaism nor Islam revere an order of saints as does Christianity. But maintaining orthodox distinctions is not the priority of Sufi mysticism, or *mulid* syncretism. In this light we will alternate between the use of the term 'saint' and 'holy woman/man' to describe the spiritual patrons of *mulids* and the sacred persons buried in the shrines visited by *mulid* pilgrims.

3 This chapter is based on fieldwork in Cairo during the festivals of Husayn and Zaynab (the most important festivals), but also during those of Yunis al-Sa'adi, Abu 'Ila, Fatima al-Nabawiya, and 'Aysha al-Nabawiya, between 1998 and 2003.

4 In particular, an unscientific but nevertheless revealing indicator of purchasing power may be found in the shoes of the participants: a large part of them (men, women, and children) wear open shoes (sandals with molded plastic or leather straps), which belong to the bottom of the shoe hierarchy.

5 A lucid remark made by an acrobat to the hero of *Sept jours de l'homme* (Qassim 1998, 170).

18

The Giza Zoo

Reappropriating Public Spaces, Reimagining Urban Beauty

Vincent Battesti

In what way does the city invite us to believe the world one more time and in another manner? Joseph 1996.

The crowd is dense, circulating around the exhibits, eddying between the monkey cages and the barriers that protect the patches of lawn. It is the second day of post-Ramadan holidays at the Giza Zoo. Hundreds of picnicking families and romantic couples get up from off lawn that is technically 'closed to the public.' Using a thick black hose, a zoo gardener inundates the area with a spray of water. "Move out! Stay outside!" But hardly has he turned his back to pick up some trash, when visitors again cross the border of this little island of green, walking with precaution toward the center of what is now a marsh in the middle of which rises a floral composition of palms and cement. Among the adventurers, two young couples: the boys are carrying cameras, and the two girls wearing head-scarves pick up their long skirts a little in order not to spot them with mud. Together, the two girls pause in front of the palms, but this is only the preliminary to a more studied pose. The competing adolescents are already monopolizing a useful part of the decor (the trunk of a dead tree): "Give me my dark glasses for the photo!" One of the couples decides to pose farther away, where the sunlight of the end of the day pierces some foliage. The boy and the girl lean symmetrically on one of the park's floral lamps; the plants form the backdrop. The girl readjusts her blouse, smooths down her dress, straightens the pleats of her skirt and, finally, immobile, both of them look straight ahead at the camera lens. A little ill at ease, the boy only brightens his expression at the instant of the flash. The girl, gently smiling, seems defiant. Following the flash, the pose is kept a few seconds too long. Then all seem relieved.

Couple being photographed and strolling in the zoo (photograph by Vincent Battesti).

The authorities at the zoo, as in most of the public spaces in Cairo, attempt to control the crowd indirectly, as a herder does his flock, by constructing obstacles such as fences to influence the flow of the crowd. Often, the crowd overflows the authorized bounds of public space. Between the initial state-designated uses for spaces and their actual arrangements, a process of popular reappropriation has taken place, conforming to the expectations of Cairo's popular classes, and to the values they give to those spaces. The zoo is, at once, the place where masses gather for big festivals, and where couples flirt in a romantic setting. It is this negotiation—the couple extracting itself from the crowd for an instant—that creates the intimacy captured in those cliché photographs that immortalize and attest to a relationship. After the photos, the two couples will cross the symbolic barrier and become anonymous again, as they plunge back into the dense and boisterous crowd.

Undeniably, green spaces provoke public frenzy in Cairo. In accordance with the contemporary desirability of 'quality of life' and its quota of greenery, many global cities have arrived at the same solution: create large parks on the periphery of the city. Urban life in Cairo, however, manages to articulate its own local responses. If some green spaces dot the landscape of the city and its suburban area, it is the not-peripheral (and quite green) zoo that the popular classes adore, especially during holidays. The popular passion for the zoo and the way it is used today were not defined in the original vision for this park. Evolving out of the garden of Khedive Isma'il's harem, the Zoological Garden was conceived within the same paradigm as the other gardens of the downtown area. During the nineteenth century, the creation of new spaces corresponded to the globalizing colonial modern urban norms of the period. Rulers of the great capitals focused on opening areas for bourgeois promenades. Over the twentieth century, however, the colonial design for these new public spaces was subverted as the popular strata of society appropriated these spaces for themselves, especially during holidays, transforming the social experience associated with those areas. Meanwhile the wealthier classes increasingly came to prefer private clubs and gated communities. How are the planned uses for these spaces arranged for the disposition of their intended publics? How do norms of behavior in public space adapt to shifts in public frequentation and appropriation? And how is the use of public order imagined and reconfigured by park-users and state authorities?

This chapter discusses certain public spaces in Cairo that respond to the imperatives of spatial openness and accessibility (Beyhum 1997), particularly the zoo at Giza (Hadiqat al-Hayawanat), with some comparison with the popularly claimed areas of *wust al-balad*, Cairo's central business district. Both spaces are very much frequented by the popular classes according to specific rhythms. These public spaces are where one goes to amuse oneself in a liberated, disinterested, and hedonistic way (a potential definition of 'leisure' that certain authors reserve for postindustrial societies, Dumazedier 1998).

In truth, we usually come here to look at the beautiful things that are here, the animals, but also the beautiful girls. The people are beautiful in the way they stroll about. It's beautiful weather out and, in fact, all the people have come today to have fun in the Zoological Garden (student from the American University in Cairo [AUC] at the zoo, 2003).

Festival Day at the Zoological Garden at Giza

Many of Cairo's residents are familiar with Giza's Zoological Garden only during its most intense moments, when it is festive and frequented by the largest mass of people, although these moments do not represent the 'normal' or daily way the space is occupied. "The ambiance is not always like this. . . . The crowds will decrease, and it will be more charming (AUC student at the zoo, 2003)."

The three-tiered ladder of usage proposed by visitors to the zoo (weekday, weekend, and festival day) represents a gradient of frequentation and a barometer of holiday ambiance. Festival days are marked by a supplemental degree of intensity that encourages people to test the limits of the use of a public space. The four days that follow the 'Id al-Fitr festival (end of Ramadan) marks an intense period for the zoo since people have been observing Ramadan's daily restrictions for a month. During the 'Id, a carnival atmosphere erupts.

During the day, the unusually deserted streets downtown hardly augur an urban fever elsewhere. But the crowds during these days can all be found at the Giza Zoo. From the opening of the doors at nine o'clock, a crowd gathers at the entrance gates and clamors for tickets. The entrance fee is only twenty-five piasters for Egyptians, Arabs, and foreigners, according to a sign, painted many years ago, at the entrance ticket-offices, and thus it is financially accessible to almost all Cairenes.

Since men seem to take charge of ticket buying, the ticket booth becomes a masculine melee as men pass their money to the women at the cash registers, through the high grates of the enclosure. The guards at the entrance try to organize a circulation of bodies that looks more like an evacuation, but one that is directed toward the interior. Colorful, varied, heterogeneous, dense, agitated, excited crowds fill the interior gardens and pathways of the zoo. The particularity of this holiday season is the large number of children that participate in it. Microbuses and packed carts discharge young boys (from six years of age) into the zoo, without parental control. The Zoological Garden becomes a vast playground. Many families also come to stroll there: married couples, fiancés or the not-yet-engaged, alone or circulating among many. An entire class of the city's inhabitants seems to show up taking only the precaution of leaving the eldest at home.

During these four days of the 'Id of Ramadan, calculations of total visitors vary wildly as bean-counters throw up their hands. "We welcome between three hundred and five hundred thousand visitors each day," noted the director of the Zoological Garden, Mustafa 'Awad (interview, 2003). Certainly, there is agreement that several tens of thousands of visitors must be here. "We made our way through hundreds of thousands of picnickers playing games, singing and dancing" (Shahine 1999). The Zoological Garden's pathways teem with people, not a single direction of foot traffic is privileged. The boys move about wandering in groups, invading the entire space given over to people, lingering; then suddenly agitated by a brusque change of regime, they run toward the larger crowd increasing its size. The object of these mobs is a fight breaking out, rather then an animal making a show, followed by nothing at all, a nonevent that fed upon the random attention of groups of visitors. The happy groups flow, occupying physical space to its smallest corners, attempting to penetrate the grottos, or spilling onto the forbidden lawns.

The crowds at the zoo during holidays (photograph by Vincent Battesti).

Boys sing and shout as they would not dare to do in their own neighborhoods. They whistle and sometimes move to music made by drums they bring along or their radio-cassettes. A small band of adolescents advances while loudly clapping their hands. In front of the banyan tree (helpfully labeled 'Ficus benghalensis'), they greet three headscarf-wearing adolescent girls, who are passing by in the reverse direction, with a low whistle; in reaction, the girls giggle, placing their hands over their mouths, lowering their heads toward their shoulders. The giant and venerable banyan, planted in 1871, is surrounded. Seated families occupy its base, children straddle the masterly branches and adolescents, bolstered by defiance, hang many meters from the ground, swinging from its giant aerial roots, at the risk of impaling themselves on the nearby kiosk.

If the boys borrow provocative attitudes, the girls are posed modestly to swap secrets and flirt. Groups of adolescents are sometimes gender-mixed and

Children climbing a banyan tree dating from 1871, Giza Zoological Garden (photograph by Vincent Battesti).

thus less oriented toward flirting and more likely to consist of couples. With the youngest 'proto-couples,' shy halting conversations are the norm, including a lot of nonverbal and tactile communications. They push one another, pinch and run after each other, boys tugging at the girls' headscarves. Despite the general press of the crowd, these mixed-gender groups struggle to frame photographs against backdrops that would breathe the calm, green enchantment of an ideal zoological garden returned to its essence. However, it seems that the entrances and grottos are the only places that might fleetingly provide this backdrop. The Zoological Garden is peppered with artificial constructions, owing to the talent of the late-nineteenth-century Italian and Turkish masons who reproduced grottos and mountain reliefs, crafted in stones and coral, sealed with a red glaze. The stonemasons have long been forgotten; but their work has always been greatly prized by Cairene visitors. Their artificiality deceives no one. To the contrary, it is their powerful romanticism (*romansi* in Cairene dialect) that excites admiration, today as it did formerly. It is not only young people but also families and small groups who have themselves photographed against the picturesque backgrounds, a decor laden with glamourous images of the past, Cairo's popularly appropriated belle-époque glory. (See El Kadi and ElKerdany in this volume for an analysis of the architecture of this period, featured in Cairo's downtown.)

It is the promenade of young lovers in search of a characteristic corner, recalling the romantic films of yesteryear. In fact, this paradisiacal place has served as the setting for many films and Egyptian serialized programs of which the most famous is the film *Maw'id gharam* ('Appointment with Love,' Barakat 1956) (Samir 2001).

The grottos, the most striking architectural structures within the zoo, have been restored, a reminder of the good old days when 'Abd al-Halim Hafez sang to Fatin Hamama as he followed her along the garden's winding pathways and bridges (Shahine 1999).

The zoo is usually a family destination. But during these few intense days, groups of youth and young couples swamp the families. However, families do not cede any territory; they bring their children with them, well dressed in their 'Id gifts, little suits for the boys and little white dresses for the girls— or wearing a complete wardrobe sold under plastic in stores, with flowered hat included. In all cases, parents have taken great care to make sure that children appear in their finest attire, costumed as angelically and child-like as possible; whereas the adolescents proudly display their brand-name 'Id gift outfits (Nike, Levi's, Adidas, etc., almost always counterfeit) and the indispensable accessories of the season. One can guess that parents, without being in their 'Sunday best,' have made a vestimentary effort as well. For men, pants and shirt are preferred. The *gallabiya* (long shirt-like garment that reaches the floor) would be gauche. Women wear dresses carefully matched with their headscarves. Women of popular quarters are identified by the way they wear their scarf knotted at the neck rather than under the chin. The appearance remains a strong marker of greater or lesser social ascension. The families circulate among the animal cages, following the children's vague desires to see the animals or to consume—ice cream, another cola, tiger or lion makeup, or an inflatable balloon in the shape of a deer or a giraffe.

Visitors to the zoo view the caged animals (photograph by Vincent Battesti).

Families and children enjoying themselves at the zoo (photograph by Vincent Battesti).

Families settle themselves on the numerous (but insufficient) benches, painted white and bottle-green, as well as in the spaces left open at the margins of the walkways. On this occasion especially, sitting on the grass is a liberty that visitors take, even against the interdictions posted on signs by the garden's administration. A tablecloth (a sheet, plastic mat, wool, or synthetic covering) performs several functions. The cloth is laid out and first, the woman—wife or mother—sits down and brings around her the children, the husband, sacks of provisions, plates, a music stand, the basket or package of food, and eventually, the football, the husband's *shisha* (water pipe), the stove for the tea, the children from other family groups. The density of the entire body renders the border between one family and the next almost unreadable. The tablecloth has an obvious function as a territorial marker whose integrity is more or less respected, particularly along the corridors between them. The other accessories are more mobile markers whose placement allows for negotiation with neighbors, expressed during the festival days through forms of courtesy and politeness: "Please, we'll make a place for you between us and our neighbors" (a space that the children already trample).

The press of the crowd demands often that the father or fiancé act as a border guard, bringing attention to invasions onto the little space of the family, or at least making a public display of it. The option of an even and maximal dispersion between families does not always prevail. The search for distance

496   VINCENT BATTESTI

Families picnicking just outside the gates of the zoo during the holiday celebrating the end of Ramadan (photograph by Vincent Battesti).

from other groups (real, without being isolated either, except for couples that are not officially engaged) is coordinated according to the requirement of finding a 'good place' (sunny or shady, dry or elevated surface, fairly near to the fountains, etc). On this small domestic perimeter of tablecloth, unfolded in a public space and refolded when one leaves, the celebrating Cairene families at the zoo manifest the signs of the pleasant and bucolic recreation of a picnic, despite possible intrusions. The mothers' and wives' first gesture is to remove their sandals or shoes, leaving them on the tablecloth. They remain barefoot through the afternoon, while regularly pulling at their dresses to avoid the immodesty of exhibiting their legs. With this space conquered, the husband can explore at a greater distance with the children, taking them to see the giraffe, for example, whose success with the children is guaranteed. Using its long black tongue, the giraffe knows how to snatch, without fault, the carrot that is extended to it amidst shouts of fright and laughter.

The public gardens are popular. These are not places a proper person could frequent. If you go there one Friday, you will see, it's impossible to go there. Cairo University student who resides in the more elite satellite city of Heliopolis, 2003.

Appropriation of zoo space is intense, a pretty confusion of generalized jostling. Practically the only beings that avoid being jostled are the animals, protected behind the bars of their cages. However, other refuge-spaces exist. The garden's administrative offices, enclosed by a high wall resembling those of the grottos, conceal peaceful small buildings. These buildings open out onto a small private garden. The entrance to this space is, however, guarded by incorruptible guards dressed in blue uniforms. The zoo's cafeterias operate according to a still different statute since you have to pay and consume to remain in them. These open-air eateries are modest, but relatively exclusive spaces inside the vast public park. There is not a door to push to penetrate this space, only a few steps, at most, to climb. The limits of these spaces are clear, 'natural,' when it concerns a reconstituted rock or a duck pond; artificial when it was necessary to enclose them with a wire netting. In these relatively chic oases, one finds tables and chairs. Here, a customer does not remain standing, and one does not make oneself comfortable sitting on the floor. In addition, one is implicitly obliged to consume the refreshment sold there (food or drink, even the water-pipe *shisha* which is *de rigueur* for the fathers of families). These products also allow the establishment to prosper, charging scandalously high prices that dissuade the majority of visitors from eating there.

Guéziret Al-Chay (the Island of Tea) is a café-restaurant that is situated at the edge of one of the zoo's lakes on which there are swans. The café is also located in the middle of a collection of very old and rare plants and trees. There, one serves you tea and a repast, at a good price. In front of you, you can contemplate the calm waters of the lake where swans, ducks, and geese of different colors splash about. And behind you, it is green. State Information Service 2001.

The price of entry to the zoo, held down to twenty-five piasters (about $0.05) allows everyone, including the popular classes, to buy a ticket. But the prices charged in the cafeterias are of a completely different order, and probably of a completely different logic. With that said, at the zoo the happy few during festival times already fill a good number of the available tables. These are families (generally nuclear families with one or two children), but also some adolescents whose pocket money allows them to enjoy this setting. Posing or seated, looking for adventures of flirting, forms of communication build on a repertoire of ironic, theatrical mimicry and gazes. The difference between the level of human density on pathways and spaces of the zoo outside the café, and sparseness of the internal space of the cafeteria, is flagrant. However, no one dares to violate these sanctuaries of relative calm without considering the steep price for penetrating this exclusive realm, only the unconscious actors of the 'social comedy.' Meanwhile, the café's waiters quickly capture those children who rush into the enclosure, attempting to contain them at the exterior of this strangely full bubble, but which seems half empty, compared to the average density of the garden. The crowd's movements can, however, overflow the cafeteria security forces. When a rumbling noise started a rumor that some lions had escaped the nearby cat compound, the panicked crowd was able to flow into these exclusive spaces without much resistance from the guards or patrons.

The crowd visiting the public and Zoological Garden during the big festival days is compact, but composed of hundreds of thousands of units, a colorful, composite crowd. What brings all of these visiting individuals together, gathered in the same space at the same time? A religious (Muslim) festival? Not really—there are many Coptic Christians among them. A holiday on the calendar is only perhaps an opportunity. (See Elshestawy in this volume for further discussion of the way popular classes use squares near the mosques of Sultan Hasan and al-Rifaʿi, and the way in which the government has tried to limit public access to them, supposedly for the benefit of international tourists.) It explains nothing about the choice of the public garden or about the practices occurring at the heart of it.

Respondent: *As for me, I come here with my family, because I find the garden beautiful. The whole entirety is wonderful: the ambiance [al-gaww], the water, the ducks. . . . It's beautiful because it is* zahma *[very crowded, densely occupied]. If it weren't* zahma, *it wouldn't be beautiful. We like to see the people. It's an occasion to see everyone, how they are, how they act, how they're dressed. . . . In fact, this is what getting out on the town is all about.*

Author: *Here in the Zoological Garden, do you come to see the animals or the people?*

Respondent (laughing): *In fact, both!* Interview in the café with a businessman in his late forties from Alexandria, visiting the zoo during a holiday, 2003.

The key word: *al-gaww,* 'ambiance,' gives reason enough. "*'Alashan nighayyar al-gaww*" (so we can change our mood, our ambiance). But "to change ambiance" in relation to what? To the quotidian, to the quarter of one's origin? This poses the question of the social and geographic origins of the users of the Giza zoo. How can we categorize these visitors without defining them simplistically? People from Cairo, the popular classes—these are crowds of anonymous people who observe one another. But this is a type of crowd that the sociologist has trouble categorizing and defining. The definition of Egypt's popular classes as a social category is a delicate matter. Should its definition be delineated in opposition to a much wealthier class, which is too easy to identify, or in distinction from the middle class, which is too difficult to circumscribe given the blurriness of consumer identities?[1]

The popular classes that use the public space of the zoo are also hard to define because they comprise an obvious diversity in terms of revenues, levels of life, social positions, educational levels, and urban-neighborhood origins. The hypothesis of Egyptian economist Galal Amin is that the Egypt of these last fifty years has provided new avenues for social mobility and that certain elements of the popular classes have experienced an ascent toward the top (2000). In Egypt, it is trendy to equate the vulgarization of public morals with the rise in power and presence of popular classes. Demographic growth, bursting of the boundaries that geographically and socially divide Cairo's worlds, public space has undergone profound change, but segregation continues.

Public Spaces: Parks and Downtown Cairo

An early jewel of the modernization of Egypt's capital city, the Giza Zoo is now marked as a nostalgic last vestige of the greenery that characterized agricultural hinterlands that once surrounded Cairo. Under the supervision of the minister of agriculture, the zoo is technically administered as fertile land in the core of Greater Cairo's downtown, submerged between apartment towers, Cairo University, and the traffic of the central avenues. Since the mid-twentieth century, the zoo has become surrounded by the neighborhood of Duqqi. The zoo is enclosed but porous; unlicensed vendors work through the bars of the iron fencing. The zoo is a destination; one moves around there. Buses, microbuses, and boat-buses serve it abundantly: mass transportation for the visitors who, in the majority of cases, do not have access to an automobile. This is another index of the social origin of the strollers who ordinarily reside in the more distant, poorer quarters. If the Zoological Garden is disdained by tourists in favor of the classic tourist sites of the capital (the Pyramids of Giza, the Citadel, the Egyptian Museum), the popular classes approve of it wholeheartedly. Egyptian interlocutors learn with amazement that non-Cairene visitors frequent the zoo, which they think of as their 'secret garden.' It is not so much the animals that draw the visitors as it is other people, and a setting in the city that offers possibilities of encounters, observations, and a certain density of people, away from the scorn of the wealthy or of immediate neighbors.

One could draw up a map of Cairo showing pedestrian density and urban ambiance, the window-shopping or lazy strolls, innocent flirtations, and children's games. It would then be necessary to take a census of all the public gardens, squares, commercial and pedestrian streets of *wust al-balad* (downtown), the shopping malls, the corniches of the Nile and its bridges, and the up-river parks and ferries to al-Qanatar where families and couples go during the weekends (see Abaza 2001, and Elsheshtawy and Abaza in this volume, for further discussion of consumer practices at shopping malls). This would be a geography sensitive to the pleasures of urban pedestrians, of strolling, chasing, and jostling.

During spring 2003, local newspapers ran headlines declaring that the Egyptian capital had taken from Mexico City the honor of being the most polluted megalopolis in the world. Cairo's residents did not wait for this record news to reclaim more green spaces. During the coolest hours of summer evenings, when public gardens are closed, Cairenes look for anything that approaches a garden. Families picnic on the grassy underpasses of bridges or meager lawns of a few traffic circles, encircled by the polluting traffic jams. This search for 'green' is global, as is its discursive manifestation, but its expression is locally specific to Cairo/Giza.[2] For example, the Japanese garden of Helwan and its design have not visibly obliged Cairo's residents to the Zen practice of quiet repose and reflection since it was inaugurated in 1993.[3]

Use of the public space by Cairo's popular classes is partially constrained by a history that should be explored briefly. Two kinds of Cairene popular public spaces attract our attention: the public garden and the downtown street. One of the most remarkable phenomena of the last fifty years directly concerns the occupation of public space. The Egyptian and cosmopolitan bourgeoisie who had occupied downtown Cairo for generations before the anticolonial revolution of Gamal 'Abd al-Nasser and the Free Officers in 1952 largely abandoned it. These downtown quarters of Haussmannian inspiration had been the middle class and elite's domain of choice since the second half of the nineteenth century.

However, the new bourgeoisie—and in particular the *nouveaux riches* of the Infitah (economic overture of President Sadat during the 1970s)— made themselves comfortable elsewhere, to the west, the north, and the south of downtown Cairo. (See Denis in this volume for a discussion of the abandonment of the city's urban more by the middle and upper classes, manifested most concretely in the explosion of gated communities in the desert.) Concomitantly, the place was occupied by the more modest strata of the population. Popular classes invaded at least the sidewalks, if not the residences of downtown. From the mid-nineteenth through the mid-twentieth centuries, the area was frequented by a bourgeois elite parading through the shopping arcades, gardens, and promenades in elegant dress under the shade of small parasols. But since then, downtown has changed into a dense and popular place of excursion for window-shopping and people-watching by another class of people.

[Families of the poor quarters] began to look at each other. They wanted to go out on the town like the others [the bourgeois]. They wanted to take walks, so they went to the gardens [gana'in], to the cinemas, the public parks [hada'iq], places like that. . . . They learned [to go out on the town]. Forty-year-old woman from a popular quarter in Islamic Cairo, 2003.

Do these practices imitate the ethos of the (former) dominant classes? Not completely, because the substance of the practices is quite different. Formerly, the accent was placed on appearance, on displays of social distinction and individuality. But what is of prime importance today during downtown strolls and walks in the gardens is more the search for conviviality and an ambiance of urban animation. One leaves one's quarter of residence to go to those parts of the city where one is sure to find that vibrancy that will be worth the trip. These Cairene residents create and seek precise ambiances and participate in a certain unique spectacle of consuming the city, which itself is watching. The excursion to the public garden has experienced the same history as that of the transformed downtown. A desire to self-segregate caused the wealthier classes to migrate to other horizons, leaving the gardens and heading for their new members-only sporting clubs. The membership charter of one of these clubs *(nadi)* of very British inspiration grants the privilege of access to reserved gardens, reserved activities, and equally exclusive ways of using these things.

Interviewer: *Where do you go during your leisure time?*
Female respondent: *To the clubs, the Nadi Gazira for example, to see friends. And I also go to certain malls to shop. . . .*
Interviewer: *Never to the zoo?*
Female respondent: *No, never to the zoo, nor to the public gardens. The public gardens are places for the popular classes. Why would we go to places, anyway, where our friends did not go? The popular classes in all ways, even if they have the means to frequent the clubs, would never dare to go there: they would not feel at home.*
Interviewer: *Why?*
Female respondent: *Because they need to enjoy themselves by having picnics with a casserole of mahshi [stuffed vegetables] and to eat on the ground. That isn't possible in the clubs, where there are tables, chairs and restaurants.*

Male respondent: *And also they would not feel at ease, because some people, not we, but some people look at them with disdain. The security agents will ask them what they have come to do there: "You, you are a member?!" By their dress, one would easily see that they are not of the group.* Interview, two Cairo University students from Heliopolis, 2003.

Criticism of the public gardens is often severe among representatives of the wealthier strata of society who express regret about the 'invasion' of public spaces by the masses who "do not know to act, who are not respectable" (*mu'addab*). All Cairenes objectively consider distinctions between classes of public space in their discourse. The wealthiest say they do not mix with the poorest of society, because they fear crime, insults, filth, contamination, and vulgarity. The popular classes say they fear feeling "out of place," standing out. For all, it is about attempting to preserve one's lifestyle among others who do not understand their codes. This social disjunction is not a recent invention. But the coming out of the populist classes is.

At the end of the 1960s people did not go outside. The people in popular-class families stayed in their homes. What does that mean? Girls were forbidden to go out. Young men went out rarely, and if they liked to go out, they went out to sit down at a café. These public gardens [hada'iq], downtown and all these things were only for the bourgeoisie. It was their own place. At the beginning of the 1970s, then people started to go out. . . . [But until then,] they did not leave their quarter [mantiqa]! Not much. They went to visit each other in their houses. That's all. But [for them] there were no public gardens; there were no cinemas. . . . The bourgeoisie went to the cinemas; the bourgeoisie went to the public gardens, and to the casinos, the cabarets—the bourgeoisie, they went there. Interview, forty-eight year old married woman from Darb al-Ahmar, a popular quarter in Islamic Cairo, 2003.

When the popular classes started going out, the wealthy strata of Cairo took refuge in exclusive leisure spaces and in gated communities. The bourgeoisie's critique of the current condition of public spaces highlights the divergence between today's popular practices and appropriations in the public gardens and their initial intended purposes, to stimulate elite national conceptions of modernism, hygiene, and morale. Historically, the first appearance of a modern public garden in Cairo, in 1837, was by fiat of Prince Muhammad 'Ali. The pasha created for the public of Cairo (in particular, the European public) a promenade above Shubra Avenue. It transformed what was a swampy lake, Birkat al-Azbakya, into a park "in the European manner." A double concern, both hygienic and moral, governed this choice: Muhammad 'Ali, very concerned with questions of hygiene, wanted to cleanse the lake, which fluctuated with the tides of the Nile. He also wanted to substitute the debauchery of nearby pleasure gardens (cafés, prostitutes, and peddlers) with a "healthy leisure activity that was both moral and modern" (Behrens-Abouseif 1985). Moral and spatial hygiene, already a global metanarrative, was one of the principal nineteenth-century arguments for creating green spaces in the urban milieu. "Trees increase air circulation, the diffusion of light and, especially, they absorb the miasma that escapes from the entrails of men and factories" (Nourry 1997). Cairo's urban promenades (gardens, boulevards) or periurban paths (the vast gardens of al-Qanatar) aimed to please and to raise to global stature the new bourgeoisie of Cairo.

In all my interviews, consciousness of the major social changes during the twentieth century, between the 1960s and the beginning of the 1970s, becomes evident. For some groups, in the 1960s they did not yet go out to the zoos and gardens, but in the 1970s they began to venture into them. For others, in the 1960s they remember strolling in the zoo and parks. But then in the 1970s they stopped going. One public replaced another, and the new users had the numerical advantage.

There is that anecdote of Winston Churchill who said that a desert entrusted to Jews became a garden but a garden entrusted to Arabs became a desert. It is quite nasty, but history has proved him right. What has become of the zoo and Azbakiya [the oldest public garden in Egypt constructed at the beginning of the foundation of the modern city]? Forty-year-old Egyptian male industrialist interviewed at his private club, Nadi Muhammad 'Ali, 2003.

The *burguwaziyin* (bourgeois) are upset by reports of the 'degradation' that these spaces have undergone. If this sometimes rises to the level of consternation, it is because the change is radical in the way that public space is occupied. The public gardens that were originally conceived in the spirit of public health, now 'function' for the populist classes only if the ambiance is good, notably if the density is equivalent to the teeming neighborhoods where these populations reside.

Al-Qanatar was not so interesting when we were there. Why? When we were there, we were alone; there weren't people! It wasn't beautiful, in fact. We weren't content because there weren't lots of people. The people give the breath of life [a soul] to the place. . . . This is the most important thing. If the place does not have people, [even] if the place is very beautiful, then it's not beautiful. You feel it. [At the zoo], there is life, that is to say, there is movement, there is life, and that's beautiful, that is very important, it means space, relaxation, it is very important. Twenty-four-year-old woman from Darb Al-Ahmar at the international garden (al-Hadiqa al-Dawliya), Madinat Nasr, a suburb of Cairo, 2003.

Even if one considers parks and gardens, to a certain extent alternative spaces to the city (Gillot 2002), the activities conducted by the popular classes there and downtown today are similar, and these places had the same fate. For the popular classes, frequenting both kinds of space represents breaking out of the constraints of cramped lodgings in their home residential quarters. The *mulid*s (festivals celebrating saints' birthdays) of Cairo are known to bring together the popular classes of the city (and sometimes of a whole province), and to be cathartic and maybe liberating. (See Madoeuf in this volume for a discussion of *mulid*s and sacred, public space in Cairo.) The life of the popularly occupied zoo and parks is less known and less described. During holidays, these venues bring together at least as many people as *mulid*s do— in particular during the two 'ids (al-Fitr and al-Adha) and the spring festival *(ahamm al-nisim)*. While the *mulid*s revisit the tissue of the old quarters, holidays in the zoo or in public gardens are space-times that occur outside of the old popular city. The urban ambiance of recreation that is created there resembles the known ambiance of the *mulid*s, and yet is at the same time different because it blossoms under different conditions.

Programs and Adjustments to the Zoo

The purview of a public space takes its substance first from its originally intended use, and second from its successive redefinitions (which never really annul the first agenda). The zoo is situated in Giza, now a residential extension of Cairo across from the Nile island of Roda. During the Mamluk era, Giza hosted a palace and royal gardens; in the late nineteenth century it became a country suburb. The Zoological Garden lies on the edge of the Nile, away from the overpopulated quarters of Cairo, but in proximity to downtown. From 1867, another garden with a lesser surface area (fifty Egyptian feddans) existed there, named the Garden of Delights. This was the garden of the royal household during the reign of Khedive Isma'il (1863–1879). The gardens were populated with animals from the royal collection for the prince's concubines (Delchevalerie 1899). By the time the zoo passed into public hands, at the end of the 1870s, it was somewhat deserted. Gradually it was reorganized in order to properly receive the public on 1 March 1891 (Keimer 1954).

The administration of the Zoological Garden attempted to adapt itself to the evolution of its public as much as it attempted to adapt its public to the zoo. Between what the administration would wish for in the behavior of its visitors and what the public offered, there was and is always a gap, as daily practices reappropriate and socially resignify place. If we follow the terminology of Isaac Joseph, we frame this process as fitting between plans and dispositions (1998). It is essential to grasp the city dweller in her/his mutually constitutive relationship with the space in which s/he evolves. We must "think together about plans (agendas or 'programs') that develop or institute the norms of usage and also of dispositions (social and technical competences) that adjust or redefine these norms of usage in a singular situation" (Joseph 1998). These adjustments, these redefinitions of the garden by its public, are unavoidable. People are always reappropriating a place, "too much" as some authorities who prefer to close the gardens, or parts of it, would say (because the public would run the risk of ruining them). Zoo authorities particularly worry about certain zones (cactus gardens, tunnels, *al-gabalaya al-malaki*, grottos) that lend themselves too easily to discrete moments of tenderness. The first authority at this level is the lock; the second, the cohort of guardians—very nice fellows actually, who enter with a blasé whistle-blow that would never really convince any picnicker to renounce his space on the lawn, and who then invites families to feed an ostrich, a sea lion, or an elephant. Police forces are present when the risk to public order is deemed to be real, during mass outings and on festival days. Tolerance (or impotence) seems to prevail but remains contained within the walls of the garden. As a policeman posted at the Zoological Garden said, "During the four days of 'Id, it will be like that. You should return after the festival. Then it will be calmer."

The zoological character of the Zoological Garden almost seems incidental to the declared motivations of visitors. However, in terms of the originally intended agenda, it is a scientific exhibit, and it seems that priority was first given to the scientific mission of the establishment rather than to the creation of a leisure-time activity for its visitors. From 1898 to 1924, under the direction of Stanley Smith Flower, (an English zoologist and son of another eminent zoologist), a policy of increasing collections was established and is still maintained. "This discourse of scientific utility is always accepted by other social groups because it theorizes and justifies, by its requirement of knowledge and of rational use, the aspiration of the elites, and then of all European society with its inventory and appropriation of the world" (Baratay 1998). The zoo is rapidly developing concerns for attracting and pleasing the public. There has developed, in Cairo as in Europe, a pedagogic will since the end of the twentieth century, or rather "a vulgarizing lens" (Baratay 1998). The interest of the public has not waned. In 1899 there were 43,567 visitors and ten years later (1909) the number climbed to 217,735 (Flower 1910). Newspapers closely witness the arrival of new animal residents (Keimer 1954).

The zoo is better than other gardens in Cairo because there are lots of people, and also because there are animals and there are really always visitors, even if one is walking in fact. Even if one has a great deal of time [to spend] in the garden he/she will not be able to see it all. There will still be a lot of things that he/she has not seen and he/she will need to return to see them. There is always something new to be seen. People and animals actually. Young woman from Islamic Cairo, 2003.

This public space, the zoo, has survived and reflects more than a century of Cairo's vicissitudes. The place has been gradually transformed; the public and its mores have mutated. Can one still talk about a concordance between the content and its containing elements? The garden was indeed conceived of as a collection and an exhibit of animals, according to the models of the last century. With that said, various ecological pressure groups interested in animal rights (in particular, American groups of this kind) exhort us to not believe this concordance and protest regularly against the 'detention' conditions experienced by Cairo's zoo animals.

Oh, there are lots of lovely cafeterias and beautiful gardens, and the grottos have been repaired. It's great—unless you're an animal. Richard Hoath, former member of the Born Free Foundation, interviewed by Ghazaleh 2000.

Today, the Zoological Garden at Giza, ignored by the majority of travel guides that prepare tourists for their discovery of Egypt, is adorned with superlatives in official discourses and is ranked among the great green spaces that contribute to the urbanity of a modern city. This is one of the world's great zoos, with a huge surface area of more than forty-eight Egyptian feddans. It is also one of the oldest (opened to the public in 1891). Without a doubt, it would have been one of the most beautiful. The zoological park of Giza is consecrated as "the most celebrated green space of the capital," for its animals but also for its plants, and for being a place to promenade and not solely to visit animals in cages:

Those strolling, tired from crossing the great expanses of the garden, may relax at the Guéziret Al-Chay (literally translated, the Isle of Tea). It's an escapade in itself, after all the excitement that usually accompanies the sight of wild and other animals. State Information Service 2001; Samir 2001.

If, since the beginning of the 1970s, practices in the public gardens have greatly changed, the relative tolerance practiced by the police services there (or their outflanking) implies a relative balance between programs and dispositions. Certainly, the initial designs of the Zoological Garden, that is its scientific and pedagogic value, have had to be reevaluated. During the 1950s, one could still write:

[A] zoological garden is no longer uniquely a place for walking and enjoyment, it is a great book of natural history for people desirous of instructing themselves, for the entire nation, as well as for school children who, accompanied by their masters, go to the 'zoo,' and for the worker, the fellah [peasant], the student, the functionary, etc.". Keimer 1954.

Today, we do not hear of didactics, but of love. The director of the Egyptian Zoological Gardens, Mustafa 'Awad, will say that he considers one of his objectives to have succeeded, because "today, there is a kind of love between the public and the animals" (interview, 2003). He wishes to explain to the public how to treat animals well and to lead the public to love them. He is not lacking in photographic resources in support of his assertions (children in the arms of a monkey, etc.). At Cairo's zoo, keepers insist that the visitors feed the animals (from the end of a stick of wood, accepting tips from visitors), while in other zoological gardens of the world, it is 'forbidden to feed the animals.' Indeed, observing the keepers, it is possible that certain animals are, for the most part, fed this way. Seals, sea lions, ostriches, elephants, hippopotami, monkeys, giraffes, and ducks are rewarded with food for demonstrating their training and for obedience to guards' cues. Surrounding visitors are impressed that the beast obeys the keeper—the hippopotamus opens his huge mouth, that the seal holds himself erect or he emits a series of groans believed to be answers to a question posed. The experience may resemble a circus show of trained animals and the keeper is more than a little proud (his falsely blasé attitude betrays him). The Egyptian zoo, is it a place for exhibiting wild animality or domesticated pets?

A priori, it is the keepers' demonstration of a level of control over the animals that is not matched by the guards' level of control over human guests (this is reminiscent of Haudricourt's reflection on the conjunctions between ways of treating animals, plants, and others [1962]; see also Battesti 2004).

"Domestication is the archetype for other types of subordination" (Thomas 1985). The zoo administration's discourse of love, the proximity between animals and visitors, the practice of rewarding trained domesticated behavior in animals—is this a 'program' thought out as such by the zoo's administration or is it an opportunistic adaptation of adjustments and redefinitions of popular contemporary uses? Even if the zoo director has abdicated a part of his authority and has offered direct access to the animals it is understandably successful, altering its mission to changing use patterns, pleasures and concepts of beauty and sociability.

Conclusion

The appropriation and 'reanimation' of the Zoological Garden of Giza marks the invention of a new kind of unique urban, recreational ambiance. The uses of the zoo have evolved under the influence of two great movements. On the one hand, zoo planners and administrators have designed a mission for the zoo, planning and directing the behavior patterns of guests, animals, and guards, guided by the metanarrative of what a zoo ought to be and how green space ought to be used. On the other hand, the zoo has come to embody the dynamic articulation of density and vibrancy, and to serve as a stage for plays of domesticity, flirtation, and theatricality. When the popular classes are at the zoo, it belongs to them. They did not reproduce the bourgeois ethos that used to prevail there; to the contrary, they have partially imported, expanded upon, and reinvented the urban models of their quarter of origin: autocontrol and urban ambiance in a festive crowd. Acting as coproducers along with the zoo's authorities (sharing readability, panoptic feature concern), Cairo's popular classes have staged and articulated new public norms of sociability, urbanity, and collective beauty that have made the Giza Zoological Garden into an icon of Egypt's newly appropriated popular public spaces.

Works Cited

Aga Khan Trust for Culture. 2001. *The Azhar Park Project in Cairo and the Conservation and Revitalisation of Darb al-Ahmar*. Geneva: The Aga Khan Trust for Culture.

Amin, Galal A. 2000. *Whatever Happened to the Egyptians? Changes in Egyptian Society from 1950 to the Present*. Cairo: The American University in Cairo Press.

Abaza, Mona. 2001. "Shopping Malls, Consumer Culture and the Reshaping of Public Space in Egypt." *Theory, Culture & Society* 18 (5): 97–122.

Baratay, Eric, and Elisabeth Hardouin-Fugier. 1998. *Zoos, Histoire des jardins zoologiques en Occident, XVIe-XXe siècle.* Paris: La Découverte.

Battesti, Vincent. 2004. "Odeur *sui generis,* Le subterfuge dans la domestication du palmier dattier (Tassili n'Ajjer, Algérie)." In *Anthropozoologica—Domestications animales: dimensions sociales et symboliques,* eds. Pierre Bonte, Anne-Marie Brisebarre, Daniel Helmer, and Hasan Sidi Maamar, 301–309. Paris: Publications Scientifiques du Muséum.

Behrens-Abouseif, Doris. 1985. *Azbakiya and its Environs: From Azbak to Ismâ'îl, 1476–1879.* Cairo: Institut français d'archéologie orientale.

Beyhum, Nabil, and Jean-Claude David. 1997. "Du souk à la place, du citadin au citoyen, Espaces publics dans les villes arabes (au Moyen-Orient)." In *Sciences Sociales et Phénomènes Urbains dans le Monde Arabe, Actes du colloque de l'Association de liaison entre les centres de recherches et de documentations sur le monde arabe (ALMA),* eds. Muhammad Naciri and André Raymond, 193–202. Casablanca: Fondation du Roi Abdul Aziz Al-Saoud pour les études islamiques et les sciences humaines.

Central Agency for Population, Mobilization, and Statistics (CAMPAS). 2000. *Household Income, Expenditure and Consumption Survey, 1999/2000.* Cairo.

Delchevalerie, Gustave. 1899. *Les promenades et les jardins du Caire, avec un Catalogue général détaillé et les noms scientifiques, français et égyptiens des Plantes, arbres et arbustes utiles et d'ornement cultivés dans les champs et les jardins et notamment dans les anciens jardins vice-royaux et khédiviaux de l'Égypte sous la dynastie de Méhémet-Aly au XIXe siècle de J.-C.* Chaumes: G. Delchevalerie.

Dumazedier, Joffre. 1998. "Loisir." In *Encyclopaedia Universalis.* Paris: Encyclopaedia Universalis France.

Flower, Stanley S. 1910. *Report for the Year 1909 (Eleventh Annual Report), Zoological Gardens, Guizeh, near Cairo.* Cairo: Public Works Department, Government of Egypt.

Ghazaleh, Pascale. 2000. "Richard Hoath: The Call of the Wild." *Al-Ahram Weekly,* 23 March.

Gillot, Gaëlle. 2002. *Ces autres espaces, Les jardins publics dans les grandes villes du monde arabe: politiques et pratiques au Caire, à Rabat et à Damas.* Ph.D. diss., Université François Rabelais.

Haudricourt, André-Georges. 1962. "Domestication des animaux, culture des plantes et traitement d'autrui." *L'Homme* 2 (1): 40–50.

Joseph, Isaac. 1996. "Les compétences de rassemblement, Une ethnographie des lieux publics." *Enquête* 4: 107–22.

_____. 1998. *La ville sans qualités*. La Tour-d'Aigues: Édition de l'Aube.

Keimer, Louis. 1954. *Jardins zoologiques d'Égypte*. Cairo: Éditions des Cahiers d'Histoire Égyptienne.

Nourry, Louis-Michel. 1997. *Les jardins publics en province : espaces et politique au XIXe siècle*. Rennes: Presses universitaires de Rennes.

Samir, Amira. 2001. "*The Tea Island*, un coin de calme et de beauté." *Al-Ahram Hebdo*, 18 December.

Shahine, Gihan. 1999. "Life Behind Bars." *Al-Ahram Weekly*, 10 June.

State Information Service. 2001. "The Tea Island, un coin de calme et de beauté." *Lettre du Caire*, 18 Dec.

Thomas, Keith. 1985. *Dans le jardin de la nature, La mutation des sensibilités en Angleterre à l'époque moderne (1500–1800)*. Paris: Gallimard.

Notes

1   Based on the Household Income, Expenditure and Consumption Survey conducted by CAPMAS (Central Agency for Population, Mobilization, and Statistics) in 1999/2000 (2000), and according to François Ireton's analysis (personal communication with author, CEDEJ, Cairo, 28 September 2004.), the Egyptian urban population can be placed in three categories: the "poor and populist classes" (less than LE12,000 of expenses per household, per year), the "middle classes" (between LE12,000 and LE29,999), and the "easy or wealthy classes" (LE30,000 or more). The first category comprises 68.12 percent of households (63.83 percent of the population), the second, 27.31 percent of households (31.41 percent of the population), and the third, 4.56 percent of households (4.76 percent of the population) in the urban zone. Thus, urban zones have a real 'middle class': real in the sense that it represents more than a quarter of the households and nearly a third of the population. However, their expenses are still limited ($1.00 was actually worth about EGP6.20 in 2000).

2   In Autumn 2004, large billboards on top of skyscrapers advertised Heineken, asserting "We need more green in the city" (green is the color of the Heineken brand). In 1992 the Aga Khan Foundation made the same observation while deciding to offer a gift to the governorship and residents of Cairo, for the anniversary of the Fatimid foundation of Cairo. It was a large public garden (but one at which one had to pay, as always). Al-Azhar Park opened during autumn 2004 (Aga Khan Trust for Culture 2001).

3   The *ginayna yabaniya* is officially named "Tokyo Garden." It is a large park, situated in Helwan, a southern suburb of Cairo. It was offered by Japan on the occasion of the declaration of the twinning of the capital cities of Tokyo and Cairo.

19 Egypt's Pop-Music Clashes and the 'World-Crossing' Destinies of Muhammad 'Ali Street Musicians

Nicolas Puig

It is the first night of the feast following the holy month of Ramadan ('Id al-Fitr), in Sa'ad as-Sawa' Café on Muhammad 'Ali Street and the musicians feel nervous. Only some of them have worked in the last weeks. Because there are no street weddings during the month of Ramadan, opportunities to play and perform are few and far between. Usually, there are numerous weddings during the 'Id so everyone can expect to go back home with some money in his pocket (between $5 and $30 according to the instrument played and to the circumstances).[1] But now, it is six o'clock in the afternoon and no one has been hired in advance to perform at a wedding tonight. Mursi, the singer, keeps pacing, traversing the same hundred steps in his very tight costume and his new haircut. He is ready to go entertain at any wedding feast in Cairo. Mahmud, the *urg* player (electric piano) is getting nervous and he calls out to Mursi, "If you get anything, I'm with you." But by nightfall, anxiety lifts among the musician's cafés of Muhammad 'Ali Street, minibuses and taxis fills the street, and musicians disperse throughout Cairo's neighborhoods to entertain at wedding feasts.

The *suq al-musiqiyyin* (the musicians' market) in Cairo refers to the social space of popular-class *(sha'bi)* urban music, the live music played at weddings but also at *mulid*s (Sufi saint's festival). This is a vernacular genre that is defined in a distinctive realm of musical training, social affiliations, and professional practices. These musicians of the *suq* have developed a specific urban subculture concentrated in a few cafés of Muhammad 'Ali Street, formerly the old prestigious center of Egyptian music during its golden age in the twentieth century. Yet, these musicians are quite stigmatized by the rest of Cairo inhabitants as a group of outsiders with very low social status. And the music they perform circulates at the 'bottom' of the market through cheap audiotape sales. This artistic form is linked to an old urban culture combined with some rural musical influences dominant in the Cairo of the popular classes, in the dense neighborhoods of the old town and in newer sprawling informal districts.

This market of musicians is composed of not only specific urban places but also a system of relationships and interactions that define it professionally, reproducing certain trades, skills, and economic interests. It is also an urban culture, or subculture, anchored in urban spaces like Muhammad 'Ali Street, in places where the wedding ceremonies are organized, and on stages where musicians play. This world of street weddings and *mulid*s represents an 'endogenous' culture developed through its own training networks and professional musical practices. These networks depend neither on the international Arabic showbiz market nor on the Egyptian government's validation that prefers to select different kinds of regional and popular music for integration into 'official' Egyptian folklore. Institutions of the Ministry of Culture such as *al-Hay'a al-'amma li-qusur al-thaqafa*, (the National Agency of Culture Palaces) promote folklore that has been sanctioned by the state. These Culture Palaces are found all over Egypt and employ civil servants and musicians who perform and represent local musical folklore and popular arts (music and dance).

State institutions maintain a substantial influence on the cultural destiny of popular music. Their presentation of musical styles, through controlled mass media or cultural promotions, results in the 'folklorization' of rural music and the stigmatization of urban music and of popular-class musicians in general.

It is this struggle for collective survival, recognition and markets in a spatially fragmented and class-segmented city that this chapter will discuss. How are these different urban cultures combined in the restricted space of the town where one finds "the greatest variety of subcultures, the most elaborate cultural apparatus, and a number of contrasting but interlinked modes of managing meaning" (Hannerz 1992, 173–74)? Indeed, the landscape of musical performance and promotion reflects the dynamics of urban society in Cairo, in the context of social differentiation and spatial conjunction. This chapter analyzes the changing roles of *sha'bi* musicians, their 'subculture,' and their relationship to the rest of Cairo's spaces and inhabitants; the rise of the booming cassette-recording industry in the last thirty years; and the 'problems' this low-scale industry raises in the national and Arab-regional public sphere of culture.

The exploration of the musical subcultures of Cairo is based on fieldwork I have been doing since the year 2000 on the musicians of Muhammad 'Ali Street, based in one of their rallying-point cafés, and joining them as they performed in weddings, engagements, and street celebrations throughout the capital. In order to shed light on the uncertain destinies of popular musicians in Cairo, first I will map out this space and its 'publics' and then describe the career of Muhammad 'Ali Street musicians. Second, I will consider the place of popular-class musicians' self-organization, promotion, identity, and performance in the public sphere of urban culture in order to understand the relationships of endogenous music to an official culture within the Cairo urban scene.

Street celebrations take place in Cairo's popular neighborhoods, in the *'ashwa'iyat* (informal housing districts), the Islamic quarter, the old city of Fustat, etc. These celebrations include "artists' nights" *(laylat al-fannanin)*, organized as benefits for a musician with financial needs, activating reciprocal relationships of obligation within the profession. Such relationships are also reinforced during other kinds of street ceremonies like weddings.

On stage, the band is usually made up of an electric organ *(urg)*, some percussion instruments *(tabla*, two kinds of tambourine named *ri'* and *duff)*, a singer, and one or two women dancers. Sometimes there are also an accordion and drums. The *nabatshi*, or master of ceremonies, is also on stage, in charge of collecting money and complimenting the donor publicly on the microphone. For the sake of the ceremony a section of the street is appropriated, creating a private space in the residential community. Large red-colored and ornately patterned tapestries delimit the space reserved for the ceremony while leaving a narrow passage for the pedestrians, transforming the street into a festive space serving contradictory functions—as a space of transgression on the one hand (where alcohol, marijuana, and scantily-clad women dancers often circulate) and, on the other hand, as a space where the deepest social and community norms are reproduced.

Two dancers and a band from Muhammad 'Ali Street onstage at a street wedding (photograph by Nicolas Puig).

The Reference Point of Muhammad 'Ali Street

Muhammad 'Ali Street today is the reference-point place for popular-class musicians performing in these weddings. Until the 1970s, the street was the center for all musicians, including the classiest ones. Nineteenth-century initiatives infused the core of the old Cairene neighborhoods with a dominating form of modernist urban rationalism, one still visible today in the design of many of downtown Cairo's streets and public spaces. The plans for the urban development of the city drawn in the middle of the nineteenth century, under the reign of the independent-minded Ottoman Pasha Muhammad 'Ali, included breaking open new avenues and widening older streets, to construct a new diagonal vector, "like a surgical incision through the densely packed residential areas between Azbakîyah and the citadel" (Abu-Lughod 1971, 96).

Muhammad 'Ali Street was to be located between the mosque of Sultan Hasan and the al-Rifa'i Zawya and the park-cemeteries of Azbakiya and Munasira (Mubarak 1980, 247). Muhammad 'Ali seized the grounds, demolished the existing buildings, and moved the debris and human remains toward other cemeteries (Imam al-Shafi'i's in particular). However, the two cemeteries kept being used until the last years of his reign (1805–1848) since the building of the street was interrupted for a time. The street was completed in 1873 under the era of the Khedive Isma'il (1864–1879). Muhammad 'Ali Street became a two-kilometer avenue that bisected older Islamic Cairo, symbolizing the reforming, penetrative will of the ruler and his aggressive embrace of modern urbanism. It was one more of the monumental public works of the khedive, who strove to make his city a second Paris by building a new downtown zone, renaming the central district Isma'iliya to bring glory to his name (Arnaud 1998, 173; Abu-Lughod 1971, 100–112).

[Muhammad 'Ali Street] was considerably wider than al Sikkah al-Jadida and unlike that prototype, was provided with wide sidewalks, shaded in part by trees and in other sections by the arcades of buildings that were swiftly built to line it. Gaslights were installed along the entire length of the road which, being the pride and joy of the monarch, was compulsively swept thrice daily to keep it immaculate. The dream of Muhammad 'Ali was thus finally realized. Abu-Lughod 1971, 113.

In the new urban configuration, the street was a major axis plowing through the old city, connecting the Citadel (the residence of the Egypt's viceroy, rulers of the country in the Ottoman era) to the 'Abdin Palace (the new military and administrative center), and the new cosmopolitan park and leisure zone of Azbakiya.

The reforms taking place in the second part of the nineteenth century in Egypt also influenced music and its norms. The bandstands of the new gardens of Azbakiya were used by Ottoman musicians throughout the century, invited by the members of the khedivial family and by Sufi brotherhoods (Lagrange 1996, 70). An elite set of 'court musicians' centered on the palace of 'Abdin, whose most famous representative was the singer and composer 'Abduh al-Hamuli from Tanta. European music was at that time well represented in Cairo, including military bands and the orchestra of the Cairo Opera House, inaugurated in 1869.

Egyptian music gradually acquired autonomy infused with a characteristic spirit from mixing Turkish, local Arab, and European cultures. Al-Hamûlî traveled to Istanbul with the khedive's court and brought musical innovations back to Egypt, integrating them into the local context. And "music was affected by change dictated by social conditions" (Vigreux 1991, 58).

By the start of the nineteenth and twentieth centuries, musicians and string-instrument workshops settled in Muhammad 'Ali Street. Musicians gathered in cafés according to the type of instruments they played and their musical style. Cafés were located in this place that symbolized the khedive's power and enabled proximity to the European town (Isma'iliya) and its new cultural focal points (the opera house, cabarets, and the bandstands of Azbakiya). This privileged relationship between urban spaces and artistic practices throughout history not only made Muhammad 'Ali Street an emblem of Egyptian music and an artistic center with influence throughout the Arabic-speaking world, but also, for a time, a prestigious space in downtown Cairo.

Musicians' cafés were initially the urban crossroads from which the musical and professional norms of the time were disseminated. Musicians from Upper Egypt and the Delta who were launching their careers in Cairo had to frequent these cafés to establish their reputations and win recognition from their peers. The cafés are public spaces, open to all men. As one customer explained to me, "Muhammad 'Ali Street does not have doors. There are cafés which welcome

Sa'ad as-Sawa' Café on Muhammad 'Ali Street (photograph by Nicolas Puig).

anyone who can afford to pay for a cup of tea." However, one still has to be recognized by others to begin a career as a wedding musician. The newcomer must become a regular visitor to the café and a figure of the group thanks to his talent and his adaptability. Both immigrants and newcomers had to become regulars in one of the cafés and gain the respect of older musicians, allowing them to integrate into the profession and begin their careers in the different musical venues in Cairo. A musician had to become a *sahib kursi* (a chair owner), someone who occupied a place in the café regularly and legitimately, with the consent of other musicians. For nearly a century Muhammad 'Ali Street was the gateway to the Egyptian capital and to its greater work opportunities for aspiring musicians coming from Cairo, Egypt, and even other Arab countries (Puig 2001).

A witness to the history of the cafés explains:

*In this café everybody can sit: he occupies a chair [*sahib kursi*], he occupies a space. He will become somebody who has a 'name,' somebody 'famous,' known. When I want a player of the* qanun *[an instrument in the zither family], I say I want so-and-so. Like this he occupies a chair, he gets a reputation. It is similar to the shaykhs who taught in al-Azhar in the past who always sat with their students next to the same column, and were known as the* sahib 'amud *[owner of the*

A musician's 'chair' in Halawithum Café, Muhammad 'Ali Street (photograph by Nicolas Puig).

column]. Who is the best qanun player? This man. Who is the best 'ud player? This one. These men occupy a chair, they get a name thanks to their talent and their technique. Sayyid, interview with the author, Halawithum Café 2000.

However, since the 1970s the vocation of the street has changed. It has been marginalized in the subjective hierarchy of city places as well within the musician's community. The street has lost its centrality and renowned musicians have begun to congregate and manage their careers in other more attractive places. To sum it up, "The heritage of the 1970s—that is, the end of the monopoly of the Muhammad 'Ali Street performers and their growing individualization, combined with the recent economic recession—has affected the entertainment market in several ways" (Van Nieuwkerk 1995, 57).

The marginalization of the street has not benefited any other area in particular. The less geographically concentrated and distinctive new spatial organization of the music industry in town reflects the diversity of aesthetic styles and artistic waves that also arose in the 1970s. The sprawling urban recomposition of Cairo and the increased mobility of all classes have also influenced the town's musical spaces. These urban changes are accompanied by a renewing of centralities and a polylocalization of cultural practices.

Along Muhammad 'Ali Street these days, there are only the 'lowest' ranks of popular-class musicians who perform in weddings and *mulid*s in a few cafés and workshops that manufacture and sell traditional musical instruments like the *'ud* (Arabic lute) or percussion instruments. One can also find workshops where tailors stitch the belly dancers' costumes. Some belly dancers live in hotels around the street and wait for evening engagements in weddings or cabarets.[2] It is not considered proper for females, even belly dancers, to hang out in the cafés, which are still predominantly gendered as male spaces.

This destiny of Muhammad 'Ali Street reflects the rise and fall of the nineteenth-century European urban center founded by Isma'il Pasha, grandson of Muhammad 'Ali. The prestige of the street and its surroundings had declined by the end of the twentieth century, as did the whole of the belle-époque downtown center, which is now frequented by the popular urban classes during festive moments. (See El Kadi and ElKerdany in this volume for further analysis of the heritage of the 'belle-époque' downtown area and recent efforts to revive it.)

Furniture sellers and mechanics' workshops are gradually replacing musical spaces, but there is still a small but dynamic music market. Wedding-party promoters, cabaret owners, and impresarios can go there to find musicians. On the typical nights for weddings (mainly Thursdays and Sundays), Muhammad 'Ali

Street is a lively and vibrant place, combining varied new commercial activities with scenes of musicians leaving the cafés for parties in Cairo's neighborhoods. These cafés are the heart of what musicians call *suq al-musiqiyyin*, a gathering place, a center for maintaining the musical traditions for weddings, and a space for economic transactions. As singer Hakim declared:

I didn't earn any money [in Muhammad 'Ali Street], but I learned a lot just by dealing with musicians. Even today, I always say that the musician who never worked on Muhammad 'Ali is not a musician, and I cannot trust them to stand behind me. Anyone who has not tried playing on the streets is no good. Muhammad 'Ali Street is the ultimate academy. Wahish 2002.

In spite of Hakim's assertions, street cafés are no longer the prerequisite gateway to success. Apart from some exceptions like himself, the street leads to a dead-end for most musical careers and appears to have lost all of its cosmopolitan ambiance. In the earlier period, local residents and the artistic elite of the country and larger region met in these cafés and interacted with each other, but today, the clientele of Muhammad 'Ali Street's cafés has narrowed to a local one and the street has lost its cosmopolitan nature. The street is the center of the *'awalim*, a pejorative word which now refers to groups of musicians and dancers that perform in street weddings. Nowadays, the street is identified with the 'slums' of Cairo and its inhabitants.

The market for musicians has shifted and now the urban focal point of cosmopolitan Arab music and dance performance has relocated across the Nile to the riverside hotels as well as to the cabarets of Pyramid Road, which have audiences made up mostly of Gulf and Saudi Arabs (Zirbel 2000, 126). (See Abaza's and Elsheshtawy's chapters in this volume for further analysis of the ways in which Gulf financial flows and consumption styles have been influencing Cairo.) Older musicians have recently developed nostalgia about the glorious past of the street:

For approximately thirty years, Muhammad 'Ali Street at night was completely different that it is now. It had an aspect of 'carnival.' You found musicians smoking, their shoes shining. They were astonishing characters that made people happy. I liked to go down to look at them and I aspired to become one of them. Ahmad, interview with the author, Darb al-Ahmar 2000.

Grounding carnival-style play in regularized vernacular institutions, Muhammad 'Ali Street cafés serve as sites of professionalization and masculine sociability deeply rooted in the urban landscape, and resemble the artisanal guilds of other professions. In this profession, men interact with women due to the nature of their craft. Musicians often work with female belly dancers or singers and thus remake some of the norms of gender segregation in public and work spaces. This gender mixing also gives their entire profession and avocation a slightly racy or sexually provocative reputation.

Halawithum Café on Muhammad 'Ali Street (photograph by Nicolas Puig).

The Career of a Muhammad 'Ali Street Musician

Observing dance musicians in Chicago, Howard Becker notes: "The antagonistic relationship between musicians and outsiders shapes the culture of the musician and likewise produces the major contingencies and crisis points in his career" (1997, 102). As in Chicago, musicians in Cairo also develop a strong consciousness of group specificity and solidarity and thus feel that they are a distinct group. They are very much in demand for entertaining at wedding parties and other functions, but people have mixed feelings about them. On one hand, they feel jealous of them, because of the 'freedom' they reputedly enjoy, and on the other, they despise them because of their supposedly licentious way of life. "Though their activities are formally within the law, their culture and way of life are sufficiently bizarre and unconventional for them to be labeled as outsiders by more conventional members of the community" (Becker 1997, 79).

Due to the lack of valorization of this profession, most families try to stop young men who embark on this type of musical career. Many musicians join the *suq al-musiqiyyin* after they fail in school and then begin to hang out in these cafés. An older musician sponsors the novice and teaches him his skills; and then the novice gets 'on-the-job training' at his teacher's performances at weddings and *mulid*s. This training does not highlight musical theory but trains the ear by practice and experience.

They learn a large repertory which ranges from the highly classical songs of Umm Kulthum or 'Abd al-Wahab to the latest pop or *sha'bi* hits. At street weddings, music is played in an entirely different way from the classical tradition to showcase the greetings and compliments that the *nabatshi* (master of ceremonies) directs toward the guests. The music is punctuated by frequent interruptions, sound saturation, echo effects, and frequent improvisations from the master of ceremonies praising the financial generosity of the guests. This music is quite different than the *dhikr* [spiritual chanting of the name of God] found in local *mulid*s (see Madoeuf in this volume). Nevertheless, beside the shaykhs' tents at *mulid* celebrations, one will find several places where musicians perform urban popular music (cafés, tents, *theatro*, etc.).

Ahmad Wahdan, singer and 'ud player who was trained on Muhammad 'Ali Street (photograph by Nicolas Puig).

In mainstream culture, the marginal and even shameful reputation of these musicians is reflected in pejorative colloquial Arabic words such as *mazikati* ('ill-trained musician,' as opposed to *musiqar*, 'maestro,' or 'highly-trained musician') or *alati* (pl. alatiya, 'instrumentalist,' synonym of cunning, craftiness). These connotations of *alati* come from the resourcefulness of popular musicians who manage to make a living despite the numerous problems they have to overcome. From a more historical perspective, this meaning refers to the official distinctions enforced between the *alati* and 'modernist musicians.' The Cairo Congress on Arab Music held in 1932 highlighted this opposition between members of the Institute of Arab Music, founded in 1923, and the *alatiya*. Members of the institute posed as reformers, criticizing the ignorance and 'backward' musical practices of the *alatiya* based on orality, that they claimed caused musical disorder. Nevertheless, *alatiya* remain members of the Musicians' Union, founded in 1920. Philippe Vigreux represents this contrast by a series of oppositions: trade union (syndicate) versus institute; common people versus beys, pashas, and aristocrats; amateurs versus professionals; *alatiya* versus *musiqiyyin*; 'traditional' versus modern musicians; space of immorality versus space of morality; attachment to an Eastern legacy (Persian then Ottoman) versus the purified and paradoxically classicized and modernized 'Arab music' (1992, 232).

The evolution of the term *'awalim*, which refers to popular-class musicians and dancers, highlights the stigmatization. First of all, *'awalim* is the plural of *'alima*, 'erudite.' It comes from the term applied to female singers and dancers who performed only for women in the Ottoman aristocratic households (Rodinson 1975). At the time, because they played in the segregated world of women, they enjoyed a respectable artistic and social reputation during Ottoman rule (Ghunaym 1998, 9). When the French invaded Egypt in 1798 they transcribed *'alima* into French as *almée*, which came to mean 'woman singer and dancer from Orient.' Flaubert popularized the term *'almée'* in his famous Egyptian travel story but he confused *'alima* with *ghaziya* (pl. *ghawazi*), a quite distinct type of female artist performing lascivious dances in front of men and singing with a mixed band, thus transgressing prevailing norms of gender segregation.

According to Karin Van Nieuwkerk, "the heyday of the *'awalim* was at the beginnning of this century" (1995, 49). At this time perfomers and *'awalim* were in great demand because many new entertainment places appeared in Cairo in the European model, such as café-concerts and cabarets, while there were still many opportunities to play music at festive occasions like weddings.

But, in the present context, the word *'awalim* refers very derogatively to musicians and belly dancers performing in street weddings *(afrah baladi)*. As an example, when I interviewed Hasan Abu Sa'ud, the president of the Musicians' Union, he complained about an article I wrote in Arabic entitled "Cairo, Capital of the *'Awalim*," arguing that it was like identifying Paris with Pigalle! However, some musicians in Muhammad 'Ali Street play with the meanings of the words and connect *'awalim* not to *'alima* but to *'alam* (pl. *'awalim*), meaning 'world.' The plural of both words sound the same in Egyptian Arabic; they have the same spelling with different meanings. Musicians therefore argue that the word *'awalim* could refer not to the dubious milieu of popular musicians and female dancers but to the different (social) worlds they enter, integrate, and confront when they go to entertain in Cairo's neighborhoods. Because they perform for many different social milieus they consider themselves privileged witnesses of urban diversity. Their ability to perform for very different audiences is frequently celebrated by the professionals of Muhammad 'Ali Street. Their musical dexterity and social sensitivity—'to read' any audience and what it wants—is seen as essential to their trade.

I work everywhere, in popular neighborhoods, informal housing areas, slums, fashionable districts, with robbers, pickpockets, 'beys,' doctors, and engineers. My work enables me to go everywhere and I have to interact with all these people. If it is a high-class audience, I raise my level to be able to speak with them. Among the lower class, I diminish completely my level to be able to interact with them. . . . The job requires me to adapt my musical style to the audience. It's not judicious to perform "Ruba'iyat al-Khayyam" [sung by Umm Kulthum] or 'Abd al-Wahab songs in front of people with very plebian cultural tastes. They will not understand what I'm playing. So, I go down to their level, and I play rubbish. Midhat, interview with the author, Darb al-Ahmar, 2002.

Ethnomusicologists like Martin Stokes recognize the importance of this cultural and musical dexterity for musicians:

Musicians often live in conspicuously trans-local cultural worlds. They travel; their social skills are those of people capable of addressing varied and heterogeneous groups, and their value in a locality is often perceived to be precisely their ability to transcend the cultural boundaries of that locality (1997, 98).

Muhammad 'Ali Street musicians share this vision. Moreover, they consider the ability to move in different 'worlds' the specific quality of a good Muhammad 'Ali Street musician, a quality that other local musicians that are not from the street, as well as classically-trained ones, do not possess because they are not as competent and their academic training keeps them from improvising and adapting to their audience. Even if some of them have had formal musical training in a school (typically the Institute of Arabic Music), musicians of Muhammad 'Ali Street do not consider themselves *acadimi*. In the Egyptian context, this word signifies the legitimate official circuit of musical training and performing in state musical institutions (like the Cairo Opera Orchestra). Popular musicians are the ones who take themselves among the people at feasts, weddings, and *mulids*, while the public would have to leave their worlds and travel into more official or exclusive spaces and adopt proper behaviors in order to hear *acadimi* musicians.

I go to a lot of places, I'm sahib kursi *on Muhammad 'Ali Street. There are musicians performing music inside the borders of their neighborhood, but they never leave it. They are not very good artists and musicians. They are not able to entertain at a party at the Sheraton Hotel or in Aswan or in a* mulid *or in a place outside of their neighborhood. They can just play music at street weddings where they live. That is all. Because they know what neighborhood inhabitants like, they are the local musicians. But those from Muhammad 'Ali Street, the one who is associated with street cafés, is ready in the morning when leaving his home to go to Alexandria, Aswan, Isma'iliya, Luxor, the Sheraton Hotel, a* mulid, *a puppet show, or a birthday party. He can manage all situations.* Ahmad, interview with the author, Darb al-Ahmar, 2002.

Yet, wedding musicians who perform in wedding processions are still considered lower-status professionals than other musicians in Egypt and very few of them are members of the musician's syndicate, especially those who play only in their immediate neighborhoods. Therefore, Muhammad 'Ali Street musicians adopt professional strategies to improve their reputations and to distinguish themselves from those even lower on the professional totem pole. In densely populated neighborhoods, where one's reputation is critical to one's moral authority and even economic position, musicians are rightly concerned about maintaining their reputations (Puig 2003).[3] For instance, a drummer confided, "How could my son say at school that his father is a *tabla* player (drummer) on Muhammad 'Ali Street? That wouldn't do; it's shameful" (Mahmud, interview with the author, Darb al-Ahmar, 2002). Many would argue that a musical career on Muhammad 'Ali Street is antithetical to family life, and some musicians give up their careers when they start a family if they have another career opportunity. For others, they simply try to avoid performing in their own neighborhood, in fear of diminishing their social capital.

There are, however, a few successful careers available to those few musicians who regularly perform in prestigious places such as Ramadan concerts or embassy parties. If musicians escape from street weddings, they will try to never play at them again because it would mean a loss of prestige. Each one carefully guards his prestige *(biristij)* and strategizes to distinguish himself from his colleagues and prove his excellence. Like numerous neo-*mawwal* singers, Ahmad 'Adawiya began his career on Muhammad 'Ali Street. These singers are closely related to the milieu of Muhammad 'Ali musicians. Transcending anonymity, they become a name on a tape and retain a degree of fame in the wedding market, becoming labelled a *nigm shubbak* (a star of the ticket booth). If they get enough offers, they employ a business manager settled in a fancy office, located in a district better than Muhammad 'Ali Street, to promote their career. The market of anonymous musicians *(suq al-musiqiyyin)* waiting for hypothetical engagements is quite different than the market for more famous singers who have well-known agents. Few musicians and singers of Muhammad 'Ali Street have significant financial success unless they can have a hit on the cheap *sha'bi* cassette tapes that are produced locally and make the professional leap to perform in more prestigious places.

Hugely popular singer Hakim is an emblematic pioneer of this trajectory thanks to his ability to break out of the 'microbus circuit' (so called because these low-budget cassettes are played in the microbuses that ply the transportation routes between poor neighborhoods). His success is due to his ability to mix romantic sentiment with *sha'bi* tradition by singing 'neo-*mawwal*,' a modern musical form elaborated from improvised popular songs sung particularly at weddings (and mislabelled as '*sha'bi*' in *World Music: The Rough Guide* [Lodge 1994] and in the *Dictionnaire thématique des musiques du monde* [Bours 2002]). According to Michael Frishkopf, "This style is the musical response to rapid ruralization of the cities: low-brow, appealing to inhabitants of popular districts. Performers such as Ahmad 'Adawiya, Hasan al-Asmar, and 'Abduh al-Iskandarani updated older traditions of *mawwal* and *zagal* (genres of folk song), and risqué wedding songs, by modernizing the instrumentation and addressing urban life without losing a folk feel, full of improvisation and flexible interaction" (2002, 10). In today's Egypt, Hakim performs at five-star luxury hotel wedding receptions, appears on television and in big concerts with international stars like the English singer Sting. Popular cassettes of 'neo-*mawwal*' are a commercial success even though their stars performed first at street parties, weddings, and *mulid*s (Puig and Belleface 2003). The increased popularity of audiotapes in the last thirty years has led, in Egypt as well as in India, to the emergence of huge alternative popular "cassette culture" (Manuel 1993).

For a long time, Muhammad 'Ali Street was the gathering place of prestigious musicians. Those who are now in the street try to draw upon their nostalgic history to increase the prestige of their profession. But according to these musicians, unfortunately "Egyptians like music and dislike musicians" (Ahmad, Darb al-Ahmar, 2000). These words remind us of Dwight Reynolds' comment about the epic songs of the Egyptian Nile Delta: "a respected art form transmitted by disrespected performers" (1989). Nevertheless the epic tradition is probably much better integrated into the official culture as a result of rural-music folklorization than is popular urban music. Indeed the relationship between the world of music and the public sphere of culture in Egypt is constantly changing.

The Public Sphere of Culture and Illegitimate *Sha'bi* Music

The musicians' position in the music world depends on the musical genre they play. Public sentiment, as well as acceptance and tolerance of these genres by the media and the state cultural apparatus, highlights debates within contemporary urban society. This is best understood by first examining the division and fragmentation that exists among different genres and social groups inside the world of Egyptian music. In the last thirty years, there has been a relative diversification of the artistic range of modern Egyptian music. Musical production today is dominated by two major currents: slick, sentimental, studio-produced pop songs, and popular-class *(sha'bi)* neo-*mawwal* urban music. The first includes a wide variety of pop music, from dance hits to ballads, heard on Egyptian radio and sung by stars like Amr Diab, Mustafa Qamar, Ihab Tawfiq, and Hani Shakir. Neo-*mawwal* music, banned from the airwaves because of its so-called vulgarity, is best known these days through its rising star, the highly publicized Sha'ban 'Abd al-Rahim. Designed for a large audience in the Arab world, the sentimental pop form of Egyptian music takes few risks in its originality, its lyrics, or its music. Composers mix basic oriental rhythms with light melodies taken from diverse sources such as simplified Eastern melodic modes, Spanish or Latin-based pentatonic, and Nubian traditions, among others (Frishkopf 2002). The marketing of pop Egyptian music is mainly directed to the Gulf and the Levant, quite the opposite for North African singers such as Cheb Mami and Cheb Khaled, who are marketed to Europe.

The Cairo-centered Arab-region showbiz industry broadcasts its pop music through the state-controlled as well as private satellite media and revolves around the launching and replay of all-important high-fashion music videos. (See Sadek in this volume for a discussion of the links between Cairo's music industry and the larger region.) Meanwhile the street music and neo-*mawwal* forms of the popular classes have developed their own networks and media of distribution. Considered illegitimate by the guardians of normative culture, neo-*mawwal* finds its audience through the huge market of cheap audiocassettes and is heard in noninstitutional public spaces such as microbuses, kiosks, and a wide range of street parties. Although this kind of music finds no official support, however, it does not mean that its practitioners lack media attention—although lately this attention has been largely negative since much of the media is hostile to this musical genre and issues polemics against it, particularly on cultural grounds. Focused on the social legitimacy of popular music, these polemics reflect the tensions of a strongly hierarchical urban society. Sha'ban 'Abd al-Rahim, who has enjoyed stunning success for a few years, is probably the most representative singer of this musical current. In 2000 he sold a million and a half audiotapes, equal to the sales of Amr Diab, the biggest 'respectable' Egyptian pop-music star.

Like Ahmad 'Adawiya, for instance, who was the first successful musician in this style, Sha'ban belongs to the core of urban popular singers. They learned their art twenty or thirty years ago at street weddings and *mulid*s. Most of them come from Muhammad 'Ali Street and have set an example for others. They never studied music academically as Ahmad 'Adawiya pointed out to *Al-Ahram Weekly* newspaper, "It is my singing experience in *mulid*s and tents that founded my entire career. My own

Ahmad 'Adawiya, neo-*mawwal* singer who bagan his career on Muhammad 'Ali Street (photograph by Nicolas Puig of audiocassette cover).

talent, combined with such a life, has qualified me for the equivalent of a Ph.D. in music. I never studied music, except through feeling, listening and a tough life" (El-Kashef 2001). Leading a tough life is an asset for popular musicians. Sha'ban used to work at a laundry as an ironer *(makwagi)*. "He personifies the honor of the *makwagi*," an admirer told me one day at the Halawithum Café on Muhammad 'Ali Street. Unskilled workers, craftsmen, and young unemployed men and women can identify with the lyrics of his songs. In his songs, he is a chronicler of daily life evoking images of life in popular quarters, a recent disaster like the crash of the EgyptAir plane, the housing crisis, or the war in Iraq.[4] His songs are an open appeal to lower-class sensibilities as well as to a sense of place, deeply-rooted in the inhabitants' consciousness. Indeed, as with other singers of this trend, he often mentions very emblematic places within Cairo's popular neighborhoods. Although he reflects shared meanings and produces them in some respects, Sha'ban is unacceptable to the educated elite. For the *cognoscenti* or simple detractors, his music is meaningless: "Sha'ban . . . is to Egyptian pop culture . . . an exercise in bad taste," according to journalist Muhammad El-Assyouti (2001). Media critics are completely insensitive to the inhabitants of the poor quarters and oblivious to the social irony of his lyrics. In the same way, Sakina Fouad, an *al-Ahram* jounalist, asked, "How can we build culture in Egypt in the presence of the likes of Sha'ban 'Abd al-Rahim," demanding official intervention "to put an end to this farce" (Mursi 2001).

Sha'ban infuses his *mawwal*s with social and political content. He layers his lyrics over chords and melodies on the electric piano—the characteristic instrument of wedding music, which gradually replaced the accordion in the 1970s. The content of his music is fitting of a genre of nationalistic protest music born in the seventies. However, such content is inoffensive for Arab states because it mainly contains denunciations of Israel and support for the Arab leaders (e.g., his "*Bakrah Isra'il wa-Shumun wa-Aryal Sharun wa-bahibb 'Amr Musa*" [I hate Israel, and Shimon [Peres], and Ariel Sharon, and I love 'Amr Musa [the former foreign minister of Egypt and head of the Arab League]). His music keeps alive the spirit of Arab-nationalist protest but does not directly challenge the Egyptian state, except perhaps by implied sarcasm. Thus, Sha'ban's tapes are not banned, although other songs of his were banned in the early 1990s. In his song "*Kaddab ya Graysha*" ("Graysha, You Liar!"), he celebrated and mocked the solidarity of the musicians' social world, full of manual workers (car painters, barbers, wall painters). A singer quoted in the song (who was referred to as a manual worker) complained to censor Hamdi Surur, who imposed a ban on Sha'ban's music (El-Assyouti 2001). It is not uncommon for the government to ban music. For example, Ahmad Fuad Nigm's poetry critiqued controversial political, social, and cultural issues in the 1970s and 1980s, and his views reached a large audience when the very popular and revered Shaykh Imam sang and recorded his poems in spite of official censorship.

From Urban Music to Popular Society

Contemporary urban music has developed with the growth of the city. It accompanied urbanization as in other towns in the world: "The rise of urban popular music is thus a reflection and a product of the emergence of vast new urban societies that scarcely existed a century ago" (Manuel 1988, 16). This music is strongly linked to these neighborhoods as we have seen with the evocation of music centers such as Muhammad 'Ali Street and at the urban-street settings of popular-class weddings. In Cairo as well as in India and in numerous cultures worldwide:

One of the remarkable features of the evolution of popular music is its association . . . with an unassimilated, disenfranchised, socially marginalized class. . . . They share a common status on or beyond the periphery of stable, 'respectable' society—the economically and socially assimilated working and middle classes. Manuel 1988, 18.

Accordingly, in many respects, cultural elites and others who criticize and deplore the genre of urban popular music deepen the stigmatization of the people who enjoy and support this musical genre: the inhabitants of vast lower-class neighborhoods, especially informal ones. In other words, neither the favorite music of residents in these areas—nor even the residents themselves—are considered legitimate in the eyes of middle- and upper-class Cairenes. Walter Armbrust has suggested that his Egyptian friends "frequently recommended al-ʿAtaba (just next to Muhammad ʿAli Street) as a place to buy things cheap; the media often denounces it as a wild place where stolen goods are fenced and bad taste runs rampant" (2001, 2). In the same way, Shaʿban in one of his songs ("*Habattal al-sagayir*") speaks about Wikalat al-Balah, a popular clothing market next to al-ʿAtaba, often evoked in the media as a center of bad taste.

The condemnation of this music followed the explosion in cheap cassette tapes in the 1970s. Armbrust notes that Ahmad ʿAdawiya "is scorned by the official media as hopelessly vulgar" (2001, 2). In addition, when Shaʿban was frequently invited to perform on TV during Ramadan in 2001, intellectuals and politicians met at the Media Committee of Parliament and unanimously condemned his appearances on widely watched TV shows during Ramadan, explaining that he would have a bad influence on Egyptian youth. ʿAbd al-Salem ʿAbd al-Ghaffar, director of the Media Committee, argued to journalist Muhammed Mursi that Shaʿban "does not represent any artistic or cultural value" (Mursi 2001). In the same article, Nagib Surur, the censor of broadcast media, justified the ban on Shaʿban's songs "to preserve good taste and fine arts," but added that on the other hand he has "no authority over programs on television in order to ban his appearance."

In the debate about the cultural legitimacy of *shaʿbi* music, we find some public stars such as ʿAdil Imam supporting Shaʿban. Egyptian cinema is mainly a popular one and ʿAdil Imam is its emblematic actor. Moreover, Shaʿban ʿAbd al-Rahim has made some appearances on cinema screens, such as in the recent social satire *Muwatin wa-mukhbir wa-harami* ('A Citizen, a Detective and a Thief') where he played the thief who moonlighted as a singer at wedding parties in Cairo's popular neighborhoods.

However, in mainstream culture, *sha'bi* singers are considered 'backward' or traditional, in fact the opposite of modernity. The same critique, of course, is launched against the people who love their music: the popular classes or *sha'b*. A poster sponsored by the Ministry of Culture and entitled "A Hundred Years of Enlightenment" caricatures twenty-three assorted Egyptian artists and intellectuals, plus a few symbols of the people: "These were the state-approved icons of authentic Egyptian modernity, the short list of cultural heroes with whom all Egyptians who had been through the educational system should be familiar" (Armbrust, 2001, 192).

According to the same author, the modernism portrayed in the poster "makes perfect sense to Egyptian nationalists trying to establish the ideological underpinnings of a state that can compete with Europe without being European" (2001, 194). In this nationalist project, linked to a promotion of rationally ordered progress, popular urban culture is denigrated and abused. Its messages are too far removed from "the view of unbroken modernist evolution" (Armbrust, 2001, 194). The same criticism is voiced about the lower classes who are accused of not submitting to the smoothly mobile, harmonious, and faceless ideal model of urban modernist order. This modernist view of the urban order seems unpracticed in real life. By contrast, the popular crowd's celebratory mass-frequenting of Cairo's downtown streets during Ramadan nights does not correspond to the modern urban order that the Cairo governor wants to promote in the city center. This order goes back to the notion of the capitalist town as a machine for free, smooth circulation, identified with Paris in the nineteenth century. In order to become modern, Cairo authorities are trying to regulate chaotic traffic, to forbid stalls that encroach upon public thoroughfares, public gatherings, and the endless bargaining in the market. "Hatgann," a well-known poem of Bayram al-Tunsi, a renowned Egyptian colloquial poet of the twentieth century, describes in a satiric but effective way "the defective civilities" in Cairo in comparison to modern behavior in London and Paris.[5] Cairo authorities still reproach the inhabitants for their anarchic manner of consumption which makes use of public space. Conversely, popular music like that of Sha'ban claims a presence for urban popular society not only in the public space of communication but also in the public spheres of traffic circulation, as his songs are noisily aired in microbuses and roadside kiosks.[6] Downtown streets and public spaces are typically filled with Cairo's popular classes, particularly as they stroll and shop when the stores are open late during Ramadan. Yet, like their 'vulgar' songs, the middle and upper classes consider these throngs vulgar and somewhat threatening, so they have begun to retreat to more protected spaces like malls, clubs, and gated communities with their family entertainment.[7]

(See Abaza, de Koning, Elsheshtawy, and Denis in this volume for these new constructions of upper-middle-class consumerism.) This contestation within the public sphere around music, as well as the use of public spaces, reflects tension between 'official' and 'endogenous' versions of Egyptian culture.

Conclusion

Midhat, an electric organ player performing at street weddings, revealed to me during an interview that he was playing the "music of the people" like Ahmad 'Adawiya had done. He argued that this kind of music was different from music nowadays. "These new *sha'bi* songs have meaningless lyrics and are very poor musically." In the same way, Hasan Abu Sa'ud, composer of numerous 'Adawiya hits in the 1970s and now president of the Musicians' Union, distinguishes his musical style that he calls "Egyptian pop" from *mawwal* or 'true' *sha'bi* music, while the local mass media do not make such subtle distinctions (interview, Musicians' Union, 2004). Seeking social legitimacy and respectability, wedding musicians make a distinction between musical currents and separate the old genre of *sha'bi* music from the new genre of Sha'ban's music. Thus, they redefine musical styles and their boundaries in order to build strategies of legitimation in a music world straining under the pressure of official validation. The issue at stake for these musicians is how to transfer skills acquired in an illegitimate social world (street weddings, mulids, or the *sha'bi* audiotape market) in order to access the resources and publics of Cairo's other 'worlds.' Performers in the endogenous culture have different goals and strategies, and some of them try to find validation by integrating their contributions and sensibilities with official and legitimized genres.

Following Hannerz' analysis of culture, French Sociologist Alain Battegay wrote about what he calls "microcultures," which is quite similar to my notion of endogenous cultures: "Unlike official cultures they always build and 'un-build,' and even if some of them can last for a relatively long time, they are always at risk of dispersion and disappearance" (2000, 246). Popular-class, vernacular 'street' Egyptian music always runs such a risk of dispersion and disappearance, particularly because it depends primarily on cassettes and stages at wedding parties as a broadcast medium. This music is repudiated by educated people and state cultural institutions, and this stigmatization mirrors the denigration of the 'backward' manners of Cairo's popular classes and neighborhoods themselves. Official state and corporate cultural establishments mistrust these classes and do not want to share the public sphere with them. They fear the political potential of this music, in spite of the assumed political allegiance of singers like Sha'ban 'Abd al-Rahim. They are not really concerned about the lyrics of his songs but the way in which his popularity reinforces the cultural presence of the urban masses in the public sphere. From this perspective culture works to "invest aesthetics with ethics" (Constant-Martin 2000, 179). In other words, music can symbolize an aspiration to social recognition through cultural expression. The same aspiration can be heard in many poor or informal housing areas, where the people often say, with a critique of government policy and the reigning economic paradigm implicitly understood, *"Ayzin na'ish bi-karama"* (we want to live with dignity). And in pursuit of dignity, pleasure and celebration, Cairo's *'awalim* will continue to cross between and articulate together Cairo's divergent worlds.

Works Cited

Abu-Lughod, Janet L. 1971. *Cairo: 1001 Years of the City Victorious.* Princeton: Princeton University Press.

Armbrust, Walter. 1996. *Mass Culture and Modernism in Egypt.* Cambridge: Cambridge University Press.

Arnaud, Jean-Luc. 1998. *Le Caire, mise en place d'une ville moderne 1867–1907.* Arles: Actes Sud, Sindbad.

El-Assyouti, Muhammad. 2001. "Man on the Street." *Al-Ahram Weekly,* 8–14 February.

Battegay, Alain. 2000. "L'espace commun, entre mythe et reconstructions: variations." In *Cultures en ville ou de l'art et du citadin,* 241–54. La Tour d'Aigues: Editions de l'aube.

Becker, Howard. 1997 [1963]. *Outsiders: Studies in the Sociology of Deviance.* New York: The Free Press.

Bours, E. 2002. *Dictionnaire thématique des musiques du monde.* Paris: Fayard.

Constant-Martin Denis. 2000. "Cherchez le peuple: culture, populaire et politique." *Critique Internationale* 7: 169–83.

Danielson, Virginia. 1996. "New Nightingales of the Nile: Popular Music in Egypt since the 1970s." *Popular Music* 15 (3): 299–312.

Flaubert, Gustave. 1986. *Voyage en Egypte, Octobre 1849—Juillet 1850.* Paris: Editions Entente (Impressions de voyage).

Frishkopf, Michael. 2002. "Some Meanings of the Spanish Tinge in Contemporary Egyptian Music." In *Mediterranean Mosaic: Popular Music and Global Sounds.* New York, London: Routledge.

Ghunaym, Muhammad Ahmad. 1998. *Jama'at al-ghuna' wa-al-tarab fi Shari' Siyam bi-madinat al-Mansura: dirasa anthrubulujiya.* al-Mansura: al-Markaz al-Hadari li-'ulum al-insan w-al-turath al-sha'bi bi-Jami'at al-Mansura.

Gillot, Gaëlle. 2002. *Ces autres espaces, Les jardins publics dans les grandes villes du monde arabe: politiques et pratiques au Caire, Rabat et Damas.* Ph.D. diss., Université François Rabelais.

Gordon, Joel. 2003. "Singing the Pulse of the Egyptian-Arab Street. Sha'ban 'Abd al-Rahim and the Pop Politics of Fast Food." *Popular Music* 22 (1): 73–88.

Hannerz, Ulf. 1991. *Cultural Complexity: Studies in the Social Organization of Meaning.* New York: Columbia University Press.

Joseph, Isaac. 1998. *La ville sans qualités.* La Tour d'Aigues: Editions de l'Aube.

El-Kashef, Injy. 2001. "Ahmed 'Adawiya: The King is in the House, This is History and He's Making It." *Al-Ahram Weekly,* 8–14 February.

Lagrange, Frédéric. 1996. *Musiques d' Egypte.* Paris: Cités de la Musique, Actes sud.

Lodge, David, 1994. "Cairo Hit Factory: Modern Egyptian Music: al-jil, shaabi, Nubian." In *World Music: the Rough Guide,* eds. Simon Broughton, Mark Ellingham, Richard Trillo, 184–87. London: Rough Guides Ltd.

Manuel, Peter. 1988. *Popular Music of the Non-Western World.* New York: Oxford University Press.

_____. 1993. *Cassette Culture, Popular Music and Technology in North India.* Chicago: University of Chicago Press.

Mubarak, 'Ali Pacha, 1980 (1888). *al-Khitat al-tawfiqiya al-jadida li-Misr al-Qahira wa-muduniha wa biladiha al-qadima wa-al-shahira.* Cairo: al-Hay'a al-Misriya al-'amma li-al-kitab, Volume III.

Mursi, Muhammad. 2001. "Sha'ban Rules the Airwaves." *Cairo Times,* 6–12 December.

Puig, Nicolas. 2001. "Le long siècle de l'avenue Muhammad 'Ali au Caire: d'un lieu et de ses publics musiciens." *Egypte/Monde arabe* 4/5: 207–23.

_____. 2003. "Habiter à Dûwîqa au Caire. Dedans et dehors d'une société de proximité." *Autrepart, Dynamiques résidentielles dans les villes du Sud: positions sociales en recomposition,* 25: 137–52.

_____. Forthcoming. "Variétés urbaines, Perceptions des lieux et positionnements culturels dans la société cairote." In *Manifestations de l'urbain dans le monde arabe,* ed. J.L. Arnaud. Tunis, Aix-en-Provence: IRMC, Maisonneuve & Larose.

Puig, Nicolas and Jean-Francois Belleface. 2003. "High Notes: The Sentimental Holds Sway." *The Encyclopedia of Modern Egypt,* 81–85. Cairo: The Egypto-File Ltd.

Reynolds, Dwight. 1989. "Tradition Replacing Tradition in Egyptian Epic Singing: The Creation of a Commercial Image." *Pacific Review of Ethnomusicology.* 5: 1–14.

Rodinson, Maxime. 1975 [1960]. "Alima." *Encyclopédie de l'islam.* Vol I, E.J. Brill, Maisonneuve et Larose.

Stokes, Martin, ed. 1997 [1994]. *Ethnicity, Identity and Music.* New York: BERG.

Van Nieuwkerk, Karin. 1995. *A Trade Like Any Other: Female Singers and Dancers in Egypt.* Austin: University of Texas Press.

Vigreux, Philippe. 1991. "Centralité de la musique égyptienne." *Egypte/ Monde Arabe* 7: 55–101.

———. 1992. "Le congrès de musique arabe du Caire dans la presse égyptienne, janvier-juin 1932." *Musique arabe, le Congrès du Caire de 1932,* 223–35. Cairo: CEDEJ.

Wahish, Niveen. 2002. "Hakim: From Muhammad 'Ali Street to Radio City Music Hall. The Business of Pleasure," *Al-Ahram Weekly* 607, 10–16 October 2002.

Zirbel, Katherine E. 2000. "Playing It Both Ways: Local Egyptian Performers Between Regional Identity and International Markets." In *Mass Mediations: New Approaches to Popular Culture in the Middle East and Beyond,* ed. Walter Armbrust, 120–45. Berkeley: University of California Press.

Notes

1   This is for musicians playing at street wedding feasts. But a big star like Egyptian pop star Amr Diab can earn up to $10,000 for a wedding.

2   For a specific discussion about female singers and dancers, see Van Nieuwkerk 1995.

3   Popular neighborhoods are "a major place of socialization and normative regulation. They represent a space of moral and social control of some over others, the proximity (physical density like cultural, economic and social proximity) is the privileged operator of this relation between spatial and social dimensions" (Puig 2003, 150–51).

4   His lyricist is Khalil Muhammad, an Arabic teacher.

5   *Hatgann ya rayt ya ikhwanna maruhtish London walla Baris*: "I'm going mad, o my brothers, I wish I had never gone to London nor Paris" (Puig forthcoming).

6   French urban sociologist Isaac Joseph explains that the public space of communication (discursive space) and the public space of circulation (among anonymous people) are two dimensions, closely dependent, of public space (1998, 42).

7   G. Gillot notes: "In a logic of separation and refusal of making use of public space as spaces of setting the scene of the social differences, the upper classes give up public spaces to the poor"(2002, 225). So for the upper-urban classes "the structuring of daily space is characterized by an ensemble of gated places whose protection is often problematic. . . . So all displacement is just a shift of the private sphere from one place to another" (2002, 234).

Cairo
Afterword

Afterword

Whose Cairo?

Nezar AlSayyad

Whose Cairo? This collection of essays by scholars of contemporary Cairo raises this important question. Which Cairo do we talk about and in whose name? As this volume indicates there are many Cairos, and many other Cairos in metropolitan Cairo itself. Indeed, there is Cairo, the city of migrant workers; Cairo, the city of informals, who occupy much of its space; Cairo, the city of unique urban pockets whose residents feel that they live elsewhere; Cairo, the city of gated communities and exclusive urban malls that transport their visitors to another world; and Cairo, the city of expatriates and experts who spend lifetimes trying to figure it out.

As the introduction of this book clearly indicates, the editors have strived to deconstruct the two most popular myths about Cairo; the city as a tomb, a dead or hyper-passive entity more like an open-air museum of monuments occupied by a population of quiescent serfs; and the city as a bomb, an entity of grave contradictions that harbors the explosive 'Arab street' that will detonate at any moment. I was writing these afterword notes during a recent visit to Cairo when I decided to share these supposed myths with one of my Egyptian friends, a Cairene architect and planner who works for one of the ministries. Invoking the traditional Egyptian sense of humor, my friend disagreed. He responded, "Cairo is not a tomb and it is not exactly a bomb; Cairo is a bomb within a tomb." He continued to explain as we were driving by what is known by many as the City of the Dead, but for many poor Cairenes it is a functioning urban district. "In Cairo we are like mummies, we all live in coffins. But ours is a death that is well-preserved, even celebrated. Perhaps one day we will wake up from our deadly sleep. It may require a bomb for that to happen." Rather than being insulted by the idea that his city is either a tomb or a bomb, my Egyptian friend seemed to embrace both metaphors as a starting point toward an understanding of his city. This made me think that perhaps the myths of Cairo are useful not only as urban imaginaries, but also as interrogative tools, that is, instruments that allow us to delve more deeply into Cairo's urban experience.

No book since Janet Abu Lughod's *Cairo: The City Victorious* has succeeded in capturing the complex dimensions of late twentieth-century Cairo as much as this one. As I read the various contributions to this volume, I was reminded of Edward William Lane's exhaustive early nineteenth-century account of "The Manners and Customs of Modern Egyptians," but here we read subtle portrayals of the lives and practices of late modern Cairenes minus the orientalist lens that tainted Lane's observations. I share the optimism of the editors of this volume as they designate the approach of the "Cairo School." There is no doubt in my mind that the future of the urban world lies not in London, New York, and Tokyo or other global cities in the north, but in the cities of the global south like Bombay, Cairo, and San Paulo; this is what makes this book and its method significant. If the study of Chicago in the 1920s and 1930s led to the evolution of the Chicago School of Urban Sociology, and the study of Los Angeles in the 1980s and 1990s led to the emergence of the L.A. School of Urban Geography, then there is hope that the new Cairo School of Urban Studies will offer both substance and methodological insights to decipher the logic of urban articulations of late capitalism in the global south at the beginning of the twenty first century.

So, is Cairo truly cosmopolitan? The contributors in this volume rightfully offer various and contradictory answers to this question. However, their main contribution lies not in falsifying that proposition but in questioning the meaning of 'cosmopolitan' in the global south. While some may argue that there is a world of difference between the 'true' cosmopolitanism of a First World city like London and the 'apparent' cosmopolitanism of Cairo, this volume attempts to reverse this assertion. It demonstrates that there is indeed a project of active citizenship in Cairo and that Cairenes themselves—

possibly in contradictory ways—are articulating, outside of the traditional institutional arenas, a unique modernity and are cognizant of global and transnational currents. They are rewriting Egypt's history and identity by employing global and transnational strategies. However, the questions that still remain unanswered include the following: why is Egypt (and Cairo, which constitutes one-quarter of the Egyptian population) unable to develop a new political culture and spatial manifestations that reach beyond the slogans of traditionalism, religious revivalism and anti-modernity; are new claims to citizenship simply a response to the perceived threat of a rising American empire with its alternative democratizing models—hegemonic as these may be? These exclamations, however, should not undermine the enormous ability that Cairenes have always demonstrated in negotiating their social world and remaking their public spaces.

Cairo, like other historic cities, is not exceptional in recasting its history, manufacturing its tradition, and facilitating the consumption of its heritage. Anyone familiar with the more modern history of Cairo will recognize that it has always been fashioned for the tourists' gaze. Perhaps the only difference today is that this refashioning process demonstrates a new dynamic between the state, its people, the emerging institutions of civil society, the agencies of international development, and the forces of global capital.

Change in Cairo often comes slow and sometimes, goes unrecognized for a while. On a recent visit to the Great Pyramids in Giza, the quintessential Egyptian monuments, my foreign guests and I found ourselves surrounded by a group of public school students from a somewhat poor district in Cairo. Listening to the remarks of the students as they descended upon the plateau convinced me that ordinary Egyptians no longer consider the Pyramids as the primary symbol of Egyptian heritage nor do they relate to the pharaonic past as part of their contemporary identity (as was the case in the early- and mid-twentieth century). For many Egyptians, the Great Pyramids of Giza are simply relics of a bygone era, whose significance has not yet been problematized for the modern moment. This is not necessarily a new phenomenon: the great medieval historian, al-Maqrizi, observed (more than six hundred years ago) that his Egyptian contemporaries felt a similar sentiment.

This raises for me the final and possibly the most important issue in studying Cairo today, namely its modernity. In *All That is Solid Melts into Air*, Marshall Berman brilliantly illustrates how the modernity of Paris and Saint Petersburg in the mid-nineteenth century was based on urban encounters in the newly opened boulevards—which were often cut out of the traditional fabric of the medieval city. These new public spaces allowed the rich and the poor to come together in physical contact in new and unprecedented ways. Berman showed how this apparently similar modernity in both cities captured very different meanings; in Paris it was a modernity of inter-class encounters grounded in particular liberal traditions, while in Saint Petersburg, Berman argues, it was a "modernity of underdevelopment" bearing the apparent forms of the modern but lacking its processes; marked more by a mix of mimicry and envy. These contradictions beg the following questions: are the exclusive malls of Cairo today, where the women in *niqab* mix comfortably with those who are skimpily dressed, the new boulevards of its modernity? Do these spaces define a unique or an alternative Egyptian modernity that may represent the larger Middle East at the beginning of the twenty-first century? Can we term this new articulation 'Medieval Modernity?' Perhaps the answers to these questions will be addressed in another volume.

Finally, we must recognize that as scholars we construct new myths even as we try to contest old ones. Indeed, the contributors to this volume have illustrated how the "making of worlds" in Cairo is also the making of words on Cairo. In the end, Cairo remains not a tomb, nor a bomb, but simply a living entity that will always change its skin with the passage of time.

Works Cited

Abu Lughod, Janet. 1971. *Cairo: 1001 Years of the City Victorious*. Princeton, N.J.: Princeton University Press.

AlSayyad, Nezar. 2004. *The End of Tradition?* London: Routledge.

AlSayyad, Nezar and Ananya Roy. "Medieval Modernity: Citizenship in Contemporary Urbanism." *Applied Anthropologist* (Fall 2005), 25: 2.

Berman, Marshall. 1982. *All That is Solid Melts into Air: The Experience of Modernity*. New York: Penguin.